From the
Playing Fields
To the
Killing Fields

Alan Hudson

ISBN:
ISBN-13: 978-1482605396

THE QUIXOTIC MAESTRO
AT THE HUB OF THE MIDFIELD

Alan Hudson was the darling of Stamford Bridge, the quixotic maestro at the midfield hub of Chelsea's supreme team of the seventies. He was England's prodigal genius, the rebellious young man about the Kings Road at its trendiest. Now Mr. Hudson is an author whose glittering instinct for the beautiful game and indulgence in the good life is making an extraordinary transition from the playing pitch to the printed page. Never orthodox or predictable in his passing, Hudson's writing is also a genre of its own. In his own way idiosyncratic, off-the-wall, quirky, often bizarre, sometimes surreal, he offers the weird and wonderful insight into the world of flowing football and life in the London fast lane during the roaring seventies. It is as much a perceptive social document as it is a kaleidoscope flashback to the heyday of Osgood, Cooke, Tambling, Baldwin the Sponge, Bonetti the Cat, Chopper Harris and... Alan Hudson.

My good friend, arguably the greatest ever English defender and captain once told me that: Alan Hudson could have conquered the world, perhaps for a time, he did?

Jeff Powell

CONTENTS

1 BIOGRAPHY

Born and brought up near the Kings Road, Alan Anthony Hudson was rejected by boyhood club Fulham as a schoolboy before signing for Chelsea Juniors. Injury denied him the chance to become Chelsea's youngest ever player aged 16 and he eventually made his senior debut 9 months later on 1 February 1969 in a 5-0 loss against Southampton.

Hudson found himself in a Chelsea side noted for its flair and skill, complete with equally flamboyant footballers such as Peter Osgood and Charlie Cooke. It was during the 1969-70 season that he established himself as the team's playmaker, in the midfield of a 4-2-4 formation alongside John Hollins, who was more defensive, creating goals for Osgood and Ian Hutchinson, and enabling Chelsea to finish 3rd in the First Division.

He played in every match in Chelsea's run to the FA Cup final in 1970, but missed the final itself due to another injury when they beat Leeds United 2-1 in a replay at Old Trafford, having drawn 2-2 at Wembley. He did, however, play a major role in Chelsea's replayed European Cup Winners Cup final win against Real Madrid in Athens a year later.

The debt burden caused by the building of the then new East Stand at Chelsea resulted in the sale of key players, and a spiral of decline began. Chelsea lost 2-1 to Stoke City in the 1972 League Cup final at Wembley, whilst a falling-out with manager Dave Sexton resulted in both Hudson and Osgood being placed on the transfer list in January 1974. Within a month, Hudson had joined Stoke City for £240,000, and his career with Chelsea was over at the age of 22.

Stoke manager Tony Waddington saw Hudson as the final piece of the jigsaw that would turn Stoke City into genuine championship

1

challengers in 1975. Hudson played some of the best football of his career under Waddington's shrewd leadership as Stoke finished just four points away from eventual champions Derby County in his first season with the Potteries club.

Owing to a ban from international football after refusing to tour with the England under-23 side, Hudson didn't make his England debut until 1975, when sparkling performances earned him two call ups by then England manager Don Revie. He starred in the team that beat World Champions West Germany 2-0 at Wembley, and then in the 5-0 destruction of Cyprus. However, injuries and clashes with Revie meant that those two caps were the only ones he earned.

Financial troubles at Stoke forced Hudson's sale to Arsenal in December 1976 for £200,000. He helped Arsenal reach the 1978 FA Cup Final, which they lost 1-0 to Ipswich Town, but differences with the Arsenal manager Terry Neill meant that he moved to the Seattle Sounders of the NASL for £100,000 at the age of 27. In the fall of 1979, he signed with the Cleveland Force of the Major Indoor Soccer League. Some sources claimed that Hudson played for the Hércules CF, although the Spanish team denied this.

Hudson returned briefly to Chelsea (then in the Second Division), although illness and injury denied him the chance to play for them again. There was also a nostalgic return to Stoke, where he helped the club avoid relegation from the old First Division in the 1983-84, season.

In that final season you might say that if his first season was although sensational, finished in devastating fashion and, therefore in his last season, although there were no sensations there was devastation, as when he boarded the Manchester bound train is hopes of becoming the next Stoke City manager were as high as that Potteries smoke, but by the time that train pulled into Stoke-on-Trent station, that smoke had vanished, for the man, Mr Frank Edwards, who was going to offer him the job had died in the middle of the night.

Hudson tried several other clubs but they all ignored him to a point of not even allowing him an interview. It seemed that Hudson had more enemies than even he thought.

When he had, in fact, become the total football outcast!

Retirement:

Since his retirement, Hudson has suffered a series of setbacks. He had problems with alcoholism and was also declared bankrupt. In December 1997, Hudson suffered multiple injuries when run over by a car. He spent two months in a coma and the doctors treating him were doubtful as to whether he would walk again, but he eventually completed a full recovery.

His autobiography The Working Man's Ballet was a critical success and led to work as a columnist on the Stoke Evening Sentinel and The Sporting Life. A further book The Tinker and the Talisman was self-published in 2003. In 2004 Hudson appeared as himself in a cameo appearance in the British film The Football Factory.

In June 2006, Hudson joined Radio Napa in Cyprus, where he commentated on the FIFA World Cup in Germany. In 2008 Alan Hudson released his 3rd book titled "The Waddington Years" which described his great friendship with former Stoke City manager Tony Waddington.

It always surprises me that certain sites document that I played for Hercules, but as I always say, the day Ken Friar called me into his office at Highbury and told me of an interest in Spain and, although I hadn't been playing, I had been on-the-run, in fact - I thought he was going to say Real Madrid or Barcelona, but he said, to my amazement, Hercules.

As soon as he did, I thought of Harold Steptoe's horse.

You'll soon read what Michael Parkinson says about both George and I and, there is plenty of truth in what he says, however, those were the sign of the times and in my case, when you admire and try to emulate your idols, you might just get caught up in it all. It is so simple, especially when you are born in such an outgoing environment, in which I was. I would like to think that along with George and the likes of my favourite players such as Osgood, Currie, Bowles and Worthington, we gave more pleasure than those that took more than it gave to the game, for you only have to look at what Bobby Moore gave and what he received in return.

He was ignored whilst the likes of David Beckham, who was a total disgrace in one World Cup, is seen with Prince William jetting off to represent us in our attempt to bring the event here. Absolutely disgusting behaviour by not only the Football Association, but the country in general and, he loves England that much, he names his kids after places in the USA.

George and I, like Bobby, were treated shabbily, anyhow whilst reading Michael keep the following in mind.

2 BEST ON HUDSON

Only a few years back Alan Hudson spent many months in hospital after being knocked over, by a hit and run driver in the Mile End Road. This was very close to the London Hospital, which was handy because if they hadn't got him there so fast he probably would have died. I first heard about the accident when I saw the headline in the paper - HUDSON SMASHED - and thought this to be one of the cruellest headlines ever, as he lay on his deathbed. But maybe just to upset journalists like that Huddy refused to die and over many weeks and months fought himself back to consciousness and then to mobility. He suffered terrible injuries and amazed his doctors with his stamina, strength and determination. They went on record as saying he was extraordinarily fit for a man of his age and that his body was in excellent shape - a statement that was one in the eye of the perceived wisdom that Alan Hudson was a drinker who did not take care of himself. He was actually a drinker who did take care of himself. When in hospital and on the road to recovery a TV team interviewed him sitting up in his bed and the camera zoomed in on a bottle of vodka standing amongst the medicine bottles on his bedside table. "I only drink cranberry juice with my vodka these days. I have adopted a healthy lifestyle," Alan explained in his defence.

I do not believe for one minute that Alan was drinking vodka or any other form of alcohol while in hospital, although knowing him, he probably does believe that cranberry juice does offset any ill-effects of the vodka. He probably would have placed the bottle there to wind-up the interviewers and the audience up. He really does not care one iota what the press or the public think and if they want to perpetuate and believe a certain image of him he will play up to it. It was that obstinate quality of his that led to him not fulfilling his potential in the game, not his drinking or lifestyle. He was possibly the greatest English footballer I played against. But he didn't suffer fools gladly and had no time for imposters or bull-shitters. He wouldn't call a manager 'boss' if he had no respect for them and, if a coach was talking bollocks he'd tell them. Alan has had his differences with Ken Bates although there has been spells over the years when they have got on better. On one occasion Bates was showing Alan around the Stamford Bridge complex when the ground was being redeveloped. Ken was pointing to certain structures and constructions while trying to help Alan visualise how the new stadium would look. "We're determined to recognise the history of the club," said the Chelsea chairman. "Over there we're having a bar named Bentley's after Roy Bentley, the 1955 League Championship hero, and over here is going to be Tambling's after Bobby." Alan was starting to think that the old boy wasn't so bad after all. "And here we're building a bar called Huddy's," Ken slapped Alan on the shoulder as he looked to gauge his reaction. Pride welled up inside him and for once Alan was lost for words, until Bates added that, "I've always been a great fan of Roy Hudd."

3 HUDSON ON BEST

It was in the upstairs bar of Harvey Nicholls - The Fifth Floor Bar - one afternoon whilst enjoying a drink in the company of my two great pals Tommy Nicholson and Malcolm Molineux when a copy of the Evening Standard was brought in. George was on the front page, only this time there was no mention of football or Miss Worlds. It was serious, in fact, very, very serious.

I was still going through my trauma - something that doesn't show. I had been through my early skirmishes all the painful news and emotion that my medical report shows. It is daunting read, but in reality they are more than words. It is not something you can explain to someone who has never been there and, that is what was going through my head at that precise moment, his initial reaction. I knew that George would be going through hell, something I also knew about. Why? Because, he had always been used to having everything fall into place. The best player in the entire world is not something that too many people can boast. Add dating and bedding a few Miss Worlds to this and, you'll find it is not something any man can wake up and call an everyday experience. But this wasn't any man, it was George!

Walking into a bar or restaurant without people staring was not something he was used to. Right now, he was, as I was to witness, all alone and as vulnerable as the man who nobody ever knew or cared about. There were no 60,000 screaming fans adoring his every touch. That was now a blur. It was like watching a movie, one which had gone from an A-listed classic to an unrated Horror.

They even made a movie of him, but once again, they were way off line and, they're always, when making them for all the wrong reasons. Money!

I experienced a similar setback in 1998. I found out just who really cared and just who didn't, however, it was a great experience in so many ways. Maybe that has changed me? The one thing I did learn was that everything has a price. And more importantly, nobody has the divine right to escape death. When I was in hospital and unable to function properly, both in body and mind, I was given the morning newspapers and the front page hit me hard. It read: SINATRA DEAD!

I became numb. A thought flashed through my head. Maybe I'd go with him. I also thought that our paths had crossed whilst in my coma, because I dreamt of him, amongst others. But these dreams were so real. But I couldn't trust my mind around that time, because it was filled with so many things that I have never experienced. I knew one thing though and, that I had been close to death and that was where George was now and, again my mind raced back to first facing him at the Bridge as a young scallywag.

George Best was a freak of nature and, Francis Albert - who also died at birth - was something of the same. Freak may not be the right word, but I cannot think of any other. A one-off or a complete genius, what do you say about such people?

Going back a step, what Tommy said to me, was not an issue. I thought of George on the field, in the Duke of Wellington and Slack Alice in Manchester and, again leaving Ron Harris lying in the mud. How many people could boast that?

It seemed that when he put his mind to it, he could do anything, but the big question and toughest decision now was still to come. All of what he did before was simple, because it was natural.

My strength is my weakness and my weaknesses far outweigh my strengths and, although my strengths may be fewer, they outweigh my weaknesses!

I prefer to think the best of people and, in the main, talk of them. That is why I begin with George Best, who without, my life would be so much lesser, in terms of reaching the stars. Without great people we are nothing. Some people - something that astounds me - love art, as in a gallery. I am the complete opposite, I like to see action. The slow motion of Best flooring Harris, Moore dispossessing Tostao, Jairzinho and Pele, then there was Sinatra unloading a song!

I look at people today with pots of gold and know that the world is upside down. I have no time for talentless people who strike gold and think they are special. Those who talk a good game and get fortunes for it annoy me. Or as young Marcus Kipling wrote to Cameron, "I get cross when I hear how much footballers and politicians get paid." 26.6.2011

He also said, "Do they risk their lives for their country?"
Meaning, those politicians!

And using the word "special," George was just that, whether with the ball at his feet or one Miss World or another on his arm. Well, entering his room, I knew that he was going into his second life, one that was totally new and, one that he would not be able to handle. I can talk of this, because I faced something very similar. After having some tests, a nurse said to me, "You don't want to end up like your mate, do you?"

I walked to the nearest pub, which was the Sporting Life - if you come out of the back gate of the Chelsea and Westminster Hospital, once St Stephens Hospital - you'll literally walk straight into the bar. It was where we used to go after a match on a Saturday, which was then The Red Anchor, where I'll always remember the ravishing Jane Seymour joining us.

On this particular day though, I had a decision to make and, it was simple!

Yeah, I hear you say, how about hearing that you have contacted cancer and, you are right, George was blessed, but as I have said many times, he never asked for this talent, he was given it. But let's not forget that, what he was given he shared with millions of us. There are multi-millionaires and billionaires on this planet of ours who have never shared a penny-piece!

As he did with me, I found out through a newspaper that he was in serious trouble, only there was no driver involved. I read that he was rushed into the Cromwell Hospital with a liver complaint. This not only shocked me but seemed weird, if only for being so close to my favourite nightspot - apart from The La Val Bonne - that being The Cromwellian.

As we stood having fun, George was having tests about a half mile away.

'Everything we did seemed to revolve around pubs and night clubs,' ran through my head. But those good old days were long gone and after my experience in the Mile End Road, it hit home that the Playing Fields had now become the Killing Fields!

My mind then quickly flashed back to when I last saw George. I went to visit him one lunch time in his local pub The Phene Arms, where he was with his new girlfriend. I can't remember her name. I only remember that she was an air-hostess. He seemed reasonably happy, "I feel fine Huddy but a couple of people have said to me that I look a little yellow," he said looking a little confused.

As I left I really never gave it a second thought. Because it never entered my mind that he was unwell. I just thought, George being George, he'd had a heavy one the night before.

However, once reading the piece I turned to Tommy and said, "I must go and see him in the morning," and was quite taken aback when my little friend replied, "But he never visited you once when you were in."

But as the saying goes, "Two wrongs don't make a right," because that is the way I am. The following morning I walked through the doors of the hospital only to be told that George was not allowed any visitors. I understood, and just said to the nurse "could you tell him I called in to wish him well."

As I turned to walk away a chap came towards me and said, "Alan, you can have five minutes." Phil Hughes - a Manchester United supporter - was his agent and he adored his idol, client and good friend. I walked into his room which brought back so many memories of my time in the Royal London and St Bartholomew's and saw the sorry sight of the man who was once the envy of all living men who followed his career.

George sat in the corner in an ordinary cheap pair of tartan-like pyjamas as if waiting to go to the electric chair and, I felt sick, vodka sick, Peter Houseman sick. I bet it was the first time he'd ever worn anything to sleep in, that is if he ever slept?

I asked myself many a time.

But trust me, George looked terrified!

I knew exactly what I wanted to say and, also that I did not want to stay too long, for I knew that when you're in such a place you need time to work out your future and, knowing George, he too needed to be left alone to do so.

Phil was the exception, for he had George's best intentions at heart and, had always looked after him and respected him. All I said to George was that he should - to kill time and take his mind off the inevitable - write a book about his life. There have been several books written about him, but I felt the man on the street wanted to know more about the man himself. We have all heard of his off the field conquests and jokes about "Where did it all go wrong?"

I also told him that I was talking for all of those who adored him in Chelsea!

I would have loved to have written such a book. After all this was the man who had it all, for he was the best player in the world and to go with that, those looks that drove girls wild and, they weren't just girls, they were the most beautiful women in the world. On top of all of that there was his surname. I mean there were, and still are, many icons in Hollywood who have changed their names. He didn't need to because he was if you'll excuse the song, which I'll mention more than once, 'Simply the Best.'

Yeah, George had it all, now all of all of a sudden he was faced with a brand new world where he had many difficult decisions to make, the most important one being, if he did get a donor would he, or could he quit the Demon drink?

I had faced many of such Demons in my time from 15 December 1997 and found them unlike the ones I faced on the playing fields, mainly in white shirts and, I don't need to tell you who they were.

I also had similar decisions to make in my time when my legs were close to being amputated. But thankfully the C-Clamp came to my rescue, aided by David Goodier, or was it the other way round?

I get really annoyed when people don't show him (George) more respect. It was not his fault that he had so much going for him and, then was struck down by what was although self-inflicted, something that was for someone like him almost unavoidable.

He wasn't someone you'd expect to sit in and watch Crossroads, Coronation Street or Eastenders for God's sake.

Going back to Marcus again, it makes me cross when I see those today earning fortunes, especially those with not an ounce of such a talent!

George had entertained millions and now he was paying the ultimate price. Don't get me wrong, I feel for those suffering from the same complaint and those who he skipped in the queue, but put yourself in his place, would you refuse? You also must take into mind the trauma, I know in my early days although I thought I was all there, I look back now and realise I was living in a daze, those magnificent drugs keeping the reality away from my, by now, very sad existence.

On a brighter note, after reading what George heard of me and Ken Bates, I feel I must tell you of a story you probably have heard, but however, here goes: When George was sitting in Vancouver being interviewed by a very naive Canadian journalist he was asked "How did you end up here?" George as quick as he skipped many a tackle said, "Oh, I was just sitting at the bar in Heathrow Airport and was contemplating a trip to Spain. Then as I walked to the restroom I saw a sign saying: DRINK CANADA DRY so I thought I'd give it a go."

Can you imagine how difficult it was for him to give up a habit of a lifetime?

Not like putting a patch on your forearm to stop smoking. Trying to keep it light hearted, it would have been like Frank Sinatra being told he could not sing anymore and, then he had to spend the rest of his days listening to Des O'Connor. I mean...

Like he said about those cruel journalists, the ones who are the biggest hypocrites on earth, for we have seen them boozing and adulterating on many a trip, yet get back home and write about us.

We were very much alike and loved the same things. We even shared the same local pub at one time or another, me in the Seventies, and he in the Eighties when he was wooing them at Craven Cottage for the team I once supported as a kid, Fulham.

The Duke of Wellington in the 70s was like George, the best!
But that was only because of the Petros family who ran it for the Mercer's and, they were a brilliant bunch who we shared many a happy hour with.

But, unlike me, he was hardly ever plagued with injury, which for someone who, like Lionel Messi today, weaved his way through so many flying boots, which was something close to miraculous, but then again, that was George Best, arguably the greatest entertainer this country will ever have the pleasure to see.

The other special quality he had was that I never heard him say anything bad about people, for there are many people who I have come across, who are pretty good at that. He also never boasted about his conquests on or off the field. Although at times we quizzed him when in his Manchester Night Club after we had mugged them again at Old Trafford. The funniest Miss World story was about Marjorie Wallace, who went to his club with a chaperone and left without her fur coat. We'll never know what else she left without, but that's George and, I'll leave that to your imagination!

To George, life was like a dream, only he lived it.

But now, we were both in the same boat, although, I was getting over the trauma, whereas he was experiencing it at this moment in time and, if we shared the same boat, it would no doubt have been the Love Boat, because we both loved life.

We even had surgeons of the same name, and like George they were geniuses.

Their names were Williams!

4 BLUE MOON

HIS EARLY YEARS

Matthew Harding was born in Haywards Heath, West Sussex, the son of Paul Harding, an insurance executive. He attended Abingdon School in Oxfordshire, but did not enjoy the school ethos. He did however return to the school just weeks before his death to speak to a small group of sixth formers about his road to success. He left school with a single 'A' Level in Latin and went to London.

MAKING HIS FORTUNE

Through his father's friendship with Ted Benfield, he joined the insurance brokers Benfield, Lovick & Rees and it was in the insurance industry that he made his fortune, starting out by making the tea and going on to be a director. By 1980 he had acquired a 32% stake in the company, becoming a millionaire and one of Britain's 100 richest men.

FORTUNE

The inheritance will be divided according to instructions left with two executors, Mark Killick and Margaret Nugent. Their instructions are to include provision for his twin sons by his wife Ruth and for Ella, his daughter by girlfriend Vicky Jaramillo. In the will Mr. Harding, aged 42 at the time of his death, also names Jessica, MS Jaramillo's daughter from a previous relationship. The shareholders in his former business, The Benfield Group, will also benefit. Mr. Harding organised a successful management buy-out of the company in 1988. The will was witnessed by England football coach, Glenn Hoddle and by a London taxi driver called Grant Davis.

CHELSEA FC

A lifelong Chelsea fan, Harding responded to Chelsea chairman Ken Bates' call for new investment in the club in 1994 and invested £26.5m and joined the board. However, his time there was marked by frequent clashes with Bates, club chairman and majority shareholder, a man in many respects Harding's antithesis, over the new direction to be taken by the club. Ken Bates eventually banned Harding from the Chelsea boardroom and effectively limited his input and influence over the club. The dispute between Bates and Harding was continual and was only stopped after his death in 1996. However Bates would not let it rest, by causing more controversy which he was well known for now, by upsetting many Chelsea fans, friends and family of Harding in 1997 by calling him a vile man, just a year after his premature death.

PERSONAL LIFE

Mr. Harding had 4 children with wife Ruth, and later on a daughter named Ella with Ecuadorian girlfriend, Vicky Jaramillo.

DEATH

Harding died in a helicopter accident in 1996, after flying back from a Chelsea match away to Bolton Wanderers, along with the pilot and three passengers, including the journalist John Bauldie and Raymond Deane.

OUR LUNCH

My son, Allen, and I dined with Matthew ten days before this tragedy. He was a true gentleman and, rare breed of football director, who truly loved his football and his football club. Chelsea Football Club was his life and soul and, he lost both through that love. I would go further than that, saying that he wore his heart on his sleeve, for it was more like on his forehead, with the worlds of his beloved team etched classily for all to see, he was that proud. The last words out of his mouth to me was "Alan, I'll just have to wait till he dies," and, he was talking of Ken Bates, who he was having absolute murders with and, as with my tragedy, I truly believe that there could have been a case of "foul play."

I am not the only person who thinks this, but as usual, the only one who would openly say it.

The story I liked was after his death Ken Bates tried to employ his driver, as to "pick his brains" but the chap refused his offer as for his respect for Matthew.

The reason I like the story is because of just how it all came about. One lunchtime Matthew was in a rush coming out of the front gates of the Bridge and hailed a black cab and, and the cabbie asked "where to Guvnor?"

Harding replied without hesitation, "Brighton," jumping into the back seat without a second thought.

I think that is where he was living. Anyhow the driver took him there and as requested, he wasted no time. When getting to his destination Matthew was impressed so much, that he asked the cabbie "why didn't you want to see my money, as you have no idea if I had any," in which the man said, "You have an honest face, mate." Matthew then asked if he liked his job and once hearing his reply told him to put his cab away and gave him the money to buy any car of his choice and, from there on in he became his personal chauffeur for the years to come.

Matthew knew - because he never forgot where he came from - that this man could be trusted. He was a "working class hero" himself and, was going to one day run the club. He could have set his sights higher and gone into the FA offices with his fortune, that was still growing, but there was - like with Tony Waddington - only one club (team) for him. I said some time ago, that, along with Tony Banks and Allan Phillips, who'll you'll hear of later, that had they have been Stoke City supporters, for later on down the road - when the roof blew off the stand at the Victoria Ground - I would have introduced them to Tony and, along with Matthew, they would have built a wonderful heart-warming relationship. But crazily, they all died and left me here - although I was the one more likely to do so - to tell their story.

Now Matthew would take an entirely different route and kept Greenhoff and me, just as he would have done with me and Osgood, which would have saved the club from the disaster that actually happened.

It's basically called common sense.

And, he would have done so with his own money. You see, that is the big difference here. Everything he did, he did with HIS money and, he is the only man I've ever known in all my life in football to do such thing. Those at Chelsea, Stoke City, Arsenal, Seattle Sounders and England (FA) are football vampires, but Matthew stood alone and, that is why I admired him so much.

The saying, "it always happens to the good guy," springs to the forefront of my mind and, as I said, alongside Waddington, not only would he still have been alive, but would have kept Stoke City at the top of the pile, with his money.

I mention still being alive, because since I first saw the wreckage on GMTV I had the gut feeling that this, like mine, was no accident!

Today the club (Stoke City) is run by BET365 and ran well, but this man was much more than just an owner, for his passion went beyond belief.

Like I say of the likes of Stan Bowles, Tony Currie, Frank Worthington, Peter Osgood and myself, in those days, we gave much more to the game than the game gave to us and, like Mathew, never boasted about it, whereas Bates boasted that he bought Chelsea Football Club for a £1 - the stingy bastard - and was very lucky that the Russian came along in his hour of need.

Matthew was a man of great stature and standards and, his greatest asset was not his money, but his love for not only the team but the fans that stood by his side in the old North Stand and in The Imperial Arms, never forgetting his roots.

Had Abramovich had come along and Matthew had been there, I can assure you he would have been turned away, for there was no way he would have allowed an outsider to claim that title above the door.

He told me over that lunch that "I always had a cheque made out for £6million in my inside pocket just in case I received a call from the club saying they wanted to sign a player and, if he agreed with the player the cheque would be signed personally from his account. Even when Bates banned him from the tunnel area, which was so totally absurd!

That was as low as one can get and, Matthew did not deserve such treatment...

For instance he loved two players who he would have loved at the Bridge, one was Matt Le Tissier and the other was Glenn Hoddle, who he eventually lured to his football love nest.

Had Matthew been at the club as a director in the early 70s there was no way you would be reading what is to follow. He, like I still do, would have thought it unthinkable to sell both Peter Osgood and I. He would have given the manager full backing along with an ultimatum, "sort this out, or you must go," of that I am certain, because like the man I was to join, he knew that allowing your best players to leave would not be in the best interest of the football club.

I would call Matthew Harding a football saint, sent down from above and, that was what was so very tragic, for they took him back there far too soon. As when Betty Shine told me that when I went flying by my father and Leslie on that cloud, they laughed at me, as to tell me they were not ready for me and I had some unfinished business and, if that was the case, it is a total mystery as to them taking him, for he had, I believe, much more to do than I have.

Although, I never knew him as well as I would have liked, because of my contempt for the club, I would dearly have loved to have been around to have seen him take over, if only to experience his deep desire to make Chelsea Football Club something they can never become. They simply are not a part of the Chelsea where I was born and, therefore no club with a Russian owner and American chairman could ever be a part of such a community.

There are some things that money just cannot buy and, that was the big difference Matthew already had the love and was building his fortune to add it to such a love.

Those before, and since, were and are not in the same league as this man, a man I never knew existed in our game and, this is what made it such a tragedy.

The reason I write this is because he is the only man at Stamford Bridge that I have met, since a 13-year-old, who put the club before himself.

When I was first introduced to Matthew, in the Chelsea dressing room, someone said to him, "You've met Alan Hudson haven't you Matthew?" In which he replied, of course, I've known him for years," although I had never came across him or seen him in my life. What he meant was that he knew every single player that passed through those gates and pulled a blue shirt over their heads. I was no different than any one of those and, once they left, including Greaves, Osgood and me, they were, although still in his heart and memory bank, were now gone and lost forever. He was only interested in those that were currently wearing his shirt.

In a cynical world that the world of football is, Matthew really did stand alone as a football fan come director and, the closest man ever to come close to him was a wonderful chap, Vince Coluccio, the owner of Seattle Sounders. I don't like football people on the top floor, but these two men, not only put them to shame, but walked with all comers. They're as comfortable in the Board Room as they were in the local pub amongst their fellow pilgrims.

The most hurtful thing for me about Matthew's passing is that long with Tony Banks he was the last person I liked there and, someone worth going there for.

And nobody will ever know, that had that tragic day never come along, Roman Abramovich would have landed at his original destination, White Hart Lane and his name would never have been linked with Stamford Bridge, for Matthew would have never have allowed that to happen. Chelsea belonged to him and those from Chelsea, those he drank with before matches in the Imperial Arms. But again, like with players, spectators never give him a second thought. He was the man that carried that £6m cheque around in his inside pocket for Chelsea Football Club, not Russian money or Sky Money, but his own hard earned money, that was Matthew.

I sometimes think about going to the Bridge and having lunch with both Tony and Matthew on a match day and then the reality of it all hits me...

I am quite proud to be able to include this piece at the beginning of my book and, keeping in mind that he was going to read The Working Man's Ballet and give me his views, regretfully I never got to hear his verdict. His death was not only tragic, but cruel, in a world, where people like him only come along once in a Blue Moon.

What you are about to read next is the beginning of my second life, eight days after putting pen to paper for my saviour Tony Waddington and, about three weeks after I had a complete nightmare against the same opposition. This was the day I knew that I met my maker and, the man who would turn me back into a real player, the one my dad groomed as a young boy setting out looking for a future in a game he loved so very much, but I never knew then that love would go beyond that by meeting this man and, one of my great regrets is that their paths never crossed, for if they had it would have been like a clash of the Titans, only one in red and one in blue and, although in two different offices, in the same world of both football and humanity.

Along the way I use the word jigsaw puzzle and to piece together the perfect football club. These would have been the first two pieces to fit into place and, then there was me and Osgood, who both men would not have ever allowed to leave.

Anyhow, this was the match that started my love affair with both Tony and, the Victoria Ground:

RIDGWAYS		HANLEY
RECORDS AND		GARAGE
RADIOS	**Evening**	WOLSELEY – MG
80 PICCADILLY,		and VANDEN PLAS
HANLEY		Telephone S-O-T
		25523

No 34,010 Telephone Stoke-on-Trent 29511 SATURDAY 19 JANUARY 1974

SOCCER RESULTS AND MATCH REPORTS in BACK

HUDSON'S THE BOY!

Crowd rise to Stoke's new signing

BUT 32,789
SEE
LIVERPOOL
STOKE CITY

By Peter Hewitt

Soccer began to boom again in the Potteries with Alan Hudson, £240,000 midfield capture from Chelsea, the magnet as Stoke City challenged League champions Liverpool before their biggest gate of the season at the Victoria Ground.

Hudson stepped out for his pressure debut to form a new midfield partnership with John Mahoney and Alan Dodd as Stoke set out to end their run of five games without a win at home against Liverpool.

Liverpool still eight points behind in their challenge to pacemakers Leeds United had an unchanged line-up, with Tommy Smith, who almost joined Stoke on loan, retaining the right-back position for injured Chris Lawler.

Hudson, who earned a standing ovation from the crowd as he stepped out, was playing his first game for three weeks since his last appearance for Chelsea against today's rivals.

Teams:-
STOKE CITY: Farmer, Marsh, Pejic, Dodd, Smith, Bloor, Robertson, Greenhoff, Hurst, Hudson and Mahoney Sub: Hazlegrave.
LIVERPOOL: Clemence, Smith, Lindsay, Thompson, Lloyd, Hughes, Keegan, Cormack, Heighway, Waddle and Callaghan Sub: Boersma.
Referee: Mr. Siddle of Bristol

Bloor stepped in to stop Heighway following a good cross-ball by Callaghan and then Hudson showed his skill as he turned neatly in the middle to find Pejic, whose high cross was easily held by Clemence.

18

Hudson then combined swiftly with Mahoney to find Greenhoff, only for Lloyd to win the tackle and, then a long ball from Tommy Smith saw Waddle heading down to Hughes who powered over.

Clemence snatched the ball away from Greenhoff following a Robertson cross and two superb passes by Hudson.

A Hudson free-kick flicked on by Hurst was headed into the hands of Clemence by Greeenhoff with Stoke beginning to play with more confidence up front although the game was evenly poised.

Hudson raced back to tackle Waddle, with Smith completing the clearance, and it seemed that Stoke's expensive newcomer was settling down easily and was always looking ready to set up a move.

He had the crowd applauding after 25 minutes when a quick burst in a short one-two with Greenhoff produced a clear shot, that Clemence finger-tipped just round a post.

A mistake by Pejic allowed Keegan to break clear and find Hughes, whose powerful drive from the right was angled rather too much to the relief of Stoke.

Hudson had to concede a corner to cut out a cross by Waddle with the Stoke defence appealing in vain for off-side, while at the other end Robertson made a promising left-wing run and forced a corner off Lloyd. But there was still little to choose between the two teams.

Hudson was directly involved in a series of short passes which ended with Hurst shooting over from a Robertson cross, while Pejic had to dive full length to clear a Callaghan cross in an evenly matched first half.

Half-time: Stoke City 0 Liverpool 0.

A right-wing run by Robertson, when he took on Lindsay and Hughes, produced a free-kick against Hughes. Robertson swung the ball into the box where Hudson darted in to try a first time shot that ricocheted out of the packed Liverpool defence to Hurst who flashed the ball home.

The Stoke crowd were rising to Hudson with every immaculate pass, but then City were caught in trouble when Cormack beat a hesitant Marsh on the left and Hughes came up to take the ball on and drive into a crowded goalmouth. The ball bobbed around, with Dodd only half clearing, and eventually Keegan netted but the goal was disallowed for hands against Waddle.

Stoke had a fierce fight on their hands to hold out and their defenders were tackling bravely. Then Robertson forced Liverpool back to produce yet another corner. Robertson had a fine chance to score in the closing seconds when he was sent clear by Hurst, but aimed his shot past the post.

Then came a final fling by Liverpool in injury time and it was Tommy Smith who levelled the score. A high cross by Boersma was a shade too long for Farmer, who could only fingertip the ball behind him, and Smith was on the spot to turn the ball home. Former Wolves manager Stan Cullis was heard on the BBC radio saying that it was "The finest debut I've ever seen."

Below this match report was a picture of Peter Osgood with the words: Peter Osgood - the subject of intense transfer speculation - leaving the North Staffs Hotel for this afternoon's match at the Victoria Ground - exclusive picture taken by Sentinel's Chris Coxon.

That point moved Stoke City up to 7th from bottom, level on points with Chelsea and Tottenham with 22 points. Below those three were West Ham, Birmingham, Manchester United and Norwich.

Stoke City were to play Manchester United in the very last match of the season, which was two days after City had beaten Chelsea on the Saturday to keep them in the running for a UEFA Cup place, while United were relegated on the same day when a Denis Law back-heeled goal sent them down at Maine Road, Manchester.

On this particular day the back page of the Sentinel showed there were eight draws in Division One….Everton 0 Leeds 0 - Man Utd 1 Arsenal 1 - Chelsea 1 Derby County 1 - Southampton 2 QPR 2 - Newcastle Utd 1 West Ham 1 - Birmingham City 1 Man City 1 - Norwich City 1 Wolves 1 - with only Tottenham taking both points against Coventry City. Burnley v Sheffield United and Leicester v Ipswich were late kick-offs.

Leeds United were top by seven points. They went on to win the championship and we were to play them in the first match of the following season, that match being Brian Clough's first in charge, after Don Revie had taken the England post. Tony Waddington had been offered the position at Leeds before Clough, but turned it down recommending Terry Venables, Tony was also offered the Manchester United job.

Page 5 read: ALAN HAS PLENTY TO LIVE UP TO! "He has everything a class player should have - skill at speed. Not goal hungry enough." That was the George Eastham file on Alan Hudson when he compiled a dossier on Chelsea before the 1972 Football League Cup final.

At 22, Hudson has the soccer world before him. In the last four years he has packed enough experience to satisfy most players in their life, with five under 23 caps, a Wembley League Cup final appearance and a European Cup Winners Cup winners' medal in 1971. He has had the heartbreak of injury when Chelsea had their two incredible FA Cup finals with Leeds United and a permanent reminder from Sir Alf

Ramsey of his ability. Sir Alf pitched him into the under 23's after only 30 League matches at the age of 18. One year later his Chelsea manager said, "If England want an outstanding midfield organiser, Alan is a natural. He has so much going for him he's going to be world class. He has a tremendous physique, skill on the ball, strikes it quickly and accurately and has stamina and pace. He is the fastest fellow on my books and we have a few who can shift. He has a powerful shot and we encourage him to use it more. Under pressure he does not disappear and he is back there defending, for he is a team player." The tribute is remarkable, but that is why Stoke paid £240,000 for a complete player. He has had a nightmare two years when his career stood still as Chelsea bought Steve Kember from Crystal Palace, hoping for more skill and control but they did not blend. A three year England ban, now lifted, hardly helped, neither did a series of injuries. As for the Osgood saga, he came into the area on Thursday evening and contacted Hudson through Geoff Hurst. The three of them shared a night out in The Place Mate in Newcastle-under-Lyme, last seen leaving at 2am on Friday morning. Hardly the perfect preparation for Hudson's debut against the English champions, but that was him. Hudson always said that Osgood is the best centre-forward he's ever seen and wanted him desperately to follow him to Stoke City. That was no doubt the topic of conversation on Thursday 17 January 1974.

Ted Drake, the first manager to win a championship with Chelsea back in 1955, said of Osgood, "He has that exceptional flair that lifts him above ordinary players. He is at last realising his full potential and, I think the time has come to establish himself in the England side and develop into a truly world class player." Drake should know, for he played centre-forward for both Arsenal and England and was rated very highly.

Alan has the last word: I know it is strange to begin a book in this manner, but if ever there was one match that was life-changing, it was this match against Liverpool. I had only played against them three weeks earlier and, on that showing I was not worth £24 let alone adding a few zeros onto it.

As for my mate, I truly believe had Osgood joined me at Stoke City - and Tony Waddington in particular - as Alf Ramsey once said of me, "There was no limit to what he might have achieved." I agree with Ted Drake he would have conquered the world and, had he had listened to me Stoke City would have won their one and only championship in 1975, and that really would have been something more to build on. I think had Gordon Banks not had that car accident - losing an eye - it might have swayed him!

Just might?

You might say, just another one of those mysteries in this book.

5 WHEN IS AN ACCIDENT NOT AN ACCIDENT?

Since the 15 December 1997 I now live from day to day. After that night in the Mile End Road, that is exactly what this experience taught me. In fact, whilst I was still under the knife, I should have been preparing for a meeting. Instead of being carved up. I should have been talking about getting more work in a job I was now enjoying tremendously. Working for Tom Clarke at The Sporting Life was like working for Tony Waddington and, for the first time for a very long time I was enjoying waking up. Although many a time, I wondered who was next to me. My wife had several personalities. The one I loved was hidden most of the time. The saddest thing, like in any relationship, she'll never know how much I loved her and, I find that something in life so sad.

My Editor Tom Clarke was always of fantastic help. If I ever needed a reference he was only too willing to assist me. Tom was cute, knowing that it was also good for his newspaper. I had been the special guest of his on that dreaded day at a Sporting Luncheon. When I say special, I mean I was fortunate to be sitting next to him. With Tom on one side of me and Jamie Osborne, on the other, I left all of the problems at home and, that was the only place I had any. Once walking out of Annie Besant Close, I can only imagine what it was like being freed from an asylum. It seemed that apart from being on the playing field, this was where I was happiest. I loved being amongst great people. When around such people, I simply forgot about all of my problems and at this particular time I had many.

As I go over this, for the last time, Jamie Osborne has just won the Cesarewitch with Never Can Tell with the magical Frankie Dettori aboard his horse. I'm delighted for him!

Working for Tom was different, for as I say he was like Waddington, he gave me carte-Blanche and, like Tony loved the way I played Tom loved the way I wrote. I remember one day he called me into his office and said, "Are you trying to get me hung?" before laughing his head off. I knew I was doing well because whenever I went racing, race- goers would pull me up and compliment me, unlike with football fans, as they're so fickle, never seeing past their own team. Only just the other night 6.9.2011 they were at it again. The media and fans were screaming about how "we were this" and "how we are that," when in the last minute Welshman Robert Earnshaw missed a glaring chance.

That would have made it 1-1 and once again the excuses would begin and, oh how boring they get and, this is mainly because I have been listening to the same old stories since 1970.

Tom, like my Professor, Norman Williams, always reminded me of Tony Waddington. They were both wonderful to work for and socialise with, although I never had the pleasure to buy the Professor a drink. Whilst on the medical side of this, I had several wonderful doctors, consultants and surgeons work on me constantly - mainly to keep me alive in those early exchanges - and here were people being so negative.

I have no time for such things.

My good friend Malcolm Molineux always comments that:
"If you taught me one thing, it was to be positive."

I once wrote in his diary - although not remembering the date - just remembering it was not long before my near fatal experience. What more, when I wrote it, I had no reason to be upbeat about the future, for I was on my very own downward curve, but only my positive outlook got me through such hard times and, incredibly, would finally get me through what you are about to read about.

Apart from losing my parents, my three worse moments in life have involved the game that I was born to play. The game my father breathed life into me. I took his breath, his words, his knowledge and his passion and added it into my small frame and somehow made it to the top.

Those three moments all included finals. The first was the 1970 FA Cup final, which I missed through a wicked (devastating) chronic ankle injury, which led to my missing my second final, this time on much more serious and larger scale (stage), the World Cup finals in Mexico. Last, but not least, was the most incredible thing that has ever happened to me and, was not only life threatening, but changed my life in the kind of way you had to live through to believe. I was close to where I nearly had to toss a coin to decide if I wanted to live or die. I was so nearly faced with such a decision after coming out of that coma in the Royal London's Intensive Trauma Unit. The decision however, was made for me by a machine called the C-Clamp. It was sitting in the corner of the Operating Theatre, without a plug, left by a rep of a company, who had brought it in just a few days prior to my arrival.

David Goodier was quickly running out of options, with the next one being amputation.

The last one would have been a different kind of final, had they taken my legs off. Isn't it scary, to think one moment you're crossing the road, after a lovely day out, and the next you're fighting for your life and, with the help of those brilliant surgeons and consultants that life was now on a knife-edge.

Anyhow, having tried with all of his endeavour and expertise it seemed David was unable to stop the bleeding and all seemed lost when he asked, "What is that machine in the corner?" He was told it was to be used on someone with a condition like mine, although nobody knew entirely. After a telephone call to the company - whose name was written on the front - David asked if it was I working order and, was told, "That is why we left it with you."

So the decision that I would have faced was made for me and, I can only tell you quite seriously and honestly, had the machine not worked and David had taken away my legs, I would have gone ahead with my plan of action to commit suicide. This would have been the easy part, by collecting my drugs for a couple of months and, finally once having collected enough, I would have thrown a party in my room and went through with what would you might call, or Frank might have sung, "My final curtain."

I even worked it out in my mind when learning of the amputation. What with having so much time on my hands all through those dark scary nights, I went through such a plan in my head and came up with committing such an act on my birthday, the 21 June 1998. This would have been halfway through the World Cup, where I was supposed to be working.

I would not, like so many ignorant people, have seen this as a cowards' way out. I think that people who take their own lives are quite the opposite. It takes a brave person to take his life, sick yeah, but brave.

As I go over this book Gary Speed, the Welsh manager, who played for several Premier League teams, has hung himself under the most bizarre circumstances. He was found at 7am by his wife hanging in his garage. The morning before, he was sitting in the BBC studio as a pundit for a match involving one of those teams, Newcastle United.

He looked well and had everything to live for. He had a superb playing career behind him that brought him much fortune and fame. He was, in fact, set-up for life. I have been on the dole queue and know about the other side of life. He was also very well respected by his peers and the tributes from those that knew him made it all the more bizarre. So, that is what I am talking about, nobody knows the state of your mind, the kind of state that would see you hang yourself. To commit such an act is one thing, but a personal hanging, simply terrifying.

And had I woken up after those 59 days to find that the two things, that had been responsible for everything great I had done in my life were all of a sudden missing, would have been totally devastating. I have said it before, although a great pal of mine always called me "brave" throughout my hospitalisation, I am not one for heroics or the Special Olympics - I think those boys and girls are so courageous - I cannot even watch them. If only thinking about what might have been?

The police would have finally had their way and been right, although lying from day one, for on waking I would have been what they put out to the media on 16 December 1997, "legless."

But let's get back to the three things I missed most in my life. I mentioned those two main events I missed through going down a hole in the Midlands, which was nowhere near as dangerous as in the Mile End Road all of these years later. But through Ashgar Fatehi making such a mess of me, I missed the second World Cup that I was going to be involved with, only this time it would not have been alongside my heroes Bobby Moore and Alan Ball. It would have been in a corporate capacity.

I had attended the new French stadium for the following years' 1998 finals with David Brown the man who was employing me. It was for the actual draw. It brought back many great memories, if only for coming across two wonderful players I once played against, the iconic Pele and the majestic Bogecivic. One rated the best player of all time, the other a Yugoslav who was possibly the greatest inside forward I'd ever locked horns with. Both had become legends in New York (with the Cosmos) because of their times hypnotising those who were fortunate to go to Giant Stadium and witness such greatness.

Anyhow, it was great to see Bogie especially at this time, because I needed a lift and just the sight of him elevated me to a different level, if only for all those wonderful matches that came flooding back. Matches where we went head to head and were always not only incredibly tough and energy sapping but enormously enjoyable in so many ways. There is no better feeling coming off the playing field, knowing you've held your own against the very best in the world. It, I can only imagine, would have been like taking Sharon Stone to dinner and, all through it, looking at her and whilst doing so, hoping that something wonderful was going to happen. I just love the foreplay and, I know there is the other side of it, the disappointment, but that is what makes life what it is!

That, like playing against the world's best, is what dreams are made of and, more importantly, fulfilling them!

So from June 10 to July 12, instead of roaming around Paris, I was planning my future - or what was left of it - from my hospital bed in the Frederick Andrews Ward just up the road from Holborn. This place had become quite a central part of my life. It was a few minutes from Fleet Street, where I met my friends from the press and, it was a few m minutes from where I met my second wife and, also another few minutes from where I nearly met my death.

The intended killer had no idea of the history of all of this, for all he knew was that he had to end my life.

A few minutes before Ashgar Fatehi came to commit such an act, my friend Henry and I were in Jamies Bar talking about the upcoming Christmas. He was very upbeat and looking forward to it, telling me that he could not be happier with his partner, whereas I was dreading going home to mine!

Had anyone listened in to our conversation and, then switched the radio on the following morning they just might have believed the police.

Anyhow, on that July evening, instead of being surrounded by 80,000 fans in the Stade de France for the final I was surrounded by my family friends who were forever at my bedside. But even then, I still did not know what kind of fight was ahead of me?

Many thought that once leaving the ITU, I had won my battle.
But as Karen Carpenter once sang, so famously, "We'd Only Just Begun."

The first hurdle was to get into my wheelchair and, in those days, it took my uncle and two male nurses to finally get me there. Walking looked like a haze in the distance and although doctors said I'd never walk again and, being in serious danger of that being true, I could always see through that haze, if only for my single-mindedness. I was never one to give up, even when I knew I was beaten. I have always tried to salvage something out of defeat. A crumb to me is more than the next man's fortune. I had to remind myself that I could have more fun with a hundred pounds in my pocket than the man walking down the Kings Road and unlocking his Bentley. I have seen them and what torments me is that they don't know how to enjoy their wealth and, I come up with the obvious answer. They haven't earned it, whereas we did.

As I said earlier about George, those exchanges with your inner-self can be so very dangerous. A split second decision, in the wrong frame of mind can be a very fine line, especially when the odds are not only stacked against you, but you are going into unchartered waters.

After running the football fields for so many years - not forgetting the many streets - in the early hours of most mornings, there was no way I was going to be beaten by this. After coming through against the likes of Bremner and Giles, there was no way Fatehi was going to get the better of me.

So, by the time I was thrown out of hospital, I had missed my first ever FA Cup final at 18, two World Cup finals at 19 and, now my first ever Christmas. Call me lucky, I don't think so!

Some people feel they're hard done by when they miss a bus, but I have found that my life has become an accumulation of near misses and, those that happen at a time when I was facing some of the most exciting times of my life.

As I have said so many times and something that should be on my headstone "Just when I was...."

It is those misses that convinces me that there are them and there are us and, they will never, ever know....

Fifteen years on, The Working Man's Ballet was seen on E-Bay, where it was sold for forty pounds and, one I saw on there for a grand, please don't ask me why?

That is because of a lack of them being printed after my being hit by Fatehi. What I am about to tell you is that just after the original publication, because of being hospitalised for all that time, I could not promote it, for being in a coma didn't help matters and on waking, after those 59 days, *The Working Man's Ballet* was the furthest thing from my mind. In fact, I had no idea I had written it.

Having said that, slowly - after coming down off the morphine - it started to matter once again, if only for all the wonderful memories inside those pages that kept me going through my darkest days and blackest of nights.

When people compliment me on them enjoying it, I ask them why they thought it to be so good. And everyone says, "Because we know that it was you who wrote it, no ghost writer and nobody putting into their words," and that was the way I wanted it.

One of the things I enjoyed most about writing *The Ballet*, at that time was our game was yet again, on a downward spiral, which made it simple to write. The reason I say that is, once again, my words rang true, as if like a bible, with everything I said then and since, repeatedly coming back to make this book a rare commodity. Why? Because, you, the public, are led to believe throughout all of the years that have passed, that this country still has a chance of winning something. If they couldn't win something with the likes of Bryan Robson, Glenn Hoddle and Paul Gascoigne - our last three world class players since the 60s and 70s - you certainly aren't going to win it with this lot.

The only thing that these players can boast is being filthy rich!
And then there are those lies, cheats, frauds and imposters, who have ruined our game - and some are still in the game - others having walked away with bulging pockets and empty heads. They have destroyed our game. Since Ramsey introduced the 'Wingless Wonders' and Charles Hughes used Lilleshall to brainwash incapable "fools" who attended this building, which had it been in the war, would have been compared to something out of Schindlers List. It was from within these walls they walked away with the dreaded coaching badge. These badges that sent our game back into the stone-ages. The badges that had us failing to reach any World Cup finals in the Seventies.

These were the badges that the likes of Busby, Clough, Waddington, Shankly, Nicholson and Greenwood would have scoffed at. Although the West Ham manager, I think, was a man who believed in such a thing. Okay, somewhere along the way, they might have needed a piece of paper - rather like a driving license - but that was where it ended.

I remember being on show on SKY one night and Dave Bassett said that, "England should play the way clubs play and, use their long ball tactics."

Well, I have never heard such trash. That is the reason we are in the basement of world football. When you think even Denmark won a major competition since 1966 and, we haven't reached a final, I think I need say no more!

However, these great men are gone and all we are left with are the ones still in possession of our game, which is still in decline. As I go back over my notes Real Madrid, Barcelona and Bayern Munich hold three of the four Champions League places with Chelsea being the other, although on Death Row, having to face Pep Guardiola's Catalonic football machine in a daunting two legged semi-final.

I will cheat a little here, because I have come back to tell you that how they beat the Spanish giants, is something, that has me now believing in miracles. Barcelona hit the bar and post on several occasions and Lionel Messi missed a penalty and, apart from that, if you swapped Petr Cech over with their keeper, Chelsea would have been on the end of a landslide defeat.

What I enjoyed most once finishing my first book, was it being hosted by my pal Tony Banks at the House of Commons, but more about that great man later. And then of course, there are plenty about those inside the walls of such a place and their counterparts from across town in Soho Square.

I felt that is was obviously the kind of book that needed rewriting, although I never imagined around that time that it would be because of what you will soon read about, but that apart, according to the E-Bay, the sale of the original book read like this:

The Description: Alan Hudson tells his remarkable story, as unorthodox and inspired as his unique style of the game. The quintessential cockney rebel, Hudson's career was marked by clashes with authority and the establishment. He oozed the kind of hip romanticism, a crystal cool, an essence distilled from Mini Coopers, maxi skirts and the Union Jack lunacy of the Kings Road. If Best was the Beatles, then Hudson was the Rolling Stones, the ultimate Beau Brummel.

Alan has signed this copy of the book on the full title page with the inscription 'To Nick with Best Wishes Alan Hudson.'

In the years to follow, I have not sold one book without it being personally signed!

This new book was to be a follow up and rewritten edition of that particular book, which was very well received of which I was really pleased about. Those reasons being, it was not only my first ever book, it was also because I was under the most immense pressure around that time. But as I was soon to find out, there are so many different kinds of pressures. The pressure to come face to face with the unknown, like most things you'll read about, simply puts everything into its rightful place or into perspective.

And once again, as I said, the most pleasing thing is that when asking people why they enjoyed it so much (the book), they tell me that not only did they love those times, but they knew that it was me telling the stories, no ghost writer, no third party and, more importantly, no punches pulled!

The other reason to write it was only a few months before I went to print I learned that what was called an accident for so long - one that almost cost me my life - I have always thought, was not that at all and, I have been proved right. There is no feeling like a gut feeling and, that apart, I can remember clearly my walk home. I can not only remember my every step, but my absolute feeling of not knowing what my future held. I know my alcohol level was high, but so what, I was not behind the wheel of a car or abusing anyone, in fact, it was me who was to be abused in such an incredible fashion. Whilst enjoying a leisurely walk home on a beautiful December evening, I was scythed down by Fatehi, in a way that never happened to me on the playing field. I had been hit a couple of times from behind in a nasty way, but that was my fault for turning my back on an opponent who was known for his thuggery, but here I was hit from behind by someone who had been paid to do so.

As I mention later, ever since coming out of the Intensive Trauma Unit - after eight-and-a-half weeks - I knew for certain that this was no accident, but nobody else joined me in my believing that. The problem being, ever since being wheeled into the Resuscitation Room in the middle of December 1997 and being wheeled out of the ITU in the second week in March 1998, absolutely nobody, but me, suspected foul play.

If it wasn't for my determination to push myself to the absolute limit you would not be reading about what David Goodier is about to tell you and, this is what he wrote on the 14 December 1998, exactly one day short of a year of being wheeled through those doors of the Royal London Hospital.

6 SOMEONE SAVED MY LIFE TONIGHT

One of my all-time favourite Elton John songs, which he sang in front of me on 21 June 1975 at Wembley, I say that because I was with him the night before and said to him, "You better be good tomorrow mate it's my birthday!" His reply was "Alan, what's it like playing there," in which I told him, "You'll be alright Elton."

This patient was admitted to the Accident and Emergency Department at the Royal London Hospital on 15th December 1997, at 21.15 hours. He had been brought by the London Ambulance Service having apparently been a pedestrian struck by a car. The Trauma Team was called. They saw and assessed him immediately on arrival. It was obvious he had severe multi-system injuries and was confused and thrashing about on arrival. He was immediately anaesthetised, intubated and ventilated. Initial examination noted him to be shocked due to blood loss with an extremely unstable pelvic fracture. There was massive local bruising around his pelvis and into his groin. Various X-rays and CT scans were performed. He had injuries to his head consisting of a frontal extradural haematoma with a depressed frontal skull fracture. He had various fractures to his face consisting of a left blow-out orbital fracture, supra-orbital fracture, a severe Lefort Type III fracture of the maxilla and nasal fractures.

His chest! He had a fractured sternum with multiple rib fractures on the left bilateral haemoneumothoraces.

His abdomen! He had a ruptured left kidney with massive retroperitoneal and pelvic haematoma. His pelvis displayed multiple pelvic ring fractures with complete separation of the right hemi pelvis. His bladder had been severely lacerated.

The most immediate problem was the bleeding from the pelvic injury. There is a complex network of blood vessels at the back of the pelvis which had all been shredded by the fracture and could not clot off as the hemi pelvis was completely unrestrained.

In an attempt to provide some stability, an external fixator was applied to the front of the pelvis with pins driven into the iliac bone connected by two bars running across from one side of the pelvis to the other. It was, however, impossible to control the posterior elements of the injury and the bleeding continued.

He went to theatre where the blood clot was evacuated from his brain but, he continued losing blood and by the morning of 16 December he had had more than 30 units of blood transfused.

By a bizarre coincidence, just a few days earlier, I had been shown a special external fixation clamp by a company representative that was designed to combat the blood loss in precisely this sort of pelvic fracture. The principal was that by applying a force at the back of the pelvis, the blood loss could be contained and active bleeding could be stopped. When I arrived at 08.00 hours on the morning of 16 December, I learned about Alan in our Trauma Meeting. Out of interest I went round to theatre which was being set up to try and block the bleeding vessels by arteriography. I realised immediately that Alan had already lost masses of blood and was no longer clotting properly because of it and decided to use the demonstration model clamp that we had available to try to help.

There was immediate concern as the frame itself said 'sample only' on it, but rapid consultation with the manufacturers confirmed that it was a working model. We applied the C-Clamp in theatre under image intensifier control with dramatic effect in that the bleeding appeared to stop and he was able to maintain a blood pressure without pouring blood into him.

After consultation with the Urologists and Vascular Surgeons, it was felt that his urological injuries should be treated by a catheter. The Vascular Surgeons opened his left groin to perform arteriography via the right femoral artery and this showed no active arterial bleeding with the C-Clamp in situ.

He was admitted into the Intensive Care Unit at 12 o'clock on 16 December 1997. He continued severely unwell and his legs swelled due to deep venous thrombosis. The pressures in the compartments of his legs rose dramatically, jeopardising his circulation further and it was obvious he would need to return to theatre for decompression of the swollen legs by fasciotomies (slitting the entire length of the upper thigh and both sides of the calf of both legs to allow the muscles to swell).

I recorded in my notes that I have spoken to his wife and said: "the head injury may cause brain damage but it is too early to tell. The chest is very likely to get infection with adult respiratory distress syndrome. The kidneys are damaged, will need dialysis. He may require laparotomy. Will need external fixation of the pelvis and internal fixation of the face and will need further surgery to the scrotum."

I explained the procedure necessary to relieve the pressure on his legs and told her: "He may die if he gets sepsis or multi-organ failure." It was felt by all involved in his care that this was highly likely at this point but that we should continue doing everything to try to prevent this.

The only positive side was that the monitoring bolt left in his brain to keep an eye on his intracerebral pressure was not showing signs of severe brain damage.

He went to theatres on 17 December for his fasciotomies but during the procedure had severe lung complications probably due to blood clot from his legs travelling to his lungs. Despite being on 100% oxygen forced in at positive pressure, he continued with poor oxygen saturation. To prevent further blood clots, Dr. Otto Chan, Consultant Trauma Radiologist, was called and inserted a plastic filter into the inferior vena-cava to prevent blood clot going up to the lungs from the legs. This procedure was normally performed via the groin but as there was so much local swelling and clotting in both legs, Dr. Chan had to position the filter via a vein in the neck, passing it through the heart into the inferior vena-cava. When the filter was in place, he was able to return to theatres on 23 December where his C-Clamp was removed and the internal fixation of his pelvis performed. Screws were passed across the sacroiliac joints under image intensifier control avoiding the nerves to his legs and fixing the posterior pelvis securely to the sacrum on both sides. Normally a plate and screws would have been applied anteriorly also, but due to the severity of the bladder injuries we felt that it best to leave the anterior external fixator frame in situ here.

All the way through Christmas there were recurrent problems with widespread sepsis which by the 27 December became overwhelming and was affecting the function of his heart and lungs such that it required copious doses of inotropes (drugs to maintain his blood pressure). The pressure of the blood clotted within his pelvis caused a sore to develop over his sacrum on 27 December and it was felt that he had probably perforated his rectum and that infection was spreading from his rectum into the massive amount of clotted blood behind his abdomen. He continued going downhill and discussion centred on whether or not to divert his bowel contents away by performing a colostomy."

The choice rested between performing a colostomy which would require a major intra-abdominal operation and, in the words of the

Consultant Surgeon was 'likely to be fatal' or leaving him alone, in which case it was almost guaranteed to get further sepsis and I commented in my notes that 'unless he is very aggressively managed there is a very high chance that the infection around his pelvis will be fatal. I also realise that intervention in the form of defunctioning colostomy may result in abdominal wall or visceral complications which themselves may be fatal.

He continued on broad spectrum antibiotics and in a conference with his close relatives on 31st December, they were told there was a very good chance he was going to die, but the only option was a defunctioning colostomy. This was performed that day. The large haematoma in his scrotum continued to cause concern and required drainage, but the surfaces continued. He continued very unwell but at a seemingly relatively stable level.

On 5 January 1998 all his wounds from his fasciotomies had healed over but the skin on his scrotum was not looking very well. As he had been sedated and ventilated with a tube for so long it was felt that his throat would be at risk and therefore he had a formal tracheostomy performed on 7 January 1998. This was done in the ITU as he was far too sick to be transferred to theatre.

By the 8 January 1998 he seemed to be improving slightly. The supportive drugs were cut back and the ventilator was maintaining good oxygenation. The colostomy was working and his various wounds were healing slowly. He was on dialysis for his kidneys, had two catheters into his bladder, one via his urethra and one through the anterior abdominal wall. He was on massive doses of antibiotics and had a tracheostomy and required further surgery to his scrotum, rectum, bladder and face, but all in all appeared to be turning the corner and looking less likely to die suddenly.

His infection continued to cause problems. He had a large collection behind his abdomen, and his legs had been opened down the entire length. He had a colostomy and had previously had bilateral chest drains all of which were potential sources of infection.

He was well enough by the 13 January to go to theatre for exploration of the various wounds and draining of the large collection of old infected blood from his pelvis fracture lying behind his abdomen. On 14 January the anterior fixator was slackened to assess the stability of his pelvis. Despite the front part not having healed completely, was stable enough to allow removal of the external fixation and a CT scan was organised of his pelvis. The blood clot filter was removed from his inferior vena-cava on 16 January. He had further debridement of dead tissue around his scrotum on 20 January. At this point he was reasonably stable from a cardiovascular point of view but still with severe wound problems. On 22 January he was reviewed by the Neurophysiologists who diagnosed widespread damage to the lumbosacral plexus of nerves due to his injuries.

It was felt on these results that complete recovery was highly unlikely and that although he might regain some upper limb function, it was likely that the lower involvement to his legs was so severe that he would probably never walk again.

He returned to theatre many times for clearing out septic and dead tissue from the pelvic space, but on the 4 February 1998 his sedation was stopped to allow him to gradually wake up. Over the next few days he gradually awoke and started speaking still with his tracheostomy in situ. On 12 February 1998, after 59 days on the Intensive Care Unit, he was transferred to a regular ward. The speech therapists, dietician, renal team and general orthopaedic surgeons and urologists all still maintained a close watch on him.

His upper limb function continued to improve and some gross movements were starting to return in his lower limbs. The neurophysiological studies on 26 March 1998 showed that he still had severe damage to his lumbosacral plexus of nerves but there had been significant recovery, although some nerve damage, particularly to the nerves to his feet, persisted and was likely to be permanent.

He was transferred to the Specialist Urology Unit at St Bartholomew's on 3 April 1998 where his rehabilitation continued slowly. He continued with problems with his colostomy, the wounds in his groin area, his bladder rupture, his urethral fistula and the nerve recovery in his legs.

I last saw him in out-patients on 24 November 1998. His memory of the accident and his time on the ITU was understandably virtually non-existent, but despite some weakness and particularly loss of nerve function in the right foot, he managed to walk into clinic.

I doubt he will ever get complete nerve recovery on the right and will probably have an area of numbness affecting this side of the calf and the big toe with inability to lift up on the foot on the right side. The left side is recovering but may take another year before it does so completely and he is left with stiffness of his hips, knees, ankles and feet which will require a lot of physiotherapy to overcome and also will not recover completely. He has further surgery to his rectum and bladder, but overall his recovery thus far has been nothing short of spectacular, but in no small amount of this is due to the dedicated team of Anaesthetic and ITU consultants, Registrars, Senior House Officers, Nurses, Physiotherapists, Speech Therapists, Dieticians, Urologists, General Surgeons. Colorectal Surgeons, Orthopaedic Surgeons, Microbiologists, Renal Physicians and many other specialists of all grades and qualifications who had an active part in his management.

David Goodier MBBS FRCS Orthopaedic
Consultant Orthopaedic Surgeon

Since all of this took place, I have lost my mother through cancer and it is something I cannot believe I took so well. I think maybe because I died a couple of times in the ITU, I think that dying is okay? I really don't know? Or was it because I thought I could be seeing her sooner rather than later? It is that living from day to day syndrome, as if it were your last, just maybe? Not long before, my cousin Harry Yewings went through the same illness. He was a great bloke and, like my best friend Leslie, who died tragically before my tragedy, they were, as I mention very soon, the people who made Chelsea what it used to be. I'll mention Leslie later.

On the 23 of February 2011, I received a telephone call from the wife of a very dear friend. It was Irene Nicholson. She rang to tell me that her husband Tommy had died the night before. I was stunned, shattered and numb, although I knew when I heard her voice, for it was the first time she had ever called me.

When I came round from the ITU he would tell me of how he held my hand and spoke to me and how I responded by opening one eye. The way he told me cracked me up, but that was nothing new, because that was something he had off to a fine art. I will never know if he was kidding me?

To ease the blow, but only slightly, I can't begin to tell you of the laughs we had together. The times we spent were precious. I visited all of his pubs since being lucky enough to have been introduced to him. The Cartoonist being the most famous - the place where I got back together with Ann, the wife who left me in my hour of need. She worked as a barmaid both in his pub and an afternoon club around the corner run by John Mullally - I liked him, even though I think he was part of their plot? - and a cop, ex-CID in fact. It was, I must say, as good a club as you'll ever frequent and I liked John. He was full of himself and very loud and brash, but I find in certain people that is sometimes a weakness in their character. I prefer the man who says little, but whilst doing so, says so much, Tony Waddington-like.

Vagabonds always had good looking girls working the bar and Ann was one of them. In fact, she was by far the best looking, which made her very popular.

She caught my eye immediately, although I was on my best behaviour, even though my first wife Maureen was miles away. I was visiting London from Seattle and that was where Maureen was at that particular time. I returned to Seattle thinking about her, but never let on that I fancied her, something that was totally innocent and, any hot blooded man worth his salt who would have told me different would have been a liar. And then things were going wrong in my marriage and I wrote to her.

Of course I was not easy to live with, mainly because I am addicted to enjoying myself.
My biggest problem, I think, is in believing we should be happy no matter what.
Once again, my strength is definitely my weakness!

I think a part of all of this, looking back, is when leading such a wonderful life, which was all down to my natural ability to play the game, I never once heard her (my wife) say "thanks." It may sound quite silly, but I don't think I ever heard her say that I had played really well. Like the Liverpool match I mention later I was walking on air after Shankly paid me my finest ever compliment, however my wife said nothing. Had it been her, say performing at the Palladium with Sinatra, I would most certainly have let her know my feelings. She never once said that she was proud of such a performance, maybe it's me, but I feel you must let the one you love know. Unless I only thought she loved me?

But back to Tommy, who I would get together with in this place almost every afternoon and, we had some quite memorable times, that I can promise you. And incredibly, I also shared time with the manager that I walked out on. It was the place where he apologised to me, but more about him later.

Tommy, who was a character and a half, also helped him (Terry Neill) out when moving into his bar just around the corner. He and Irene - who spent her life in the kitchen of all of their pubs - also ran pubs in other parts of London which I frequented whenever I could. One was in Kinnerton Street, just along from the famous *Nags Head* where he also stole the show.

Anyhow, it was Irene who put the call in and, it stunned me in more ways than one, for Tommy and I had been talking about getting together and, I think my last words to him were, "we must Tommy, because you know what will happen?"

And it did, the only difference was it was much more likely to be him coming to my wake!

This is not an obituary, it is me just saying how sorry that we never got to get together beforehand. I loved Tommy. He was one of those men when someone dies it hits you, 'Oh no, I'll never see him again!' I felt exactly the same way whilst sitting at the bedside of Tony Waddington, only it was different, if only for being with him just before he left us.

And like Tony, Tommy was such a joy to be around. He carried the kind of joy that was so infectious. If you did not like Tommy, then you did not like life…

I promise you that I never saw him down, miserable or dejected and, I might be right in telling you that he is the only man I can say that about. He lifted me on many occasions. He would outdo me on occasions and, even did so when I invited him to help me - I only wanted his company - in a coaching school that I put on with Don Shanks, Frank Worthington and Chris Garland. He was not only brilliant company in the bar afterwards, which went without saying, the kids took to him like a fish to water. He was, you might say, "A Man for All Seasons," and, I can only imagine Irene will miss her soul mate.

I started this by saying about my mother dying of cancer. My friend (Tommy) was fighting the same terrible disease when finally beaten by a heart attack.

I went to his funeral (3.3.2011) in Birkdale. It was strange. It was quiet. I was disappointed. It was the only time I went to visit him and it was gloomy, dim gloomy. In the church, the thought of his laughter helped me hold back the tears. I prefer funerals (wakes) to weddings for they are a celebration of someone's life and, if you had lived a life as Tommy had done, you most certainly deserved a celebration. Right up to the final moment of being inside the church, I really was waiting for the coffin to open, that was what he was like. But it never happened and my sadness and disappointment grew further. I only wished that I could have organised his service and departure, although he will always be with me. As I write I look on my sideboard and see his face with the words: To Celebrate the Life of Tommy Nicholson…well, they didn't!

The tear I shed on that morning seemed like my last.

On the way home I said to my friends, Jim and Sheila that I could not believe how sedate the affair was - and it was. I expected a real big celebration and, as I just told you, when they carried the coffin out, I thought Tommy would push the lid up and start singing. When he didn't, it hit me that he was gone. And he was, but never to be forgotten.

My final memory of it all was his mate Gerry Marsden singing the incredible "You'll Never Walk Alone," one of the greatest songs ever written and performed by Gerry, although sang quite beautifully by Sinatra!

I said to Irene, "isn't life strange love, thirteen years ago there was he thinking he was about to attend my funeral and here I am, at his?"

He was passionate about his football and his music. He loved them both, although his first love was Irene. He loved life itself and, that is why he was a big part of the Working Man's Ballet. It would be absolutely stupid to say that I am glad he died when he did, but I am glad it wasn't a few days after I went to print because I want everyone reading this book to know what a special part of my life he was. He stood alongside all the great people mentioned inside these pages. And, unlike today's media, managers and players, I don't use the word "great" loosely.

I go on to talk about some very special people in my life, some very famous, some who were well known and then some simply wonderful people. Tommy was one of them, in fact, all of them!

The one thing I'll always remember him for is when in Tampa Bay, Florida, when he and his pal went off to play golf. On the way back they dropped off at the bank to change some money. When in the queue, his mate John told him he was bursting to go to the toilet - of the serious kind. The problem he had was that the only toilets were behind the other side of the counter. John was desperate and pleaded with his mate. Tommy coolly stepped up to the counter and said to the young girl, "excuse me love, but my mate wants to make a deposit." The girl then passed him a deposit slip and a pen. He then told her it was a deposit of a completely different kind and whispered to her.

She pressed the buzzer.

They walked into the bar afterwards and you just knew that Tommy had been mischievous.

He was so quick, always ready with that quick one liner. For that alone he will be missed.

As you read on, I tell you of having to ask myself many questions after coming out of that coma. If this was the last tragedy, of which I doubt, my first would have been as an apprentice when a knee injury threatened my career. Had I not recovered, my career would have been over at the tender age of 16. So, the direction of my life would have changed dramatically.

When I say this, some people think I mean in football terms. But I mean football took me in a direction where I met such people. Some people look at football as a means to earn money. I saw it as a love affair with all of these good things and people in life and, Tommy is a great part of my way of thinking. When you hear the saying that, "Football brings people together" it is true, but then there is the ultimate, because for every so many thousand people I have met through the game, they equate to one Tommy.

Whilst in the darkness of my hospital bed, I thought about all of these things and after experiencing everything that this brutal attempt on my life brought with it, I asked myself, 'would I have given up all of my wonderful memories and experiences not to have gone through the last 15 years?

It is the most difficult question I would ever have been faced with. Rather like the one had they amputated my legs?

I think of Papillon, whose life was made hell, all through injustices that destroyed his soul and his heart, but never his spirit. I feel that my life has been pretty much the same. Again, as you read on, you will find that just when I was about to enjoy success and happiness, someone had other ideas.

When I mention that about Charrier, I say it because it destroyed him, like me, because people were so despicably dishonest, yet they walk the streets unscathed.

The reason I decided to write a book which includes so much of The Working Man's Ballet, was because this all happened to me within six months of bringing the original autobiography to you and, after my last throw of the dice, to find happiness with my wife of six months.

I would have been better off going to the casino, at least it was safer?

The one thing that I will never, ever understand is how it all came about? As I write, I still search for an answer. You might say that my jigsaw puzzle is incomplete and as long as it remains that way, I will try my utmost to piece it together, if given time. The only thing I know for certain is that the secrecy of it all is no more. Alcohol can be such a friend and, at that particular time it became mine, that being when a stranger thought it safe to say, "Alan Hudson was really lucky....well, we'll see?

There is so much more to come…but for now, what you are about to read led me to not only writs another book, but be able to hopefully do something about it. If nothing comes of it, at least I've tried with the greatest will in the world, unlike David Beckham going to represent England with Royalty for a World Cup situation, and - as I write - hold the Olympic flame 18.5.12 it puts my flame out.

Is there no limit to where some people go?

I speak of Bobby Moore and how he was after leading us to our greatest moment in our sport and, look at Beckham and he turns all that greatness and gold into the ashes of a desperate November 5.

I am just so absolutely thrilled that I knew Bobby Moore, for I knew the man who made you once proud to have worn the same shirt and, now that shirt is absolutely meaningless, with bad players, foreign and inept managers and, of course, those faceless and heartless complete fools who continue to bring our game to its knees from Soho Square.

Anyhow, from the men with their pockets full, to those who fight for them, without knowing the kind of people who represent them, which was the main reason I began writing Don't Shoot the Taliban…..You'll Wake the Locals!

7 THE SNIPER

Whilst on being like those I've just been talking about, here's something that brings a new meaning to your life, but only, like me, if you come out alive.

Sometime after leaving hospital and between operations, I spent a lot of time in Northern Cyprus where I was fortunate to meet several people who made my time there worthwhile, for without them, life there was something I look back on as having a dream upbringing in Chelsea.

One or two of them were from an island that I had visited some years earlier, in fact, whilst on an end of season tour with Stoke City. However, I mostly made friends with those who were from closer to home. One, incredibly, was in the same class as my brother in Fulham way back in the 60s, him being Philip Trusty. Another was the doorman of my favourite night club, Jake, which is documented later in this book. I want the majority to remain nameless for very personal reasons. Theirs, that is.

Before I go on to tell you the reason for such a story, I must mention a great man who was born in Famagusta, or, as they call it, Magusa. I was told of him being a Chelsea supporter and that he would like to meet me. I agreed. I was at that time losing faith with those living around where I wrongfully chose to stay. The reason I say that is because I thought I would go and see an old friend of mine. I was worried about him and through my stay in hospital thought it would bring back memories of the good times we shared together. Maybe it is something to do with what I said earlier, those things in your mind that take you somewhere you know nothing about, but think you do?

I was wrong and it became another one of my on-going disasters.

But back to Okan, who asked a mutual friend if he could fix up a meeting.

So, because of things that were going on in and around us, I thought that one more disaster would not affect my life there. However, I was pleased to find he was delightful.

We met in the Salamis Hotel which, as the crow flies, stood less than a quarter-of-a-mile from where we stayed on that trip, in the beautiful Golden Sands Hotel on the famous Golden Mile.

One day when going to a football match, to my amazement, I saw it standing there derelict after the battering it took from a war I am about to tell you of. This war began on the very morning we were about to leave this island. And you can imagine, after coming out of a night club, on a club trip in such great company, war is the last thing you'd think of.

We had the most wonderful of times, in fact, as good if not better than any of those unbelievable trips with my old team-mates at Chelsea, if that was at all possible? But then again, our manager fixed these trips up so you could enjoy yourselves after a long hard season. Mr. Waddington, that is. Dave fixed them up for something I don't understand. He had the club in mind, whereas Tony had the players in mind, plus he himself loved all of the things I loved. I always say that travelling is the most exciting and rewarding of all experiences.

But it seemed nobody understood one another in those heady times when we had such a great understanding and, again as I will repeat many times, it was only the players that understood each other.

When the first bomb dropped I was sitting alongside Jimmy Robertson and Tony Waddington in the wee small hours waiting for a taxi. The place shook. Well, the pavement shook. The strange thing is today, looking at the news on TV everyone takes war for granted, and here we were at the beginning of one without knowing anything about it. Just a few minutes earlier Jimmy was smashing plates over the heads of a couple of our players on the dance floor. That was fun. I know for sure Jimmy enjoyed one particular head he bashed.

Whilst he was doing such a thing, nobody inside this club could possibly have envisaged that there was a bomb hanging overhead.

It was much like in the Mile End Road, where one minute you are looking up into where the fresh night air which was so very calm and refreshing and, the next - be it 59 days later - you were looking into a different kind of space.

But back in Famagusta, I can remember thinking, 'nobody mentioned anything about earthquakes.' However, this was no earthquake. I had been through all of this at the Bridge without knowing it, the bombshells that is.

Again, never knowing the biggest was still to come.

This was the furthest thing from the Working Man's Ballet!

As I just said, on our last night of this most wonderful of trips, the place shook as Jimmy, Tony and I sat on the pavement waiting for a taxi outside our favourite night spot. What we thought was an earthquake was, in fact, we found out years later, the first bomb of a war that when returning horrified me. In that time, I met the man who wrote the Genocide Files, Harry Scott Gibbons, and the stories he told me, from his first hand experiences, sent shivers down my recently shattered spine (pelvis). Harry, who was a very nice and incredibly brave man, was working on the front line for one of the top broadsheets in Fleet Street and was somehow free to go where he wanted without ending up in a ditch with his head cut off. This was something that happened to so many innocent people in the most horrifying of times on a daily basis. Before I go any further, I want you to know that the opening of this book is not me being dramatic, the Genocide Files documents this in exactly the same way Harry told me, and several other people. Since meeting Harry and reading his accounts, I have visited the local villagers and saw this to be true. It was written all over their faces. What I noticed most was that they looked a lot older than what they actually were. In their tiny hut-like homes you could smell the remains of such a war. Nobody talked of it, but it was almost as if they were still thinking of it. I wanted to ask, but....

We were, I think, the last flight out later that morning and right up until the day I returned to the old city of Famagusta, I did not realise what kind of impact it had on those who live between the now badly shattered surroundings right down to Bogaz.

Chelsea's newest signing David Hay was not so lucky. He and his family were smuggled out on a naval frigate after missing the first half-a-dozen matches of the season. Little did he know that he was lucky to get out at all!

Anyhow, back to the man I'd like to mention, Okan Dagli, a very well respected doctor and politician, with a lovely wife and two very well brought up boys, who are also obviously Chelsea fans. He is the kind of man you only meet once in a blue moon. The downside to all of this is that I am truly not happy about them supporting my home club, for they don't deserve such support.

With that out of the way, I move on to several of my neighbours, including the Golden Girls, and I can tell them that they were the only bright spot in a country which is riddled with all the things in life that really disturb me. Once you have read of my upbringing, you will understand my feelings about such a place. I am not a person who gets on well with cheating, corruption, lying and deceit.

That is probably the main reason why I received only two international caps.

Outside of my very special circle of friends there was one person who is behind the opening of my very important story and, his name is Alfie Fisher, who I met in a bar on the south side and, there I found out that he supported my old club Arsenal.

Alfie invited me to a match on the Army Base not far from the great divide, where the war has left two bloods still running high. At times it gets to boiling point, but luckily it is under some sort of control, which is great if only for the likes of Okan's young children. For those living and visiting there it is not quite so great, for there always seems to be something in the air, rather like going back to Elland Road or Elm Street, both of which are a big part of my story, but that is later.

On this particular day, I was to give the Man of the Match award to the best player out of two teams who face such a daunting task each and every day of their young lives. Our team, run by Billy Miller, was the Army and the first half was not going well as the Navy, their fiercest enemies, were two goals in front.

Let me go back a fraction, where the pre-match build up was better than any seen at Wembley Stadium, when you see all of those nobodies walking across that red carpet along with today's multi-millionaire impostors dressed in white shirts, and then there are those from Soho Square.

Here we had real captains, real sergeants and real generals flying in from overhead, with the choppers falling out of the sky like a scene from Mash, only they were not the incoming wounded.

They had either been flown home on a stretcher or in body bags.

The most important part is realising that there were so many team leaders, those who lead young men, into a different kind of battle. Billy's team had just returned from the front line in Afghanistan and, although they had been trapped in combat for many days and nights, they looked remarkably fresh and ready for a completely different war.

I was welcomed with much more warmth and gratitude than before my England debut against the world champions, West Germany. One General in particular wore more stars than I had played against throughout my entire playing career!

Whilst all of this was going on, my mind flashed back to those first few weeks whilst coming out of my coma. Although my legs were numb, paralysed numb, the rest of my body tingled with a feeling that I had never felt before.

But the biggest problem I had and, which led to my problems today, was the bottoms of my feet, where they had both dropped whilst in the Intensive Care Unit for those eight-and-a-half-weeks and, they tried to put some kind of splint on them. This was to keep them upright and, once I could or would ever walk again, stay that way. I cannot begin to tell you how painful this was. In fact, even after telling me of the importance of putting them on, because of the danger of foot-drop, I would not let them put them on me, I couldn't. It was the most excruciating pain that I have ever experienced, making going down that hole in the Midlands seem like a simple, well, not even a head cold.

I felt different about being alive. I thought back to the time when I had to decide about my future, as to whether to fight or not? Do I give it my all, or feel sorry for myself? That feeling was soon to disappear. It took a little while for all of this to sink in, because it also took a little while for me to realise that this team were different from any other I had ever seen. When pouring my coffee at half-time I felt, rather like being on the side lines at Wembley and Old Trafford, that there was no way back. By the time that coffee had turned to a vodka and orange these lads had done something that they obviously did not see as special, unlike Chelsea beating Leeds United in that second match. Although like ours, their comeback was impressive. The way they fought back was something that they obviously thought nothing of. It took me a lot longer than usual for it all to sink in. I don't think it ever entered their minds, for they were used to these matches, playing them as if it really was a matter of life and death.

These young boys inspired me!

They actually inspired me so much I decided to write another book called Don't Shoot the Taliban….You'll Wake The Locals!

It also reminded me of the way players today cheat in the penalty area, something these lads would teach them a lesson or two in the art of playing with your heart on your sleeve. There was no shirt tugging. There was no rolling over. And when you hear the commentator say, "He rolled over as if he's been shot" is an insult to these players.

Sometime later that evening I called my son, for me being so glad that he had not been alongside these incredibly brave kids a few days before. That emotion stayed with me throughout the evening and, with my new friends, we partied all through the night celebrating a breath taking comeback. Not from Afghanistan, but from being two goals down to win 5-2, with their two front men grabbing all the spoils and adulation. I had the unenviable task of now choosing the player to get the award. There were not enough medals to go round, for they had only brought the one and I had to do the impossible by leaving out ten heroes. I did so by presenting it to the Sniper, who grabbed two of the five goals. And although his partner up-front bagged a hat-trick, I think what might have swayed my decision was that he had shot eighteen Afghans from a thousand yards - whilst holed out alone in a trench for the best part of a day-and-a-half. Not a great preparation for any match, especially when you look at today's modern so-called superstar.

And there was Rooney carrying his very own pillow onto that luxurious aeroplane, the one taking all those losers to South Africa.

But what caught my eye most of all was the way the Sniper and his strike partner worked together, in unison, as if watching each other's back just in case the enemy crept up and tried something that could be fatal.

Those body bags entered my head.

But it was the furthest thing from theirs as they were far too busy enjoying the freedom of space. I know what it is like to enjoy such freedom since leaving the Royal London and St Bartholomew's Hospitals, which was rather different from what they had experienced. My freedom now is away from such dangers that surround the operating theatre.

Each and every raid, or attack on the Navy goal, was looked upon by me as if it was the difference between life and death for these lads, something I will never know about, for all of my most dangerous moments were whilst under the heaviest anaesthetic in the Intensive Care Unit.

And so it ended and my heart started beating normally once again. My only regret is that I never had time to truly thank each and every one of them involved on that day as the choppers disappeared slowly into the distance; but more importantly to thank them for everything that they allowed me to experience, that is something they take so much for granted.

They were simply flying back to a war that our Government regard as just another day.

I mention later about David Cameron heading our 2018 World Cup bid. He should be addressing this issue instead of adding to an already shameful state of affairs at Soho Square.

There have been many people who saw me in the ICU and fighting thereafter and, where the word bravery has been used on several occasions, which I thought of whilst standing watching these young men, enjoy themselves without fear of it being their last day here on earth.

Whilst reading through this book you might understand my reasoning about certain aspects of this beginning, a country that was once ours, one that certainly doesn't appreciate or deserve such courage and bravery of those who carried away the trophy in such wild jubilation. It was if those bombs had stopped in mid-air. I think of those nights when I could not sleep before a big match, and then I think about the Sniper and all of his pals (team-mates), those who would die for one another. He ran for miles on this day, as if at times he was chasing that speeding bullet, the one I hope he will never catch. The only advice I gave the Sniper and his strike partner afterwards, was that if they continue to watch each other's back as they did on that day, we will not be reading about them, or watching them on our TV sets crawl slowly through Wootton Bassett.

Or be reminded of them whilst listening to that wonderful song The Angel Flight!

I could not sleep that night after swapping stories with those young soldiers. I wanted to know more about them than they did about me.

I thought of my apprenticeship at Chelsea when - although already having learned the game through my father - I would train every morning at Hendon (The Welsh Harp) and, my mind flashed back to when I was working on all my skills these boys were working on theirs. Only difference mine was keeping possession of the ball where theirs was keeping possession of their lives and, those of their mates.

Mine was cleaning my boots whilst theirs was cleaning their rifles. We had a lot in common though and, the main thing was what I said about Chris Hutchings, we helped our team-mates when trouble appeared. The one outstanding thing in watching the Sniper play alongside his strike partner was that the both of them worked closely side-by-side without it being coached into them. Some things are taken out of context in football, but the one thing that is not, as in our matches against Leeds United and, that is when the whistle blows - as with these boys - it's war.

You cannot coach people to fight together on a training field, like Osgood and Hutchinson, in those early days. When they went onto that field, they were ONE.

When you see today managers and coaches say that so-and-so (Torres £50m) and Drogba (un-buyable in May 2012) can't hack it together up front for 90 minutes, I say that they have a weakness, for on this day the Sniper and his sidekick make a mockery of such people.

The coaches, managers and players that is!

After that match when introduced to me, they hadn't a clue as to who I was?

But after returning to their dormitories and a quick telephone call home they came to meet the three of us, I was now their hero. I have news for them and, that is they have it the wrong way round!

In my new book, Don't Shoot the Taliban....You'll Wake the Locals.....they are at the forefront of my mind and my inspiration to write such a book. I hope before I die, again, I would love to come across the Sniper and all of his team-mates and hand them a copy of my book, as a thank you to them for allowing me to realise what is going on (wrong) in our country.

Recently, my son, Allen, was attacked by two Polish immigrants in Wood Green and, on my return for Majorca, showed me his scars. I thought of the Sniper as Allen said had I had my baby, Nancy, with me I would have got my Stanley knife (he had his tool - working - bag with him) and knifed the b******s And he would have had every right, however, he would have got a life sentence, how can that be right?

We are now not safe in our own home, how can that be? I asked, "Were there any police around?" Of course not and, he even went into Wood Green Police Station to report the incident.....nothing, they simply did not want to know.

Had anything had happened to our little Nancy, I can promise you with all of our contacts from Chelsea to Bow and Stoke-on-Trent, unlike England in the 1974 World Cup, the Poles would have been beaten badly.

Some Pole is walking the streets of Wood Green not knowing how lucky he is to be alive because of our little Nancy not being with her Dad when attacking him.

There would have been another war to go with every other one that is going on in this country today and, as I write I see the enemy pass our window and, we can't give £81 to the newest,

Let me elaborate on this problem we have here: I met my friend Tony Banks - the Sports Minister at the time - in the Big Easy, before heading for a match at the Bridge. One of my friends, Gary Shepherd, had a mate with him who was rather *Schindlers* and mocked Tony about reading that he was mugged by four black youths over his manor, Newham, and it embarrassed my friend. I looked at Gary with daggers and, before I knew it Tony replied by saying, "I hope they try it again," and pulled up his trouser leg, showing the kind of knife that 'Crocodile' Mick Dundee would have been proud of.

Remember the scene when he pulled it out on a would-be mugger saying, "No mate, that's a knife!"

.

8 BLUE MURDER!

Once I came down off those incredible drugs, I had to start trying to piece my life together yet again, although it was to be a completely different kind of life, due to that incredible night of 15 December 1997. As you will read, my life covered in the original Ballet was one of a roller coaster, but since that fresh December night, it puts all before it very much in the shade. This incident had turned that roller coaster ride into a leisurely walk down the Kings Road, whereas the Mile End Road had become a minefield, with the only difference being, the mine had my name on it.

I have had many challenges throughout my life, but this one beat all. But before I headed into all of this, there was one thing always on my mind. How did this all come about?

I knew that when I crossed that road I was okay. I was then, and still am now, very sure about all that happened. That is why I have always had more than a seed of doubt as to whether this was pre-meditated. I was almost certain that this was something waiting to happen, if you know what I mean?

I have often thought about all of this and always come back to it being a definite attempt to kill me, but I guessed that we'd never know. Or would we?

For if I have anything about me, it's not letting them get away with it, call it my competiveness, for you only have to look at so many comebacks, for the want of a better word?

There hasn't been a day go by without my wondering just where this driver came from?

Just as in the Matthew Harding case, I believe there was foul play!

The only tear I ever shed whilst wearing a Blue shirt was when I could not be on the field with my team-mates at Wembley and Old

Trafford against the loveable Leeds United in the FA Cup final of 1970. There will be quite a few things I miss when I finally do leave this place, but if I could relive one moment before I go, it would be beating Don Revie once again, only with me being on the field with my mates.

I am a person who goes by first impressions with people. Of course you are not always right, mainly because there are not many people as you go through life that are completely straight. When I finally came face to face with him, after he chose me in one of his England squads, I froze. I knew immediately that this was a man I could not and would not have anything in common with and, could not and would not ever like. I was almost right. Almost, because he was worse than I ever imagined a man could be. It was a nightmare for me, knowing that for a little while I had had my ban dropped only to hear the incredibly bad news of Don Revie taking over. Talk about, "Out of the frying pan....

My international career you might say, even at such an early age, was in turmoil. At 18 Ramsey praised me highly, telling the nation that I was a certainty to play for him and then he banned me. I was devastated. However it touched such a nerve, that later on I reached the heights that only something like this could spur me onto. I'm quite certain a lesser man would have accepted it and, play dead. But it, once meeting Waddington, inspired me, to such a degree that, like a love for a woman, I put it so far to the back of my mind that it could not possibly return. And, it was only facing Franz Beckenbauer that had me excited about playing for my country.

Otherwise, I don't think I would have bothered, honestly!

What still astounds me is, how can the country, with all of its players and supporters be put in the hands of a man like his. The only explanation is that those at the FA are very consistent at choosing such bad, bad managers, people who should not have the power to do so.

Much like politicians, I must add.

I will mention this more than once, as this was at a time when there was, the likes of Tony Waddington and Brian Clough at their disposal. Waddington would have been the perfect choice, because he could mix with the best and the rest. He wore several hats, if you like. But his special hat was more of a cap. It was a thinking one and, that is why he chose so many thinking players, those wonderful inside-forwards.

Our game is a national one, from Exeter to Blackpool and Scunthorpe to Bristol, and here was a man (Revie) who cared for Leeds United - and Leeds alone. That's fine by me, but if that was the case, and it was, he should have stayed there. It was a world that he built and lived in, one which only he and his disciples understood. Players of that day never left his Leeds United because they were cloned by Revie. And as soon as Clough arrived after Revie took the England job, all of this came out. It was simple really, for Revie should have stayed put and Clough given the national job.

But no, those frauds at Lancaster Gate were all frightened of their own shadows, let alone the shadow of Clough in the hallways of Lancaster Gate.

If anybody can honestly stand up and tell me that Trevor Cherry was a better player than me, then I obviously have learnt nothing from my past in the game.

Revie thought so, I wonder why?

The problem was that Revie was a very strong character, meaning there was no way in the world I could turn it in my favour, not even by playing so fantastically well in my first match against the world champions - West Germany in 1975. And the realism of what I am telling you was waiting in the Wembley dressing room as we entered it victorious. At one stage I thought I was in the wrong dressing room. I have said to people, and documented elsewhere, that when first entering that famous tunnel a few minutes before kick-off I looked at Franz Beckenbauer and got a chill. There he stood in all his glory. Bobby Moore sprang to mind, thinking of these two giants of the game walking to the halfway line for the tossing of the coin.

This was 1975, nine years on from England winning in 1966, and we were in the middle of the biggest slump in the history of English football - and all because of our winning the World Cup.

No more wingers. We were now known as The Wingless Wonders!

Can you imagine the Brazilians doing away with wide players? And inside forwards were soon to become mid-fielders. No more Carter. No more Shackleton. No more Haynes. No more Eastham and, over the border in Scotland, no more Baxter. They were out. Coming in were to be the likes of Carlton Palmer, David Batty and Trevor Cherry and, from over that border, nothing!

In Stoke-on-Trent, there is a monument of Stanley Matthews and in Preston, Tom Finney, and now they were becoming extinct.

I wonder if Ramsey would have selected Finney or Matthews in 1966!

Or would he have stuck with his Wingless Wonders?

The last great wide player we saw was Jamaican John Barnes, who was phenomenal in the red of Liverpool, but once putting a white shirt on he became a shadow of that wonderful player that had those brilliant fans on Merseyside adored and respected. When I hear people slag Barnes off, I become like young Marcus, "have you ever put your life on the line" meaning playing for England was just that, getting a decent pass from your full-back was like asking Jesus to turn water into wine.

As Perry Como would sing, quite simply, "It's Impossible."

Why? The system stank. At Liverpool he would be given the ball early, to his feet, to weave his magic, whereas for England he was like a magician looking for his wand. He was, like a few others inside these pages, the epitome of the title of this book, a sight to behold.

That night preparing for the biggest match of my life against the West Germans, I simply blanked Revie out and focused on enjoying the moment with Alan Ball. He was the best in the business in those days - and there has been nothing like him since - and another we'll never see the likes of again. My only regret, to this day, is that I did not walk out of that Wembley dressing room, up the tunnel, throw my shirt at my father and never set foot there again. As an England player!

At that moment I wanted to be wearing that beautiful green German jersey and actually be playing against Revie. And on that particular night that is what I did. I played against those Germans....and our manager.

This, like at Stoke City, was the only time I had played not only against the opposition, but others in my own dressing room.

Anyhow, The Working Man's Ballet was Tony Waddington's idea, and description of a game that brings so much pleasure to so many people; therefore, there should be no place for the likes of Revie. As you read on, if you don't know already, even Brian Clough agrees. But I have to get it out of my system, because there are two sides to every coin. This is one tossing of that coin that comes up with Tony Waddington's head on it each and every time, and it would have been absolutely tragic had Tony taken over at Elland Road once he (Revie) had taken the job offered by those total morons at Lancaster Gate.

You - even the most ardent fan or potent football lover - will never know that feeling and, that something inside, when you look into their eyes as the referee puts the whistle into his mouth for the very last time. It's like being told you have only 90 minutes to live.

You have simply got to make the most of it.

I gave everything as a young player and got nothing in return, so that is why as you follow my story you'll understand my love for the Potteries.

Only yesterday 19.09.10 I was with a couple of fans from the Seventies. We met outside Stamford Bridge, in the old Britannia pub, and they were going on about me and Chelsea. I tried to explain about what I did for the club, yet still could not get a ticket for the match - Chelsea and Blackpool - and they were shocked.

Chelsea supporters don't know the half of it.

As I said, some time ago I wrote to Richard King, who is the Chairman of the Chelsea Pitch Owners, also attaching a copy of the back cover. He once accused me of causing trouble at Stamford Bridge and, my reply was that he was not only being totally Chelsea Football Club biased, but so brutally ignorant.

You'd really have thought that it was him who played in those matches at Old Trafford, Sofia, Bruges and Athens, I'm just so happy that he didn't, only because he was like those England players of today who talk a good game. In a nutshell, he is a nightmare. If he stood with Mourinho, the man would simply shrug and ask him, "What do you do?"

I only mention King because these are the people who are walking round as if they have got the club where they are. Did they ever play?

As Marcus says again, "did you ever put your life on the line?"

Where was King when we were 1-0 down at Old Trafford?

Was he the one who took the ball across the halfway line and clipped such a wonderful pass into Osgood's path?

Of course not, he was the one saying "when I was playing...

Anyhow, I never knew him when I was trying to get my Chelsea career going.

Who the fucking hell is Richard King?

And then there's that one armed spy - the one Bates gave Italian lessons to, so that he knew what Ranieri was saying about him - who is still there, in fact, he was on the Champions League winning bus 22.5.2012, which is simply wonderful and, I can't get a look in. However, if they sent me a private plane (or yacht) I'd rather go down the Labour Club in Kidsgrove - my local where Lesley Whittle got murdered - and watch it. At least I can turn it off. And if I waited for them to get the ball off of Barcelona and Munich I might have well have been asleep. At least our team tried to get the ball and play, well we had Charlie Cooke, Peter Osgood and myself - never forgetting those that were just as good as us in other departments.

It's much like Bobby Moore winning the World Cup and they send Michael Jackson's monkey to pick the trophy up.

Fulham have a statue of Michael Jackson outside their ground, after having had one of the all-time greats, Johnny Haynes play and remain so loyal for so long. The Brylcreem Boy could have taken his pick at any club in Europe, but stayed true to his club, yet they have a statue of one of the Jackson Five, work that out?

Did You Know?

Johnny Haynes was the first footballer to appear for England in every class of football available in his playing era - school, youth, Under-23 and 'B', before making his full international debut.

Footballing legend Pelé once described Haynes as the "best passer of the ball I've ever seen," which was an accolade that was again made by England's record top-scorer Jimmy Greaves.

Haynes became the first player to be paid £100 a week, immediately following the end of the £20 maximum wage.

I used to play opposite the Cottage - Barn Elms - for my school in the morning and, as soon as the whistle blew, Bill Boyce - my little black pal - and I, would head across Hammersmith Bridge to see the great man play.

Anyhow, getting back to that fraud King, I for one/ was born a couple of hundred yards away from Stamford Bridge: two/ I was a 12-year-old schoolboy when my father first took me and my home-grown skills to them: three/ I was 19 when they won their first ever FA Cup final: four/ I was 20 when they won their first ever European trophy: five/ I cost them nothing and they earned £250,000 out of my transfer: six/ they refused to pay me my 5% transfer cut after lying about me asking for a move: seven/ whilst I lie dying in the Intensive Care Unit - and the 10 months afterwards - they weren't decent enough to send me a get well card or even telephone my panic-stricken family (especially my poor mother) who sat outside the most terrifying part of any hospital for eight-and-a-half weeks. It wasn't until about three months later, when coming off the morphine, that I realised this.

I might have told you that when I finally opened my eyes in March 1998, the first thing I remember was the walls being covered with dazzling colours, well, that was what it was like to me. It was probably something to do with the morphine. I also remember doctors coming and going but always having a look through them. I recall one of them saying "You have some friends out there?"

Well, little did either of us know that there was not one from the club I had served so well for ten years, but even though, I hadn't looked through them by them, if you'd ask if I would have been surprised to see that there wasn't one from Stamford Bridge, my answer would have been quite simply...

Some players got Testimonials, Ron Harris I think got two, however I never even got a get well card, So, Richard (King) don't talk to me about mending fucking bridges!

Whilst going through those hundreds and hundreds of cards and letters, it dawned on me that there was nothing from the club I had done so much for. Okay, I didn't care and I wasn't surprised because I only had one thing on my mind, and that was getting my life together again. Where would people like Richard King be if it wasn't for the likes of me? You would think that they were the ones who were out there against Leeds United, Real Madrid, West Germany and Bruges.

Again, as young Marcus says, "do you risk your life every day?"

I also had another problem, and a massive one, one I did not need at a time like this, and although I did not know at the time, I did not think anything else could possibly go wrong.

It was that my wife of six months did not fancy pushing me about in a wheelchair for the rest of her days and that hurt much more than Chelsea Football Club. I will tell you of her rejection later, and of course, the accident that wasn't. As for Chelsea, here we are 15 years on and still they ignore the most local player in the history of the club. Instead they give all the adulation and loving to strangers, who cost them an obscene amount of money.

So much for those days when the 'Local Boy Makes Good.' I write this for the local people of Chelsea and those most faithful supporters from our area who need to know all of this. I also need to tell you that both Peter Osgood and I never asked or wanted to leave, although we both felt along the way that we needed to get away from the manager. We were simply used as two scapegoats for a bad business plan, bad management and directorship.

I am proved right by the history of it all. The record books don't lie.

Stoke City went from third from bottom into Europe in my first five months, whilst Osgood helped Southampton beat Manchester United in the following season's FA Cup final in 1976. Chelsea got relegated!

That is why I say, it was bad management (and directorship), for if it was good management that clot on the brain (through an almighty bang on the head) must have done more damage than my surgeons could detect?

9 THE AUTHORITIES

Along the way you'll find out what an 8-year-old (Marcus) thinks of these people!

Those who you will find at the end of all of my writing have once again made not only our game, but our nation a complete laughing stock, Is it a wonder that John Lennon left these shores - not to mention Tom Jones and Engelbert. We get a genius every pancake day and when we do, we toss them in a very different way.

Or, are we scared of them?

The people in charge, I mean!

In the end it was the great JL that tossed them off, he did so by sending his gong back.

Before I found out about it being an attempt on my life, this was what I wrote: At 9.15pm on 15 December 1997, Ashgar Fatehi roared through the Mile End Road and changed my life forever. Having crossed one of London's widest roads, I can only presume he overtook on the inside and, without seeing me, he took his eye off things. He then sucked me into his windscreen, before throwing me into a big old tree on the side of the pavement. A passer-by was stopped by the driver and told that he didn't realise he had hit something and, then asked if it was he who had been hit? He replied, "No, you hit him lying under that tree over there."

The police arrived and kindly let him go. Three hours later - after having gone through the resuscitation procedure and now surrounded by several surgeons in theatre - they finally contacted my family. My wife of six months lived literally a five minute walk away. This was three long hours after I had been ventilated by Frank Cross and all of those wonderful consultants, who were fighting to keep me alive whilst those policemen were about to question my family in the waiting room of the Royal London Hospital.

Why did it take so long?

I was about to miss the first Christmas in 46 years, however, not knowing it could have been so very much worse. And then, eight-and-a-half weeks later, plus a few more weeks of coming down from the morphine, I learned how close I was to losing my legs!

My uncle George - who was with me every day in hospital - and I returned to both the Intensive Care Unit and the Resuscitation Room some months later.

I found, the latter was the more frightening of the two.

I visualised them wheeling me in under the most incredible circumstances, but that was only after reading my medical report!

At 4.30am on 18 February 2010, Ashley Cole put in a call to his local police station telling them "Come quick, please, someone is breaking in," after he heard voices at his downstairs window. The day before his wife had been photographed in the Sun newspaper leaving for LA, without both her engagement and wedding rings. He was therefore being robbed and the cops took five minutes to get to him.

Now, that's quite a difference, wouldn't you say!

When seeing me lying on the pavement, only a block from their station, the police took it on themselves to ignore the situation, thinking that I would not last out the night. Frank Cross and David Goodier had other ideas. Along with Otto Chan (the radiographer) they slowly devised a plan that kept me alive. Their first concern was that blood clot on the brain, my shattered pelvis and those fasciotomies, which is behind so much of the pain and discomfort I carry with me over the last 15 years.

Please trust me when I say each day has been sheer hell.

Although it struck me like lightning at first - I was devastated - in the end, my wife walking away was also a great help. Like playing against the Germans knowing Revie wanted me to fail and my wife wanting me to not pull through, I used this to turn around this situation into my favour.

I can't really tell you of how she felt initially, but I did know as time went by that she was leaving me and, that was partially after she learned that my incredible surgeon's main fear was amputation. Although the damage they did to my body was caused by, as I was told, simply keeping me alive.

This meaning, whilst they were cutting into my legs, as one consultant told me, there was so much blood pouring out of me that they could not see what they were doing. That is the reason I have all these problems right now. So when I am struggling, I simply think back to that time when they were cutting into me blind.

One of the Professor's assistants told me she was responsible for cleaning up the mess and that she had never seen anything like it, the stench was breath-taking - only a different kind of breath- taking.

What I am trying to tell you is that the police wanted me dead, along with someone else, whereas these people wanted me alive. All through the night, along with me, they fought for my life and it was no different for the next 59 days as I lay in a near coma. If everything I went through in my life before was a disaster, falling out with the authorities at Lancaster Gate, Stamford Bridge and Highbury was a completely different ball game. This was close to devastation - I had now replaced Alf Ramsey, Dave Sexton, Terry Neill and Don Revie with Frank Cross, David Goodier, Otto Chan, Norman Williams, Claire Strickland, David Badenoch and David Ralph, they were to change my life like those managers but in a very different way. They were skilled at everything they did. No bias, nothing but sheer dedication to doing the best of their abilities, like what Mar. Goodier said in one morning trauma meeting: "If Alan is going to get through all of this, he needs stronger management."

I never met David until after he saved my pelvis, my legs and then my life and for s short while we became friends, my respect for him as a man and consultant/surgeon is immense.

And, like when moving to Waddington, I finally got it!

You will read of my playing days under the finest management of the incomparable Tony Waddington. I thought of Tony a lot whilst being treated by these people, for it was the only time in my life I respected management and, that was the management of those in the Royal London Hospital. These strangers became my heroes, my life savers and my friends like Tony before them. As for the police, they allowed the driver to walk away into the fresh, but by now, cold chilling night air. Again, why?

When I look back and think about my relationship with these great people, so brilliant at what they do without shouting about it and, then those like Ramsey, Revie and Neill in particular, I feel privileged to know them I let Sexton off the hook here, because I did not class him as a manager, for he was a coach in the wrong job. He should never have gone into management, although he did very well at QPR, but they had a bloody set of players there, players that had lots of experience and great ability. People like Frank McLintock - who had won the Double at Arsenal - knew all about winning football matches and, then of course, there was Stan Bowles.
Who could coach such genius?

I have mentioned about Dave not being a manager, so if you doubt me, listen to what Frank had to say on the QPR website:

How did Dave Sexton styles compare with Bertie Mee?

FM: Totally different, Bertie was never a real football man at least not when it came to coaching and tactics. That's not to demean him at all it's just he was a physio at the club and before that an ordinary player at Derby County. He never reached any great heights as a player but he was an excellent physio and very disciplined man.

When you got injured at Arsenal it was horrible, he would have you in at 9am through rush hour traffic, give you one hour for your lunch and send you back home at five o'clock. You never got a cup of tea off him, you couldn't read a paper. It was just treatment and work all the time. So no one ever wanted to be injured at Arsenal.

When he took over the manager's job we were astonished, we thought we would get Alf Ramsey or Don Revie but we finished up with Bertie. But he was very clever he allowed people like Dave Sexton and then Don Howe to completely take over the coaching. He never interfered in that, he just ran the club. It was all very professional and he had strict discipline about dress code and how to properly represent Arsenal football club.

Dave Sexton was a quieter man, you could talk to him more he was more like a friend or an ally he was a lovely person but he was a fantastic coach too. He was full of ideas, always going abroad to pick up new things and he ended up getting us playing similar to how Barcelona do now. That's just how we operated, as soon Phil Parkes got the ball Dave Clement and Ian Gillard would run up the halfway lane, Dave Webb and I would go left and right of the six yard box, I'd normally get the ball thrown to me as I was a former midfielder and perhaps a bit more comfortable on the ball and then I'd have so many options. If Dave Clement's man came towards me I'd chip it over his head to Dave who'd now be free. Stan Bowles would drop in deep and that would cause so many problems for the opposition because they'd want to clatter him, it was constant rotation of players and it was mind boggling for the opposition because they couldn't pick us up at all.

Some years later, I studied Henri Charriere, the one and only Papillon, and he got similar treatment from his enemies in black. He somehow went through it all, including the dreaded solitary, after being wrongly convicted of a murder he did not commit. Like me, he was not only the innocent party, but survived the kind of trauma that other people bring on so despicably.

15 years on, I still suffer from the multiple injuries brought on by Fatehi - while this man roams free. Why? How comes?

Charriere springs to my mind every time.

10 PAPLILLON

Charrière was a native of Ardèche, France. He had two older sisters; his mother died when he was 10 years old. In 1923, at the age of 17, he enlisted in the French Navy and served for two years. After leaving the Navy, Charrière became a member of the Paris underworld, and later married and had a daughter.

According to his autobiography, Papillon, on 26 October 1931, Charrière was convicted of the murder of a pimp named Roland Le Petit, a charge that he strenuously denied. He was sentenced to life in prison and ten years of hard labor. After a brief imprisonment at the transit prison of Beaulieu in Caen, France, he was transported in 1933 to the prison of St-Laurent-du-Maroni on the Maroni River, in the penal settlement of mainland French Guiana. According to the autobiography, he made his first escape 42 days later, subsequently, he was adopted by an Indian tribe in Colombia before being recaptured and put into solitary confinement for the next 2 years.

While in French Guiana he spent 11 years in prison, including the two years in solitary confinement, and confinement on Devil's Island itself. During that time he made 7 more escape attempts before his final escape in 1941, when he sailed for miles on a bag of coconuts. He arrived in Venezuela, where he was imprisoned for one year.

He was, of course innocent and, the Gendarme knew it, they also knew who did this particular crime, but wanted Henri because he was a good human being and had more class than anyone around. It was, as you know in so many cases, a simple issue of being jealous.

The same thing happened when they nicked Osgood after our League Cup win at Tottenham in that brilliant semi-final, for absolute nothing. They came down on the four of us like we were the Great Train Robbers, those who nicked the Queens money. How about those in Parliament doing the same thing, only they don't have to hold up a train. They simply go for lunch and do so...

Anyhow, that night in the Kings Road, they saw it was Osgood and thought 'Oi, we can have a laugh over nicking him. And, like my case in the Mile End Road, they can go in their local pub – which I knew they did - afterwards and tell one another that, "Guess who I nicked today?"

From time to time I wonder just how certain people live with such a conscience, the police included, although I know they don't have one. Like those at the FA, certain things are hidden, for over the years and with this World Cup coming up, I realise nothing changes. I got my three-year England ban for missing an under-23 Tour, whilst Rio Ferdinand got nowhere near that for skipping a drugs test, you might understand just why people like me find it difficult living with such grievances. So that is why I became so rebellious, a non-believer and supporter of English football no more. When England disappoint, once again, I chuckle while some other clown gets rich.

My ban was outrageous, when you look at the behaviour of several of our big star names today. When I hear the word loyalty I think of people like Don Revie, who walked away from England for the big bucks with the Arabs and that just confirms what the FA is all about, they are complete idiots. The likes of me get a three-year ban and he gets paid a fortune for wrecking the nation, plus he was allowed to bring in Admiral Sports - who he also earned a fortune at Leeds United. He put a brilliant team together at Elland Road, but in doing so became the first football gangster, one that would have fitted in well with the Kray Twins. They just spring to mind because of my time around Whitechapel. With The Grey Maurice opposite and The Blind Beggar up on the corner, it was so sinister once the sun went down. If you see a London-born street trader about there in these times, it would be as big a miracle as me surviving Christmas and getting through to March.

I take strength from the other side of it all, the wonderful times that got me through my darkest days in the Royal London and St. Bartholomew's, when I had to make the biggest decision of my life. Did I want to spend the rest of my days in a wheelchair, or would I fight? At first it was quite daunting, but my decision was to fight like I had never fought before. The treatment I received from the managers I mentioned compared to that of the consultants is the one big difference in this story. That difference is the reason that I chose to re-write my autobiography for not only you, but also for me, to finally get it all out into the open hoping that along the way some things just might change for the better, although I very much doubt it. For nothing in my life, so far, ever has.

When Betty Shine told me of my late father and Leslie laughing at me, as I sped past them on my cloud - a little bit of the Rolling Stones flies to mind - her explanation was that they were telling me that they were not ready for me. In other words, I still had things to do here. The only thing I can think of is writing this book.
Either that or share the pain of so many others.

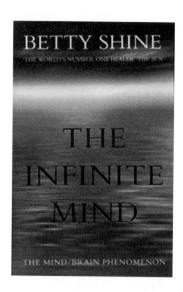

Betty asked if she could enter my case into this wonderful book (Chapter Two), after she dispersed the blood clot on my brain. That was two weeks before doctors told my family that they were not sure about it?

When I finally met her, I knew immediately of her wonderful ability to heal people, something she chose, so unselfishly, over becoming an opera star. She was rated, in her early years, right alongside Maia Callas. Can you imagine a footballer or manager today, giving up such a thing for the needy?

As if I hadn't had enough in my playing days. Anyhow, I have no reason, none at all, to challenge Betty. The latest fiasco regarding John Terry, Ashley Cole and Wayne Rooney, and the handling of it, typifies the complete hypocrisy at the Football Association. They are incredible at passing the buck and, if our players could pass the ball as well as they could pass such things, we would waltz the World Cup every four years.

Like what they say about my mate Stan,

"If he could pass a betting shop like he could pass a ball, he'd be a very rich man."

In my early days in the game it was unheard of to have a Swede or an Italian having to try to get us back on track. Ramsey, Revie, Taylor, Hoddle, Robson and Keegan were all failures of one kind or another and got pretty wealthy whilst becoming so, but bringing in a man from a different country is definitely not the answer. I have not heard or seen of one quality that they have that an Englishman has not. How can Eriksson expect loyalty from a young English player when we are playing against Sweden?

Ramsey and Revie, of course, were responsible for us not qualifying throughout the Seventies - we, a nation who supposedly invented the game. This was at a time when Brian Clough and Tony Waddington were at their disposal along with Peter Osgood, Jimmy Greenhoff, Frank Worthington, Stan Bowles, Charlie George, Colin Todd, David Nish and I, as players.

These were the players who could, and should have, been the backbone of our game, but we have that uncanny knack - like no other nation - to never select our most talented players. Ramsey chose no wingers while Revie chose former Leeds United players. Such bias is something that has made us a laughing stock. Whilst standing in The Grapes, my friends' pub in Newchapel, Stoke-on-Trent, whilst Germany were wiping the floor with us in the 2010 World Cup finals - the look on the locals faces summed it all up. 'Here we go again' I thought, as I stood there with a white German top on. I will soon explain that to you.

The reason is quite obvious for those of you who know me. I loved my England debut for several reasons and, no bigger one than playing against Franz on that memorable night in March 1975 and, I only know that because I watched those fantastic thoroughbreds running up that Cheltenham hill under my conditions, very heavy ground. I knew whilst watching them slogging it out it up that hill, that I knew that my ankle would be fine. The heavier the better, like when Waddington got the Stoke-on-Trent Fire Brigade in at the Victoria Ground, the result the best performance of my life against the best team in Europe, Liverpool.

Anyhow, this was the next time at that great old ground....

11 LOOK OUT HUDDY'S BACK

On the back cover of The Waddington Years - my favourite book - at the top of the page was a sign saying 'Look out Huddy's Back' which was for my second Stoke City debut against Arsenal. As you'll read, we were 14 points adrift when I arrived back at the Victoria Ground on a month's loan from Chelsea, for a second time. Although my first move there was for a record £250,000, this was not an anti-climax in any way shape or form. In fact it was just as daunting, as I had never been in a team faced with relegation. As I ran down that tiny famous slope, I looked up to my left and immediately got an almighty adrenalin rush.

As the Beatles sang: Yesterday, all my troubles seemed so far away!

And they were, as I went through that morning with nervous thoughts of everything going wrong.

But this massive banner gave me something I'd not experienced in a long time.

It was better than any booze or drug I had ever taken!

Although I knew my legs were no longer the ones that could get me all over the field, this lifted and inspired me to the point that I knew I could make an impact and, more importantly, get a much, needed result.

These players today, who people talk of in such glowing terms, could not join a club in such dire straits and boast of what I did.

Here's just three examples of what I am saying, Torres at Chelsea, Cole at Liverpool, and Adebayor at Manchester City (now at Spurs, he's even worse).

Why is it that all of these fantastic players, who cost vast amounts of money, need time to fit in?

To sign on a free transfer for a club seven matches behind the rest and turn the whole thing round, I can't even imagine it. For instance, take Ronaldo, he left Manchester for Real Madrid - the biggest ever transfer - and won nothing. United collected all of that money and won nothing either. Another example is Beckham, Manchester United to Real Madrid. He then went, like Revie before him, for the big bucks to LA Galaxy before realising that there was more to life than money. He then chose AC Milan. Would he have left America if the World Cup wasn't on the horizon? Don't get me wrong, but is he that impressive? He is not Messi, is he? Loyalty was lost when the incomparable Bobby Moore left us and, of course, the one and only Johnny Haynes. They were simply giants, both on and off the playing fields of the world.

And then there was Jimmy Greaves. I could not resist adding this piece for you that he told the Sunday People: I had a nice little cuddle the other night with an old flame I used to score a lot with. That's right, a football, the Adidas Jabulani, the World Cup ball which has caused a lot of people so much trouble. I was on the James Corden show and they handed it to me. I caressed it and it felt just great to me. I reckon I could have done a lot more damage with one of those. I used to like to stroke a ball, flick it and swerve it - rather than just welly it - and this little beauty would have suited me just perfectly. Before the tournament started (June 2010) everybody reckoned that the Jabulani would cause nightmares for goalkeepers, but I've not seen too much evidence of that. It's been more a problem for forwards with a lot of free-kicks and other long range shots ballooning over the bar, as well as a huge number of over hit crosses. But, to me, that's all down to poor technique, because I notice a lot of players seem to lean back a lot rather than get their head and body over the ball. The ball is the main tool of our trade - so important we named the whole bleedin' sport after it - but it has not often been the subject of such debate....until the Jabulani came along. But footballs have changed a lot over the years, and pretty much always for the better. For the first couple of years of my career we were still playing with the old heavy, lace-up ball - and that was a horrible thing, believe me. You would often see players come in at half-time with horrendous cuts to their face where they had connected with the lace, which could have the effect of a razor. Worse still, the ball got so heavy with water and mud during a game that it was a nightmare to head it. When the great England centre-forward Nat Lofthouse was asked who was the better winger, Tom Finney or Stanley Matthews? Nat said it was a tough call, but it had to be Stan because he always seemed to cross the ball with the lace facing away from you. A lot of players, a little older than me, suffered from premature dementia because of heading those balls. When you think of all the head tennis and heading practice in training, as well as matches, they suffered more damage to their heads than a boxer. So when they brought in the first lace-less balls, in the late 1950s, it revolutionised the game for the better. It was only those old-fashioned hatchet-men, who used to like to take the player as well as the ball, who were unhappy when the lace less balls were introduced and the game sped up and became a more attractive spectacle. A year or two after the lace was done away with, they started laminating footballs. That was the second great progression as it made them waterproof and, therefore, lighter on pitches that were often like swamps. Balls have got lighter and lighter and I cannot understand why a lot of old pros complain about this. I was doing a promotional gig for Burger King in Leicester Square the other week, volleying balls out of the doors of the restaurant at startled Japanese tourists (well we've all got to make a living). I reckoned with modern footballs I could still do a decent job, even at the age of 70 - and that's with two replacement knees! Apart from the Jabulani, another major World Cup talking point has been, of course, the vuvuzelas. A lot of people seem to hate these too, claiming the sound of a giant beehive is distracting during matches. Me, I love them. They drown out the sound of all the commentators, for starters!

I just love Jimmy Greaves and agree with everything he says, especially about the commentators. Just before I married for the second time, to the one who abandoned me, I took her to Ocho Rios in Jamaica just down the road from Montego Bay. It was an all-inclusive deal, which meant you don't really have to leave the hotel, which was superb. The hotel that is! However, we did and on one excursion into town, as I do, started chatting up the mini-cab driver. I asked if he liked his football, he said he really loved it. He went on to tell me that he used to pick up a footballer named Jimmy Greaves, who was always the last one left in this seedy bar in the wee small hours of each and every morning. I was dumbfounded. It was not a known thing in the game that Jimmy was a boozer and after him becoming clean and reshaping his life. I still find it really hard to believe that he was an alcoholic.

Like Moore and Haynes, he still remains at the top of my list as a player and a man.

My favourite story, along with the one where he visited his great friend Bobby whilst locked up in Bogota, was as a 16-year-old at Chelsea. Jimmy had just scored seven goals on the Saturday for the youth team, and on the Monday was confronted by the daunting figure of Ted Drake, the manager. Now, in those days the first-team players hardly ever saw him in training, let alone the youngsters. But on this Monday morning Drake walked straight up to Jimmy and said, "You're young Greaves aren't you," to which Jimmy nodded. "I hear you scored seven goals on Saturday. Let me tell you something, I once did the same thing." Jimmy interrupted by saying, "I know Mr. Drake, it was at Aston Villa, and you hit the bar twice and also should not have played through injury." Shocked, Drake said, "How on earth did you know that?"

Jimmy replied, "I know because I love my football."

Drake said, "Every time you go to bed at night say a little prayer and always remember what you did, because you'll never do it again."

On the following Saturday young Greaves scored eight!

12 WHETHER IT'S A QUARTER-OF-A-MILLION OR A MONTH'S LOAN...

Later on you will read about that second spell at Stoke City. The odds of escaping relegation were not even on the board, they were doomed for the drop and this famous old club was heading for Second Division football. And just five-and-a-half years earlier we were top of the First Division on the run-in - just around Easter - when only a couple of goalkeeping errors cost us the championship. But for those errors, I would be limping around with a League Champions medal on the end of my chain instead of a European Cup Winners Cup medal. That was at a time when I was playing the best football of my life - and how close we were to pulling off what would have been talked about today as something close to a miracle. In those days only Brian Clough did such things. Like Derby County and Nottingham Forest, Stoke City is a small club surrounded by the likes of Manchester United and City, Everton and Liverpool, Tottenham, Chelsea and Arsenal. We were the backstreet gang of the football world and winning the best league in such a world would have been quite astonishing. In fact it would have been as close to Moses parting that ocean. And we did it with such style. Anyhow, that back cover I sent King read like this:

Apart from being abducted by Aliens, there is nothing dramatic that hasn't happened to Alan Hudson but give it time. His has been a life lived as a soap opera with equal dollops of glory and despair. He has spent the last 12 years in rehabilitation with an accident that nearly killed him. He has battled a painful recovery with Great Spirit and the

optimism which kept him buoyant throughout a turbulent
:r.

He was a footballer who moved Sir Alf Ramsey to fulsome praise
which nowadays would be like Sven Goran Eriksson telling a joke. Sir
Alf said there was no limit to what he could achieve. His team-mate
Peter Osgood, himself a player of great skill and grace, said that, "He
is one of the greatest players I have played with or saw, and had
incredible skills, great brain, and great stamina."
So how come he only played twice for England?

He will tell you he had problems with Ramsey, who didn't pick him
at all, and Don Revie. But that doesn't explain how possibly the most
gifted player of his generation ended up without a job in the game.
There were injuries, cruel ones at crucial times, which interrupted the
flow of his career.

But the trouble was alcohol. In the seventies football liked a drink.
George Best set the pace but Hudson and his team-mates were not far
behind him. And like George, it did it for Hudson in the end. It
blunted his talent, dictated his personality and thwarted his career.
What it didn't destroy was his ability to cling to the wreckage of his
life.

Anyone who saw him when he was young and intact will remember a
talent to amaze and will feel sad it was so willfully squandered. In the
final analysis the greatest calamity to befall Alan Hudson is one
suffered only by greatly gifted people who take their talent for
granted; he will never know just how good he could have been?'

Sir Michael Parkinson

The first time I met Michael was at Stamford Bridge. He was with
George. I liked him immediately and, then some years later to
promote the original Ballet he had me as a guest on his radio show,
again, I found him charming. And, of course, he was the best in the
business at what he did. There was not anyone in the world that was
at the top of their own trade he did not interview and, interview with
the kind of class that had he played our game, he would have been in
the same side as George and I. I cannot pay him any higher
compliment. His likes today, are sadly missed on our TV screens.
He might find that odd being a Barnsley supporter.

On that first meeting he came along with George - the same one
when the legendary Monte Fresco took that wonderful photograph of
Osgood, George and me together in a Chelsea blue shirt. It was the
only time George pulled this particular shirt over his head. He so

wanted to do so many times after that, but Dave Sexton would have none of it. Incredible management!

Incredibly bad management, I should have said.

This book is like a jewel for me with some wonderful stories and incredible names, talent-wise, but had George signed for that Chelsea team it would have been maybe the most incredible ever written.

The dressing room stories alone. The matches with George, Charlie, Oz and me doing their donkey work, or more like, watching the magic of such a trio, would have given me such joy to write about. The thought of it all has just made my hairs stand up.

I had a very special relationship with George. We respected one another, to an extent that when both living in and around the Kings Road we never attempted to ruin such respect, we kept our distance. The last time we had a drink together in the Kings Road was by accident. I was with a few friends and walking into The Big Easy, spotted him sitting all alone eating lunch. He was like a naughty schoolboy, as I walked round to see him, because he had a bottle of wine on the table and, he maybe have thought I objected. Because, at that time he was wrongly being accused of accepting that liver and, of course you know what followed. I would always give him the benefit of the doubt, because Joe Public just doesn't know what it was like to be George Best. I know because it is hard enough being me. So I invited him round to meet my friends and to his delight it was Happy Hour - two for one - and we shared the joke. He drank one and left the other to show that he actually could. Different class, well I thought it was and that is all that matters between friends!

It was always a great pleasure and honour to be in his company, if only for him sharing his wonderful stories, those of his escapades with one Miss World or another, but there was never a time when we talked of the game we both loved - and that was not too often - he put himself above you. As you read on you'll discover that my favourite part of anyone I have ever come across is modesty. It is a 'gift' not to flaunt, to have such an incredible talent and share it, is the biggest talent. George, along with Haynes, Moore and Greaves are just four such people. So vastly talented, yet so vastly modest, and it goes with the talent because like that talent, it is natural!

Fast forward. I have been through hell, coming out of that 59 day coma and then spending the whole of 1998 in hospital. I suppose after being so close to those wonderful surgeons and consultants deciding - with the help of the C-Clamp - that I would just about avoid the amputation of my legs, I should count myself lucky.

But, however, I don't. I feel quite the opposite. What happened to me in the Mile End Road just about summed up my life playing our game!

My missing FA Cup finals and World Cup finals through an injury that I carried throughout my entire career was a nightmare alone. The ban from playing for England was another dream wrecked. I thought that things had changed when so close to getting my dream job at Stoke City, yet the chairman died just a few short hours before. Still, I thought I'd had, as Frank sang, "My share of losing" but that split second in the Mile End Road that was to follow just about put the topping on it all.

And then George entered my world in a different way. He came in and joined me and realised just what I had been through, by having his own fight against his demons.

I was the first one out of all of his mates and colleagues at his bedside, if only to tell him how much he was not only admired, but much loved. It was far from sweet, but after what I had been through, I suppose in some ways I was showing him I was telling him how much worse it could have been. But that was not why I did it, far from it. I did it because I knew from my very own experiences that it is lonely out there when you are on the opposite end of the kind of scale we had been on. The love, adoration, adulation and all the rest that goes with what we'd been through - him more than I - you must cherish, but only by keeping it all in its rightful place.

The one big question I ask myself after all of my life threatening injuries which Mr. David Goodier tells you about is: "Would I have swapped all of my most wonderful moments that are in this book with living a life without where that car sped down the Mile End Road and ruined so many things that we take for granted? I am stuck for an answer. It's really tough giving up all of my wonderful experiences on those football fields (those Killing Fields) all over the world. My happiest moments were in a football shirt, especially amongst the elite and on special fields such as Giant Stadium, which I think was my favourite of all. I mention that because it is the place which I would chose if given one last trip. Not just to play, but disembark, book into our hotel and, then go with the flow. The pre-match build-up, the match, the Piano Bar, the memory of all of that is something special.

As I go back over my notes, only last week, the death of Giorgio Chinaglia reached me and, it rocked me.

Some people can boast money, some can boast being phoney, I can boast playing against these three Superstars of our game. You'll read of many "greats" between the pages and every one of them would love to be in this photograph. Today, these players would be priceless and rightly so!

I suppose it is a combination of the whole surroundings. Sinatra, Chinaglia, the Piano Bars at three in the morning and, the remembering of where I came from to the city that never sleeps. I often wonder if it's anything to do with my problem with sleeping. The near post at Shepherds Bush always springs to mind, though, something I'll tell you about.

These were the memories that got me through my darkest nights in that most daunting of buildings in the Mile End Road. I would promise myself that I would fight, although never play in New York again, to get the strength to return and take it all in one last time.

13 I WAS HIGHER THAN THE SPACE NEEDLE

I paid this place a visit on my first night and although it was breath-taking, I never knew that the city I was looking over would gave me the best four years of my life and, my only regret was I did not have certain people there to share it with me.

Before I go back to where I started 15 years ago - to the beginning of The Ballet - I'd like to show you the impact that us English players had over in the NASL. But what a lot of people forget is that it changed so many people's lives and, I was one of them, also like many of them I wanted to remain there, but again, it was not to be. But the strangest thing with me, it seems as if it's all because of one man or another....anyhow this is what I left behind. They have and never will reach such heights again and, to give you some idea when you read about David Beckham playing for LA Galaxy, our team, as would the New York Cosmos, would have wiped the floor with them.

14 1980 SOUNDERS HELPED BUILD WINNING SOCCER TRADITION IN SEATTLE

Thirty years after the 1980 Sounders had a great NASL season, Sounders FC continues Seattle tradition. The next time Qwest Field is rocking with a sold-out crowd for a Sounders FC match, give an assist to the old guys with the short shorts and long hair who laid the foundation.

In the summer of 1980, Seattle's popular soccer team was cheered on wildly by record crowds. Top talent from all over the world meshed seamlessly to create high-scoring entertainment, with a charismatic coach of high standing, who barked instructions from the side lines.

Thirty years later, it's happening again. But it's important to remember where it started. A generation ago, Seattle experienced an extraordinary soccer season. The 1980 Sounders won more games than any team in the history of the North American Soccer League, finishing 25-7 in the regular season.

If not for an unexpected exit in the playoffs, the squad might be considered one of the best in the history of American soccer. A handful of players from that team and their larger-than-life coach, Alan Hinton, recently took time to reflect on that memorable year. They vividly recall the big games and shared moments in the locker room. But most of all, they wonder where the years have gone.

The legacy of that great team, they say, is hard to pin down.

"I'm not sure I know what it is," says Sounders FC assistant coach Brian Schmetzer, who watched the season from the bench as a wide-eyed 17-year-old defender. "The legacy could be that that group was the one that started the support of soccer in Seattle that we see here today."

A Dream Season

The first victory of the 1980 season came well before the games started. Hinton, a first-year coach in Seattle recently dismissed by the Tulsa Roughnecks, built a roster based on his own experiences as a standout left-sided midfielder in the English Premier League. Using tactics he learned from legendary Derby County manager Brian Clough, Hinton brought in an influx of extraordinary talent with the support of owner Vince Coluccio.

A particular coup was purchasing the vaunted trio of forward Roger Davies, defender David Nish and goalkeeper Jack Brand from his former club, Tulsa.

"At the end of the day, X's and O's are very important, but the most important thing for every coach is to know talent. And I knew talent."

The list goes on. The midfield was led by exceptional playmakers Tommy Hutchison and Alan Hudson - the latter a favourite of a kid named Adrian Hanauer, who grew up to be Sounders FC General Manager. A rigid defence was led by Ian Bridge and Bruce Rioch, not to mention Brand, who recorded 15 shutouts that season. It didn't stop there. There was Jon Ryan, a second-team All-NASL defender, versatile Frank Barton in midfield and crafty Steve Buttle.

No wonder home crowds at the Kingdome averaged more than 24,000.

Davies, in particular, had a magical season, scoring a league-high 25 goals ("and with a smile that lit up the Kingdome," Hinton says) to earn the NASL most valuable player award.

"Most importantly, it was one of things where everything and everyone just clicked," says Mark Peterson, the team's second-leading scorer as a 19-year-old forward from Tacoma.

Seattle quickly caught fire. Through 23 games the Sounders had a sparkling 21-2 record - the best start for any team in this city until the Storm of the WNBA started 22-2 this summer.

"Everything fell into place," remembers forward Bruce Miller, who was injured (broken ribs, punctured lung, torn diaphragm) in the season's second game in a collision with the San Jose Earthquakes goalkeeper.

But euphoria came to a quick halt in the playoffs. Seattle's season came to a startling end in the National Conference semi-finals with an agonizing loss to Los Angeles in a mini-game.

Jeff Stock, a 19-year-old defender from Tacoma, says it was particularly shocking "because when we walked out on the field, we thought we were going to win every game. It wasn't a question."

Work hard. Play hard.

Almost half of the 1980 roster, it seemed, was English and, that was credit to Hinton's recruiting across the pond. Many of those players, who brought with them a playing pedigree from the top leagues in Europe, also provided a sense of professionalism.

"Those guys came in and worked hard all the time, they never slacked off," says Miller, a Canadian. "The typical English player at that time had the attitude of "work hard, play hard." They worked hard as they could and, played hard in the games, and then afterwards they went out and had a good time. They liked their beer, that's for sure, but they never slacked off."

An affinity for pints and pinpoint passing might best describe the complex Hudson. A carry-over from the Jimmy Gabriel-coached team in 1979, Hudson needed convincing to stay in Seattle and play under Hinton. Hudson later battled alcoholism, declared bankruptcy and was in a coma for two months after being hit by a car. He eventually made a full recovery and has written three books.

Potential issues and distractions from an eclectic mix of personalities, however, were eliminated by leadership, says Stock, who now owns Omni Properties in Federal Way and Caffe D'arte.

"If you look at the guys that we had, they were all captains on the teams they came over from," Stock says. "They were all great leaders."

The locker room was close but had its share of playful ribbings. Americans, especially the young ones, would get sarcastically taunted by the English about playing "football" the proper way. Rioch would get teased for being an Englishman on the Scottish national team.

All in good fun!

Hinton said, "I used to tell all my teams, 'let's get along because if we don't, coming to practice will be tough. If we win some games and get along, the season will be over in five minutes."

Planting a seed

It was always about more than just soccer for the 1980 Sounders. A self-proclaimed group of working-class guys felt they were part of the community. They nurtured an unusually open relationship with fans. Training clinics and youth camps were as common as picturesque

Hutchison assists from the wing. Call it cliché, but it wasn't all about the money. One generation later, the fruits of that labour are seen in the Qwest Field stands.

"When I first started playing, parents didn't understand the game," Peterson says. "Finally, it's catching that wave. People that played and understand the game are making it a major sport. It's been a part of them all their life."

Hinton marvels when he sees the crowds for Sounders FC games - the best in Major League Soccer - and can't help but think of the old days.

"We have been waiting for this to happen again," Hinton says. I wake up and say, "Wow, 36,000 people." That's down to the love of soccer here and it's all going to get bigger. It was real privilege to be here and be amongst the great people. Now that I'm 30 years older, I just love the way the game has taken off.

"Here's to the next 30 years."

We did not help build a winning tradition in Seattle, for we built our very own winning tradition. Players came and went on a regular basis, but that team was a very special one that will never be equalled both on and off the playing fields of any stadium they wish to build. On my first evening there I dined with Jack Daley in the wonderful Space Needle, which was the equivalent of our Post Office Tower and, I stayed that high over the next four years, right until what I call 'A Big Fat Yank' of the worse kind come along. Bruce Anderson shattered all that was built, like, you might say, "A Bull in a China Shop" and. I think I could not put that more aptly. Like I write of the likes of Don Revie, one man should not be allowed so much power, Seattle may have recovered financially, but that's not difficult in the USA, but they'll never see what those fans, both young and old, will never experience what those back then experienced.

And like Chelsea, Arsenal and Stoke City they disappoint me with their ignorance of it all….for it is never the achievers that get the rewards, it's always the followers who live off the scraps….the names that followed us could never have gone to Giant Stadium and did what we did and, there will never be another team that will show the fans a 22-2 record, and break the record with six matches remaining.

I can recall having dinner with Alan and Joy Hinton, Ray and Sandra Evans and my wife Maureen in a restaurant in Bellevue when the news came through that we had won that our record could not be touched after one of our rivals failed to win. Well, I've no need to tell you of our reaction….for not only could we play with the best we could….

15 THE WORKING MAN'S BALLET

So fifteen years after originally writing the Ballet for you, I live to do begin my new book with this chapter. Nobody could see me doing such a thing as I lay paralysed in my hospital bed once coming round. However, I told you way back in 1997 that my life story was a roller coaster ride with many twists and turns, never knowing that the last would not only be the last, but fatal!

Unlike where I begin my story saying these were the happiest times of my life, sitting in my bar in Seattle, lying under that tree in the Mile End Road and then the Intensive Trauma Unit of the Royal London Hospital is something more out of a Stephen King novel than The Ballet, however, this is how the original started….

It was 3.30am and I was, as usual, feeling melancholy. I love being out with my mates, but a moment like this afterwards reflecting on such wonderful times is something to behold. It was moments like this I felt so lucky, yet my life was far from that. I did not know, obviously, at that time that my life would become threatened in the kind of way you only see in a movie. This was Godfather stuff. But for now, I thought of my family and best friends, mainly Leslie, and my thoughts were simply that I wished that they could share these special moments with me. After all they had brought me up to experience such times, they educated me more than they had planned, you might even say, I had taken enjoying my life onto a different level. I was, after all, over all of my troubles and woes at Chelsea and Arsenal, and although missing my love affair with Waddington, I had found a different kind of love affair that I could never have imagined. The difference was this affair was with a place.

This is the man who named my first book, or you might say I stole it from his heart and, oh boy did he have one. One of my greatest regrets is that he never managed so many of the great players in this book. Had he, he would have been talked of in the kind of terms that would put today's managers firmly where they belong. As Tina sang of George, she also sang of my boss, mentor and great friend, Tony Waddington, was Simply the Best!

If only he could have been there with me. I had shared great times with him all round the world including his humble surroundings of Abersoch, so as I sat drooling over my future, I dreamed of repaying him for such magical and memorable times. There are no words to describe just how delighted I was that Chelsea booted me out and into his capable hands. What makes it even more delightful, is that they thought that Chelsea would thrive and Hudson and Osgood would wither and die. I just wish I could have been in their boardroom on the day of their incredible relegation, just for that one moment when that final whistle blew for their last match in the old First Division. However, I bet it did not stop those directors cracking open another bottle, yeah, the one we paid for. By this time though, I was with Waddington.

Some people win the lottery, I found Tony, like Seabiscuit found Tom Parker in his hour of need, without knowing coming across such a person would mean and, it was only in my later life, especially in my hospital bed trying to piece this all together that I realised just who was who and, the importance of such people. Special people are so difficult to find. I had one whilst going through my worst experience and that was George Mason, my uncle. Like on a football field you need someone by your side, like Bremner needed Giles, Osgood needed Hutchinson and I needed John Mahoney, in hospital George was the same. It is pretty much like a wonderful love affair, a fling if you like, where you can let yourself go knowing someone is there if things get really daunting. I remember at Stoke City when Leeds were doing a job on us leading 2-0 and beginning to swagger we needed to do something about it, and quick. Although no words were spoken between Josh (Mahoney) and I we knew just by the odd glance that we had to get to grips with the two Leeds playmakers, if we were going to both get back in the match and get out of the Victoria Ground with our pride intact. Nobody inside that wonderful, sometimes spooky, old ground knew what needed to be done, but I'm proud to say that it was the Welshman and I that swung it our way. Others who contributed to a near miraculous fight back might disagree, but I feel, as always, a match is won and lost in midfield and, that is why Barcelona are the greatest club side in the world today and, that is why Tony Waddington's remarkable achievements were getting so close to the kind of heights that would have been talked of forever and a day, had that roof not blown away all of his dreams. Like getting hit by that car, one freak gust of nature blew everything down the A40. The reason Waddington was so special, id because he did it alone, like Tom Parker.

When the chips are down, you can rely on the one next to you and, that is a wonderful feeling, but to go it alone is more so, look at Maradona, Pele, Best and Messi, they were blessed with such a talent that, although they played in great teams, they lifted the greatness to another level. And this was what Tony looked for in a player.

Where would Arthur Daley have been without Terry?

I felt like this at this time of the morning, arriving home after a long day out with my team-mates, where I was fortunate once again in my life to help build such a great team spirit. This was the first time since that horrific moment at The Hawthorns (WBA) that at last all my bad times were behind me. Having been out of work for six months prior, I was now captaining a club which had broken all records in this part of the world. A part of the world where I truly wished I could have spent my entire life. You could say I had found my niche.

I sat down at my bar, fixed myself my favourite tipple, Crown Royal Deluxe, ginger ale, with a slice of orange on top of a crystal glass full of crushed ice. It was absolute pure Nectar.

Overlooking this great city, I then let Sinatra take over.

Had Frank have been a player he would have had to share the billing with those I just mentioned, whereas with being such an artist of song, he stood alone.

I must break into the story because this is the only part of the book this can fit, much like that jigsaw puzzle that I get out of the box every now and then.

Just recently 15.12.2011 I have had contact with Max Clifford, that brilliant PR man who frightens people, the wrong people, that is, or is it the right people? He is like a great footballer - a sport he loves - and, that being he keeps his business simple. And, one of the reasons he has been so highly successful is just that, unlike so many people, he can keep a secret. That is his secret to success.

He has no ego!

Then, all of a sudden I was introduced to his book READ ALL ABOUT IT and was stunned when I learned that I sat only a few seats away from him back in 1971 at the Royal Festival Hall. Anyhow he tells it like this and, the memory of that wonderful night came flooding back - My best and most memorable recollection of him was the gala concert he gave at London's Royal Festival Hall in 1971, a year after I set up on my own and the same year he announced one of many retirements. It was a star studded black-tie occasion. Sinatra was introduced by Grace Kelly, his co-star in the film High Society, Bob Hope, Prince Rainier, Nelson Riddle and Princess Margaret were also amongst the host of celebrities present. I had a great seat near the front behind Paul and Barry Ryan. Paul was with his girlfriend and Barry was with Princess Mariam, the daughter of the Sultan of Johor, then one of the world's richest men, who he married in June 1976. Sinatra sang some of his old favourites including "I've Got You under My Skin" and "Strangers in The Night" and then about halfway through the show he announced, "Ladies and gentlemen. I'm now going to sing a new song, by a wonderful British songwriter, Paul Ryan. It's called "I Will Drink the Wine" and I'm about to record it. Paul had decided to quit performing to write songs, and was desperate for a big name to sing one of his compositions. He'd sent a few songs, including "I Will Drink the Wine" to Sinatra about a month before the concert. Sinatra would probably never have known about them, except that unbeknown to Paul, Harold (Davidson) mentioned the songs to him. He then looked through them and picked out that particular melody. When he finished singing, he pointed to Paul and asked him to take a bow. A spotlight followed Sinatra's hand and settled on Paul, who was so taken aback he was rooted to his chair. I leaned forward, gave him a push and said, "Get up, get up." He did and the entire audience applauded him. It was an amazing and unforgettable moment and very generous of Sinatra. There he was, the biggest star in the world, thanking Paul a young songwriter. It was an example of Sinatra's generous side and showed how kind he could be when he wanted to."

Max was one of the select few to be invited to the intimate post-concert. Well that brought back some very exciting and incredibly emotional memories, there was my all-time favourite songster and, there was my uncle George and I sitting within touching distance, just like Max. Elsewhere in Max's wonderful book of incredible meetings with such stardom he mentions a party thrown at Annabelles in Mayfair, where the doorman there was a big Chelsea fan and friend of mine - and a lovely man - named Joe McKay, who I bought those two tickets off and, who started my pal Danny Gillen on his way when introducing him to Victor Lowndes of Playboy fame. It was not until picking up Max's book that this all seemed like a jigsaw puzzle that had been left on the sideboard with the box waiting to be opened and the puzzle to be finished. I walked past the Festival Hall just about a month ago, for only the second time and my hairs stood up thinking of such a night.

This was Sinatra at his supreme best!

Harold Davidson was married to Paul and Barry's mother Marion Ryan, a well-known English singer in the 50's and 60's. I met Harold in the early Seventies through a friend in the music business, but never knew the connection. Every time I put Sinatra on, whether a CD, a plastic album (which I had in Seattle) or on a pub jukebox, I still see Frank standing there a few feet away. There may be two or three people in this book that oozed such class, but as I speak of him, he stands alone.

15522 South East 48th Drive, Bellevue, Washington, was the house of my dreams. Many miles, dreams and nightmares from our Chelsea prefab. Along with Sinatra this was my inspiration. It gave me a feeling of achievement. I did not have much else to show for all that I did in the game. When you think in my first two seasons I had achieved something that not even Johnny Haynes had done in his entire career. I had won both the FA Cup and European Cup Winners Cup. The FA Cup even eluded George.

However, it seemed that apart from my incredible experience at Stoke City under Mr. Waddington, it all went sour.

All through, initially an injury that crushed most of all of what I set out to do and was then followed by an accumulation of events that you will soon be reading about.

My career in England was behind me and I was once again forgotten. All I had to show for what looked like being a glittering career was an FA Cup winners' and losers' medal, a European Cup Winners Cup winners' medal, a League Cup losers' medal, runner-up at the Football Writers Footballer of the Year Awards, The Most Exciting Player of the Year Award in 1975, two full and several under-23 England caps.

Something that I don't understand is when these pundits (former players and media) speak of experienced international players - I call them experienced failures - as they did in South Africa once again. Before they took the field against Germany in the last World Cup they were talking of us being more experienced than our most illustrious opponents. Franz Beckenbauer had it right when saying we were burnt out, whilst the Germans were fresh and had more desire. Going back to the experience of such players, I made it very clear that these players are what I call, 'Experienced Losers.' Take David Beckham for instance, had he not got injured he would have played in his fourth World Cup, which would have been a record. That to me was a negative, for if he could not win, or get to a final whilst at his peak, what chance have we got when on his last legs?

Just look at England managers. If you judged them the same way, you would be stupid enough to believe that Keegan, Eriksson, Hoddle and the two Taylor's were more cut out for this job than Clough and Waddington.

Once again, I don't think so.

Before I go to print Eriksson has just been sacked by Leicester City.

Before that he was at Notts County.

At one stage he was being paid off by the FA and at least one Football League club at the same time.

But what has he achieved whilst entering this country?

It seems the most success he had was with a weathergirl and that FA office girl. Both affairs fitted quite nicely into my other book, along with several of his former players, John Terry, Ashley Cole, Peter Crouch and Steve Gerrard. Can you imagine him still being the manager when John Terry was brought in front of the FA when he was doing the same thing with a certain very attractive young lady by the name of Faria Alam?

This was the most success he had as England manager and any other job he has had over here:

FARIA ALAM REVEALS ALL

Sven Goran Eriksson is a master in the art of lovemaking according to former FA secretary Faria Alam. The 38-year-old Ms. Alam has finally revealed the sordid intimacies of her affair with the England coach Sven Goran-Eriksson and the former FA chief executive Mark Palios. In interviews with the Mail on Sunday and the News of the World she has described in graphic detail their sexual affair and reportedly she even intimated she would not be averse to marrying him. In the report she says that she vowed that she would never marry again but now she was so in love with Sven, that if he did propose she would most likely have said, "Yes."

Faria Alam has also revealed how she first fell for Palios and said she was attracted by his aura of power. Regarding Eriksson it was at a Christmas dinner, she was seated at a table for 10 people with Mr. Eriksson on her left and Mr., Palios on her right. The newspaper reports that according to Ms. Alam Sven soon signalled his intentions by as she says, fondling her at the table. Claiming the England coach rubbed his leg against hers and she whispered back to him and asked him what he thought he was doing. Her account goes on to say that he just smirked and put his finger to his lips and said shhh!

In the report Ms. Alam recalls she was shocked by former FA communications director Colin Gibson's proposal that if the News of the World left Mr. Palios out of it she would have to tell them all about Eriksson.

Following the revelations both Palios and Gibson have resigned but Eriksson still survives as the FA found he had no case to defend.

According to the newspapers Ms. Alam says she flatly refuses to lie for them and their disgraceful plot has been exposed. Further saying Sven has done nothing wrong but the FA was willing to sacrifice him to get Palios off the hook, he was hung out to dry by the FA in a similar manner as she herself had been.

So, although you cannot knock him, he earned a fortune for being a great lover. Well, I know that George Best couldn't have been that bad, but how come he never got such financial reward for entertaining the entire world?

And then there was, of course, Bobby Moore and, how shabbily did those same people at the FA treat him, the man known as God amongst his peers.

It seems nothing has changed after all this time. But back to my story, although what I have just told you about me, I still felt this had been a successful journey. On the night that I decided to write my life story, again it was the longest day on the calendar, 21 June 1981. It was 30 years to the day of my birth in Elm Park Gardens, just off the Fulham Road, Chelsea. There's something about thirty years…

As I sat listening to my all-time favourite songster, looking out over one of the most beautiful of cities in the world, it hit me that the time was right to write the Ballet. In the wee-small hours I thought of several titles, but there was only one. If only because of the greatest man I've ever met in this game of theirs. Yeah, theirs, it's not ours anymore, although I still have the inkling to wrestle them at times!

I felt this because I had come so far, travelled many miles, visited so many wonderful places and had met more than enough famous, infamous and other interesting people. However, it was the "others" that always irked me. If they had just left me alone, anyhow, that's the way I see it.

I am also proud to have known Waddington because he was always in control, the kind of control that was so assuring, it is a just a crying shame he could not control the weather and, because of that he one day had to being in the Fire Brigade, for that is how much he cared and how far he'd go. But that was a long way down this long road, but I tell you early on because until I got to him nobody else had such a wonderful insight into things that to others were an everyday occurrence, but to us life shattering.

Do people ever turn around and mention about Jimmy Greaves feelings about missing that World Cup experience, no, of course not, they're too busy patting themselves on the back and counting their money. Did anybody really care about Bobby Moore in Bogota or when he called it a day, no mate, well, Jimmy did, but Jimmy did not have the kind of power that those sitting in their high powered offices have.

You just must watch when Jimmy met Bobby; you can see it on Google!

I also felt I had come to the end of my life, in football terms. I truly wanted to stay in Seattle for the rest of my days. The most important thing about all of this, though, was the special people who you will read about. The downside to this story never entered my mind at this time, especially the experience in the Mile End Road which was, without me knowing, going to soon be a big part of this story. Not only that, but so close to, as Frank sang, "My Final Curtain."

I had experienced many setbacks and heartaches throughout my career, but what was to follow years later threw a completely different light on things.

When feeling like this, I used to call my best pal, Leslie - remembering there was an eight-hour difference - and we'd talk about life on both sides of the pond. Oh how I wanted him to come and experience this life with me. This was, apart from my playing under Waddington, the greatest time of my life in the game. My experience at Chelsea was fantastic, but that was only because of the players I shared it with. As for the club, they were and still are something that leaves a very bad taste in my mouth, and several deep regrets.

Had I only been allowed to have played for Fulham, my life would have taken such a different direction and, one I feel for the best. I loved playing with players like Cooke and Osgood, but I would have given it all up to play down the road with Johnny Haynes, who was just running out of petrol at the Cottage. I could have put a few more gallons in his tank, with my young legs and extra-special eagerness. In those early days I could - through my training regime - run through any kind of barrier. Some players like Alan Ball were blessed with such a thing, but I had to work at it and, because of the lifestyle I chose to lead, I had to work even harder, so much so, it became an obsession. Thankfully, it helped save my life.

I suppose what I am trying to tell you, is that all of what we went through was wasted on people who actually believe they were a part of it all. They, of course, were not. I have no time for impostors and that is the category that I put them into. They criticize us years on, but deep down, they have not got a clue what the game is all about, even the ones who know, don't really know, they are simply caught up in something that they know nothing about.

If you were to ask them the real question about a player they could not tell you why he was special. Take Harry Redknapp - who had just left Seattle at the beginning of this book - for example, he said not long ago (in 2011 as I write) that Joe Cole was the best young player he'd ever seen, when Joe can't even play football, he simply hasn't got a clue as to when to pass a football. And Harry was wanted to run our national team, not that he would not have done a good job, but don't make him out to be some kind of Football Messiah, please! That would be like taking Alan Shearer, Iain Dowie, Mark Lawrenson and Gary Lineker seriously and, as the great John McEnroe used to tell the line judge of referee, "you can't be...

To think my upbringing was all about Chelsea, all the good things, the football, the friends and later on the growing up in and around at such a time, was breath-taking. Each and every day was a different experience, but that was when it was Chelsea. The comings and goings of the likes of Bates and Abramovich is simply a sign of the times, but the people of Chelsea are no longer important. After my coming out of hospital - and my wife having walked away - I moved in with my mother, only to find after her death that I would be kicked out of her flat. I went to see Michael Portillo and he was more interested in Elton getting married to his live-in boyfriend. Even a gay politician was against me. So you might say the worm had turned and the Con Man was definitely one of those worms. As I say, Chelsea is most definitely a place to be remembered as a kid growing up.

I try my best to keep at arms' length, sad for the most local player in their history and, as Frank sang once again, "my story is sad, but true." But as I mentioned somewhere else, history stands for nothing. I remember Ken Bates once saying that, "Chelsea didn't exist until I got here."

No, it didn't, not his Chelsea that is. My Chelsea was knocked down long ago, much like the Cage being replaced by Chelsea Harbour. Much like The Chelsea Drug Store becoming MacDonald's, The Markham Arms turned into the Halifax Building Society and more importantly, for those Chelsea supporters, The Stamford Bridge Arms, becoming The Butchers Hook.

The crying shame of it all is that there is nobody inside Stamford Bridge that would not have a clue about the history of what I have just mentioned. These were all there when I was growing up at Park Walk Primary School and when I left for Stoke City eleven years on, but when I returned from Seattle, it was if there had been a Third World War, the place had been obliterated.

I thought that Adolf had returned from his bunker.

I truly feel sad for those that gave so much to the area in my short trouser days, making it a place where and when the sun seemed to shine for longer periods and, much brighter. There seemed to be much more delight and happiness in winning then and, I put that down to the fans and those surrounding Stamford Bridge and Fulham Broadway being local.

If you had taken a survey of who came from within five miles of this place after their recent Champions League triumph, you'd need to check their visas.

It seems to me that Stoke-on-Trent is now much clearer with the smoke and smog of the pot banks seemingly having travelled down south. I was asked some time ago by a friend, "Alan, why do you spend more time in Stoke than you do in London?" My answer was as swift as Greaves latching onto a loose ball, "I prefer Stoke because the people in Stoke are from Stoke." It is as simple as that and, if those living from where they're bred then they'll have more respect for the place and, I respect that in them. Don't get me wrong their politicians are as big an "arsehole" as in London, but that is the world over, after all someone has to cheat, don't they!

Where they used to be one big happy family, they are now insignificant and the minority in their own environment. I think what sums it up more than anything is Chelsea Harbour.

Although it stinks of money, it is classless. It is, in fact, like me now, homeless.

But here I was, living a completely different life and at that precise moment I wanted it to be, as I said, my resting place. It was the place I had been looking for although never ever contemplating I would find such a place and, all through nobody in my own country wanting me. Surely I could not have been that bad, after all, we hadn't qualified for a World Cup for eight years and, just before I left I was selected to play against Brazil. Please don't ask me to work that out, because if I did, it would give you the exact answer to all of England's problems since Bobby Moore lifted that tiny trophy above his golden locks.

But back to Seattle, being the only love I have ever lost and truly miss, apart from my family and a two year-old filly named My Lifetime Lady, but more of her later. Although I made the mistake of leaving one other beauty behind, the kind of girl I think I would have found complete happiness with. Hindsight is the most mysterious of things and there were so many times when I thought I had it cracked, and then The Man upstairs intervened.

Born Alan Anthony Hudson on 21 June 1951 - the longest day of the year - I was the second son of Bill and Bubs, I had the most wonderful upbringing and I put those successes I mentioned earlier down to that alone. The appreciation of all the good things in life, appreciating my father working all hours sent to put clothes on our backs and shoes and football boots on our tiny feet. My brother John - also a very talented player - was just over two years older than me and we shared a tiny room until he moved out of our prefab to marry Pauline Thomas in my first season as a professional. My sister Julie came along after a couple of years of us being in Upcerne Road, where the prefab stood. I defy anyone to tell me that they had a better upbringing, although Bill worked all hours and his fingers to the bone, something you don't really appreciate until it's your turn. This I suppose made it even more special as his hard work was not, unlike today, for his needs, but ours.

I look over this again - before going to print - just after the Tottenham Riots and after hearing the excuses given by those in Parliament, the media and other authorities and organisations, I am proud to say that Chelsea was the safest place on earth, despite the poverty and lack of what kids have today. When we weren't playing football in the streets we were racing our go-carts made out of a plank of wood with four ball bearings as wheels. The pole to push these contraptions might have been from the washing line, whereas today it would no doubt be a weapon of some kind?

My dad began on the Asphalt before turning to cleaning windows and painting and decorating. He also played Amateur on Saturday and for the Chelsea Old Boys on a Sunday morning. These were the generation us youngsters looked up to and, what I remember the most is there being the most wonderful characters amongst them. The main meeting place was the Worlds End Cafe. It was where the Chelsea and Fulham supporters ate, drank and exchanged many memorable antidotes (abusive slang) with one another.

That turned into a Greek fish and chip shop a few doors away from Paddy Power which used to be the Wetherby Arms, where the Rolling Stones used to play. Opposite there I can still see Tommy Steele waiting for one of the lads to give him instructions before a Sunday match. The air in those days seemed like it was so much lighter. The sky seemed brighter and there were so many more smiling faces. When I go back now, the faces are a different colour and the smiles on them are gone.

I'm not trying to make this sound all doom and gloom but that is the way I see it and, I think I see it with the kind of vision I once carried with me onto the playing fields, that was Arsenal apart, but nobody can go through life without a nightmare or two, or in my case at Highbury, three.

Bill, my dad, was not only a very good player, he also knew about the game. He could put it across to you, unlike those I mentioned a few pages back. I don't know where he got it from, to this day, but he certainly had it. The game was different in those days. I think people understood it more. Today there is too much written in newspapers. I was once close to Harry Redknapp and, thought the world of him. But he talks in The Sun newspaper as if those of us far less fortunate don't know what we're looking at. With the greatest respect, Harry once spoke down to me and, I wasn't too pleased. I had just come out of a coma and he was the West Ham manager. I could have run that team - that included Di Canio and John Hartson - from my coma. He had Joe Cole, but never had the know-how to complete his progress as a player. People like Ferguson and Mourinho - which he did for a while - would drum into him the other side of the game. The game is not all about showboating. If it was, Joe Cole would have been in the Italian's class. Paolo was the absolute business in those days and had Joe had an ounce of what he had, he might have made a real player, but instead of making a player he made a fortune!

I do understand however, that Harry is from that part of London where, along with Allison, Bond, Brown and Sexton, they thought that football was invented there, but as you read on you'll find that to be a load of bollocks. How many times have they won the League Championship or Premier League?

Their fickle - and sometime unbelievable fans - still walk around saying that they won the World Cup.

And in this first part of the book you'll read of them never having a Cooke or an Osgood. Or a Hudson come to that, probably the nearest thing to me was Alan Devonshire. Oh, and they never in those early days had a keeper anywhere near as good as Bonetti, although Phil Parkes was a fantastic keeper, but that was in a different era. So someone somewhere has it all wrong. As I write in another book of mine, Don't Shoot the Taliban....You'll Wake the Locals, there are managers and there are managers. Ron Greenwood and Arsene Wenger are two Academy addicts, who love attacking, flowing football going forward, but when the other team gets the ball, they are simply clueless. Plus, both men have not got a clue about goalkeepers and centre-halves, if they had....

Without Bobby Moore, West Ham would not have won the FA and Cup Winners Cup and England would now still be wondering when they'd win their first World Cup?

George Graham left Wenger an incredible back four and if he hadn't the Frenchman's cabinet would be even more like Old Mother Hubbard's.

As I say, people get carried away with themselves. That is what I am talking about with my father, for he knew the game, now all of a sudden it becomes rocket science with these people. Not long ago Harry was trying to offload Bale and Pavlyuchenko because he didn't fancy them and, the next thing you know he's spouting out that they are incredible players for him.

My dad once told Sexton not to try to teach, or tell me how to play, as Waddington said a few years on, "I never told Alan how to play, he already knew. When I signed him, I just sat back and watched him play."

That's management!

So my father, Bill, Brought me and John up well, although John was one of those who did not listen to him as I did. Maybe his reason was not being as hungry as I was and, although my hunger was deep rooted, I still never dreamt I'd make it to the very top. It wasn't a lack of confidence, it was simply, I was just a happy-go-lucky young kid, who loved life and, that was what got me in trouble in later life. I trusted people too much, the wrong people, I thought at an early age that the world was a good place. I thought that everyone outside of our prefab were like those inside of it. I know I was naïve and, because I mixed with good honest people, it was to become my downfall. I suppose it all sank in, finally, when I met Ken Bates and realised that I lived in the wrong world, or was it the right one?

There were other Ken Bates=like figures that stood in my way, one was in the Potteries and one in Seattle and, it was when coming across them, the power of money was too much for me. They knew nothing about what I have just been talking about, but they had the power (money).

If only I could have got into the game as a manager, I know that I would have been up there with the best of them and, the reason I know that is because I have the ability to takes the bones out of the good, the bad and the ugly.

Who are they?

Waddington, Neill and Revie in that order, as for Alf, he was the luckiest manager ever to put on an England tracksuit. I'll give you four reasons and they are Banks, Moore, Ball and Charlton.

There would have been five had Jimmy been fit for those matches outside the group stages. However, had he not got that injury, I have a funny feeling that we might not have won it.

I think it was destiny. Geoff Hurst was destined to become the only man to ever score a hat-trick in a World Cup final, just as Chelsea were destined to somehow knock out Barcelona, however they didn't need a dodgy Russian linesman, they relied on a Cech, a goal post, a crossbar and, then of course, how on earth could Lionel Messi - the greatest player since Maradona - miss from twelve yards, when he's been chipping goalkeepers from closer in.

Forget all you hear and read in the newspapers, if you want your son to become a footballer, simply sit him down and show him a video of Lionel Messi. He defies everything that has ruined our game from Lancaster Gate to Soho Square. I remember seeing Alan Ball at 17 and, when they question a player's size, forget it. Messi, Maradona, Ball are all magicians in their own right.

Some people are just born lucky and, had Bobby listened to Jack Charlton, who was screaming at him, to do what defenders do today - kicked it into touch - that ball that hit the bar and did NOT cross the line would have made the final result even more controversial. But Bobby was the only one in Wembley Stadium, just over a 100,000, who kept his head and his composure before coolly clipping the ball over the oncoming Germans for his mate to finish them off.

It still hurts, knowing how Bobby was treated....

You see, when I talk about Bobby Moore, had he played under Waddington for so long and, so marvellously, Tony would have made sure that he stayed in the game at the very top level, as he did with George Eastham, a man Tony admired and appreciated. Tony knew that if George could pass just a morsel onto me in training - which he did - then he was worth his weight in gold, although George didn't weigh that much, however, he was like most of the most talented players you ever have seen, only frail, but not when in possession. I suppose frail is not the right word, but you know what I mean, today's players are big and strong, but can they do what Eastham used to do? I don't think so!

It is not all about physical strength it is all about mental strength.

As a youngster I was frail, but things would change, but it took a very long time, in fact, I never grew up until I reached Waddington, for he made a man out of me. Why?

That is because he gave me a license to kill (play). The difference was, when I played against Charlie George, as a 14-year-old schoolboy, he played as if it was a formality that he would go all of the way. There wasn't anything about his play, his body language or his attitude that seemed to have any doubt. And he was so talented, or gifted, I think gifted, because that is what it is, a gift!

Not something that Santa might bring you, that is called making money for the enemy. I real gift is from one man to another, with no middle man involved and, as with Tony, there was no middle man.

It much like falling madly in love for the one and only time, there is nothing else in the world that matters and, that was how it was with Waddington. He was my gift from out of nowhere. Like Parker with Seabiscuit. I have felt this way over a woman, but somehow there seems something missing, that is why I understand more than most about gay partners, I watch them and they give everything to each other.

"YOU MAKE ME COMPLETE" - YOU DON'T EVEN HAVE TO SAY IT!

As in the elevator in Jerry Maguire the dumb boy signals to his girlfriend that, "you make me complete" and, when I put my red and white striped shirt on and looked at Waddington, that is how I felt. No wonder they sang that I could walk on water. There were times at the Victoria Ground that I thought I could fly and, I am frightened of heights, unless I am sitting holding a drink in one hand looking out of the window.

Anyhow, back to that prefab where my brother left Chelsea under a cloud and after a row with Tommy Docherty, Bill threatened to take me from the Bridge, but was told in no uncertain terms that if he took me away my future would be in doubt, in fact, very much in doubt.

You see, football is no different from any other trade and, when you're walking into the unknown you don't have the time to dither. It's like dithering on the ball, in the end, you'll get caught.

I was just fifteen then. So my brother left and joined Guildford before being transferred to Bexley.

He was a terrific player, more skillful than me and, he was a rare talent, that being he was left-sided. And, how our country needed such players, for they are a rare breed and, the type we don't seem to inherit.

After all of these years waiting for a Gareth Bale, he comes along and, he's Welsh.

In all my time here, we have only ever had two natural left sided players, who could play wide and, they were Peter Thompson and John Barnes and, they were both brilliant players.

Yeah, there were several others. I mean players who would have fitted into any other national team on earth. The problem with Barnes was that he was too good for England, for they just did not know when or how to give him the ball and, he had a problem, he was Jamaican and a very talented one. When he had the ball you could put music to it and dance, The Ballet, I suppose, again, Tony was right!

Both of these would not have figured in Alf's World Cup plans. In fact, Thompson didn't and, Alf thought he could justify that by boasting winning it. He was wrong, however, because in 1966 he took our game back years.

Four years later Brazil showed that Ramsey was wrong by boasting Rivelino and Jairzinho in their World Cup winning side and, one where they didn't need the help of a Russian linesman or the sending-off of the Argentina captain. Ramsey called them "Animals" yet had Nobby Stiles in his team...

Martin Peters played on the left side in the World Cup and, was basically right-footed. Years on, Emile Heskey played there also, but I am not saying he was anything like the great Peters, in fact, nothing like him at all. Peters was a superb footballer. If this book does one thing, it gets across comparisons pretty well. Joe Cole for instance, although the same size, could have done with a lesson or two from Alan Ball, as could all of our modern day midfield players. Bobby Charlton is another that will never be seen again, unless you dig Tony and Brian up. They simply loved talent.

I live in Stoke-on-Trent and often I walk through the streets and ask myself where have all the young players gone?

It is quite simple really. There's nobody bloody looking for them, well, nobody with the ability to spot a player. I go to Stoke City training ground and I ask, "Who that?" Oh he coaches so and so...then, I'll ask, "Who's that?" Oh he's a scout...My mind goes spinning and, I laugh thinking of Tonto...you ask why English football is in a state, read on!

Up front we've never had anyone with the know-how of Geoff Hurst or the brilliance of Greaves. In the last World Cup Robert Green, I mean, how could you speak about him in the same breath as Gordon Banks?

We would have been better digging up Hughie Green.

And as for captain of our national team, since our greatest ever, Bobby Moore, only Bryan Robson can be talked about in such glowing terms and, as world class. A word slung about today as if at a wedding.

Billy Hudson once went on a coaching course - to Lilleshall, I think - one Sunday morning and, was back in our prefab by supper time. When my mum asked him what he was doing home, he said that they told him to do the washing up. He walked out, saying "I'm here to coach." You see, my dad never, ever did the washing up in his own home, so the FA had no chance of getting their dishes cleaned. They have the wrong people in the wrong places. They actually do have square pegs in round holes and they made them at Lilleshall.

OK, he lost out, but all that the FA ended up with was a clean kitchen and a load of coaches that would soon rubbish our game!

It was whilst playing in the Southern League that my dad spotted Ian Hutchinson, but that is all to come. Like me helping Frank Lampard get a move to Chelsea and Steve Bould to Arsenal, two fantastic signings, like my dad, I got nothing.

My brother became a little bit of a celebrity, where he and his partner, Tommy Trevatt, could be seen on the ITV, advertising Mars Bars. With the message being: Work, Rest and Play....which was something that would never apply to me. I worked hard and played hard, but the only time I got any rest was in all of my hospital beds!

The most famous story I knew of Mars Bars involved Mick Jagger and Marianne Faithful, but I was young and impressionable and it was, of course, allegedly!

On John's 11th birthday, the 20 May 1960, a 23-year-old Alan Hudson was to fight 18-year-old, Cassius Clay, in a Light Heavyweight bout in the USA. After a brave beginning hard man Hudson, was badly beaten by the man who would soon become the greatest boxer on the planet.

Oh how glad I was the other Alan Hudson!

Little did I know then, that one day I would fall in love with his country, as did George!

Like George and me, in some ways, Clay had a falling out with the authorities by refusing to go to war, whereas I refused to go on an unimportant under-23 trip. I would also have refused to fight for this country, for I have learned only to fight for people who fight for you, although I learned far too late, as I have said, I fought for Chelsea Football Club, but whilst I lay dying, they could not have given a fuck about me. You live and learn.

However, had I died - which I did - only had been buried, they would have had a nice Memorial for the local boy and all had a good time. But I would have been looking down on them, knowing that I was with far better people, for those living inside the walls of Stamford Bridge are a little like those in the basement of The Royal London Hospital. Did I say a little?

By not going to war it became his platform for the incredible fame he was about to achieve, Clay that is. However, my career took a turn for the worse, to say the least and, that was only a meaningless under 23 tour, not Vietnam. When he did so, Pele and George Best were on the same level as him in our game. In cricket - my second sport - that wonderful Jamaican, Garfield Sobers was the equivalent, in horse racing Lester Piggott, whilst in music Frank Sinatra was charming the millions with his velvet like voice. In England we were so fortunate to have the incredible Beatles, who along with The Beach Boys ruled the charts on both sides of the pond and, as I found in the States, Supertramp, who will come more into my story later. Their lyrics are a big part of my life, especially, "When I was young I thought that life was so wonderful, beautiful, magical, then they took me away…

These were all my favourite artists. This was all taking place when this world - well, my world - was a far better place than what it is today. Sadly Clay was struck down with that disease caused by too many blows to the head - much like many footballers heading those laced-up balls in those times - and today he is a very sorry sight, just as the world has become - but they still use greats like him. He was seen here in the Potteries only a year or so ago at a function that I refused to attend. The people who used him should be ashamed of themselves, but it seems nothing changes, for they don't seem to have what Clay had in abundance - class!

I was told, after the event, by more than one person, that the great man looked a very sorry sight, as I was when leaving the ICU just under seven stone. Whilst using him as the main part of their circus reminds me of another "great" of those times, who took the part of another circus act The Elephant Man - and like in all of the parts he played, he did it so magnificently - him being John Hurt.

You might think that I am making this up, but just yesterday, in fact a few hours ago, I approached the great Hurt outside the Green Man in Berwick Street and, as I have always stated strongly the greater the performer the greater the person. He was delightful. He was Bobby Moore, Jimmy Greaves, Johnny Haynes, Pele, Lester Piggott, Graham Bradley, David Nicholson, Phil Collins, Viv Richards, Tony Bennett, Jack Jones, Ray Winstone, Reggie Dwight and, I bet John Lennon, the only one of those I have not only had the pleasure to have met, but be in the company of and be a part of the occasion.

I really don't like dropping names, honestly, but when you're in the company of such wonderfully gifted people, I get a thrill. When there is so much bad going on in our world today and so many nasty people, I feel really good about writing about people who have entertained so many millions of ordinary folk over the years and, I mean ordinary with the greatest respect.

So my latest thrill was to meet John and, like on several other occasions I have regretted not approaching someone to tell them that they are so very special - which they certainly are - I missed that opportunity a few years ago. We were both in a pub somewhere in the City of London and I was nursing a rather nasty hangover and was down on my luck - what's new I hear you say - so I allowed the chance to pass me by. But yesterday, I told him, and he must have thought me mad, that I knew that our paths would one day cross again. I really did feel this and, when my mate said to me "John Hurt's outside" I knew then, that it would not happen again.

I mention this, because when I came out of my coma I was taken to Treves Ward, the one named after, Frederick Treves, who was the doctor who treated and was responsible for John Merrick himself, The Elephant Man...is this weird, or is it me?

So it looked like I would end my career, and my life, in the USA, and on this particular evening my mood was so great, I felt I was at peace with a world that had not been kind to me and, I had the feeling that I would never see the country I was born and bred in, ever again. I truly felt I had reached my destiny. I was totally in love with the United States of America. Again, though, The Man upstairs had other ideas, although it wasn't for the first time and most certainly wouldn't be the last. His last idea was a fraction away from taking my life.

The crazy thing was that I was here for all the wrong reasons.

At 27 years of age, in 1978, there was not one single football club in the world that wanted my services, when only six months prior I was, as I told you earlier, picked to play for England against the best team on the planet, Brazil. I declined!

Maybe had I played and performed as I did against the world champions of 1974, there would have been a host of clubs after my signature. Well, that was not to be, there was one who showed little interest. That was a Spanish second division club who I'd never heard of. For that reason, when the Arsenal secretary Ken Friar told me of such interest shown by Hercules FC. I immediately thought of Harold Steptoe's horse. Even they lost interest and I never found out the reason why. I would have loved to have played in Spain, especially with the climate being one of great warmth. Having said that, the grounds (playing fields) may just have been too firm for me and, I doubt if they would have had the aid of a Fire Brigade to take the sting out for my chronic ankle injury, but that will make more sense to you a little later.

On the 29th December 2010, I was invited to a great charity raising function in West Drayton, somewhere near Heathrow Airport, by Joe Smith, a famous local gypsy, bare knuckle fighter, professional boxer and professional golfer. Lionel Platts, a Ryder Cup golfer, wrote, "To be a fighter of such brutality and play golf to his level is incredible."

Anyhow, I was to see a man there I had met before and enjoyed his company immensely, he was John Fagan, and Joe said of John, "His claim to fame was that his father was the owner of Hercules (the horse), whose real name was Sally."

This not only brought back such memories, but made me chuckle! Hercules, the team, not the horse, has recently beaten Barcelona at the massive odds of 33/1
(Sept 2010).

When you have had as many setbacks as I have had throughout this life, it is extremely important you never lose your sense of humour and, that was something I needed more than ever before, twenty years on as I came round after 59 days from my coma. The morphine got me through those early days before finding out that my condition was one close to horrendous and it has become a never ending on-going nightmare. Other pills have replaced the morphine but quite the opposite of what Frank sang again, "too many to mention."

I think the most important drug I took was the anti-depressant, Amitriptyline, although I never knew how important until I stopped. It was a complete accident, in fact. I went away on a holiday with my mate Malcolm to Jerba and the day before returning I was beside myself. I was miserable - and we were having such fun - for some unknown reason. I then got to the airport and as Malcolm went for a smoke I was in a terrible state. I tried to telephone the wife that walked away from me, to apologise, but thankfully I could not get through. Once having a couple of drinks on the aircraft I cheered a little, but was still in need of help. We reached Victoria Station from Gatwick and caught a black cab back to Chelsea. At around six in the morning I walked into my bedroom and there on the sideboard were my tablets. Believe me, it is the one drug that I know definitely works.

The other one is a large Smirnoff vodka and Orange.

Those doctors were spot on as they told me, 'you'll not get any better.' I live my life now as if I died and come back to a far inferior one. After all, in my first life I could run, and I mean run. I would run while the world slept. I would go to bed - even after leaving the game - take a sleeper and, if it did not take effect after half an hour, I would slip into my running shoes and take off into the darkness. Had I not, I think I would not have survived the Mile End Road incident. Well, as I say elsewhere, my very last training session, I believe, may just have kept me alive, no, I know that it did, because it was that close and that session was one I got stuck into as if I knew what was waiting for me. It sounds bizarre and dramatic, but I truly believe that my last session in that gymnasium was the difference between me coming out of that hospital in a wheelchair or in a pine box.

They feared throughout that my heart would not hold out, but there was never any fear of that, if only for my training routine. No man with an 'iffy apple' could put themselves through what I did to myself and, that was after a good day out in great company. Only difference being, while they were sleeping it off, I was running it off. The booze, that is.

It was such a relief leaving all of this behind me. What I left behind was a catalogue of wonderful times and complete nightmares. The nightmares were brought on by people who I could no longer believe in, but the problem was, I never saw it coming. And, that wasn't the car. It was my wife walking away, it hurt so much. When I was at my lowest ebb, I needed her love and comforting more than I have ever needed anything before. I was scared after just getting over my paralysis and needed to show her that I would not be a burden and I would fight it all the way, the only way I know, but she disappeared into the cold night air just as that car drove into it and, I was devastated. However, although it is not a happy ending, the consolation was it gave me the strength, like playing against Don Revie, when he was my manager, to win this battle. I thank her, even though she doesn't deserve it. I say that, because had it been boot on the other foot, I would have put her first and taken care of her for the rest of our lives, that was unless, she didn't want that. That was what brought on the hurt and pain, the kind of pain no medicine can touch.

But let's go back to the beginning of the happiest period of my life. My eldest son Allen was six. I found after arriving in Seattle, I had more time to spend with him and loved every minute of it. I will be the first to admit in those early days playing the game you could not really call me a good father. It wasn't that I was a bad one, for it was because I was so wrapped up in my early days of great excitement and pleasure in not only playing the game, but being around such fantastic characters, playing against the best players in the world and being around beautiful girls in the kind of atmosphere that seems to have got lost in time.

I'm sorry, but the world was a far better place back then.

Some people go to work each and every day and it's a chore, I just couldn't wait to get into that training ground, every day. It was hard work and each day brought a new meaning to having fun. There was a story every day to cherish. The Osgood/Channon one, although I wasn't there, being a classic example.

The United States suited me and me them. It was a dream. And like all dreams, they either end, or turn into nightmares. Well, my biggest nightmare since missing those finals came in the shape of the worst kind of American - although I don't want to talk about him right now.

I was saying how I enjoyed my new life and I most certainly was. It was a wonderful new beginning. And the added bonus was that I was spending more time with my son and, once again, without planning it, was waiting on the arrival of a second one - son that is. As I said, I was not what you might call a good father, but that depends how you define one. It was a special time, especially for our kids, because the players could bring them into training to enjoy the beautiful surroundings and mix amongst some of the finest players of the Seventies. It certainly did young Jamie Redknapp no harm.

Allen and Jamie were the same age. Allen is now a painter and decorator in Chelsea, whilst Jamie, of course, a former international, is now doing a great job as front-man for Sky TV. Had I the good fortune of say, his father, my son would have followed in Jamie's footsteps. He maybe even had him walking in his shadow. But as I repeat several times, Frank sang: That's Life!

Sight and sound: I was fortunate to see and hear the best of both when seeing Frank and Grace Kelly on stage at the Festival Hall. Frank's immaculate voice matched her incredible beauty, however I never got to hug Princess Grace, but I did the gorgeous Shirley MacLaine.

I never met Frank Sinatra, but I was fortunate to have a hug and kiss with one of his close friends, Shirley MacLaine. It was at Earls Court and I was just going into Elton John's dressing room, after yet another wonderful concert. However, I missed something. It hit me later that I should have taken her hand and took her in with me. She was standing alone and looking beautiful, therefore I would have invited her to Franco's, my second favourite restaurant. She could have only have said "no." But I was caught up in the atmosphere and excitement of it all, which is easily done. I was playing quite brilliantly at Stoke City and was down in London celebrating with my uncle George and Leslie, by taking them to see Elton, as I said earlier about using the gift. I was flying high, when my football was going well and, at this time I cannot think of anywhere on else I'd rather have been. I know there words to a song and the fit perfectly.

Had that transfer had not gone well, I might have become the youngest manager in the Football League. I was at Chester Races one afternoon and drinking champagne with the Chairman of Blackpool and he offered me the job. I said to him, that if I had not been playing for such a brilliant manager and enjoying my football so very much, I would have jumped at the opportunity.

Looking back, it was the first time in my life, I regretted being so happy, for it cost me the one opportunity of getting into the manager's office. The next opportunity I got was as eerie as anything that has ever happened to me, but that came later, much later.

But back to Elton, who was simply magnificent and, although I had met him before, I found the experience quite something. I don't know if he'd feel the same way of entering our shrine once beating the West Germans at Wembley or standing there watching Bill Shankly walk into our Victoria Ground dressing room to congratulate me on an incredible - like his - performance. I can't answer that, but I can tell you to walk into Elton's dressing room after such a performance was quite something. I think that is most definitely my passion and love for the wonderful performance. I watch Messi now and feel a chill.

What I loved most about the USA was that you socialise more at home than in England and I loved nothing more than hosting parties in our lovely home on top of the hill. Anthony Patrick was soon to become an American citizen, although at this time we were waiting for him to arrive into this most perfect of settings. I could not be happier to have him born in the best country in the world. He was to become the youngest Head Coach in the history of professional soccer in the United States of America, which is absolutely astonishing. He is now coaching Bahrain under-21s.

Astonishing because his brother was far more talented and he is doing something that he, his father and grandfather were far more cut out for. But that makes it all the more impressive, as he has knuckled down and achieved something that only a couple of years before you would have called an impossibility.

More like miraculous and, it just proves that the wrong people in the game more times than not and, that's not knocking my son. I am simply being very honest.

As I just said, that is the game. If you would have said Harry Redknapp would go on to achieve more in the game than Bobby Moore, you would have been strapped up into a straightjacket and admitted into the Cuckoo's Nest.

As you read on, you'll find that I knew both Harry and Bobby very well, and also I'll tell you of how I miss the latter so very much. He was one of the most impressive men I have ever met and so important in my life without ever having known it. He was also so very influential in a life where I cherish such friendship. In fact, he was the main reason I decided to write this book from such a wonderful place. Any time I came into his company something special happened, maybe that is why he will always remain the only captain of this country that carried it off. The World Cup that is and, as I state more than once, I said that would be the case when they boarded that plane back from Mexico, in 1970.

I remember vividly thinking, as I sat watching Alf make changes against West Germany, that this was the beginning of the end of the English game and, my prediction was chillingly accurate, but still I couldn't get a job in the game.

Like in any walk of life, you will find some people never achieve what they are capable of, then there are those who get the best jobs and become, rich and famous with less than an ounce of their ability. You only have to look at the Seventies when all the best players never got selected for our country. When asked why have we never won anything since 1966?

That is the one and only answer I ever give!

Then there were the so-called good coaches and managers. I say this because I played for the best. The others have made a bloody good living out the game whilst taking it backwards. My manager lived and died in poverty in comparison, living on expenses, a meal here, a meal there, a taxi here, a taxi there, and a shack in Abasoch, somewhere in the outback of South Wales. He was actually too good and too loyal to those who used him and, without him, Stoke City would not be where they are today. I have known a lot of their managers since, some personally, some not, but there are none who compare. He was, as that singer screamed: Simply the Best!

However, Tony never screamed!

Those at the Football Association, along with those in Parliament, are the two greatest examples of what is wrong in our world. Look at the FA employing Sven Goran Eriksson, for instance, giving him £5m a year to fail miserably. They are just the people in a job who are not capable or worthy of such a position and, then there was a bloke named Adam Crozier, who ran the place like it was Fawlty Towers. He came from Saatchi and Saatchi, and went on to run the Royal Mail. It is common knowledge that when the females in their offices were a little uneasy about working in Soho Square, they approached him. They felt that way for obvious reasons - prostitution and pimping are just two things that spring to mind in that part of the world. One young lady was propositioned in the surroundings, which was nothing new for the locals (call them what you will), but they worked for one of the biggest organisations in the world.

Adam Crozier made it very clear that they get on with their jobs or they had better look for other employment.

That is the modern-day Football Association, yet they expected to host a World Cup while employing the likes of Crozier. Then there was the affair the Swedish manager had with the TV weather girl and also one of his staff, which was laughable. I know I mentioned that earlier, but it was worth another mention, if only for tickling me.

Not bad if you can get away with it, whilst earning such a vast amount of money. As I go back over this book, the World Cup is six days away and that Swede, who was sacked by Mexico in the group stages, was given the job with the Ivory Coast. You have to question those who employ such people?

How do they keep getting such jobs?

How can these same people keep employing them?

Had I been lucky enough for our chairman not to have died on the morning of me taking over at Stoke City, I would have been in such a job - and that is not arrogance or stupidity, it is something that I knew would have happened. I look around at managers since and it churns my gut.

Not a single final of any kind since 1966.

As I will mention more than once, in the Seventies the two best English managers were Brian Clough and Tony Waddington, but they never made the short list for a job they were absolutely tailor made for. The result, as I just said, is not a World Cup or European Championship final for 46 years. Even more damning - as I mentioned earlier - they never even qualified throughout the Seventies, a period when we had our best players.

But back to my boys Allen and Anthony who have a step-brother Adam, who they never really had much time to get to know - neither did I come to that - for his mother decided it was over between us before he reached primary school. He is now a very talented chef on the outskirts of Leek, Staffordshire. He is also a staunch Stoke City supporter, whereas Allen is Chelsea through and through. Strange, isn't it, how things turn out, looking back at the 1972 League Cup and, all that happened afterwards?

There is a very good saying that sums up life, it says simply "Live a Little - Die a Little."

I think I heard it last in the Shawshank Redemption. I have done both.

I have lived in some lovely places, once leaving the prefab in Southfields, which is close to Wimbledon, our first home as a family, a lovely home which today would have been my pension. But being so young and full of love for life, allowing it to sweep you away, you lose sight at such a young age. It's just we were so wrapped up in playing, that things like becoming rich never entered our heads and, as I say later, for completely different reasons, Tomorrow Never Comes?

Just take a look at Beckham today; he must have the greatest team of advisers around him. Plus, agents were only just coming on the scene around that time. George had the first one, in Ken Stanley whereas

Ken Adam was next and signed the finest array of talent around. He had several of the biggest names in the country, which included me and Oz, and then he had George once George left Stanley.

Frank Worthington, Peter Shilton, Rodney Marsh and Gerry Francis were amongst his clients and I was his first, in fact, that got him on his way. I haven't seen Ken since Tampa Bay, Florida where we shared some great times in the Sunshine State.

Here's a rare moment with another Frank (Worthington) a great bloke, player and entertainer. He once told me every time he walked onto the field, he took Elvis with him. Now as the other Frank sang, "You've either got or you haven't got style?" It just so happens, both Frank's had it!

In those days we had to sell our home when moving, whereas today they have no need to sell such things, they have several homes and cars in their drives, and their cars cost more than our homes. Today, I would have had an agent who would have done the deal and that house would still be mine. Wonderful at the time, but as the Mary Hopkins sang, Those were the days my friend, I thought they'd never end?

I was fortunate to have lovely homes for someone who rarely had two pennies to rub together. Once arriving in Stoke-on-Trent, Barlaston was my home which stood in the lovely countryside of North Staffordshire; I found another place to die for and, to live for. Isn't it strange that when finding a nice home with terrific surroundings, the thought of moving on never enters your mind?

Well, this was just another case. When I moved into Sispara Gardens, we had just won the FA Cup and were on our way to lifting the European Cup Winners Cup. Chelsea could not possibly think of getting rid of a local 20-year-old who had helped break new ground, could they?

It was a lovely home where my father, helped Brian Harrison build the most beautiful of fireplaces. It was a brick and marble affair with a drinks cabinet in one side and music cabinet in the other. Leslie and I would spend many an hour on either side - me on the drinks side, of course - in the wee small hours. Coming from the prefab this was like being in Hollywood, never knowing Seattle was still to come. I never thought at that time that I would ever see one like it again, the fireplace that is. I paid £23,000 for that home. It is now worth a lot more than £500,000. I moved from there to the Potteries and bought a home for £35,000. The last time I passed that first home it was worth £250,000, the amount I left London for. Now I haven't got a home. The gist of me telling you that is we could not afford to even rent the London home out. As I just said, today they have three, four, five homes, with as many cars in the drive and, in the most wonderful of places and, even Harry's dog has an apartment in Marbella? Allegedly!

Having said all of that, my football was the most important thing in my life and, like with my marriage, it was all going to go pear shaped. And, it could not have happened at a worse time. Or, as it turned out - football wise - a better time, but I did not have any inclination of that once stepping off of that Euston to Stoke-on-Trent rattler.

My initial memory stepping onto the platform of the station at Stoke was one of horror. Was it the booze wearing off and reality setting in?

But soon that horror was to change thanks to the man I owe so much to. But that's all to come!

ON MY OWN

This is such a wonderful song, beautifully sung by Michael MacDonald and Patti Labelle.

I listen to this song - which I love - and it captures everything about my life. It is hauntingly true. When it plays on the jukebox I go numb, even if someone is talking to me. I simply go into a trance.

So, I moved in on my own for the first time since being married and, it would not be my last, Maureen refused to leave London on two counts. Firstly, she thought I was having an affair and, secondly, the Potteries did not hold the glamour of London. Can you imagine Posh Spice walking around Burslem, Tunstall or Kidsgrove?

Some things never change and this was long before the term WAG arrived and, my missus could wag. Unlike today, a million pound place here, a two million pound place there, my home in this beautiful village came to thirty-five grand with a mortgage which, if I were still playing today on my wages, could never have been paid off. Especially under Dave Sexton, something that will make more sense to you later.

It was a tiny village, with a row of four or five shops, a paper shop close to the railway track, a petrol station and one pub, The Plume of Feathers. My boozer was the Duke of York, run by the lovely Lenny Bacon, up the hill towards where Josiah Wedgwood had his place. They were really nice people around these parts and, it was actually heaven from the hell of London. Only problem was there were no mini-skirts and hot pants, although I would soon find out that there were enough pretty attractive young ladies to take my mind off my marital troubles.

Although I loved my first home - it was so special for many reasons - and years later Seattle was the ultimate home, this was also special home with many special memories and, it was the dynamic concoction of the two things in my life and, the two things I had always loved most, playing football well and enjoying myself to the extreme.

And then there was my mate Leslie who was as 'good-a-lad' as you'll find and the thing I loved most about him was his absolute straightness. If he didn't take to you, you would take too long working it out. He was blunter than blunt and it did not matter who you were, he had no time for poseurs or impostors, now you know why we were so close. He had one problem though, and that was that he was too stubborn for his own good, like me again, with his strength being his weakness. In the end we ended up not speaking for a while over nothing, but I truly did not know how ill he was, for I would have walked from Stoke to see him and, that 150 miles would have meant nothing. I adored him.

That first home was very special, because people in those days didn't move out of Chelsea. But this was different, because I was now the first teenager to win an FA Cup in a Chelsea blue shirt, in fact, one of only fifteen or sixteen players in the history of the club to do so. So you might say I was Moving on Up if only towards Wimbledon Village. Okay, it was not like today in Cobham, Elvis's place or Michael Jackson's funny farm, but I can tell you it was for us then, wonderful, when you come from a prefab.

Those four incredible years in Seattle - the most special and enjoyable of my life - were still a long way off, but the only problem in the Great North West was there was no Tony Waddington to share it all with. He would have loved living there close by to his mate and, our parties would have been even more sensational. He would of loved the likes of Steve Buttle, Mike Ivano, Roy Greaves and David Nish and, make no mistake, they would have loved him. There was never anyone better than holding court than him, I never have come across anyone quite like him before or since and, to be even more honest, there was nobody in his class. I believe that Busby, for sure, held him in the highest regard wanting him to take over the reins at Old Trafford and later on, I found out that Clough loved him.

Need I say anymore!

There was another kind of home even further off, one that you don't go looking for, the Royal London Hospital - where I first died. A home where I first came into contact with morphine and, oh boy, how I needed it. It was also where I experienced trauma, and I mean real trauma. On finding this place everything I had experienced before changed. I used to be able to put things in what I thought were their rightful place, but this re-arranged everything.

It was to become my greatest test of not only character but a test of trying to keep your emotions on an even keel. When people judge you after such an experience they need to step back and count to ten, before they make it nine-and-a-half.

This is the first time you really do have to make the kind of decisions that are the most difficult you have ever imagined. And with the addition of drugs and mind games it complicates your state of mind and blurs your vision so much that the people around you, although they love you, simply don't understand.

You see more than they do, however, you are not sure if it is real or not. Still, to this day, I look back and wonder just what I did? Whether I was right or wrong?

The only thing that I am certain about is that I was prepared to fight.

I made the most of what I had, to not only give it a go, or survive even, but set myself impossible targets. I wanted it all. I wanted to get back into the mainstream or, as the Eagles sang, The Fast Lane.

My time, although I didn't realise it then, was just a blur in the Royal London Hospital. Through all of this time I am telling you about I was paralysed from the waist downwards and, the word going round, quietly, was that I would never walk again, something I have to remind myself of on many occasions.

My days now are like I have said, taking one at a time, like each careful step where, through my foot-drop, I have to watch every single step, and check out every paving stone along the way. But that was after I got over my wheelchair days, which kept my uncle George as fit as he'd ever been.

What I can remember of that hospital, was that the staff were magnificent and, then they shipped me out to St Bartholomew's for nine months, and a little more, they too were like family to me. That was another fantastic experience and, when I think of Henri Charriere serving all that time in solitary, I must have been, in comparison, the luckiest man who ever lived.

Two innocent men serving sentences like that, when there are people accepted into this country who will not be happy until they have blown us all up.

Again, Parliament has so much to answer for whilst our kids are being blown apart in Afghanistan!

The English people who cared for me are terribly overworked, vastly underpaid and totally ignored by those on the top floor. They kept me alive when I was contemplating the opposite. They were vital in my every move towards trying to live a normal life once again, totally oblivious of what I would have had to do, had David Goodier, along with that C-Clamp, not have saved my legs. What I am going to say next is mainly because had I lived in these places now, I would not be able to walk those hills, let alone put my trainers on and fight such a daunting fight.

Just before Fatehi came along I'd run the parks with my mate John Westwood and my most favourite of all running escapades was - without a shadow of a doubt over Greenwich Park and what John called 'Plum Pudding Hill' which to look at was nothing daunting at all, but running it was a different proposition. After running around this most exquisite of landscape parks and getting to the peak of it all, it was as if you had climbed Everest. On reaching the top, overlooking the whole of London, I felt like Rocky, when he reached the top of his stairs and, I say that looking back as I now miss such things so very much.

I have just helped a young lad with a project in University, his name is Alex Dean and, I think he will have a very, very good future in film. He did small film of me and called it The Forest Gump of the East End of London and, I thought that very apt.

I look forward to making a DVD with Alex, in the hope it will kick-start a wonderful career for him and then, of course, I need to get some very important points across, for surely you be fed-up with what you hear and read every day. I certainly do!

But back to Greenwich, where, whether you liked it or not, you would without hesitation take the deepest of breaths, for the air seemed so clear and the view so immaculate. You can, it seemed, see forever and ever…and, although I told you I don't like London these days, this was a simply a sight for sore eyes. I'd take that deep breath and take on Plum Pudding Hill and, am I glad to tell you the story, one that had a happy ending for a change, I beat it.

Again, it was all a big part of saving my life, especially as John only expected me to run this little intimidating beast just twice. I don't think so, John!

Anyhow as we passed through to our starting place we passed the famous Cutty Sark, which there were two of, one the famous boat and then this: Welcome to the Cutty Sark Tavern. We are a long established Free House on the south bank of the River Thames in Greenwich, London. Built in the early 19th century, you can immediately feel the history of the tavern. Its imposing external Georgian façade and wood beamed interior give it the feel of days gone by. Like the TARDIS that it is, the look and feel of the tavern contrasts starkly with its views over the modern day River Thames; you can see and almost touch the legacy of the turn of the last century, the Millennium Dome and the new city of London, Canary

Wharf. As a family business in the same ownership for over 40 years we welcome everyone through our doors from local residents and families and businesses to visitors to Greenwich and London.

I can only thank John for introducing another hill that I conquered.

This is why I go back to such things as my lovely home in Southfields, which stood just off Putney Hill, which leads you up to Wimbledon Common. I go back because all through my hospitalisation, I relived all of this because it kept my mind active. I was trying to take my mind off of 'just say, I never walk again?'

And by going over all my past it gave me the strength to get out of that bed and, then that wheelchair and back on my own two feet.

I would think about leaving home and heading for Wimbledon Village, Sandown, Kempton and Epsom Racecourses. Wimbledon Dog Track was within walking distance and, thank God it was, for the times I left there with holes in my pockets!

Plus, I could get to Chelsea's Mitcham Training Ground and Stamford Bridge in 15 minutes. Then, of course, in five minutes you could drive to Putney High Street, which is just across the bridge from my beloved Craven Cottage.

Well, it was as a schoolboy.

For that period in hospital, all of these places were a total blur. As I slowly came round, watching people come and go from my room as I just seemed to lie there, still wondering what had happened to me. And also, why? Doctors would walk in and spend time looking through all of the cards and letters that covered the entire four walls, before getting down to the real business. I dread to think what it must have been like for John Merrick, the Elephant Man, who was under Treves in that hospital. This really was the weirdest period of my life. What made things worse, was that I was an outgoing person. There was no in-between with me, for it was training, by pushing my body to the absolute limit or making arrangements for a day out, like the one I experienced, when nearly taking my very last breath.

It was also strange, as it seemed like Christmas, although I had missed it for the first time in 46 years. There seemed so many people coming in, going out and making such a fuss about it all, almost as if I was a little kid.

I was like one, though, for I couldn't walk and talk. At this time I had a tracheostomy inserted into my throat area, which meant nothing really because I had so many injuries and doctors coming to treat them that I didn't know what one to worry about most. Although, I can honestly say, that I was totally at ease with it all. I had also made myself surgery-friendly, meaning I loved going to the operating theatre. My family simply could not believe my excitement. However, that was the way I was, I really psyched myself up for each and every trip to theatre. I saw it as a massive step in the right direction and, that was the way it turned out. My build-up was like going into a big match, the preparation precise. From my first meeting with my anaesthetist to finally putting out cold, my preparation was like clockwork. As George said earlier a camera crew came in and focused on a bottle of vodka on my sideboard. I would sit up all night on my laptop whilst enjoying a few vodka orange and cranberry juices and spend the evening relaxing, knowing that tomorrow I would be having yet another part of my body improved and, there was always the importance of being positive.

I suppose the majority of most of this was the aftermath of all of the trauma suffered leading up to this period, although even now, I don't understand. So, the best way to fight the unknown is to fight it with the unknown. I knew how to approach a football match, however, this was something very new to me and, I worked it out as if it was new to me, then it was new to the opposition. My attitude going into the skirmishes in theatre was as positive as I've ever been in my life.

This might look just like any other building, but trust me, it was as sinister as those that surrounded it in those times leading up to the arrests of the Kray Twins. Those who have travelled half the world to watch the Olympics just a couple of miles up the road don't know the half of it!

The Americans think it is our Disneyland.

Well, Walt Disney could not have made a film of something that might have even have equalled The Godfather?

The worst time though was those first 59 days, but not for me.
I can only imagine what my family went through?

I saw going through an operation like travelling and, if I loved my time living, I loved travelling even more so. I looked forward, and still do, to flying the skies, it really excited me before this experience and that feeling remains. It takes me away from everything, from the very first moment I set foot into the place itself.

As I board my mind wanders. Who will I meet? Especially when travelling alone. As soon as the passport is checked, I am straight to the bar. I loved the airport bars in America like no other, so much so, that I welcome a delay. Then once boarding and settling in, awaiting take-off my adrenalin rushes. The sound of the door locking also clicks something in my mind as well as my heart, as once again I know I'm leaving my demons behind, you might call it relief, for I can now sit back and enjoy yet another journey. And, to totally confirm it, the sound of the engine starting up and the wheels rolling followed by them being pulled in below gives me the feeling of going under. The anaesthetic has worked wonderfully well and I go into a deep state until the place comes alive again, only it's not those 59 days. This time it's a brief fix which puts the past into its rightful place, for it tells me once again that it's only the future that counts. I am obsessed with it all, I truly can't get enough of being in space; the Operating Theatre taught me so much about travelling and travelling well. I feel so safe once above where it all happened to me, looking down on so many special times, sprinkled with so much pain, or these days, is it the other way round?

Being a big Elton John fan, you might say I could be his Rocket Man? Isn't it strange how every time I look up to the sky and see it this way and my nightmare below is not being able to run the streets anymore and, I think that is why, more so since those days in that coma, I am so much more at home amongst the clouds and I ask myself again, is it because this is where I passed my father and Leslie? Only Betty will tell me that when I finally see her again, hopefully it will be quite a long way off, for I still feel I have so much to do!

Anyhow, by now, in mid-air my blood levels out and I cannot take my eyes off those clumps of cotton wool outside my window. My laptop comes out and the next stop a vodka and orange. Within half-an-hour of my journey, I am completely and totally relaxed with not a care in the world as, 'they can't touch me now' slips, as usual, through my mind.

I am still waiting to find out what it is?

The heartbeat that once pounded was now like the surface of the mildest and stillest of lakes. And the lake I love most is the pond, the one that you look over once reaching the USA. My favourite touchdown - if you'll ignore the pun - is coming into Tampa Bay, where you head for the water and can almost see into your hotel room in the Bay Harbour Hotel. This was the first hotel I visited in Florida and it sticks with me today and will forever. My memories of George Steinbrenner's - of the NY Yankees - place are untouchable, from taking on about a hundred of their Army at the bar - just back from the Falklands - to Terry Bate setting the piano player on fire with his ciggie.

As The Beatles sang: Yesterday, all my troubles seem so far away…

Going into the Operating Theatre reminds me of all this. It has been my most enjoyable experience, not just seeing places, but experiencing every single moment. And again and again, the excitement of the airport lounge, the boarding, the mystery of those clouds below (those I just said that reminded me of floating clumps of cotton wool), and the expectancy of what was at the other end of the runway, never forgetting the looking forward to pastures new. The meeting of many different and interesting people, nice people, lovely people and ones I could finally call my 'dearest friends.'

In fact, as I go back over this, I look forward to Chris and Anne-Marie Bennett visiting me from Vancouver, Canada, to celebrate the 12th Anniversary of my ordeal in the Mile End Road. Chris visited me from Vancouver about two months into my wheelchair days. What a truly great bloke he is.

Chris and Anne-Marie epitomise all of this!

Because if it was not for my ability to play football - which I am truly grateful to my mum and dad - that gave me so many opportunities to travel, I would not have met such wonderful people.

Take a Look at My Girlfriend she's the only one I got…..
Supertramp 1978/79

And then there is the enchanting Melissa who escaped me in Tampa Bay….if she was not such a lovely girl, I would have married her. I used to look at her and think, 'how could anyone ever hurt you?' And, I would be the last to do so. I thought about asking her, but I was always enjoying myself too much and, I would never or could never have been unfaithful to her. When I first met her husband, I thought he was a "jerk" and that she was far too good for him, I was - I am not happy to say - right. When I asked her some years later who she never married me, she said gently, "But Alan, you never asked me." So, she knew two "jerks." But, I jest, I would never have married her, simply because she deserves the absolute best although, now I think with my 'Playboy; days behind me, I would be her perfect partner, mainly because my love for her. But would I put her in front of flying? Of course not, she'd have to come with me or….

And, once again, if it weren't for football and travel, I would not be able to sit and write with such delight, and definitely not have as much to tell you. I loved, along with those many fantastic places, meeting fascinating people from all walks of life. Then there were all of those beautiful women I was fortunate enough to boast being not too far behind my mate George Best, if at all. You'll read a lot of the one-time best player in the world very soon. Although my two marriages failed, with a live-in lover tucked in between, although we had our problems, what those girls didn't lack was beauty, which is quite fitting because they thought I was the beast.

I can only say that it takes three to tangle

Whilst I was in hospital, all three loves disappointed me, for two didn't visit when they had moved past reading me my last rites, while the other one who should have been by my bedside was - like I was doing with her, unknowingly at the time - Sleeping with the Enemy.

Regrets, I've had a few, but then again, too many to mention.

And this was one of them. The most hurtful thing about my second wife walking away was that had it been the other way round, I would have looked after her forever, but I've told you that already. But it's worth telling you again, because that is possibly the most hurtful part of my experience on that dreadful December night of fifteen years ago. Why? I loved her. Ouch!

Is that the Gemini in me, or is it that I am too loyal for my own good?

That loyalty has worked in my favour though. I have loved the same friends and family since my short trouser days, while those that came along afterwards can vouch that I am a man of my word. The biggest problem I have had throughout my life has been a financial one and it is incredibly difficult to function as the person you set out to be, in such traumatic times. Since my disabilities I have found that although money counts for nothing, the £1.9million compensation cheated from me, thanks to the Old Bill, ouch again!

It really would really have made my life far easier to live. Mr. Bernard Clarke, my brilliant solicitor, had done a wonderful job, only to see it all turn to ashes, thanks to those I just mentioned. I also believe somewhere along the line that they had a part to play in my near demise.

Something similar happened to Henri Charriere (Papillon) who, like me, was innocent and yet was locked up for a crime he didn't commit. He was like me also, totally abused by the police, albeit in France. He was told by a certain Monsignor, "What has happened to you has happened for a good reason. You have been put through the most severe test of character and come out the other side, although wrongly done by, a better person. Now you can get on with your life and enjoy the rest of it. You have passed the ultimate test."

Papillon - well known for his Butterfly - was mistreated in such a way. He would have been well within his rights to succeed in his revenge, which he set out to do. But he met the love of his life and she talked him out of it, unlike me. I have never met such a woman. Or maybe I have, but never realised. I think I have, but will now never know, for leaving her behind without the opportunity to prove it.

I know I mentioned this earlier, but every time I think of injustice, I think of Charriere.

But going back to the police, some years ago, when I was in the Potteries working on the Sentinel newspaper, I had my England cap stolen from my friend's lock-up. I put an advert in our paper saying that if they returned my cap I was not interested in pressing charges. All that I wanted was that they return the most important thing I had ever won in the game. It meant that much to me and was absolutely no use to them. That was my memory of the West Germany match. That was my most valued possession.

The meaning is pretty difficult to explain, because it covered such a vast period of my life. It was everything you play for and more, because when I finally got my opportunity to show I could play against the best in the world, I proved so many people wrong.

The feeling inside me on leaving Revie in that dressing room, knowing he cursed me, was absolutely exhilarating, I was not any particular cloud, for at that time, I think I was on them all!

Then I received a call from the CID in Newcastle-under-Lyme and over the phone he gave me some great news: "I know who has your England cap."

I was absolutely delighted. We arranged a meet in the local hotel - The Borough Arms - and over a friendly drink the cop ask me how much I was prepared to pay to get it back. I said, "Do you think that after my father had brought me up to play this game, I then reach my goal by representing my country and, after doing so, I'm going to pay a thief to get it back?"

The answer rocked me, by telling me that this thief was more important than I was. "He is our biggest and most important fence in the city," were his words.

I can happily say that I have replacement which belongs to my first and, one and only grand-daughter, the beautiful Nancy - with The Laughing Face!

One day she will find out what it meant to me and also, what she did also - by her coming along and giving me another motive to not only live, but get that replacement. It was only Nancy coming along that triggered it all off again.

Because, of course, as I said, I fear each day and live it as if my last, whether out trying to break all records or bringing this to you. I prefer the first part, because, if it weren't for that, there would be no second, would there?

The relevance of the police here is that they changed my entire life. My Barrister made it very clear that he had never experienced a case where the victim had been so victimised. He added that if I went to court and fought them for the money I deserved, I would get nothing. After what had happened in my football life, was I getting paranoid about everything being against me?

After all, had I knocked Fatehi into oblivion in the Mile End Road, they would have banged me up and thrown away the key. They may have even screamed "racial" such is the manner of how they treated my case.

Wealth comes in many shapes and sizes. My wealth comes from deep down in my heart and, those emotions created most of my troubles, both in and out of the game, but in the end saved my life. My will to beat those Demons was incredible. I cannot even begin to tell you! It made playing against those white-shirted Leeds United thugs seem like a Cinderella pantomime. I also had a very good record against them - Leeds United that is!

Love affairs are just like our game, they are unpredictable, building you up, knocking you down, fulfilling your dreams and then giving you living nightmares, just when you think you've got it cracked....

Frank sang that he did it His Way. I most certainly did it Mine!

What you are about to read is a roller-coaster ride, the road that led up to my home on the top of that hill, so incredibly steep and very dangerous. However, little did I know then, that there was one road somewhere which was the opposite of the one I have always searched for, the Yellow Brick one, this being in the Mile End, the road which changed my life in such a dramatic way, only this time, it was a change of a very different nature.

I don't imagine that anyone in that Intensive Care Unit would have dreamt that I would one day bring you another book. In fact, I'm quite certain of that. But if there was one person, it would probably be Miss Betty Shine, that wonderful medium and faith healer, who dispersed the clot on my brain, although some people out there will say that I have never had one. A brain, that is!

Anyhow, let's get on with my story, a true one, a happy one, a sad one, but most importantly an honest one; something of a rarity in those around me in my life, and then there's what is going on in today's football.

And one of the reasons I have never got a living in the game that has been such a big part of my life, you will find along the way, is that

I detest cheats and frauds. The saddest thing is I came across so many in our game, so many less talented people who have made a fortune out of it. I just could not go along with it all. Of course I regret it now; we all do as we get older, because it begins to eat at you and when you are at your lowest ebb, it churns your gut to a level you never knew existed. It was a different kind of sick than the one that I experienced after that night in December 1997. What hurts most, is watching lesser, much lesser mortals getting paid big money for something they're no good at. You see with me, I can't turn my back on the game I love. If I could, it wouldn't hurt so much, but I have tried unsuccessfully.

As I go through this again, Capello has just proved all of this to be true (18.6.10).

From time to time I will, without apology, swing back to the 15 December 1997 which changed my life dramatically. Ever since, I have been chasing time. It is time that I will never get back. Those eight and a half weeks in a near coma was hell for my family. As for me, the problem was wondering where all this was going to take me, once coming out of it all. I was totally confused, paralysed from below the waist, without knowing if I had any legs. Unbeknown to me, I was to learn later, that I was minutes away from losing them. I was used to losing things, like on the dogs, the horses and in cup finals, but my legs. Again, ouch!

I found that what you are about to read, got me through it all. Those wonderful memories of my times, both on and off the playing pitches of the world, would make me realise that like in my past, I had to fight to stay alive. I had to dig deep and, realise that life was a combination of glory, heartache and pain.

Today's players, with their massive pay packets, don't realise they are born. We played for peanuts and, maybe that is why sometimes we acted like monkeys. And that's why many of us, ended up a little nuts. It was just the way it was, there was no money and there are no regrets, not even a few to mention.

Leaving home in mid-December and waking up in early March is a strange experience. It is definitely one I don't recommend - now, not even sleeping pills work - but what was even stranger was working out what was going to happen in my new life?

This was to become my third!

Being paralysed from the waist down was a new experience for a man who had run for miles that particular week and cycled for many more on the morning of my near-demise. As I said, they were only a few minutes from taking them off, those legs that were responsible for everything that is between these pages. There is absolutely no doubt in my mind that I would have had to have taken my life, of that I can assure you. Without my legs I would not have been Alan Hudson, I would have been a sorrowful sight that people would have looked at and said, 'He once was....

For once in that life, I really did drop lucky. A stranger walked into the Royal London Hospital with a machine called the C-Clamp - it was a sample - with not even so much as a plug attached to it. But with the assistance of the brilliant David Goodier it worked the miracle he and his assistants had been looking and hoping for.

Before they put me in the wheelchair they tried carrying me out in a sling. They'd put me into it and carry me, crane-like, to wherever I was going. But I nearly fell through the side. Had I done so, I could have been even more seriously threatened. The reason I nearly fell through was because I had lost so much weight. I was seven stone. When I came back from Spain after missing the FA Cup final and Mexico I was 14 stone and trying to lose it. This was not the way to do such a thing!

When I try to explain how damaging missing the 1970 World Cup was, I think this photograph tells the whole story. Just to be on the same field at this moment would have been worth living for. Pele acknowledging that Bobby was the best defender in the world....

The wheelchair that awaited me was only short term. Well, that was my aim. I am sure there are certain people going around in one of those contraptions, who are in nowhere near the state I am in. My balance as a player was perfect - not like Charlie Cooke's outside Barbarella - but that has now gone. I cannot jog, let alone run. Sometimes when a bus comes along, it hits me when I stand in horror and watch someone run to catch it. It seems as if time stands as still as me. It seems that no matter what an injustice, nothing waits for you. If you are disabled, you have to learn to live with it. The authorities certainly don't give a damn and then there was Portillo. Maybe I was born the wrong colour?

I just have to wait for the next one, life that is, not bus. Something I never had to do in my former life. The foot-drop being my biggest concern, through them cutting into my nerves in the ICU, it causes me to take the odd tumble. The fear every morning once leaving my front door, of hitting the pavement can be traumatic, which leads to paranoia.

The strangest thing is that I walk better when under the n=influence of alcohol and, I think that is because of it talking away the fear. Dutch Courage, you might say?

The only thing I am thankful for is that the erratic (or as we know now, unsuccessful) driver, Ashgar Fatehi, did not come along when I was in my late teens or early 20s. It would have been simply devastating after tasting what I tasted in my first two seasons.

Had I been struck down so wickedly after what I experienced as a young teenager in my first full season, it would have been something that I truly could never put into words. I often think about it and wonder if I would have ever recovered my sanity. I don't think that I would have overcome such a thing, so for that I am truly thankful, although I have nothing to thank The Man for. He is the one who has given me and my family so many different life-changing illnesses.

I'm approaching the 15th year of my third life - although you've read that I've already done so - that is because of going over this manuscript to try to make sure I got it right for you.

My first (life) began in Chelsea which took me into my second, which started after one meeting with Tony Waddington in the park at Russell Square.

I came through their yesterday and my heart skipped a beat as my memory of not only the occasion, but him touches me so much. I truly think that our relationship = player and manager - was the most special of all time and, something that I am so really proud of and, one of those motives I spoke of earlier, to live. When I go to the Britannia Stadium and into the Waddington Suite, as I did at the back end of last season, I told those supporters, that if it weren't for him, they would not only be not sitting in such a place but watching Stoke City play Mongolia United and, that was his worth to such a club.

I may mention elsewhere that a journalist, Keith Elliott, once interviewed me in Crewe a few weeks after Tony had passed away. He told me I looked "awful" and "haggard" and he was right. He said that it was as if a part of me had died with my former boss. I know that to be true. Of course you die a little when losing someone so special in your life. This was so different, though. Every time I look at a bottle of Gordon's Gin I think of him. Every time I see a special player, I think of him. Every time I see a beach, I think of him. Every time I hear of the Pope, I think of him. Every time I visit Stoke City Football Club, the same.

So you could say he will always be with me….

Every time I raise my glass at midnight on 14 December, or 9pm the following night, I always have Tony in my thoughts. I remember being by his bedside when he left us, it was a paralysis of a much different kind. There you are fully aware of what is going on yet, being helpless and hopeless. If I can say just one word, I was "empty."

The first thing that sprung to my mind, apart from his looking so weak and ill, was 'I will never enjoy his company anymore.' The same can be said of Tony Banks and Allan Phillips, whom I touch on later and will make a little more sense because I always have wished that people such as these should be together. But they are now and, that was possibly the one reason I wasn't afraid of dying?

Strangely enough both of these men, like me, were treated shabbily by the club they loved. The only difference being, with me, I had no love for such a club. They had used and abused me in 1974 and that was when I learned that the club I grew up at was no good. In another society you might call it rape. They took my best, most innocent years and spewed them down the River Thames. And, all of that because that stupid bunch of so-called coaches at Fulham turned me away for being "too small" it was just as well, Lionel Messi didn't turn up at Craven Cottage at such a young age. He'd be with Peter Knowles now, stacking shelves in Sainsbury.

I am absolutely thrilled to still be alive to bring you these latest experiences along with some from The Working Man's Ballet, which is all about a young kid from the back streets of Chelsea fulfilling his and every other kid's dream, dreams that, as I said, come in different shapes and sizes.

For me at the end of the dream, the ultimate goal was to be like the two players I am about to mention, who simply made the hairs on your neck stand on end.

Well, they did for me.

Like queuing up to watch Frank Sinatra, it was also a special occasion going through the turnstiles to watch two football legends, Jimmy Greaves and Johnny Haynes. Along with Bobby Moore, they had that 'Something' (a love song written by George Harrison and one that Frank says is the best ever written). He says that because, although it is so terribly romantic, it never once mentions that magic word, the word that was the reason behind my near demise.

Again, I remember going to see Sinatra at the Royal Festival Hall and left the auditorium mesmerised. He was also dying while I was so close to a similar fate. On coming out of my near-coma, I learned that he was in one himself. The only difference was that he was at his home with his family, while mine surrounded my hospital bed. It was incredible that the biggest influence and inspiration in my life should die at the same time as me. Although at that time I never knew that I had died at least once before him in the ICU?

Who said or sang Working Class Hero? It was, of course, John Lennon, who was one himself. Like Frank and George, he was also a genius. His song Imagine fits in here perfectly. More about the Lennon genius later!

As I go over this piece it has been 30 years to the day of his shooting and the footage from outside his New York Apartment is spooky. New Yorkers were crying, people in complete horror whilst his music played on - and it has ever since!

In my early days of experiencing such a thing, dying that is, I could never have imagined the Intensive Care Unit, the coma, the unlimited pain and wasted time. It's all time, as I have said, I'll never get back. And in the end of my time hospitalised, I experienced the worst kind of rejection.

Rejection is sometimes, though so hurtful, so helpful. At first it crushes your heart and soul, but if you have anything about you, you turn it round in your favour. It gives you an opportunity to work out where you are going in life. I found out, in my case, nowhere. Although in time, I realised and could appreciate why all of this happened to me, be it so terribly wrong and unjustifiable, in fact, completely out of this world.

It also pulls your heart strings and gives you a warning; can you remember the song by the Searchers: Don't Throw Your Love Away! It's been a big part of my life!

One of the reasons I understand all of this, is through Papillon, who was a magnificent man, a man who beat away one Demon after another. He was the only man to escape from Devil's Island, sailing those shark-infested waters on a sail boat made of coconuts. I think it was him who was responsible, in the end, for them closing it down, because they thought escape was totally out of the question. Well, it was until Henri put that bunch of coconuts together.

"I've got a lovely bunch of coconuts"....And he did!

Being sent there was the ultimate one-way ticket, a little like mine, but like him, I also had other ideas, although nowhere near as dangerous and incredibly daunting.

Papillon, as I mentioned earlier, was just like me. He was the innocent one who spent years suffering, whilst the real villain walked away. Oh, how I know how he must have felt, the only difference was his escape route was far more dangerous and courageous than mine.

I reached somewhere near the top by playing against the very best, but I can tell you that I have definitely been in the basement. The lowest floor in the Royal London Hospital was running wild with rats. If I sound a little bitter at times, please forgive me, but in those early days in the Treves Ward, I did not know that the basement was not the only place where they were, for those in Parliament were only a stone's throw away and, then there was Stamford Bridge who ignored my grieving family, as for me, where there was no love, there will never be love....the only thing that rankles me is that they cheated this young kid from the backstreets where they had taken over, which is much like a Gangster movie where they muscle in on your patch and abuse the locals.

The Krays spring to mind!

When I go back to London now to see my son and grand-daughter, I steer well clear of those parts. The stench of the Thames has cleared those once proud walls. Although me and my son play "Spot the White Man" in north London, at least we are far away from my worst memories of such a place. The day I walked out of those gates for the last time as a Chelsea player, back in 1974, it was a little like coming out of my coma. Like coming out of my 59-day period under heavy sedation, I was in a complete and utter state of confusion. My father had walked me through those gates ten years earlier, as a schoolboy, and after becoming the most successful local player in their history - here I was walking a tightrope without any protection below. The boy who was given on a plate by Billy Hudson had now put a quarter-of-a-million-pounds in their bank account. And what did the boy and his father get in return?

Nothing, in fact, they were also cheated out of the 5% of such a transfer fee.

Talking of rats at this time, my wife was planning on leaving me. The timing was completely wrong and the way she did it incredibly cold. I thought at first it was the shock of it all for her and that she would come through it, but no, the reality of it all soon hit me. For when I was in the ICU she told my uncle that, "If he pulls through George, I will never give him a hard time again."

When I told him of her intentions, he told me this and also said that I was imagining it all, or it was the drugs?

But I knew I wasn't because every time she sat at my bedside, her chair was moving further away by the day. This was something that could have ruined my chances of getting through it all because I was, at first, completely devastated.

This hurt me so much I cannot put it into words and, again, I learned of trauma, a new deep trauma of a very different kind. You need as much love from your partner as humanly possible when you wake up to find that your life has been totally devastated and, even worse, is that you don't know how or why?

I can only imagine how cancer victims feel when they first get their prognosis, although I shudder to think of such hurt, pain and trauma and, I would be lying if I told you how I first felt when coming round.

But the hurt disappears in time, although that time has, I found, been although hurtful, helpful if only for all of this being because of a love for one woman. Although I still ask myself, was it love? There is such a fine line between it working and not working out. This was living proof. She became my toughest ever opponent - you could see the likes of Bremner and Giles coming - whereas with her, you never knew which one you were either waking up with or going home to.

As I said, I had been 'Sleeping with the Enemy' without ever knowing it!

Talking of that fine line, next to living and dying, comes success or failure; the greatest example in my lifetime is that I'll never forget talking to Dougie Thompson, a member of that wonderful band Supertramp, and in his own terribly lonely way he admitted to me that "If this album doesn't sell, we'll have to disband."

I tell you this whilst on the subject of love and, the heading of what you just read about Melissa and, also it takes me back to that most incredible experience of travelling the world. To think I had to go all across the world to meet these boys from where I came.

I first heard of them through another girlfriend, when they were musicians…..but now they sang and did it so beautifully….

The scene was the Seattle Coliseum, the stage was dark and, as the crowd waited anxiously they flicked on their lighters, and then slowly the auditorium lit itself.

"When I was young, I thought that life was so wonderful …."

The hairs stood up as my childhood flooded back. I remember thinking 'If this doesn't sell, I will become friends with Don Revie.'

They could not, they would not and they did not disband. Thank goodness! Breakfast in America became one of the biggest-selling albums in the history of such music. When I saw Dougie a couple of years later at Earls Court, he seemed a little embarrassed that he told me of his near failure. He needn't have, he was honest. Every time The Logical Song comes on, my hairs stand up, eyes fill and then a feeling that has you almost in a state of hallucination. I am so proud that I was the one he told and, I can stand in my local and listen to the song filling the room knowing that they were a whisker away from this song not reaching the jukebox. It would have been like George Best and Johnny Haynes not playing in an FA Cup final at Wembley and more so, even worse in George's case, not playing in the finals of a World Cup!

Everyone in the pub is singing and dancing, never knowing that this most wonderful piece of music was so close to not reaching their jukebox. Well done boys, you deserve the kind of success your genius brings. Some fine line - and they have many of them.

George didn't do songs. He tormented defenders and pulled Miss Worlds, in his spare time, instead. Who needs George Best?

The Beatles certainly didn't - although they named him the fifth Beatle after torturing Benfica in Portugal - they had Lennon, McCartney and Harrison, just like Manchester United had Law and Charlton alongside George himself. Dave Sexton didn't either, or so he thought, it still seems so crazy. George was a great inspiration to me and would have been to so many who swarmed into the Bridge in those days. That was just another reason why I have this thing with Dave.

Does he actually know (understand) just how many people he cheated out of seeing George every Saturday afternoon?

To watch him play as a kid, then be on the same field as him as an 18-year-old, and finally becoming his friend, is something I cherish. I was the first to visit him in the Cromwell Hospital on hearing of his liver transplant and looking at him sitting in the corner made me shiver. Nothing like the kind of shivering he gave defenders, this was of a completely different kind. The reality of it all was shocking for me, but the look on his face told the true story.

I once read of someone saying, "If God hadn't made him, someone would have invented him."

That was George!

What tormented him, like he did those defenders, was the fact that he was born Irish and in those days there weren't enough of them who were anything like him - Pat Jennings the exception - to help him fulfill one of his dreams and, that was to actually play in the World Cup finals. He could have anything he wanted in life, including a string of Miss Worlds. However, he would have swapped a few of them, if not all, to show the world his genius in the finals of the Greatest Show on Earth. And what we were about to experience in South Africa made this even more obscene. Some of the players that can walk around boasting that they played in the finals of the World Cup, I find this mind-boggling, when you think that George was sitting in Spain every four years by a swimming pool with this or that blonde. It was simply incredible. And whilst he was there we have to suffer the also-rans and the riff-raff of our game.

Can you imagine Frank Sinatra never playing at the Royal Albert Hall?

Can you imagine the Beatles never leaving the Cavern?

Can you imagine Cassius Clay being abandoned in Louisville?

Can you imagine Dolly Parton with tiny breasts?

Again, the mind boggles!

Sinatra and Bruce Springsteen choose Presidents. Had Bobby Moore been born in Kentucky, Ohio or Nashville, I think he would have made the White House also.

Why?

This is because Presidents are Ambassadors, though Bobby might have had far too much class and honesty for such a place.

Out of the last four people I have just mentioned, only Bruce lives. I have experienced his concert and he lived up to his nickname, The Boss, for he was simply sensational.

Some may say I'm a dreamer, but I'm not the only one, some thought me a schemer, but again not the only one. Some say I was both. I think they are more likely to be right. As you read on you'll find that I did dream a lot. How can you go so far if you don't have dreams?

But my crazier ones were when under heavy sedation, for those 59 days.

As I told you, I saw my Dad, Bill, and Leslie, my best friend since school, float by. They passed me by on one of those clouds you only get to see from the window seat of that aeroplane I love so much.

When I actually did wake up, I saw my old man in the corner of my room. He was a coat hanging on a peg and, around that time I was complimenting the nurses for their excellent choice of wine. It was, of course, water.

I can still see my Dad and taste the wine, for that is how real it was.

Back down here as a kid, I watched the kind of players that Sinatra would have been, had he been born in Ilford or Belfast instead of Hoboken. The kind of player who filled the terraces like Greaves and Haynes did. Now they were my kind of players.

When you look at the players of today, they really are not in the same class, or you might say, are not even good imitation.

They just don't have what we say is "a real touch of class." Today is a little different, though, because there are not so many working-class heroes. They are breast fed. They are spoilt. They believe their headlines and wage packets. They are driven on by the greenback.

I go over this as Joey Barton is sentenced with a 12 match ban, do you think he cares? He's getting obscene money for bringing thuggery onto our football fields and, at a time there are terrorists walking amongst us, there he is bringing our game down to a new level of gutter=football.

With Drogba throwing himself over every time a number 14 bus passes the front gate, it is bringing our game into a state where cheating seems to have taken over from us waiting for a touch of inspiration. Having said that the big Ivorian has a little genius in his locker and, like a magician, can have us asking, "How on earth did he do that?"

Barton looks a useful player, but if they kicked him out for good, would he be missed?

I don't think so, somehow!

I have a great deal of admiration for Mark Hughes and, he should know better, than to allow him to bring his attitude to our screens. If we want to watch that, we can buy a video and watch Steven Segal...

The managers are no different, in fact they are worse because not only can't they manage, they could play either. This is sad, but true. And the thing I detest most is they have too much to say for themselves and, when the big one comes along, nothing. I will tell you later of their chances in the upcoming World Cup and we will see if this is so. I actually don't think so, I know so.

I was told that I could not have this published after the event, but trust me, this was written well before that total disaster in South Africa, if you know me, you will disregard this, for it being true!

The one thing that never changes is that first step. That being, first, become an apprentice professional and then step two - which is the toughest - reach professional. Once you've achieved that, your next goal is to play for the first team, followed by playing in an FA Cup final and finally the ultimate dream, to play for your country. I did it all in eight short months. Or so I thought. The Man upstairs intervened once again, although that was for the very first time. The last time was far more daunting, in fact a completely different kind of scary.

The man responsible for all of my football dreams coming true was the man who this book is especially for, my father Bill, without whom I would not have so many wonderful things to write about. It's also for Tony Waddington, the man who confirmed to me that there was more to life than just football, but get it in the right order. He gave a new meaning to performing to the very best of your ability....hence the title of my first most important book, which had a great title and of course, it was his title.

My funniest story of Tony was when taking Stoke City to Rome for a match against Roma. He was asked by the guide to tell him if he needed anything to help him enjoy his stay more, not to hesitate to ask him. Tony, tongue in cheek, said, "I wouldn't mind an audience with the Pope." After a stormy match the guide told Tony that his wish had been granted and the Pope was expecting him the following morning. Tony at first thought it to be a joke, before realising it to be true. He shook Mr. Henshall, our chairman, out of a drunken sleep - more like a coma - and off they went to the Vatican. He was told by His Eminence that he had better keep his team in order and then asked if he realised just how responsible his position was?

Tony left a little stunned, not believing how much the Pope knew about our game. He gave it great thought, although he never stopped his back four from knocking seven shades of the other stuff out of the opposition. The following season they won the only trophy of any significance the club had ever won, the League (Carling) Cup, beating us 2-1. Not long afterwards, his team experienced a very bad start to the season and after a lengthy chat with the chairman in his office, Tony had, had enough of it all and told Albert that it might be best sorted out over a Gin and Tonic in the Boardroom. As they were heading up the stairs, Henshall said, "Tony, I think I have the solution."

Tony looked over his shoulder at him and said, "Don't be so ridiculous!"

It was soon after that he signed yours truly.

Thirdly, this book is for Leslie May, who was with me through most of this. A friend I could never replace, we were inseparable. We lost Leslie under the most terrible of circumstances and, in the months to come after the heartbreak and torment of losing her son, his mother followed him. I believe to this day, that is the way she wanted it. I sat with her many times as she poured her heart out to me, never coming to terms with losing him. She told me one morning of him calling her from the top of the stairs and, on walking from the kitchen, looked up at him and nearly collapsed. "Al, he was green, it wasn't my Leslie." My heart went out to her, more than I can tell you. I hope his brother Peter will read this new book and be reminded of all the fantastic times we shared together, and we really did.

Those times are still talked about by the locals when I visit Chelsea, well, that was before they closed down the Chelsea Conservative Club - where I first came across Portillo - the people who ran that club would have fitted perfectly into those walls surrounding Parliament.

They let Chelsea down "big time" by doing something good thieves don't do and, that is steal from their own and, they don't need me telling who they are, although David Lloyd, Jimmy Whelan and Bobby MacDonald were as guilty as Cameron and his counterparts.

The only regret here is that my mate 'Millwall Mick' got involved with such riff-raff. The club that is, not the people, he was far too superior to them.

The last time I saw Leslie was in this Den of Iniquity. But back to the good times and Leslie and, I will never forget one particular day in St Ives, Cornwall when we were with our girlfriends. We use to stay in the Heatherbell Motel. We left there one morning, where we were down to our last few quid and, headed for that wonderful village, where we found a betting shop. Just before leaving I had been told by the head lad of Michael Jarvis that he fancied his three runners. The rain lashed down similar to my greatest night at Wembley, when the ground was "bottomless." We had three £5 doubles and a £5 treble and they all obliged. The Heatherbell ran out of champagne more than once. That was after Leslie and I had to wait for the small town bookie to go and fetch our winnings from a few friends. This was a couple of years before I saw this stuff poured into a bucket and even longer before my old man acquired a taste for it, but that was ten years on, in Seattle.

And then there were times when, after a match at the Victoria Ground, I would jump on the train back to London with Leslie just to spend some time together. We'd have drink on the train, then in Knightsbridge, in The Magpie and Stump or The Imperial Arms (Matthew Harding's pub) the following day and then I'd get the late train back to the Potteries. All on £200-a-week!

George Benson sang, "Everybody's searching for a Hero," and my cousin Anthony Mason is mine. He has been to hell and back since his teens but has kept his dignity and wonderful sense of humour through it all, in a life that so many people take for granted. He has charmed people. He has touched people.

He has been a credit to our family. I am very proud of him, for all that he got in return is heartache and pain, that makes my case seem like a mere case of the sniffles!

If Anthony was my hero, Bill and Tony were my inspiration, my motivation and my mentors, two men I played the game for along with George Mason - Anthony's father. My father brought me up to play the game properly - an art I always tried to hand down to my younger peers - before passing me over to Tony. He did so, to take me to the next level. My title is theirs, my game is theirs and my reaching the heights I reached is theirs. As I just told you, I played the game for them. Without Bill, I would not have made a player. Without Tony I would not have played for England. Without them both, my life would have been so much less. They were, and still are, the two most knowledgeable people in my football life. Their passion was that of a Sinatra song. Their love of life and humorous outlook on it all, to go with that passion, was quite uncanny. Two men coming together that had me thinking that 'There is someone up there.' And along the way, I am even more convinced, although that is only when I think of such glorious moments.

When my father first shook hands with Tony, I could not help remembering that he didn't shake hands with people. When he shook hands with Tony he meant it. I simply left them together. I am proud that not only did I have great love for them both, but actually played for them both and, therefore, I had to keep up my standards to earn their respect. I look at managers today and know that I am right.

Best, Cruyff, Haynes, Greaves, Mackay, Baxter, Pele and Bobby Moore all came from working-class backgrounds. In the Seventies, greats such as Bowles, Osgood, Worthington and Currie, all my mates, were the same.

My first visit to Wembley was to watch Billy Digweed and Johnny Fennell play for Hounslow against Crook Town. This was the day I knew I just had to make it. I just had to play at this marvellous stadium. On returning home and telling my father of my experience, he promised me that I would one day return there, but not for an Amateur Cup final. Teddy Weston, Paddy Long, Bobby West, Buddy Herbert, Harry Yewings, Charlie and George Mason, were just some of the very talented players of that time around the Worlds End.

So, it was something special alone to become the first player from the Worlds End to ever get, not just into the first team, but get such unbelievable success at an early age and, of course there's always those who just "might have been?" or could have been?"
Well I could sing like Sinatra and Buble.

A little later Bobby Eyre, who could play and, was as good as Ashley Cole and Graeme Le Saux, David Carter and Rodney Udall (who my father felt was a certainty to make a player) were three players who could have gone all the way. Mickey Sheehan was another talented player of those times, but once again he needed a father like mine to guide him. That was just how good my father was.

Chelsea was an area where football was rife. Football was second nature. Saturday morning, afternoon, evening, then came Sunday morning, afternoon and so on. Even parties in our prefab were split into two, with Sinatra in the tiny front room and my father holding court in the even tinier kitchen.

My uncle George must come in for a big mention here, for he has been the most consistently wonderful person in my lifetime. A man who would look after you no matter what, but at that time I didn't know just how far that would go. You'll hear of that later, very much later. He became a rock once my father moved on and has been such a very special part of my life, it's no surprise his son is my hero.

I am told on good authority that Billy Hudson could play a bit. He played at Wimbledon before they changed the rules. He also played at Wealdstone before ending up playing with most of those names I just mentioned, in a very well-known team called the Chelsea Old Boys. Thanks to him, I could make that quantum leap, not only to the stars, but to play both with and against them.

Bill Shankly once said to me, "I thought I'd seen the greatest performance of all time, but today you surpassed it." If I tell you this more than once, it is because of the weight it carries. The previous was performed by his hero Peter Doherty at Preston North End, who he played alongside - he was obviously the greatest player he had ever seen. I could not have put in such a performance without these two great men.

I don't apologise for mentioning this several times, there are a million and one players who would love to boast such a thing!

This is the man who changed Merseyside in so many ways, bringing his wonderful humour to a city that never sleeps in that department, but along the way those comedians flourished because of him and, my first memory of this was seeing Tarbuck with him in the famous Boot Room in 1969/70 season. I know Jimmy adored him!

Quite a compliment from quite a man! As I write, Sky News comes on and tells us that it was 50 years to the day that he became the manager of Liverpool, the club into which he breathed new and extraordinary life into. There was only a few men who such a compliment would have been worth savouring, those being Tony Waddington, Jock Stein, Brian Clough, Bobby Moore, Alex Ferguson, Matt Busby and, of course, the old man. Although as you read on, the fantastic Len Shackleton gave me ten-out-of-ten on more than one occasion.

I suppose Pep Guardiola and Jose Mourinho would fit in there somewhere.

And, as I write the former Barcelona boss, looks like becoming the next Chelsea manager, having changed his mind about taking a year out of the game, to recharge his batteries. I really wish him well, he is a man of incredible class and fantastic integrity and, I hope the Russian Oligarch treats him with both. He is going to need it, however, because he is going from a top team to a Sunday pub team in comparison. This first job will be to get the team go from a team who are better without the ball to a team who are better with it, as Barcelona showed them in that incredible semi-final, which will still have me wondering how Chelsea won, well into my third life.

Helmut Schoen, the West Germany manager, remarked after my England debut in 1975 that "England have at last found the next Bobby Charlton," Gunter Netzer said, "Where have England been hiding this player?

Tonight he was world-class."

That was, of course, just after my international ban was lifted, thanks to Mr. Waddington banging the drum. Mine that is.

Those words coming from such giants in our game are my CV and, I owe it all to one Billy Hudson. As always, my mother took a back seat on the football side of things, she was responsible for getting me prepared for my matches and telling Bill not to get too excited. You see, my father knew that I would go to the top, whereas my mother only dreamed about it. That was two dreams fulfilled, mine and hers.

After mentioning Brian Clough, who was as well as being a football God, was eccentric, that fine line once again and, this story is an example. My boss in the USA, Alan Hinton, told me of on a very hot summer's day at Craven Cottage he had him stunned. I can remember this match, if only for being a Fulham supporter and, it was nearing a hundred degrees, when Clough had a bottle of Watneys Pale next to their plates at their High Street Kensington hotel, about three miles away. As they all looked at the head of the table, where Clough was seated, he lifted his bottle up and said, "Cheers boys" and put it to his lips. They were all stunned and waited for the first one to follow suit.

In the end Alan was the only one not to partake and, Brian said, "What's up Alan, is the company not good enough for you?"

Clouseau, as I called him, said, "Boss, I don't drink on a Thursday night before a game, let alone three hours before."

Clough said, "It's a hot day, you're going to need fluids inside you and they are sponsoring this match. If you don't drink it, you'll not play."

Alan drank it and was pulled off after five minutes for being drunk whilst in possession of a football. Well, not in possession, a ball slid under his left foot right in front of the dugout.

That was Clough letting him know who was boss and, it was brilliant in some ways for he chose a match that he saw as a pre-season friendly, against Manchester United.

In those days the Watney Cup opponents were the two teams that scored the most goals the previous season and, that was all that Alan saw of it, I'm very fortunate he never played that trick on me, I might not have left the hotel.

Hinton that is, in Seattle!

As I have said, my elder brother John, younger sister Julie and I had the most fantastic upbringing and they were the happiest times of my life. This being so important when you have to go out into the great unknown on your own. Whenever things go wrong and I feel that I didn't deserve such a bad break, I think of my times in our prefab and things more than levelled themselves out, although years later, I had to think hard about that, more of that later also!

Our prefab was my father's Lancaster Gate. The Cage, in Upcerne Road, was our Wembley and my mother was the woman of whom they used to say, "Behind every great man...."

I thank Chris Willsmore for originally talking me into brushing the cobwebs from the original manuscript which I began writing from my beautiful Seattle home. Then there was Martin Knight, who popped up to give me great help and encouragement and, more importantly much later he brought me that laptop to my hospital bed and, I could not begin to tell you how much that helped me through such torrid times. He also, along with Bobby Eyre bought me that cross to hang round my neck once that crucifix appeared burning a hole in my sister Julie's wall, something I will explain later. Then there was Ian McLeay, who in the beginning was so very helpful with his research. Last but not least of all, Malcolm Molineux, a man who put this project before all else, by helping me get the best possible product to the publisher. It is not an easy thing to do but what is, if you want to do it well?

All I can say is that later when I bring you my thoughts about Barcelona, it brings a new meaning to expressing yourself on a laptop.

I must give a special "thanks" to Jeff Powell, for influencing Jeremy Robson of Robson Books to publish it originally. Jeff has been a giant in his field since our days around Fleet Street. He remains a special man in my life and, my respect for him is on a par with all of the many wonderful names inside these pages.

All I can say is that my experience of writing this is the next best thing to actually playing the game. Not just because it has brought back so many happy memories, but allowing me to use my ability to bring it to you in such a simple way. As you will find out later, it also saved my life while I was holed up in hospital for the longest year of my life, all of this at a time when, as I said earlier, I was close to losing my mind (and my legs) through such an experience. I had lost almost everything else. My body was in bits, my mind not far behind it, paralysed below the waist and, in time I would find that I had lost total control of my balance and of course, lost my wife, but after plenty of deep soul searching and asking the one great question of "why me?" I looked around the hospital and saw people not only a lot worse off, but lonely. I had a wonderful family at my bedside and, although my partner was moving slowly away by the day, however hurtful it became, I had no option but to replace her with my laptop. Without that, thanks to Martin, I may have just gone over the edge, for it kept me in sane and, in touch and, as I had to drill it into my head constantly, life certainly goes on with or without you.

And then one Sunday afternoon, I broke new ground - something I was used to doing. The surroundings of St Barts were like a Ghost Town on a Sunday. Looking back from my wheelchair, as Anthony pushed me, I saw a building that seemed to be lying dormant. When I say that, if you are going to be ill, don't do it at weekends anywhere near this place. Finding a consultant would be like finding a black cab, or the Green Man, in the Sahara Desert. Anyhow, crossing the road there was not a soul in sight, as we headed for this little boozer around the corner just opposite the Smithfield Meat Market.

It was there that I planned my move. I waited for my cousin Anthony to go to the bathroom, and as soon as the door closed behind him, I grabbed the bar with all the strength I could muster and, counting to five, I hauled myself to my feet. My legs buckled. I clung to the bar for dear life and, as I did, ordered myself a large Jack Daniels. To my absolute amazement from over my shoulder came a round of applause from the table behind. Anthony, who had by then returned wondered what all of the fuss was about.

And then he looked at me as if I were a ghost. Maybe I was for those few seconds!

I was still trying to put weight on around this time and, was down to between seven and eight stone, so I thought Jack might help.

There was definitely one thing for sure during these times and, that is I found out just who was who in my life and Martin Knight was right up there on the leader board.

You'll hear from Martin later. Without knowing it, he has been a massive help and, one of the funniest men I have ever come across.

Just before Fatehi hit me, Paul Miller was another who was really good to me when things weren't going my way. But the one thing I always had was my mask. That brave face, without that, there was only the mirror that would tell you the truth. Although for the first few weeks in Treves Ward - and then Frederick Andrews - I refused to look into the one thing that would have surely have frightened the living daylights out of me.

After all, as I just told you, I was down to just around seven stone, back to my playing weight as an inside forward at Park Walk. This was place that led me to the playing fields of my world and then, into the killing fields!

As I say, it also helped me through those early times when returning from the depths of despair in the Intensive Care Unit. What you heard and what you read was nothing like what it was. There are no words that can explain the pain, grief, despair and complete disbelief of it all. It was on the other end of the scale from the Working Man's Ballet.

It is amazing how your entire life can change like switching on a light, though in my case it was like switching it off. And that is something they were close to doing in those early days as they continued to cut me from head to toe on a daily basis.

But David Goodier came to my rescue and demanded that they gave me stronger management - something that is a big part of this story - thank God they listened.

I owe David so much, if not my life!

Great management was something I had only experienced under Tony Waddington, so you could say that there are people out there who don't need a coaching badge to get the best out of you. David Goodier along with Frank Cross and Norman Williams were such a fantastic coaching team and then there were Otto Chan, David Badenoch, Claire Strickland and, much later, David Ralph. They made the mugs I had been around for so long, look just what I had always thought of them. Mugs.

As my mate Ray Winstone said to bloke in the pub in Love, Honour and Obey when seeing that the word Mug was written on his forehead, "And that is what you are, a mug, you mug." It brings it all back to me when seeing that piece of the film, now Ray might know how I felt in my career?

Well, he should, because he's watched West Ham enough over the years…

So this is part of the reason that I have decided to rewrite The Working Man's Ballet - to put the record straight once and for all.

What many people tend to forget is that players of my era - especially the more talented ones - were brought up in an environment which was all about drinking, gambling and womanising. But I think you'd have to agree that compared to today's equivalent, there is no comparison. You only have to look at the behaviour of today's players. Rio Ferdinand missing a drugs test, the John Terry, Peter Crouch and the Ashley Cole affairs - there will be others to follow, you can be sure - and, worst of all, what players now are proud to boast about, the 'roasting' of young girls.

When I look around at my old team-mates and the trouble we got in with the management we, in comparison, were pussy cats!

But what's new?

16 A WHITER SHADE OF BLUE

The summer of '95 was a hot one.
I was having a drink in the pub opposite the front gates of Stamford Bridge.
It used to be called 'The Rising Sun' back in the days when my great pal Danny Gillen ran it, two lifetimes ago. I was about to go and see Ken Bates about writing a foreword for this book.
What was I thinking?

After I had been in to see Ken Bates about writing the foreword for the original Ballet and, though receptive - maybe because I had my future wife with me - he was his usual arrogant self, although I could swallow that because I thought somewhere along the line it might benefit the both of us.

Bates wasn't as clever as he thought he was, so therefore, I go along with it all, you merely let him think he was and, in all fairness I've met worse people - though not many - than him in my lifetime. The bloke at Stoke I mentioned earlier was one of those and the next to him was in Seattle, two men of little ability but lots of the kind of power I talked of earlier.

Anyhow, he said he would take the manuscript on holiday with him and if he approved of it, he would give me his answer, which was fair and understandable. While we were there he insisted on showing us the new ground and said that he was thinking of opening another bar with my name above the door, it would be called, he joked 'Brandies' something different from what George said earlier, although it was humorous.

However, I was not one for this man's humour at the best of times and, this was no exception. What also surprised me was that he showed us the ladies toilets which he said he was proud of designing. Something I found a little weird. But little did he know that I had been told by a certain person who knew him that after a few drinks he would be quite rude to the opposite sex, this someone was once involved with the club and a personal friend of Captain Birdseye.

Am I surprised?

People will come and go and they will run the club and move on, then someone else will do the same, whether it is for the one pound that Bates boasts, or the initial £120million invested by Roman Abramovich.

Whatever the case, I can always boast about being born and bred in Chelsea and, when I say boast, I only say it because, of those people around those parts in my schooldays.

Today, forget it.

My new friend Phil Shaw, who warned me about publishing with my World Cup predictions, visited the Bridge (4 June 2010) to interview Peter Shilton and, said he was absolutely shocked that there were bars all around the ground with names on them, which had him thinking 'why no Hudson?'

The day I was kicked out of Chelsea by the Mears organisation holds the key to such a story, the kind of story that outsiders will never know. I don't see why, all these years later, we still suffer, having done what we did for the club, yet those who have done absolutely nothing are rewarded for all of what we actually achieved. There is so much mediocrity at the Bridge. They walk around the place like they are the ones who put them on the map.

This is why I distance myself from not only them, but the place itself.

That is why I admire Sir Alex Ferguson so much, for my mate Jimmy Greenhoff tells me that he has so much time for the real players, those who are the history of Manchester United. Directors of football clubs have so much to answer for and, when I look back at the way Brian Clough treated them, I now understand why. The way he was treated at Nottingham was scandalous after all he did for them. Just like those directors at the FA over the years who have earned fortunes for destroying our national game.

They employ to destroy and get a fortune in doing so!

As I have said elsewhere, in the Seventies the two best managers were overlooked, and the outcome, is there for all to see. How could Revie have been given the job in front of Clough and Waddington?

To give you an idea of what I'm talking about, Waddington could have had both the Manchester United and Leeds United jobs, but turned them down. He went to meet Manny Cousins and all of his friends in the Elland Road boardroom and left unimpressed and, knew that Stoke City were in better shape, even though there board were a complete joke. They would have been alright in Vaudeville, in fact, I thought at times, they were.

So the point is that Revie left both Leeds and England in a complete mess.

The likes of Revie and Eriksson - not to mention Capello - waltz in and waltz out and, after taking our game back into the dark ages and, never had to worry again.

As Supertramp sing, "Money here, many there," well they earned money everywhere, but did a brilliant "fuck-up" whilst getting it. I nearly said earning it?

They should get paid on results, not on how much time they are there. When are these idiots in Soho Square going to see that?

They gave Capello a two year extension on his job before we even got to South Africa, now what other job can you get such a bonus and, when getting the sack for failure get paid up for those two years. Absolute nonsense!

Eriksson still waltzes through this country like a terrifying landslide, leaving devastation behind whilst moving on to his counting house.

Did I say house?

Oh, and gets his leg over along the way, it can't be bad, can it?

I mean, leading up to the World Cup he played a different team in each half in those all-important friendly matches.

What was he thinking?

This was the most ridiculous situation I have ever come across by an England manager!

Why?

Because when I played I based my game on getting better as the game wore on and, I prided myself on that. When I say, get better, I actually mean stronger, as I worked very hard on my fitness. I may have said this elsewhere, but I had to train hard, unlike others who were naturally fit, but I think my way was better, because when you work that hard in training, especially after enjoying yourself, you get greater satisfaction after a match when you have put in a good performance.

I trained for a two-hour match, therefore I was running on whilst my marker was flagging say, with 16 minutes to go. That is why the better tea and stronger teams were, or are, the ones who always score late on, it's not a coincidence, like Barcelona they don't go breakneck from the beginning, they simply wear their opponents down and, in the last twenty minutes of matches you'll see massive gaps in their defence.

I think Tony appreciated this also and, that is why he gave me Carte blanche in our team. People still come up to me and ask how I did it?

How I would go back and get it off the goalkeeper and keep everyone waiting. It's very simple, for the game is simple 'complicated by idiots,' as I always say, for possession will always be as the saying goes, "nine tenths of the law."

When Tony Waddington turned down both Manchester United and Leeds United to stay with his one love, Stoke City, they were the worst decisions he ever made. His love and loyalty for such a club was as mad a love affair as my second marriage. You get no better thought of. And like a love like mine, the better you are to and for them, the more you get abused.

What Osgood and I gave Chelsea and what we got in return was nothing short of scandalous. I touch on this right now after telling you about my training regime and, what I put in for this club and, although Osgood never did such a thing, he did not have to, because he gave them something, as Jeremy Vine states on Eggheads, "something that money can't buy, their reputation," although his was both that and, his expertise and, his wonderful knack and ability to score wonderful goals and, more than that, very, very important ones.

What odds would you have given this just three weeks ago?
Stoke City v Southampton at the Victoria Ground and Oz on the end of a 4-1 hiding. But I think our look tells a different story, as if looking for the nearest pub!

Although I am not a lover of him, you can put Drogba in that category, but unlike Osgood, he spends far too much time rolling on the lush green grass and play-acting and, as I said already, this is a job for Stamford Bridge not Covent Garden.

But back to Tony's misfortune and, then you look at someone like Harry Redknapp for instance. Talk about falling lucky, with West Ham, Portsmouth, Southampton, and Portsmouth again and then Tottenham.

Dave Sexton once said to me, "When you can put six international caps on my desk, you then have a case to demand," what did that have to with playing for Chelsea?

He then kicks you out, gets the sack himself, goes to Manchester United and QPR before getting a lovely number at Lancaster Gate. The game and those who have earned a fortune out of it, sickens me. Don't get me wrong, if they were that good, I'd say "good on you," but I've worked with Harry, Dave Sexton, Don Revie and Tony Waddington, and the wrong ones fall firmly on their feet. Waddington would blow those three out of the water when it comes to real management, yet ended up with next to nothing to show for it. Plus, had he earned like those today, he just might have lived longer, through getting better treatment for his illness.

But back to the start of my career with Dave and, the story that I am about to tell you, that is a sad one, for three of that famous team of 1970 died far too young. A couple are in poor health and, of course, I experienced a near fatal car ordeal, in what I always suspected, was an attempt on my life.

I am still in the early stages of finding out just who was behind it?

Then there are two famous Scottish internationals - both of them being in a completely different class from those of today - who have both 'dried out.'

Few of us made the fortune we should have or would have today and, few of us tasted the lasting success also, yet, it is an uplifting story of hope, courage and all-too-brief glory; a group of young men who lived a dream!

That, for me, was just another dream in my lifetime that turned out to be a nightmare and, if only Fulham had listened to my old man and, then if only my dad had took more notice of Wilf Chitty at West Ham?

But that was before we knew that Bobby Moore was going to be so influential and important to me!

If only I had met Bobby a little earlier, for he would have changed my life, because although he gave me some valuable advice I never listened and, that was because of Alf.

Like I told you about Dave and those caps, Bobby told me once, "Alan, forget about your club, put your country first, because that is where you get your recognition." He was right and although he had the love and respect of all of his peers, it didn't really do him much good with the hierarchy, did it?

And how ironic, after all that time in our lives, he ended up at my beloved Fulham and, as you already know although I was a Fulham supporter, I was to fall in love with Chelsea, not the club but the players of that time, never knowing that I was going to play a big part in such an incredible success story. And we had so many good times, great times, but that was nothing to do with the football club. It was to do with that wonderful team spirit that was built within the walls of both the dressing rooms of both Stamford Bridge, and the Mitcham Training Ground and, of course, the pubs and clubs surrounding them.

The only reason I wear my Cup Winners Cup medal around my neck is to remind me of our wonderful team spirit and those great times although when I came out of hospital I had the cross hanging from that chain.

Once that stand was knocked down - with the long bar that haunted Sexton - it seemed and, as it turned out, that it was like knocking the heart out of the club.

And, it definitely showed on The Playing Fields.

Two people dominated my football life early on. My father, Bill, and my surrogate father, Tony Waddington. Both have been taken from us and the world, especially mine, will never be the same without them. As for the game, what happened?

Just look at some of the managers throughout the Seventies and Eighties. John Sillett, Dave Bassett, Richie Barker, Gordon Lee, Geoff Hurst, Ian Porterfield, Bill Asprey, Terry Neill and then there were those England managers. The latest being Fabio Capello, who is just as bad as Sven and his sidekick Steve McClaren, who only got handed the job because one/they could not pay the Swede and, two/he was already on the payroll, so because they could they not afford to pay him - as an out of work coach - they instead, decided to keep him on. All very confusing, but what isn't at Soho Square?

As I have said, the word is that they are still paying the Swede today, along with two other football league clubs. Great jobs if you can get them. I don't know how to put this, but whatever way you look at it he's getting paid for doing nothing and, whilst achieving nothing!

Can someone please tell me what Ray Clemence does?

The other thing that gets up my nose is how they make such a pig's ear of the job and, are seen on television giving their opinions on a game they know absolutely nothing about. The other year, I saw Alan Shearer along with another joker, Iain Dowie, bring Newcastle United to Stoke City. They stood on the touchline shaking their heads. I made a point of watching them throughout and pointed it out to my pal Ranvir. It was quite hilarious. They simply did not know what to do, yet sit on television analysing and criticising afterwards.

They get them relegated, and then return - after getting a fortune - to the comfort of that BBC armchair. Do they really think, along with those that employ them, that the public actually take any notice of them?

It's the same with Sky. Okay the coverage is brilliant, but the 'faces' on there are on the wrong set, for there is a Comedy Store on the other channel.

If you heard them before England reached South Africa, you'd understand what I am talking about, for they talked the same utter trash as years gone by.

They lack the knowledge and the common sense and are embarrassing, so much so, if I didn't drink, I would have to turn to it. They, as Brian Clough said to John Motson - about John himself – you are not qualified to do such a job!

In the 1969/70 season, I had to change from white to blue and it was difficult - for I was a big Fulham supporter - but the thing that made it possible was that I had been around all of my new team-mates throughout the period of my crippling and career-threatening knee injury. In the dressing room were four world-class players and I was soon going to be playing alongside them. Peter Bonetti, Eddie McCreadie, Charlie Cooke and Peter Osgood were those four world class performers, whilst Marvin Hinton, who if having a little more self-confidence, would have been alongside any international defender on the planet.

These were my heroes within the walls of Stamford Bridge.

In time to come we all became heroes together.

I'm talking each and every one of us, all heroes in different ways rather like in a jigsaw puzzle, each piece fitting perfectly into place.

Before I had reached my 19th birthday I had faced the three best players on the world stage - Pele, Cruyff and George. And then there was God himself, Bobby Moore, the greatest of them all, for what he was both on and off the playing field. In recent years players Kung Fu the fans, fight outside night clubs and talk of roasting young girls and, there was I thinking that Kung Fu was a TV Show, a Night Club was for going out for the night to enjoy and celebrate and that a roast was what you went home for at 2-o'clock on a Sunday afternoon.

I wonder how they would have stood up to the white heat of that '70 FA Cup final replay between Chelsea and Leeds, when there were no prisoners taken, and certainly no love lost.

Those were the days when we never talked about what we were going to do, unlike today, players then simply got on with it. They never told the fans, they showed them. And those were the days when the fans applauded the players - nowadays it is the other way round. It is almost as if through guilt. It is quite incredible, for as I write, Didier Drogba - who always has a lot to say - has just been involved in a situation that could cost him his place in the upcoming World Cup in SA. He went into a tackle with a Jap and broke his elbow, but it was as he was writhing in agony that it flashed through my mind 'Here we go again,' only this time it was the real thing. I have absolutely no time for play-acting in our game, (and that is what actors get).

And then Chelsea and Barcelona flashed through my mind, those unforgettable child-like tantrums, uncontrolled acts of near violence, trying to terrorise referees and television viewers. Who on earth do they think they are?

Whilst watching the Tottenham Riots (August 2011) I thought about Chelsea.

Also, watching those in The House of Commons, who act like complete yobs themselves, balling and screaming at one another, whilst some even have the odd kip (sleep) whilst people who pay their taxes are watching them on their TV screens.

If we can't have any discipline within the walls of Parliament how can we expect any on the streets of our capitol?

Talking of such complete discipline and total control, I return to the great Bobby Moore in Mexico when under siege from those brilliant and ferocious Brazilian attacks. He not only stood firm and tall in that incredible heat, but kept his head, unlike that shambles against Germany in 2010. He was what Frank sang of A Man Alone as firstly Jairzinho took him on, then Tostao, then Pele himself and, had it not been for Gordon Banks incredible save from Pele's header, the match would have totally belonged to Bobby - I mean totally.

Although it did anyway, for Gordon's was a super reflex effort whereas Bobby's performance was 90 minutes of a sheer master at work!

There has been nobody in his class before or after and, look how they treated him after all of his achievements and, I don't apologise for repeating this several times.

Let me explain something. Do you think that the wonderful Diego Maradona would have got to Peter Shilton had Bobby been at the heart of defence? I don't think so!

But back to possibly the greatest ever FA Cup final - the first ever replay - where Tommy Baldwin and Terry Cooper, two of the quietest men in football, were taking lumps out of one another as the battle began at Old Trafford. Tommy, better known as Sponge and, my replacement when I missed both those matches because of injury, was a prolific scorer when given the opportunity. In these two matches he was given strict orders not to allow the most skillful full-back in English football to cross the halfway line.

I fit this in here, because this was a different kind of discipline showed by my mate Tommy.

Ron Chopper Harris didn't need any telling. His discipline was taking discipline to an entirely different level and, I will never know just how he prepared for such displays of sheer destruction.

His early scything tackle on Eddie Gray was chilling and, that set the pattern for the rest of the match. It was the only way we could have won it, by fighting white fire with blue fire and, the outcome was there for all to see. The colour blue was everywhere you looked in the Manchester night air, as those assassins in white shirts left the place empty-handed, beaten by a group of players who were more famous for being a team of Goodtime Charlies!

On that particular evening, we showed that we could have a good time both on and off the pitch against our most bitter of rivals. As for Charlies, it was Cooke who set up our equaliser quite brilliantly for Osgood, and for me, it was the brilliant striker's most important ever goal for Chelsea and, one carved out from nothing by Cooke. I can't think of anyone in this country since who could have served up such a feast, so delicately floating a teasing chip - Tiger Woods like - into that sinister Manchester night air, as Charlton, Hunter, Madeley, Cooper, Giles, and Bremner all stood there as if in Madame Tussauds. And then coming out of that air was Osgood to stab Leeds in the heart (that would have been had they had one). However, it bled and. I would just have loved to be in Revie's shirt pocket as the big lad from Windsor connected. As he did, although it was the third equaliser, it was in fact the winner as we took a deep breath to inhale victory into our lungs, as it had never been inhaled before. We knew right then, we were taking the FA Cup back to London for the very first time in the clubs' history. It not only won us the FA Cup, but the European Cup Winners Cup as well.

That is why I call it his most important ever goal for the Chelsea.

It's moments like this that make me sick to the pit of my stomach. Such genius performed for a club and, yet there are those who hold onto their false positions within it. As I just told you Osgood gave Chelsea something "money can't buy" and here was the greatest example of such a thing. If it were a painting, Nat King Cole and our very own London bus conductor, Matt Monroe, would have sung about it.

You've got it, Mona Lisa!

It was Peter Osgood and Charlie Cooke who made Chelsea the club it is, never forgetting Greaves, Bentley and Gallagher before them.

I just wish people within those walls were not so blind, so ignorant and so incredibly unreal. There are so many people who still live off this goal, that is why I keep away, for when I do go there and watch them swan around, I can't help but show my contempt and disgust.

Today (5.9.2011) I watched a clip on U-tube where Eddie scissor-kicked Billy Bremner head-high in the area. The referee was only about five yards from the situation, but waved play on. They say it was the roughest match of all time and that is something our boys can take with the most incredible amount of credit. It showed that we could not only play, but mix it on the playing fields as well as in the bars.

This night we mixed everything and, it also stood us in good stead for our following years' European escapade!

We were, after all, good at mixing things, over the years I'd mix my vodka with tonic, coke and now orange, whereas at the start of The Ballet, I told you of my love for mixing the best Crown Royal with ginger ale with a slice of orange, whilst in a crystal glass. But that was when I was getting paid more money than Chelsea, Stoke City and Arsenal paid me all together, in Seattle.

I will remain Chelsea's their most local ever player, being born within an Ian Hutchinson long throw-from Elm Park Gardens, although we actually crept closer to the ground when we moved to Upcerne Road. This was the place where I would learn my trade. Number 23 in fact, which was our prefab. Now I bet a lot of you have never heard of a prefab, let alone been inside one. It had two bedrooms - one I shared with John - a tiny kitchen, which led to a small living room and, an even tinier toilet and bathroom, where only a small passage split it up. As the saying goes "You couldn't swing a cat" but it was home and a very warm one. And we never had a cat we had a dog called, no not Rosie 47, but Ossie number 9. Unlike the number nine, Oz was a poodle whilst the more famous Oz was like a bull in a china shop, although he could score amazing goals without breaking a piece of Wedgwood. However if there had been a nose or a leg it might have been different, you see, he loved the other side of the game as well, just ask Frank McLintock and Mike England over in north London.

Opposite us lived the Champ family and, just around the corner Bob and Ray Eyre, whose mum Rosie was my mum's mate and, no she was no relation to Harry's dog.

Next door to us was Annie Hitchcock, whose son Henry would push round the streets of Chelsea in a wheelchair. Some nights our mothers would peep through her window where they saw her and her Henry dancing as if on Strictly…

I wonder if she'd had got her benefits today?

No, I doubt it, Annie Hitchcock was a local woman and…

My mate Bob was, and still is, the loveliest bloke you could ever wish to meet. We two and Mick (Champ) would get up to some tricks. I remember one Bomb-Fire Night we had some bangers and' some bright spark - if you'll excuse the pun - came up with the idea of lighting one and putting it through letter boxes of our dear neighbours. Bob and I looked at one another and said "whose house should we do first?"

Mick as quick as a flash said, "I reckon we should do mine." It was a classic!

This was our football HQ as well as home sweet home, from where another Hutch throw would have landed in our Cage. This was the size of a six-a-side training pitch surrounded by barbed wire. The Moulton's, who had the house on the corner, would spend quite some time throwing the ball back over their fence, which stood about eight feet tall. There were some wonderful characters surrounding our prefab. And then just about a couple of hundred yards down the Kings Road was the place that should be the Chelsea milestone, the Worlds End. That is quite appropriate, if only for me once leaving in '74, it became the end of my world in Chelsea, although I returned to live with my mother after coming out of hospital to find my marriage was defunct. This was not long before my mother died and those friends of Portillo had me thrown into the streets without re-housing me. Again, I am a different colour to those I met in court to fight this case and, to fight for my mother having lived there since her birth, it was sad, hurtful and fucking annoying, but once again, it wasn't like a Leeds and Chelsea contest, this was no contest, you simply cannot beat these people in high places.

I had represented my country in front of a hundred thousand England supporters, yet here they were from another background putting me on the streets. Don't you think I have the right to feel annoyed?

Now, as I said, the Chelsea Harbour dominates the skyline and overlooks where I once dwelt and spent many long hours dribbling, juggling, passing and working on my overall game. Michael Caine, Elton John, a one-time big hero of mine, Terry Ramsden and my ex-wife Maureen all owned properties there. Yeah, she owns property there and I'm homeless and, she's Irish?

Terry was once the Walsall chairman and a racehorse owner. He was said to have lost £52 million on the gee-gees, and I thought my pals Don Shanks and Stan Bowles were big time.

Donald and Stanley - as I call them - were the greatest ever double act in our game. It is a shame that, like me, they have been 'labelled.' Both of them had so much to offer, especially Donald. He worked with me in many coaching schools and clinics and was great value. Stanley, on the other hand, worked mainly in Hills, Corals and Ladbrokes and, like his great mate, never had much luck. Donald also did a great job abroad, with the black nations before the boom set in. He always told me of such talent, not that I needed telling. I had seen them over the years through touring in those countries which are now thriving. Don believes in that great old adage, 'work hard play hard,' just as I do. There is absolutely nothing wrong with that in my book.

As I said, I was born in 1951, under the influence of the star sign Gemini, which is represented as the Twins, Castor and Pollux.

Egyptian astrologers symbolised them as peacocks. Characteristics include being quick and restless, mutable and not to be depended on. I was definitely sleepless and, always have been, although Seattle made me even more so and, as for depending on me, only when it counts. In 1951 the most popular songs were 'Because of You' by Tony Bennett, 'If' by Perry Como, 'Be My Love' by Mario Lanza, and Mocking Bird Hill' by Les Paul and Mary Ford.

I signed apprentice in the only year of World Cup success, never thinking, or dreaming, that one day I'd play against every one of them, bar one, George Cohen, who played for the club I supported at that time, Fulham. Not only that, but I would even play alongside two of them, Geoff Hurst for Stoke City and Alan Ball for England.

In '68, after my serious knee injury, I signed professional and within a year I would incredibly be facing Leeds United for the first ever Chelsea FA Cup winning side. But like the Man says, as Paul McCartney sang, he had other ideas.

But going back a few months, my first match for Chelsea came about in the most peculiar of circumstances, circumstances that were to become far too familiar in my career. It was on the last day of January '69 that Dave Sexton had been tipped off that four of his first team players were Schindlers in the nearby restaurant, Barbarella. This was on a Friday, barely 24 hours before they were due to play Southampton at The Dell. As far as the four lads were concerned, they were having a quiet lunch in the restaurant that still stands between the Main and Millennium gates. It's actually on the Fulham Road opposite the off-licence, where the wine connoisseurs amongst the Chelsea crowd were known to congregate before all of our home matches. It was a fine Italian restaurant that I frequented many times. I knew the owners well through my friend Peter May, Leslie's brother, who was responsible for the arrival of their daily vegetables. It had that lovely ambiance and atmosphere that you'd see in those wonderful gangster movies The Godfather and Goodfellas. The owners are supposed to run a superb establishment down the street from Puerto Banus these days, and you can bet your life that it is superb.

I had so many wonderful times enjoying all the good things that the Italians do best. The food was spot on - although second to Alexandre - the wine tasteful and the women on a par with the rest of the place. When in Barbarella, you could have been anywhere in the world and, there were many times that I was. Anyhow, every time I frequented this most lovely of places I would stand there with a drink in my hand and, think of that 5-0 thrashing at Southampton, but only for a short while.

For it was here that these four were well and truly 'grassed up' by one of Dave Sexton's spies and the manager was quick to pounce. The afternoon on the eve of a big match - Dave would not have allowed it four days before a friendly in the Outer Hebrides. The story goes, and I did get it first hand from one of the boys involved much later, that Ron Suart, Dave's assistant, was closing in on Charlie Cooke's breath. And as the brilliantly balanced midfield player backed away, he lost just that and, went flying backwards over the tiny wall outside the hotel next door. It was as if he had been hit by one of Paul Reaney's flying tackles. That is if the Leeds United full-back could have got a blow in at him.

Charlie, the same Charlie who bamboozled Leeds, lay flat on his back as fans were passing in complete shock. They were just coming away after getting their match tickets for the following day's game. As I said, Charlie was one of the most perfectly balanced players I have ever seen and, had, had the pleasure to play with, and more than that, he was famous for his great control.

But 'Prince Charlie' not only lost that wonderful balance, but all control.

The other three who made up the lunch table - Peter Osgood, Tommy Baldwin and John Boyle - were in fits of tears, but little did they know though what all of this would lead to?

Oscar Wilde said that:

"We are all in the gutter but some of us are looking at the stars."

Those passers-by, on this day, would have seen it the other way round. In what was to mirror the tragic break-up of our great dual cup-winning team, Sexton axed these four rascals for that match and the rest is history.

Three of these four made up the Athens Hilton Drinking Party 18 months later.

A star is born - more like a star is torn. At the time of this fiasco taking place, however, I was directly opposite Barbarella, lying on Harry Medhurst's treatment table. If those buildings would have been glass, I would have had a birds-eye view of Charlie hitting the deck. All of this led to the telephone ringing in Harry's medical room. I was having treatment for an injury that would have seen me miss the following day's reserve match. Harry sat there by my side - cigarette on - making the room more reminiscent of a Pot Bank in Stoke-on-Trent than one where you received treatment.

He was a lovely man and a great target for those who loved a bit of fun. But at this moment, without me knowing, the manager was on the other end of the phone and, all I heard was his usual strange grunts. Little did I know, either, that he was talking about my chances of being fit to play for the first team when, as I said, at that precise moment, I wasn't fit to play for the stiffs (reserves) and, little did I know that was what the conversation was all about. Harry would stand over you and when asked by the manager what the chances were of the player being fit, he would just look at you and wait for you to answer. He didn't have a Desilu - but that wasn't his fault, because that was how the game was then.

One of our funny men, John Dempsey, would take the rise out of Harry something chronic, the former Fulham centre-half being such a nuisance around the place. He would come in and put on his white medical coat and go round looking at all the injuries. Like I saw on many occasions, years later in both The Royal London and St Barts, he really looked the part on his rounds. His verdicts went from "forget tomorrow son, amputation" to "no chance son, stay with Harry and have a cup of tea and a few woodbines."

He was fantastic for the dressing room. He was a breath of fresh air. I often wondered how he signed for Dave, having had him as manager at Fulham. It was a little like Pat Jennings signing for Terry Neill after playing under his management at Tottenham. The mind boggles!

There was a funny story about John at Fulham whilst Vic Buckingham was manager. It was said that he was always late for training, something that I never noticed with us, which knowing John I found suspicious. Someone told me, that he did it on purpose, even going as far as waiting in his car until a minute after 10.30. One morning he was called into Vic's office and fined. The following morning he walked into his office and paid him out in halfpennies. I love John Dempsey, as I do several others of this particular bunch of loveable rogues and, never forget, winners.

As I said, when our team, and club, was falling apart, Demps was worth his weight in gold. He was a great bloke and such an under-rated player. Staying on Johnny, I must tell you of one of the funniest things I have ever heard regarding one of my team-mates. We were coming back from a pre-season match in Holland and were talking about the funniest things we'd experienced in a match. Stories ranged from the one-armed Luxemburg captain to my 'goal' against Ipswich. Then Johnny said, whilst playing for the Republic of Ireland, "We were playing against Norway who had just been awarded a corner and, as I was getting ready to man-handle their centre-forward I got a whack over the top of the head. I turned round to retaliate and, as I did, I could not believe my eyes. A little old lady was standing there with her umbrella in her hand ready to strike me again." We fell about laughing. What I would have given to be there, and even better, if only it had been televised.

Since retiring he has worked with the handicapped for those peanuts and halfpennies I was talking about and, it seems some things never change. But I have seen him recently and he loved every minute of it. He certainly is a special kind of bloke, with a wonderful outlook on life. I only have to look in his eyes and I can't help myself, for he cannot be serious, unless he's taking care of those who are handicapped!

Anyhow, Harry had finished both his cigarette and telephone conversation by now, and as soon as he placed the receiver down, he said, "If you're fit, you're playing at The Dell tomorrow?"

I can remember thinking for a split second that I was dreaming, then realised this was for real. So I said immediately that I was fit. I wasn't, of course, but there was no way I was going to pass up such an opportunity. However, I never knew why. Had I, would I have said I was fit? This was crazy, one moment I was not fit for the following days reserve match, the next I was fit for first-team duty. How could I turn down such an opportunity?

But, oh boy, did I live to regret it. The other problem that I had was that I was not playing well in the reserves. This was not really the way it was supposed to be, or was it?

Anyhow, once again, the rest is history. I made my first-team debut against Southampton because four of the regulars were Schindlers. The following day we got as smashed as the players the day before, only it hurt more, for we were completely sober. 'Welcome to the big time Al,' I thought immediately, a five goal thrashing, alongside one of my old Fulham heroes and, it was that man John Dempsey again. We both made our Chelsea debuts together, and got walloped. Two Fulham supporters getting whacked for the team down the road.

I also loved Demps when he played for Fulham, with the great Johnny Haynes. He was masterful, consistent, reliable and, a player who was never fazed by any centre-forward that came his way.

So, as I say, here we were, two Fulham supporters, never knowing that we would soon be going on the greatest and most exciting period in the history of their local rivals.

Chelsea had a history of washing their dirty linen in public and here it was, all over again, only unbeknown to us, over the next twelve months it would get so much worse. But for now, it was just the beginning and, what a beginning it turned out to be.

A couple of years before, Tommy Docherty sent eight players home from Blackpool, including Terry Venables and George Graham, just before a vital league match at Burnley. My brother John was in that squad and almost got his first-team debut the same way as his younger brother. Wouldn't that have been something?

Even more amazing was that the score-line wasn't much different. The Doc's boys got hit for six that day.

From then on, the tabloids had a field day with the Playboy image of the club and very soon I was to become a big part of it, plus in that same year that club became a big part of my social scene - The Playboy Club that is!

I was on my way to becoming the George Best of the south, although never knowing we'd soon become great friends!

When I found out the circumstances for my sudden call-up, I just had to chuckle, never knowing at that time that I was going to be quite a big part of that particular social scene. I was at that time already aware of the night life around Chelsea. I was brought up amongst the likes of Joey Baines, Peter May, Brian Harrison, Peter Millard and Johnny Fennell. I loved the night life, but now I had to find a way to juggle it with football. At that time, I still thought I would not become a player, which makes what was going to happen over the next eighteen months all the more extraordinary.

I knew that I would not stay in the side at that time for Charlie Cooke was at the top of his game and, when he was in such form there was no better sight. The last laugh, however, was nearly on me, as I recall thinking that this disaster - and I was to have many of them - would end my career before it got off the ground. The newspapers were full of it, although one headline did read:

'LOCAL BOY MAKES GOOD'

At the very least I had got further than anyone else around our area, which often amazed me because Chelsea was full of some very talented players, some of whom I mentioned in my introduction. The picture next to the newspaper article was one of me with a French crew cut holding our poodle, Ossie, whose hair at that time was not far different, from Oz that is!

Mine was quite different from the image that was to follow once getting back into the side, this time though earning it and, not having to rely on anyone getting Schindlers!

As I said earlier, I honestly believe that I will be the last local-born Chelsea boy to play for them. Not that they produced me, for as you have read, my father was responsible for that. I had my teacher at home. I can also never see Chelsea producing a youngster who will be good enough to achieve what I achieved in those first two seasons.

My early days at the Bridge were spent around a couple of players who went on to become real giants in football management, George Graham and Terry Venables. Chelsea fans used to moan that while these two were harvesting trophies across the other side of town, the Stamford Bridge cabinet was like Old Mother Hubbard's under much lesser mortals.

Not forgetting the preposterous decision to appoint Geoff Hurst, someone that was not cut out for it and, I use him as an example of their incompetence when it came to finding the right manager - much like the FA you might say.

To say I was bitterly disappointed that he took over, just as I was going to sign for a second time under the management of Danny Blanchflower, is something of an understatement, but that was eight years on. This was just another case of sheer bad luck, or was it that Man once again?

He was becoming a real pest, yet in those early days, I did not know to what extent?

15 December 1997 was a long way off and, as I say elsewhere, just how glad I am that Fatehi did not come along around this time!

Going forward to that day with Danny, I left the main office absolutely delighted that he was keen to sign me. His last words were "come in to see me in the morning and the forms will be ready for you to sign." I then headed for The Town House to celebrate that great feeling of being back in work. But once again, what was about to happen could only happen to me. I hadn't even finished my first drink when Frank Upton came in and broke the news that Danny had been sacked. Where did that leave me?

If you look at the Stoke City chairman dying, although that was three years later, you might think that I had done something that Glenn Hoddle had talked of, being bad in my past life. Only difference is I am disabled in this one and that just seems to be my luck. I know you might say, why didn't you sign there and then?

And, I'd agree with you, but what difference does a day make? In my case, plenty and, never top my advantage. Well, all I know is that it made a lot of money as a song, but as for me, that day has twice cost me very dearly and, in particular when Mr Edwards died, for that would have been the beginning of my managerial career.

Frank (Upton) who had been a decent former Chelsea player, thought he was getting the job, but they gave it to Hurst. This was the man I once lived with. He knew me inside out and, therefore I think he was afraid of me. There is no other reason for him not signing me. He knew exactly how I could play and, the man also knew I was a bloody good trainer. He also knew I liked to enjoy myself, just as he did - I write biting my tongue - yet here he was, frightened of me. Now a frightened manager is not a good manager, or will never be a manager and that proved to be right.

Look at Ferguson and Mourinho, are they frightened of anyone or anything?

However, I was completely stunned, no, more than stunned, devastated. No, furious, knowing that he knew me so well, yet here he was believing that Chelsea was his club and because he scored a dodgy hat-trick in a World Cup final - just like Alf - he could move the goalposts, well it might have worked for him at Wembley, but this was Stamford Bridge and, they don't take kindly to those in east London. There was no love lost between the two clubs. As for me, I knew he would be a disaster and was proved right once again, but the powers-to-be obviously know more than I do, fucking idiots, more like it! The funny thing was that Frank told the lads to now call him boss, not Frank.

They never got the opportunity.

Like I said about me being in hospital, it is so important that you don't lose your sense of humour and, this was just another case of that. And, with Frank doing, or saying that, I had to laugh.

The following day I was dazed and obviously choked, especially knowing Hurst well and knowing he knew I'd have been a good signing. After all, he had absolutely nothing to lose, I was a free agent and because of that there was no fee involved and, I wasn't going to want the earth. When I did finally sign it was only for about £250-a-week, just enough to cover my bar bill in the Stamford Bridge Arms, forgetting The Tin Pan Alley, where TD and I would be entertained by young Frank Frazer, Mad Frankie's son.

Anyhow, as I said, I was both choked and dazed by Hurst's decision, so as I was walking through the Earls Court Exhibition with my dad and my uncle George - where he worked with my cousin Harry Yewings - I decided to put in a call to the only man to score a hat-trick in a World Cup final. His attitude was just something that told me he would become yet another failure in the Chelsea managers' office. I told him that Danny was going to sign me and he said, "If you turn up for training every day for the rest of that week, we will see?"

I told him what I thought of him and that was it. That four-letter word that can get you into so much trouble had done so again. I was wrong though, for I should have done as he asked and, saw what was going on, but he called my bluff and I, because of being insulted, bit the bullet. Instead, I should have used that bullet. I should have seen him off, but I was so hurt by his insult. I should have just gone in every day, signed, and waited for the inevitable.

What hurt most was the fact that Hurst knew that I was a great trainer from our days together at Stoke City and, as I said, when I first moved there I lived with him and Judith. I think probably, though, it was a case of him being not only unable to coach me and afraid of my lifestyle, but also his inability to manage people like me. Mickey Droy made me chuckle. When the new manager began changing things around the place, he suggested he leave things as they were, telling

Hurst, "I will be waiting at the front office to shake your hand when you leave, for you will be out of here before me."

It was simply a case of, 'Don't bring West Ham to Stamford Bridge.' He was a disgrace as a manager and, if that sounds a little too harsh, what you are about to read proves my point.

But before that, when I was living with him in Stoke, I was disappointed, because I wanted to stay in the hotel, however Tony Waddington insisted, for he didn't want me running around town. The irony of it all was all too familiar, as I found out that by me staying at their home, instead of paying my hotel bill, Geoff and Judith's carpets and curtains were paid for in their lovely Madeley bungalow.

Now the reason I'm telling you this, is because I see that as using me - and after what he did to me at Chelsea - and, they all gained once again, all except me. It might have turned out that Tony was right because, those early matches, especially my Liverpool debut, were so important and, that changed things completely. Had I been in the hotel and I had not done the business in that match questions might have been asked. Well, not might, definitely.

But back to the comparisons between Hurst and Terry and George, who had relatively short careers at Chelsea and were tremendously popular and, very impressive in a team that I felt could have been the best Chelsea side of all time. I was sure that they could have gone on to break the northern stranglehold, established mainly by Liverpool. They went to Anfield in the FA Cup and knocked Shankly's team out with a breath taking display. Add a young Hudson and Osgood (although Oz actually played that day) along with the brilliant Charlie Cooke and you can understand my way of thinking.

What would that kind of squad be worth today? But both Terry and George were to fall out with the Doc, which led to their exits. This was something that changed the whole direction of the team and, of course, the club itself. Terry's battles with Docherty seemed to look like a warm-up for what was about to happen between him and Alan Sugar. They also paralleled mine and Oz with Dave Sexton. What goes around, comes around, you might say, not quite a circle though, more like a spiral, a continuous curve.

I would truly have loved to have got into that side and played alongside Venables. It would have given me such great pleasure. He was a player I watched, studied and admired. Although at that time John Haynes was in a different class over at Craven Cottage, Terry was pretty decent himself, as he was always conjuring up something different. So it was no surprise to see him become so successful in management. His confidence was the "key" to his overall career. He was a thinking man's player. I was a tremendous fan of his, but John was a more complete inside forward. Today he would be priceless. They talk today of players being "world class" well, that was John. There is no player today that can compare!

George Graham was a real piece of work. I always thought the nickname Gorgeous was appropriate. He was a class act both on and off the playing field and a proven one also. Who can doubt the credentials of such a man? I listen to the lads who played under him at Arsenal and they could not speak too highly of him. My mate Steve Bould - his best signing - tells me he was brilliant to play for and work with. His nickname was actually taken from a famous American wrestler on whom Muhammad Ali, another superstar, modelled himself in the Sixties. All of his Leeds United, Tottenham and Arsenal boss's faults became his virtues and I admire him for that. He had seen it and done it on both sides of the fence. I always enjoy seeing George, he is warm and forever flashing that smile of his.

George's record as a player and manager is incredible. Whilst Chelsea employed all of these foreign managers, apart from Jose, George would have been the perfect man for the job. But he would not have stood for Abramovich poking his Russian nose in.

It is, as I've said to George, one of the great mysteries of Stamford Bridge is either him, Venners or both never taking over, for they would be a better team and a far better club for having them there!

A lot of people under-rated him as a player, for he was very deceiving in his all-round game and, as a manager known for being a disciplinarian. However, he stood by Paul Merson and Tony Adams through all of their problems with the drink, drugs and gambling. It was something that Dave Sexton could not have handled. One out of those three would have been enough for our manager, but all three, I don't think so!

For those two players were both self-confessed alcoholics, who would have had Dave swinging from Battersea Bridge by Mickey Droy's bootlaces.

Terry would also be right there alongside George, had he been interested in taking over under Roman. The other side of Terry was the archetypal London John. Would you buy a car from this man? Sergeant Bilko meets Budgie! The TV character he created with Gordon Williams, Hazel, was his alter ego. This programme captured the mood of the times so well.

I played against Charlie three times, twice when he was in these colours and once in Seattle when he was with Celtic and, it was at Highbury that he showed his brilliance against our struggling Stoke City team, however, what a fantastic talent!

I love this story if it is true.
Around the time George managed Millwall, he would frequent this afternoon club, drinking champagne with that great Arsenal player Champagne Charlie Nicholas. They were spoke of in those circles around London as you can only imagine, George was still a class act and, Charlie, of course, was a brilliant player at Highbury and, one

with such flamboyance. I also love this because of my growing up with the brilliant Charlie George; was there something about Charlie's and George's about Highbury?

And then George got the call after doing so well over on the dockside of London. It was for the Arsenal post and, with his wonderful CV as an Arsenal player, surely he was tailor made for what was ahead. There was nobody else, when you look at it.

Anyhow, his first job was to call his drinking partner into his new office. Charlie thought that it was a meeting of a completely different kind, but he had misread his mate. George was a different proposition in different surroundings and that was the end of Charlie. "But I was drinking with you George….but GG would not see any of his players drinking in such places, especially when he was there. Charlie is now my favourite on Sky TV each and every Saturday afternoon. He has that undeniable knowledge, passion and that something that made him such a wonderful player, who had it all, but as Tony Waddington said, "There's nothing wrong on doing those things, as long as you have them in the right order."

Charlie didn't, he misread George, but that was a simple mistake which we all make. You might say don't mix business with pleasure and, in this case, it was exactly that.

When I went drinking with my boss it was different, because he bought me and we loved each other's company and, not only that, he trusted me not to let him down on match days, which was something I very rarely did.

I can promise you, that I think I only let him down on two occasions and, one was inexcusable while the other was something that happened with one of his coaches, not the ones with the wheels on, but the one wearing a second hand tracksuit.

As for the first occasion, all I can say is any one perfect?

But I am just giving you that because these things go on, but in many different situations. I remember the story about when Jimmy Greaves was worse for wear on the morning of his West Ham debut and he said to himself, 'what have I done,' his words, anyhow he score twice, well he would wouldn't he, he's Jimmy Greaves.

Another case was at Liverpool, where the players hated Emlyn Hughes because he was close to Shankly, but unlike me, I never grassed any of my team-mates up and, that was obvious because, I was worse than any of them when it boiled down to breaking the rules, but I feel I gave more than the rules I broke and, never hid the fact. Tony knew he could sleep well, when it came to me doing the business for him.

Anyhow, back to a totally different proposition, where the bottom line, however, was that there was no way that he (Charlie) would fit into the George Graham system. If you had to choose between Alan Smith and Charlie Nicholas to lead your attack, who would you choose?

I would have Charlie every time, However, George chose Alan and that was why he was so successful and, it was absolutely brilliant management on his part.

Here is what they say about the man on the official Arsenal website: A hero of the Double-winning side of 1970/71, Graham returned to Highbury in May 1986 after a successful start to his managerial career at Millwall. Arsenal were treading water in the mid-80s - they had not won the title since Graham himself paraded the trophy 15 years earlier - and needed someone to shake things up.

Graham was that man. He revitalised the Club, bringing through a talented generation of young players such as David Rocastle, Michael Thomas and Tony Adams and supplementing them with a raft of astute signings including Lee Dixon, Nigel Winterburn and Steve Bould. That trio, along with Adams, became the Back Four, the bedrock on which Graham's success was built. The Scot had been known as 'Stroller' during his playing days, a nickname which reflected his laid-back approach in the middle of the park. But if Arsenal's players expected a relaxed, easy-going new boss in 1986, they were hugely mistaken. Graham was an uncompromising manager and instilled discipline and a strong work ethic from day one. His methods were rewarded with a fourth-place finish in Graham's first season and, more importantly, the Club's first piece of silverware for eight years.

Charlie Nicholas was the hero at Wembley with two goals as Arsenal came from behind to beat Liverpool in the Littlewoods Cup final, but this was the triumph of a cohesive team unit - and more was to come. The title returned to Highbury for the first time since 1971 when Michael Thomas struck in stoppage time at Anfield, of all places, on 26 May 1989. It is a game and a date etched in the memory of every Arsenal fan and Graham was the architect of that famous victory. Liverpool were technically superior to Arsenal but Graham won the tactical battle and, with it, the biggest prize in English football. Graham's ability to foster a siege mentality within the dressing room also helped. Arsenal were docked two points during the 1990/91 campaign following a brawl with Manchester United players at Old Trafford but they took that blow on the chin and went on to win the title by seven points, losing just one match, while conceding only 18 goals.

That final statistic owed so much to the famous Back Four and new goalkeeper David Seaman, who Graham insisted on signing in the summer of 1990 despite the fact that John Lukic was a favourite among the Highbury faithful. "I still think John Lukic is one of the best keepers in the country; I just think David Seaman is the best," said Graham. He was proved right.

The inspired signings continued. Ian Wright's arrival early in the 1991/92 gave Arsenal a steady supply of goals and he went on to break the Club's scoring record. However, Wright's arrival was soon followed by a change of tactics. Perhaps influenced by a European Cup defeat to Benfica, Graham swapped the flair of Rocastle and Anders Limpar for a more workmanlike midfield. That made Arsenal even harder to break down but they lost some flair going forward so, despite having won the title so comfortably in 1991, the championship eluded Arsenal for the remainder of Graham's reigns. Instead, with Wright always capable of grabbing a goal and the Back Four bordering on impenetrable, Arsenal started to dominate the cup competitions.

They became the first club to win the FA Cup and League Cup in the same season when Andy Linighan and Steve Morrow emerged as unlikely heroes in 1993. The Cup Winners' Cup followed in 1994 - Arsenal's first European trophy for 24 years - after a stubborn rearguard action against Parma in Copenhagen. 'One-nil to the Arsenal' was born.

Within a year Graham had gone but he had brought the good times back to Highbury and left plenty for his successors to build on, not least that rock-solid defence. These days the fans are well aware that 'Arsène Knows'. But 'George Knows' came first.

I was never given any credit for the signing of Steve Bould from Stoke City, as Steve was being chased by Howard Kendall at Everton when I was in my pub and night club and, Steve would come in after matches on a Saturday. On this particular early evening he told me of the Everton interest and, I told him in no uncertain terms that Arsenal would be his rightful move and, that I had told Stewart Houston - George's assistant - exactly the same thing. Steve listened and he went on to become one of the greatest Arsenal defenders of all time.

I'll leave the last word with Paul Merson who I went to see in Leek last year as he summed up that match at Anfield telling the audience that that he (George) detailed the win incredibly, from the first minute to the last. He told the players it would be 0-0 at half-time and that they would score their first goal around the hour mark, and then finally go on to score the all-important winner in the last minute. And that's how it panned out.

It was George Graham who was responsible for Arsene Wenger getting his only successes at Arsenal. Since George's defence broke up under Wenger, the Frenchman has shown his true qualities in his knowledge of getting his players to stop the opposition scoring. He seems simply totally ignorant when it comes to stopping the opposition and, I am not exaggerating. It was the former Arsenal manager that formed the best back four Wenger has ever had the pleasure to have picked. Since they have dismantled, the Arsenal manager has not had a clue how to put together such a marvellous unit, Wenger needs a Graham or Don Howe for when the other team are in possession!

El Tel once paid me a great compliment in saying I was a better player than he was and, I will not argue with him on that one. But I don't think he knows how influential he was in my becoming so. Tommy Docherty has gone on record as saying that it was when he saw my potential starting to blossom that he began planning to let Terry leave Stamford Bridge. I cannot believe that entirely, for Tommy brought down Charlie from Scotland and it looked pretty obvious he was his replacement. However, it was quite something coming from Docherty, for if anyone knew a player, it was the Chelsea manager. He also never got the credit he deserved for producing three great managers in those two and Eddie McCreadie.

Sexton, however, got rid of me with the same thing in mind, if what he says is gospel. He kicked me out to make way for Ray Wilkins. It backfired on Dave though because Chelsea were relegated, he got the boot himself - what a mess the directors made of all of this - as I went on to help Stoke City qualify for Europe with an incredible run of just two defeats in my first 25 matches. We went from third bottom just after the New Year to fifth from top.

The question on everyone's lips was and still is: "I wonder what would have happened had Alan Hudson joined them in the summer?"

Tony Waddington pulled off some kind of miracle, getting an alcoholic to ignite such a feat at the Victoria Ground. Well, that is what Richard Attenborough called me and Osgood. Oh, now how I wished I had chatted up his daughter-in-law, she was far too good for his family and would have fitted into mine perfectly. But that was the film business!

Wilkins came in and fulfilled all of his promise. He was a very good player. But Charlie Cooke and myself, I don't think so. To think I had just turned 23 with all of my best days ahead of me, which was, unthinkable.

However, I did not know right then that my best days were ahead of me, for I could not have dreamed that Waddington was exactly the man I could not only play for, but could talk to and more importantly, because of his experience with more experienced and other excellent and players who had "been-there-and-done-it," he'd understand me totally.

Can you imagine Chelsea allowing John Terry and Frank Lampard to leave, at the same point of their Chelsea careers? This was all as preposterous as the Geoff Hurst appointment - no wonder the club over the north side of London laughed at Chelsea. Whilst Chelsea was employing a World Cup winner, they had won the Double with a physiotherapist in charge. Management! Is it that difficult?

The Mears household had so much to answer for!

Ray Wilkins has followed Sexton into management and has made a right hash of it. But he will always get jobs because of his demeanour and his seeming to agree with the hierarchy. His record as a manager leaves a lot to be desired, and to make things even more ridiculous he has been back at Chelsea. As I have told you, he was working alongside Ancelotti after seeing first Luiz Felipe Scolari and then Guus Hiddink leave for entirely different reasons. He was brought in to work with Scolari - why? I can only think because of his position on television. As a TV pundit he sits on every fence available and, that is why he is no good in the coaching or management department. With great managers, there are no fences.

Players liked giving managers nicknames and still do to a certain degree, so it is not surprising that sacked Chelsea manager Felipe Luiz Scolari picked up the name Popeye Doyle from the French Connection.

Here he is doing his impression of Gene Hackman sleeping!

Like Venables, Wilkins exudes the corporate image demanded by the FA as a pre-requisite for the post of running the national team. He is also as sharply dressed as Terry and George, but he hasn't got the strength that goes with it, or their special presence and charisma. The assistants in Armani must break into the broadest of smiles when any of these three approach their store, much like the scene from Pretty Woman when Richard Gere does his number on the assistant when kitting out Julia Roberts.

El Tel learned how to cultivate the media many moons ago; he had the perfect teacher in The Doc and to some extent Malcolm Allison.

A line in The Godfather always sticks in my mind and, these words could have been Terry's, as Marlon Brando tells his son to, "Keep your friends close, but your enemies even closer."

Terry learned this very important lesson well, and I often wonder if he's seen the movie as many times as I have.

When he took on the England job, his first step was not the football, but the media, the Fleet Street Gang as he knew them and, as I would also get to know so well. Whereas Gordon Taylor tried to take them on, Terry lured them into his Den. Arthur Daley could have learned quite a few things from Terry.

The last time England had anything that looked like a decent team it was Terry that assembled them. It didn't take a lot of doing, but it never does, but Terry had the simple answer to a question that is always asked, "What's going wrong?"

Well, the simple answer is, select your best players available and, that is all that he did and, Teddy Sheringham, Alan Shearer and Paul Gascoigne were the three main players who could rise to the occasion. He knew Teddy and Gazza well as players and, they were magnificent and a blind man could tell you that Shearer would have got a game in any nation in the world at that time.

That was Terry's strength, for he knew players and, like Waddington, he could motivate them, plus was it a coincidence that when Tony turned down Leeds, his was the name that Tony put forward as the best young upcoming manager?

Leeds United didn't listen and have never recovered and, that is something I'm not too sad to say, because it's those in boardrooms that define the future of their clubs. The only time Leeds come anywhere near returning to the big time, was through George Graham.

But back to his mate Terry, I remember one evening at the Waldorf Hotel. I was standing talking to Tommy Wisbey - that Great Train Robber - when Terry approached us. Tommy said to Terry that he had a job for him, but it may require a mask. Terry, in a flash, just pointed to his own cheek. We howled!

His personal persona is absolutely superb. To the press he is always marvellous copy, always ready with a little quip and smile. As I just said, managers like Graham Taylor were not so media friendly and very naive, finally paying the ultimate price. He not only lost his job but was dragged through that horrid cabbage patch, or in this case the turnip one.

I have always believed that Chelsea suffered at the hands of the media because Ken Bates ruffled so many of their feathers. Thirty-odd years ago chairmen never talked to the press, all of a sudden they were controlling them.

The Chelsea fans were always portrayed as something out of an Oliver Stone movie, which was in stark contrast to fans of other clubs that also had a dangerous, albeit small, hooligan element in their following. If Chelsea had been involved in the Heysel Tragedy, I wonder what the outcry and punishment would have been.

The most exquisite (if Ray Wilkins doesn't mind me using his favourite word) time of Venables life, in my view, was when he captained Chelsea at that particular time, when barely out of his teens. No team in the history of the game ever caught the imagination and the mood of the times as Chelsea did in that period.

From the early Sixties to the break-up ten years later, they were the talk of the town.

It all started in the Swinging Sixties. The trendy Kings Road with its baronial rock stars and air of decadence threw out vibes that were to change society. As I said earlier, it was us that set up what they have today, not before us and not after us, but us. Anything and everything seemed possible and, there was a strong feeling that something unique could happen. The tremendous bond between the fans and the team were forged then.

As Martin Knight says, when he started following Chelsea and, through his Shed Years, the introduction of the players before matches was something that had him hooked. That led to him becoming a staunch Chelsea fan for so many years - right up to three or four years ago - when it lost its great appeal. He feels that now Chelsea, HIS Chelsea, has gone forever.

In the Seventies when it all went sour, a lot of Chelsea fans were lost, never to return. They still had great affection for the team and, what it had and should have done, but not the club. None of them started supporting other teams. They had just had enough. Venables, it seems, had it sussed. He always maintained that the biggest potential in London was at Chelsea. That cliché, Sleeping Giant, is trotted out every so often. I just wonder how it would have worked out had Tommy Docherty and then Dave Sexton seen it differently and, somehow worked together. The best of both men's Chelsea teams would have swooped the prizes, of that I am convinced. And let's not forget George Best was itching to play for us.

I often think to myself that in a perfect world, instead of me leaving for Stoke City, we would have been far better off swapping managers, Dave Sexton for Tony Waddington. Tony loved talent like the names I will be mentioning and would have insisted on keeping us all together, until we were all as old as Sir Stan was when he brought him back.

In doing so, the crowds rocketed from 6,000 to 35,000 at the Victoria Ground and, if Sir Stan could make that kind of impact by filling those terraces, then Chelsea would have had to have built another ground and, quickly had we signed George and, Tony would not have slept until he got him.

That is what you call management.

Another of Venners ideas was a dream of a London team playing in a stadium, with all the power of a one-city team. In the future it is not hard to visualise a global league emerging. Countries such as Japan are developing in a big way. Could that be the reason Terry took his England team out there?

Soon the Gulf will follow, just like all the other small countries that have caught us up and in many cases overtaken us. When I first wrote the Ballet, we had witnessed the Euro '96 and, saw the Swiss give us a good run for our money, whereas 30 years earlier they were part-timers. In that opening match there were times when it looked the other way round. Although there was one outstanding display from Sheringham, Shearer and Gascoigne against the Dutch, however overall we weren't good enough once again and, the future looked bleak and, to think that that was the best team we've had since 1970.

Plus the Dutch were going through their very own turmoil, a shadow of those before them, for they had gone from Total Football to Total Disarray and Turmoil.

It seems every time a big tournament comes round there is trouble in the Dutch camp, this time I think Edgar Davids was behind it?

This was at a time there was nothing like Docherty was building, although at Ajax they had been producing tremendous talent from around the Johan came through, I mean, I this country the raising of great young talent was beginning to freeze. I saw it when I was coming through, for the youngsters were just not there.

The part played by Tommy Docherty's in that explosion at Chelsea, which is still an influence in the game, should never be overlooked. The combination of him and Sexton would have been as great as any in sport, but as individuals they had flaws.

I would have loved to have played under Tommy the manager and Dave as his coach. In that role I liked him and, was comfortable with him, however in his office he was completely different animal.

As a coach he was comfortable and confident. To me, he seemed to dislike many aspects of management and, so did we. It was much like Don Howe, who was fantastic for me at Arsenal as the everyday man on the training ground. But put him and Dave in an office and they were like Jaws out of water.

All of those personality clashes, blown-up egos and "one of us must lose" syndromes seemed a far cry from The Cage, where we could just go and express ourselves without a manager causing a problem out of nothing.

Alan Ball once said to me that when he was at Arsenal they did not need a manager; for all they needed was someone to keep them fit and let them go out and play. It was one of the wisest things he'd ever said. More was the pity, however, that Alan wasn't quite as shrewd when he went into the hot seat himself!

As I mentioned, I was a Fulham supporter as a young lad. My hero was Johnny Haynes and, along with Bobby Moore and Jimmy Greaves, he still is. When you look at today's England players you might understand why I think this way.

In my other book I'm writing at this time, Don't Shoot the Taliban....You'll Wake the Locals, although it is about the injustices that our soldiers are experiencing, it touches on so many comparisons of what I am talking about here. The difference between Moore and Terry and Ferdinand, Charlton and Ball to Gerrard and Lampard, Banks to Green and Greaves to Heskey is not only the reason for England's on-going disasters, but totally mind-boggling and, the wrong players got the fortunes they deserved.

They were players I looked up to, admired, respected and used to try to emulate and, then George came along to bring the "film star" element into the place. George changed the face of English football. If you were a bloke, you wanted to play like him and, if you were a girl, you fancied him, so he had it all, the ability, the style, the looks and the name, nothing could possibly go wrong, no matter what the little Irish night porter reckoned.

With Haynes, I was fortunate to see him at a few functions after writing the initial book and he still exuded the magic. He has the one quality that always impresses me in a person who is a truly great performer. Modesty!

I have seen and heard people boast when they are less than average human beings, so to be great, which he really was and, play it down like Bobby, Jimmy and George, is a real special quality. John had that quality. Sadly he died after a terrible accident, much like mine, the difference being, unlike mine, John was inside the car and, it was fatal.

It was a very sad day for a lot of people and, his wife in particular, for John must have adored her - and her him - as he uprooted and moved to Edinburgh for her.

My great pal Tony Millard put on a Testimonial Evening for me in his Ealing Studio Bar and, without me knowing, put in a call to John.

He travelled all the way down from Scotland to be there. Sheer class!

Tony did something Chelsea, Stoke City and Arsenal could not be bothered about and, that tells you something, not only about my friend, but the strength of the supporters in those days.

There were and still are not many footballers who can carry such ability around with them. I see players who really are second-class citizens in our game, who think they are the 'real deal' but they cheapen the game. This is one of the reasons why we have never lived up to that day at Wembley in 1966. The problem being that they are too busy counting their houses, cars and money in one hand, whilst blowing their trumpet with the other. Once again, it really gets to me and, as I told everyone, it would happen again in South Africa, which it did.

While Chelsea was blazing under Docherty, Johnny Haynes was as Leo Sayer sang A One Man Band at Craven Cottage, surrounded by Tommy Trinder's cast at the London Palladium. When Tommy went on stage he should have taken Jimmy Hill with him. They would have been a match for Morecambe and Wise, only their humour would have been one of something a little different. Where with Eric they laughed at him with his Luton Town gags, with Fulham they alone were the joke and, if it weren't for Haynes, they would have drifted down the Thames never to be seen again. But you must give it to Trinder, whether he knew anything about football or not, he made John the first £100-a-week player. If he knew about football, good on him, if he didn't he had a good adviser, either way well done Tommy. I wonder what Dave would have done had John asked for a oner-a-week?

As for Hill, he got away with absolute murder and, that is all I have to say about him. But before I dismiss his ignorance, a few years ago I applied for the Fulham manager's job which could have led to a dream coming true - being the only club outside of Stoke I wanted to manage - but the reply from Hill, who had become the chairman, was that he would prefer someone like Dave Bassett. No wonder Fulham were in the doldrums for so long and, how I feel for their local supporters, of which, along with my family, I was one, right up until I reached the Chelsea first-team.

I received a call from my old mate Bobby Keetch, an ex-Fulham player and co-creator of the impressive eating establishment Football! Football! He told me that there was no way Hill would consider me. And although I was not surprised, I was deeply disappointed. I was also disappointed for all of those Fulham fans, including my old school pal Bill Boyce, who has been following them through thick and thin and, then having to sit and watch the Chairman spouting irrelevant nonsense.

I can recall so vividly how Hill, on his BBC laugh-in, MOTD, ignored one of the best performances I ever put in for Tony Waddington against Newcastle United at St James' Park. At that time,

I was playing the best football of my career. I really was on top of my game and, our team was going great guns. After the match, before going to my local pub, I rushed back to my Barlaston home to put on the video recorder. I wanted to watch the highlights the following morning. I was that delighted with my performance. I had talked about the match in the pub and if anyone had watched it, they must have thought that I made it all up. It was a simple case of Hill not liking me. Or was it that he does not know as much as he thought? Which is more like it, or maybe a little of both, or maybe a lot of both?

The following morning, I spoke to my dad and he was livid, but then he said, "I wouldn't worry about Hill, get the Sunday People and you'll see that Len Shackleton (one of the greatest players of all-time) has given you 10 out of 10."

Now that just tells you one thing, who should be on the TV?

The same applies today, as I said earlier. Just look at them today 19.6.10 Hansen, Shearer, Lawrenson, Keegan and several others, at the beginning of the tournament talking of great success, yet once England fail once again, they change their minds. Yet, they still get employed. The watching millions expect to hear something that they don't already know; but these people on the panel are not capable of doing such things.

In my second season I was told by a People reporter that I held the record for maximum points in one season, beating none other than Johnny Haynes himself.

Not bad for an alcoholic, was it?

John Haynes 1934-2005

The brilliant number 10 was Fulham's best ever player and was capped for England on 56 occasions, 22 as skipper.

His greatest game for his country came against Russia in 1958 when his hat-trick helped England to a 5-0 victory, He was also inspirational when Scotland were beaten 9-3 at Wembley in 1961. Pele described Haynes as the "best passer of the ball I've ever seen."

I was just beginning to get to know John pretty well, when he was involved in a fatal car accident. I sent him a manuscript that I had based on him, which was all about Fulham searching for the next Haynes and, after reading the manuscript he sent it back and, very modestly said that I was totally nuts.

John will always stand alongside the Moore's and Greaves' of this football world, a true giant!

On the Monday after that Newcastle match, George Eastham told my old mate, Michael Carter, when asked what the match was like, "Your mate was absolutely brilliant. He is the best inside-forward I have ever seen."

Now, who would you listen to, Jimmy Hill or George Eastham and Len Shackleton, two of the best inside forwards ever?

Another Londoner I was disappointed with was Gerry Francis. When we roomed together before my England debut he did nothing but slag players off.

But I, of course, said nothing. Gerry used to live a long bus ride from me in the early days when we were both doing the business at Chelsea and QPR. And he weren't bad at it either - he was a bloody good player. I won't go too strong about this matter, if only because he was held in such high regard by my mate Stan Bowles. He was a big fan of his old team-mate and, loyal to the core. If only people like that were just as loyal to him.

I also didn't like the way he was getting cosy with Revie, as if some kind of spy and, if he thought that, he was more dafter than I thought, because The Don had the best spy in the world, Les Cocker.

Earlier, my career was thwarted by Alf Ramsey, when banning me for three years for refusing to go on an under-23 tour. Stan turned down several trips, but that was because of his fear of flying. He once walked out on Ron Greenwood when he took over the reins as international manager, but the former West Ham boss, being the good man he was, didn't take the kind of line that Ramsey took with yours truly.

Bowles and Hudson were always labelled as being rebels, yet here was Francis walking out the back door on his country and colleagues. When I woke up on that afternoon, before the German match, Gerry was gone. There is one thing about the great events, not only in the history of football but in life, you must always stick together. Gerry didn't see it that way, although he should have for he played in that exceptional QPR side with fantastic characters like Frank McLintock, who had by then, showed his strength and quality, by captaining that great Arsenal side to the Double.

I find it sad that there are people like him, and then there are people like me, again they always come out on top. He played for the team I once followed - QPR but as you know, Fulham were the one team who were in my heart in those early days, although they rejected me when I was only 13 and still growing. This was around the time Alan Ball had played at the Cottage for Blackpool and was magnificent in his size six boots, had they not watched?

I was rejected once again. I wondered what it was all about with Fulham and the Hudson family. After all, look at all the mugs that they have had within their walls. At that age I was shattered, although obviously I didn't know any better then. All I wanted to do was, "go play ball" as the Americans put it. But I had no problem. My father was brilliant. He explained everything to me whilst continuing to build me up both physically (with the help of mum's cooking) and, of course, mentally. And then there was the confidence factor, which he built up wonderfully. He did the job by coaxing me through all of these experiences until he finally passed me on to Tony Waddington.

He was adamant that once I had filled out, I would overcome these knock backs and, then go right to the very top. I still had many doubts because I was just happy kicking about with my mates in and around Upcerne Road, whilst never really thinking about playing professionally. What helped me, I suppose, thinking back, was that I wanted to play for Fulham and, when I watched them, I thought they had so many average players.

However they had some good ones, my favourites being Haynes, Mullery, Barrett, Dempsey and Leggatt. What odds would you get that years later they'd have two players called Hudson and Dempsey? And, even weirder, one coming from the USA.

So although we were a Fulham household, against everything he believed in, he took me over the bridge into Fulham and, through the gates of Stamford Bridge. Yeah, even the Chelsea stadium is in Fulham and, as Michael Caine might say, "not a lot of people know that."

How different things would have been had that stupid coach at Fulham let me through their gates. I would have followed Haynes and, that would have been such a thrill - pulling his shirt over my head. Although it was quite something wearing Jimmy Greaves' eight shirt at Chelsea and much later the number ten of Eastham at Stoke City.

So it wasn't to be at Craven Cottage and, because of them turning me away, it all started for me at the Bridge. I began training two nights a week with the likes of Terry Venables and Eddie McCreadie and, of course, my soon to be youth coaches Tommy Harmer and Frank Blunstone. This was the first time I saw the talented Venables in the role of a coach, although the reason he was there is as follows: Docherty was a smart cookie, for he would have the players come in on those Tuesday and Thursday nights, just so he knew what they were up to. It was much like years later, when he was carrying on with Mary Brown at Manchester United. He had her husband work all hours God sent, so he knew where he was and, of course, what time he was getting home.

And by the time he got back there, Tommy was home with his wife Agnes.

It made me chuckle years later when I heard about George taking over at Spurs, for one of their problems was that the treatment table was nearly always full, so in his great wisdom, he put it on the notice board that there would be evening treatment. It worked a treat!

Back to the Doc, having said that about his players, it was a revolutionary idea, having established players come in and mix with the schoolboys who were potential players and, the future of Chelsea Football Club. Not only was this so valuable for those kids and, good for team morale, but what better place to have his players, just where he wanted them. Especially on a Thursday night, two days before a big match. This is just another reason I rate Tommy so very highly and, I tell him whenever I see him, but he just chuckles, if only for knowing I am right.

Docherty started that kind of thing, now clubs are employing their former players, be it on a very different level. I think this was why Tommy had such an exceptional bunch of players, his production line of players then was simply incredible. Which is why when you look at today's situation, a good local talent finds it very difficult to get in front of Joe Foreigner. It just goes to show that the people inside the club are not up to the job at hand.

Surely the local player must always come first?

Every time I go through Stoke-on-Trent, I think exactly the same way, 'where have all the local talent gone?'

It's the same in Chelsea, as it all comes flooding back. In those days there were so many brilliant prospects, but not now and alright, they won the Champions League, but like the 1966 World Cup it might be the worst thing that ever happened to them, well, not ever, Sexton did that.

When I hear Abramovich say "we can win the Champions League eight times" I think of what Michael Parkinson said about booze blurring my vision, well, if that is true, oil (money) must have the same effect.

Where under Mears, the players Docherty had, went on to become household names and, to reshape the future of the modern game, but look at them now....

And in those days, I thought that my size would be a deciding factor in just how far I would go, but my father nurtured my natural talent and the next stop was West London and then London Schoolboy trials. It was after the latter that my world had been shattered once again, as I did not get a look in. But Bill, once again, picked me up and told me in no uncertain terms that I would reach the heights that he always maintained I would reach. I just had to work hard and be patient. I may have said elsewhere, that there were so many talented kids around, but they never had such a father, one with so much knowledge of our game and one who always knew about the limitations of others in the game. He once told Dave Sexton, "don't ever try to tell my son how to play the game." Then years later, as you will read later, Tony Waddington, once buying me, said that he never once told me what to do or how to play, for I already knew.

The whole thing seemed so unfair, so ridiculous. How could these morons who ran such a show be put in charge of all of these youngsters who dreamed of becoming a professional footballer?

Of course, since coming through and seeing the larger picture, I now know. It is no different in any other walk of life and, if you look at Parliament, you'll understand it even more.

My dad told me to simply "forget it and continue doing all the things you've been doing," which I did and, although I got through that period, there were many very difficult times still to come. In fact, right up to my second debut - you can't count Southampton against Spurs - I never thought I'd make a player.

I must tell you that I was horrified when leaving that trial, because I thought that was the end of my journey. It was all because of my size, but my dad insisted continually, that once I grew I would leapfrog over all those kids that were chosen in front of me. I couldn't see it that way, but persistence overshadows everything in life, even talent. It is, in my view, the most valuable resource we have.

Alan Ball was a very special player to me and, the perfect example of one lacking size but more than making up for it with ability, desire, honesty and sheer determination. Pound for pound, along with George Eastham, he was the finest footballer I ever came across. On that night that he scored a magnificent hat-trick for Blackpool against Fulham, as did my mate Dave Metchick, I knew I had just seen a player who would become a true great. Dave was also tiny, but even though he's my friend, Ball was on a completely different planet, But

Dave, unlike those today, knew this and, never made out that he was a superstar.

Dave was better known for his film star good looks.

If you looked at one of those James Dean photographs you could be looking at Dave and, that is a compliment to the American legend.

The last time I saw him was at the table with Terry, George and Jeff Powell in Langans, he was just overcoming an illness. I hope he has maintained his good recovery and, his health is much better, for he's one of life's diamonds.

I didn't realise he wasn't well until I heard Terry and George talking of it in the Butchers Hook (The Stamford Bridge Arms) on the night of Chelsea's 100 Year Celebration, which was another disgrace, even if for there being no Jimmy Greaves. But there was Gordon Ramsey - yeah, Gordon, not Alf - Bernie Ecclestone and Claudia Schiffer, now what the hell have they got to do with the Chelsea Centenary?

Talking of Alf takes me back to Ball, who defied his size and, I go back to him because he was so influential in Ramsey winning the World Cup. He worked tirelessly, which helped to create a myth that he was just a hard-working, busy midfield player, who relied on that work-rate. In fact, he was one of the greatest one-touch players I have ever faced, or for that matter, seen. He, like me, always put his monumental success down to his father, who taught him that football, like Shankly said, was more than a game. It was a way of life.

Alan and I it seemed were destined not to play together sat club level, after Terry Neil bought me to replaced him, unknowingly to both of us, however I can still dream about spending time in the same team as him. He was probably the most under-rated player in the history of the game – 0h, but only by those that didn't know!

He possessed such energy and fire - maybe it was something to do with that red flamed head of his - with a desire to not only win, but win by being the best player on display and, I think I saw him become that on so many occasions.

The one thing I didn't like about that was that he did it against me on more than one occasion, oh, and the other thing I fell out with him about was he promised me a job with him at Stoke City before he took over the manager's job there. What was so disappointing about that was that I thought he would stand up to anything and anyone in the game, but he did not stand firm with those mugs at the Victoria Ground.

Like him, I had this in my locker at a very early age – that special desire to be the best. If I wasn't the best player on the field, no matter even if we had won, I would not be fully satisfied. As you will remember in that '66 World Cup final, Alan ran those German defenders ragged. He never stopped chasing the ball down that line, giving Karl-Heinz Schnellinger an absolute nightmare. But as I said, there was more to his game, much more and, his appetite was like watching those sharks surround an upturned vessel. He approached the game in absolutely the same way as I did. One of my great regrets was that Terry Neill allowed him to leave Highbury just when I had signed to actually play alongside him. Once I knew that Stoke no longer wanted me and Arsenal moved in, it was playing alongside Alan that made up my mind.

People who tried to kick me and Alan, we loved. The same applied to the likes of Currie and Bowles. Alan and I, though, would wear them down. I knew my fitness level would get the better of my marker as the game went into the latter stages, like I said about Eriksson earlier on - and he was exactly the same.

He would not only run them ragged, but one-touch them to death. I would take them all over the field as if on a cross-country run, until I saw them flagging and, that is when you can impose yourself on the game in a much more damaging way. Your extra ability then shines through. You have that extra time and space to make the most of, which is why - as I said earlier - the best team nearly always come out on top with very late goals.

Up to the moment he left Manchester City's managerial position, Alan Ball was the only Premiership manager who possessed a World Cup medal. It is incredible how he could not hack it as a manager. Well, not incredible. I think the reason is his strength as a player was his weakness on the other side of the fence. If you look at someone like Wenger or Mourinho, they weren't great players, so that never affected their managerial skills; whereas the likes of Ball and Glenn Hoddle, it was the other way round. Alan couldn't understand why players could not do what he could as a player, or so it seemed. It was just as well Alan was not in charge of the Titanic because he would have been famous for two very important moments in our history. Glenn wasn't much better. He didn't get clubs relegated, but he did the most bizarre things, things he would not have agreed to had he been a player in his own team.

Matt Le Tissier was the player who saved Ball at Southampton and after Alan left The Dell, he forgot to take him with him. That is, if the great Sir Matt would have left his beloved Saints. Le Tiss was one of the game's great Mavericks, who kept Southampton afloat single-handedly, not to mention scoring one of my all-time favourite goals.

Picking the ball up in the centre-circle at Ewood Park, he elegantly and easily jinked in and out of three Blackburn players, before unleashing a 40-yard thunderbolt that had poor Tim Flowers tangled in the net, almost upside down. The keeper looked like a flapping piece of cod after being captured by that dreaded fishing net. He flapped and thrashed about as if fighting for his life whilst losing total control, such was the ball hit from so far and with so much pace (venom) and direction. As soon as it left his boot, it was like something coming out of Cape Canaveral. It was my favourite Le Tissier goal and, he scored so many amazing individual solo efforts, which made a mockery of the saying, "that one player doesn't make a team," because when playing at Southampton, he certainly he did. I can only think that he didn't want to leave Southampton and, if that wasn't the case no wonder Alan got fired. Matt was the perfect example of the Big Fish in a small tank, although he would have cracked it wherever he went. The only problem he had was him fitting in with a "mug" manager, because they don't have anything to tell or say to him.

I interviewed him one day for a magazine and he told me a story of an England training session, where in a practice match a ball went out of play without him chasing it. The coach pulled him to one side and said "you have to chase those balls." He replied casually, "Don't you think it pointless chasing a ball you can't possibly get?"

This was what great players were faced with, whereas the average ones chased lost causes. Like Matt, I certainly cannot see the point. That is why he was overlooked so much and, that is why so many average players got picked instead of the two of us. Carlton Palmer would have chased that ball and, those coaches would have applauded him. His name would have been scribbled on the team-sheet, whilst Le Tiss would have found himself left out. That is why you hear certain people say this player is "lazy." Players such as him, Stan Bowles, Frank Worthington, Peter Osgood and, Berbatov today, were the same. These people could not be more wrong. It was simply because they were not prepared to waste energy by chasing a ball that Linford Christie would not have reached.

Nobody worked harder than me and, I make him right on that one. And, although as that coach said, "Those fans want to see you chase everything," I say they might, but the real fans don't want you making a complete fool of yourself and don't expect you to. That is why England have struggled and laboured over so many years. They have chosen players who chase lost causes in front of those who have the requisite ability, such as Matt Le Tissier and, it is not until they are let down once again, that they realise that this country have an uncanny knack of never picking their best players.

We are the only country to do so on a continual basis.

The summer of '69 was famous for the Charles Manson murders, the one that Bryan Adams immortalised in song.

It was something that had me concerned some years later whilst in Seattle. Why?

The Manson family would cruise the I50, which ran from California to our Seattle home. Okay, Manson was locked up by then, but his family was still very much alive. Each and every night, I locked my doors and windows double tight, whereas I would usually leave them open in this wonderful part of the world. Having said that, it was where Ted Bundy began his path of destruction, by killing all of those young College girls.

But back to Charlie, who incredibly has been kept inside for so long, which makes a complete mockery of their judicial system. I was in the middle of reading his book and was scared like never before. On Friday 9th August - the start of our season - the Manson family visited 10050 Cielo Drive, Bel Air in California.

The result being that the beautiful pregnant wife of Roman Polanski, Sharon Tate, and three friends were brutally murdered. Manson was behind these murders, he was the most dangerous man on the planet. On the other hand, when Bundy was finally taken to the chair, it was broadcasted on air and, everyone in the entire USA were told to turn off all of their electrical gadgets in their kitchens, bathrooms and garages.

If you thought that Ronnie Harris was scary, you had it all wrong!

It was coming to the end of the most fantastic decade of all time. It was also when Tommy Baldwin's drinking exploits earned him the name Sponge. It suited him perfectly, though I never called him by that name. He is simply Tommy to me and, always will be. He was, and still is, one of the nicest individuals you'll ever have the pleasure to come across.

He will drink with you, run for you, laugh with you, fight for you and score goals for you.

He is a Gem. The fans who sang, "His name is Tommy Baldwin and he's the leader of the Gang" think that this nickname belongs to him because of all of the miles he ran and all the punishment and work he soaked up, but the truth is that Tommy was a great socialiser.

By early '70, Leeds were looking at winning the first-ever treble….the League Championship, FA Cup and European Cup and, they won nothing!

So this was a good year, Leeds got nothing and Charles Manson got several life sentences.

That first match at Southampton still haunted me, but my father once again told me to remain patient. He made plausible the idea of me becoming a real first-team player. By the start of what would prove a monumental season, 1969-70, I was in the reserves in the Football Combination side. Although I wasn't burning any bridges, I felt that if I could get back into the team I could stay there given a long enough run to settle in. I recalled that when Docherty brought in Osgood to replace Barry Bridges, which the crowd were not happy about, he told them, "I am playing Peter Osgood for a dozen matches no matter what."

That was what I needed, and then one day that is what I got, although Dave never went public with such a statement.

My dream at that time was to captain Chelsea, just like Venables, even though I was still a great Fulham fan. I had captained every single team that I had played in up until now. Park Walk Primary with Mr Robertson, Kingsley Secondary Modern and West London Boys with Mr Tranter, Chelsea Boys Club with Mr Hudson and Chelsea Youth Team with Mr Blunstone. Now I wanted the first-team armband with Mr Sexton. It sounds simple. It wasn't and, it wasn't ever to be. I so wanted to be captain of Chelsea. I loved the responsibility on the field. I thrived on it and I never got it until I reached Waddington.

But in those early days just getting into the team was quite something with the likes of Osgood and Cooke. But it was before that, that I realised what Charlie was all about and, I had never seen anything like it. Watching him when he first stepped on to the Stamford Bridge turf in front of the entire Fleet Street snappers, it seemed Docherty was losing the plot and changing his club into a circus. Charlie was like a seal with the ball, he could do absolutely anything and everything with it and, I remember thinking 'is that what you have to be able to do to become a first-team player?'

Charlie was simply off the wall - this just could not be true. I was watching something from Outer Space and, whilst watching him perform his act in front of the media, I thought that my talent would not be enough. I truly had never seen anything quite like it. It seemed to me like there was another way of playing the game and, that was Charlie's way, never knowing at that time I would - within a couple of years - be playing alongside him, have to play it. I'd only ever seen anything like this on Sunday Night at the London Palladium when young Brucie was the host.

Although I had seen the other first team players in close-up action and, played in that one match, albeit disastrous, I still felt that if I could get a recall, I could surely do better. I had been working hard on my fitness level as well. I knew I had to work harder to make up for the gap in ability, after watching Cooke. For when he was in the mood, it seemed it was impossible for anyone to get the ball from him.

It was almost as if it were part of his anatomy.

Yet he seemed so unimpressed with this God-given talent and just what he could do with the ball.

Little did I know then, that it would soon be my job to make sure he got as much of it as humanly possible and, that became my pleasure.

The sweet smell of success that was to come still seemed light years away, for the season started badly for Chelsea. It had been a long, hard, dry summer, rather like the one when I first started writing the Ballet. The hard-baked grounds were anathema to a player like Charlie. He could actually play on any surface, especially the ones I hated - but that was after going down that hole in the Midlands. And then there were those icy pitches on which he would be like a ballet dancer, literally gliding across, as if born to do such a thing on such treacherous conditions. I recall him playing on such a pitch at Selhurst Park one bitterly cold afternoon, whilst others were making total fools of themselves.

Charlie gave a performance of such perfection that it actually made a mockery of the weather and the underfoot conditions. He was skating across South London, as others were falling around him like in a Bowling Alley.

It would have made Torville and Dean, look more like a couple of Hod Carriers!

I wonder if today, he would have entered Strictly?

I've seen two former goalkeepers on there and had to laugh and, if only the girl knew that she was taking her life into her own hands by allowing Peter Shilton to skate around whilst holding her.

But that was in years to come, when I found out about his handling, but at the moment we had no problems with Bonetti, he was still in tip-top form, for he was as consistent as a Sinatra song!

Chelsea's opening match of the season could not have been more difficult, or as they say, "an easy one to start with," a nice trip up to Anfield. Unlike today, this was the toughest match on the fixture list.

This fixture was to leave such a fantastic memory for me, but was performed in a red and white striped shirt, well, two of them in fact, for my two best ever performances both came against the best team in England.

But for now, I was in the reserves and watching our boys struggling at this early stage of the season, but as I said, this really was the toughest match to open up your season with and, to make things worse, the conditions didn't help. It is tough enough chasing shadows, but on a blazing, red hot day, chasing the same coloured shirts was daunting.

I was just pleased that I did not start the season with them, as all I need was a roasting to follow that Southampton one.

Liverpool ripped Chelsea to shreds, winning 4-1. So, had I played my first two matches in a first team shirt would have been 0-5 and 1-4, which really would have had the manager ask questions about me, well, maybe.

However, I was not yet a Chelsea supporter, so for now I still looked at it as Chelsea, not us, that was all to come. Ian Hutchinson, in his first full season, headed our goal, but what I remember most was John Hollins getting a pasting by Peter Thompson. But in all fairness to John, he wasn't a full-back and, how many full-backs didn't this winger make a fool of?

I remember watching Match of the Day one evening and felt so sorry for my old coach Don Howe, as Peter did exactly the same to him. I bet Don sat down afterwards and thought long and hard about how to stop such a genius whilst flicking through his coaching manuals. When he got to Arsenal he would use my mate George Armstrong to be his first line of defence. Not that George needed telling, for he was a workaholic on the football field and, a player who would see that as second nature.

These were the days when there were some magnificent wingers and, looking at Thompson, when you think we have been struggling for many years to find such a player, it makes you wonder and, all of this was down to Alf.

People really don't know the damage Alf caused by winning the World Cup with no wingers....

Thompson was as good as any Brazilian winger we have seen since '66 and, that is as high a compliment, as one could give to any mortal. Since, only John Barnes, whilst playing for Liverpool can be talked of in the same breath. His problem playing for England was once again, the system.

I love Barnes, for he oozed class on the field and off. I had to chuckle some time ago (January 2010) at a function in Manchester. Whilst we stood there swapping stories, he saw Tony Woodcock and they laughed as they hugged one another and, then told me why. He said that, that incredible goal - and it was actually more than that - he scored against Brazil was all down to Tony. For as he was about to shoot, his team-mate got in his way, so he delayed it and, whilst regaining his composure, beat yet another Brazilian. He then waltzed round the keeper and slid in a beauty, George Best-like.

Greaves also, at his best, could score such a fantastic goal!

At Liverpool they were told to give him the ball early, whereas with England he would have to go looking for knock-downs and scraps. Nothing has changed, although we have nothing like him today!

So Liverpool mauled Chelsea as they were capable of doing to the very best of them. Tommy Smith was kicking lumps out of Peter Osgood, while a young Hutch was having a right old ding-dong with Ron Yeats. Hutch articulated his unhappiness to Smithy and suggested that they swap partners. Not in a dance way, but one where when changing you knew there was something rare and dangerous coming up. And that is the way it panned out. But before the all the fun began, as they were crossing, Osgood said to Smithy, "Tom, did you hear what Hutch said about you? He reckoned someone put a tin of peas on your face and not one fell off."

The rest is history, for Tom, who is a blinding bloke, quiet and placid beyond belief off the field, was an animal on it. On this day it was memorable as I can only tell you that in the modern game I dread to think how this would have been received. There would have been no time or need for the yellow card, which was a simple booking in those days, for this was a 'straight red' confrontation. And you would not have seen any of that diving around. There was no play-acting, no shirt pulling and, certainly a case where both players were fully committed hard cases. In those days there were some pretty serious front twosomes and, these two ranked right up there with the toughest of them.

Two nights after playing on Merseyside, the chaps travelled across London, where my hero Bobby Moore and his two World Cup winning mates were waiting. Again, the team was ravaged by injuries, so Marvin Hinton - Suave Marv - wore the shirt I would soon be wearing, the one Jimmy Greaves made famous and Bobby Tambling, aka Jumbo, who was now towards the end of his glorious Chelsea career and was to play one of his last games for the club and, like a couple or three other of our players, he would soon join Crystal Palace.

As they did so often, Martin Peters and Geoff Hurst got the goals.

Hutch's header then won us our first two points against Ipswich Town, a team I would soon come to detest. Meanwhile, I was playing for the reserves down in Bristol for the Combination side. Allan Birchenall was in the side. I once saw Birch play at Craven Cottage. He played up front with another blonde striker Mick Jones and, to this day, I am absolutely convinced that Dave Sexton went north and came back to Chelsea with the wrong player. Jones was by far the superior striker. Was this a cock-up by our manager? I was to ask myself that question many times over the next couple of seasons.

The big Leeds striker was to try to put Bonetti out of the biggest match of the season at Old Trafford, but that was all to come, but at this moment in time, it was all a distant mystery. The mystery being, if you saw us in these first few matches you'd never have thought we would turn into such a force.

Two more draws left Chelsea in 16th position with five matches gone. On 27 August we were away to Tottenham in another midweek fixture, for what I thought was going to be, as Paul McCartney sang Just another Day.

I had been training in the morning with my mates in the reserves and afterwards was invited along for the first-team match at White Hart Lane. I thought it to be something along the lines as I was doing just before Sexton got there with that Osgood Schlatters Disease, but was I in for a surprise.

I was no stranger to White Hart Lane on a Wednesday night! This was the ground that I was to make my own, or so I felt. I have so many great memories of the Lane and, sitting on the team bus, they all came flooding back as we got closer to the ground, even though my dad would take John and me by Underground.

I was happy to be amongst all of the players I had been around for so long in the home dressing room after that lengthy knee injury. But to my absolute amazement, at just after 4-o'clock, Ron Harris approached me and handed me four complimentary tickets.

At that precise moment I realised that I was back in the big time.

I was in a daze, obviously hoping there would be no repeat of that most terrible of days at Southampton, but there was a difference here, all of our players were sober.

I was to have many thrills that season, both on and off the field, but on this night facing Jimmy Greaves was by far the greatest, before coming face to face with George, Pele and Bobby Moore just a few short weeks down the line.

Jimmy was the greatest finisher I have ever seen. Was this why I was in a daze?

Then it was six o'clock and team-talk time and, with Dave Sexton running through every single minute detail I would not be telling you the truth, if I told you how I felt. The only thing I can remember is him telling me that I was responsible for another one of my boyhood heroes, Alan Mullery.

I had been on this ground so many times with my dad - and my brother John - watching that great Double winning team and, now here I was being thrown into the deep end with no life belt. Unlike at Southampton, we took to the field like a real team even though we had injuries to a couple of our main players. And I am delighted to tell you we played like one. This was probably the match that changed my life - before my debut against Liverpool for Stoke City - for had I put in another performance, like at The Dell, it could have curtains for me. But I didn't and, as it turned out, it was actually the beginning of something that nobody this amazing ground could have seen or visualised on this particular night.

I can't think that even Dave could see that this was going to become a record breaking season?

I had played against a man at Southampton who would one day be my boss, Jimmy Gabriel of Everton and Scotland fame, now here I was up against another wing-half of great stature, Alan Mullery.

I regarded this as the day that - although still only eighteen - would be crucial to my immediate future. I knew that I could play and most of the first team also had faith in me, but there are some kids that look good in training, but when it came to the big time they either weren't good enough or didn't have the desire and big match temperament and, on this night we were going to find out about both. Playing on the same field as Greaves was beyond my wildest dreams. It was like walking on the moon.

And going head-to-head with Mullery not only gave me a great thrill but also a massive challenge, one that I knew if I could live up to, would help me in my quest for a regular first-team place. Along with Haynes, Cohen, Dempsey, Jim Langley and Graham Leggatt, Mullery was a great part of the Fulham I had grown up supporting and adoring.

Les Barrett, Steve Earle and Stan Brown would follow and, then came Marsh and Allan Clarke, two men I could have never become friends with, firstly Marsh was responsible for me not making my fortune in Florida and, Clarke was to leave Fulham and team up with Mick Jones at Leeds United and, you cannot become friends with any of those can you.

Having said that, Ken Bates, Gus Poyet and Denis Wise, but they weren't our Chelsea, they were Bates' Chelsea.

Oh, how I wanted to play for them, Fulham, that is.

Alan Mullery became the first player to be sent-off playing for his country, but on this particular night there was no such thing and, the only thing I can tell you about this match was that I remember David Webb scoring a trademark goal and, the other Dave giving me my first bollocking and, like so many of the others, I don't think I deserved it,

But it did make a change from Osgood being on the receiving end of such a thing.

But it would stand me in good stead.

This evening was also more than an ordinary thrill as I was a regular visitor at White Hart Lane because my father saw it as a great part of my football education. Being taken to watch Greaves, Gilzean, White, Mackay, Jones and Blanchflower, was like a student going to the best college. Now, here I was walking out to face such legends, on a ground that I had watched the first English team to win the League and FA Cup Double.

They really were up there with any of the great club sides of my time in the game.

As he did on many occasions, as I just said, David Webb gave us an early lead, which helped settle my nerves no end and, I remember thinking, 'thank God for that' as it stunned the locals and sent our fans into a frenzy, something I'd experience several times on this ground.

It was the first time that I had been in a team that were winning a match in the First Division and, we so nearly kept it that way.

I got through it unscathed, although as I just told you, I got my first bollocking from the manager, for in his eyes I gave the equaliser away. I threw a ball into a team mate on the halfway line, only for it to be intercepted by Jimmy Pearce. The Spurs winger incredibly hit an unstoppable shot past Peter Bonetti from full thirty-five yards for their equaliser. I was completely gutted as the ball sailed into our net with such venom. Little did I know then that I would be involved with so many important goals on my favourite ground; that is before joining Stoke City, although I scored a goal there that clinched the first ever win in the clubs' history, which was 100 years.

Later that year we'd put five past Watford in the FA Cup semi-final and, then score two more in another important semi-final - both that saw us to Wembley - and then I scored the only goal that saw Stoke City win their first ever match in this wonderful football stadium, as I just told you.

That gave me as much pleasure as that last minute winner that took us to the League Cup final.

You might say that this is the "real" Jimmy with that cheeky grin, a happy-go-lucky, wonderfully warm human being with an ice cold temperament in the penalty box. He will remain the greatest goal scorer of my time growing-up, watching and playing the game. When Chelsea voted Zola their best ever player it was an insult to Jimmy, he was without doubt the exceptional one and, even Osgood bowed to him!

I would have settled for a 1-1 beforehand, after my previous call-up, although a 1-0 win would have been a brilliant return to the big time, especially with Jimmy on the other end of such a defeat.

Little did I know on that night that this was going to become my favourite ground, until I reached the Victoria Ground, it just seemed that I excelled there. It literally was the first fixture I looked for at the start of every season.

Anyhow, I took my first bollocking on the chin and, was happy to be kept in the side for the next match. I had no choice. Very shortly, I came face to face with one of those giants I just mentioned, Dave Mackay. He was one of the greatest players to ever play our game. But now he was captaining Brian Clough's Derby County and, I found myself on the famous dog track that surrounded our home pitch face-to-face with the Great Scot. I was just about to pick up the ball to take a throw-in, when Dave grabbed it telling me, "Go away son, you shouldn't even be on the same pitch as me," which hit home quickly, making me think, 'Oh, that's what this game's all about?'

Some years later, I got to know him well and introduced Martin Knight to him. My great pal then wrote his book. But some time before that I was at Haydock Park races and, whilst I was in the bar, I was told that Dave was in a corporate box with Tommy Docherty. I went to say hello to Tommy and, whilst talking to Dave, told him of the story on the Dog Track.

He simply said, "Don't take it personally Alan. I used to say that to everyone."

He was an absolute giant in our game, or was it his game?

Can you remember that famous photograph of him having Bremner by the scruff of his neck at White Hart Lane?

It was a classic and, might tell a story about how the game was beginning to change. Dave was one of the last real tough players and, I mean genuinely tough, fair tough, going for the ball tough. He was probably the cleanest toughest, hard-nut ever to play the game.

When he finished with me I ran away like a naughty schoolboy who had just been given a telling off by his Head Master. And that is exactly what he was. Confidence is everything in life and Dave had it in abundance. I had just been given a great lesson from him. People like Mackay would like to shake your confidence, whereas the likes of Bobby Moore would increase it with his manner. My father, and then Tony Waddington at Stoke City, made me aware that I could control my response to events, even if I could not always control events themselves.

On that particular night I did not have time to think about the outcome, as to what if we got another beating?

That night at White Hart Lane was my biggest yet, with 47,396 supporters reminding me of what I had always wanted to be. I had been at Chelsea when there were 72,000 against Spurs in an FA Cup replay. I had been amongst something like that before at the Lane - on my fathers' shoulders - when winning their first Double.

I was on his shoulders when they beat Crewe in an FA Cup replay and don't think I saw a goal, but it didn't matter. It was the atmosphere!

It was sensational. It was electrifying and, tonight I was in the middle of the action, not in the paddock. I simply loved the atmosphere, the experience and, after that particular night I wanted it more than ever before.

In my favour was what I just said, I did not have time to think about things. I am a bad sleeper as it is, so that was another bonus, for I never had the opportunity to toss and turn all night playing the game over and over in my head, something a lot of us do.

The following day Tony Frewin, my best mate at Chelsea, and I walked the Kings Road looking to improve my wardrobe even more. My love for wearing the best clothes was soaring higher than my wages, but I thought that I had to be as smart off the field as on it.

Today, with all of the money these players earn, I am absolutely astounded when I see them walking around like tramps. Dress casually, of course, but scruffiness, definitely not. Even the Chelsea manager Hiddink warned his players about their dress code and sense and, he was spot on. He is old school. It's called respecting not only yourself but your club. When I went to Stoke City there was no dress code, which was fine, because I liked the laid-back approach to matches there. However, I would always be "suited and booted" as Del Boy might say. To get dressed up, even for a match made me feel good and, I felt that "feel good" feeling carries onto the field.

I simply loved getting dressed up and wearing the best there was to wear. I even paid over £250 for a suit at Major when I was earning only a quarter of that a week, without taxes and other incidentals. And there were lots of those about.

I bought a suit from the Squire Shop. It was a shop owned by a bloke named John Simons who still has a shop in Covent Garden, or he did when the original Ballet was being written. Tony and I would frequent his shop often, which used to be owned by a butcher. It had an amazing Tudor interior. In those days John was selling a three-piece French look with wide lapels on the jacket and high waistcoat. I think it was from here that I bought my velvet suits. I had figured I had to look my best as I had no intentions of returning to the Stiffs - which is what we called Combination football. I hoped that was a thing of the past for young Hudson. After Colchester United and Gillingham, I had now tasted White Hart Lane, played against Jimmy Greaves and Dave Mackay and, wanted more of it.

It was much like another hero of mine, Henri Charriere, Papillon, who escaped from Devils Island and I'm sure never wanted to see it again, well, I never wanted to go back to these places.

I wanted to face George Best, Denis Law and Bobby Charlton in Manchester, Billy Bremner and Johnny Giles at Leeds, Alan Ball at Everton and, the man who would make such an impression on my later life, the one and only Bobby Moore. He was by far the most impressive man in football I have ever met, alongside Waddington.

The next match was another win at Crystal Palace with Oz scoring from a long diagonal pass from Eddie. We kept playing Crystal Palace that season, or so it seemed and, Oz kept scoring against them, so it seemed. At Christmas we swatted them like a fly, 5-1 at Selhurst Park, with him scoring another four.

After forcing myself into the side that Autumn I was just beginning to pick up the pace of it all. I found I was getting more time and space than I could have ever imagined. But after a match against Leeds in the League Cup, I realised I needed to step up my training schedule. I was run off my feet by Paul Madeley. He was a big, tall, loping figure who was far too strong for me and doubts crept back into my mind. My dad questioned my lifestyle on this particular night and, it was something I had to address, and quick. I had to work harder on my long distance running, so from there on I would run the Embankment, or as my mate TD says, 'The Five Bridges!'

The next match up was yet another drawn one, after leading Wolves by two goals we threw away a golden chance of two points. We were leading by a couple of goals with only a few minutes remaining, when the legendary Derek Dougan popped up and made both goals. I liked The Doog from the moment he knelt over me when I was down with what we kids called a dead-leg, the nest time I received one of these was in Athens. He was sincerely concerned and years on I was not surprised that we became great friends. After the match, I recall limping to my brother's wedding reception. John married the lovely Pauline Thomas from Victoria, which led to them having two great kids, Billy and Claire. Billy was at Tottenham under Venables before I took him to Crewe to work for Dario Gradi. He now has his own carpeting business. Like my eldest son, Allen, he could have made it. I think had my dad not died, it might have been different.

I found it difficult, and still do, speaking to people who I see as inferior, especially when they think they're superior. My dad had the right idea, for he would allow nothing to get in his way. He was brilliant. As he told Sexton in those early days, "Don't try to tell him how to play, he already knows, I taught him."

Next up it was Leeds, in that League Cup replay that I just told you about, where after missing the first match through injury I was to come face-to-face with Chelsea's greatest enemies. The last time I was involved in this fixture I was blitzed with coins thrown by their loveable fans at the back of The Shed.

That was the last time, I told myself, for it was nearly as dangerous as the Mile End Road, if only for not seeing them coming and, that was what happened, I would never return, for The Shed was a very dangerous place in those days.

I'd much rather be on the field with the most feared team in England, if not Europe, Leeds United were nothing if not dangerous all over the field, but I preferred it that way, because you knew you had to have your wits about you at all times.

We never realised on this evening just what was going to come at the end of this incredible season and, this was the team it involved.

However, that was to become my greatest heartache in my short career and it led to so many heartbreaks.

But, I could never have dreamed of one such wonderful match that would put an end to their near record breaking run. But that was once reaching the Potteries, after so many changes in my life, where so much had happened by the time I was to move, but for now, this was my first encounter with the most hated team in the country. You can hear about such things, but to be out there in the heat of such battles was incredible and, I can only tell you they were the ultimate football matches.

I cannot tell you just how delighted I am to tell you that we won the two most important matches from 1970 to 1974 and, although I missed the first one, the second was truly memorable, also. It did not win Stoke City the FA Cup, but it did leave the people of the Potteries still talking of such a match.

I never knew at this particular time also, that my move would very much make me the player that was hidden inside of me. This was the player I was as a kid playing for my dad's team.

But right now we, Chelsea, were playing our best football so far that season and, we ran out 2-0 winners, but it took a tactical change at half-time from the manager. As I said, I had been up against the strong and powerful-running Madeley in the opening period and he was becoming too much of a handful for such a young player. I was a young lad who was still not only feeling his way, but still a little on the frail side. I knew through that first half that I had to step up on my fitness and, do more cross-country runs, and more box-to-box training. The latter would hold me in good stead for years to come.

If you were to study Frank Lampard over the past few seasons, I bet you'll find that he uses this training regime. His box-to-box running gets him his goals, whilst keeps him fit enough to get back to perform his defensive duties. I have watched Frank train at West Ham and, am not at all surprised at his mammoth success at the Bridge and, like with Steve Bould, I had some say in his move also. However, once again, I got nothing for doing so. So, my record is not bad, two players recommended, both of them turning out to become internationals and win League and FA Cup Doubles. How many scouts can boast such a record?

My best moment in a Chelsea shirt to date came in the second-half of that match, when facing my favourite English full-back, Terry Cooper. I was on the by-line in front of the East Stand, when a ball was played into my feet. The Leeds player confronted me and, as I feigned to knock it inside, I just rolled it through his legs for my first Nutmeg in English football. Terry was on one knee and one hand, rather like the picture I had of the exact same thing with Keith Newton, the Everton and '70 England World Cup full-back who took over from TC. The photo showed me on the ball looking forward, with the yellow shirted Newton leaning on the same two parts of his anatomy. Although that was great, it did not do me any favours because Dave seemed to think that I could play out wide and, he was wrong again, for I was about as good out wide as chocolate fireguard.

This reminded me also of when Charlie gave Emlyn Hughes what we called The Rollover, leaving Emlyn clutching the Stamford Bridge turf. This was something he had perfected and something we in England had never seen before. All he did was get the ball under his foot and pretend to pass it inside to an imaginary team-mate, but when his marker - Hughes in this case - went to intercept the pass, he stopped it at the very last moment and dragged it back, leaving the defender on all fours. I sat watching Charlie do this for the first time that night against Liverpool and along with fifty-odd thousand people, tried to work out what we had just witnessed?

17 IT'S RAINING GOALS, HALLELUJAH

*By the Christmas of '69 I was established in the team and looking forward to my
first experience of the FA Cup and, that was my next great achievement. I was
brought up to love cup football, winning many of them at both school and Boys
Club level.*

It seemed as a young kid every match was a cup-tie.

I suppose because if you were on a losing team, you felt knocked-out!

After that Leeds victory, we were desperately unlucky to get knocked
out at Carlisle in the next round and, although that was the Football
League Cup it was a body blow. It was a match where we played some
beautiful football, but as in many cup-ties, if you don't take your
chances you'll pay the price and, that is exactly what we did.

However, there was some consolation, for this was my best
performance to date, on a pitch rated as the best in the country, along
with Ipswich Town.

Jimmy White would have been very much at home on it.

The next time I played here, was in '75 with Stoke City and, put in a
display that earned me another 10 out of 10 in the Sunday People,
which had their manager tell Tony Waddington that it was the best
performance he'd ever seen on that particular ground.

But here it was not a good night, even though we had played
tremendously well, for Peter Bonetti went to ground after having been
hit on the back of the head by a coin thrown from the crowd. This
was the first time I had witnessed a coin being thrown since standing
in The Shed against Leeds United.

Carlisle scored in the confusion and Oz said Catty was still looking
for the penny when the ball hit the net.

Can you imagine if it had been a Chelsea fan who chucked such an object?

I felt after this performance that I was more than just another player in a team that was quickly improving and gaining great momentum. We had now given up drawing matches we should have won and were going to absolutely steamroller the opposition, although we lost this one, which was a complete one-off. The signs were that this team was going to do something special, though we really had no idea just how much so. Charlie had been moved wide right and, I was now teamed up with John Hollins, running the middle of the field. Charlie was not an out and out midfield player, inside-forward, as such. He was an individualist who loved getting players on the line. Out wide, he could go inside or outside them and, when on song, not only was it easy for him, there was no finer sight. He wasn't the kind of wide player that would use his pace to go by his marker. Charlie would totally bemuse them.

They say as a defender you must always keep your eye on the ball, but with the likes of Charlie and George that was not such a good idea.

I have never seen a wide player so at ease. He was so composed on the ball. Wingers would get the ball and run at full-backs. Charlie, it seemed, would tease them. As Waddington said of Matthews and me, some years later, "he would frighten defenders into thinking if they tackled him, he'd make a complete fool of them." That was Charlie and, again, the only other player I saw with such immaculate close control. Barnes.

Well, that was until reaching Highbury and played alongside Brady!

It was wonderful being surrounded by such talent. We really had the most incredible blend of players. We had a Cat in goal, four defenders who would not be out of place on the frontline in Afghanistan, a midfield of such skill, grace, craft, graft and, two front players who would in that first season scored 50-odd goals between them. There were just 12 of us throughout this run. Then there was Marvin Hinton, the classiest 12th man who ever lived. Tommy Baldwin, who you could always rely on to get you goals when coming in, and Johnny Boyle, a player who would burst a gut from any position he filled. Although I talk of these as players that came in and did a brilliant job, when it came to our other team, the social one, they were very much a part of it, especially Sponge and Boilers, whilst Lou Hinton was what you might say, the wily Fox.

And then there was Allan Birchenall from Sheffield United who, as I said, Dave went to watch and brought back the wrong one. I remember seeing Sheffield United at the Cottage and it was obvious Mick Jones was the player out of the two of them.

These players were a fantastic part of our squad, great characters who would come in and always be relied upon. When you think Marvin came on sub in the two '70 FA Cup finals, Tommy replaced me in both those matches and, then Johnny Boyle came in and did brilliantly in Athens the following season.

The reason I say this is today, manager's talk of small squads. Around these times all clubs had about sixteen players to choose from. With the pitches, the balls and the injuries far more serious than today, it still astounds me how they complain. Plus, we played three matches over four days at Easter and, never thought anything about it. I was also amazed when Gullit was in management and, asked for a break at Christmas. Is he for real?

I was now playing like I did for my school and Boys Club teams, enjoying the freedom that I was making myself and, enjoying setting up so many chances for Osgood and Hutchinson, who was also a revelation in that season. He was strong. He was tough. He was brave and, he was fearless. He was simply Hutch, the player that would become a walking disaster, through self-inflicted damage.

He shirked nothing and that would become his downfall.

I now wanted to be our best player week in, week out. I always did, since my very early days in the streets and, in the Cage. This was my goal and my aim. It was since I first remembered kicking a ball. I was not happy just winning. Some years later when I was playing for Seattle Sounders, our right-back John Ryan said to me, "Huddy, can I tell you something? Playing where I play, I can see the whole playing field, everything that goes on, the whole picture and, in these last four matches (this was our last of four in 10 days in Boston); you have not lost possession for us once." I drank a toast to that, as one does and, thanked him for bringing it to my attention, although obviously I was already aware.

There is no higher praise than from a colleague....

Those four matches came against the likes of Franz Beckenbauer, Giorgio Chinaglia and Igor Bogicevic in New York, the Peruvian Teofilio Cubillas and Gerd Muller in Fort Lauderdale, plus some other very talented players who you would not have heard of. This was what was so special about the North American Soccer League.

You were always pitting your wits against every type of player.

John also mentioned that he had never seen such consistency.

Those compliments, coming from team-mates and peers, are what it is all about.

That is one of the reasons I loved the NASL so much, but my favourite one was that you packed your bags and head away on what you might call a working holiday, well, that is if you loved all of this as much as I did. To get good money, play against those players I just mentioned and, stay in the best hotels all over the greatest country in the world. But more of this later and, the only reason I bring it up now is because of the difference between travelling to Carlisle on a Wednesday night and, then returning for a match at the Bridge on Saturday.

Flying cross America from Seattle to Boston, onto New York then down to Florida was a dream and, on top of that the social side of it all was so much better than we enjoyed here in England.

To sit on an aeroplane with a drop of your favourite Bourbon in front of you without facing trouble with your manager was something to behold. American expected this of you, whereas in England, if you did such a thing you were "out of order" and, I think the USA had it right.

But this was all to come and, for now I was still earning my stripes. By now, my new Chelsea mates were not only accepting me, but appreciating what I was bringing into the team. They could not have been more encouraging, especially once we had gotten over that shaky start and were now Moving on Up a notch or two. I was playing my natural game, although it would not be until I reached Waddington that I really flourished and showed another side to my game and, my greatest regret that he weren't on that aeroplane next to me.

The most outstanding and satisfying thing about me at this moment in time was that I was getting stronger. It was taking time, but I could feel it coming, although I was what you might call the Dogsbody of our team. I was the young legs and, although I knew that I would one day become an accomplished inside-forward, only time would tell if it was to be here or elsewhere?

When players like Marvin Hinton and Eddie McCreadie began showing you respect, you knew you had arrived. I knew that Oz and Hutch would always hold the ball up when I played it through. I also knew that they would get on the end of anything hit aerial or otherwise and, they were both so hungry for goals. When first writing the Ballet, I used Mark Hughes as an example of who was doing this at Chelsea at that time. He was absolutely brilliant at holding it up for his team-mates to get up and join him. The other great exponent has been Teddy Sheringham, in fact, I believe Teddy was the very best and, the reason I say that is they questioned him when he followed Eric Cantona, but Teddy not only silenced them, he was a ;part of the team that won them their first ever treble, which included conquering Europe.

I have been a massive fan of Teddy's since his Millwall days and, saw him go up the ladder of improvement at each level he took and, improving with his every move. He has that wonderful confidence in his ability, something so vastly important in a player like him. I would have loved to have played with him.

It would have been like playing with Greenhoff!

It is very rare to come across a player who seems to have the same understanding of how the game should be played and, I was fortunate to find two in Osgood and Jimmy, but right now Osgood, it seemed, was just flexing his muscles.

There were not many in Osgood's class, in fact nobody, he was simply the best around this time and, the '70 World Cup in Mexico was waiting for him - for the bigger the stage, the better the player - and he was that player. He was the ultimate big match player. As for Hutch, he could hurt defenders and, he did in more ways than one, which led to him hurting himself far more.

The one thing I also loved working on, were my corner kicks, if only knowing we had such a strong hand in that department. I could hit them anywhere, depending on who was heading into which part of the area. Hutch was the easiest target and, I also knew that even if I didn't hit it perfect, he would turn a not so good one into a good one. Then you had Dempsey and Webb piling into the box. Plus, what was so exciting about taking them was that when I hit these balls in, I had the very best view in the house. I would float them, hang them or drive them and, then fall back onto my heels and watch the fireworks.

We had as much air power as a squadron of B-52s. They were easy to pick out. The goal that stands out most came when Hutch scored from one I drove hard into the near post - at Highbury at the Clock End - and, from my vantage point, where the band used to play in the paddock, I leant back and watched him get to the ball so early, it seemed he was above the bar, hanging like a glider with poor old Bob Wilson looking up at him. The Arsenal keeper was seen going back on his heels, as if wondering what he should do. The answer Bob is that when Hutch was like that, absolutely nothing. I remember this goal being in the Chelsea programme and, it most definitely confirmed that the former Burton Albion and Cambridge United striker was above the bar, which made a change for him as, like so many of us, he was usually hanging onto it.

As I have said, my career could have been over before it began. Between the ages of 10 and 15, I would suffer terrible knee pains after the slightest of knocks. At the beginning of my second year as an apprentice, I was finally sent to see a specialist and, the x-rays showed me to have a serious complaint called Osgood-Schlatters Disease. I was given the news that it might take up to five years to actually fuse. The only way this complaint could have been stranger, was if it had been called the Osgood-Hutchinson Disease. That was one I would get some time later after some lengthy drinking bouts with them, especially when we went on the Amos and Andy.

I was told at 16 to do absolutely nothing, no jogging, nothing - never dreaming that all these years later, I would be in the same position - only this time I couldn't if I tried. The only difference then was, I didn't need telling. This all came from the pounding on streets and, other surfaces that jar your joints. In my case the knee joints didn't fuse. So, as I said, I was faced with a situation where I could have been out of action for five years, in which time I would have been finished. There was no way I could have been absolutely immobile and, then got back to a state of fitness where I would have been able to compete at this level, for it was difficult enough as it was. Plus, with what I was learning about life in the Kings Road, I would have been so unfit that I can only imagine what sort of condition I would have been in.

That was at the start of the '67-68 season the summer of love, hippies and everything else that was flirting down the Kings Road, and I was right in the middle of it. So I spent eight long months cleaning the showers, toilets, floors, boots, shoes and anything else that was in that home-team dressing room at Stamford Bridge. This was harder than a million cross-countries and, the equivalent in doggies. Although at that stage I knew nothing of doggies. The one consolation was that Tommy the Tyke Docherty had recognised my early talent and, decided to take me as skip-boy to all the away matches. That was a great eye-opener to say the least. No, it was more, it kept me interested. It kept my appetite alive. In fact, I fell in love with the game more, being so close to the action. I experienced what my mates, although I was still a teenager, were going through week-in-week-out and, I wanted to be not only part of it, but amongst them. To win with them and, enjoy the after match celebrations, without knowing that there were going to be so many of them coming up and, of such immense proportions. So I'd gone from almost going out of the game at such a young age to breaking new ground in a team that had such incredible characters. It was almost something like Stephen Spielberg would put together, it was that incredibly unbelievable. It was a time when I thought that nothing could possibly go wrong and, I don't mean just on the playing field, but anywhere. West Bromwich Albion was still some way off and, I sometimes look back and wonder how something so simple could cause so much trouble for me. That one incident would cost me everything that you will read about that went wrong in my life.

My weight troubles, my falling out with Dave and the doctors, my trouble with Ramsey was all brought on through that one incredible twist of fate and, it obviously affected my training routines and day to day training in general.

Unlike today, we never got such information about such an injury and, it was as if nobody was aware of it. Looking back, I was fortunate to have this diagnosed, for I can imagine, like I experienced several times later on, even when established, that the clubs trainers (physiotherapists) and doctors were not worthy of their job titles. It was definitely that way when I had this injury and, then that chronic ankle injury. The club simply was incompetent and, that led to me drinking more through frustration than anything else.

In those days how could we know, if the physios and doctors never knew?

Now you can go online and find this: Osgood-Schlatter's Disease can be very painful and, if your child is suffering then you have found the perfect website. Osgood Schlatter's affects almost a third of active children, typically aged between 8 & 16. As parents ourselves, we understand how worrying it can be to see our children in pain and suffering. We hope that you find lots of information on our website which is dedicated to Osgood Schlatter's Disease and treatment of it.

Allow us to introduce you to The Strickland Protocol. This proven cure can be reviewed on Wikipedia's article "Osgood-Schlatter's Disease" where you may also view the clinical reports.

So, as I told you through an injury such as this, where I was in such terrible pain and discomfort from my days at Park Walk right through to my early Chelsea days, I could have been finished by the time I had reached seventeen.

So through all of this time, I was carrying the skip to away matches, cleaning their boots and helping Harry about the away team dressing room. It was an absolutely fantastic experience, because although I was around the players each and every day, now I could get a birds-eye view of the travelling and, what goes on in preparing for an away match. This was invaluable to me at such a young age and gave me such a lot to work on.

I think that was where I began to perfect my pre-match preparation, which stood my in good stead also, for my trips to the Operating Theatre, where I took that as seriously as preparing to face Leeds United of Liverpool.

The most exciting match I was involved with was a 7-0 mauling by Leeds United. It was, as they say nowadays, awesome. Leeds United surely had never had a more magnificent 90 minutes and, unfortunately they chose us. However, Chelsea were in turmoil, for it was a couple of days after Tommy Doc was sacked and, I remember it well, for Oz playing one of his first matches since breaking his leg.

Ron Suart - who did not have a clue - was in charge of the first team on this particular day. I sat on the touchline at Elland Road and saw this mean machine put on a superlative display of pure football. I would like to say that they made up for their fans, but I cannot. There is one thing you could not take away from Leeds United, when they played like this, they were brilliant. They were nasty, crude and dangerous in every way, but they could most definitely play. And Giles and Bremner on this day told me that if ever I was fortunate to get into the first team, I would have to work harder than ever before, for on this day they were, as I said, totally awesome.

It was very similar to the match they show on TV where they put a record amount of passes together against Southampton and, I think the score was similar also. This was special for me, because I was the closest to the pitch that I'd ever been and, it was probably the greatest lesson I was to be given, if I really wanted to be a part of it all.

It had everything that you did not want to see as a youngster and, watching such a demolition job helped me no end. There was no way that I ever wanted to be on the end of such a humiliating defeat and, there was only once that I came close, but that was to come, in fact, three days before my worst ever day on a football field.

Mentioning that 7-0 drubbing, I watched a recording of our 4-0 thrashing of Leeds on the first day of the 1971-72-season. Whilst watching I thought, 'If only we could have been reminded of that match, we really would have gone for their throats. We were that superior we could have hit double figures. Wouldn't that have been something to look back on?'

Had I been the manager on that day, I would have used that match as my team-talk. Nothing like what Revie said when leaving the dressing room against those Germans, "Remember what those bastards did to our chip shops?"

I would have got that match and showed the lads on the Friday and, reminded them in the dressing room as the buzzer went.

I talk about this and, bring it forward, if only for it being as close as to the kind of bashing that would have wiped away the memories of that 7-0 humiliation. But, as I said, Chelsea had nothing going for them on that day and, they were in the worst possible state, if you took into consideration where they were just a few days after the Doc' got sacked.

Anyhow, the main reason I mention that 4-0 win, was that I think it was the best that Charlie and I had ever played together and, we had Leeds chasing shadows, much like they did Chelsea at Elland Road. In midfield you usually get one of our main players "having it off" and then the following match it's your turn, but here we both sang the same tune and the music, although sweet for us, must have been really off tune for them.

In this form, you could not help but drool over Charlie.

I did not take much notice on the day, but to my great delight when watching this video I saw Don Revie sitting in a pink plastic raincoat and he looked exactly what he was a ….

This still reminded me of all of my time and those chores in that great big old dressing room, but no matter how busy I kept myself, I ached to get back out there with the rest of the lads. When I was not cleaning off the mud and shining boots and shoes, I was scrubbing the showers, toilets and the big bath. And then there were the floors when everyone left.

The only good thing was it got me out of cleaning the mess on the terraces, which was part of the apprentice's job each Monday morning after some fifty or sixty thousand fans had left two days prior.

My respect for several of those players was immense, after spending those nine months virtually looking after them more than their wives. Those nine months I spent in the home-team dressing room, compared a little to the year I spent in the Royal London and St Bartholomew's, if only for the frustration of not knowing if I'd ever play again, whereas, almost thirty years on, I had the harrowing experience of wondering if I'd ever walk.

I had several different types of relationships with these players, beginning with firstly respect, because only a few short months ago, I knew of them as Chelsea, a team taking on Liverpool for the title. Now, it seemed I was a part of the happy family, or so it seemed, because this dressing room was something that gave me my first taste of such a bonding. I took this with me through my entire career for a happy dressing room is the backbone of a good team.

Before joining the club my respect was for the players such as Bonetti, McCreadie, Hinton and Osgood, remembering when I joined Charlie hadn't arrived just yet. But being around the dressing room you get to know them in a very different way and, those that treated me like I treated other youngsters, I would do anything for. I mean, when they were out training they'd come in and could not believe how shiny their shoes were. I never said a word.

Oz became my first room-mate and we became very close both on and off both the playing fields and pubs of England, and then Europe. Again, it was interesting to see just how he prepared mentally the night before and right up to kick-off. I was interested in what made him tick?

To actually see how a master at work got ready for a big match. It wasn't rocket science by any means; he just had such incredible confidence in his wonderful ability. Nothing and nobody fazed him at anytime, anywhere, hence his out-of-order sessions such as in the Athens Hilton. Real Madrid meant nothing to him, we might as well have been playing that team from Luxembourg, when we hit that record 21 goals and he got eight of them. Osgood had the most extraordinary outlook on the game and, in fact, life itself. I think the first time he fell below his standards was whilst trying to "woo" Raquel Welch. He failed miserably and, I told him so. But even though he did, he did not know it, he truly believed in everything he did was right and, I think that is what made him such an incredible player. He had tunnel vision. Had he been a boxer he would have been the Ali of our country. His pre-match weigh-in would have been something you dare not miss. Even if he was going to get bashed up, he would still believe that he'd win the fight and, would be organising the post-match celebrations whilst doing so. I have never seen anything like it and, I can't tell you about Bobby Moore, because I wasn't fortunate enough to play alongside him, thanks to both Alf and that hole in the Midlands. I was to learn one thing from Osgood and, that was confidence is almost everything and that is what he had. He was as perfect a centre-forward as I have ever seen and, when people question me, I stop listening to their opinion and, views on the matter, there is no point, Osgood was without a doubt the very best of all-time. He let me down on several occasions off the field, but I always forgave him because of all of what he did on the field, when either lifting a dull match out of the doldrums or turning a losing match into a winning one with one of his untouchable and astonishing goals.

Here's Tommy in a Seattle Sounders shirt, a shirt that not many
people knew we both wore.

The only consolation I take out of missing those two FA Cup finals
against Leeds United (1970) was that Tommy replaced me, for had it
been someone I didn't care for, it would have been even more hurtful!

When Oz or Hutch was not available, who better than Tommy
Baldwin to come in and cover, although he covered for me at
Wembley and Old Trafford, of which every time I look at him
reminds me of the pain. But I love Tom so much it almost made
everything alright. But, of course, it didn't, I was completely
devastated.

Whilst speaking of Tommy, I was at a Stoke City match - in fact it was the match where they won promotion to the Premier League - and afterwards met the man who was responsible for a lot of the writing of Upstairs Downstairs. I was introduced to him by Terry Conroy, whose house we were celebrating in and, the chap told me that the characters of the butler and the cook were named after both Tommy and I. Gordon Jackson played Hudson and the woman in the kitchen was Mrs. Baldwin. My first thought was, 'If only my mother knew all of those years ago, she would have loved telling everyone at the Fulham Broadway Bingo Hall.'

But before we go into the competition that was to change the face of Chelsea - I will explain that more in a few minutes - I must tell you of the importance of how close I was to becoming a non-runner, before the race had come under starters' orders.

So I had just a few weeks before a decision was made, as to whether I would get a full-time professional contract. I was terribly nervous. The team was due to go on tour to Mozambique, but before they left they were to play a match at QPR for Mike Keen. These were the days when a player would get a testimonial for 10 year service. I think Ron Harris got two of them. I never got any, even though I was at Chelsea for over 10 years, had cost them nothing and earned them close on £250,000.

I had watched Keen play many times. That was around the time of them winning the League Cup as a Third Division side in '67. They did so by beating West Bromwich Albion in an extraordinary Wembley final after being two goals behind. I had lost a lot of valuable time in the last few months and had some catching up to do. Dave Sexton threw me into this match to have a look at me. I remember arriving at the ground thinking this really was my big chance. It was a complete mud bath and my initial worry was my fitness level, having been out for so long.

What Dave saw that evening was enough to offer me professional terms. Then there was another match at Wimbledon and again he must have been impressed. After signing, to make things even better I was on the aeroplane to Mozambique for an end-of-season tour. This was the place where the great Eusebio was born and bred. However, these trips were soon to lead to terrible problems in the camp, but I knew from that first trip that this was the life for me. Although I had already been on a Youth Tour of Switzerland, being away with the first team was a different ball game, it was incredible.

In those days of The Osgood-Schlatter's Disease I was thankful for having Tommy Harmer and Frank Blunstone as my youth-team coaches and of course Tommy Docherty, who always helped me along when it was always in the back of my mind that I was never going to get the opportunity to fulfil my dream. It had been a constant nightmare when unable to train. But now things were beginning to change. I was also fortunate that I got on very well with the manager's son Michael. We had a wonderful football understanding in the youth team and I thought that if I had made it, maybe we would get the opportunity to crack it together in the first team.

I still think about it, but obviously, we'll never know?

I was also fortunate that before reaching Chelsea I had the terrific Tom Tranter. Tommy was our Kingsley and West London sports master, our football coach if you like. But my biggest ally was always, of course, the head of the Hudson family, Bill.

At that time, having been quite a prolific goal scorer throughout my short trouser years, I saw myself as a Jimmy Greaves and Johnny Haynes rolled into one. I was always top goal scorer and maker at school. Jimmy was the supreme goal-taker, while John was the most fantastic distributor of the football.

Although later, in my first spell at Stoke City, my role was changed to a deep-lying inside-forward. I will always use the term inside-forward as I was brought up on the likes of Haynes, Jim Baxter, John White, Luis Suarez and Gianni Riviera of AC Milan. Then there was George Eastham, who one day I would follow to Stoke City.

I watched the old films of Ferenc Puskas, who helped rip apart both Eintracht Frankfurt at Hampden Park and England's Billy Wright when Hungary won at Wembley.

Wright was a player I had a laugh with at the opening of the rebuilt Wolverhampton Wanderers stadium. I knew him from my playing days at Stoke City when he was working for Central TV.

On this particular night, Wolves were playing the Hungarians, the team they played years ago at the old ground. After the match, standing at the bar with Kenny Hibbitt and Phil Parkes, I saw Billy approaching. I pulled him to one side and said, "I see nothing has changed then, Billy?" He replied, "What do you mean, Alan?" I pointed to the other side of the room, where Puskas was standing. "You still can't get anywhere near him, can you mate?"

It no doubt reminded him of that night of the famous Drag Back, something I saw and added to my game. Puskas was a complete genius, a complete one-off and, a player that Tony Waddington brought over to play in Stanley Matthews farewell match at the Victoria Ground, but nothing surprises me about that.

I recall being in The Lord Palmerston in Fulham and the landlord, a Hungarian wrestler named Tibor Zakash, told me he had a bar/restaurant in Hungary, where Puskas and all his international team-mates would have the place to themselves on the odd afternoon. Now Tibor knew of my drinking exploits and reputation and, with that in mind whispered, "Alan, they would have drunk the modern day footballer under the table. And whilst doing so, be surrounded by the most beautiful women." This was music to my ears. I only wished that Dave Sexton had been there to hear of such a thing. Wonderful stuff!

It was so wonderful because it was all of a sudden Dave Sexton against the world, or so it seemed.

The team that he wouldn't want to be a part of would have consisted of George Best, Pele, Frank Worthington, Peter Osgood, Alan Ball, Igor Bogicevic, Eddie McCreadie, Charlie Cooke, Tommy Baldwin, John Gidman, Stan Bowles, Carlos Alberto and leading them out, Bobby Moore. These are just players of the Seventies that I played with and against.

When I eventually came on the scene, the game was beginning to change.

Lilleshall was becoming more popular for the young coaches and track suit managers and, that was the turning point. All of a sudden we were being coached by the likes of Mike Kelly, the QPR goalkeeper and, as I'll mention in a moment Ray Clemence coaching the present England team, not the goalkeepers, but the actual players. If you see him with his piece a paper on the touchline showing outfield players what to do, you might understand a little more where it's all going wrong.

Coaches like Don Howe were brilliant, but in general, coaches are the main reason we are no longer a force in world football. Today people blame the lack of opportunity for the young English player, but it goes well beyond that, read on....

For instance, one night at the Footballer of the Year awards, Malcolm Allison was holding court at the bar and I was just standing there listening to the man, who for me was simply unimportant in our game. He looked at me - champagne in hand - and said, "At first I did not fancy you. I didn't think you could play, but I have changed my mind."

I really didn't need someone like Malcolm telling me, my father knew and right up to that night where I was runner-up as Footballer of the Year, he was spot on. I got this far, playing against George and Pele without coaching and, now they wanted to coach it out of you.

Thanks Malcolm, but bollocks. I lived in the real world where people like him lived in the fantasy one. I will tell you a story later which will explain this a little more. The West Ham contingent that included Malcolm, John Bond and Sexton himself, thought they had come through some kind of coaching time-tunnel which was well known as The Academy. Later in my NASL days there was Bobby Howe in Seattle, a nice bloke but still stuck in that time-warp with their philosophy on the game - and still believing West Ham won the World Cup.

Then there was Geoff Hurst, whereas Bobby Moore was in a completely different league to not only him, but all those impostors at the FA. At Soho Square our game depends on spineless individuals, who hide behind the greenback, always saying what the suits want to hear and, you, the public keep asking what is going wrong. I'll give you just four such reasons beginning with Hurst and, onto Ray Clemence, Gareth Southgate and ending with Trevor Brooking.

England could make a fortune out of those four alone, if they brought them out as that dog that sits in the back window of those cars. Just looking out nodding their heads!

He was just miles apart and, dare I say it, like me, one of the unlucky ones.

How can Hurst manage Chelsea whilst Bobby managed Southend United?

There is something seriously wrong here. Bobby should have been given the England job and been allowed to bring in the best coach in the business, no matter what nationality, colour or creed. I am all for our national manager being English because he needs to be passionate and want this country to overcome our enemies. But as for coach, it is entirely different, all he needs to do is organise the team that the manager has chosen. For instance, if I were England manager, I would employ Jose Mourinho and, we would discuss how we were going to play and what system and then I'd hand him the ENGLAND team. That is why Bobby Moore, like Beckenbauer with Germany, Cruyff with Holland and Maradona with Argentina would have been ideal. If he had one weakness he, unlike those that run the FA, was far too straight and honest and more than anything, he was a million-per-cent patriotic and cared more about the country than they did him and, so it proved.

Players would have respected him and, apart from him being the only player ever to carry off the Jules Rimet, he simply had the class, the aura and knowhow, something the national side has lacked since '70.

Only Bryan Robson could possibly be put in the same category, but even Bryan was way behind Bobby and that is not a knock at the brilliant Robson. It's just that Bobby was unique, a complete one-off. Look at today for instance. John Terry has just lost the captaincy for having an affair with his best mate (and team-mates) girlfriend. It was handed to Rio Ferdinand, who had been banned for dodging a drugs test, and been filmed in a very dodgy holiday video involving young girls. They could not possibly hand it to Wayne Rooney because he has been caught coming out of brothels. And Steve Gerrard, who has finally been handed it, will soon be in hot water for a potential bombshell that the media are sitting on.

I can only think that it has been hushed up for now because of the timing of the World Cup 2010, because the newspaper would be held responsible for our demise. In recent weeks there has been plenty in the news of the break-up with his model wife. This is behind it all. What would Bobby Moore have made of all of this?

There was, of course, the other side of the game and, that being the 'social side' with which Malcolm fitted in very nicely - when it suited him. He, in fact, looked at himself as football's equivalent of The Godfather. Sporting a big fedora and his overcoat hanging over his shoulders with a massive cigar dangling from his lips, this was Malcolm. However, since speaking down to me, I got to know him years later and liked him and, was very sad to hear that he was unwell and, has in fact, now left us, which is very sad, because as I say underneath his exterior, I'm quite certain he was alright.

In my last spell with Stoke we played a match in Tampa Bay and, Malcolm was having a working vacation with his mate Marsh. We were by the pool and, he turned up unannounced, and when he did me and my mate Foxy immediately went to work and before you could say "vodka and orange" the poolside was buzzing with glasses, ice buckets, beers, gin and vodka everywhere. We offered him a glass but he rejected by telling us that they were training a little later. At this moment the players of Tampa were planning a revolt and, were going to give Marsh an ultimatum as to either Allison goes or they go on strike and, this was told to me whilst my mate TD and I were staying over in Florida, after the boys left for home and, that following week we read in the Tampa Bay Tribune that Malcolm had been nicked for DWI (Driving While Intoxicated). I rest my case!

This team who I would end my career with was tremendous both on and off the field and we owed that to that dressing room I told you of earlier.

I told you just now that I'd come back to how this period destroyed the club and, the main reason was the our chairman, a nice man named Brian Mears admitted to me that he got so caught up in our success he lost sight of it all. He actually thought that he was one of the team and, told me that. It cost him not only the club but his marriage to the lovely June. June would knock spots off any of the WAGs of today, she was a good-looking woman and, one all of the boys would make a fuss off, especially on tour. So her husband Brian got caught up in the hype and instead of seeing the big picture saw the one that was to destroy the club. And, as I say, after I blamed him for selling Osgood and me, he was so taken aback, that he admitted his mistakes and, I only enter that in here because those Chelsea supporters slaughtered us two for leaving. They simply sold us for two reasons, one/they were in debt and two/Dave could take no more of his run-ins with Osgood and, I was a pawn in the game.

But back to the greatest part of that time, for these was the sign of the times, times that had everything. And compared to today, there was absolutely no comparison and, their players might be able to boast having millionaires whilst winning the Champions League, but apart from their absolute fluke - combined with the brilliance of Petr Cech and that Messi penalty miss - we beat better teams than Napoli and Bayern Munich in Bruges and CSKA Sofia.

And off the field, the sight and sound of Hari Krishna, the movement of The Flower People cruising the Kings Road and, then my favourite, those beautiful young ladies in the mini-skirts and hot-pants made London and, Chelsea in particular the most visited place on earth. On a summers day the pavements were packed outside the pubs with their punters overseeing the greatest ever catwalk in the world. My heart still pounds and, again, going back to the Royal London and St Barts I would lie paralysed thinking of both sides of this ridiculous life.

And then there was over east where Bobby Moore had become God. Some years later I would attend his opening of the Blind Beggar pub right opposite my hospital there. They were still filling in the bullet holes as we arrived. It was there I got teamed up with John Conteh, who, had he been a player, he would have become the first black player ever to pull a blue shirt over his head. Conteh was a real darling, who was always being lambasted for him being politically incorrect. When someone told him how much greater he could have been but for "women and drink." John's answer was simply, "The only reason I did anything was for women and drink."

It has been revealed that, whilst at his Pomp, Ali was quite a womaniser.

Different motives drive different people. Dave Sexton could never grasp that. There are those people who do not drink themselves, who fail to understand that in some cases it enhances performance by giving confidence and insight. In the case of the group of players I mixed with at Chelsea, and then later at Stoke, Arsenal and Seattle - the social side forged that deep bond, team spirit and camaraderie that was us. That I have already mentioned and, I can't stress enough of the importance of such a thing.

Dave had a very quiet personality. He was in a state of perpetual inner exile, very edgy. Looking back, I can see it was not personal, just a lack of communication. The terrible thing about it is that I really liked him a lot and, once forging a strong bond with Tony at Stoke

City, it made our relationship look even sadder. But, as I say, I truly liked day from the first day I met him and, often wonder just what life what had been like had he been a little like Tony?

Being a Gemini, I always place great store on my first impressions. The first time I was introduced to Dave was by Tommy Docherty. It was on a Tuesday evening behind the goal at the Shed End. I saw a man who was totally involved with football and nothing else. Sexton would soon replace Tommy and, as I suggested earlier, I felt it was the breaking up of what could and should have been a brilliantly successful partnership. But, the powers-that-be at Stamford Bridge, though I did not know at that time, had that wonderful ability to simply 'fuck things up' big time and this was a prime example.

The playing career of Dave Sexton was always shrouded in mystery to me also. To this day, I have never met anyone who saw him play. He was a part of that coaching mafia that I spoke of earlier, along with Malcolm Allison, who also played for the Hammers before his career was cut short by TB. John Bond played in the same side and they formed a mutual admiration society called, as I mentioned, The Academy.

His son Kevin - who was a team-mate in Seattle - is now on the brink of being the England coach, along with Harry, Joe Jordan and Rosie.

I was to come across his father some years after playing against his Norwich City team. I was captaining Seattle at a time when Bond was visiting his son and, whilst doing so poking his nose into something that was none of his business. He thought that he was above us, because he was or had been the manager of Manchester City and, we were NASL players. I told you about the Gemini in me and, with this in mind I did not like him from my very first blink and, after all we would have beaten his team wherever and whenever.

After all, who the fucking hell is, or was, John Bond?

He is one of the problems there is such a lack of good, great or useful managers in this country right now. The very best being Ian Holloway at Blackpool who puts teams together to go out and play the proper way and, does not make a song and dance of it all. He puts the best players, he can afford, together and gets the best out of them. That is the greatest talent one can ask for.

The problem with people like Bond is because you have never managed and, they feel or think that they can talk down to you and, you'll remember what I said earlier about approaching inferior people who think their superior and, here was just another case.

Well he picked on the wrong one on this day, as we stood talking and watching a training session. I was injured at the time and had just come off the bike in the dressing room and was watching the boys train when he turned up. We were having a chat, when he brought up a match at Norwich, saying, "I heard that when you played against us at Carrow Road for Stoke City, you and a couple of other players were in the pub the night before the match and, in knowing that, I felt you could have done a little more."

This was music to my ears because I had played tremendously well, controlling the match throughout a very important 1-0 win. I told him, "I don't know how you could be disappointed with my performance. Not only were we out the night before we played you, but were out at Brighton on the Wednesday, we had a night out there and were in that pub in Norwich on Thursday as well as Friday night. Yet we still beat you and, I had the ball the entire match. I followed that with, "where were your players on those three nights, if that's the best you could do?"

After that conversation it got back to me that he had said something about me, so I called Kevin to fix up a meeting in Dukes Bar - you might hear Frasier talk about this bar on his wonderful show. I got there early and waited, but his father failed to show. I don't like that. I was prepared to at least have it out with him, just for the sake of his son who at that time I liked and, had a lot of time for.

The last time I saw Kevin he was managing Bournemouth - and he blanked me - before driving Harry about at Tottenham, a job he held as some kind of smokescreen. You can read into that any way you wish, but all I know is that you are either good enough or you're not.

The thing with Harry, like with Rosie's bank account, is that everything can be swept under some carpet, but the only thing is that this particular one is not magic, it is, in fact, flying to nowhere and, those at the FA were in so much trouble, after their preposterous decisions of hiring the likes of Eriksson to McClaren right through to Graham Taylor and Capello, all of them absolutely useless, that had they appointed him they would have had one more inside the walls of Soho Square, much like Parliament bringing in Ronnie Bjggs. But by hiring such people, they hide behind a different kind of smokescreen, one which somehow keeps them in top jobs. What I mean is that they are never questioned.

When I was eighteen and in the England under-23 team, I saw these people carrying one another onto aeroplanes in such a state it was laughable and, I knew then that Lancaster Gate was about as serious as Butlins. They should have worn red coats they were that outstanding.

So, when I received my three-year ban, in the early Seventies, I thought about those days. It was like Ted Bundy charging Charlie Manson, or Freddie West putting Leslie Neilson away.

Yeah Kevin Bond blanked me and, now you'll see what I mean about these managers and, the one of the things that really gets up my nose, is that I would not mind if they could boast about being successful.

I sat and watched Bond, Harry and Joe Jordan sit motionless as Jose Mourinho's team tore them about and, all that Harry said was that his team had come a long way in a short space of time.

When he (Mourinho) took over Chelsea, he won the first championship in 50 years in his first season in charge.

That is the difference and, why he boasted he was The Special One and he had every right to boast that, because what he did was very special to those Chelsea supporters and, after those managers Bates employed along the way from Hurst to Porterfield and Campbell Mourinho is a footballing Messiah.

So, going back to Bond, at that particular time, our manager knew exactly where we were and when it came to the Saturday, we simply tortured the opposition. However, Bond can walk with his head high because his team was tucked up in bed at an early hour after a nice cup of Horlicks.

That is why those in charge never picked the best players throughout the Seventies, well there was that and, they could not tell them how to play.

Can you imagine Graham Taylor telling Peter Osgood what to do?

Yet there he was (Bond) questioning my professionalism, when surely his coaching and team tactics should be questioned. I had similar fall-outs with Bobby Howe at Seattle. He was our assistant coach and, although a good one, he carried that stigma around with him and, one night it nearly got him in big trouble. I let him off with a brush of the forehead. It would not have been the right answer and, definitely would never have made that stupid stigma disappear. All that tells you is, for me to do that, I must have been as wound up as Snide Rolex watch, because that is not me and, you'll probably know now why I don't get mixed up with such people.

Shame, because like with Dave, I liked Bobby Howe.

It's almost as if when Chelsea and West Ham people come together - Two Worlds Collide!

West Ham had those three World Cup winners in their side, led by Bobby Moore. Rather like Chelsea, though, at any given time they had a bewildering mixture of brilliance and mediocrity. Both clubs were and still are under-achievers. And it was only Roman Abromovich's riches and Mourinho's genius changed things that had been so horribly wrong for so long

The only chance they had since we left was the one that Matthew Harding gave them. While Bates was taking all the pats on the back it was Matthew that was wheeling, dealing and feeling his way through such bad times.

Matthew Harding would have been the greatest chairman in this country had his helicopter not gone down under the most suspicious circumstances and, like with me, there was more than a hint of foul play!

If Chelsea were the upcoming team of the south in the Sixties and Seventies - even though there was so much in-house trauma - West Ham with their Academy had a huge influence over the game. I found it narcissistic, although Allison's partnership with the late great Joe Mercer was one of the most exciting pairings in English football management. They actually put together a wonderful team at Manchester City. Only Brian Clough and Peter Taylor matched it and surpassed it.

Having said all of that, it just goes to show what Waddington did, all alone!

Clough and Taylor fell out, however, like Ike and Tina, John and Paul, Charles and Di, Chelsea with me and Oz, quite often the sum is greater than the parts. Allison and Clough never rediscovered the glory they had with their partners, which told a story itself. In Damned United, if this part was true, it showed Clough, after his sacking at Leeds, going back to Taylor to beg him to come back to him. It was hilarious, while at the same time humiliating.

I still say that had Tommy not gone on a destroying mission with Manchester United, QPR, Aston Villa and Rotherham, he and Dave Sexton would have fitted into the category I just mentioned. I truly believe they would have built something so very special and, with that conveyor belt coming from Dickie Foss at Hendon (The Welsh Harp), which was moved onto Mitcham to Stamford Bridge Chelsea Football Club, would never have seen the likes of Roman Abramovich.

Why?

Because at that time Harding was making his way through the City with only one thing in mind and, that was to one day be the Chairman of Chelsea Football Club and, please believe me when I tell you there would have been no greater man to see the job through. With his contacts that he was building up in the City the Bridge would not have needed an America, Arab or Russian and all of its body guards.

Chelsea would have been run by the City of London without knowing it and, with friends and allies like Tony Banks - who was to become Sports Minister - the backing was all there, waiting to make Chelsea Football Club the best in Britain.

And, I think Bates knew this and, that is why Matthew is no longer with us?

Back in the late Nineties I was drinking in Terry Venables' watering hole 'Scribes' and had the pleasure to meet Craig Johnston. He is a very likeable bloke and, now very successful in television in his native Australia. He also brought out his own design for a football boot, which I believe was very successful. Anyhow, he made a special point of saying how, although he won five titles, a European Cup and a host of other honours, he considered me to be the real player.

Just a little story to show the esteem our Seventies Chelsea team was held in.

But back to '69-70 where and when the FA Cup seemed to arrive at just about the right time for us, for we were just beginning to really click. Dave had tinkered with a few things before finding the right blend for the team. I think it came right because it gave me time to settle and, Dave time to finally organise our midfield.

The only obvious part of our team that season was the Osgood and Hutchinson had formed quite a formidable partnership up front. If formidable is the right word, no, I don't think so, more like awesome, for in that season there were times that teams just couldn't cope with them. With the kind of scope there, simply incredible, when you look at the skill, guile, know-how and that confidence that bordered on complete arrogance, quite frightening, whilst Hutchinson was, you might say, an extra arrow to his already lethal bow.

They were like two heavyweights going into the ring, only there were no boxing gloves. What they possessed, again, could not be coached and, there was no other partnership in the country, if Europe, like them. Do you remember what I told you about the advice I gave The Sniper about watching each other's backs. Well these two epitomised exactly that.

If Osgood was a combination of that 'Raging Bull' in a china shop, whilst at the same time being the lead of The Working Man's Ballet, Hutch was the one you didn't want to come across down a dark alley. When he arrived he was far from street-wise, he was a leather jacketed motor bike rider, who never imbibed and was true to the woman at home. Within a few short months after mixing in this band of scallywags, I can only say Doctor Frankenstein could not have done a more frightening job on this man from Burton-on-Trent.

Put Osgood and Hutchinson in a bar or on a football pitch and the repercussions were something that you would have to be present to believe.

When they ran the pub together in Windsor- which Oz thought they named 'Royal' after him - it was the main event from Heathrow Airport to Amsterdam and, they didn't need a red light.

So with Bonetti's name glued on the team sheet, Ron Harris like Frasier's fathers armchair in the living room, Eddie McCreadie always in charge of the left side of that defence, we needed to iron out the two-from-three situations, which was between Dempsey, Hinton and Webb. This was not too difficult, if only when Lou Hinton was left out, Dave would have not have to answer his office door, so it was the height and intelligence of Dempsey and the swashbuckling competiveness of DJ Webb at the centre of defence. When people ask about the game today and how it has changed, I cannot begin to give them four reasons and, the answer is what I just gave you. These four, on their day, you could put in any zoo and they'd scare the living daylights out of the inmates and, whilst doing so humour the hyenas.

That left us in midfield, so playing 4-2-4 which would change to 4-4-2 once losing possession - which was rare that season - the team literally picked itself. The very left-sided Peter Nobby Houseman was like Catty glued to Dave's notice-board, while Johnny Hollins - our Man for all Seasons - was the player who would try to cover every inch of every field on the planet, with his energy endless and, I would like to say that was the reason he couldn't make our drinking team - for not having the energy - but I can't. John, like John Mahoney at Stoke City, was the perfect part of this particular jigsaw puzzle, now that Charlie was happy running the right touchline. Me, I was at last a fully pledged member of not only the squad, but the team and, was the final piece of that wonderful puzzle.

On the downside, although that was a little way off, was that when a puzzle gets broken up, it leaves the kind of a mess that leads replacing it with one easier to piece together and, the easy ones are the ones that have absolutely no substance.

I once shined their boots and several of their shoes, now my job was to do their running, but I did not mind, for compared to playing at Gillingham and Aldershot in the reserves, it was an absolute pleasure, plus I could get a close-up view of Osgood and Cooke in action, whereas I used to have to watch from the faraway Shed. My job was to, as they said in the old days, fetch and carry and, that suited me fine, but only for the time being, for I had bigger fish to fry. Now I was in the side and improving I had my eye on Bobby Charlton's England shirt. Sounds crazy, but I had come so far in such a short space of time, I had no intention of stopping right there.

I learned this from Sinatra and Moore, if you're going to be something, aim to be the best!

That time had come and, the one that little did we know then, would be the beginning of an historic period of this once great football club. The 3rd Round of the FA Cup and it was kind to us, as it was to be all along, in what was unbeknown to us then the most exciting time of all our lives. Birmingham City at home suited us fine.

We wore yellow, a colour I loved playing in, although my favourite strip was our change kit of red shirts, white shorts and green stockings. So it was yellow shirts, blue shorts and yellow stockings, a strip that became lucky to us, as it was to Everton who won the title that year. The following year Arsenal went one better, winning the League and FA Cup Double while using the same combination as their away strip.

Birmingham wore the famous Real Madrid all-white strip which Leeds United had become almost as famous for and, I stress almost without there being any real comparisons. Incidentally, Leeds football credibility has gone downhill since the Revie era, for it was he who was responsible for all the good and bad (not to mention the ugly), inside and outside the club (and, of course as I said his disgraceful running of the national team told an entirely different story about the man).

Wearing white on this day, though, were two Chelsea favourites, one being Albert Murray, known by the supporters as Ruby, although to us he was known as Satch. Albert was an absolute diamond and, he showed me he had so much more class than many of my other team-mates when visiting me in my hospital bed, once getting past the ICU. The only others to visit me were Johnny Dempsey and Ian Hutchinson, although Oz came up much later when I was told he got paid £500 (a monkey for a monkey) for doing so off the Sun, allegedly.

The other was Tony Hateley, who I think was possibly Tommy Docherty's last signing. They also had a player who looked a little like a mini-Dave Lee Travis, called Trevor Hockey and, he was as usual, busy although there were plenty of them in those days. Wingers were either in a different class or run-of-the-mill. Although that was no reason for Ramsey to do away with them, for that was done merely to spoil the game and get the result needed. What people never grab is that, had England not had everything go their way Alf would have got slaughtered for such tactics, however, success hides a multiple of sins. You only had to look at our team to know had it been outside of England we would still be waiting to win our first ever World Cup and, as I said in 1997 in the original Ballet, I told everyone in 1970 that, it would be the last time we stood a chance and, when we did get it right on the field, Alf got it wrong from the bench, in fact, more than once!

The tension on the terraces was running high, for there was history between these two sets of fans. A Chelsea fan had been chucked under a bus a few years prior and I always recalled trouble at St Andrews.

It would be tempting to add little had changed - just look at Millwall. Some things, disappointingly, never change and, after watching the problems going into the European Champions, if what we saw on a BBC documentary on 28.5.12 is anything to go by, this will be seen as a re-run of Mary Poppins.

The first half was tight, with no quarter given by the away side. In fact, it was a little frenetic and needed slowing down, which a goal would do. And so it did. I picked up a ball wide, close to the dog track just under the East Stand and, headed for the by-line under the North Stand, where Matthew Harding was sitting. Having got there, I found the time and space to look up to see Oz lurking dangerously at their back post.

Remember that Raging Bull?

All I needed to do was put it in the space between him and the keeper and, I knew he would do the rest. I have watched this on video and it shows Oz come crashing in, like he did that night when the police attacked him in the Kings Road - that China Shop again. He never thought twice in these situations. Much like when Dave singled him out. It was simply a red flag to a bull. This was why he was that good. He never thought about it, he just did it. Like in Athens, "Go home to bed son, leave it to me," he had incredible confidence. That reminds me of George, the self-admitted alcoholic and genius who would not pass to the great Bobby Charlton because, as he admitted, "I could not resist trying to beat as many defenders as possible."

As in The Godfather, "It's not personal, it was business," with George.

This was personal though, with Pele, the man who always said that George was the best player in the world.

Once the ball left my right foot, I just watched the big centre-forward crash a header through a crowd of players and into the Birmingham net: 1-0. It was right on the stroke of half-time and, the best time to get your heads in front.

Little did I know we were heading for a memorable first FA Cup final replay at Old Trafford where tragedy awaited me.

That was the much-needed breakthrough, the first of so many FA Cup goals in that extraordinary season and, the scorer would set a record of scoring in every one of them, right up to the final. And then of course, keeping that record going by scoring at Old Trafford in the FA Cup final replay, which was my favourite all-time Osgood goal. I cannot stop myself mentioning that one particular goal. It was (whilst I was still in a state of trauma watching from the stand) possibly the most important goal in Chelsea's history.

Have they ever thought about what might have happened had Leeds gone on to win the FA Cup?

We would have been like Harold Steptoe's horse drinking down the Nags Head, not on the open top bus in the Kings Road. Nobody looks at it like that. As Brian Mears said to me all those years later, "I was so wrapped-up in it all myself."

Pity he wasn't so wrapped-up in my transfer deal.

As I was one of those players who got him wrapped-up.

This one settled us down which made the second half comfortable, as our visitors never troubled us. We added two more on the way to breaking the record amount of goals scored in that FA Cup-winning season. Thirteen minutes from the end, a little inter-passing move out on the left near the West Stand between myself and the two Peters, Houseman and Osgood, led to Hutch scoring in typical style from close range. He went on to bag his second and our third with a last-minute header from a Johnny Hollins cross.

We were on our way!

I remember my jubilation as I sat in the Kings Arms with my parents, dreaming of Wembley, even at such an early stage. I told you about my dreaming.

And to celebrate, the following day, I bought a new jacket from Take Six. It was a Prince of Wales check. It was the jacket I would wear on the day I stepped off the train at Stoke-on-Trent Station three days after signing in January 1974. I've loved clothes for as long as I can remember, so you can imagine what it was like when becoming friendly with Peter Wyngarde, who was then none other than Jason King. All the rascals in the area were top dressers with Brian Harrison - who was immaculate - probably topping the lot of them. Clothes were such a big part of our lives in those days. I have always thought you could tell a man or woman by their attire and, like George, I found a well groomed, good looking woman irresistible!

How times have changed in both players and supporters. I see photographs of players today and am astounded with all of their big money salaries at how their dress code and standards are so low. They don't match their flash cars. Can you imagine James Bond getting into his Aston Martin dressed shabbily? I don't think so and, then there was Bobby Moore. You would never see Bobby less than immaculate. He dressed as if he was leading out England at Wembley, if you saw the difference between him walking out the tunnel at Wembley and then at Upton Park you'd see what I mean.

As I mentioned earlier, just a couple of seasons ago the Chelsea manager, Guus Hiddink, gave his players a dressing down - if you excuse the pun - telling them they needed to clean their act up both on and off the pitch. No more tracksuits and tatty denims. He even went to the extent of fining anyone who did not straighten his tie.

It was really exciting going to work on a Monday after an FA Cup win, I think, with me, it was the anticipation of who was coming out of that bag and, just who were next? We would train at the Bridge on these Mondays, where a transistor radio was switched on five minutes beforehand the draw, so we could hear our number. This would interrupt our five-a-side for a few minutes before getting back to the job at hand. This day was also a good one for us, another home draw, this time it was Burnley. A team who were a real tough nut in the Sixties and, although all of their best players were finished, they still had some really talented youngsters. Their youth set-up was looked upon as one of the best in the country. Tommy Docherty even sent his son Michael there after he and I had worked out a really good relationship both on and off the field whilst apprentices. I liked playing alongside Michael who, like his dad, was a tough-tackling Scot who took no prisoners.

I was really disappointed to see him leave.

The problem with this match was that we scored a couple of goals inside a minute or so and, then took our foot off the gas. It was human nature, but Dave took it a little too far and, found it difficult taking his foot off the gas when it came to Osgood. He entered another phase of winding up his most dangerous player. I still stand alone sometimes, trying to get my head around just why he constantly made a bee-line for the King of Stamford Bridge. Was it because of that? Could he not handle him getting all the glory and all the accolades? I could go on asking myself questions and, know if I entered a fourth life, I'd never find an answer. Did Dave know? Just what was it with him and Oz?

Why?

Well, although Oz had scored again, after a brilliant piece of play by yours truly. I gathered the ball on my thigh, from a throw-in under the shadow of the West Stand and, after flicking over my marker's head, without looking, flipped a ball high over everyone to the far post. It was like if you were in a crowded train station - say Liverpool Street on a Friday night - and if you were in doubt, if you knew Oz was amongst them, you'd simply throw it in the air and, there's good chance he'd get on the end of it. Oz was no 'Nearly Man.'

And as I suspected, the former builder from Windsor was right on cue. With Peter Mellor stranded at his near post, Osgood got to the ball before that Liverpool Street crowd, or so it sounded like and, did what he did best.

Although I could not see through the crowded goalmouth, I knew it was Osgood, because as I ran towards The Shed he was there blowing kisses as normal.

But what was to follow, was behind the Sexton/Osgood on-going fiasco. The man that Oz had left for his goal popped up at the other end to score twice, therefore taking it to a replay, which meant it would be the first and only time we'd leave London on the way to FA Cup glory.

Martin Dobson was that Burnley player and, he'll never know the trouble he so nearly caused?

These were both from dead balls and it was the reason that Sexton let Osgood know in no uncertain terms that he was to blame. I believe this was the beginning of the Sexton/Osgood saga that ran right up until our departure in the January of '74.

But again, Dave didn't mention his goal, again, why?

But going back a few minutes, Dobson headed home once and, then the horror show began in the final few minutes and continued into the first 45 at Turf Moor in the replay. Burnley, were tough, very tough, and there was no doubt about that. Turf Moor was daunting and with no Osgood, even more so. I cannot tell you why Osgood never played but what I can tell you is that the mist was like a scene from a Stephen King film, falling out of the night sky like it was taunting us, until finally disappearing into the dead distance, however, leaving us to hang on for dear life. It all seemed a part of the show. For a while I thought that Wembley was disappearing with the mist, as we faced our biggest onslaught of the season. That two goal lead at the Bridge, with ten minutes to go, seemed a lifetime ago. We looked in big trouble as Steve Kindon and Ralph Coates run both flanks like Olympic sprinters. Then there was Brian Buddha O'Neil biting at our ankles in midfield. For the first time that season, we were on the receiving end of a battering. We just could not wait for half-time to come. When it did, there was such a sigh of relief and, part of that relief was that we were only one goal behind.

I would be telling you a lie if I told you what was said in the dressing room, but I wouldn't be lying if I told you we were stunned, rocked and on the ropes. Having no Osgood, we wondered where a goal was going to come from.

But surely, thinking back, they could not possibly keep that pace up?

And so it proved, when around the hour mark the game had changed somewhat, for we had clawed our way back into this pulsating match with Charlie and me getting more possession. Yet we were still a goal short with a quarter-of-an-hour on the clock. It really looked like our Monday mornings when listening to the radio were over. Our fans from The Shed were absolutely magnificent and, it seemed then, that they lifted us into the next round, as Peter Houseman, our unsung hero, was responsible for getting us back into this match. He grabbed a hold of the ball, ghosted past a couple of claret and blue shirts before hitting a sweet left footed shot inside Mellor's post. My heart stood still. I can honestly say, even now, that the relief of being back in the match was absolutely incredible. I suppose in some ways, it would be like coming out of that coma. One minute you're close to losing your legs and, then they find the C-Clamp sitting there in the corner. However, the only Clamp I ever heard of in our game was Eddie. And who signed him? Tony Waddington at Stoke City.

From the moment Nobby's shot hit the back of their net, it seemed that the match had turned into a home match, with The Shed silencing (numbing) the home fans. They were delirious. In the final minutes after that equaliser at Turf Moor we were like lions in the Ben Hur arena and, Burnley were running scared. Not that Three Lions rubbish of today. We were real lions and, we knew then that Wembley was back in our sights. Although the referee blew for extra-time, we knew the match would be ours. Burnley looked to be falling to their knees, totally knackered. They had given their all and, were like that boxer who had smashed the hell out of his opponent, but just couldn't put him on the canvas.

And just when he thought he had won on points, the sucker punch came.

It was the nearest thing to the Bruges match - but that was a year away - for they also had us on the ropes' in Belgium, but had not finished us off and, on this night Burnley battered us for most of the match, but soon would be paying the ultimate price. However, I often wondered what might have been, had they got a second goal?

This was everything I loved about cup football and more unless, of course, you were on the opposite end, which was all to come, but for now we were finding our rhythm once again!

However, this was my first taste of the FA Cup, well an FA Cup hit-and-run job.

I'd watched this competition as a kid and always dreamed about walking out of that tunnel in an FA Cup final, could this be it in my first full-season?

We were now looking for the winner, whilst they were absolutely punch-drunk. How refreshing to see that we were the sober ones for a change and, we were, although I could see intoxication in the distance, on the horizon!

Speaking of intoxication, it is absolutely amazing how a game can change and, swing your way, if you had a great spirit and, we had that in abundance. Along with that spirit, our supremacy paid off with another goal from Nobby. And then Sponge, put daylight between us. Our first trip outside London in the FA Cup was now a job well done. The shock of being knocked out was now replaced with jubilation. Charlie and I should have scored as we tortured the home side in extra-time.

That goal was like being given the morphine handset in the Royal London, were one second you're in big trouble and after one press of that button and, you're on top of the world. But the fans didn't need such a drug, they had their unbelievable faith in us throughout, however now their cries were one of joy, not ones that were try to lift us from the jaws of defeat.

They all of a sudden knew that they were on their way to Wembley. We showed them in those latter stages that we would not let them down. Osgood, or no Osgood, we were on our way. To think, only just over half-an-hour ago, we were in such big trouble.

Again, it was like what I said earlier, one moment you're staring at something completely different from the outcome. Unlike in the Mile End Road, this was absolutely delightful and my God, so relieving.

I always look at the "what might have been" had Burnley held on and dumped us out?

What would have been the repercussions? That Martin Dobson double would have eaten at Sexton and, given his on-going feud with our main player that extra spice. Only this spice was always to leave a nasty taste in our mouths and, in the end, it was what was behind the breaking up of this incredible bunch of players.

But, that was what it might have been, had Houseman not have come up with the goods in our hour of need, but we could now look forward to Monday without cringing at the 5th Round draw.

Looking at the Chelsea match in Munich a month ago, as I write, this was pretty similar, but the difference was that we tried to get back at Burnley, whereas the present side had no intention of going into the German half until they fell behind with four minutes to go.

The hero of the night was Houseman, who was now relishing the FA Cup. Peter had great balance, control and was very deceiving when in control. His trick was that once he got past his man, he never gave him the opportunity to get a second bite of the cherry. As soon as he got that space to cross the ball, he whipped it into the near-post, mostly like he did for Tommy's goal. He was Sexton's personification of what a footballer should be. He was an introvert. He did not join our crowd when out drinking. He was one of those who you would not know had been at the party, but as he showed at Turf Moor he didn't need to be noisy to spoil one.

The fans saw him as Bill Wyman to Osgood's Jagger.

I will not include Keith Richards in this analogy.

The irony of it all was that Peter and Sally Houseman were killed in a car crash. If any other of the Chelsea forwards had met with a similar fate, it would have compounded the legend that sprang up about us and, curiously still seems to be spreading. River Phoenix was born that year. If any Chelsea player had died at a similar age, the legend like that of Monroe, Dean and Presley, would have been complete. Houseman made a massive contribution to us winning the FA Cup that year. He seemed to be pumped up for each and every match and, got stronger the further we went. It was as if he knew what the future had in store for him. Although his death was not straight afterwards, it was as if this FA Cup run was to be his Swan Song.

Let me say this about Nobby - and I really don't know how he got that nickname - much like Chopper, he was a diamond. He was warm, always smiling and, as genuine as another Genuine Snide Rolex. When initially writing this book, I came across some folk who knew him from his Oxford United playing days. I was not surprised at all that they held him in such high regard and, with so much affection.

I played in a Chelsea reserve match on my second time around where I asked a couple of people there about him.

I was not surprised to find that they loved him as much as everyone at the Bridge, even more so, in fact!

This was the night when Mickey Droy, Dale Jasper, Peter Rhodes-Brown and I were in Rocky's Wine Bar in Putney High Street after the match. TD was there also. Tony Davis was and, still is, a fantastic friend of mine. He is a man that has always been there for me. The only time he didn't turn up, I got nicked. It was the Friday after the '78 FA Cup final at White Hart Lane, my favourite ground, but on this night it proved to be the opposite.

We had arranged that I drove to the match in order that I could have my last drink with the lads, because I was about to tell them I was leaving. TD, who was coming by train, so he could later pick my car up and drive me home - well, that was the plan.

My little mate was as reliable as Oz scoring when he said he would. On this night he did not turn up and me, like the fool I am, drove home and, got breathalysed. It is funny looking back, but then, not really. I was lost in this part of the world and, whilst driving into oblivion, I noticed on the back of one of those big red buses that it was heading for the West End. I followed it thinking I'd be okay from there, not knowing it was a bus lane. The yellow light flashed right behind me. As Jim Davidson would say 'Nick! Nick!'

The cop was great though. He threw me across the bonnet, once I told him that I had just been playing in a testimonial for Arsenal. He was no doubt a Spurs fan.

Funny thing was, I bought my Toyota from a chap in Gravesend named Colin Gay and, when I spoke to him later, he told me that a copper had telephoned him and, wanted to buy my car.

Can you imagine that?

It would be like waiting for your best friend to die, so you could have his wife…and I'm not going into the John Terry story of last season.

You have cops like that doing those things, but when it comes to catching these fucking nutty terrorists they're nowhere to be seen. He could have helped me out, but he chose to manhandle me, I was to find out later through my Mile End experience that these cops get a kick out of telling their colleagues and friends, "Guess who I nicked the other night?" Big fucking deal!

I was livid telling Colin, "Why didn't you sell it to him and fix the brakes?" I seriously meant it. Because as Betty said, "What comes round goes round."

So, did it shock me years later that they cost me £1.9million?

Did it shock me they wanted me to buy my England cap back?

Funny thing is, I have been drinking today 7th June 2010 with a couple of cops, great lads these are though. Refreshing, is life getting better?

Though I don't think anything has changed, in fact, it's got and is getting worse, much like the UEFA, FIFA, the FA and referees.

I used to play in the same All Star XI as stuntman Rocky Taylor in the days of my second spell at Chelsea and, it was in his Wine Bar where one of the funniest things happened. In all of my time playing - at any level - I have never come across a player who never knew the final score. About 3am we stood at the bar having the usual crack about life in the stiffs when Peter (Rhoades-Brown) interrupted our conversation by saying, "It's just hit me, how on earth could we not beat that team tonight. Just look at us Alan Hudson, Mickey Droy, Dale Jasper and me, how could we not beat a poxy Oxford team?"

We all looked at one another not knowing whether he was serious or not?

And then, finally we cracked up knowing that he never knew the score. Now, the funny thing here is, can you imagine him going home and telling his missus that we drew 2-2 and, then the following day she looks in the paper and sees 3-2. She's going to ask him "where were you last night?"

Funny bloke, Peter, I hope this finds you well mate!

The other thing was on that night although he was not following the game he must have done something right, for Oxford signed him not long afterwards.

Those were our days in the Chelsea reserves and trust me, they were hilarious and, they had to be, otherwise you'd go nuts!

But from Oxford back to Burnley and, our supporters - who did us proud - went to the motorway, surely hoarse and, we were delighted and, relieved that after an early scare, we were in the hat for the next round. Our victory at Turf Moor made people up and down the country sit up and take notice. Earlier Chelsea sides may have crumbled under such a siege. That night we showed an incredible will to win and, also the kind of resilience that was to weld us into a very tough unit. We were incredibly together in those days, with that spirit which cannot be coached, but you can coach it out, without knowing it.

I sometimes think that Dave maybe felt left out, you know, like looking in from the outside. Rather like watching people enjoying themselves at a private party through the pub window, totally left out in the cold.

Also, a little like wondering what has been happening whilst you've been in a coma.

Although our minds were firmly on the FA Cup, we were playing well in the League, however, I don't know if it was because it was Hutch and my first season, but it seemed something in the air, like something big was on the horizon?

We did our usual, listening to the draw in the forecourt of Stamford Bridge, taking out five minutes from a very tough five-a-side. This was our Friday morning training venue but since the FA Cup began we for some reason started training there. I think, no, I know Dave was, as Blind Stevie might sing, "very superstitious" because it was noticeable he had worn the same blazer for our first three matches of this cup run and, what made it more definite was that he had a button missing. Dave Sexton would not have done such a thing, he dressed as well as any man I'd ever seen and, now here he was wearing a smart blazer without a button.

This was before he lost his marbles, or was it Brian Mears?

Anyhow, the most important thing was that we had been lucky once again by being drawn in London and, this time at Peter Osgood's shooting range, Crystal Palace.

I can only think that their goalkeeper, John Jackson had either gone to his GP or asked his club doctor for some sleeping tablets. Oz had stuck four past just a few weeks earlier and, I don't know, but his record against Palace goals-per-game must have been second-to-none.

Had they lived in the same street as me and my second wife it would surely have been named Elm Street, with both Jacko and I having the nightmares.

The fifth-round match at Selhurst Park saw us take a field which could have been mistaken for Cheltenham Racecourse - only it was early February, not March - on a rainy cold winter's day in South London.

But we were not bothered about anything at that time; it was a case of 'bring 'em all on' because at that time we feared nobody. Charlie missed this match, which meant Sponge took over his No 7 shirt and, Oz had his No 9 back. I was becoming a very close pal with Tommy - he was a lovely, lovely man - well mannered, good looking, always happy-go-lucky and, much to the dismay of Dave loved a drop of the other stuff. We were ideal team-mates loving all the good things life brings and, of course, football was in our blood. We also had the other stuff in our blood, the Dave didn't like, but that never stopped us. We lived as we played, as if the sky was the limit.

We remain great friends to this day.

Although we were concentrating and, totally focused on the FA Cup, because our matches were so very exciting, we were still in with a shout for the League Championship. Chelsea had been beaten in two semi-finals under Docherty before finally getting to Wembley in '67, only to be beaten by Tottenham, who were captained by none other than Terry Venables on that day. So we wanted to win this trophy and, become the first team in the club's history to do so and, the feeling in the camp was that we would.

I was beginning to get plenty of media coverage, the press seizing on the Kings Road connection, the long hair and, the trendy clothes image. This was a heady cocktail for Fleet Street. But On the morning of this match, the newspapers were full of Osgood and, his earlier goal spree when facing Jackson, that poor Palace keeper. As you know now, our family dog was named Ossie and, I was photographed holding him in my arms outside our prefab - the dog that is.

The crowd was 48,000 (or 12 times an average Wimbledon home gate at Selhurst Park in '98). The gate receipts were a record £22,000, hardly the Brinks Mat job but solid money then, when I was earning £25 a week. Palace's top player was Steve Kember, who would be joining us a little later, but he was out injured on this particular day.

The story behind Sexton buying Steve was a little mystifying, for he had played really well against us not long before, but the reason he played so well was because I had been out on the tiles the day before. Sorry Steve, although that was the greatest favour anyone has ever done you, but on that particular day, I had been out drinking away a big problem I had at that time. Anyhow, on waking I found myself rather the worse for wear. After our pre-match meal, I even went over to the Adelaide an hour before the kick-off for a livener, but it didn't work and, so I spent all afternoon in a daze. I would have been better staying in the pub and, getting a ban, a fine or anything else Dave wished to hand out. I regretted turning up and, playing so badly and, that's putting it mildly. It was unlike me, but I was going through a real bad time. Anyhow, I did Steve a big favour. The crazy thing was that before he signed Steve he told me one morning at Mitcham that it would not affect my position at the club. Of course it would, because, as I told you, Dave always knew as an outlet he could switch me wide and, when he did I went into a shell. I hated playing out there, for I found it like waiting for a bus to come by. I needed to be involved all over the pitch, in the thick of things like most great inside-forwards. With the greatest respect wingers are a breed of their own, you are either a winger or your nothing at all.

Peter Osgood was about as popular at Palace as Eric Cantona became.

It was poetic justice that he put us in front from a Houseman corner, almost on half-time, which had Palace complaining that it was a foul, but the goal stood. Oz would have a running battle with Mel Blyth - a player he later teamed up with at Southampton to win the FA Cup - and was booed throughout the match, something that he absolutely loved. It is great when an opposing crowd gave you that treatment, for it shows you are hurting their team and, he certainly did that in more ways than one.

However, he never resorted to Kung-Fu!

Palace equalised early in the second half, which gave them a lifeline and, us a kick up the backside. A boy called Hoy scored it, something he had done at the Bridge earlier on in the season. They then threw everything but the tower at us, but we stood tall and, hit them on the break with two devastating attacks. John Dempsey scored a rare goal by heading home a towering cross from Holly. It was his first cup goal for Chelsea, never knowing his last one would be in the European Cup Winners Cup final in Athens. Talking of towers, John was a tower of strength for us, the most consistent performer in our defence, one you could rely in no matter what.

The atmosphere at the club at his time was electric, with absolutely no signs of the trouble that would follow. We were winning matches for fun then.

John was a great character and, a fantastic buy from Fulham, which later had me wondering why Bobby Robson had allowed him to join us. But Robson was not as canny as they make out.

He also missed a great opportunity to have two of the best young players around. And they were Hutchinson and Hudson. My father pulled him on a train coming back from Highbury one evening and, told him about this young centre-forward playing for Burton Albion.

However the rest is history as, Chelsea bought him from Cambridge after someone went there after being tipped off about a goalkeeper and, came back with a rough and ready centre-forward sporting a leather jacket.

Anyhow, Robson's loss was our gain, big time, and now he was enjoying the kind of atmosphere at this club that was absolutely electric, with absolutely no signs of the trouble that would follow. It was incredible how two young men from completely different backgrounds were now going on such a journey together. I was a natural footballer who would in time, possibly go on to be a top inside-forward, whereas Ian was that rough diamond and, as my dad said about him, "he could be absolutely anything" and, the way things were going that rough diamond looked like turning out to be a jewel.

Right now, we were beginning to win matches for fun.

Perhaps Robson was right.

Who wanted a young, talented, up-coming leather-jacketed motor-biker?

I'm sorry, but I can't see people like that so impressive in the game. He was a great footballer but was lucky as a manager. He only chose our best player when his Plan A didn't work in that World Cup in Italy.

Why in the first place, was Gascoigne not first choice?

On the England front, Osgood was playing superbly and, must surely have been playing himself into the Mexico squad and, although I was playing well, I thought that my game still needed more substance and, was still a little short of such a stage. I was not dominant enough, but maybe that would change when I stopped becoming the "new kid on the block" who was still looked at as the boy who was only cleaning the boots a few months ago.

But it was up to me to get rid of that stigma and, the only way to do such a thing was to try to take more command of the game.

Goals seemed to come so easy for us around this time. Oz should have scored just after Dempsey, but his shot flew through a crowd of players and, struck a post. Our crowd was now in full swing as a free-kick by Webb found Dempsey again, he headed it down for Nobby to add a third.

In his first fight with Sonny Liston, the great boxer known as Cassius Marcellus Clay would yawn to show his contempt for his opponent. The ability to score almost at will was a similar act of arrogance. Although not arrogance as such, it was simply great confidence in your ability. Like when I tell you elsewhere, when Oz beat both Banks and Shilton in 7 days and turned to me and said, "Who's next?"

My theory about the apparent inconsistency of the club was that we were more vulnerable against lesser teams, because we considered them to be below us and, therefore, not so much effort was put in to obtain a result. But isn't that human nature?

Anyhow, at his moment in time that wasn't the case, we were burying teams and, poor old Palace must have been sick of the sight of us, especially Osgood.

I read about carbon molecules which could have the hell beaten out of them yet bounce back. Chelsea was like that in those days. Hutch grabbed a fourth, but the game was already over, out of their reach and, Palace knew it by playing out the rest of the match as if on Prozac. They were simply devastated by the savagery and, speed of our attacks. Bert Head's team was wrecked and we were turning the screw, as we did on all our cup opponents around this time. We were simply devastating.

Incredibly, we were drawn in London again for the sixth round. This time, though, it was a much tastier affair, with more grudges than in Parliament. A trip to Loftus Road, where Dave Sexton had first seen me play, was our next assignment and, we could not have been happier. I told you earlier that I wanted to play alongside Terry Venables. That wasn't to be, but now here I was facing him. He had just finished an unhappy spell at Tottenham and, was strolling around west London at Shepherds Bush.

QPR suited Terry because that meant there were three car dealers in that part of the world, Jim Gregory, Webby's mate in Warren Street and, of course Terry himself. Would you buy a car of this man?
This is where Webby got that Roller from, but more of that later.

There were some really tasty match-ups here, including Marsh and Osgood and Hudson and Venables. Also playing was Venables alter ego Hazell. Playing at right back was Dave Clement, who sadly committed suicide after being told that he had cancer. And after finishing it all, it transpired that he had been misdiagnosed. What a horrific thing to happen to such a nice bloke and, fine player, one of those one-club men which were so very rare. Looking back, I suppose I should thank my lucky stars, on the other hand...

As I said, it was built up as a grudge match with the biggest talking point being who was the better player, Osgood or Marsh? I think Ron Harris would have a say in this one. It was again like a home match for us, with our fans seemingly filling the place. Behind the goal opposite the Shepherds Bush End they piled forward leaving hardly any space to take a corner kick. It made the atmosphere absolutely electric, like something I'd never seen before and, it was strange because less than a year ago, I was playing in a friendly here and, this was so far from being one of them.

I had also followed QPR right through their League Cup exploits when winning it by beating West Bromwich Albion at Wembley after going two goals down. There was one thing for sure, if we got two in front there was no way they'd repeat that.

I could remember everything about that League Cup winning season and this was how it read...

On the first day of the 1966–1967 League Cup on 23 August 1966, QPR played Colchester United at home, winning 5–0

In the third round, they knocked out Swansea City on 12 October by two goals to one.

They were then drawn against Leicester City in the following round where three quick-fire goals in the second half saw them come back from being 2–1 down to win the match by four goals to two. The first of these goals was a rebound off Leicester goalkeeper Gordon Banks after a shot by Rodney Marsh. Les Allen snuck through a packed Leicester goalmouth, and the final goal came from Mark Lazarus in similar circumstances to the Allen goal.

Until the first leg of the semi-final against Birmingham City, Rangers had not won an away match during their League Cup campaign. They were one goal down at half time and, again were forced to stage a comeback during the second half. In the 55th minute, Marsh scored his 34th goal of the season, heading the ball home after a corner kick from Allen. Marsh was involved again in QPR's second and third goal as he set up Roger Morgan for the second and, then hit a back-heel pass through to Lazarus for the third. QPR's fourth and final goal saw Marsh head a free kick to Allen, who slotted it home.

The second leg secured QPR's first trip to Wembley and, marked the first time that a team from Division Three had reached any Wembley final. They won the game 3–1, but waited until the last twelve minutes to score two goals to take the win on the night. Marsh initially took the lead for QPR, but Birmingham came back with a goal from Eric Barker, but QPR struck twice through Marsh again and, a goal from the club captain Mike Keen.

As I said, I watched all of those home matches plus the away match at Birmingham. My only regret was that I missed the final and, that was because I had to play for the Chelsea Youth Team on that morning and, then report at the Bridge for the first team match in the afternoon. I will always remember though, where I was when Rodney Marsh struck the winner at Wembley. It was a few yards away from the exact spot where I signed for Tony Waddington on that life changing Saturday morning in January 1974, just by the main door of those old Stamford Bridges offices.

I told you about my love for cup matches!

So, I included this, to remind you of my love for not only cup football, but big matches and, this one in particular. Plus, although I was a fan of Marsh, he turned me over for a multi-million pound deal in his beloved Tampa Bay. Had I known then I might have had a special word in Chopper's ear. Hindsight!

But once again, I can look back on this win and think of what might have happened had we been beaten?

But as you'll hear and, for those of you that weren't there, we were simply magnificent and, it meant so much to me one/ for beating the team I watched five years earlier turn everyone over and two/ move one step closer to the Twin Towers, those that can be seen from this tiny ground.

Before telling you about this match, yesterday I wrote to the editor of the Daily Mail asking if I could write a piece about the upcoming World Cup (we are three days away). I put in this e-mail: Isn't it about time someone stopped misleading our fantastic supporters. Every two years, all you read and hear about is us winning the upcoming competition. I want to tell it how it is. We have absolutely no chance and, after knowing that, those fans will not be so disappointed when it all goes pear-shaped once again.

Why do we have this most terrible of habits? Please don't tell me it's the Bull Dog spirit!

That spirit is not needed and found in South Africa, it is in Afghanistan. This is football, not fighting, not bloodied headbands. It is all about technique, Lionel Messi, Diego Maradona, Johan Cruyff, George Best, Stan Bowles etc. Not Paul Ince, Carlton Palmer, Tony Adams or Terry Butcher. The Bull Dog spirit is old hat. Blood and guts is not enough to win a World Cup. Did you ever see Bobby Moore or Franz Beckenbauer smothered in blood?

Also, going back to the Sniper, can someone tell me why all these famous people played in front of 73,000 at Old Trafford the other night and are giving the money to Kenya, whilst our boys are getting killed in Afghanistan through lack of funds for proper protection. Then I see the England team board an aeroplane with fifty-odd top class beds. Wayne Rooney walking around with a pillow under his arm is not really a very good sign, not when these young lads are fighting a war and sleeping so very rough.

Their wives live every day in fear, whilst these WAGs stroll around in Sun City.

Let's get it all in the right perspective and, that is what I'm trying to do with my other book, Don't Shoot the Taliban....You'll Wake the Locals!

This is the front cover of that book with Peter Rayner who was killed in Afghanistan.

His wife Wendy kindly gave me permission to use this photograph and I thank her!

But in 1970 there was a mini-war going on at Shepherds Bush and, I call it a mini-war because the real one was awaiting us in May, in the shape of Leeds United.

Once again, in the muddiest of conditions, Rangers tore into us forcing us back, almost into our fans who, spilled onto the tiny surroundings. They almost drew first blood through a former Chelsea favourite Barry Bridges, but that blood got spilt all over them as the yellow and blue shirted Chelsea scored twice in as many minutes. The opening goal was breath taking. With seven minutes gone, David Webb won the ball deep in our half and slogged through the Loftus Road mud-heap, exchanging passes with first Charlie and then John Hollins, before sweeping the ball high into Mick Kelly's net. It was, you could say, a great training ground goal. You win it, give it and, off you go and, that is what he did, stopping for no-one, like an express-train coming in on the end of a delightful cross from Holly and, once again Webby's timing was far better than any Manchester to Euston train!

Mind you, that's not difficult!

Before the crowd and the Rangers players could get their breath back, it was 2-0 as Charlie picked up another loose ball and, looking up saw Oz making a run down the left-hand side. And before you could blink, the "Wizard of Oz" had buried his first of three goals in brilliant fashion. It was a typical Cooke through-ball and Osgood finish, with Oz latching on to it, nonchalantly controlling it with the outside of one foot and dispatching it with the other, all in one sweet movement. Most of his goals had a touch of sweetness about them, for he hardly scored an ordinary one. It was something Osgood did so often, so brilliantly, one touch with the outside of his right foot then sweeping it in with his second touch, delightful!

This was yet another sell-out and record crowd, this time 33,000. It seemed as if we were breaking every record in the book now and, that record crowd gasped as McCreadie brought down the ever busy Bridges. Bridges was electric quick and, although Eddie was his equal, he got first run on him and Eddie clipped him from behind.

Penalty!

Ron Harris and Peter Osgood disputed it for what seemed an eternity, but it ended with Venables stepping up and hitting the kick to Catty's left. It was if our keeper knew exactly where it was going, as he dived and saved it with ease.

There was further controversy as Kevin Howley, the man in black, pointed back to the spot ordering it to be retaken. To this day we don't know what for. I have watched it on video and I am still amazed. Was it because Peter moved before the ball left Terry's foot? Was it because a player encroached?

But as I have been saying for thirty years, this was just another case for bringing in The Third Eye!

Chelsea ended Manchester City's impressive unbeaten run at Stamford Bridge just recently 12.12.2011 thanks to the referee missing David Silva blatantly fouled inside the box. Where was the referee? A mere ten yards away, in clear view!

Whatever, Howley was lucky that he wasn't playing, as Chopper would have seen to him. I say that because as he ran to the edge of our box having pointed to the spot, Ron ran at him as if going to perform one of his specials on him. He went totally berserk and Osgood was a fraction behind him, after his blood. I stood behind them listening to the kind of language that you would not hear at 3am in a night club.

Whilst there was mayhem, the coolest man in the ground stepped up and coolly slotted a sweet right foot shot into the opposite corner with Catty completely flat-footed. He was a great penalty taker, cool, calm and decisive, even after missing the initial kick he didn't flinch as he stepped up and fired past his old team-mate with ease!

It rather reminded me of the Peter Storey penalty against Gordon Banks in that very controversial FA Cup semi-final when my mate Josh Mahoney handled on the goal-line seven minutes into stoppage time. It was not a great penalty by any stretch of the imagination, but Gordon was simply rooted to the spot. He was wrong-footed, as if paralysed for that one vital moment.

And I know what that is like. I was like it for several months!

I always regarded Venables as a pretty limited player, although a bloody good one, but when it came to dead-ball kicks, penalties and free-kicks, he was masterful. He was a great scavenger of ideas, always picking things up from those around him, asking questions and listening to anything and everything, then piecing them together - a great football mind.

But now he and Rangers began asking us serious questions for the next few minutes, piling players forward into our box. A back header from Vic Mobley flew high and wide. And then that man Bridges grazed the angle of the bar and post with a pile driver. Oz was booked for a foul on Clement and the home crowd growled. That was the way our goal-hungry centre-forward liked it. He was already waiting on an FA appearance over three bookings, but that didn't bother the big striker in the heat of battle. Then to get up the noses of the home crowd even more, he slammed home his second and our third as Kelly went down in a heap, trying to save a fierce shot from Holly. Once spilling it, Oz was there to smash the ball into an unguarded net.

At 3-1 we were surely home and hosed, but they fought like lions all the way. Osgood, in front of Ramsey, was proving that he was not only superior to Marsh, but better than anyone around. He was, as I said earlier, and before Tina sang it: Simply the best!

That goal was seconds before the half-time whistle, which saw our goals tally rise higher than a stack of Guinness Book of Records and, we were breaking plenty of them.

Rangers began the second half as they did the first, throwing everything at us, but we were always in control of the situation. In previous weeks we had squandered two-goal leads against both Burnley - in that cup match - and Derby County. In the latter match, I scored my first League goal and it was a beauty, striking a volley from about thirty yards over the head of Les Green. At that time, he might have been the shortest keeper in the country, though I am not saying the two things are connected. After the match Terry 'Tex' Hennessey, that great old Welsh wing-half, was on Grandstand and, told of one of the best prospects he'd seen in years.

I mentioned about White Hart Lane being my favourite ground, well the Baseball Ground weren't far behind it. This was my first goal for the boys in blue and, then I played against Scotland in an under-23 match there when Tony Currie and I toyed with the Jocks and, then there was another terrific performance on the Saturday three days after my England debut, well, it was not just the match it was after the combination of the build-up knowing, Revie wanted me to fail - which was so very evident - the 90 minutes against the best team in the world, three hours in La Val Bonne, three hours in The Candy Box and another special couple of hours with a beautiful blonde. Apart from being with the blonde OI was with Alan Ball and three Germans, so you might say we beat them twice that night, both and off the field. Ball was a brilliant socialiser who was as good at both sides of our game, something we both prided ourselves on.

Alan said in his book ALAN BALL written by James Mossop: Don Revie came in and I knew there was history between us after my reluctance to play for his transfer game when I was a lad at Blackpool and he was managing Leeds United. To be fair, he seemed to hold no grudge and I captained England six times for him, winning three, drawing three. High among my memories was that nigh in March 1975 when we defeated West Germany 2-0 at Wembley. With Alan Hudson and Malcolm MacDonald rampant we blitzed them, but Revie never played the three of us again in the same side.

Well that was the night and, although Alan had it wrong, because we all played against Cyprus in the following match when Malcolm scored all our goals in a 5-0 win in the European Championships. He was right, as I said, for it was certainly memorable!

As for the blonde she was merely the icing on the cake and, I could not have asked for a more beautiful bonus. So, that was my England debut, where you might say it had a little bit of everything and, you know what they say about a little bit of everything....if I had one regret on that night, well two, one was that I wished Waddington had been our manager and the other was if only Bobby Moore had been playing.

The only downside was that it was where I received my broken leg - at The Baseball Ground!

But that was still to come and in a red and white striped shirt!

I got to know Terry quite well in the States through him and Alan Hinton being team-mates at Derby at that time. We talked of that match as it was incredible one and, I remember when 2-0 up the Baseball Ground created the kind of noise that was new to me. They forced us back to a draw, only because of the crowd reaction. This would also become a good ground for me right up to when Bruce Rioch broke my leg in the year of the heat wave of '76. I mention that because having to go out each morning running the back lanes of Barlaston, I remember the first day only reaching as far as the corner of our street. The following day a little further, and so on. When I did finally get to where I set out to get, by the time I turned up for pre-season training, I found myself like a long-distance runner, very one paced. For the first few weeks of that season I was lacking sharpness and, it showed in my play. But initially, it was a different kind of discipline, something the public don't see. Again, they remember you in the pubs and clubs, but not in the back streets of Barlaston, Wedgwood and Stone.

More about that tackle later and of the part he played in our great NASL success.

There was no doubt that Osgood had not only impressed, but most definitely had played his way into the World Cup squad and, I felt that I would not be far behind him.

He must have been impressed with me, as I was covering every inch of this mud bath, skipping tackle after tackle, making it more of a 'mud lark.' He had watched me earlier on, when I had played really well against his old club Ipswich at Portman Road. I felt that I was playing really well but, sometime afterwards I watched a video of the performance and was disappointed. But Alf wasn't, as he told the waiting Fleet Street gang, "There is no limit to what this player can achieve in the game."

And the most important thing was that I was getting stronger and, the difference between when I was totally overpowered against Leeds United in that League Cup match, and here, showed that my training regime was paying great dividends.

And not long afterwards he included me, still an 18-year-old, in his provisional 40-man squad for the Mexico World Cup. Anyhow, we were not finished yet and, although Rangers piled forward, we were always dangerous on the break. On the hour, I fed Nobby who hit a raking cross towards Oz. Ian Gillard got to the ball first, only to get it all wrong and, to his horror, the ball ended at the feet of Osgood. At this moment in time this bloke didn't miss. He just collected it, gave a little shimmy and struck for his hat-trick, putting the match out of their reach: 4-1.

The Twin Towers were looming and, the script could not have been written any better. It seemed to be written in the stars and, with each match our stars were coming more and more to the front. Although Charlie was just going beyond his peak, he was still some player in possession. Bonetti was second only to Banks, Dempsey was flawless, Hutch was awesome, Nobby was saving his best for the FA Cup and I was like a little kid in a sweet shop - being the baby of the team!

It was just a matter now, of who we drew next?

Now here I was, along with Hutch, only two matches away from a Wembley FA Cup final. Again, my mind flashes back to George and John Haynes.

And, of course Bobby Robson, who could have had the both of us!

The Marsh and Osgood debate was no longer and, I had run Venables ragged. You could say that made it 6-1, but our performances warranted more than goals. It was an excellent one under the most horrendous of conditions.

Although they fought to the bitter end, Rangers FA Cup final aspirations were truly over, while ours was nearing reality. Near the end, Bridges pulled a goal back and, that is no less than he deserved for all of his hard work and endeavour; he had given our defenders a difficult time, been their best player and, worked tirelessly. Bridges was a big part of the Chelsea that was being reborn with this new team, before Osgood came along. I liked him as a player and a man.

If Ron Harris had pockets in his shorts, Marsh was in one of them. The same can't be said of Mobley, who could not come to terms with Osgood. Cooke found enough space to cause havoc. Houseman was making the FA Cup his main event and, Hollins as always, ran forever. All in all, it was a brilliant performance, a fantastic day out for our fans that took all of us another step closer to Wembley. On this day, Osgood showed Ramsey that he was head and shoulders above Marsh however, what did he have to do to show the England manager he was better than Astle?

He got chosen in the World Cup squad on the strength of this performance, which was also not only flawless but breath-taking.

There was not much more Osgood could do to prove his worth to us and, with the ever-improving Hutchinson alongside him, they were forging an awesome partnership. Between them, they simply had almost everything and, that made it so easy for us in midfield. You could pick them out blindfolded. Osgood could score goals out of any situation, whether in the air or on the floor, where he simply glided across any conditions and, this day proved it. His goals were classics, and, nothing was beyond him, headers, half-volleys, volleys, curlers and, of course, benders and, he and I went on plenty of those!

What Ramsey had told the media about me would soon become absurd, but that was still to come, although I touched on it much earlier, a three-year walk into international wilderness was a bit out of order and, something I believe led to Ramsey's downfall. Firstly he got rid of our wingers and, then Colin Todd and me. And in the end they were three massive mistakes, mistakes that eventually saw him sacked and, keeping in mind his decision to play Astle in front of Osgood that made it four.

If I wanted to dig deep I could muster up a few more, but the problem was like with Sexton winning those two trophies, which were massive, considering what he took over, winning sometimes clouds directors and supporters judgments and, I think you'll see that with Chelsea's latest Champions League success. It was a bigger robbery than my mate Tommy Wisbey, only he got caught!

So we were one step away from Wembley and I celebrated by going to my favourite all-time restaurant Alexandre with my girlfriend Maureen, mum, dad and pal Tony Davis, only this time the owner,

Camilla was even more delighted to see us. His first match was at Burnley and even he was catching the bug. He and the other boys (waiters) loved the players and every time we left the place the story book thickened. Each waiter had their very own pin-up boy, with Webby being on more than one of their bedroom walls, I can only imagine. David was "Very Butch" as he was screamed across the floor on many occasions and, he loved the attention. In Alexandre it was all good clean fun and a laugh a minute, except for when Oz and I were waiting on a call from all of those clubs wanting to sign us, but that was three-and-half- years down the road.

The funniest night was when the boys were down there after stealing Pans People from the BBC studios at White City after terrorising every artist on Top of the Pops. They still play OUR Blue is the Colour at Stamford Bridge and I am certain they have no "rights" to do so. They shouldn't anyway. They should not be allowed to play out song, one, because it is not theirs and two, it was not made for that club. It was made for our team. My blood boils when I hear it on, if I go to a match or on BBC Match of the Day and, I bet the Russian don't even know anything about the history of it all. If you don't, it was made for the 1972 League Cup final and, was to be the reason for our break-up. The match not the record, the record got to Number Five in the charts, where we were ten places lower in the First Division. It was published by Larry Page on the Penny Farthing label and once again, like them playing it before every home match we never got a farthing, let alone a penny, for our efforts, once again. But, again, all we have are the great memories of doing so. The song reminds me of the music selected to play at a funeral as they carry the coffin out.

The only problem was they never had a coffin big enough for Alan Hudson and Peter Osgood.

But back in Alexandre, everything tasted so much sweeter and, from that night my time looking forward to the FA Cup final in my first season was like walking on the Moon. This was a little different from drinking in the Man in the Moon, which stood on the corner of Park Walk School, where I began my football career. That tiny little school playground was the breeding ground for every young player in Chelsea. Mr. Robertson was responsible for our year and, we won all our matches at Eelbrook Common which stands opposite Fulham Broadway and at the bottom of Wandsworth Bridge Road.

I heard years later that Suggs frequented such a school. I like him and, met him at the Bridge one day and introduced him to my Book Launch of The Working Man's Ballet which was held at The House of Commons, with Tony Banks as the host and, he did it brilliantly. I was to have many an enjoyable lunch with Tony at The House, even though I can't stand the smell of Politicians, but Tony was different, he was certainly, no doubt, one of the chaps.

But as I say, it was now time to relax and enjoy ourselves now we were at Wembley.

I had to keep pinching myself, that within twenty-odd weeks I had reached the FA Cup final, been selected for the England under-23s and, without me knowing at this time there was much more to come. The only problem was that it wasn't all going to be good.

I mentioned the pub nearest my school, which I only used once or twice, so for you Chelsea fans now, here was the Chelsea Football Club Pub Guide....But first there, was only one night spot and that was the one and only, The Cromwellian, which we frequented after 11pm. Our main afternoon watering hole was The Town House, which is now a recording studio. Others were Susans in Beauchamp Place, The Green Rooms in Sloane Square and, years on, my pal young Frank Frazer's (Mad Frankie's son) place, The Tin Pan Alley in Denmark Street.

There was always a terrific blend of my favourite players, friends and family. There would be Oz, Chris Garland, Sponge, Eddie, Johnny Boyle, CC, Leslie May, Tony Davis and George Mason; a great mixture of all that was great about Chelsea. My best mates all earned better money than me. Leslie was a greengrocer, Bobby worked at Stowells of Chelsea and Tony Davis was a tipper-lorry driver. They would all have loved to have been a part of our side, but this was the nearest they came to it and, like I said earlier, Bobby could have made it but he was not fortunate enough to have my father to guide him.

Not only did we have the best players and socialisers, we had in Harry Heart, the absolute best bartender you would ever have been served by and, I mean anywhere in the world.

Heart is gone, along with The Cromwellian, and was last seen in a bar in Brighton.

They might both be gone, but certainly never forgotten.

Nowadays, stories of players swilling champagne at over £200 a bottle - remembering in our day you could get a bottle of Moet for £5 - meant that both the players and the fans could afford it and, more importantly, drink it together.

After matches we would use mainly The Red Anchor - which was on the next block to our school - and, would have a pint in our hand whilst Liverpool were still hammering away at their opponents goal at the Kop End. It was a great little pub where we were once joined by Jane Seymour, who was then married to Dickie Attenborough's son. She was something a little special and, so it proved by going on to be included in the catalogue of the James Bond leading ladies. She is now Medicine Woman that incredibly successful American TV show.

Had Jane been my nurse in St Barts, for the whole of 1998, I might have stayed in longer, especially knowing my wife was soon to be on her toes. She could have been my medicine woman all day long....
The Red Anchor is now the Sporting Page, where young Frank sometimes frequents.

I wonder if Frank realises what a favour I did him by telling his father that he would be committing football suicide by joining Leeds United instead of Chelsea!

Another famous pub - although that was before I got into the side - was The Ifield Tavern. You'd walk down from the ground and turn first left past Brompton Cemetery. It was a very popular place run by Bill Tidy. This was about a hundred yards along from Billings Road where we sometimes used The Fox and Pheasant. Leonard Rossiter lived down there along with Britt Ekland, who I saw the other week at the NEC (March 2011). I asked her about my hairdresser friend, Steve August in Sloane Square, but she seemed to have lost not only her looks but her memory. However, she was, on her day, as beautiful a woman you'll ever set eyes on. She was no doubt the most beautiful of Rod Stewart's scrapbook of Blondes Have More Fun. Although according to her their relationship was far from fun, for she totally detests him right now. Rod should worry!

As for Rigsby I was driving through the Fulham Road one morning on the way to London Colney, our Arsenal training ground and, he pulled out. The traffic was horrendous. As I sat in the traffic I looked up and saw him sitting waiting to get out of that turning. I couldn't help but start laughing as I waved him out. He signalled a 'thank you' to me and, as he pulled out he stalled his Volvo, I think it was. He looked up at me and gave me the look he used to give to Miss Jones and, waved me on as he shook his head. But I would not move until he got out. I chuckled all the way up through Baker Street to the A1 and onwards. I loved him, for he was a complete and utter genius.
They really don't make them like him anymore, much like players!

And as for Baker Street, every time I turned the corner outside the station, I'd wind down my window and, turn Gerry Rafferty up full volume, those crossing would not know what was going on. Gerry sadly died about a year before this book will be published, but again, his music and, that song in particular will live on with me.
Only the English collared on (to Baker Street), but that said, there wasn't many!

These were the pubs closest to the ground. Well there were them and, then if you stayed in Fulham there was The Adelaide, The Imperial and The Lord Palmerston, the pub ran by the Mancini family, who were better known for the boxing knowledge and involvement. Tony would run the corner for many a big name fighter.

One night I recall seeing Terry Downes fall through the door hanging on to Joe Frazier, or was it the other way round?

From the Worlds End, where the pub stood - and still does - there was The Wetherby where the Rolling Stones would play on the odd occasion. They lived just across the road from that flat my mother died in - and I got .

The Wetherby was also responsible for Ian Hutchinson's first ever alcoholic drink as a Chelsea player, although he wasn't yet in the first team. He walked in not knowing there were such places and when falling out, the last thing I remember was watching him chase a number 31 bus up the Kings Road. It was not long before he was chasing more than buses, because no woman was safe with Hutch around.

This made us fair prey for Fleet Street. A lot of people, including those around one of the most famous streets in the world, said that my generation of players were a waste. The problem was that we had so much talent to waste. Perhaps we were seen in terms of presence rather than achievement. The Chelsea team of '70 crystallized the era and, more importantly excited and, had those supporters flocking through those great big blue gates opposite The Stamford Bridge Arms – the one where I first met Danny Gillen.

This was no doubt he most exciting era of Chelsea. I went there for a match this season 2011/12 and, at 3.30 walked past the Shed End and, I thought I was walking through the cemetery next door.

Some years later Bobby Moore's son, Dean, ran this pub and, only last year 28.7.2011 he was found dead in his flat. They documented that he had a medical problem and, probably died of natural causes. My son could tell you more of the truth though. He was due to meet with Dean, who was 43, only a couple of days prior to his death. My son thought the world of Dean as I did his father.

I don't think I'd be out of order by saying his death could have been prevented, but that is all that I can say on the matter, for one/it won't bring him back and, two/I'd rather think of his father and, all the great things the Moore name stood for.

To finish this chapter, rightfully I think, is to mention all the other places that used to love seeing us coming through their doors. Going up from the Worlds End was The Birds Nest - where I met my first wife - then The Trafalgar, which was Sponge's favourite, going further on was the pub of all pubs, The Markham Arms, where the girls would flock on a Friday night and, was my first experience of those in hot-pants, although the min-skirted young beauties would knock todays WAGs into orbit.

I think this pub took more cash than any other in England on that particular night and, I wonder if, that is why it is now a Building

Society. Going even further you'd end up at Sloane Square and The Duke of Wellington, which would one day become George's local before finding The Phene Arms. Anyhow, The Duke however was absolutely fantastic, ran by a family from Iraq, The Petros clan. Our families became very close and, they were magnificent people, who were adored by the whole of both the Hudson and Mason families.

If all those morons who talk so much about this racial had of seen us all together they just might have thought twice. Of course there is discrimination, but it is a two-way-street and, of course Don Revie was racial against Londoners, so just take it in its right context and, give more attention to those in Afghanistan than two footballers squaring up to one another - like two Nancy's - on a football field.

Eddie and George Petros were the best show in town in those days in The Duke. Anthony Hopkins, Martin Landau - Mission Impossible - could be seen there, along with Richard Green - the original Robin Hood - who I did see bring his empties back one Sunday morning. It's true, Eddie told me he'd do it on a regular basis, but I had to chuckle when I saw it for myself and, I thought we were hard-up and, it would have been even more amusing had he done such a thing in my local in Bow!

And, even though we were I cannot imagine taking it that far. I was surprised Richard Green drank in there though, because they never had a dartboard. So the Duke was the end of the line for us, although there were a few pubs scattered along the way to Buckingham Palace, but the closer I got to there and Downing Street, I got a nasty feeling of nausea. These days though, I think that those two young sons of Diana have brought a little sunshine through the windows of the Palace. Harry is an absolute credit to not the family, but those of us that live life and, put it on the line, unlike those that hide behind their wealth and watch us doing so.

As the son of Tony Kipling of the Yorkshire Regiment so boldly put to the leader of such a place:

Dear Prime Minister....

I am Marcus Kipling and I am eight years old. My dad is in the Army in the Yorkshire Regiment I am writing this letter this letter because I am angry about the wages of a soldier.

I think soldiers who go to war should get more money in their wages: they risk their lives for their country.

I get cross when I hear how much footballers and politicians get paid - do they risk their lives for their country?

Why do soldiers sometimes have to buy their own equipment?

If you are a good Prime Minister you will answer my questions.

Yours sincerely, Marcus Kipling

Let's just hope that young Marcus will one day get himself into a position where he can use his insight and guts and, like his father his bravery. But judging by the talent that I have seen get either ignored or overlooked by those inferior, I doubt it very much. It is those inferiors that do the damage, because they get themselves into such a high position and, once there see us - of which Marcus is the future - as a threat.

I would have liked to have introduced Marcus to my all-time true hero and friend, Bobby Moore, who was not only an icon but a legend beyond a legend. Have you heard the saying, "He went where no other man would ever go," well, that was Bobby, whose middle name was Chelsea. That was the Man we called God and, here was all they had to say about the sorry way he ended his life, when you look at those...

Robert Frederick Chelsea Moore, OBE 12 April 1941 - 24 February 1993 captained West Ham United for more than ten years and was also captain of the only England team to win the World Cup in 1966. He is widely regarded as one of the all-time greats of world football, and was cited by Pele as the greatest defender that he had ever played against.

He won a total of 108 caps for the England team, which at the time of his international retirement in 1973 was a national record.

After football.....Moore retired from playing professionally in 1978, and had a short relatively unsuccessful spell in football management at Eastern AA in Hong Kong, Oxford City and Southend United.

He became manager of Southend United in 1984. In his first full season, 1984–85, they narrowly avoided having to apply for re-election to the Football League amidst severe financial difficulties. However, the side was gradually rebuilt and in the 1985-86 season and, started well and were in the promotion race until the New Year before eventually finishing 9th. His successor, David Webb built upon those foundations to win promotion the following year. Moore agreed to serve on the board of the club and held this role until his death.

His life after football was eventful and difficult, with poor business dealings and his marriage ending. Many saw Moore's acceptance of a role as a columnist for the salacious tabloid newspaper, the Sunday Sport, as a sign of how low he had been FORCED to go. Moore's supporters said that the Football Association could have given a role to Moore, as the only Englishman to captain a FIFA World Cup winning team. Moore himself kept a dignified silence.

Moore joined London radio station Capitol Gold as a football analyst and commentator in 1990.

In April 1991, Moore underwent an emergency operation for suspected colon cancer, though at the time it was just reported that he had undergone an "emergency stomach operation".

On 14 February 1993, he publicly announced he was suffering from bowel and liver cancer; by this stage the cancer had spread. Three days later, he commentated on an England match against San Marino at Wembley, alongside his friend Jonathon Pearce. That was to be his final public appearance; seven days later on 24 February, at 6.36 am, he died at the age of 51.

He was the first member of the England World Cup winning side to die, the second being Alan Ball 14 years later. Moore was also outlived by the coach of the side, Harold Shepherdson, who died in September 1995, and the manager of the side, Alf Ramsey, who died in April 1999.

Bobby Moore's funeral was held on 2 March 1993 at Putney Vale Crematorium, and his ashes were buried in a plot with his father Robert Edward Moore (who died in 1978) and his mother Doris Joyce Moore, who had only died the previous year.

His former England team-mate, Jack Charlton, on a BBC documentary of Moore's life in and outside of football, said of Moore's death:

"Well, I only ever cried over two people, Billy Bremner and Bob. (long pause) He was a lovely man."

On 28 June 1993 his memorial service was held in Westminster Abbey attended by all the other members of the 1966 World Cup Team. He was only the second sportsman to be so honoured, the first being the West Indian cricketer Sir Frank Worrell - the Dean of Westminster.

That was my friend Bobby and, how he was treated after all he did for those at the Football Association, yet they live off all that he not only did, but achieved. Whilst he was ignored by them under house arrest in Bogota and, then sweating through that Mexico heat in such fantastic style, they were having a fully all-inclusive month in the Mexican sunshine.

Yet once he had given his all, they disregarded him and allowed him to go through all that you have just read about. Can you imagine Germany allowing Beckenbauer undergo such humiliation? I think not!

There is one thing that comes to the top of such murky waters after so long and, that is those at the FA do not deserve any better than what they are served up on the field, but the shameful thing is they don't care, whereas it hurts those that do. However, with another European Championship coming up, as I finish, all the wrong people will be packing their bags and filling their pockets with it all coming out of the kitty, that kitty that has made Soho Square a complete laughing stock - just as it did Lancaster Gate, in my day.

And, just as I go over this Roy Hodgson, the newly appointed England manager has said, that he is not too bothered about The Euros. That's nice, because, if he's not, why should the rest of us be and, I'm not even an England supporter, in fact, quite the opposite. I'm still laughing at our failure throughout the Seventies when I was banned for some of it and, we failed to qualify, so, as I say, be prepared for another early aeroplane ride home.

18 THE WORLD CUP WAS MY LOBSTER

Chelsea 1969/70 season

From Wikipedia, the free encyclopedia

The 1969-70 season, was Chelsea Football Club's 56th of competitive football, and the club's 43rd in the English top flight.

The club began the season having not signed a single player. Defender Paddy Mulligan, who joined in October for £17,500, was the sole recruit during the campaign. Bobby Tambling, still Chelsea's record goal scorer with 202 goals, had his final season with the club, signing for Crystal Palace on loan in January before leaving permanently in May.

The season proved to be a success, as the club won the FA Cup for the first time in their history with a hard-fought replayed win over Leeds United. The club also finished 3rd in the First Division, their highest placing since 1965. Chelsea were for a time in title contention, although an indifferent start and heavy defeats at the hands of rivals Leeds and Everton ultimately ended their chances.

Midfielders John Hollins and Peter Houseman did not miss a game. Hollins was also voted Chelsea's Player of the Year by the fans. Peter Osgood finished as top scorer, with 31 goals in all competitions, and became the last man to date to score in every round of the FA Cup. The average home attendance for the season was 40,342.

As you read, John Hollins was the Chelsea Player of the Year, yet I was runner-up in the Football Writers Footballer of the Year behind Billy Bremner, something that tells a story of its own. If anyone should have won that ward at the Bridge it was, of course Peter

Osgood, for as you just read he scored 31 goals in all competitions and, that was apart from setting many others up for his strike partner, Ian Hutchinson and, also knocking defenders about with his fiery will-to-win attitude that went beyond belief at times. He and Hutchinson were tailor made for one another, reminding me a lot of Starsky and Hutch, who run around the town in a red and white mustang, whereas Osgood cruised from Epsom to Chelsea in a black X-J6. Had it come to a fist fight I think the other couple would have been in big trouble....

The spring of '70, River Phoenix was born. Jack Walker - the one in Coronation Street - died. Raymond Douglas Davies, born on the same day as me, changed the lyric of his song Lola from Coca Cola to Cherry Cola to avoid a BBC ban.

We were to play yet again in the London area, this time Watford, whose devoted fan Elton John was making a big impression on me, beginning with Your Song. The venue was very much to my liking, as White Hart Lane, was the place I was in love with at such a young age.

We were immediately installed as the bookmakers favourites as Manchester United and Leeds United were paired together. This one would go the distance and further, as George Best looked for his first FA Cup final appearance. I often wonder if the incredible Chelsea and Leeds United final was meant to be?

The hatred between the two teams was on a par with not only both sets of supporters, but Clough and Revie.

It was like a red hot local derby although we were two hundred miles apart!

So the dream final that everyone wanted with Charlie, Ossie and me against George Best, Bobby Charlton and Denis Law was still on the cards.

This was the one that caught the imagination of all football lovers.

It's amazing how two of the world's greatest ever players, John Haynes and George Best, never walked out from that most famous of tunnels for the Holy Grail of cup football. They did more or less everything else, but I bet they would have swapped anything and everything for an FA Cup final appearance.

John, some of his England caps and, George some of his Miss Worlds!

John actually dated Petula Clarke around the time he became the face of Brylcreem, taking over from another great, Denis Compton.

It seemed that I was the only Chelsea player who wanted something different, a final against Leeds United and, I wanted it because they thought they were invincible. This was what I wanted and, it made this match all the more compelling. That Mean Machine from up north against the southern Playboys, or as some say, Southern Softies. So we had more than one point to prove here and we showed over those two long matches that we were anything but a soft touch, in fact, quite the opposite, but there was the final hurdle to get over.

It looked a foregone conclusion, but people had forgotten that Watford had knocked out both Liverpool and Stoke City along the way.

My all-time favourite photograph of Dave Mackay, letting Billy know just who is the boss.

I loved playing against Billy, because like Ball, his standards were so high. You know what I said about players of such a size.

It was something ironic that I received a letter whilst in hospital saying that Billy had died. It was from a Chelsea fan, who said something about beating Leeds again. The Leeds/Chelsea thing of those times lives on and always will, even though Billy's probably drinking with Oz and Hutch high above us.

Cooke and Hudson against Giles and Bremner, whom I had a score to settle with after the Scot had just edged me out of the Football Writers Footballer of the Year Award, was what I looked forward to more than anything. But, like talking or writing about it at this moment, as if it was going to be an easy ride and, although our confidence was as high as The Oxo Building on the Embankment, we still had to finish the job, that meaning, the job of reaching the Twin Towers. You hear of FA Cup banana skins and, there was always that being the outcome, however, it never entered our minds that we would not be on that bus taking us down Wembley Way come May, the month that would hopefully lead into Peter Osgood, Peter Bonetti and yours truly boarding that aeroplane for Mexico and, what a prize to take on board with us....On top of everything, the carrot of such a final was something out of the ordinary. George had never played in a final, Bobby and Denis had of course, but still they had a far tougher test than us. It was no secret that with that Manchester United team running out of legs, this would be the last chance that these three had of playing in an FA Cup final together. But we could not concern ourselves about their semi-final, for we had to be completely focused on Watford. Man for man it was absolutely no contest, but as I have said about that banana skin, no football match has ever been won on a team sheet. My favourite ground was full to the rafters and, had this ground been able to hold double or treble its capacity I am sure it would have.

Like you might expect we started as we left off at Loftus Road - even though Rangers pulled back a late goal - we were very much on the front foot. We began to batter Watford from the very first whistle. I have since watched the opening and, it was as I remember it so well, for the match started explosively and, once again the pitch was a quagmire - making porridge look like soup. White Hart Lane that day, made Loftus Road and Selhurst Park look like the first day at Royal Ascot. In the first 10 minutes, it looked like we would run up a cricket score. In our very first attack I went through, after swapping passes with Nobby and, only a Watford toenail stopped me giving us a first-minute lead. That surely would have been the quickest goal in the history of FA Cup semi-finals?

I scooped up the ball, placed it on the tiny patch next to the corner flag and, looked up to see our Fleet Air Arm, David Webb, our express train, chest bulging out; Dempsey, making himself look taller; Hutch, a hungry looking mean machine and, Osgood, a man that just stood out in any crowded goalmouth. I chose to clip it into the near post, giving it just enough air so that any defender deciding get into that area first would struggle defending it. You have to whip it in where the defender has two options, an own-goal or another corner, however I was relying on Dempsey and, that was the way it turned out, as he arrived bang on time, as did Webb at the other post as if like clockwork, sliding down to put us in front.

That end of the ground was going crazy as The Shed, who had been magnificent throughout this amazing cup run, went totally ballistic. This was the goalmouth where he (DJ Webb) put us in front on that first night that started all of this for me. Webby was absolutely brilliant at coming in late, strong and quickly, making it almost impossible to defend against. He was like an oncoming Manchester to Euston Inter-City rattler, only as I've mentioned before, he always arrived on time. The floodgates would surely open?

But it didn't work out that way and, I can't to this day tell you why. I at first thought it was that sauna the day before, but that was something all in the mind. Their big midfield player, Terry Garbett, hit a long hopeful shot that seemed to bounce awkwardly in front of Peter Bonetti. This was on a pitch that you could have mistaken for Brighton Beach, with the ball bouncing like a beach ball before squirming into the corner of our net. We were stunned. The Shed were stunned, and, I think even Watford were.

The next and, last time I saw Garbett was when my Seattle Sounders side played at New York and he was on their bench. It was one of the things that had me dazed. There were so many fantastic players from all over the world - and then there was Terry, which had me thinking immediately, 'was it because of that particular goal?'

How else would the New York Cosmos have heard of him?

He would not get any goals like that in the Big Apple because their pitch was Astroturf, which meant every bounce was a true one. But that was the great part of our game. Well it was in those days - you don't get pitches like that anymore - and many of today's players would question playing on them.

Shortly after they scored, the tiny Scullion put their other winger away, his name was Owen. I'd never heard or seen of him before or since. He skipped past Webby, who was not the greatest of defensive right-backs, before getting a cross in. It looked for a moment like it would evade Catty and fall for Barry Endean, who got the goal that knocked Liverpool out in the previous round. But this time our keeper did not have to worry about any dodgy bounces. As usual, he claimed it into his chest, making a difficult catch look easy. I only ever saw this in Banks and Jennings, although years later a certain Peter Fox, another great Stoke City keeper, comes to mind. Making the art of goalkeeping look easy was no different from making pass look the same, where most of today's players make it look as if they had just pieced the most incredible jigsaw puzzle together.

Simplicity is genius - springs to mind!

That was the last time they really bothered us. It actually sprung us into life. I suppose like taking one on the jaw and, then realising that your opponent was no mug - you react. I smashed a shot that their keeper Mike Walker dropped on. Webby with another one of his great runs burst through to set up Nobby, but he hit the crowd. We were going through them like a knife through melting butter. Houseman again went close, although he should have scored. As Walker saved, I looked at Nobby and, he smiled that innocent smile of his, as if apologising. Not long after, he would be making up for it, but for now, the half-time whistle blew and, we walked off looking like we had just taken a massive blow to the chin, the Cooper and Ali scenario comes to mind, for we were stunned. You know when you hear the saying they'll be happy to hear that half-time whistle, well that applied here.

Both semi-finals were level - although it never entered our minds at that particular time - much to the surprise of everyone who was inside White Hart Lane. Those 15 minutes in the Tottenham dressing room seemed the longest of my life, until I reached the Royal London Hospital, but that was many years and ups and downs away. Players were edgy, wondering if the next 45 minutes were going to see us involved with one of the greatest FA Cup upsets of all time - that banana skin.

Sexton spoke but I am certain nobody listened to a word. We just knew we had to get back out there and finish them off, just as we had done with all our earlier opponents.

Now this brings me to the most important point up throughout this entire book. If you studied our overall FA Cup run and, that is before we got into Europe, where we were involved in a couple of epic encounters.

In our second half and late on in matches we were always finishing by far the stronger, now the point is, we were preceding our reputations all the way through this, for every man and his dog knew us as Good Time Charlie's, Playboys and, any other unpleasant name that could be aimed at us and, yeah, I cannot give you the reason why, but we had an inbuilt substance or ability that cannot be summed up totally. No man can tell the next just what we had. All I can say, through being an insider, is that there was something between us, whether it was because we all had something on each other, as if to say "if you're going to go out like you do, go out on a limb when we need you."

We could dig deeper than any JCB.

If you looked at the pitches we played on to get to the final, at Crystal Palace, QPR and, now White Hart Lane in London, whilst Burnley was no snooker table, you would truly not believe that we could play such exciting football and, score so many stunning goals. We beat Palace and Rangers by four and, now we were on our way to the final with a five-goal show, but you would not have thought so at half-time.

I can only imagine those listening millions on their transistor radios were as stunned as everyone at the Lane?

I know our dressing room looked like we had been watching the latest Stephen Spielberg movie and, I don't mean Jurassic Park.

Jack Charlton was in the other semi-final.

However, what we were about to serve up was a feast that Pepe in Alexandre would have been proud of, although the Hors D'oeuvres were a little stringy. But that was soon to be forgotten because this main dish was not served cold - that was waiting for Leeds United - it was piping hot stuff from the moment Gordon Hill put his lips to his whistle to start the second half.

It was really quite impressive, mostly brilliant and sometimes breath-taking.

Watford's star player that day was that tiny little winger, Stewart Scullion. He was a lively and tricky customer who had given Eddie McCreadie a hard time. The Eddie of old would have nailed him early, but I think he was in decline. Eddie was at one time the greatest full-back in the world. That was undoubtedly because of Tommy Docherty, who constantly reminded him that any opponent's right-winger (including Sir Stanley Matthews) should not cause Chelsea any trouble at all. Eddie was clued into what Tommy meant, Thou Shall Not Pass.

Eddie cost £5,000 from East Stirling, what an incredible signing!

The buzzer went and we were on our feet as if it were a new day. Bang, bang, bang, we tore at them like a raging bull. We started exactly the same as the first half, only this time we didn't take our foot off the gas. Had it been a boxing match, it would not have gone into the last quarter-of-an-hour. The lethargy that hung over us in the dressing room had disintegrated. The fatigue that I saw in that dressing room, for the first time in that cup run, was gone. It was like a cloud was lifted from our backs, it was sheer imagination. Now it was reality and Watford would suffer.

The 16th century swordsman had a saying,

"No matter what state your mind is in, make the cut."

It was if he was talking to us. We must have confused our manager at the restart because we were a different proposition and, I began feeling sorry for this team in yellow shirts. We played the kind of football that we knew in our hearts only we could play. The only time I remember a performance so impressive was against Bruges a year later when that swordsman, it seemed, had spoken again, however the Belgians were a far, far superior side than Watford even though they did knock both Stoke City and Liverpool out in previous rounds.

We battered Watford into submission with sublime football and movement. Charlie sent over a high cross and I witnessed Hutch hanging in the air, almost in slow motion, as only he could. Like all great headers of the ball, he had that gift. The ball flew from his head like a steam hammer. Walker threw himself after it like a maniac and somehow scrambled it clear. The defence that found it easy in comparison before the break couldn't cope with it all. We were everywhere with balls being pinged in and out, back and forward, and over the top. We were now ripping poor Watford apart. Their brave, energetic chasing had now become increasingly anxious.

I remember being all over the pitch, looking to put people in. Oz, was always my first option, Hutch was next and then Nobby. Charlie was also now dominating with that great art of dribbling. When he was like this I felt like a spectator. He was majestic. I could sense that the game was ours and it was just a matter of time. I also knew that the next time we hit the front, we would stay there and, on the hour, we got our just reward. After jinking in and out of a couple of challenges, including a nutmeg, I found Nobby alone on the left. He gathered the ball, sidestepped his full-back and hit a cross that Oz couldn't resist. The big No 9 kept up his record of scoring in every round with a powerful header. He was one of only eight players ever to do so.

Hutch, alongside his mate, hammered the rebound back into Walker's goal, where Oz clung like a giant octopus that had been unfortunately caught in a fisherman's net. The breakthrough had been made and, as at Palace and QPR, we could taste blood. Our game was so strong, it was exhilarating. Like all great teams, we could punish mistakes and make the cut. In the first half, the switching of the Watford wingers seemed to unbalance Eddie and Webby. They were now non-existent. Now, it was our wide players causing havoc, with Charlie and Nobby giving their very own renditions of how the game should be played and on a completely different level.

This was The Working Man's Ballet played on such a surface made a mockery of all clichés.

I just loved chasing the game, getting the ball and feeding such players. The ball was still whizzing through the sand dunes of a pitch and, I can recall jumping over tackle after tackle. Then we hit them again, bang!

A fantastic solo effort from Nobby as good as booked our one-way ticket to Wembley. He turned three defenders inside out before lashing a shot inside Walker's near post. It was nearly as important as his first goal at Burnley when for the first time we were in Cup trouble. It was also one that he regarded as his best in a Chelsea shirt.

Hutchinson was by now winding everyone up, no matter what shirt they were wearing. I believe it had just hit him that in 12 short months he had come from Burton Albion to the brink of an FA Cup final. This was quite extraordinary. My father was right and, Bobby Robson wrong.

By hitting and hurting defenders he was also making space for the likes of Charlie and me to run into, although he was never aware of this. He was as unselfish as any player could be. When you look at people like Marsh, who would go hiding after being stunned by a Harris tackle and, then look at Hutch, you knew just how important he was to us. If Chopper hit Hutch he would suffer the consequences. Once, Sammy Chapman (a proper hard-nut at Nottingham Forest) hit Hutch and within minutes he was stretchered off. Hutch walked alongside him with a broken arm.

Defenders knew they were doomed when they came across a fired-up Ian Hutchinson and, right now that was what Watford were experiencing. It was as if they wanted this match to end. We showed them no mercy and, unlike the first half, we were not letting them back in this match for a second time. I looked around and it reminded me of one of those war films in the Deep South. There were bodies everywhere, bodies that did not want to be there and, as I just said about that "something" the most terrible thing for those poor yellow shirted soldiers we were not unloading our guns or pulling in our bayonets.

We had been scoring for absolute fun and the taste, like the aroma of Pepe's cooking was still swirling around White Hart Lane and, we were still hungry, unfortunately for Elton John and his players. Even a Pinball Wizard, A Rocket Man and Benny and the Jets would not be of any help for Elton on this particular day.

And looking back you might say it was Goodbye Yellow Brick Road from I Guess why they called us the Blues.....sorry Elton!

What did it no doubt for them was that we hit them three times in six minutes and, the last of them made it five and, that was Nobby in the 79th minute, that was just four minutes after Hutch put the match a little, you might say, out of their reach.

Yeah Hutch was a handful and more, he was tough, real tough and, you simply did not mess with him. I remember vividly going back to the Bridge with Stoke City for, funnily enough, A League Cup tie and Hutch hit John Farmer from a corner, which left our keeper completely motionless.

As we walked away I said to Hutch, "What the hell was that all about?"

He glared at me and replied, "Tell him the next time he comes for a cross he'll get it again," and he said it in a way and with a look as if he'd never seen me before. That was Hutch, who wasn't a bully, he was nowhere near John Farmer who stood 6feet 2inches in stocking feet!

The game was now beyond their reach. As Osgood fed me, I played it into Hutch on the edge of their box. He then turned his man, changing direction by feigning to go inside and after twisting his body, like a hungry python, he lost his marker before unleashing a stunning drive. The big question that followed was, "Just how great Ian Hutchinson would have become if he hadn't been too brave for his own good?"

His injuries were all self-inflicted.

His bravery was on the edge of madness!

His love for a battle was almost over-saturated. He was definitely the man you'd want to be in the trenches with. Like me, in many ways, he lived to the extreme. His love for a drink was the same for a woman. He wanted it all and, he wanted it now, almost as if making up for lost time.

Ridiculous!

He was only in his early twenties. When he arrived at the Bridge he was a teetotaller and, went home straight from training. Now you might say that we "had bred a monster."

Without Hutch, our Chelsea team was not the same. Oz was not the same. It was like that dumb girl in the elevator - though she was far from dumb - in the magnificent movie Jerry McGuire, where she signalled, 'You make me complete.'

That was how important Hutch was for his strike partner.

Ten minutes from the end, with Watford screaming for the final whistle, we scored our fifth and again, it was Houseman who finished it in great style. It was the fourth goal in a devastating spell of attacking football. It was football at its best on a pitch that wasn't worthy of it. I could see openings in their defence that you wouldn't get in the Biggest Whore House in Texas. They brought on another defender to try to take the sting out of our play, but that made no difference at all. We were getting stronger as they got weaker. Now this wasn't bad considering we were basically a team of Playboys - well, eight of us!

Charlie got the ball wide, played a one-two with me and then Hutch picked out Nobby on the edge of their area; this time on the right-hand side of the box. He turned his man delightfully and crashed another stunner past poor Walker. We scored yet again, only for it to be disallowed, so instead of six we settled for another five. This had become a lot easier than the match we should have had in the car park the day before, but only in the last 45 minutes. However, it was only easy because of that first-half shock.

It was a shock that shook us into another life.

Looking back the closest thing to that was the morphine handset, where one moment you're in so much pain and, then with a long press of this button you were off the runway and taking towards those clouds, pain free.

At this moment in time though I don't think even that would have saved or eased such a pain for Watford, in fact, there was nothing that possibly could. Looking at it another way again, I imagined sitting in their dressing room afterwards, because not only had your Wembley dream come to an abrupt end, but you were sitting there wishing you had got knocked out in the third round.

Much like a boxer who had taken a pounding for fifteen rounds when he'd been better getting knocked out in the first, why take all of that pain, if you're out anyway?

Our fans were singing of Wembley. They had been there three years earlier to see their side beaten by Spurs, but this was different. This side were hungrier and, we'd make sure we'd get to bed a lot earlier than that team. We had Hutch, who not long ago was at Cambridge United, and was now not just going to turn up for the showpiece, he didn't do things in halves. And then there was me. I was the new kid on the block who had just been given the keys to all the pubs in the Kings Road. I was heady at the thought of reaching the Twin Towers in my first full season.

Little did I know then that the Man had other ideas!

I still cannot remember an FA Cup Semi-final of such dominance.

Six would have maybe reflected the difference between the two sides or, based on the second-half performance, maybe 10?

That night I celebrated in the pub next to my uncle George's flat in Fulham, before taking our party, as usual, to Alexandre. I remember it well for not only reaching my incredible dream, but for seeing my first love Irene for the very last time. She came to say hello and disappeared, just like Watford, in those last breath taking 45 minutes. The last time I cried was over her leaving me and, now I was soon to do it again in the very same place. But for now, it was the furthest thing from my mind.

That tragic day at the Hawthorns was still to come.

The following day Nobby and I were guests on The Big Match with Brian Moore. I wore a Squire Shop suit and, obviously looked like I had had a much later night than my mate. But that was understandable and, this time I was expected to do so and, I was going to make sure everyone in the Kings Road knew it.

At the start you explain the steps you take in our game, getting in the door at your local club, signing apprentice, then professional, then first team football and, the dream of an FA Cup final and, I had just achieved that. Now for an FA Cup final against either George, Bobby and Denis or Johnny and Billy all of them absolutely fantastic players and, had someone told me I'd been playing against the likes of these players at Wembley whilst sitting on that bus travelling to White Hart Lane, of all places, way back in September, I would have thought them absolutely crazy.

But all of this now seemed crazy, for this to happen to both Hutch and I, did not make any sense.

I began the book by telling you that there would be many twists and turns and, we are only at my nineteenth birthday. I had overcome some eerie moments already, some that just might have gone the other way.

I cannot give you any comparisons and tell you of anything or any place I'd have rather have been.

As I told you, I had celebrated by going to where else but Alexandre with Maureen and the rest of my family and, although I frequented this place on so many occasions, I cannot remember anything about this one. Was it because everything had happened so quickly?

I can only give that as the reason, for I was buzzing, whilst at the same time a little numb. My head was filled with all that had happened over the last few short months. But the strangest thing was that they had flown. The great euphoria was something new after experiencing so much over those days and weeks leading up to all of this.

I thought of George in the other semi-final and, hoped that although I badly wanted to face Leeds United that if he could have made it what an occasion it would be. The build-up alone had so much potential, as did the celebrations. There was one thing for sure had we met George, Denis and Bobby whatever the outcome there would have been hugs all round at the final whistle, whereas with Leeds United…

And then I thought of John Haynes and, how after all of his magnificent career he never did what I had done in such a short space of time.

I had also achieved something that no other local Chelsea boy had ever done. When you looked over east side of London you'd find dozens of them, but not from this neck of the woods.

Why?

I am not usually lost for an answer, whether right or wrong, but here I am. I recall a local lad called Johnny Key playing for Fulham and, later Coventry, which was probably the Jimmy Hill connection?

That's about it, so this was a little different, in fact, something pretty fantastic and, a far cry from that unbelievable day at Southampton.

The big question right now was who would come through the other semi-final, but in all fairness, I could not have given two monkey's, as I sat back enjoying the moment in the greatest restaurant I'd ever set foot in.

There were three League matches that followed in quick succession and we won them all and, I suppose that is what happens when the pressure is off?

And incredibly, we were still in with a shout for the First Division title.

Against Stoke City a fantastic Charlie Cooke strike saw Gordon Banks wondering if the Scot was Brazilian. It was struck brilliantly. A vicious arrowed low volley was hit with such venom, although you could put it down to brilliant timing. Charlie now works with Rivelino and talks about him as if revering him, I'm afraid that he underestimates himself.

I can only think that in that match Tony Waddington was obviously making notes about the player for whom he one day pay a record £250,000. On the Saturday, Hutch weighed in with two goals that beat Manchester United in front of 61,479 at the Bridge. The gates were closed by the police 40 minutes before kick-off. Now can you imagine what sort of ground we would have needed had we signed George?

He was their most impressive player that day. United, you could see, were coming to the end of their tether, with some very important legs beginning to buckle. This was a sign that they could not get past Leeds in the other semi-final, which went to two replays. Also at that time, George was under more and more intense media pressure and, it was beginning to show. He was losing those dashing good looks of his, or was it that he could see that his club were falling apart?

That night in Benfica, where he tortured them, seemed light years away.

Without George, like Oz without Hutch, Peters without Lee, Morecambe without Wise and Rodgers without Hart, Clough without Taylor and my Crown Royal without Ginger Ale, United would never be the same. Players like the brilliant Pat Crerand, the irreplaceable Bobby Charlton and, the stunning Denis Law were all coming to the end of fantastic careers. We would surely take over from Manchester United, if only we could sign George!

Now my thoughts were with my father, Bill, wondering what he must have thought about both Hutch and I reaching the final, for it was he who discovered Hutch and, he had been adamant that I would make it to the top - despite what everyone in Chelsea thought. Bill was a little different from all of those he played with in the area, if only from coming from Walham Green, in Fulham. He was most certainly his own man. He was a little bit of a loner in many ways and, a little mysterious in more ways than one, coming from a completely different upbringing from those in Chelsea.

Although there was a small dividing line between Chelsea and Fulham - that line being in the middle of the road on Stamford Bridge - people were different. They rarely mixed and, the Worlds End was a place where a stranger could be spotted a mile off. Today, it seems, it is the other way round?

The memory of walking through those glass doors at White Hart Lane will stay with me forever. It was like winning the lottery - I can only imagine - and being on your way to pick up your cheque.

As like Lionel Richie would sing - Oh what a feeling!

I walked out into the air and was faced by several journalists, all who I knew from my days socialising in Fleet Street. Their one big question was "Who do you want at Wembley?" and, without hesitation I said, "It's got to be Leeds." They told us that they were in extra-time and, heading for a replay. I could not have given a damn, all I knew was I was playing in the 1970 FA Cup final, in my first season.

Had I won the Football Writers award, the FA Cup and boarded that plane to Mexico for that '70 World Cup, it would surely have been the most amazing first season by any young lad in the history of the game. As Arthur Daley would say to Terry McCann, "The world is your lobster, young Terence." Well had my name been Terry this would have fitted perfectly.

Dennis Waterman was in the box with me on the day that Bobby Moore accepted my invitation and talked me into going to Seattle.

Lovely bloke Terry, I mean Dennis!

I met Den at a Luncheon at the London Hilton, where we were both guests on the same table, and we cracked it off immediately. He is one of the "greats" of our times both on and off the screen.

Despite the fact that we were smashing all scoring records in the FA Cup, our League form was not suffering; we were still impressive and, had an outside chance of the championship. To add to what I just said, maybe the League and FA Cup Double. That would have been a season that one could only make up.

I scored only my second League goal of the season at Highfield Road, the home of Coventry City. I clipped the ball over the outstretched body of Bill Glazier, after running from the edge of our penalty area without anybody else touching it. It was pretty similar to the one Maradona scored against England, only I ran further, though his finish was something a little more magical and, it was against my mate, Peter Shilton - I jest!

Whenever I returned there (Coventry), I was reminded about it by those old enough to remember and, it is a memory I will cherish forever. Peter Osgood, however, said it was almost as good as the one he scored at Turf Moor in the Sixties and, he didn't waste any time doing so, it was before I got back to the halfway line.

He was never the one to be outdone, but I'll let him get away with that, but only because of his total brilliance!

This was not only a special goal, but a special performance by both me and the team, as we crushed another opponent by three goals. At this particular time we were playing brilliantly, as individuals and collectively. On this day, it was like a walk (today a limp) in the park as our football was flowing like a good wine in Alexandre, and that was the place I was heading for, to celebrate once again.

Our team spirit was higher than most pop stars - although we couldn't afford their drugs - and there was still no hint of any troubles ahead. There had been signs of trouble - only between Sexton and Osgood - but it wasn't to snowball any further down the line, which was when it all reared its ugly head once boarding that first aeroplane and going into the unknown, the unknown, being the European Cup Winners Cup, the following season.

But right now, we were sweeping all before us in the biggest and best domestic cup competition in the world. Our celebrations were becoming a great part of our existing as a team. The winning was fantastic, but the celebrations that followed were more than just the icing on the cake. Dave Sexton, it seemed, turned a blind eye to all of this. I can only suppose because of the way we were playing. And I can only imagine that if he liked cake he would have scraped that icing off.

How did he celebrate so many marvellous successes?

Dave was only seen at the training ground or Stamford Bridge on match days, although it was as if he was always hovering above us. But not like that free spirit watching out for you, but counting your drinks?

He was like an accountant, commuting back and forth to Brighton where his wife and three children shared his home. He did have favourites, or so it seemed. The only three players who lived a similar life to him were John Hollins, Peter Bonetti and Peter Houseman, but we still looked at them as great friends and team-mates of ours. And of course, they were a big part of our great success.

I also recall someone telling me that he took the Harris brothers to see that amazing Cooper-Ali fight at Highbury. Some would say that Ali's jab to Our Enery's eye was the best ever seen at one of my favourite grounds, although Frank McLintock might disagree.

His tussles with Oz were notorious!

Talking of this, a little way down this most famous of roads, Sponge and Charlie would arm-wrestle Richard Harris in one of their haunts, whilst taking on the likes of Oliver Reed at his favourite pastime. I tell you this because this was the dressing-room gossip each morning before we started training. Can you imagine the additional stories, had George joined us?

Around this time I was way ahead in the clothes stakes, for I was born on the manor, although Oz, of course, liked to think that he was untouchable, which had me roaring. Let me give you an example of how Peter Osgood would be. We were dressing after training one morning at the Bridge when he asked if I would show him the best shop to get a new Whistle. He really should have had his suits made to measure, because he had such long arms and, getting them off the peg was almost out of the question. He was one of those people, who could not be kitted out in one of my shops, but somehow it was done, but then he could do anything. As I said earlier, he thought Windsor was named Royal because of him and, I can't argue because he must have been the most talented person ever to come out of there.

Anyhow, I took him to Take Six, where I knew the staff well and, told the lads to "Look after the best centre-forward in the country." I then wandered off over to the Markham. I was sitting there with a couple of pals of mine when he came in with three suits in his bag with a look like the cat that had just got the cream. He was absolutely over the moon. The Windsor Boy tried his hardest to upstage me, but there was absolutely no chance of that.

I was simply born to be the main man in Chelsea, even though it wasn't Royal.

I was buying suits for £300 a time from Major whilst he was still in his bricklayer clobber.

Anyhow, we drank our drinks and went downstairs and lunched with Camilla. This was out sanctuary. It was that great divide. We could be ourselves by having the best of everything even though we were had nothing. How we got through living like this, is something I will never, ever know. I have tried working it out, but I'm afraid you can get the best contestant on Countdown, Who Wants to be a Millionaire or University Challenge and even they be foxed.

We enjoyed a lovely lunch as usual and, he went to Epsom, whilst I returned to my humble prefab, still waiting for the big day and, it could not come quick enough. The excitement that filled the streets around Chelsea leading up to that final was chilling. It was like everywhere you went you were being talked of, or scrutinised. And then there was the magic of Fleet Street, which intrigued and, delighted me. I would have been one of those chaps if not one of ours, even if it had been doing what I did for the team in those early days and, that was scouting for the afternoon drinking dens.

I was perfect for Fleet Street.

But back to Oz, who was now Beau Brummel, with his new gear. The one thing you had to love about him, like the goal at Coventry - was that he wasted no time. The following morning I came from the shower and overheard him telling the boys, "If ever you need any clobber, just go into Take Six and mention my name." He was now top man. Whatever I did he had to try to get one over me, but because he was my mate and, I loved him so much as a player I let him get away with it.

We were the young Princes of the Kings Road, although he was the King of Stamford Bridge. Hutch was not yet into the scene, but that did not bother him, for he had his own love nest in Worcester Park. He was still fretting about having been told to get rid of his leather jacket and wheels. We were afloat in the libertine Chelsea life in the debris of the Sixties hitting the Seventies. Osgood wanted to obtain some of the Kings Road style, but being a country boy at heart (that is why he would later renege on a deal to join Stoke City with me) he was unclear how to go about this. I always figured he had to prove himself in London first. It didn't mean anything to me. It was already my town. I grew up in the pubs and clubs at a very young age, so I had nothing to prove to anybody on or off the field.

Some people say I burnt out quickly because I became too close to the environment that encouraged it. I refute that. I was part of the scene already. There was a book out called The Joy Luck Club in those days - this was us. We played with joy. We had spirit that had the joy of living, and, we also rode and, to a lesser extent made our own luck.

The media portrayed me as someone who liked a drink, partying with a different kind of crowd. Players like Keegan were always more their cup of tea. He had the iron will to succeed. He aspired to live in a huge house and get mobbed in the streets - I call it the Noel Edmonds syndrome - and after a while people forget their limitations as players. He is also one of those lucky ones. The Geoff Hurst and Ray Wilkins crowd, who keep coming up trumps in a life that seems to be tailor-made for those that continue to amaze me. Ray Clemence being another. Ask of their achievements in the game since hanging up their boots and, you will get an answer that is written on a bank statement.

Keegan still lacks it as he sits as a pundit, unsure, unclear and hesitant, plus incredibly way off the mark. I might mention elsewhere when asked his prediction about our match against the United States in South Africa, he without hesitation said we would win 4-1. We, of course, drew 1-1.

Just how far out can one be?

Can you imagine just how many fans watching the television built their hopes up?

These are the people those mugs at Soho Square give the job to. They have absolutely no idea of what is going on and when the other stuff hits the fan they all run for cover.

But of course, they take the money first!

So we had beaten United yet again and, in doing so it hit me that I was the one player who could now claim Charlton's England shirt, once his international career was over. But first, there was a little matter of Wembley before Mexico, and, of course, Leeds United. It does not come any tastier! I was itching to get out onto that Wembley pitch to come face to face with Bremner and Giles once again. This would become my greatest test as a player. Just like years on in the Royal London Hospital would become my greatest test as a person. When you look at things such as this, it about sums up what kind of life you have experienced.

Though George was troubled he made a mockery of, "A worried player is not a good one."

George was what it says on the tin and his birth certificate. Best!

Our match with them came two days before the second of United's third battle with Leeds to decide who would be walking out on the hallowed turf alongside us. Although we would soon find out that the Wembley pitch was far from hallowed on that particular day. Not that it would really matter to me, but that was the furthest thing from my mind, for it didn't matter to me that Harvey Smith and all his mates saw to that, in the Horse of the Year Show. By the time I reached Wembley on FA Cup final day nothing mattered to me, much like coming out of my coma, you simply try to look so far ahead, having missed such a massive part of your life. I have now minimised this though, by trying not to look back and forward too far and, that is why I decided to write this.

Wembley being like most of the pitches we played on in this FA Cup run was all down to those fucking idiots at the FA, once again.

Have you ever seen an FA Cup final played at Epsom or Royal Ascot?

Once again, it was that Mighty Midget Billy Bremner who settled that other semi with that all-important winner. How many times did he pop up and do that for his team?

The answer was that he was inspirational and, when the chips were down he would roll his sleeves up and, wander into the other teams' box almost unnoticed. Not because he was small, but because that was his way, he would walk in there with such a great belief in his wonderful ability and, when you have that, like Osgood, it seems luck does actually fortune the brave.

He was a fantastic player, in fact, a giant in dwarf's clothing. That can also be said of his sidekick - the silent assassin Johnny Giles. Giles, though, was more cunning than Bremner. Billy would show his deepest emotions with every tackle, however high, whilst Giles was more like a secret agent. You really just wouldn't see it coming.

Someone like Mike Tyson would mug you in a telephone box in the darkest hour. But these two would mug you in front of 60,000 people in broad daylight. The problem was they were brilliantly talented too and, they were the two players I wanted to mix it with at Wembley. For I wanted not only to win the FA Cup, but do it by beating the team everyone feared, everyone hated and, the team who loved and wanted it that way.

Had we won the FA Cup by beating Manchester United those in Leeds would have said, "We'd have beaten Chelsea" and, that was one of the reasons I wanted to play them, just so they never had that opportunity.

As I may have mentioned elsewhere, Brian Clough pointed out, "Leeds didn't win things they cheated." He also said, "Throw all of your cups, saucers and medals in the nearest rubbish bin."

They broke every rule in the book. I will tell you later about when Revie chose 80 players for an England get-together and left Osgood out. I just wonder if he would have done the same had he thrilled all of those fans at Elland Road over the years. I somehow don't think so. Had Leeds United had a Peter Osgood he would have been capped more times than all of those Leeds players put together, The Don would have seen to that and, he would have loved Osgood because he was as nasty as his players.

After that Revie episode where Revie left him out, I saw it as a great time to wind Oz up even more about the Leeds boss. Over a drink,

I'd pick my moment. I'd choose a conversation and bring Leeds into play, then I'd hit him with, "what's it like being the 81st best player in the country mate?" He'd go crazy.

People ask me, "He couldn't do that, could he?"

I tell them that you can do what you want in such a position and, when you have such incredible belief. People simply forget that football is absolutely no different than any other occupation. They think that these people are straight, when they have no scruples and, are not bothered about individuals who they dislike. Not of their personalities, but what they did against Leeds United and, after Osgood scored that mind-blowing equaliser against them at Old Trafford, although there was no sign of Revie leaving Leeds for England, if it ever happened, Osgood had absolutely no chance of getting chosen.

Later on at Stoke City, the same applied to Jimmy Greenhoff a player that Revie had already sold from Leeds to Birmingham, all because he would, or could not leave his foot there once the ball had gone.

In other words Jimmy was a pure footballer and, whereas Waddington wanted the players who could play, to play, Revie wanted everyone to be able to commit the unthinkable.

As Clough told him, your disciplinary record speaks for itself, you were bad champions who cheated and, he was correct on each and count.

Clough won the League and European Cup with three henchmen in his team, but won those trophies with an immaculate record in that department.

Revie was biased and, he was not a nice man - and he wore pink raincoats and, I cannot tell you just how happy I was to see him sitting in one. Had he been the Chelsea manager, he would have been laughed at all the way to the dugout.

It surprised me that Revie never brought out a line of these, Mackintosh's through Admiral, for he had such a good thing going with them. He even talked the FA into changing over to them as part of his deal, but more about his underhandedness and that Manchester episode very soon.

Back to Manchester though and that semi-final defeat against Leeds which spelt the end for one of the most wonderful football teams put together by Busby, after such tremendously traumatic times that followed the Munich disaster in '58. I have looked back at the footage and seen it as nothing short of stunning. Like when I was in hospital for that year I had to try to work it all out or in other words simply, why?

What must have gone through Busby's mind when coming round?

I once spoke to Billy Foulkes about that terrible time and, although he was very cool about it and, I could tell that it had affected him. It obviously would. I just wondered just how much it went towards him finally carrying off that European Cup.

Where Revie used the war to try to inspire and invigorate us - which it never did - I wonder if Busby ever mentioned those who didn't survive?

I doubt it ever entered his head, for it etched too deep!

To recover from Munich - after losing the likes of Duncan Edwards and Tommy Taylor - and, of course others and, then build a side to conquer Europe, was the greatest achievement in football history. Take into mind the terrible trauma of those that died and, those who lived through it. The deep hurt is still seen on the face of Bobby Charlton, if he doesn't mind me saying?

Quite phenomenal!

I also wonder how Sir Alex must feel as he takes his club into one battle after another, for he unlike all the rest, carries such pride with him and, therefore deserves as many accolades thrown his way.

Matt Busby's suit fits him well!

This defeat was, in fact, the end of a golden era. A Bremner goal finished them (much like our defeats against Leyton Orient in the FA Cup, Swedish side Atvidaberg in Europe and Stoke City at Wembley a year or two later). That might sound a little bizarre but a defeat like that can change the complexion of everything. Instead of a manager seeing it as a blessing in disguise, he presses the panic button. That is what Dave did, whereas Busby saw it as his team being a little OTT.

How many times have you see teams grown too old together, well here was the perfect scenario, with George left to carry the team all on his own, for this would have been the closest thing to Maradona carrying Argentina through not only the World Cup but winning it. The only difference here was that George would have to have done it for 42 matches a season, whereas Diego did it for a month.

This was to be George's last opportunity to reach an FA Cup final, with Manchester United that is and, all I can say is that was his destiny. Not even he could break through that Leeds defence once in three matches. When you think that we did it four times in those two fantastic matches, shows you how special our performances were. The first was no classic, but it was a final that had everything but magic. It was like a warm-up for the real thing. Like a weigh-in, with Gray slaughtering Webb followed by Harris slaughtering him in the follow-up even more so and, in an entirely different fashion.

The one real piece of magic came in the shape of Osgood in the replay and, it turned the match on its head. After the ball nestled in the back of Harvey's net the Leeds players stood there staring into space. They could not cope with Charlie's ball in and, then that wonderful flying finish. Osgood came through the air as if on a wire. Strange how it was Osgood again, Dave, I mean Don, no Dave, okay both!

But that was all to come. Our next match in the '70 run-in was a home one, which saw us beating Sheffield Wednesday 3-1. Jackie Sinclair, a nimble Scot, shot them ahead but Hutch and Osgood put us in front before I scored a replica of my goal at Coventry. As I always point out, I didn't score many, but when I did...

Like at Coventry, I picked it up deep in my own half and went on another mazy. Matthew Harding, who was sitting just above me as I slotted it past Grummitt, says it was his favourite Chelsea goal. But then again, I wondered what he told Oz?

On the way back I was given a standing ovation and, as they did so, I couldn't help thinking of how they would have responded had they been at Coventry?

Scoring these two wonderful goals and, so identical was as if someone was telling me something about this season. It was not like I tried this on a regular basis, like a player shooting a hundred times and, scoring a couple of great goals and, the others ending up in the Kings Road. I ran at these defences just twice and scored two beauties.

Anyhow, not long afterwards there was a lull as Ron Harris - for the first time ever - went down injured. He once went down against George, but that was a different kind of injury, it hurt his pride, for he never missed his prey. This was such a rare sight that it had the Stamford Bridge faithful falling silent. As I looked over, I thought about him missing the final, never dreaming that it would be me who the unlucky one.

He missed our next few matches but made Wembley. Eddie was also out of our next match, against Everton who would eventually become League champions. He made Wembley also. On this day, Everton played like champions. They simply tore us apart from limb to limb, with Alan Ball, in particular, awesome. In such a one-sided match, I realised just how teams felt when we had been hammering them. With half-an-hour to go, we were five goals down and, if the ground had opened up, I would have been the first to hold out a hand to whoever, to pull me out of this nightmare.

I can't even make an excuse by saying that Bonetti was out, for even if Tommy Hughes, John Phillips and Catty had all been between the posts together, we still would have been thrashed. It was one match where you are totally embarrassed to say that you were a professional footballer. To make things worse, they scored the quickest goal of that season and, any other I can think of, as Howard Kendall netted after

15 seconds. Ball scored not long afterwards. Unlike Howard, Alan had a nightmare in management as did another superb player, the third Everton midfield musketeer, Colin Harvey, who fitted in so well with Ball and Kendall. On this day they had us chasing shadows, they were the complete midfield trio, the very best in the business and, what a day they chose to remind us. Alan Ball was at his absolute best. He was here, there and everywhere, doing what he does best, playing one-touch. Joe Royle - who proved he was also a good manager - banged in a couple and, then Alan Whittle got a fifth in front of 60,000 mental Everton fans. This was a game where I got my second right-hander, although it was not a punch as such, it was more GBH of the elbow. Johnny Morrissey - of whom they say his sisters are harder than most of the blokes in that part of the world - belted me from behind.

I tell that story on Merseyside and the audience smile in agreement for it is a well-known thing there, so I have to count my lucky stars that one of his sisters was not marking me. She probably would have brought a new meaning to one-touch?

I was crawling back to our half semi-dazed after being floored to the cinders. I really didn't know what had hit me, or how. All I remember was seeing was a blue shirted number 11 running away into the distance and, looking over his shoulder as I got to my feet. Anyhow, it was not as painful as the punishment we were receiving from their overall performance. Everton were fantastic and, on this display, showed that they were more than worthy champions. Well they were more than that, on this day they were, in boxing terms, Ali at his best and, in musical terms, Sinatra. Alan Ball was the greatest English midfield player I have played against, with and ever seen.

They, unlike Leeds United, had a manager who was not known for an attitude of "winning at all costs," Harry Catterick was quite the opposite. He was like Waddington, one who realised that you needed to stop the opposition, but when in possession play and, their midfield trio were the best at that time, and all English, something you could not possibly get today.

I heard some time later that Tony wanted to buy Alan Ball, but could not afford him. What a great shame that was. He would have been absolutely brilliant under Waddington and, looking back it looked like, although I was quite a bit younger, I was destined not to play with one of the greatest inside-forwards ever produced in this country. However, like me and Currie, they were already players before reaching their respective clubs.

But my dream was to come true five years later, but until then I had to be patient and come across him twice a season. I loved playing against the best players, but there was one setback, possibly, as you had to be at your very best when coming up against the likes of Alan and TC.

WHO WAS REVIE KIDDING?

It was fitting that they won in the championship this season, as it was us the FA Cup. Leeds ended up with nothing, but they had been champions before, but as Clough said about them, "they have been champions, but not good ones. They hadn't worn the crown well."

Plus, when he took over at Elland Road, he said to those players, "Well, I might as well tell you now, you lot might be internationals and, won all the domestic honours there are to win under Don Revie, but as far as I'm concerned they are worthless."

I watched another of Revie's interviews with Clough on U-Tube the other day, when he tried to put Clough down for his running of his beloved Leeds United - after he took the England job - telling him on national TV, "You had world class players like Terry Yorath, Frankie Gray and Mick Bates at your disposal, but instead, you brought others in."

But the funniest thing was, as he mentioned "world class" Clough's face was a picture of not only amazement, as mine must have been, but astonishment. But that's how biased Revie was. If he thought that those three were world class, then what chance had England got of reaching a World Cup final under his management?

The answer to that is obvious, for whilst he was making sand castles - and counting his Arab pocket money at the same time - we were all watching a World Cup without us being involved. Don was, of course, on holiday relaxing - on their money!

After watching that interview I looked up Mick Bates on Google - although I had played against him in my first season. He was a pretty decent player. I must stress decent and, I found the following: "But looking back at things I knew my place. Johnny (Giles) and Billy (Bremner) were different class. They were world class players. There's a difference between those and players like me, I wasn't capable of turning a game, where they could, the difference being they were world class."

If Mick Bates - who you see disagrees with his manager - as Revie said, was world class, why did he not pick him for England, he picked Trevor Cherry and, his buying Roy Ellam from Huddersfield Town was if he knew he was leaving Leeds United and, if that was the case, he would be leaving them in a complete mess.

Bates was, in fact, saying that he was not "world class," which he was not!

So, there you have it, Revie was talking absolute rubbish in front of millions of viewers on national TV. His intent was to simply try to belittle a man who was his superior. And in his own mind, he did. But his mind was riddled with self-opinionated bullshit. What he was in fact trying to tell (brainwash) the entire country was that everyone who put the Real Madrid white shirt on for Leeds United was world class. I don't think so, do you?

It is quite remarkable looking back at those tapes and, it all comes flooding back, the way he tried to put people down. Clough on the other hand, it seemed, was simply play-acting with the game. When you look at today and, all of these top managers, Ferguson excluded, they all talk a good game, but Clough won the big trophies, without doing such a thing. He had a lot to say, but everything he said came true - much like Mourinho.

He never had the millions of today, when just recently, with such vast amounts of money, clubs like Manchester United, Manchester City and Tottenham have been knocked out of Europe before Santa has even put petrol in his sleigh. It's far too cold and dangerous for reindeers. Most of the players - unlike years ago - have gloves, undershirts and polo neck jumpers on. They'll want fires lighting on the sidelines next and, little do they know, the way things are going, that could happen and, if luck might have it, it might lighted up those who run the line. You've heard the saying, "He needs a rocket up his…

That's our officials!

So, Revie was the man those idiots at FA thought was the best man to run our country.

The result: No World Cup in the Seventies and, that is one of the reasons why today, we have had to go abroad and, employ those Swedish and Italian clowns, when we have our very own - clowns that is!

My ideal of an England manager is Ian Holloway, no shouting about what he's going to do. He simply gets on with the job and, he is the only man in the country who could have done what he did at Blackpool 2010/11.

What a match the final would have been if they (Leeds United) were going into it with the possibility of them winning the League and FA Cup Double. The treble even, for when they won their FA Cup semi-final, they were still in contention for the European Cup and faced the great Jock Stein's Glasgow Celtic. Jock had knocked out Revie and, now we were about to so the same come May!

Before that though just a reminder of what Clough said again, before the first training session, "Well, I might as well tell you now, you lot might be internationals and won all the domestic honours there are to win under Don Revie, but as far as I'm concerned they are nothing. They are worthless, because you cheat and, you can't play with a smile on your face."

When questioned by Revie about winning and, how he could improve such a thing Clough, said, "My aim is to win things, but do it better." What Clough meant was that, without saying it - which Revie would have boasted - was that his team won things with the best disciplinarian record. He had some of the toughest players around, but their record was immaculate!

As I mentioned earlier, Clough managed Larry Lloyd and Kenny Burns and later on, the rock-hard Stuart Pearce. You just can't get tougher than these individuals!

The wheels of Leeds United's machine were all of a sudden falling off, which seemed to be the case every year and, they were to become bridesmaids more often than not!

It seemed even the Man upstairs hated them!

The answer to all of this is obvious, although for the life of me I never heard how it came about. The first thing that the FA should look at is the character of the man, something that I cannot really say they didn't do, because I truly believe they don't know and, don't have that ability to do such a job. The one thing amazes me is that these people get a job they're not qualified to do, much like Parliament. The people that run everything that is important in this country are simply morons and, who suffers?

The public suffer while they get fatter...

I had played against the Germans - picked purposely by him to fail - but it rebounded on him (Revie) and, the result, he dropped me and got us knocked out of another World Cup.

Why, if he thought Mick Bates was world class, didn't he pick him for England instead?

So, there you have it. Revie was talking absolute rubbish on national TV - as our national manager - just to try to belittle Clough. And to make him look more stupid, even one of his players agreed.

Anyhow, back to that Everton defeat where the news spread like wildfire after that dreadful afternoon at Goodison. Dave, like Revie, had his spies and, this one spotted John Dempsey and Dave Webb gallivanting through the hotel reception at 3am on the morning of this catastrophe. But judging by the way Joe Royle had performed, I am inclined to believe such an interesting rumour. The strangest thing though, is if you are facing Big Joe on that kind of form, an early night is definitely required.

The story I like about Joe was at that Revie get-together in Manchester. Revie introduced those eighty players - the morning after a very late night in George's club - to the new club doctor and, this bloke got up and spoke about the importance of pre-match meals, In the early days it was steak, steak, steak and more steak, or so it seemed in Joe's case. But seriously, my first experience was steak and toast, which was quite obvious wasn't god for you, for it took too long to digest and gave you no energy.

The doctor got his point across by saying that pasta, cereal, poached eggs etc., gave you the necessary nourishment to get the best out of your body for ninety minutes of top class football. To be fair, although this seemed obvious it was about time someone did something about this. But then, just as he was waiting for us to applaud Joe stood up and said, "In 1970, I would eat my steak, and all the leftovers on every plate at the table (there were about fourteen players at the table) and, finished the season the top scorer in the country, can you explain that?"

The room fell about as the doctor sat down like a man who had wished he hadn't have been there.

Quite a few years later Peter Fox, Tony Davis, George Byatt and I were in a bar in Palma Nova and Joe walked in. After a few pints of beer Joe attacked a dozen hamburgers!

So that gave the new England doctor food for thought on his very first day in charge of Don Revie's squad and, although Joe would never be a part of his team, it was something to think about.   There was no way in the world Joe was going to change a habit of his football lifetime. He was one of the games great characters and a terrific bloke. It was much like when Tony Waddington agreed to sign Geoff Salmons in a Famagusta hotel at four-in-the-morning at the bar and, Sammy told him, "I must tell you now that I go to my local every Friday and have eight to ten pints, and I am not changing for anybody." Tony said, "If that is what makes you tick, keep doing it."

MY WORST LIVING NIGHTMARE

If that Everton defeat was my first taste of being real pain on a football field, the worst was still to come. On Monday 20 March 1970 in front of 31,207 football supporters I found the biggest hole in the Midlands.

It was, before the 15 December 1997, the worst day of my life - never knowing what was in store all of those years later, which put all of this into its rightful place. I went into this match looking forward to repairing the damage done at Goodison Park, but it went from bad to worse, only this time it was in the shape of a brutal ankle injury at West Bromwich.

It would change my career forever, just as that car would change my entire life forever.

It was me now, not Ronnie, who that old Wembley Jinx had struck. I was so excited about facing Leeds that the disappointment never, ever left me. As I say, it was only when I came round after being in the

Intensive Care Unit after eight-and-a-half weeks that it slowly disappeared. What was the greatest setback of my life, which cost me so much in playing terms, would become all so trivial, as my life-changing ordeal in the Mile End Road, put everything into perspective.

Like with Ashgar Fateh, I never saw the hole even though it was right there in front of me and, I remind myself here to stop saying that Fatehi didn't see me, which I was under the impression, before having it confirmed that it was no accident. He simply messed the whole thing up, thankfully.

However, in this case, there was a ball involved and, not a car. If there is one thing you must always do in any sport which concerns a ball and, that is never take your eye off of it, whether it is when batting, bowling or fielding in cricket, teeing off and putting in golf or, striking the white on the green baize in snooker.

However, they are completely different ball-games as you don't have to watch your opponent and, where you're going to land it looks easy, much like an airplane touching down smoothly, but if you hit a pothole, you can be in trouble and, that is exactly what I did.

It did not hit me at the time, but what also disappeared down that hole in the ground in the West Midlands was the opportunity to walk out beside my hero, Bobby Moore in Mexico. Little did I know that when I hurt my ankle at The Hawthorns with no Albion player anywhere near me, my long-term objectives, along with my heart were totally shattered in one split second.

Although it was the end of my upcoming dream, it was to become the beginning of an accumulation of tragedies. It was quite the opposite of the Yellow Brick Road which was within touching distance. One of my all-time favourite songs came to haunt me with the words ringing loudly all around me:

"When are you gonna come down, when are you going to land, should have stayed on the farm, should have listened to my old man. I know you can't hold me forever, I didn't sign up for you. I'm not a present for your friends to open I'm much too young to be singing the blues....so Goodbye Yellow Brick Road...

From that day on, my football life was damaged in a way I really could not put into words. But put alongside what happened on 15th December 1997, it really did not compare, not when it came to every tragedy I had experienced even in my early life. This was not just an ankle injury, for although it left a scar in my head and my heart right, it really didn't compare with coming off of that ventilator 59 days later and, when I am low, I just think of how close they were to taking my legs from me.

That's when I look at the big picture and...

The depression disappears and I come alive, if only half a man!

However, the hurt, pain and the 'not knowing' stayed with me for 27 long years. I carried that pain from West Bromwich Albion to Seattle and back to Stoke-on-Trent for my last hoorah.

I watch my every step since Fatehi came along, watching every paving stone closely along my way. I have clipped a few. I have hit floors from the Kings Road to Palma Nova. I have been brought down in penalty areas at Stamford Bridge and the Victoria Ground but never one so dangerous one early afternoon in Beaufort Street. This must be the most dangerous crossing I have ever had the displeasure to have attempted to cross, even more so than the Mile End Road. I know that might sound bizarre but it is true.

There is traffic coming from three ways, one from the right another from the left and, the third blindly from behind that big red bus turning right into the Kings Road. When looking right you cannot possible see the cars behind it and, they cannot possible see you. I had got halfway across this road when my foot dropped and, clipped that floor, crash...

As I hit the tarmac, I was there for the taking and, all I could do was lie waiting in hope that this third automobile was not going to swerve out from behind that bus, which had gone from a shield to something like a wall that you might see on a football field. A goalkeeper is blinded by such a wall as the kicker advances towards the ball, never knowing what was coming next. I was that goalkeeper, only if anything had been directed my way it would have cost me more than a goal.

My heart leapt into my mouth.

There was absolutely no way that an oncoming motorist could have avoided me and, the consequences can only be measured by your imagination. I was given a helping hand and, walked stunned to my destination and, once there my heart had got back into its normal rhythm, but before entering The Big Easy, I looked skywards as if looking for my father behind that cloud. Phew!

So the most I've told you about, apart from those wonderful matches and players, has been about tragedies and, on the lighter side, not having been able to play alongside Moore for England, the holders, in the biggest and the best World Cup of all time was just another. It would have been something which would have made the Ballet a far better read. In fact, something I would have been able to write a book about alone. It would have changed my life forever, but instead this ankle injury led to that three-year ban, something that ruined any chances I had of playing in a World Cup. Having said that once playing the best football of my life, England decided to employ Revie just after my ban was dropped. Replacing Ramsey, which I was delighted with, and replacing him with Revie was like jumping out of the frying pan and…

Like Chelsea getting relegated after allowing me and Osgood to leave, the FA were also blind here, but what's new?

If my injury was a hindrance, Revie was incurable.

Had I been in Mexico, I could have brought you everything that happened out there, including Bobby Moore being ignored whilst under house arrest in Bogota, by both Ramsey and, all of those conmen in Soho Square which was, of course, Lancaster Gate then.

The one thing you might have gathered by now was how totally amazed I was, and still am, at Ramsey overlooking Osgood. Was it because he got away with leaving Greaves out in '66 and, thought he could get away with it again?

I mean, Roger Hunt or Jimmy Greaves?

Then there's Astle or Osgood?

Today, it would be like comparing Heskey to Defoe. The latter being in a totally different class, however he is never first choice and, then there's the omission of Adam Johnson in the European championship squad.

Again, no wonder we never win anything!

Here's Alf's other side, he took lessons to improve his speech to get the England job, do you think he missed something out?

He called the Argentine's "animals" in '66, when he was picking Nobby Stiles, Jack Charlton, Norman Hunter and Peter Storey.

Ability and talent does not come into it with some managers, it means absolutely nothing and, winning becomes such an obsession they are blinded by the light. I don't think since I first watched England we have selected our best XI and, if we have I have been missing something. I could give you an England team in any year or decade where our best player is left out and, that remains the case today. Just about eighteen months ago, Scott Parker - who is however, not our best player - who has played at Charlton Athletic, Chelsea, West Ham, Newcastle United and now Tottenham was left out of Fabio Capello's squad for South Africa and, then once the Italian walked, his right-hand man Stuart Pearce made him captain, now if you can explain that to me....no, don't bother!

But back to Bobby and, to have been on the same field as him when putting in the best defensive performance I have ever seen against the Brazilians, would have been an absolutely incredible experience. The way he broke up the waves of Brazilian attacks was impeccable. His overall performance majestic and, the photograph of the wonderful Pele embracing him at the final whistle was all that was needed to tell the entire story.

Moore lived up to his name and reputation on that day - God!

But it was not to be. I had been taken under the wing of the man who for some reason had a middle name of Chelsea and, was touched, inspired and honoured. I got to know Bobby early for liking the same things in life. This one in particular was in the shape of a songster named Jack Jones. He was the son of the very famous American artist that sang Donkey Serenade....Alan.

It was backstage at the Victoria Odeon where I first met Bobby socially and knew immediately that we had much in common. He was immaculately dressed, which was the first thing that impressed me. I don't use that word loosely, if Osgood thought he was Mr., Brummel then Bobby was something from a different planet.

I knew on that evening that Bobby was in a different class, for I had been around the chaps in our dressing room, but nobody had anything like his class and charisma and, even Jack Jones, who had Susan George on his arm, was taken by him.

Footballers in those days left these modern day millionaires so far back in the shade it is too ridiculous for words, although that is not a knock at them. I think it is simply the change of attitude and money. Having said that, they still don't dress like they should or am I being very Sixties?

Looking at it from a different perspective, I think that it was we who should have dressed as those today dress, for when you think of the Flower Power and all the other weird and wonderful changes that were taking place.

When you dressed like Bobby, George Graham Terry Venables and George Best the sun shone. Footballers in our day walked with Sean Connery (James Bond) with only the cooler than cool Steve McQueen in the same kind of class, with his well-cut grey suit, powder blue shirt and dark tie, he reminded me so much of not James, but Bobby himself, if only for his chiselled good looks and golden locks. His image in The Getaway sticks in my mind whenever his name leaves anyone's lips. Plus, he could be Bond in the Thomas Crown Affair, a different one than the England players of today boast; it's more like the Sven Goran Eriksson.

REVIE AND MOORE

Can you imagine Revie talking down to Bobby?

But back to that particular night in Manchester - the night of the get-together- we were told there would be an 11 o'clock curfew. We all looked across at each other and chuckled. How can you have an early Saturday night after having played that day?

When you're amongst Alan Ball, Tony Currie, Stan Bowles, Frank Worthington, Chris Garland, Geoff Salmons, Bill Garner and several other rascals?

This, we all knew was just a test by the manager, I mean, how petty. How childish. If it had been Waddington, he would have come round to everyone's table, welcomed them to the squad and, then told them to enjoy a good night out and, he'd look forward to the talk the following morning. After all, there was no match. It was simply a gathering of players. In fact, it was a bloody waste of time, because there were eighty there of which at least half never had a chance of getting chosen, sixty even.

Garland and Garner were two of them. They would not have got in front of Osgood at Chelsea if Oz had a broken leg, a patch over one eye and was nursing a hangover and, yet here they were in front of him in the queue. Don't get me wrong that were both bloody good players but Osgood.... That is why it was a test or a get-up, not get-together. He just wanted to get a lot of chaps together to eliminate them and, or even more important, eliminate themselves and, looking round the restaurant there were many.

And the other one was my room-mate, Geoff Salmons who on leaving George's club, actually got in the elevator with Revie at almost 4am. I was outside the club waiting for both Sammy and a cab, but after about 15 minutes I gave up on him and went back to our room. Then about twenty minutes later he walked through the door and said, "Well, that's my international career over." And, it was!

Earlier on though, on walking into George's Night Club there stood Allan Clarke, leaning larger than life, with a drink in one hand and a bird in the other, he looked us up and down and simply said, "What are you lot doing in here, Don will have your guts?"

Well, it was okay for the Leeds players to be out after 11pm but the rest, no way. How could the FA employ such a man?

This is a job that is supposed to be beneficial to all of the country. What about those supporters who travel the world wanting to see the best team in their country perform and perform well?

And hopefully win something for once and, here we were with a man who was, as I said, both racist and biased!

After watching that film of Revie and Clough 'The Damned United', I realised what an evil piece of work I played under in '75. He even had the Admiral Sports Company under his spell. They dressed Leeds United and later, when he took over, they dressed the national team. I wonder how much he got out of that deal.

What made it even worse was their gear was tatty, just like the whole set-up!

It was well known that he used to look after all the staff at Elland Road. If the tea lady's daughter was pregnant, Don would give a gift. If the washing woman's husband was laid off, a few quid to see him through. He was seen as the other Don, when really all he was doing was buying everyone... and that included referees. One referee once told me that he absolutely hated refereeing matches with Leeds involved, because rules and regulations went out of the window. They harassed referees and, they intimidated them throughout the entire match. It was almost like a three-way match between Leeds United versus Chelsea and, then the man in black. The verbal assault was not fit for a kitchen discussion. Again Clough said, "Play clean, play good football, play with a smile." He then told them, as I just said, to "throw all of their medals in the trash can because that was what they were, trash."

Would have chosen George had he been English?

George was not much bigger in size than these two - Bremner and Giles - like Alan Ball, which takes me back to my father's point earlier that, "He will grow." There is just no substitute for that kind of skill.

Can you imagine Manchester United, Arsenal or Chelsea, Arsenal turning Lionel Messi away because of his size?

George once wrote to me after my three-year international ban, telling me not to worry because I was the best player in the country. This was like Sinatra telling Bennett he could sing a song and Lennon telling McCartney he could write one.

You know by now that I loved George. He just oozed class just like Bobby Moore. His career was something from a higher plain. He was the white Pele. Today, Barrack Obama would have introduced him to the White House, as he does his other heroes, which includes Stevie

Wonder. That would have been perfect for George, for he could have given his rendition of: Isn't She Lovely, which would have been quite fitting for the world's best puller!

The greatest match he ever played - George not Stevie - was at the Stadium of Light in Lisbon. United beat Benfica 5-1 and he brought the place to a standstill. The worlds press all agreed that there was a fifth Beatle, except that he played so many different tunes. However, they were all on the same wavelength.

That semi-final defeat against Leeds spelt the end for the most wonderful of football teams put together by Busby, after such tremendously traumatic times that followed the Munich disaster in '58. I have looked back at the footage and seen it as nothing short of stunning. Like when I was in hospital for that year, I had to try to work it all out, or in other words, why?

However, I'm not happy with Busby, because he backed Sexton and Chelsea against me at my tribunal over my signing-on fee. He was out of order. Did he mistake me for George or see something in me that reminded him of his greatest ever player?

I had no chance in that room, for there was me against Sexton, Busby and Chelsea. Waddington was there to back me and, on the train journey home from Birmingham, I sat at the table with both Busby and Tony whilst Tony held court and, Sir Matt was hanging onto his every word. I could see right there and then that the Manchester United supremo wanted Tony to take his job when he stood down and, when Tony refused Sexton took it. How ironic is that?

There were two losers here, both Tony and I, all because I was too young, naive and honest and Tony too loyal to Stoke City. However, that was what brought us together. I played my heart out for him, something I could do no more for Dave.

I had the last laugh as we qualified for Europe as Manchester United got relegated that season and Chelsea were struck by the same fate the following season.

Can you imagine that happening today?

Going back to our semi-final with Watford, there was something quite extraordinary nearly happened. Well, extraordinary had Watford had added our scalp to those of both Liverpool and, strangely enough, Stoke City to their giant killing acts of that season.

I told you about our 5-a-sides in the forecourt which now is more like Millionaires Row. We would have the toughest match of the week there and, the crowds would stop and watch the lads kick lumps out of one another. There were a few vendettas, one in which I think might have led to the departure of Keith Weller, but I'll tell you about that in a little while.

Fans loved it also, because where on a Saturday they'd watch their idols from so far away - remembering we had that bloody dog-track around the pitch - on a Friday morning they have a close-up view of Cooke's dazzling footwork and, Chopper's leg breaking tackles. And, all for free!

But going back and, why was this extraordinary?

Well, I used to tell Dave Sexton about my trips to the steam baths in Jermyn Street - years later I'd frequent the one in Bayswater - which was also superb. I'd go regular on Sunday lunchtimes, mainly to try to sweat out the booze from the night before and that lunchtime, which was a ritual to me. I would go with my pal Danny Gillen, who was a big lad and, one who could handle himself admirably. You might say he watched my back...

Just a pity he weren't there on 15 December 1997, but that's by-the-by, in fact, it was nearly "bye-bye" literally.

Danny, as I might have told you, first ran The Stamford Bridge Arms - before it was named that - before going on to work for the Playboy Club through my friendship with Joe McKay the doorman at Annabelles. He then followed that up by looking after Richard Burton and Tony Curtis before ending up the right hand man to Phil Collins. I met Phil on a couple of occasions and, what a lovely, lovely man he is - Phil was another who was mesmerised by Bobby Moore. Always remembering that my favourite asset (quality) in a star; is their modesty and politeness. He has both in abundance. Sinatra also, always asked for Danny's Rolls Royce when landing at Heathrow Airport. I think Danny also admired Bob Monkhouse very much after driving him to and from a show. Dan told me a funny story and Bob, by saying that he asked him to pull over at a Service Station to get a drink and sandwich. Danny told me one of the cleverest men in show-business, was sitting in the back in just his shirt and boxer shorts relaxing. When he pulled up Bob said, "stay there Daniel, I'll go," and simply stepped out and, walked in without his trousers, yeah, of course it was intentional. Danny laughed his socks off, if you'll excuse the pun...

But back to that Friday when Dave had different plans for our big match the day after. He took us to a sauna bath in High Street Kensington. I still don't know if it had anything to do with me continually telling the lads about my time spent in the Steam Baths in Jermyn Street?

Why? I never asked and never found out. The only thing I can think of was that he did not want any last minute casualties. However, at half-time it entered my mind that maybe the sauna had something to do with us flagging after the opening twenty minutes. How the mind plays tricks on you at such a time. To show how absolutely ridiculous that theory was that in the second half we simply got stronger and stronger the more the match progressed.

But going back to me saying I sweated it out, I bet you think that, 'yeah, it would have taken more than just one afternoon in a steam room to sweat that out?'

This sauna could not possibly do anything like a steam bath, whereas after three hours in a steam bath I could knock off three pounds, which around that time was the cost of three pints of lager.

The Jermyn Street place was situated at the back of St James' Square, by the side of a tiny cheese shop called Paxton and Whitfield. Sounds like Ipswich Town's full-backs. George Best used to live nearby, just around the corner in a flat by Fortnum, which he shared with his last Miss World, Mary Stavin.

In that same street, he was a regular in Tramp.

I felt sorry for George, living in the heart of the west end of London. He was shacked-up with the most beautiful girl on the planet, revered wherever he went, dropping into the casino and then Tramp. What a dull life! As that tiny Irish waiter said to him as he brought champagne to his Dorchester Hotel room and saw the bed filled with £50 notes and, with Mary coming out of the bathroom with just a towel covering her stunning body,

'George, where did it all go wrong'?

Now keeping all of this in mind, George wanted to become a Chelsea player. I know this is true, because he loved our company - as we did his - after Wednesday night matches in his club in Manchester and, more importantly he loved our style on the field as well, but the problem here was that the manager would or could not have handled such a move. Now I ask you, who in their right mind would turn down the opportunity of signing George Best?

Mr. Waddington would have walked (limped more like it) the M6 to sign the greatest player on the planet and, that about summed up the difference between the two managers and shows you the problem with the game, as England wanted players who were, you might say, dull and uninteresting.

This, you might agree, showed on the field and, still does!

My admiration for Tony's management skills lives on as strongly today as when he was at the top of his trade. After all just look at this: Gordon Banks (World Cup winning keeper), Peter Shilton (ouch!) Jimmy Greenhoff (how did he end up cap-less?), George Eastham (World Cup squad member with Gordon), Geoff Salmons (he had no chance after getting in the lift with Revie at 4am), John Ritchie, Jimmy Robertson (Scotland international), Roy Vernon (Welsh international),

Dennis Violett (a Busby Babe), Jackie Mudie (Scottish international) and, of course me and Sir Stanley Matthews.

There were then the unsung heroes such as Terry Conroy (Southern Ireland international) and John Mahoney that Welsh international, who was a pleasure to have by your side when facing the likes of Leeds United. Then Maurice Setters (Manchester United) and Tony Allen (Burnley). Waddington shuffled his pack uniquely and beautifully and the people of the Potteries will never see the likes of not only him, but those players again.

But back to Sexton, I know we were over the top at times, but imagine George in our line-up! It surely would have been the Greatest Show on Earth? In 2009 Manchester City offered £150 million for Kaka and, he is a churchgoer.

Maybe Dave would have preferred him? Why did I say maybe?

If Dave was a bundle of nerves when the trouble began, we would have heard of him swinging off Battersea Bridge from Mickey Droy's bootlaces within two weeks of signing George. But that would never have happened. I'm still in a daze when thinking about such a thing happening, I mean, George Best, come on, Dave…

Right, I mentioned about vendettas at the Bridge and, where you might see one or two of them go a little bit too far. One was between Weller and Ron Harris and, to this day I could never really put my finger on exactly why?

But there was one hell of a clash and, the two lads from the east end of London made it quite clear there was absolutely no love lost in their relationship. Why on earth did Dave Sexton sell Keith?

Around the time I left, I heard that Dave was interested in re-signing the former Millwall and Tottenham winger, but that was allegedly.

I liked Keith a lot although he he were not close, he was a little bit flash and, full of himself in a harmless way, but that was what you got from east London. Venables was exactly the same and, if you look about that side of London, it is simply a part of their make-up.

One night before my wife, allegedly, was to instigate my near demise she said to me that I was not accepted on that side of the water. I told her that I had several many good friends - who still are to this day.

This was around the time which led to my near death!

Keith Weller will remain a mystery, as to why a player so gifted could be sold on. But that was further down the road, although very appropriate here, as to Dave's way of thinking. I mean Weller, Hudson and Osgood were top players in anyone's collective album.

I met a chap yesterday 15.4.2012 in Macclesfield who supported Leicester City and, he told me that Keith was his favourite player both there and at Chelsea. Maybe he would have been a better manager than Dave?

The fans at the Bridge loved Keith. His nickname was Sammy after a character in a Charles Dickens novel. He had a short Chelsea career of just over a year, in which he played more than a small part in our first-ever European success. The more I think of it, the more I realise how preposterous his transfer was.

In his early days, when running the line quite brilliantly, he scored 10 goals in the first ten matches of the season, but was carpeted for allowing their full-back too much time and space going forward. He changed his game which led to him only adding about another two for the rest of the season. Coaching? With players such as Keith, you just let them get on with it. He was a superior copy of Theo Walcott today - in fact, he was in a completely different class, because he knew what he was doing. Walcott must surely go down as one of Wenger's worst signings. Come to that, anyone's worst signing and, he has that trait that I hate so much today, along with all the big names, spouting off of how they're going to do this and, going to do that, when the outcome is always the same, coming home early from World Cups, no, I cannot stand reading such trash!

By curbing his natural predatory instincts, Dave blunted his game.

It's like, 'girl meets boy, falls in love, gets married and then tries her hardest to change him!'

This is why I mention my slant on Dave as a manager and as a coach. Why buy him in the first place?

Surely he knew his strengths and weaknesses?

That is part of being a manager. When Waddington bought me, he gave me one piece of advice in saying, "Go out and enjoy yourself." By that he meant go where you want, pick the ball up from anywhere you see fit and, play your natural game. "That is what I have paid all that money for." When he was asked a question by Les Scott, who is a very good writer, "What makes a good manager?" Tony struggled to answer. Les then said, "I once asked Bob Stokoe the same question and, he said that being a good manager is all about signing good players. Once you have done that, your job is easy." Tony then smiled and told Les, "Yeah, Bob is right, that is all I have done over the years. For example when I signed Alan Hudson, I just sat back and enjoyed watching him play. I didn't need to tell him what to do, he already knew."

If I have mentioned this before I don't apologise, for I love looking back at such a time and love my memories of playing and, living in the same world as Waddington. He brought a new meaning to playing the game I loved so much.

To be the best player on the field was like a gift from me to him.

I think also, Keith would also have been his kind of player, for like Salmons he was direct and, to have two wide men like that would have given the opposition far more problems.

However, Keith left for Leicester City and, was joined by Birch (Allan Birchenall), who was better known for his double-act with Joe Cocker in the Penny Farthing in Sheffield. He was followed by Chris Garland or vice versa. Chris was a great lad and, an underrated player, who has suffered for so long with Parkinson's. The great news, though, is he is winning one battle after another, just like I knew he would. Ray Kennedy, that great Arsenal and Liverpool player, suffers with the self-same illness. I once went to see him in Newcastle and, I felt that I was the luckiest man alive, even though I was on the floor myself. It was terrible, awful, sickening. Chris ran the likes of Hutch very close when it came to the Crumpet Stakes and, being fearless, although Sponge wasn't far behind, if at all.

He fitted in perfectly at the Bridge and, the Kings Road in particular, with his golden blond locks and dashing smile. It was as if he was born to be a Chelsea player. Chris once told me of all of the unrest and aggravation amongst the London Johns at Leicester and, their clashes with the locals. They had quite a useful team there, including Lennie Glover, the former Charlton winger, and Jon Sammels, a player I liked, who escaped from Arsenal as he became, for some unknown reason, a target for the Highbury boo-boys. He could not have played any worse than I did in my time there, so I can only think there was something else going on.

In the end Leicester City had half of our team: Webb, Kember, Birchenhall, Weller and Garland were decent additions to Jimmy Bloomfield's team, whereas I think Frank McLintock signed Webby, keeping in mind their time at QPR together....

To this day, I cannot understand the stick Sammels got.

As I say, he could not possibly have played worse than I did for them.

Peter Shilton was in their goal, but more of him later. Although before I go back to him, I was told that he and Sammy had a set-to in the showers at half-time. What they were doing in there at that particular time I dread to think, but Sammy put up a good show. I last saw Keith in Seattle after we had beaten his Fort Lauderdale team in the play-offs. He came into the match at the Kingdome and, reminded me of just how good a player he was and, I remember winking at one of our defenders and pointing at him, as much as to say....

One of the most asked questions of me, is who was the toughest, well, I I'll give you a clue, had Chopper hit Hutch he would suffer the consequences. Once, Sammy Chapman (a proper hard-nut at Nottingham Forest) hit Hutch and within minutes he was stretchered off. Hutch walked alongside him with a broken arm.

Defenders knew they were doomed when they came across a fired-up Ian Hutchinson and, right now that was what Watford found out in that semi-final, just as Leeds United were to do at Old Trafford.

When arriving at Stoke City I learned - although Denis Smith was known for being the tough-guy - it was Alan Bloor who was as the main man, when hitting an opponent. The man known as Bluto, if he hit you, then you remained hit. Like a heavyweight boxer catching an opponent with a perfect hook, he'd hit the ground and see stars. Well, Bluto was not supposed to be a star, because he was like Hinton at Chelsea, a laid back introvert of a character, as was Greenhoff, however not ones you could ever underestimate and, that apart, Bloor could play the game as well, unlike many a hard case.

I have seen many stars, but thankfully not after an Alan Bloor blow. He admits to this day that when he hit Garland at Wembley, that today he would not have seen stars but a red.

Talking of hard players brings me back to my dad, Bill, who when coming to play for the Chelsea Old Boys from one of their fiercest rivals, it was the talk of the town. He most certainly was a hard nut, but also one of the gentlest men you'd ever meet. Although the right hander he gave me when I left home because of my relationship with Maureen was far from gentle. It sent me further than any tackle I was on the other end of throughout my career. After striking me though, he went back to the prefab and sobbed. I could understand then and, can now, as he was right. Maureen wasn't for me. Having said that, I thought he should have let me find that out for myself.

He had done absolutely everything for me and more. He had worked his fingers to the bone to give me everything I needed to go all the way. Not just material things, for when he wasn't working, his time was given 100% to me and my brother John. And when Julie came along he doted on her completely. In the early days, he worked away on the asphalt before turning his hand to window cleaning and decorating. As my mate Peter Millard says, "He was a wizard with the pin," meaning he could have worked for Fagan, being able to pick a lock as well as he picked his teams. He wasn't like the man who finished work and went for a pint. In fact he never drank until he reached Seattle, where I got him on the champagne and orange. He then became a different man. By that time he doted on my Allen, who still dotes on him, even though he's been gone such a long time. In fact, we had a couple of hours talking about him to my son's girlfriend the other day. Allen, it is clear to see, totally adored him. Yeah, we talk of him as if he is still around, my sister swears to it. In fact, when she received that first call to tell her that I was in the operating theatre, she cried out for him immediately.

This was the time when on receiving the call from hell she became hysterical and cried out for Bill. As she was doing so, a crucifix came up on her front room wall. It actually burnt a hole in the wall and, whenever I had a relapse, it would appear once again.

Betty Shine said it was a sign of peace with my Dad telling Julie everything was going to be fine.

As for picking locks, he actually got nicked one day for breaking into our own home. He left his keys in the house and, on getting to our front door he found that my mum had taken John and me to the ABC Cinema in the Fulham Road. I remember sitting in the picture house when the doors at the back swung open, the film went off, the house lights went on and, he stood at the back with an Old Bill an each arm. He was screaming at the top of his voice for my mum to get up and come and tell them it was our house. My mum could have died of embarrassment, whilst me and my brother, only about six and eight, couldn't understand what was going on.

He was our hero from there on in and, I think of that when I watch Bruce Willis and Sly Stallone.

I thought of all these times when lying in hospital, wondering how he would have reacted to my being in a coma, then hearing of the amputation and then the aftermath. And then there was the aggravation with the police and the questioning of how all of this came about. My dad would have left no stone unturned and, he would have painted every room in every one of my surgeon's homes.

Was that why, after coming out of that coma, I saw him standing in the corner of my room?

It will live with me until I do finally go, as to just how he would have reacted to this all, it really is the one and only thing that still stays on my mind. My dad weren't like anyone else; he reacted in the kind of way that was very unpredictable.

On their first visit to Seattle, he, my mum and sister Julie, after meeting my friends, he got very close to a couple named Ken and Grace who were Japanese, or some race like that. They were marvellous people.

After about three days my mum turned to him and said, "We're going into Bellevue, can you be ready in half-an-hour?"

He turned and replied, "I can't, I'm going to work."

My mum said, "We've come half way round the world to see our son and, you're going to work?"

He said, "Well, it's not work as such, Grace's front room and passage need decorating."

It was stunning.

And then he started painting the outside of my house and on the day my mum was leaving for home - I talked him into staying - he was up the ladder painting my roof. Maureen called him at least three times to say, "Bill, Bub's leaving and we have food on the table."

A car pulled up for my mum and she got in and left for the airport. My dad got down from the ladder and sat with me at the kitchen table, I was screaming with laughter inside knowing what was coming next, when he said, "Where's Mog?"

I turned to him and said "She's gone home, dad," and he went berserk saying, "She couldn't even be bothered to say goodbye."

Maureen said, "But Bill, I called you three times," in which he said, "But I had some touching up to do."

Again, stunning!

Like with me, I think I have never seen him as happy as he was in Seattle, it was a country that suited us just perfectly. The people were great and appreciated you. As I might have said, even my next door neighbours were perfect, with their surname being, Barman, yeah, Bob and Jean and Bob Barman.

Now Osgood would have thought they'd changed their names just for him…

19 LET THE HEARTACHE BEGIN

At West Bromwich Albion I went for a harmless looking ball with nobody in touching distance. Asa Hartford, that great little tenacious Scottish midfield player, was the closest player to me.
He could probably tell you what happened better than me.

All I can remember is my life passing me by as I knew immediately that Wembley was completely out of the equation. I knew as soon as I hit the floor that Wembley was no longer a dream. Isn't it strange, how the mind works, quickly telling you that your dream was now a nightmare!

All I can remember was the immediate pain and knew straight away...

I first played against Asa in the FA Youth Cup at the Bridge in my last year as a youth team player. He was the player Revie tried to sign, but he failed the medical under the strangest of circumstances. They said they detected a hole in the heart, but he went on to have a long and distinguished career.

This was very strange. I mean, what would Don Revie know about a heart?
Had they not detected a heart at all, Revie would certainly have signed him.

Looking back, this was quite incredible, if only for in a roundabout way. The Don Revie connection, which being, he was going to sign Asa from West Bromwich Albion until finding out about his heart condition and, then Asa being the closest person to me as I went down this hole. I have played against him since - but never knew him socially - where if I had, I would have asked his recollection of it all. A little like that bloke who saw the car hit me and, the one that the police scared away just after he told my friend, Johnny Westwood, that he saw it all happen. He was my only witness and the police threatened him into not taking it any further.

There was another player at that time that looked like making a big name for himself and, that was Len Cantello. The last I heard of Len, who I met through the England Youth trials, was that he went out for the Sunday papers one morning and returned home on the following Thursday, empty-handed and, rather the worse for wear. So it wasn't only Chelsea who had such players. He probably would have fitted in well at the Bridge!

My ankle was to become my Achilles heel, as stupid as it sounds and, would cause me the kind of grief that nobody would ever understand. I had seen specialists all over London, had all different types of treatment, but all to no avail. Even when I woke up in hospital all those years later, although they had cut me from head to toe, my ankle was still a major problem. The biggest problem was that I could no longer play on hard pitches, the kind I had learned my trade on, but in 1998 that wasn't a problem at all, because I could hardly walk anyway. Whereas in those days I prayed for rain on a Friday, today I need it dry, because of my bad balance and slippery surfaces are as dangerous as the hard grounds were all of those years ago.

This is the most bizarre jigsaw puzzle of all-time!

I felt jinxed to the hilt.

I would wake some Saturday mornings, jump out of bed and, look through the curtains hoping to see puddles outside my window. It seemed the only time I had a piece of luck was before my England debut when it lashed down and, the time when Tony Waddington got the Stoke-on-Trent Fire Brigade in to flood the Victoria Ground.

But back to that match at the Hawthorns. It was going from the ridiculous to the most bizarre as bodies were coming and going from the pitch like a scene from Mash. What started out as a confidence restorer, turned out to be a complete nightmare as Hutch was next, damaging his hip when scoring.

Then it was Bobby Tambling, Jumbo as he was known, who came on for me and also left the field through injury.

I think it was one match where the score-line was immaterial, for all seemed to be going against us and, by now my ankle was wrapped up and my heart broken. I knew that all of those great matches I have just told you about now meant nothing to me. I was out of the biggest match of my young life, the match that every kid dreams of playing in.

I knew the very moment I went down that I would be out of the FA Cup final. It was the last time I cried, well, that was until I wrote The Ballet.

The pain was excruciating, not through the pain, but through missing that final. It felt as if someone had taken a chainsaw and, was trying to hack my ankle from my leg. It may have been better if they had. Today, players are treated with so much more sophistication - travelling to the other side of the world to see specialists. My trips were behind closed doors with Mr. David Montague at Sloane Square and, a fleeting visit to Sir William Tucker in Harley Street. Years later I found out that he was part of the Tucker family (Tucker Town) in Bermuda.

He tried putting me through some wax treatment. It didn't work. Nothing did!

And all of those years later I had a nightmare of a different kind in Bermuda, well two in fact, I got married there and, spent my wedding reception alone drinking pink champagne on my balcony. It seemed I didn't miss much because my wife popped over to try to talk me into joining her, but the damage had been done, funny isn't it how you somehow know from word go that this wasn't going to work?

That is why I have always preferred funerals or wakes, they are far more touching and heart- warming, meaning, they are something that mean so much more and, are forever!

I remember getting to Euston Station where I was greeted by a photographer, for the news had spread like wild fire.

I would miss the 1970 FA Cup final.

Although I knew immediately, it just would not sink in. I really have no idea how I coped, in fact, I coped far better in the Royal London Hospital, coming to terms with a life of misery.

When you think what I had to go through from my hospital bed, compared to an ankle injury, it all sounds quite absurd. But that was my love for not only the game, but those around me, who had put so much into getting there. After all, I was only eighteen and, even though I thought I was advanced in my way of thinking and attitude, something like this hits you like a sledgehammer.

Whereas, in my Treves Ward bed, it was like watching one of those war movies, when the soldier sits there dazed. He is, in fact, trying to work out his future, as I was.

It was nothing like anything I'd experienced before, I'd had setbacks aplenty, but being absolutely paralysed and sitting there like the Elephant Man, with people coming in and out looking at you like you were something of a sideshow. I may have mentioned elsewhere that Treves was the man who treated John Merrick - played by John Hurt - in that extraordinary movie about the man who had such an unfortunate life. Hurt, as usual, showed just why he is one the greatest actors from these shores, alongside Cary Grant, Anthony Hopkins and Richard Burton.

You see, I was the one who ran the streets. I would get up and go. I was the original Man About Town of our time. Out of all of the boys of my era, I was the one who had got a wonderful start and was not going to miss anything, from the Worlds End to Fleet Street to my first trip to Switzerland. You might say that I had the bug!

When you read the next part, it all seems so nothing.

What I found to be the worst thing about all of this was that once put into plaster, it seemed to glue everything together. When I came out of plaster, it was never the same. My mobility was never the same and I could never hit the ball long distances, hence the main reason I hardly ever shot at goal. This led to our club doctor, Bill Marshall, telling me to take a ball and, put it against the wall and, then keep smashing it like going into a block tackle. "That would break it down," he said. It never did, but it nearly caused me having one.

I can only imagine that years of fatigue would grind it into gristle. I would spend hours upon hours in the bathroom of my Southfields home sitting on the side of the bath going through the hot and cold water treatment. This still did nothing. The fear of going over on it again was always at the back of my mind, so the psychological damage was everlasting. I felt like a kid who had been bought a brand new bike for Christmas and, woke up to find I had no legs to ride it - which was almost the case some 27 years later.

In my favour, I was still a few months off my 19th birthday. It was no consolation then, like that car hitting me, I often think 'Thank the Lord he didn't hit me the day after reaching Wembley.' It just goes to show once again how The Man works, although he never worked for me. Some people have all the luck. Hurst springs to mind. The way that ball hit that bar on the same pitch way back in '66 was a great example, if it were me, absolutely no goal. And as for that car that hitting me, had it been Geoff, the driver would have stopped and, asked if he wanted a lift home.

That's the difference. Some people are just born so very lucky. I told you about Ray Wilkins, a complete nightmare in management, but he still gets a plum job with Chelsea. David Beckham gets injured before the 2010 World Cup and, there he is on the aeroplane with the rest of the lads. He also gets sent-off against Argentina and is slaughtered and, the next thing you know, he is going up with Prince Harry, or is it William, to represent us as to hold another World Cup here. I mean, it just doesn't make any sense whatsoever. The Bobby Moore thing still rankles at me and, every time I see Beckham smiling besides Royalty and, President Obama, I think of Bobby.

When Rio Ferdinand got injured a few days before the start of this competition one commentator said, "Very shrewd man Capello that is why he took Beckham along, so now he can console Rio." Well, I must be missing something here. I thought we took people there to win the bloody thing!

There were so many losers sitting about in South Africa, even to the extent of Ray Clemence always there, no matter who gets the sack. When a manager gets the boot, he should take all of his staff with him. Get them out, new broom.

England is still a nation of continual losers and, will always be so. Even, as Roy Hodgson takes over and, chooses his squad, he says "I need that blend." Well, of course you need that blend, but get the losers out, because if they can't win the World Cup at 22 or 23, they are not going to do so at 33.

If I am not getting through to you, just look…Pele, born 21 October 1940, Edson Arantes do Nascimento, in Ties Coracoes, Brazil, won the World Cup at his first attempt when 17 years and 249 days old and, was the only man to win the Jules Rimet Trophy on three occasions. Franz Anton Beckenbauer born in Munich on 11 September 1945 won it as soon as he took over the captaincy in 1974. Diego Armando Maradona Franco, born on 30 October 1960, in Villa Fionto on the outskirts of Buenos Aires, won it when captain in 1986, he was 26. He was known as the only man to win it single-handedly and was voted joint Player of the Century, alongside Pele, in the year 2000.

And then there was my man, Bobby who was born on 12 April 1941 in Barking, which made him 25 when becoming the only man to lift it for us. However his finest performance came four years later when he was, no doubt, at his peak (his very best).

Moore attended Westbury Primary School and Tom Hood School, Leyton.

He played for both schools.

Moore joined West Ham United as a player in 1956 and, after advancing through their youth set-up, he played his first game on 8 September 1958 against Manchester United. In putting on the number six shirt, he replaced his mentor Malcolm Allison, who was suffering from tuberculosis.

Allison never played another first team game for West Ham nor indeed any other First Division game, as Moore became a regular. A composed central defender, Moore was admired for his reading of the game and ability to anticipate opposition movements, thereby distancing himself from the image of the hard-tackling, high-jumping defender. Indeed, Moore's ability to head the ball or keep up with the pace was average at best, but the way he read the game, marshalled his team and timed his tackles marked him out as world class.

Bobby Moore also played county cricket for the Essex youth team alongside fellow West Ham player Geoff Hurst.

In 1960, Moore earned a call up to the England Under-23 squad. His form and impact on West Ham as a whole earned him a late call-up to the full England squad by Walter Winterbottom and the Football Association selection committee in 1962, when final preparations were being made for the summer's World Cup finals in Chile. Moore was uncapped as he flew to South America with the rest of the squad, but made his début on 20 May 1962 in England's final pre-tournament friendly - a 4-0 win over Peru in Lima. Also débuting that day was Tottenham Hotspur defender Maurice Norman. Both proved so impressive that they stayed in the team for the whole of England's participation in the World Cup, which ended in defeat by eventual winners Brazil in the quarter finals at Viña del Mar.

On 29 May 1963, 22-year-old Moore captained his country for the first time in just his 12th appearance after the retirement of Johnny Haynes and an injury to his successor, Jimmy Armfield. He was the youngest man ever to captain England at the highest level. England defeated Czechoslovakia 4-2 in the game and, Armfield returned to the role of captain afterwards, but new coach Alf Ramsey gave Moore the job permanently during a series of summer friendlies in 1964, organised because England had failed to reach the latter stages of the European Championships.

1964 turned out to be quite an eventful year for Moore. As well as gaining the England captaincy, he lifted the FA Cup as West Ham defeated Preston North End 3-2 in the final at Wembley, courtesy of a last-minute goal from Ronnie Boyce. On a personal level, Moore also was successfully treated for testicular cancer and was named the Football Writers' Association Footballer of the Year.

The FA Cup success would become the first of three successful Wembley finals in as many years for Moore. In 1965, he lifted the European Cup Winners Cup after West Ham defeated 1860 Munich 2-0 in the final with both goals coming from Alan Sealey. By now he was the first choice captain for England with 30 caps, and around whom Ramsey was building a team to prove correct his prediction that they would win the 1966 World Cup. 1966 had a mixed start for Moore, however - he scored his first England goal in a 1-1 draw with Poland, but then captained West Ham to the final of the League Cup - in its last season before its transfer to Wembley as a one-off final - which they lost 5-3 on aggregate to West Bromwich Albion. For Moore, who had scored in the first leg, and his West Ham team-mates Geoff Hurst and Martin Peters, considerable consolation lay ahead. Moore scored his second and ultimately final England goal in a friendly against Norway, two weeks before the World Cup would begin.

On the verge of his greatest triumph, details were released to the press in early 1966 that Moore wanted to leave West Ham. Moore had let his contract slip to termination and, only after the intervention of Sir Alf Ramsey and, realisation he was technically ineligible to play, did he re-sign with West Ham to allow him to captain the England team of 1966. Ramsey had summoned West Ham manager Ron Greenwood to England's hotel and told the two of them to resolve their differences and get a contract signed up. Moore was the leader of the World Cup winning side and established himself as a world-class player and sporting icon. With all their games at Wembley, England had got through their group with little trouble, they then beat Argentina in a controversial quarter final and a Eusébio-led Portugal team in the semis, a match also surrounded by controversy.

West Germany awaited England in the final.

According to Geoff Hurst's autobiography, England full back George Cohen overheard Ramsey talking to his coaching staff about the possibility of dropping Moore for the final and deploying the more battle-hardened Norman Hunter in his place. However, eventually they settled on keeping the captain in the team. Moore had not been playing badly, nor had he given the impression that he had been distracted by his contract dispute prior to the competition. The only possible explanations were that the Germans had some rather fast attacking players, which could expose Moore's own lack of pace, and that Hunter - who was of a similar age to Moore but only had four caps - was the club partner of Moore's co-defender with England, Jack Charlton.

In the final, England went 0-1 down through Helmut Haller, but Moore's awareness and quick-thinking helped England to a swift equaliser. He was fouled by Wolfgang Overath midway inside the German half and, rather than remonstrate or head back into defence, he picked himself up quickly while looking ahead and delivered an instant free kick on to Hurst's head, in a movement practised at West Ham. Hurst scored.

The West Ham connection to England's biggest day became stronger when Peters scored to take England 2-1 up, but the Germans equalised in the final minute of normal time through Wolfgang Weber - as Moore appealed unsuccessfully for a handball decision - to take the match into extra time.

Ramsey was convinced the Germans were exhausted, and after Hurst scored a controversial and heavily debated goal, the game looked over. With seconds remaining, and England under the pressure of another German attack, the ball broke to Moore on the edge of his own penalty area. Team-mates shouted at Moore to just get rid of the ball, but he calmly picked out the feet of Hurst 40 yards upfield, who scored to bring the score to 4-2.

Of many memorable images from that day, one is of Moore wiping his hands clean of mud and sweat on the velvet tablecloth before shaking the hand of Queen Elizabeth II as she presented him with the Jules Rimet trophy (World Cup).

Moore became a national icon as a consequence of England's success, with him and the other two West Ham players taking the

World Cup around the grounds which West Ham visited during the following domestic season. He was awarded the coveted BBC Sports Personality of the Year title at the end of 1966, the first footballer to do so, and remaining the only one for a further 24 years. He was also decorated with the OBE in the New Year Honours List.

He continued to play for West Ham and England, earning his 50th cap in a 5–1 win over Wales at the end of 1966 in a Home International match which also doubled up as a qualifier for the 1968

The year 1970 was a bittersweet, mixed and eventful one for Moore. He was again named as captain for the 1970 World Cup but there was heavy disruption to preparations when an attempt was made to implicate Moore in the theft of a bracelet from a jeweller in Bogotá, Colombia, where England were involved in a warm-up game. A young assistant had claimed that Moore had removed the bracelet from the hotel shop without paying for it. While there was no doubt that Moore had been in the shop (having entered with Bobby Charlton to look for a gift for Charlton's wife, Norma), no proof was offered to support the accusations. Moore was arrested and, then released. He then travelled with the England team to play another match against Ecuador in Quito. He played, winning his 80th cap and, England were 2-0 victors, but when the team plane stopped back in Colombia on the return to Mexico, Moore was detained and placed under four days of house arrest. Diplomatic pressure, plus the obvious weakness of the evidence, eventually saw the case dropped entirely, and an exonerated Moore returned to Mexico to re-join the squad and prepare for the World Cup.

Moore went on to play a leading role in England's progress through their group. In the second game against favourites Brazil, there was a defining moment for Moore when he tackled Jairzinho with such precision and cleanliness that it has been described as the perfect tackle. It continues to be shown frequently on television around the world. Brazil still won the game 1-0, but England progressed through the group. Moore swapped shirts with Pelé after the game. The shirt is now on display in a virtual reality museum called the Priory Collection.

Defeat after extra time against West Germany saw England eliminated in the last eight, and it would be 12 years before England were to return to a World Cup finals.

At the end of the year, Moore was voted runner-up (behind Gerd Muller of West Germany) for the 1970 European Footballer of the Year award

Well, there you have it and, I hope you are now on my wavelength...and, as for Alf being very close to leaving him out of the 1966 World Cup; that would have been yet another incredible mistake made by the England manager and, had he, England and, Bobby in particular, would never have put on such a marvellous display against Brazil in 1970, not to mention Alf's biggest gaffe in the match against the Germans.

But back to the story...

Had Mourinho been offered someone like Wilkins or Clemence at any of his clubs, he would have laughed. The man's a complete professional, a master of his trade, and more importantly, a winner!

What made me laugh in South Africa after Robert Green dropped that clanger against the USA was that a few days went by and I saw a clip of the three goalkeepers working out and Clemence was nowhere to be seen.

So what the hell is he doing there?

In the Seventies he was a terrific goalkeeper, but if he told me what to do as a player, I'd tell him in no uncertain terms where to go. Goalkeepers are there to stop shots and when they're not doing that they should keep out of the business of playing football.

I talk of luck elsewhere between these pages, Beckham, Hurst, a couple of others, which includes Venables, where everything they touch turns to gold, hence why David is named Golden Balls. El Tel, who is now creeping towards the top of the charts with a World Cup song - prior to the event - with an Elvis song titled: If I Can Dream. He don't need to. Unlike me, he doesn't experience nightmares. Just like when the Stoke City chairman died on the morning he was about to offer me my dream job. This can be the kind of trauma you carry with you for the rest of your life, which leads me into this incredible bout of trauma and, is in keeping with let the heartache begin.. On 11 June this appeared in the Daily Star....

Bright Vicky Harrison killed herself after applying for 200 jobs but landing none of them. Vicky 21, had 10 GCSEs and three A-levels but took an overdose of pills and left a note to her family saying, "I don't want to be me anymore."

The message went on, "Please don't be sad. It is not your fault. I want everybody in my life to be happy."

Her death came after she received yet another rejection letter following a job interview at a children's nursery. Vicky's father of Darwen, Lancashire, broke down in tears as he told an inquest how she also failed to land a job as a waitress, shop girl and school dinner lady after dropping out of a university film and media course. He also said that, "I think it was very difficult sometimes, particularly if she felt the interview had gone well." Vicky also had an on-off relationship with boyfriend Nathan Howard and had been prescribed anti-depressants. Blackburn coroner Michael Singleton was told that police investigated her claim that Nathan had hit her but found it unfounded. Nathan told them that Vicky had had a miscarriage. A verdict of suicide was recorded.

It really can lead to that, quite tragic! It takes terrible bravery to do such a thing. Some say it is a cowards way out, but no, quite the opposite.

The photograph showed her to be a very, very pretty young lady.

The two instances at West Bromwich (1970) and the Mile End Road (1997) were two brutal acts of total life-changing devastation, but then there are people who have been diagnosed with the dreaded disease called 'cancer' and, therefore I will forget my woes for now. And then there's the kind of situations young Vicky went through, a different kind of illness, the kind of depression with no cure, or just an even break.

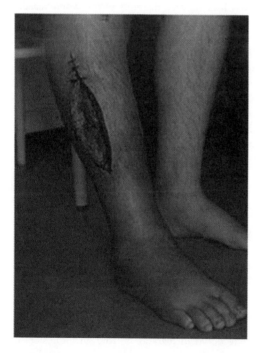

When I talk of devastation this is what I am talking of. The fasciotomies performed by those incredible surgeons left me so badly handicapped. But I was told straight afterwards that I should thank them for saving my legs, as they fought like hell under the most harrowing conditions. One lady told me that they were cutting as if blindfolded, where they could not see through the blood.

As for rejection, I can relate to that after my wife walked away when I needed her most. I don't think she understood, in fact, I know she didn't, and still don't, because I have only ever have seen her once since and, that was in the pub that Tommy Nicholson opened in the Barbican. I was with the Great Train Robber, Tommy Wisbey and, as I walked to the bar where Tommy was, my mate looked a little uncomfortable. So I looked over my shoulder and, there she stood. She, is a lovely looking woman - much to my regret - meaning, that was the main reason I fell for her, but as the saying goes, "Beauty is only skin deep" only I had to have that confirmed to me in the most hurtful way. So, although it was a little different from young Vicky's situation, I can understand her loss. I just wish I had known here and, given her some advice on the matter and, like her also, I know what it is like for so many things in your life to go wrong and, continuously.

Whilst talking of drugs, I must tell you about the damage the dreaded cortisone injection does. Although I played many times with the stuff pumped into my ankle, the worst moment (when I realised just what damage it does) came in my first match as captain of the Seattle Sounders. The carpet in the Kingdome was pretty kind, for it had a nice cushioned Astroturf, as I was still struggling with my injury. Our club doctor, Marty Kushner - what a real nice man he was - injected me with this stuff about five minutes before entering the arena. What I did not realise was that he had pumped only enough of the drug to last me just over 90 minutes. That is an hour and a half playing time and of course 15 minutes through the half-time period. You see, in the North American Soccer League, if the scores were level at 90 minutes, you went into overtime. This was where you played until either one of the teams scored, or after another half-hour you went into a shoot-out. If it goes the distance you could be out there well over two-and-a-half- hours and, that was where we were heading, when once again, 'Ouch!'

After finishing all-square with the Tulsa Roughnecks, I took to the field for overtime. About five minutes into it I felt as if someone was once again trying to hack it from my leg. The pain was absolutely excruciating. I left the field in agony. The ecstasy of my latest move had gone and, once again I was in hell.

So the lead up to my dream FA Cup Final in 1970 was the stuff of nightmares. I was now seeing every doctor, including a witch doctor, and an acupuncture specialist. We even held a séance in the prefab during the week of the final. The information we found out from the 'other side' was that I would not score at Wembley.

How could I from that famous bench?

After the first encounter with Leeds United, as I left the Field of Dreams following a 2-2 draw, Dave Sexton put his arm on my shoulder and told me that, "Had you played, there would be no replay. Let us get you into hospital."

So I was hospitalised in Earls Court in the place where my son was born, the Princess Beatrice. I felt awful from day one, all because I knew I would not make the replay. However, looking back once again, compared to coming round in Treves, it made everything I'd ever been through all look so trivial.

I could at least then walk. I could talk.

I could laugh at the injustice. But in Treves, I could not do anything. I was paralysed!

Rio Ferdinand doesn't know he's lived, crying over a training ground collision with one of his own players. The strange and funny thing is he's the only player Emile Heskey has ever put out of a game - weird!

All I did in this particular hospital was rest while people came in making a fuss and, trying to build my hopes up. The one consolation was that I was wined and dined with the best Italian food from Francos. Franco was a great friend of Camillo from Alexandre and, this was to become my second restaurant. 10CC sang that Life is a Minestrone and mine certainly was for a few days, followed by steak pizziola, my favourite steak dish and, the waiters would give me the full treatment, no expense spared. Great people, the Malts!

Well-wishers and telephone calls bombarded the Upcerne Road HQ of Football. But there was not one moment when I thought that I would make the replay at Old Trafford. People would call wanting to hear of my progress, or in this particular case, lack of it.

One day, a little old Irish lady from Victoria wrote inviting me to her home. Her family were big Chelsea fans and she was a faith healer. She was convincing enough for me to take a chance, thinking she could cure me.

I was becoming more like the horse Seabiscuit, a useless case, simply incurable!

The difference being, with one of the most famous horses of all time, it was in his head.

Mine was in my ankle.

She stroked my ankle and for a moment I felt hope. It was quite obviously false hope - and was I just kidding myself?

Later, Peter Houseman told me of someone in Wimbledon, who was a spiritualist and, someone he had great faith in. Again hopeless, I was running out of options and time.

In the first edition of the Ballet I covered the FA Cup final. I find it very difficult to do that now. I barely get through thinking about it, talking about it, or writing of it, without feeling nausea. So I will skip it if you don't mind. The best thing I can say about it is that we beat Leeds United in the replay at Old Trafford and, qualified for the

European Cup Winners Cup where although I played, I almost missed that replay as well, more of that later though.

So I never got to play against Leeds in that final and, I often wonder just how it would have all turned out in that first match. It would have suited me. The Horse of the Year Show had absolutely destroyed the surface, with Harvey Smith and all of his horsey pals making a mockery of it all. The pitch was all churned up like a ploughed field, which would have suited my young legs. What we must take into account here, was that had I played, I would not have gone through the trauma that West Bromwich brought, so I would have been injury-free and, ready for Bremner and Giles.

Sometimes I try to figure it all out, but each time I do, it always comes out differently.

Mostly I try to forget this year ever existed.

Although, on sitting up without any feelings in my legs, once leaving the ITU, this was trivial.

You see, the most frustrating thing is that these types of experiences only come along once in someone's lifetime, but having said that it happened again to me, didn't it? I have already explained what a season it had been, leading step by step not only to Wembley, but Mexico. Extraordinary!

There is something that nobody ever mentions about great moments or occasions in not only sport, but life itself and, in this case, the repercussions of a Leeds United victory. I have bumped into several of their players since, Johnny Giles most of all, in England, America and Canada and, he never mentioned those two matches. I have come across people from Leeds and, they don't either, but can you imagine them saying nothing if Osgood had not come up with that most wonderful of goals and, then Hutch hadn't of thrown that ball for what seemed like miles, before ending up in the Leeds net via David Webb's shoulder?

I don't think we'd have heard the last of it and, then there would have been Don Revie rubbing it in, especially with Brian Clough and, every time I was close to him, which thankfully wasn't often, I could see that night in his eyes.

Oh, we have had years of such pleasure, if only for them and, not us, losing...

With all of the renewed interest in Seventies football and the culture involved, the BBC ran a series called Alive and Kicking. Nearly all of one episode concerned that '70 FA Cup Final replay. Strange how they re-wrote history to exclude me from the programme at a time when I had the strongest image in the game, except for George of course. The fact that I missed that final was barely touched upon, yet had Leeds United been deprived of Bremner or Giles, I wonder what excuses would have been made?

In the intervening 18 days between Wembley and Manchester (when I was hospitalised), Leeds United had lost to Glasgow Celtic in the European Cup. So this was all they had left to fight for. They had been done by Everton in the championship race and now Jock Stein - what a man he was - and his team had beaten them. So they had to go into this match against a team hell-bent on putting the final touches to a season where at one time they looked like doing the Treble. It was up to us to see they finished with nothing, but we needed no such incentive.

One of the upmarket Sunday newspapers interviewed me from my hospital bed and one of the obvious questions was, "do you think you could lift the trophy?"

They also wondered whether I thought that Leeds were like Sisyphus. He was the one who had supposedly pushed three boulders to the top of three mountains and watched them as they rolled backwards into the Valley. Did I think that Chelsea, even without my talents, could leave Leeds empty handed?

My answer was that Chelsea would win the FA Cup and as for Sisyphus, I did not recall him playing for Charlton! At first I must admit I thought he was talking about some disease, the one you could catch around those streets in Soho where the FA, thanks to that worm Adam Crozier, are so at home.

When I woke up on the morning of 29 April 1970, I felt like a failed terrorist; the bomb had gone off and, I was the remains. I had missed the final and, after making Alf Ramsey's 40 for Mexico, I had not made the final 22. I was only cut because of my injury and many years later, at Wembley in fact, that great Daily Mirror journalist Ken Jones, then of The Independent, reminded me of such times by saying, "Did you ever know that had you been fit for Mexico, you would have played?"

Thanks Ken, but no thanks, I didn't really want to hear that mate!

I can only imagine, looking back on those final two matches in Mexico, that Alf would have had me in mind as the player who could come on when Bobby Charlton's limbs were becoming a little weary. And that's what happened against the Germans, when at 2-0 up he brought Bobby off to give him a much needed rest for the following match. It backfired!

There was no following match because of such a substitution.

As I just said about had Alf left Bobby out at Wembley and, can you imagine things going wrong, he wouldn't have got the sack, he would have got hung, especially with the World Cup final taking place in London and, bringing a Leeds United player in to replace the great man. Plus, I like Norman and, he was a bloody good player, but replace Bobby in an England shirt, this is Cuckoo's Nest stuff...

Alf had messed up twice in the heat of Mexico. The first of these was giving Franz the time and space to get forward and, in doing so, got the Germans back into the match - through bringing off Charlton. That would have been me substituting the great man and, I continue to wonder just what might have happened if it had been me replacing him?

So, I had to wait another five years to finally play against one of my great heroes, 'The Keizer.'

Had I played my part in that magnificent '70 triumph against Leeds United, then gone on to play in Mexico, on the greatest stage of all and, what turned out to be the greatest World Cup of all, the mind-boggles to think what direction my career would have gone.

All of this was caused by something so simple - a ball dropping from the sky with nobody near me. But it is the simplest things that can be so damaging. A mistimed tackle or a driver's handling of a steering wheel.

I had been in this position a million and one times before - just like crossing the road - but much like crossing that road, one second you're almost onto the pavement and, the next thing is like you're flying over the Bermuda Triangle and, you're off the radar, or in my case, on life support.

These were the two defining moments in my entire life!

Ramsey's prediction was chillingly accurate - the feeling of this all being unfulfilled was to haunt me all through life, all because of injuries to my once fit body. What had I done to deserve this?

I knew of the Wembley jinx; it used to occur each and every May, when some poor soul would miss the biggest match of his life.

But the one in Mile End Road was something a little different, for you miss more than a match.

It really hit home when standing in The Stanley Arms, which later became The Magpie and Stump on the corner of Limerston Street, watching the team bus glide by with all of my team-mates waving to those many thousands of supporters. I was engulfed in a way I cannot put into words. I was choked for a number of different reasons. How can something so joyous become so hurtful, spiteful and damaging to one so young?

I think from that day, my drinking got worse. I was drinking for different reasons. No excuses, just simply trying to work out like so many years later, why me?

When I mention my drinking and, say it got worse, is because it should get better, for you can drink happily, which I was doing before WBA and, once missing Wembley and Old Trafford, it did not taste the same. Overcoming a hangover in those days was a walk in the park, but they had gone from that, to an on-going headache and, years later, a rather continuous limp.

We all went back from the pub to the prefab for a party, which was more like a wake, one I much prefer to weddings as it happens, but this was different. There is something about someone dying that affects you and, today I had died and I found that was the difference, as you can celebrate a good person's life, but here I was commiserating mine.

I had a bath, washed my hair with a can of lager and cried into my bathwater. I cried once before in this tiny room when my girlfriend, Irene Roberts, gave me the news that she was in love with a Frenchman. I never did like the Frogs and, still don't!

In that epic thriller, I remember Billy Bremner doing what he did so many times, roll up his sleeves and, then push into the heart of the battle - the opposing defence. But it was too little, too late. Like the Samurai swordsmen, we had made the cut when it mattered.

BBC2 had shot a documentary on Leeds over the previous weeks in this, their nightmare end-of-season. Real 'fly-on-the-wall' stuff. As Chelsea went up to collect the cup, Jack Charlton stormed off the field to become the only player in the history of the competition not to walk the steps and collect his medal. Such was his rage, anger and disgust at Chelsea's triumph. I heard that he tried to kick the dressing-room door off its hinges. He caught a cab outside, refusing to be around to listen to all of those Chelsea voices singing their victory songs in the bath of the jubilant adjacent dressing room.

And, what made things worse was he would have heard Osgood, who was not only our best singer, but the one who stuck that first knife into that white shirted machine.

In seems odd saying that Leeds United had a heart?

Charlton and Don Revie could never forgive or forget the humiliation they had suffered at the hands of Chelsea on that most magnificent of nights. Revie did all he could to thwart the international careers of Osgood and myself and, anyone else who had any ambitions to become an England international, once he took over.

One moment, whilst playing my best football on hearing the news about Ramsey's sacking, I looked back at my walk through the corridor once putting the receiver down, after he told me of my fate. It was haunting, but now this was sweet music to my ears and within a few short weeks the added news that the former Leeds United manager was to be his successor, took me straight back down that corridor, only it was darker and incredibly, more sinister.

Death Row springs to mind....

Again, how can a man so bias, become the leader of your country?

Charlton went on to worldwide acclaim as manager of the Republic of Ireland, employing the kind of tactics they had used against Chelsea. It still seems so strange how he did so remarkably well. For when I was at Arsenal, I was speaking to Frank Stapleton after he had just returned from international duty and, asked how Jack was?

Frank said, "The funniest thing happened, he asked if Liam Brady was a good player?"

I don't know if Jack never knew, or was he simply testing Frank?

Like Revie allowing Jimmy Greenhoff to leave Leeds United and, then afterwards not giving him an England cap when he was the best player in the country, at a time that he and I were playing quite brilliantly at Stoke City.

Jack, it is said, like Johnny Giles - who also managed Ireland - had a little black book, with more Chelsea players jotted inside of it than any other team. You can believe Hutchinson and Osgood were two of the names, while I am told on good authority that those of my mate Eddie McCreadie and mine were etched into the pages of that pocket-sized genius, Giles. Not long ago in the Manchester Hilton, I asked Johnny whilst on stage about that book. He denied it, but hit-men do!

Perhaps somewhere down the line we lost our way. We took the Cup on that unforgettable and most magnificent of nights, which made everyone believe in us and, did so by scoring a record number of goals along the way.

But like Jake La Motta, when we were up against it in those two finals, we never went down.

However, I could not wait to get out of Manchester. There was no Slack Alice this time for me, it hurt too much. I made the last train out of there on a different kind of sleeper from the ones I became almost addicted to and, reached London Euston, the station where I was to become such a regular customer to and from the Potteries. I use it now as I write and, use it more than ever. I spend more time in the Potteries than I do Chelsea, the place that has left a nasty taste in my mouth.

I have made more friends in the Potteries since signing in the mid-Seventies and, I enjoy the surroundings there much more than my days in what was once Chelsea. I am also given more respect, both from the football club - Tony Pulis in particular, who respects the part I played in their history - and those fans, who unlike those at Chelsea, hold true players and, local ones, so close to their hearts.

Even at such a late hour, I found the place was throbbing. The problem was, so was my ankle. My everlasting memory of that torturous night was drinking amongst some very happy Chelsea supporters in the Tottenham Court Road Sporting Club. They were a lot happier than I was. I was commiserating. I was choked and felt like a leper. But, even in the mist of such glory, little did I know that one day soon, that was exactly how I would be treated by both the club and those fans, me, the boy who came from a couple of hundred yards down the road.

My mind flashes to Henri Charriere as he walks into that Leper Colony, after escaping from Devil's Island and, I feel that I will always be in good company, for if it's good enough for Papillon...

I felt so left out of it all, much like all these years later, however, looking back, I would have been better in the kind of coma that was awaiting me, one which would change my life in such a completely different way.

Those days, weeks, months and years leading to my most tragic moment had haunted me because of missing two such monumental occasions. Always keeping in mind this led to my World Cup exit.

Now, in comparison, they seem so very trivial, almost non-existent, almost to the point of meaningless.

It is only the writing of this book that gives me so much pleasure. But that is nothing to do with the clubs I played for, as you will know when running your eyes over the last page. It was, and still is, all about those who pulled the shirt over their heads alongside me and, of course, socialised and celebrated through so many happy times.

Footnote: I have always said that the only consolation in missing that final was that Tommy Baldwin pulled on my shirt; however, this was just something I was trying to cling onto. Having said that, had it been a player I disliked I would have been even sicker, especially someone lucky – as I've said and - someone who hadn't earned it - but Tommy was a great pal, who still is, and I thought the world of him. Anyhow, the reason I include this is because of the following, which I find quite spooky, for the simple reason of reading about my best friend in North America, Chris Bennett:

An English immigrant to Canada, Bennett was a member of the Vancouver Whitecaps of the NASL in their inaugural season of 1974, playing 8 games and netting two goals and an assist. Just before the 1976 season, the Whitecaps traded Bennett to the Seattle Sounders in exchange for Tommy Baldwin. In 1978, he moved to the Memphis Rogues. Prior to going to North America, Bennett was a member of Chelsea F.C. in 1970 and '71, although he never played a first-team game. He played indoor soccer at some point, likely the 1978-9 season, for the Cleveland Force.

Chris is a dear friend and, one who when people say, "You can count your friends on one hand?" he'd be one and, he is a wonderful character, who I got very close to when in Cleveland together. He flew to my hospital bed in 1998 from Canada and, yet many of my team-mates in London were nowhere to be seen and, that is to give you some idea of the man. He also flew into London and travelled to Stoke-on-Trent for the '12th Anniversary' of my 15 December ordeal.

Well, I think enough said about Chris, for that says it all, about the man.

20 THE SPIRIT IN THE SKY

Europe was going to become the breaking up of several things including marriages and, finally the Chelsea team itself. Air stewardesses were going to become a big part of our lives, although I was never one of the guilty parties. Divorces were going to play a big part in our new beginning, never dreaming, that those splits would include Osgood and I.
Me going north, Oz going west and Chelsea going down!

The club had been in Europe before and, I remember it well. It was on an electrifying night when a Venables hat-trick against Roma and, Eddie being given his marching orders, were the two outstanding events of a night of high excitement and incredible drama.

I was just a Kingsley schoolboy and, can recall standing under the North Stand and, after sitting in there in my early years, was not surprised they knocked it down, for if they hadn't it would have fell down on its own. The last time I sat there it was rocking and, tonight the whole place was, only for an entirely different reason. In this coming year I was to realise just how those supporters felt on the night against Bruges, if only for looking back on this night against Roma.

I also - although not a Chelsea supporter - would never forget such an atmosphere, never knowing, that one night I'd experience such an incredible high and, as I just said, that was to come against the Belgians about two months down the line.

But setting out into the unknown, we might have been watching a movie and, one where you might say it was: Looking into the Future...

All of what was happening on this particular evening, was nothing compared to what was about to happen to this team. What was so glamorous at the time turned out to be so damaging to so many people. Even a year later, when the boys were running around town with Pans People, everything took a back seat to all of this. It seemed that going into Europe was something that brought a new meaning to bonuses. The bonus was that two, three, four of our boys could enjoy something that to me was pretty hilarious - those lovely young things in British Airways and Caledonian uniforms.

In those days these girls were like those lovely young girls on Page 3, even today they've disappeared, nothing compares to these times.

Oz in particular was besotted with them the most and, one in particular, Miss Pippa Cook-Smith. One of the funniest things I have ever heard about him and his female companion from BA came while he was with Southampton. He had ditched his car, literally, near Heathrow and, he and his young lady had to 'Leg it.'

As usual it reached the press. On getting to the training ground Mick Channon said to Oz when he entered the dressing room, "I saw you made the nationals today mate."

The big centre-forward said, "What do you mean?" To which the horse trainer replied, "It said in the paper that a car was found in the ditch and, two people were seen running down the M4 from the scene of the crime."

Oz then said, "Well, where do I come into it?" The quick witted England striker finished by saying, "Well, it said that she was about 30 yards in front of him," which had the dressing room falling about.

On a serious note, it was sad that the break-ups really did affect so many people and, finally it was the straw that broke Dave Sexton's back, even though Osgood still wanted to break his neck. Although our problems did not begin in Europe, the sessions which followed our trips in the Cup Winners Cup were the main reasons for the breaking up of that team. You might say, the spirit was in the sky and, lots of it. He would detest our journeys home from away matches. Thursday morning we would be on an early-morning flight knowing it would lead into an afternoon out in a pub or afternoon club. This was nothing new.

But with Dave it was simply a case of him being there to watch it all begin. This was the part of the job that he did not like, but could not get away from. It was like he would have to simply sit there and suffer, as the boys swapped stories, sipped their "hair of the dogs" and, made arrangements for the rest of their day off.

This was just another reason why he should have stuck to coaching, for he would have looked at it in a completely different way?

For some reason, Thursday was the best afternoon of the week. If you played on a Wednesday night and, had the next day off (free), it would definitely lead into a session, especially when coming home from an away match and, more importantly, winning, then the drink tasted better than ever, especially knowing that there was another trip to follow. That was the beauty of playing the first leg away, for if you got that first result - which we did in every round, but one, we knew nobody would beat us at the Bridge on a European Wednesday night.

This was also what happened after England matches. I remember Alan Ball getting back from Hampden Park on a Thursday and, going on a spree. At midnight he found himself in a new watering hole where the barman warned him that, "Before you order, I must tell you that your manager (Bertie Mee) frequents here and, he might even be here any minute." So Alan took the hint and slid out. On the following Monday morning Mee called the tiny World Cup winner into his Highbury office and said, "Look Alan, you are playing brilliantly, both for us and England, but don't spoil it. Keep out of my pleasure places."

Good management!

Now, do you see about the difference between a coach and a manager?

All of that on top of no sleep on the Wednesday was not really the best preparation for a Saturday afternoon League match. It led to several showdowns, mainly with Dave and Oz, the two main protagonists. And as I said, it led to several marriage breakdowns, so all in all our European excursions were very costly in more ways than one.

Winning the European Cup Winners Cup was probably the worst thing that happened to us, if you look at it sensibly. Had we got knocked out early, we could have concentrated on our League form and, there would have been fewer distractions, mainly in several households and, of course the manager's office.

Today the talk of Europe being a distraction is a load of baloney in comparison. It is an excuse for managers. Just look at Liverpool over the past few years, absolutely hopeless in the Premiership and, so successful in the Champions League, although Benitez wrecked all of that. It didn't affect Manchester United in 2009. They won the Premier League and, lost in the Champions League final to the best football team in Europe, Barcelona.

Bad managers and excuses turn my gut.

They get absolute fortunes and, yet still make excuses, then get sacked and get a big pay-out and another lucrative job. Just look at Benitez (June 2010), he got sacked for a nightmare season at

Liverpool (where they failed to reach the Champions League), but got a £6m pay-off and walks into the Inter job.

As Willie Nelson wrote and sang so beautifully, it's "Crazy."

The directors who employ such frauds need to get their heads tested. The same goes for the FA. Again, just look at Eriksson. As if I could not have done a better job than him. And then there's Capello. Now he's got to be as lucky as anyone who ever walked through that gate, although Lancaster Gate was gone by the time he got there, thanks to that idiot Adam Crozier. What organisation would give you a two year extension on your contract before you reach the World Cup?

Not long ago Hull City employed Iain Dowie for the last ten Premier League matches. Alan Shearer also took him on as assistant to help Newcastle out of the same position. They both got relegated. Where is he now, like Shearer, a TV pundit!

I was already making enemies in the game, usually those that were in a position to do my career the maximum amount of damage. Jimmy Hill springs to mind. I recall him at the Football Writers Footballer of the Year Awards seemingly looking down on me. That might just have been my imagination, but after what I told you about his Match of the Day programme, I know I am not imagining it.

I take nothing away from Bremner, who was one of my favourite players and, opponents, but I thought that in my first season I deserved to win that most coveted award. That would have been a great consolation on the eve of that FA Cup final. At least I could have drowned my sorrows in style. And if not me, at least Osgood should have won it for a phenomenal season leading up to Mexico.

Hill is a nothing in our game, no matter what they say about his feats at Coventry City. I suppose it didn't help that I had to watch him play at Fulham alongside the great Haynes. Dave Sexton was once grilled by Hill after Chelsea had lost at Liverpool. Hill was critical of our short passing game on this day. Dave was subdued and nodded in agreement to most of it. Dave should have responded to Hill like he did to Osgood and gone for his chin and, he could not have missed.

Imagine Hill coming out with such trash to Shankly or Clough?

Or trying such a thing with Ferguson today?

And then there's Mourinho, who would tie him in knots.

I don't believe people like Hill should be given such airtime.

In the end, I would turn the TV off whenever he came on, the same as today.

A few days after we settled into our new role as the first team ever to win the FA Cup for the Chelsea faithful, we signed Keith Weller from Millwall. An excellent signing I thought at the time - and, I have never changed my mind. I went to Spain with my best pal, Leslie May, to do what George Best did in North America, Drink Canada Dry. I bought a new suit from Major on Harwood Road for about £250, which was more than a month's wages. His clobber was fantastic, a wonderful cut. He was a tailor who entertained some of the great names in show business, which included Ronnie Corbett. He gave me a pair of his slacks one day by mistake and, I walked round his shop talking like Alan Ball. Years later I took Geoff Hurst there. It was too up-market for Oz. He was still frequenting all of my Kings Road boutiques.

Spain was a complete disaster. I returned two stone heavier than when I went down that hole at The Hawthorns. What made it even worse was that whenever I went on vacation I would always have a run each morning. This time, due to my duff ankle, it was out of the question. My weight ballooned.

I made a pact with myself from a very early age - well, after that League Cup match against Leeds - that if I was going to live my life in the fast lane, I would have to go that extra mile in training and, that was what I did.

There are more lanes in The Mile End Road than any other, but he got me in the slow one!

I did not think anything of it on my return, thinking that pre-season would soon see me back to my fighting weight, but how wrong could I be?

Little did I know with that long, long hot summer and, the hard grounds, I would struggle to work it off, I simply thought that a hard pre-season would see me right. But I did not realise just how bad my ankle injury was. It simply did not allow me to perform on such underfoot conditions. Pre-season then was the toughest time of the year without such a hindrance, but here I was with what now became the biggest struggle of my life.

Again, in comparison to entering a different world in the Royal London and St Bartholomew's Hospitals, it was simply a limp in the park.

Without your complete fitness forget it and, here I was struggling to shed those pounds and, my manager was not amused. I had come back to our Mitcham Training Ground as an overweight lookalike of Alan Hudson. Then through my inability to train, I would get depressed and, then drink more. I know what you're thinking, 'as if you need an excuse.'

It became very lonely. You think that the whole world is against you and, it is easy to go into your shell. Well The Park Tavern and The Lord Palmerston were my shells, the places I took my problems to. The FA Cup final still haunted me. The Mexico World Cup too. And being the animal I am, I drifted, which would lead to my marriage falling apart.

But that was just something waiting to happen.

There were scars on my soul. People don't see things hidden so deep. Plus, you have to put on a front, something I did so well. People think that you're celebrating, whereas I was aching inside. As you might well know, the bottling up of such trauma can damage more than just your ankle. It was easier to take to the booze, mainly because nothing else was going right. The manager, the physiotherapist (trainers in those days) and, club doctors did not have a clue just what I was going through. So, what happens is that you fight against everybody. I just could not handle the injury. When you begin a season and, have to wait for the bad weather before you could even think of playing, it was extremely frustrating. As I have said, I like the best of everything, so playing badly was something that drove me off the rails. And when there is a pub on every corner, this was the place where people who, after a few drinks, made more sense than those who should be taking more interest.

The summer slipped by, played out to the backdrop of that incredible World Cup, where Bobby Moore returned from his finest moments on the playing fields of the world. Brazil had won it for a record third time to take the Jules Rimet Trophy outright. I watched as many of the games as I could, imagining being there alongside Bobby and Alan Ball and, obviously wanting Oz to come on and continue his great form.

But Alf did not see it the way I did.

Here's how it reads on Wikipedia....Quarter-finals: The quarter-finals saw a transformed Italy prevail 4–1 over Mexico after trailing 0-1. The host took the lead against Italy with a Jose Gonzales goal, but his team-mate Gustavo Pena equalised with an own goal before half-time. Italy then took over, and dominated the second half. Two goals from Luigi Riva and one from Gianni Rivera saw them go through 4-1. In Guadalajara, Peru's World Cup adventure ended in the quarter-finals, where they lost 4-2 to Brazil after an entertaining and dramatic match between two equally attacking teams.

The game between Uruguay and the Soviet Union was goalless until five minutes from the end of extra time, when Victor Esparrago struck to send the South Americans through. The last quarter-final, a rematch of the 1966 World Cup final between England and West Germany, produced one of the great matches of World Cup history. England suffered a serious blow before the game, when their great goalkeeper Gordon Banks was taken ill with food poisoning. His deputy Peter Bonetti stepped into the breach and, early in the second half England had a 2-0 lead and, seemed to have West Germany firmly in its grasp. However, West Germany pulled one back with a goal from Beckenbauer in the 68th minute. In a panic, England coach Alf Ramsey decided then to substitute the tiring Bobby Charlton.

Without Charlton, England lost its ability to set its own pace on the game and could not contain the relentless German attacks which eventually resulted in West Germany equalizing eight minutes from time with an Uwe Seeler header. In extra-time, Geoff Hurst had a goal mysteriously ruled out before Gerd Müller's winning goal in extra time after another Bonetti error, thus, ending England's reign as world champions.

Well, that sounds quite simple, however, at the time it was horrendous, as Ramsey messed up big time. As I said, Alf got it wrong against Brazil with his substitution and, then did so again, by bringing off Bobby Charlton. The one thing that we will never know is just what might have happened had he played his cards right and brought on Osgood, instead of Astle. I think the whole world, were stunned at his decision and, when the ball dropped at his feet that same world held its breath. Osgood, trust me, would have buried it. The Astle FA Cup winning goal flashed through my mind, when he hit a half-volley into the Everton net. This time though, he hit the bar with a much easier opportunity. Osgood, I would bet my life, hit the bar afterwards, but not in a good mood and, like me, must have been absolutely sick and, if he was, then so was Bonetti.

Like I tell you about certain things haunting me, well that chance that fell to the West Bromwich Albion (What is it with WBA?) striker, must have haunted Osgood from that day on and, what made it even worse, he was sitting so close to it.

They (whoever "they" are?) had got to Gordon Banks and, without going into it, I believe did the same to Bonetti, because I heard something that distressed our keeper, however, I like Peter too much, to mention anything personal. They say things happen in threes and, here is just another example: Bobby in Bogota and, Banks and Bonetti against Germany.

I'm also quite certain that Osgood would have come back from Mexico hailed as the greatest centre-forward in the world had Alf picked him. Instead, he chose Jeff Astle in front of him. Well, I told you of his first great mistake and, this was the second and, much more damaging. I know I have mentioned this several times before, but this is how much it riles me. Tell me please, am I crazy? Was Jeff Astle more cut out for the World Cup finals in Mexico than Peter Osgood? If he was honest, I don't think even Frank Skinner would disagree. He weren't even a better singer than our number 9.

Oz told me on his return that he was, "absolutely buzzing" out there and, Bobby Moore repeated that to me. The brilliant England captain agreed with me, that the Chelsea number nine was mistreated. He also said that he was the fittest he'd ever been in that Mexico heat, dropping any excess weight he had (which was minimal) and, was ready to take on the world. I told you about his supreme confidence and, the bigger the stage he could be anything. He had proved it at every level until Mexico and, it upsets me that players can be completely abused by such negative management and, Ramsey was that and, it has been the undoing of our game ever since. These tracksuit managers with badges have absolutely slaughtered our game. I have always said - since travelling the world with Chelsea - that we were second class citizens in football terms and, to make things worse our coaching system is even lower than that. This is why we have always chosen the inferior players, because the coaches are not intelligent enough or honest enough to see that they should not be in such jobs.

And then there became the introduction of foreign players and managers, not only at club level but nationally. Can you imagine a manager from another country pulling George Cohen away from that Argentinian, calling him "an animal?"

I can tell you right now that my son is going in the same direction and, my father would turn in his grave. I can only imagine my son, Anthony, telling a Jimmy Greaves, Peter Osgood or Jimmy Greenhoff what to do, totally preposterous.

My son is coaching the Bahrain under-21s as I write.

Had I been there with him, I think we would have come back two of the hottest properties on the planet, had Alf played us and, I think that there was also a very good case for Currie, Bowles and Worthington. This was still going on in my head and, what with my frustration of not being able to regain my fitness, it piled on top of me like an avalanche. After Mexico nothing seemed to go right on the international scene for either of us, it seemed like Mexico was not only the end for me and Oz but England itself and, as I said at that time, it has turned out to be true.

The craziest thing about all of this was I was 19 and Osgood 23, now what other country could that happen?

If Oz was disappointed with the outcome, then Catty was doubly so, for his worst nightmares came true against the West Germans and, although I told you without giving you a reason, there was something wrong mentally with the Chelsea goalkeeper.

Oh, how I felt for him. To this day, I can still make a case for him. I know that the Beckenbauer goal looked like a soft one, but I think it looked far worse than it was and, given what was to follow, it kind of escalated and, got highlighted out of all proportion. The defending in that penalty area when Seeler got that back-header was something out of the Duke of York Coaching Manual. Bonetti had an absolutely blinding season in our goal and one mistake should never have been magnified as much as it was. It was a simple case of being in the right place at the wrong time or was it vice-versa.

The Germans, it was said, poisoned Gordon Banks. Now could they have put something in Peter's half-time cuppa?

No it was definitely something else, for after removing Gordon that was their first job accomplished, although they had failed with Bobby. They didn't need to spike Alf's cuppa, if that is what they had in mind in Mexico at that time. Alf didn't need any assistance in completely getting it all wrong the whole tournament long and, he only got away with it because of those two very controversial decisions at Wembley four years prior. But going back to that thing called luck, which made Geoff Hurst four years earlier, it had definitely all ran out.

Osgood had no such good fortune.

Also, why is it that the Peter Shilton blunder against Poland, that got us knocked out in 1974, is never mentioned?

And then he got away with it again when leaving his line far too late when Maradona "mugged him" with his hand. I don't care what anyone else says; our goalkeeper should have been out and eaten the Argentine genius. Diego was the best player in the world at that time, but not in that department.

I recall listening to Banks talking about having an imaginary line about a yard in front of the goal-line and, that helped him scoop that Pele header out and, with that extra 36 inches Shilton would have gobbled that up and, we would have still been in the game.

No argument, once again!

It is obvious that Maradona is quicker to react than Shilton, after all he is a footballing genius. His total awareness is on a different level, but I still thought that the goalkeeper had every advantage here and blew it!

So, in effect, he cost us two World Cups!

What Alf Ramsey did with his substitution was far more damaging than anything I have ever done in or out of an England shirt. And after all, we were still a goal to the good. Then the wheels fell off and, all through bad substitutions. Since '66, Ramsey had made quite a few 'cock-ups' but, like Sexton, when you're winning it papers over all the cracks.

The incredible thing here was that England played better in their last two matches in Mexico than what they did all through the tournament, four years earlier, when winning it!

And going back to the Osgood debate and, the closest thing I have ever seen to him. When I was putting pen to paper as an apprentice in '66, England were on their way to carrying off the World Cup (where we had more luck than my mate Tommy Wisbey and his Great Train robbing mates). In that competition, there was a player called Albert. The Hungarian No 9 was being hailed as the finest in the world. If he was, then Osgood was the finest ever. And then in '70 there was the Brazilian, Tostao, who linked up the play brilliantly with Pele, Rivelino, Gerson and the rest of his pals in those bright glistening yellow shirts. Both those players were not in the same class of my old team-mate. They could ghost past defenders in such fashion, but they could not hurt defenders like him. They could not score fabulous goals like him. They could not change a match on their own. I have stood in amazement as he simply changed a match with no help from anyone. He was just simply what Tina sang about. There are many injustices inside these pages and, Oz in Mexico is certainly one. The other is that had George Best been in Mexico, he would have showed the world that he was what Pele called him. Just like Sinatra said of Bennett and, around the same time, the entire world said about Garfield Sobers. I recall running home from school to watch the West Indian genius hit a spin bowler named Nash for six sixes in one over. This took place down in Wales and, it was like being in Portugal to watch George destroy and embarrass those Benfica defenders. Also, like being at the Olympics, and seeing Bob Beaman nearly jump out of the stadium. Then there was Lester Piggott nicking a jockey's whip on the run-in, just to remind him who he was taking on. Going back to music, there was those incredible Beatles. There are certain things you can't argue with. They were light years ahead and, with Osgood there was absolutely no doubt he was the best in the world.

If only he had been given the opportunity to show everyone watching: The Greatest Show on Earth!

I really get the hump when people have a go at George. When the World Cup came around every four years, he spent his month in Spain with so many beautiful young ladies. When you look at our players today spouting off about what they are and aren't going to do around this time, it puts it all into perspective. Why don't they just take their obscene wages and, thank their lucky stars. And that is exactly what they are. That is, if you can call then stars? They should keep their lips closed tight whilst letting this country down time after time after time and, then afterwards swan around as their followers pick up the bill. They did it again in South Africa.

They should take a leaf out of George's book and, sit by the pool every four years!

How can you be so frustrated having the most beautiful women in the world?

Well take it from me, George was just that and, along with him, my other pal, Pat Jennings, like Oz and George, would have been hailed in the same way. Like I say, on so many occasions people don't know what it is like to watch inferior beings experience something you'll never get the opportunity to do.

It is rather like Frank losing his voice and having to listen to Des O'Connor for the rest of his life.

Around that time, talking of the best, there were four players from these shores that were always called up into the World XI. Two were ours, Charlie and Eddie and, then there was that other Scottish genius Jim Baxter and Denis the Menace, George's great mate Denis Law. Which always reminds me, whatever happened to the Scottish game?

Mind you, England has never boasted a player such as Baxter, so he was a total one-off in every way.

We have also never had a Dave Mackay, Dalglish, Souness, Bremner or Eddie Gray, who, as you know by now, would never have been picked by Ramsey for playing wide on the left.

Had Eddie Gray been English, Emile Heskey would have got picked in front of him, that's how it is!

People are forever talking to me about today's players not being in that class, yet earn such vast amounts of money. I am breathless for an answer. George died with just his many, many glorious memories and, of course, someone else's liver. Osgood and Baxter had to run pubs to get by. Charlie and Eddie were also very serious drinkers, which nearly cost them their lives. Jimmy Greaves was a self-confessed alcoholic, who has dragged his life together to become one of the most well respected human beings of our time. He is a great After Dinner talker, who tells it how it is and, of course, he was a little like me, being absolutely distraught when missing those final matches in our '66 success. Again, like Osgood and Astle there is the same situation about Greaves and Roger Hunt, simply no comparison.

I have told you about. Pat Jennings being an enigma, for the want of a better word; or maybe a mystery, an introverted giant of a man in more ways than one, whilst his other team-mate, Dave Mackay, remains so very well respected both sides of the border. My mate Martin Knight wrote his book and found him to be amazing and charming. Ball was a giant on the playing fields of the world, but in the manager's office he shrank to his normal size. And then there is Bobby Charlton. What can one say about this man?

He somehow got through that incredible trauma of the Munich Air Disaster and held a position at the football club that leaves others in the shade - in this country that is.

And, what is it about Scottish managers?

Busby, Ferguson, Shankly and Graham are just four examples. And now there is David Moyes, who one day will be added to such a list, a man who will surely sit in the hot seat at Manchester United once Sir Alex finally hangs up his medals and, money belt. Only difference is that unlike ninety-nine per-cent of his colleagues, he has earned every penny.

My theory is that the old adage of Scots giving nothing away may come into this equation.

I cannot leave this little statement without adding Jock Stein to such an incredible list.

Jock was going to win the European Cup that year, just as we were limbering up for our domestic one and, to do so we had follow up the Great Scot's fantastic achievement. They beat Leeds over those two matches in that semi-final, but that was over two legs, where our success was in a replay. However, at last, the Good Guy came through unscathed emotionally, that was apart from me.

Whilst Glasgow Celtic were putting Leeds United into their rightful place, all I could think about was winning the FA Cup, only this time make it to Wembley all in one piece, though that seemed a million miles from reality, taking into mind my new-found condition.

That was a dream….going back to May of 1970, did I say dream?

My father went to the Press with concerns of my future, thinking that I would not only, never be the same player, but may never play again. The problem that bothered him most was the swelling and, my inability to train. That was all caused by being in plaster for so long.

I look back on this as my Elvis period. I became like a bulimic in those times, gorging my way through the good times whilst drinking my way through my new found depression. I was sickened by the previous season and, totally frustrated at not being able to even contemplate full fitness. My form was nothing short of disastrous and, although as I gained experience, I learned to cope a little better, it never really eased the heartache and, pain of it all. I really was going through a very rough patch. It is incredible that when something so traumatic happens to you, especially one so young, people in higher places seem to turn a blind eye. They also point an ill-fated finger. Like so many years later in the Mile End Road, it always flashed through your head, why me?

To make things worse in my first gruelling 45 minutes in Amsterdam we faced Johan Cruyff, a player although pretty much unknown, was quickly becoming the new George.

He was sensational.

On a baking Sunday afternoon in July, I was feeling a little worse for wear as it was. Plus, on our arrival to this great city, we found out they had brought out a new drink. It was called Heineken.

Never realising that Ajax - better known for being a cleaning product - who were also an unknown quantity in those days - were on their way to becoming one of the greatest club teams of all-time.

We thought that a few of these would be all right on the night before a mere friendly. Well, if you'll excuse the pun, this cleaning product wiped the floor with us!

Johan turned on the style as I limped obliviously through a match that had now planted a lot more seeds in my, very troubled state of mind. The Flying Dutchman was completely unstoppable.

Not even Ronnie could lay a stud on him.

This was the new Golden Age of football and, a team who were known for playing Total Football were to emerge from the shadows of the Dutch League. We somehow equalised, but were totally outplayed and, outclassed. It wasn't such a big deal for it was only a friendly in Holland, not a European Cup Winners Cup match, something that we were about to experience very soon and, luckily they were not in our competition. That did not enter our minds at that time, because we were on our way back from a far-away tour and, simply dropping off an-hour-or-so from London for another match to sharpen us up. More like blunt us.

Around that time there was someone already playing under the name of The Flying Dutchman and, I bumped into him one evening in Alexandre, on the eve of a match on Centre Court. He was with American Marty Reissen and, I would not say they were like our boys in the Athens Hilton Drinking Team, but they looked very relaxed. I was a massive tennis fan in those days when they had such wonderful characters. Top of the Pops was John McEnroe. And then there was Nastase. Later on came The Iceman, Bjorn Borg, who became my favourite for his complete control and, for being someone who epitomises the Ballet - as did JM, who really was a Maverick of the game, therefore, had he played our game, in our time, he would have fitted in with Cooke, Hudson, Osgood and Hutchinson, sorry Nobby, you're going to have to sit this one out mate.

And I will never forget the brilliant Boris Becker win his very first Wimbledon in quite incredible fashion, although he reminded me quite a lot of another favourite of mine, Jurgen Klinsman, for he was on the floor a lot.

But back to that day in Amsterdam, where I only recall the Heineken, the Red Light District - where we were the night before the match - and Cruyff. Little did we know then that here were two reams that would win the two main European trophies in 1971 and, I was going to say that maybe it was something to do with the Heineken, but if one thing was for certain, Ajax might have slaughtered us on that afternoon, but they would have found us a different proposition the night before.

1971 European Cup Final

From Wikipedia: The 1971 European Cup Final was a football match held at Wembley Stadium, London, on 2 June 1971 that saw Ajax of the Netherlands defeat Panathinaikos of Greece 2–0. An incredible comeback in the second leg of their semi-final against Red Star Belgrade meant Panathinaikos became the first Greek side to reach a European Cup Final. However, Ajax were too strong, winning with an early Dick van Dijk strike, and a late goal from a shot by Arie Haan that deflected off defender Anthimos Kapsis and past the goalkeeper. This was the first of a run of three European Cup victories in a row for Ajax.

That really doesn't tell the entire story because the Greeks were not really a great side and, Ajax were just beginning to flex their European muscles.

If you really want to see the master at work go on U-Tube and press on The Johan Cruyff Dribbling Compilation and in hale the genius, yeah inhale, because it's simply breath taking. I am one of the players he made look daft, along with David Nish, as he did what he did so brilliantly, somehow wriggling his slim body in between me and my mate in a match in Washington, when our Seattle team were the best in the NASL.

But back to Tom Okker, you won't be surprised to hear me say JM was the main man. When you see and hear him today on TV at Wimbledon, you can understand why I think so little of those on Match of the Day and Sky. The man talks the way he played. There are no fences, or in his case, nets. He simply oozes class.

I was fortunate to bump into Jeremy Bates at the Britannia Stadium and found him delightful and, not long afterwards I watched him beat

JM at the Albert Hall, which must have been a right thrill for him. Like the good man he is, when I mentioned it to him, he played it down.

I would have told the entire world!

As I just said, had McEnroe played our game, he would have fitted nicely into our Chelsea team. The only problem would have been like Manchester United who needed two balls with George, we would have needed three with Charlie and Oz.

Only today's Barcelona can boast being anywhere near that Ajax side of the Seventies, only superior, and although they can boast Messi, they only need one ball, because their overall team work and ethic is clear for all to see!

After that match in Amsterdam it was clearer than Smirnoff Ice that firstly, I had to get my head round not only my ankle injury, but the excess weight I was carrying. I was facing another massive crisis with that injury, which was just one of many that would play such an incredible part of my life, but as I've told you several times that was all to come.

Although, looking back to think that I think about all of the trauma then and, after the 15 December incident, I truly don't know how I've done it. I have always said that the body is an incredible machine, but never really took much notice of the mental side of it and, when I see some people go into depression - like my great pal - and then, the other trauma that it brought to me, it is so totally amazing that you wake up and start again.

As I have said and, I mean it, this is my third life and, when I keep that in mind, I feel so much better, basically because my first life is a long way behind me and, with it my bad times are buried with it. My second life finished when Mr. Waddington died, however I lived on until Fatehi finished that life in the Mile End Road, well in the Resuscitation Room of the Royal London Hospital as they checked my vital signs (organs).

And, now I'm in the fifteenth year of my third and final life and, once again, as I said a little earlier, I believe in things happening in threes.

But going back to my troubles, which were beginning to rear their ugly heads - yeah, there were a few of them - which involved my new found love, Maureen.

Maureen was causing a different kind of trauma, this time though it was much closer to home. In fact, it was in that tiny prefab, a place where there was so much love. Maybe, just maybe, this is where and when all of my dreams turned into the on-going nightmares, but it would be unfair to put it all down to her, but only maybe!

This was Supertramp stuff again: When I was young I thought that life was so wonderful...

A little while after, on another sun-drenched afternoon, Everton visited the Bridge for the Charity Shield (today it is the Community Shield played at Wembley) and, they brought the same form that won them the championship. And to make things worse, Alan Ball was at it again, this time though, in his new white cut-away boots as he tore our midfield to shreds. It was so hot that Mexico sprung to mind, a mind that by now was becoming menacing.

Later on my boss in Seattle, Alan Hinton, would put in the best crosses in his white boots, I think he was the master at not only his timing of the cross, but the weight on them. John Robertson also springs to mind - funny how they were both under Clough. Players today - including Giggs - are nowhere near wingers in our day, when it came to putting in quality crosses.

It was tough enough facing the likes of Ball when you on the top of your game. I was far from that, in fact, I was going through my own personal nightmare, both on and off the field.

Ball showed on this day exactly what I thought the first time I ever set eyes on him. He was one of those very, very special players and, here he was a World Cup winner, who had just come back from playing so very well in Mexico '70.

Everything seemed to remind me of all that had gone on in that last horrifying end to the season. It was still haunting me. The pace was too much for me. I was a yard or so too slow at least and, as I just said, keeping up with Ball was hard enough when you were on your game. Keith Weller came in on the right, replacing Sponge in the No 7 shirt. Tommy had taken my place in those two finals which was the only consolation, for he is someone I love and admire. There are not too many of them in my time in the game, but Sponge is most definitely one of them. Had it been someone I did not have such feelings for, it might have been even worse. This was to become a tough time for him also with Keith coming in, although he looked booked for replacing Hutch, who was by now picking up injuries like George did Miss Worlds.

Hutch breaking his leg was the start of a catalogue of injuries, injuries that would wreck his career and almost cripple him in the coming years. Whenever I hear about the movie The Lion King, Hutch springs to the forefront of my mind. He was truly a lion. When I look at today's players with The Three Lions on their shirts, I laugh and I think 'Are you lot serious?' Hutch would have absolutely slaughtered you!

I have not seen a player since who compares with Hutch.

And as for all of this shirt-pulling!

He could set the whole team afire. Charlie and I would do so much setting up the play, but Hutch would ignite Chelsea and, take us into another dimension. What my old man said on that Sunday morning in the prefab was true, "This lad could be anything!" My mum was stunned, as he never ever spoke of any player outside of me and my brother, so he saw something very special in Ian and, was absolutely spot-on. It takes a special ability to pick out a player. Especially if you take into consideration the amount of money people like Benitez spent and, couldn't get Liverpool into the Champions League.

So between me and my dad, we recommended three players, Steve Bould, Frank Lampard and Ian Hutchinson, which is not bad for a decorator and out-or-work author/alcoholic, which I am kindly known as under people's breath, although mainly the latter. However, I was brought up on sticks and stones, which was something I warned Brian Clough about.

Liverpool had been thrashed by Ajax 5-1 with that man Cruyff behind it all. Afterwards, Shanks said that, "we could not play against defensive teams."

Shankly was the king of one-liners!

The biggest compliment of my career was paid by him. More of that match later though. In the meantime, he said of Hutch, "This boy is brave, very brave."

That one liner was a massive understatement.

Johan Cruyff could be called some kind of "freak" he was that good. He was without a doubt the greatest I'd ever been on a football field with!

As the grounds got harder, the games got faster and, I got more desperate trying to keep up, a combination of both my weight and, my chronic ankle condition. Well, that combination was growing, adding the booze to the injury, the heartbreak of the FA Cup final, Mexico and now Maureen. And there was absolutely no sign of my form returning. The early times of those fun-loving days and nights in the Kings Road were turning quickly into dim and dark lonely afternoons just off Gloucester Road, in The Town House.

It is absolutely amazing, like the dramatic saga in the Mile End Road, just how one flash can change your entire life. Where last April I would get out of bed and look forward to jumping in my car and going training, I now dreaded it and, as I say, the pitches were harder than a Bank Manager's heart and, the temperatures hotter than those girls wearing those mini-skirts and hot-pants in my beloved Kings Road.

My personal life was now hitting Fleet Street in an entirely different way, whereas I was the best young player since Jimmy Greaves at Chelsea on the back pages, I was now on the front pages for being a home wrecker, well, not me, but Maureen, but it was, as always, my fault. I suppose if I played today, I would be wearing Balotelli's undershirt.

And now I was so close to knocking George off the front pages and that day was not far off.

Today it was like John Terry knocking off Jordan, which would not surprise me - after all that went on leading up to South Africa.

And there is one thing for sure George wouldn't knock Jordan off and, neither would I, in my day, even if I had to have George's leftovers.

On one particular morning I turned over the first six pages of The Sun and every page had a Premier League player plastered across it, with of course, their WAGs in tow, well, George started all of that, only he was with Miss World.

In our day, if you wanted to read about a player you'd go straight to the back page. I wouldn't mind if their women were anything special and, I say that as I look at the Russian, Katsia Zingarevich, who is a stunningly beautiful model on the arm of the owner of Reading.

Barcelona (although losing to Chelsea last night in the first-leg) are by far the best in the world and, now we have these Russians (females) coming into our game. That is not a complaint, she is gorgeous and, had I been playing today, I think I might just have signed there, but only if I knew she'd be at every match.

Can you imagine me and George at Reading?

However, my new love affair with Maureen had leaked out. It was not so much the affair, it was my leaving home for this girl and, my parents took it badly. I remember whilst we were on that pre-season tour of Amsterdam, getting the Sunday People and, it was splattered all over the front pages. On my return the media were waiting to pounce on me. One knocked on my door and said, "If you don't give us the story, we'll write it our way," for that was the way it was back then. I gave them the true story, which led to more family grief, for this led to a marriage that was like a UFO hovering over and, looking down into those tiny windows of a once very happy prefab. My world was crumbling around me. Since going down that hole at West Bromwich Albion, nothing had gone right. And the last thing I needed was to face Alan Ball at his invincible best. Not just that, but as I said, on a red hot day and, a pitch which would to be to the liking of Jimmy White and, that was another issue, my pockets were empty!

My family turmoil led to the strangest proposal. We were in Alexandre when my parents walked in. They ignored the three of us. I was with Maureen and Danny Gillen. I went over to their table to offer them a drink, hoping to get us all back to where Barbra would sing, "The Way We Were...I was told, in no uncertain terms by my dad, "If you love her so much, marry her!"

I returned to our table and proposed - to Maureen, not Danny, well, I was that confused!

Where Alexandre was such a happy place where everything was close to wonderful, now here I was standing in the middle of this restaurant, where one minute I was asking my family if they'd like a drink and, the next, incredibly, going back to my table to propose to my girlfriend.

If it were a TV movie you'd switch it over, or off, it was that off-the-wall.

Maureen and I had only been together a few weeks and, I didn't even know if she had a middle name, now here I was asking her to change her surname. Like a fool, I listened to my dad and, I should have known better, as I know he was calling my bluff.

My life since missing that final had been a complete shambles. My once wonderful upbringing and childhood now seemed to be like Santa coming down the chimney and stealing my presents.

Or leaving me a bicycle only to find I woke up 59 days later with no legs!

All those times when I felt this was such a wonderful world were slipping away and, as I say, I even doubted the great Louis Armstrong and, as I was to find out, Supertramp had it right, and, I don't apologise for mentioning them once more: When I was young I thought that life was so wonderful...

The problem was that I had seen Maureen and fancied her immediately, but my parents didn't. They simply didn't like her, which is something I can now understand, but I believe they needed to let us make our own mistakes.

The other thing was, how do the media pick these things up?

I was still very naive to the world of Fleet Street, a place that was behind the demise of my second marriage and, crazily both times I was completely innocent. Fleet Street was where I met my second wife. She was lovely at first, very, very pretty, in fact, stunning, but as the saying goes, "Beauty is only skin deep."

There is one thing I can always say and, that is that I did love her and tried everything in my power to make our marriage work. I even asked her to marry me because I thought her problem was insecurity, but it obviously wasn't. To this day, I really have no idea just what her problem was, having said that, I had a slight idea, but it was a long shot and, far too personal even for me to talk about.

I would tell you if I didn't still love her, but that's not the case, but as regards spilling the beans about my near death that is completely different. If I can go one step further and, find out exactly who it was behind it, at least I can go and see my father, Tony Waddington, Bobby Moore, Johnny Haynes and all the others I love and admire so much and, talk it over and, of course Betty will be there to explain other aspects of it all.

I would even go as far as to say that I would maybe forgive her, maybe, for I believe she was a little unstable. That is my way of letting her off the hook and, I say that because as I have said elsewhere, had it been boot on the other foot, I would have been there for her. Always!

She was another one to knock those WAGs bandy.

The trial of one Charles Manson had begun. I followed his career as closely as George's. I was soon getting to know how George felt. We were pictured on the back pages, him on one side with a blonde in Spain, me on the other outside the Princess of Wales with my new wife-to-be. It was a glorious evening, weather-wise and, Leslie and I laughed as he grabbed the camera from what they now call the paparazzi and, threatened to throttle him and, as with that man Gillen, you didn't mess with him!

These were the times I felt at home. I loved nothing more than being out with my mate on a glorious summers' evening and, enjoying all the wonderful things that Chelsea had in store.

In those days it was incredible. In comparison to today, it was like another life.

You knew everyone.

You could not go into a pub where you didn't know anyone, whereas today you can't go in a pub where you know anyone.

Although we were having a great time, because life was so exciting and intoxicating down the Kings Road, I hadn't quite felt the full impact of my international ban. It wasn't like you might think after reading the papers, 'Oh, Hudson will not play for us for three years.' It simply hadn't sunk in. All what I had worked for and dreamed about was now something that was never going to happen. I don't think I knew for a very long time just how it affected me. I think maybe I was that bitter with all of those at the FA that it took over me. I had now become completely anti-England and, have stayed there ever since. Plus there have been no Bobby Moore's since. I have not admired an international player for so very long.

The ones I did have time for were Teddy Sheringham, Bryan Robson, Glenn Hoddle and Paul Gascoigne, who were all proper players.

Plus, I was so happy playing for Tony at Stoke City and loving my football, as England continued to mess things up, I simply thought, good riddance.

But underneath it all without me knowing it was crucifying my career.

You don't give it a second thought, a little like life itself, your career is short and, you'll never get those playing days back and, so it proved!

I hadn't slept with a team-mate's girlfriend, roasted a young girl, or intentionally missed a drugs test, but I got a three year ban, which led to much more than that, with Revie taking over.

I had genuinely told Alf Ramsey that my ankle needed a rest and, some much needed treatment and, that I was using the summer to move into our new family home with my new wife, new baby boy. Now please tell me, does that warrant such a punishment?

Joey Barton got twelve matches by bringing his absolutely unbelievable behaviour to not only our football fields, but our TV screens and, I ask myself, is that why he did it?

But whatever reason, these are the exact same people that banned me for three years and, you just can't add it all up.

Meanwhile, back at the Bridge, Keith Weller was an instant hit. He cracked two stunner's (George had many of those) past Ferguson against West Ham at Upton Park from a couple of knock downs by Oz. I remember taking the two free-kicks that led to the goals, but that apart, I was struggling to regain my fitness, which in turn led to a lack of confidence. This is something that was a big part of my game, without both of these I was simply just another player and, that was one thing I did not want to be.

I was brought up to be an outstanding player, if that doesn't sound too big-headed, yet this was a completely different script.

I would rather have never played if that was the way it was.

Like everything else I ever did, I wanted the best, the very best friends, best clothes, best food, best wine, best music, the best-looking women and, of course, I wanted to be the best player I could be.

However, I felt my game was coming back, albeit very, very slowly. I would simply have to wait for the rain without knowing right then that the rainfall would play such a big part of my life. My best matches would be on heavy pitches and my worst....need I say more?

In September we tasted our first European experience, well some of us. I think Eddie, Catty, Ronnie and Lou Hinton had been there before with Docherty. For the rest of us, it was something new and exhilarating, never knowing where it would take us. This was to become another incredible journey, especially for one so young and, born amidst everything that this was all about, the people of my home town.

I had only ever ventured out of the country three times, once on a Youth Team Tour of Switzerland, then to Mozambique for an end-of-season tour with the first team and, the other with Leslie, Jackie Brannon and Bobby Eyre to Spain and, had loved every minute of it, but now it was a totally different journey, never knowing it would lead to us winning one of Europe's main prizes.

I loved being around my new team-mates. I was to come to love and respect the likes of Lou Hinton, Tommy Baldwin, Eddie McCreadie, John Dempsey and Osgood, mainly because of the rogue element. I loved Lou - that is the only reason I included that picture of us in Athens - he was a thirty-five grand snip from Charlton Athletic and, along with the silly money Eddie cost from East Stirling, they must have been the two best buys Docherty made. Especially when you think he paid a hundred grand for Hateley, even though he scored the header at Villa Park - which I was sitting in line with - which was the goal that took us to the 1967 FA Cup final and, the goal was against poor old Leeds United again.

Did I say us?

No, I was a staunch Fulham fan in those days and still wanted to pull Johnny Haynes shirt over my head.

That semi-final was the first time I saw Jimmy Greenhoff play and, was probably the match Revie decided to sell him. He played wide on the left, if I remember correctly. And, if I know anything at all about football, it is he simply could not play in that position.

That brings me onto the final which was close to being cancelled, for our lot were in the bar of the Dormie Hotel, in Bournemouth, refusing to play until they got their allocation of 100 tickets.

These tickets went in one hand and out of the other in exchange for five grand. The purchaser was, of course, the infamous Fat Stan

Flashman. Was it a shock that Chelsea were trying to cheat them, seems nothing changes?

I think there was another ticket tout at that time and, I believe it was something to do with Marvin getting the nickname Lou?

How the club has changed. As a young lad there was Joe Mears, a man the Doc swore by. But Tommy swore by most things. When Joe died Brian took over the club, he was, as they say in management, "too nice" and far too gullible - had Ferguson had come there, I think he might have straightened Brian out. Well, I don't think, I know. The worst piece of work was still to come. Ken Bates. I need say no more. I mention elsewhere our first conversation and, that says it all. I cannot complain about the new regime can I. Or can I?

They are Russian. The biggest complaint I have with Abramovich is one day I had lunch before a match at the Bridge and, the waiters had not heard of Smirnoff vodka.

Now if the Russian cannot run the bar, what chance, have they with the football side!

At the end of it all, Chelsea is simply a front for Roman and all of his hangers-on. This is something since that has been completely overlooked. It has gone from Mears of Chelsea, to Bates of Wigan, and Abramovich of Russia. Who would have thought around the Worlds End in those days we would be ruled by a farmer from Wigan and a Russian?

The famous Worlds End café is now not only gone, but long forgotten and, The Worlds End pub is there, but only in name!

And then there have been all of the absolute joke managers employed by Bates. If you look back at our team, you could pull us from limb to limb over our social activities, but when it came to doing the business on a Saturday afternoon, a Wednesday night in Manchester or both a Wednesday and Friday in Athens we were the absolute business. Compared to those on the top floor we were true champions and, the one thing that still turns my gut is those who are still there living on what we lads did.

Talking of champions, little did we know then that our European experience would begin and end in Greece and, I don't think we even knew where the final was going to be played on that first trip?

As I just said, when travelling to Salonika for our first match, no one thought where the final would be taking place the following June, let alone our being in it. The crowd from Alexandre were excited and wanted to travel. They had tasted the FA Cup and, were now a real part of our team. Their first excursion last season was that monumental epic at Turf Moor and, they now loved everything that went with such nights, the kind that you never forget. It has your heart pounding (and stopping a couple of times along the way) and, mine pounded a few times whilst in their restaurant. There was never a dull moment with Camillo and his staff.

This was something different though. It was us going into the unknown, playing teams we had only read about and, the strangest thing was that we never looked beyond the next match. It has become a cliché, but this was absolutely true then. And after getting through, we never talked about who was left in the competition and, we never looked at the results of the other teams. Unlike today, the whole of the country can see who goes through to the next round and, get a close-up of their next opponents, but then, no way.

In fact, what was even more incredible, I could not tell you to this day who we would have played in the final had they beaten Real Madrid in the other semi-final.

I can still see the picture by the side of the aeroplane once on the tarmac, where the boys stood there, not knowing what this European lark was all about. It was like the outing put on by Del Boy, where nobody knew anything about anything. As in 'Only Fools and Horses' once reaching Margate half of the Nags Head had nowhere to stay and, on that dramatic evening in Athens - where UEFA cocked up yet again - half our supporters were in the same boat, well not a boat, they in fact, ended up sleeping on the beach.

I look at that first photograph of us all and, swear nobody knew what was going on. I also look back and think, 'If only we earned what they do today,' mainly because we truly deserved it. Why? That is simple, because we were all British and, were all in it together. The country today lacks the likes of us.

Sitting around that table at Olympia, I looked at the faces of Tommy Baldwin, John Dempsey, Johnny Boyle and Marvin Hinton and, saw so much happiness overshadowed by so much sadness, that it hurt.

I was wearing a wonderful psychedelic matching shirt and tie from Lord Kitcheners, or was it Quincy, a new shop on the manor? We used to get a little ribbing from our northern counterparts, but they did not have a clue about how to dress. Only George was up there with us and no matter how hard he tried, Kevin Keegan could never pull it off. We were the Chelsea Boys, the jet-set of the modern game.

Those who mocked were wearing poor copies, which cracked us up and, even the Windsor Boy would chuckle. To these people the appalling clothes were a link to the world which they thought they really should inhabit. When we boarded the train to take us north, I felt in those early days, that we were a team who were going to take over from Liverpool, although there was always that lingering doubt. That doubt hit home to me once joining Stoke, however, when I realised that all that we were missing was a manager like Waddington, that someone who believed in us as much as we did ourselves.

Shankly was the top man in the country. He had put this club on the map, much like Docherty at Chelsea, and was responsible for all their successes since. I could see that Chelsea - in those first two seasons when winning those cups - were the club of the future and, then, of course, there was the jet-set element, although Sexton was not too happy with that!

The pitch in Greece was awful, dusty and bumpy with holes in it. I remember thinking of West Bromwich Albion. The game was what you might, in those days, have called 'dirty' but we kept our heads, while our professionalism shone through. It was clear they would go to any lengths to get a result, but something bothered me about them. Why try all of these tricks, knowing they had to come to Stamford Bridge for the second leg?

They spat, which was rare in our game, well, in this country. They swore and cursed us, or so it seemed, but after the Leeds United experience, in comparison, this team were choirboys. We were awarded a penalty after Paddy Mulligan was dragged down. The Greeks made rather a long production of it all. As Peter Osgood waited eagerly to put the ball on the spot again, he did so once and, they punted it away, there seemed something wrong, maybe because this was something new to us. Eventually, when normality was restored, Oz took it and missed. That alone was a collector's item. Our Chelsea side were awarded so few penalties that the whole thing was a rarity. But here it was, one of those moments where you thought to yourself, 'We might have to be patient and finish them off in London.'

Looking back, when you go through matches such as this and think, 'It's just a matter of time,' it is dangerous, that will come clearer later when probably the second worst team we played, knocked us out. The worst team were the ones whose captain had one arm, but he was nothing to do with Lou - that ticket spiv.

John Dempsey was given his marching orders and, then early in the second half Salonika scored. They went ballistic. But Oz made amends for his penalty miss with a typical equaliser. He would score a fantastic goal in Greece some months later, which was far more important. This was his first in another record-breaking season for him. Nothing ever bothered or damaged his unshakeable confidence. A 1-1 draw was a good beginning. It was more of an experience for we had learned how these people approached European matches, although we were not sure what kind of team they were. In other words, how to gauge this competition, but as the saying goes, "you can only beat what's put in front of you."

I'd always thought that the Greeks are like the Turks - very highly strung and excitable - and we would soon see what they were really made of in London. I had a feeling they were wimps and, I was to be proved right. Anyhow, our first away trip in European competition was a success, knowing that is we got back to the Bridge unbeaten we were in with a good shout. If we could beat the likes of Manchester United, Leeds United and Liverpool there then Aris Salonika (who were they?) should have no chance and, that was how it worked out. More than anything it was an eye-opener for us.

However, it seemed that the troubles we were going to face were not on the field, but on the flights, with our first trip back home, was as if setting the pattern of things to come, the expectations were high and, after the year before, that winning feeling was also. You already know about our appetite for celebrating and, without looking too far ahead, I could tell we were going to enjoy this, although keeping in mind this was just a run-of-the-mill Greek outfit. So, as we had been doing for the past year, we celebrated in the only way we knew how, which was to become the start of all the troubles. The manager did not like us drinking after matches, let alone on a Thursday flight home before a League match and, the big problem here was it being after a tough European tie, unlike the usual trip down the motorway and, what we failed to understand was that it was new to Dave as well.

But we were in high spirits and, they seemed to be everywhere!

Some years later, I realised, because I was eight years older and more experienced, that it was like a working holiday. We simply loved packing our bags and, taking off and, this set of players could take off alright.

Something else we didn't know at that particular time was that we were on our way to another astonishing climax, although this was just the foreplay and, that for me is the key to everything. The build-up to matches was as exciting as it was to sex and, I think that was why I struggled to sleep?

I was not yet introduced to sleeping tablets but when I was….

But back to flying, Sexton on these trips had a face like a kite, all grim and tight.

At that time we could never envisage what lay ahead. Had it been Waddington, he would have handed out the champagne while still expecting another good performance two days later. And he would have got it. He would have sat with us and split a bottle. He would have enjoyed the moment. On the other hand if we had under-achieved, it wouldn't be overlooked. He would have let us know in his very own way, but unlike Dave, once it was said, it was done. You could see Dave bottling it all up and it didn't suit him, for as I say elsewhere, I liked him and, this was just another reason why I thought he should have concentrated purely on coaching.

The smell on certain players' breath would be like a red rag to a bull and, it was just as well in those days there was no Red Bull - which can be mixed with vodka - although Dave would have though it a simple energy drink?

We knew what Dave was going through and, we also knew he would never see us halfway, so we made the most of the greatest of times. As I say, it was like a working holiday and, although we paid our way, it was if it was all-inclusive, stewardesses and all.

One of the things that have always intrigued me is how we could afford enjoying ourselves so much on so little money?

The problem - with the manager - was that if you are told not to do something, you do it even more, in spite. Crazy I know, but true. Treat a man like a man and he'll behave like one. Our lads were a team of individuals living in the heart of the greatest action anywhere in the world. The Kings Road was the only place to be and, now we were taking it into Europe. It was like we were introducing ourselves into this world and, I believe we showed that on the playing fields of Europe, those that were to become our killing fields.

We were from the Kings Road after all. Over at Arsenal there was nothing surrounding Highbury and, at Spurs you would hold your breath coming out of that ground. Hence the recent riots....I'm not so sure they could do that much damage in the street leading up to The Lane. In those days, within a minute of coming out of the front gates at the Bridge it was like entering The Lost Horizon - the buzz was constant and the temptations endless. It wasn't our fault that we got sucked into it and, in those days what else was there to do?

What a lot of people seem to forget here, is that the Fleet Street Gang were there also, enjoying every sip along the way.

I was still trying to control my weight, because of my failure to train properly. I loved training and, I trained as hard as anyone and, now with this ankle injury making my life miserable, only the alcohol consoled me.

It was after returning home for that pre-season I became famous for something a little different, which had the rumour factories working overtime. One of those was that I was so overweight that when the team photographs for the official programme were issued, it had an inset of another player's head on my gut. This, though, was true, not very flattering I know, but true.

Mind you, there were a lot of bodies that I wanted to impose myself on at that time.

They were mostly the many lovely, leggy, mini-skirted ones always down The Kings Road.

Actress Judy Geeson was the new girl on the block at that time. I think she lived next to the Bridge, but Jane Seymour was the real stunner of them all. She joined us in The Red Lion after one match and, if you thought that tongues were wagging before, had the paparazzi of today been sticking their lenses through that pub window it would have made the front and back page news.

When you look at the difference today,

Wayne Rooney earns over a hundred-grand-a-week and visits hookers!

And there we were with one of the most beautiful Bond girls in the history of 007.

As I may have mentioned earlier, the lovely Medicine Woman was married to Richard Attenborough's son. Dickie Darling, who was just another one of the Mears clan (who owned the club then), thought he knew what was going on. However, he didn't know a football from a camera. He said to Osgood that I was an alcoholic. How on earth did he know more than one of my best drinking partners? It was such a shame he could not have said it to my face. Then again the football business is much like the film business - all false and messed-up people.

I also told you that while I was in hospital for all of those months, Jane could have been my Medicine Woman. I might have stayed longer, especially knowing my first marriage was going the way it did, I would have asked to see Jane on a different level because she was a real stunner. And like those people I talk of - the special ones - she had no edge. I think she is now on her fourth husband, something which makes my life look a little shallow, but I would still have loved an affair with her. Having said that, I mentioned today or a decade ago, Sharon Stone would have been my ideal nurse.

She could have been my Day and Night Nurse.

With the White Hart across from my hospital bed, well right opposite the A and E in fact, where that lamp post stood outside my window, and Sharon taking care of me, I might just have stayed in their forever. I could go into the gymnasium in the morning, write in the afternoon and, then after a session in the Hart, have Sharon give me the rest of my treatment.

I suppose I would not have felt so traumatised about my wife walking away!

This takes me back to Dusty Springfield. I left our prefab and headed for a pub in the Kings Road on the night she was due to come round. It was The Birds Nest and, I was with my mate Frew. I told him that when she turned up, he must leave us after the first drink so that Dusty and I could go to Alexandre. I had told my mother to tell her where to meet me, but Dusty never arrived. To this day, I question whether she was given my message. Frank told me later that this brilliantly talented singer wanted a baby and, he put my name forward. That's Frank Allen of Searchers fame; he took over from the very talented Mike Pender, who sang one of my all-time favourite songs Needles and Pins which would have been quite appropriate in the time of my hospitalisation.

Frank went on national BBC radio and told this story, only he said that I bottled it.

He could never be further from the truth!

Today, I am dating a lady named Diane, who I named Dusty, as she wears her hair up exactly the same way. It is incredible really because, I chatted her up for fun and, here we are three years down the road and, the crazy coincidence is she works at a place called Headway, an organisation that looks after the badly handicapped.

Do you think that there is something in that?

This is one of my great regrets for I would have loved to have fulfilled her and, plus who knows just how talented the kid would have been?

The only thing I may have been concerned about was getting a right hander from her girlfriend, that very talented black singer Madeline Bell, who was part of the group that had a hit with The Melting Pot.

She really was a big girl, more a partner for Mike Tyson than Dusty!

If a boy, maybe a Wimbledon champion?

If a girl, no doubt a model, a singing one with no chance of being a Singing Nun!

Dusty - Mary O'Brien - was, as I saw it, very insecure and, was searching for something in a life that outside of that wonderful voice was quite a sad one. I would have loved to have brought some sunshine into it. I once met her brother Tom at Frank's home in Hayes. That was actually on the night I was introduced to Wyngarde. He was upstairs writing songs. I cannot say who for, because their trio

The Springfields had fallen apart by then, a little like our defence was about to do.

We butchered Salonika in the second leg and, as I suspected, they were like 11 weak Greek Yoghurts in Greek Mafia attire. They were almost apologetic!

I say butchered because we had not forgotten the match over there. Once again it still amazes me why teams act like that when they play the first match at home. They had shown us all their cards in that first match and, we had showed them nothing. So when they stepped off the plane in London, they did not know just what they were up against. Strange race the Greeks, or was it that we were just a bunch of lads out to simply enjoy ourselves?

After the incredible amount of hatred of the FA Cup final a few months before, as if we would be worried about an outfit like Aris Salonika.

I had followed European football many years and, whilst doing so, never heard of them.

So although we were going into the unknown, we knew that we would beat the Greeks.

Beating Leeds United was quite something under the circumstances and, what made it even better was that Jock Stein's Glasgow Celtic beat them also. I will tell you later how much I loved meeting Jock, he reminded me so much of Tony Waddington. I would have given my all for Mr. Stein just as I did for Tony. And compared to Revie they were Football Gods, lovers of everything that was good in the game and, as Clough told his new Leeds team to, "play with a smile on your face."

Like the saying goes, 'smile and the world will smile with you.'

And that was not Leeds United.

Two blockbusters from Holly set us up early on, followed by Hutch weighing in with another two and Lou Hinton scoring a peach of a sweeper's goal after breaking from deep. This was possibly the first time Dave thought of moving him into a midfield role, but that was ludicrous because Suave Marv - as you also know now as Lou - did not have the legs or the stamina for a real midfield role. He was a superb player, but an inside-forward he was not.

Marvin Hinton was one of my favourite players. I thought he was simply magnificent.

All of a sudden, this Euro lark looked easy. I think we had a good feeling about it, if only for having no scares, unlike the previous year at Burnley in the FA Cup. However, we had no idea who we were to come face to face with next and, never knowing that we were to face two of Europe's finest.

A few days earlier I was involved in an incident, which was one of the most controversial and bizarre situations in the history of the game. I must add here, that referees then were far better than today. They were more aware of a challenge and, could read the game better and, if you take into consideration that today's are professional it is ludicrous, however, again I blame the FA, UEFA and FIFA, because incompetence starts on the top floor. The referees in those days could spot a tackle and, in those days they were proper tackles.

Mind you, a lot of the trouble is that referees maybe had it easier, if only for players have more idea than they have today about knowing how to tackle. There is an art to tackling and today's players have no idea, mainly the foreign ones. It takes me onto falling all over the place, which is much like not knowing how to tackle, for it all comes under the same umbrella, because you see one person put in a right suspect looking challenge and his opponent falling over the place, which more times than not is very comical.

I watched the Chelsea/Barcelona match last night 18.4.12 and Didier Drogba spent the whole time on the floor. They must do something about it, by carting him off and, leaving him on the side line. He'll soon learn when the manager says, "Do you realise we're playing with ten men every time you're off."

Having said about referees then, this was incredible, as we were leading Ipswich by a Peter Osgood goal scored at the Shed End. The Suffolk side were managed by Bobby Robson, who I had come to dislike for ignoring my father, after Bill approached him to recommend a young Ian Hutchinson to Fulham. As I explained, he ignored what my dad had to say, the result being that Hutch was now going great guns in our side. Dave had a good relationship with Robson through their time together at Fulham, allegedly.

Anyway, in the 66th minute I watched as Charlie and Nobby swapped passes with no apparent danger out on the left under the West Stand. All of a sudden Peter beat his man and, slipped the ball into space just in front of me and, for a change I decided to shoot. I hit a sweet drive that their keeper Best (no relation to George) could only watch sail into the corner. The only difference was that it was in the corner of the outside of the net and, yet referee Roy Capey, to everyone's amazement, signalled a goal. One of my soon-to-be Stoke City team-mates Jimmy Robertson was after my blood and, that of the referee, but what can you do?

All I knew was that two points earned us the princely sum of £60 and, would pay for that steak pizziola and a nice bottle of wine at Alexandre that evening. Funny how such things enter your mind at such a time.

I have never had a steak pizziola quite like the one Pepe made and, that night it seemed he made it with a little more spice, or was it my imagination?

He was in a different class!

Webby ran to me and said, "Tell them it wasn't a goal." You're having a laugh DJ. In my first season I scored two great goals against Manchester United, one at the Bridge where I dribbled along the by-line and, slipped it inside Alex Stepney's right hand post, whilst at Old Trafford, I blasted one in from the edge of the box to make it 3-0. This time it was Alex left hand post. When I think about those goals, I think about Eusebio who was clean through against Alex in that European Cup final and belted the ball straight at him. I'm not saying I was a better goal scorer than the great Portuguese striker but...

Both were disallowed. Why?

Only the referee knows. Well, only he knew why he gave this goal. When I see players today argue with these people in black clothing, I just can't understand why. You're simply wasting your time. Once again Brian Clough was the master. His disciplinary record was remarkable. His players never argued with officials, whereas Revie's men practically used GBH to get what they wanted.

The newspapers called it 'The Goal That Never Was!' and 'The Phantom Goal!'

A BBC replay confirmed it to be just that.

As I said I didn't score many, but when I did....

In the original Ballet, I wrote of all of the trouble it would cause today, but just recently refereeing has got pretty out of hand. Referees have simply been given too much power as well as too little help. They have become like policemen. I remember in my first season, I said to that great official Jim Finney, "fucking hell ref, you're blind?"' and, he simply ran away replying, "I'd worry about the way you're fucking playing." Classic!

It made me laugh then and still does today. A couple of seasons ago, when they (the FA or UEFA) were talking of sending players off for swearing. Football is a passionate game and, things are said in the heat of the moment. It was enough bringing in all these ridiculous rules about tackling from behind and, no passing the ball back to the keeper, but swearing. Come on, fuck off!

If you can't swear, you have no passion!

It is surely time to bring in the Third Eye, which I have been calling for since coming back from the United States in the late Seventies. To this day, I am truly amazed. Or am I?

The ignorance of FIFA, EUFA and the FA by not introducing this technology into our game is truly astounding. As Del Boy would say, "You know it makes sense!"

Something quite incredible will happen at FIFA by the time I finish this book!

Stoke City scored a goal against Spurs at the Britannia (2010), only for the referee - standing literally five yards away - to wave play on, after putting his whistle to his lips. After doing so, he then looked over at the linesman who was unsighted by at least a dozen players and, some sixty yards away. The referee for some reason ignored his first reaction - an obvious goal, and stuck with giving Spurs the benefit of the doubt, which there wasn't. It was incredible refereeing in any league, and so it goes on...from FIFA, to UEFA right down to Soho Square. I spoke about The Third Eye in 1980 and here we are with the same incompetence surrounding a game where there are more billionaires than brains. The people at the top are getting richer and fatter whilst the players and managers get richer and richer - so many under false pretences - never giving a thought to the paying customer, the real supporter and, the one massive issue they never take into consideration, the man in the betting shop who backed Stoke City on that day, only to be cheated by a referee. It seems the game is not only run by corruption, but cheats in every department from those organisations I have just mentioned, Extraordinary!

One modern-day referee whose attitude I dislike intensely is Mike Riley, the one who famously settled the Arsenal and Hull City FA Cup tie with another blunder. Riley was the man responsible for the great Manchester United and Arsenal set-to a few years back. He awarded a penalty for Wayne Rooney when it was clearer than a Smirnoff Black Ice that the England striker had not been touched. I think this ended the Gunners long, proud unbeaten run. One man should not be allowed to bring such a run to an end, especially under such circumstances. Again, just how long is it going to take those morons at the FA to realise we need to introduce technology?

Going back the Cup Winners Cup, it was great to see the back of the Bubbles and, be in the next round of the competition. I could feel another great cup run beginning, although it never entered my head we could go all the way. The old cliché comes in here, simply, "take one match at a time." I have loved cup football since my short-trouser days when winning every cup I ever played in. That was except the FA Youth Cup. But now I had tasted the big time, the FA Cup. Next, could we possibly win the European Cup Winners Cup? It never entered our minds, for we were simply enjoying ourselves too much. Going into Europe and experiencing something you could only do by being a professional footballer, was absolutely amazing. Playing against the best teams from other nations and, then there were the bars, restaurants and those stewardesses. Though I repeat, I was not guilty.

The stewardesses were a huge part of not only our downfall, but one, two or three marriages and, the night on Top of the Pops - had it been today - our boys with Pans People would have filled the front pages!

I once saw Babs - now married to Robert Powell - hobbling through the gates of the Bridge on crutches. I learned later that she was going to see Harry Medhurst and, to say I was surprised to see that she ever danced again simply amazed me.

I first met Robert - a staunch Manchester United fan - through Dennis Waterman and, when introduced, I asked how his father was?

He didn't get it, for it was just after I watched him portray Jesus of Nazareth so brilliantly. Never mind, Bob!

Our next rendezvous into Europe in 1970-71 was tough and, I mean tough. It was my first taste of yet another country and Bulgaria was all that I imagined it would be. CSKA Sofia were unbeaten at home in Europe and, were a truly remarkable team. The kind of team that played all over the pitch, with their defenders as comfortable on the ball as their best midfield players. They were one dangerous outfit. In those days we never had our opponents looked at, as I mentioned. I don't think so anyway. If we did, we were not given too much information about them. But it was easy to see that they were special and, in one player in particular, Jekov, they had the leading goal scorer in Europe.

As always, we preferred playing away first and, that is how it panned out in this tie and, it did right up to the semi-final, in fact. It was mild when leaving Heathrow, but on landing it was as chilling as another Stephen Spielberg movie. It was cold, very cold. Spooky cold!

October in London was a little chilling with those nights closing in, especially in and around Mile End Road where the Kray Twins and Jack the Ripper operated, but my operations were different as I was to find out some years later, however, I also found out that this place was dangerous for many other reasons.

The only time I heard of Bulgaria in those days was when my mate Danny Gillen mentioned it after going away on holiday there. He said in the summer it was absolutely stunningly beautiful, however, not tonight and I knew this was going to be no holiday and, as I said before we knew absolutely nothing about them. It wasn't even as if you could read up about them in their official programme - if they had one - and, I could not even tell you where I found out about Jekov.

But we were soon to find out that this was not only a terrific experience, as it turned out to be, but they were a terrific team. I only know that we played well because we not only kept a clean sheet but there weren't many scares, unlike in Belgium.

Ian Hutchinson sadly was by now missing too many matches through one injury or another. This made way for Sponge with Keith Weller again operating wide on our right. He was in flying form, absolutely devastating down that right-hand side. Tommy would cherish the kind of service that Weller provided as he would run flat out and, cross close to the by-line with only one thing on his mind and, boy, he was good at it. And that was exactly what Tommy had on his - that being the near post.

How many times do you see wingers trying to beat full-backs when they have no need to, when their job is simply to get the ball into the right spaces, those that defenders hate defending.

That was why Keith was so good.

When a striker timed his run, he knew that Keith would deliver at exactly the right time. The best I've ever seen at this was my old Seattle boss Alan Hinton and, their two main strikers, Kevin Hector and John O'Hare, would vouch for that - Derby County that is!

This was something new to us, because we were used to a more controlled wide player. Charlie and Nobby were all about close control. When you gave them the ball you knew they would keep a careful eye on it. With Keith, it was head down and off he'd go. So in many ways he was a breath of fresh air, bringing another string to our already decent bow, or a new dimension to our game, if you like.

The great thing about Keith was that he was positive. He simplified his game and, he just stuck to what he was good at. Sheer pace and putting in crosses at high speed was the name of his game. This gave defenders problems and, not only his marker, but the defender running towards his own goal. With Osgood he could hold out because he could score in so many different ways. But Sponge, this was his forte - the near post run.

He was great for Sponge.

Tommy would dart towards the near post and, that is how we got the only goal of the match.

Keith had the great knack of putting in great crosses when flat to the boards.

It was a great gift.

An art he worked on constantly and, what made it even better was that as a midfield player you could give him the ball and let him get on with it.

You would never, like with Charlie, let him have it and look for the return, as I said it was head-down stuff. That sounds a little bizarre, as if he did not know what he was doing or where he was going, but he knew alright and, his percentage of crosses reaching the right area was impeccable. I see players today - and Giggs in particular - for all of his experience his crosses were far too in and out. He seemed as if he rushed them far too much. With the likes of Alan Hinton, John Robertson, John Barnes and George Armstrong they seemed to take pride on that final ball. You always knew about great crossers of the ball by the strikers goal account.

At Manchester United, when Beckham played, Van Nistelrooy was in seventh heaven. At Arsenal, Ray Kennedy and John Radford were lucky to have Geordie knocking them into them and, at Liverpool, Ian Rush had a field day with Barnes knocking them in. Possibly the worst was when I supported Fulham where George Cohen, the World Cup winning full-back, was wayward and awful. But that was okay with England because he hardly get into the other teams half, if you watch the '66 World Cup, you might be able to count on one hand how many times George crossed a ball and, you might find that strange seeing we had no wingers.

As an inside-forward, Keith suited me, because you could have a much needed rest, especially whilst playing in Europe, against the likes of Pirri, who will enter the fray later.

Now it was Charlie who was missing, so it was Holly and me holding the middle of our team together. You could always rely on Holly. Charlie's form was becoming a little patchy with his marital problems and, the demon drink debilitating his game. I could see him drifting away. And Charlie was not a good drinker, he was an obnoxious one, you know the drunken Jock you hear about and, who you didn't want in your company. That Jock was Charlie. Every time I see him now - totally sober for many years - I still see him as he was then, but there was never any doubting his amazing ability, for at his best, a total genius. He was a complete one-off. I say that with the greatest respect. We did a chat show not long before finishing this book and, him being sober, he talked of many aspects of his game and, how he saw it. It's incredible that all these later we talked more about the game than back then.

And I'm also surprised he remembered as he talked, although he once said to me, "Huddy, I don't see how you can remember all of that stuff?"

Well, one/ was he was on the hard stuff big time and two/ I was only an impressionable kid who took it all in.

The last time I played against him was in California.

He had been off the booze for a while and it showed.

We (Seattle) had a great side and were flooring all before us, but Charlie kept his team (The Surf) in the game throughout.

He was at his majestic best. Charlie without booze was like Harding without Bates, he would have been far better off and, not only that, still alive?

In the second half CSKA threw everything except their ancient floodlights at us, but our defence stood firm. Ron (Chopper) loved these European nights. For he was always looking for new scalps (prey) scavenging for new blood. Also, these strangers from overseas never knew just what they were up against, which I think was something Ronnie also got a kick out of.

It sounds like a Sinatra song doesn't it.

But it was nothing like one, I can assure you. If there was music here, it would be sinister, like Friday the 13th, or something like that. Psycho, even, not that I'm saying Ron was a psycho, because I've never roomed with him, but had I, maybe I might have thought about sleeping with one eye open, two even. When Ron Harris had chosen his prey it was scary. Lou Hinton came in for Dempsey and, was his usual immaculate self. Europe loved his style and, he found it easier in those surroundings. He excelled against the better teams, the teams who tried to play their way through you, a little like the England captain. They were similar in the way they read moves, sharper in the mind than a world chess champion. As Oz said about me, "he couldn't tackle a good steak dinner," although, that was taking it a bit far and, that was Lou. He could read the situation and, as my father taught me, he could 'nick it' from an opponent's toe like the Artful Dodger.

This rebounded on me once though. I thought I had mugged Pele, but I forgot the great man had more than one set of eyes; either that or he had a sixth sense, or both. He simply flicked it through my legs and went off as if I didn't exist, bringing brilliance and genius to another level. Not forgetting vision!

I know a lot of people who would love to boast about being mugged by Pele and, I would never hide that as a secret. I'd rather be out there getting outsmarted by him than never playing against him at all and, the privilege was immense. It is a great experience and lesson, bringing you swiftly down to earth, that is, if you thought you were like today's players - better than you are. There are them and then there are us. And tough, Ronnie put in a tackle and, his foot flew off the great man and, like the great competitor he was, he never flinched, he simply bided his time and got Chopper with a four armed smash, GBH if you like.

To think Sexton would not entertain George is unthinkable, so if George was out then that said the same thing about this man. Outrageous!

Is it the same old story of them not being able to be coached?

And then there was the booze, of course. I mean, once that first whistle goes, is coaching a factor?

When a ball bounces and an opponent comes towards you, does coaching come into it?

I had now drunk with more than two World Cup winners - one a captain - in my first 18 months and of course, George. In fact, I had played against Banks, Moore, Stiles, both Charlton's, Ball, Peters, Hunt and Hurst, which makes it nine. George Cohen had disappeared and Ray Wilson, I believe, went Down Under.

He became an undertaker!

Amongst these were four world class players in Moore, Banks, Ball and Bobby Charlton all players that Tony Waddington would have loved to have managed.

Like me, or more like, me like him, Tony did not really believe in coaching, although we had George Eastham and Alan A'Court they didn't do much coaching of any significance. Had Tony had Don Howe, I think they might have reversed those two dramatic FA Cup semi-finals with Arsenal. Don was brilliant and with his discipline and organisation and Tony's eye and attitude in man management, for me anyway, they would have been even more formidable, although I don't think that even Don could have avoided the roof being blown of the Butler Street Stand, but that was three years down the line.

I cannot remember once listening to any instructions sent onto the field in my playing days. When you're involved in a match I don't believe that anyone sitting on a bench can see it clearer than you can.

When you see managers and coaches throwing their arms all over the place, it's nothing to do with tactics or instructions, like with Harry Redknapp, its more nervous energy they're burning up.

When I was at Arsenal, I once hit a half-volley at Terry Neill sitting on the bench at Newcastle. He was shouting out nonsense and, I just smashed the ball at him to give him my answer.

Terry once old a room full of players - who had won the FA Cup and League Double - that, he'd make them all better players. That is like me telling Lester Piggott how to pace a horse race or Jimmy Greaves how to score a goal. Terry thought because he played in the same team as George Best, he was as good as him and, I dare to think what he told strangers about those days. Terry simply didn't have a clue, but I cannot slaughter him because even though we went through hell at Highbury, I still liked him a lot.

It was only just before going to print that I received a telephone call from a lovely lad called Chris Maskery. He is a local Stoke-on-Trent lad who I tried to take under my wing at the Victoria Ground. He was my room-mate and a good one. I tried to help him in every possible way. He was a decent player, one that would run through a brick wall for you. Anyhow, he called me out of the blue and, he asked me why I did not attend meetings of all the old players, from Terry Conroy and Denis Smith right down to himself. They call themselves SCOBA (Stoke City Old Boys Association) and, I said that if I did go there'd be trouble ahead. That meaning, unlike them there are certain things I don't forget. He also mentioned that he would never forget what I told him in those days. His words were, "I remember you telling me not to listen to coaches and managers, but I did and it ruined me." This kid was too genuine for his own good. Bad coaches and managers have ruined more players than they know, but the only difference being, they don't know!

I have told several youngsters - like Mask - that had they been there under Tony Waddington they'd have had more of a chance. Plus, if they hadn't have made the first team, at least they'd improve enough to go and make a name for themselves elsewhere!

Only fools and bad players listen to coaches. I remember one morning in Santa Barbara, when Steve Daley - who Malcolm Allison paid £1million for - joined us for his first training session. I was captain and, our main midfield player. I was the one that started and, set-up the play. The quarterback, if you like, in American terms. I think that I perfected that art at the Victoria Ground under Waddington. Had I stayed at Chelsea, this couldn't have happened. I would never have been given the total freedom of a football field. Waddington, as I told you earlier, said, once reaching his seat, "I sat back and watched him play." Yeah, just like a paying customer.

And he was a paying customer, for he paid £250,000 to watch me.

I was prepared to change my game a little to accommodate him (Daley).

I will never forget looking out over the beautiful blue waters as we worked on a dead-ball situation, when I asked him, "Steve, where is your favourite position?"

He looked a little lost before saying, "I don't know." These are the kind of players who need coaches, those that need telling what to do, where to go and, when. Steve had lots of ability, but was simply a player who played off the cuff, with never any thought going into his game. If you asked him why he did this or that, he couldn't tell you. This is not a knock at Steve, all I am saying is, that this was a player Allison paid a million pounds for, whilst Tony paid a quarter of that price for yours truly. The problem, at that time, was Manchester City were falling so far behind United and the club told Malcolm to go spend a million on a big player. Now do you see why I rated Waddington so highly!

Dave Sexton seldom picked Marvin Hinton because of his lack of height, whereas Clough picked Colin Todd and Dave Mackay who weren't any taller. Maybe Lou should have gone and kicked Dave's door in every now and then, or smashed him into those hoardings in the forecourt.

That is what Sponge did when his name was not on the team sheet.

Lou, like Bobby Moore and Peter Simpson at Arsenal, was a World Cup player, not a League Cup player. There is a big difference, a difference in class distinction and all three of them had it in abundance, class that is. Years on, I found this with the likes of Alan Dodd at Stoke City and David Nish in Seattle both very classy and under-rated individuals. Dodd, like Greenhoff and Bloor at Stoke City, somehow went uncapped, whilst Revie was picking the likes of Cherry and, other of his white-eyed boys. If only Revie had flown straight to Saudi from Leeds, things would have been different for all of us and, that included the supporters.

Had he, we would have at least qualified in the Seventies!

Both Dodd and Bloor were terrific centre-halves, but there is only so much a centre-half can do against the likes of Peter Osgood, Ian Hutchinson, Joe Royle, Wyn Davies and, probably my favourite header of the ball, Ron Davies of Southampton, Manchester United and Wales fame. Ron also had a spell in Seattle with us under Jimmy Gabriel - his old pal at The Dell. Had there been a drink on the moon, Ron could have jumped up and, drank it. He might have been way past his best as a player, but he certainly wasn't when it came to socialising. Ron had that rare ability to leap and, once reaching his highest point, hang there. He was amazing. One day we were out together drinking and, there was a dispute about the way the game should be played. Ron insisted that the ball should be played in the air, "because they can't kick you up there," he said. But as Clough once stated, "If the game was supposed to be played up there the sky would have been green."

Only Clough could come up with that!

In recent times Gary Lineker said that he avoided heading the ball because he was worried about possible brain damage in later life. Now come on, what went wrong?

I look at him on the box, talking trash and selling Walkers Crisps and, think about how unscathed he is. His adverts on TV are embarrassing. There are certain things that I would not do for money, no matter how short I was and, still am. But Lineker has absolutely no shame and, more importantly, no class. He is a very wealthy man, yet he makes himself look a complete fool, doing those stupid stunts with a packet of crisps.

I did not appreciate those doing the Pizza adverts after missing penalties in the World Cup either. They looked like the KKK and, had they been in one of those South American countries and, were earning money out of getting them knocked out, they might have received a bullet instead of a pasta bake and a hefty cheque.

I really could not do such an advert and, then walk round with my head up. Southgate and Waddle are now holding down positions on TV where the supporters who watched them miss them penalties actually care and, of course, Pearce has managed England. They talk of pride!

Can you imagine Franz Beckenbauer doing such an advert in Germany?

If you compared him to Lineker, you'll understand why our game is in such a state!

I was at a luncheon once and my mate Chris Garland approached him about helping his charity, for Chris has Parkinson's. Lineker snubbed him by saying "speak to my agent." Chris was livid and, I had to calm him down. Had he offered him a crisp contract he might have taken time out for Chris. People like Lineker use the game for all the wrong reasons. He is smarmy. He is smug. He and his mates on the BBC sofa are like sewer rats. He swans round with a young bird thinking that he's God's gift. If he is a gift, I am glad I don't accept them. As for her, she is obviously tasteless. He is good for her modelling work. I was hoping that his likes would follow Keys and Gray. If they all get the push, they could all go away on an all-inclusive and count their money.

I believe the BBC and SKY have a lot to answer for by employing such people. There are no other programmes on TV that are criticised as often as those which include them. If I had a pound coin for every time one of they were laughed at in my local, I would not have to draw my fifty-odd-quid disability allowance!

Going back to heading the ball, of course there is no truth in that theory, no real shred of proof, but then I look at big Jack Charlton and, think about how many million times he splattered the ball with his forehead. And there he was, ignored by the FA, therefore taking the Irish to the World Cup instead of us. Are you getting my drift?

Okay, what I'm trying to say is that it makes you wonder just who are brain damaged?

I used to love Lineker's mate Alan Hansen, a real class act at the heart of Liverpool's defence, but it was only his height that made him a superior version of Lou. Hinton was a better player on the ball. That is a compliment to Marvin, not a knock at Hansen. The difference between the two players was confidence, something the Liverpool player had in abundance. Do you think that was anything to do with Shankly?

After all Sexton didn't buy Lou, Docherty did and, in those days it weren't like today. Today, you can swap and change players like going down Tescos, in fact, there are cases when you can buy a player and get one free.

I heard that Boro would only sell Huth to Stoke City if Tony Pulis took Tuncay.

That was, I must stress, allegedly, or rumoured!

I would much prefer to listen to Hinton than Hansen on Match of the Day. The latter drives me crackers, just like Mark Lawrenson, Alan Shearer, Ray Wilkins and a couple of others that I can't be bothered to mention.

Whilst on this subject, what a pleasure it is now Andy Gray and Richard Keys have been removed from Sky for their acts of sexual abuse to those females on our screens.

Gray said that he was gutted about the way Sky went about it. It affected him badly, not for him, but his mother, 90, wife-to-be and, daughters. Well, say that girl he asked to put that microphone down the front of his trousers, had been his daughter?

Apart from a player spouting off in the newspapers about what they are and are not going to do, these pundits are television's worst nightmare. There is nothing worse than a player telling the newspapers just what they are going to do and, then you sit in front of your TV set and watch, what my mate Paul, who runs the Princess Royal, calls A Muppet. Or, as on those panels, a puppet. I am sure you will agree with me when the European or World Cup comes around and, you hear them sitting there as if they know, saying, "We have the players who can bring back the trophy." It makes you want to vomit. What makes me even sicker is that they're getting fortunes for talking a load of cobblers and, I can't get a look in.

People follow the England team around the world giving up their normal family vacations. They spend their last few quid in the hope of seeing us win our first trophy since '66. But all they ever get are false promises, which lead to more disappointment. It is okay for those I just mentioned, for they get paid fortunes for misleading these genuine football lovers and, of course, they get first class treatment. They get paid for travelling to these tournaments and, of course, all the other treatment, one enjoys, much like the politicians, who rob the "real people" and, use their money for all the good things in life. I've seen them in the Commons whilst lunching with Tony Banks. Now there was a man with class and integrity and, how I used to love the way he fronted up Ken Bates, as much as to say, "This place is not yours, it's ours."

Two days before the opening match against the USA, Joe Cole was shouting - through a newspaper - that England would win the World Cup and, it all comes flooding back. Yeah, I've been listening to this for thirty, no forty-odd years. Get on with your football Joe. You're not Mystic Meg you're Joe Cole who people don't want to listen to. They pay their hard earned cash to watch you try to, not only entertain, but actually win something for them and, their country. These people take time off work, pay for flights, hotels, food and drink in great anticipation. The last thing they want is false hope. As I might have said elsewhere, "talk costs lives."

It really does get aggravating as the rest of the world are laughing at us. I will give you an example: They themselves were tipping us to win the World Cup in South Africa. They are not tipping themselves, which is something that takes the pressure off them and, cleverly puts it on us.

I have to laugh and, it is the fault of the media, who themselves are a shadow of Fleet Street Gang I once knew. After reading recently that a certain club are to save Joe Cole from his Liverpool nightmare. Now, unless that knock on the head in the Mile End Road did more damage than I was led to believe, I recall Cole saying that this was his dream move and, he would make Liverpool great again. Before he could possibly do that, he has to make himself great first and, there are absolutely no signs of that.

He is what we used to call a 'Tanner Ball Player,' and not a great one at that.

Harry Redknapp says he's the best youngster he's ever seen. Well, Harry should not boast that, because he has not got the best out of his natural talent.

Mourinho is the only manager to get anywhere doing such a thing.

Anyhow, these (CSKA)were a team who did not have any of those kind of players, they moved it about quickly and neatly and, had they had not caught us on a good night defensively, we might have seen an ever better team, for it seemed that all they lacked whilst at 0-0 was that first goal and, I had a feeling that whoever got it would win the match, which would have been great for us, for being the away goal and, that's what happened.

I thought that we had completely outfoxed CSKA and, did so without shouting about it. We did it in a very quiet and effective way. It's called professionalism. No shouting. No screaming. We simply slipped into Bulgaria and, slipped out with the result we needed so badly. We were like the silent assassins. We simply returned home and went about our Saturday business.

And like us, I bet that they hadn't a clue about any of our players.

Had they put one over us and played Bruges, it would have been a classic, for they were two brilliant football teams. If I had to pick the winner over the two legs, I would have gone for the Belgians. If only for such an intimidating atmosphere inside that tiny ground of theirs and, one thing is certain, I would have loved to have been there to witness it, but Bruges were still to come!

Even though it was a terrific performance and, one of great discipline - the sort you need in order to win in Europe – and, to our credit, we were still the new kids on the European block. The biggest scare on this particular night was after the match, sitting round the table with several stewards and stewardesses - they were BA - celebrating our victory. We were ambushed by the local police. They were dangerous, more so than even Jekov and, were carrying the heaviest artillery imaginable, the likes I had only seen in those black and white war films. For a fair few seconds a few bottles twitched and, then they were drunk. Much to our joy they disappeared in a flash, the police that is, and then the booze.

It must have been Dave Sexton trying to get us to bed is all I can think.

Was he getting that desperate?

On the aeroplane home we were again in high spirits. We were getting the hang of this European lark and, then there was Thursday lunchtime to look forward to finish off the celebrations. We were now perfecting these celebrations through all of our fantastic cup exploits. I can still see Sponge - our goal scorer - swinging in the aisle, "Flying high in the friendly sky," which did not go down to well with the manager. Then all of a sudden it went off. Dave Sexton and Peter Osgood began shaping up to each other. "See you behind the North Stand when we get back," was the request. I can't remember who asked who, but whoever it was, the challenge was met.

All of this left a sour taste in our mouths and for the first time it brought it all out into the open, something that had been simmering and, festering for quite a while.

Sexton tore into Osgood. He always looked for Oz when things were not to his liking.

Apart from what part two of the book will reveal, this is the most bizarre situation throughout my life in football. Still to this day, we'll never know the reason why?

Was it because the fans adored him so much?

Was it because he was so popular?

Was it because when things were getting tough or going against us, he would get us out of the mire with one of his specials?

Leeds United at Old Trafford springs straight to mind. It must be so frustrating for coaches and managers when a player like Osgood comes up with that kind of magical goal when all seems lost. That is why I could not understand this situation, for I believe Dave should have taken all the great things Oz did into account in moments such as these. No one person can take the credit for something so special, that is why I get annoyed about Osgood always taking the flak, because he was so instrumental to all of the great things achieved by our team. He was such a class act.

I recall George going into Busby's office for a dressing down.

This was because Sir Matt had to be seen to be doing something about George's social life. When George left his office he reckons he counted every flower on the managers' wallpaper. Brilliant!

He had his bollocking, but didn't hear a word.

Much like when you saw coaches screaming from the touchline. I don't think I ever heard what they were on about and, if I did, I took no notice. That is why I mention elsewhere, when Ray Clemence goes to the touchline with an England player - piece of paper in hand - and begins to tell him what to do. I would have simply told the former England goalkeeper what to do and, where to go with his piece of paper. Did you ever see a Brazilian coming onto the field with someone holding a piece of paper, pointing instructions?

If players don't know what to do, what are they doing in the England team?

That kind of stuff doesn't come from any training ground.

You just cannot coach genius!

Can you imagine someone telling Sinatra which note to hit and when?

I recall Dave coming back from Mexico and showing us a video tape of the Brazilians and, how Jairzinho made that little space to get the early cross into those incoming strikers I just told you about, yet Alf didn't want wingers. Why?

I mean, what was all this about?

Who was right here, Dave or Alf?

It made no difference to us, we watched the tapes and carried on playing our way, although Peter Houseman, no doubt took notice, but he was good at that. If he had a race with Jairzinho it would be like Bolt outrunning Osgood, but he had the "cunning" move, where he'd make just enough room to manoeuvre his cross into the near post. The problem he was having now though, there was no Hutchinson!

Dave loved Peter and, rightfully so, he was a managers dream. He'd come in bright with never a sign of alcohol or late night.

Incredibly, I bet my life on the latest night he had was when he and Sally got killed so dreadfully and, I still go numb at the memory of it all.

Dave also felt the same way about the other Peter, Bonetti, and John Hollins, which again I can understand, however, it was strange that Bonetti had messed up in Mexico and, John was going to miss a penalty that would cost us just as dearly, although it was not at international level, however, still devastating, but that was a little down the road.

If he loved them, he saw things in our personalities that he found repulsive. Sometimes it seemed as if he loved us like younger brothers; other times he hated us like we were the white of Leeds United. Someone once said that to hate someone with such spite, a part of you must love them too. I have experienced this to be true, especially as I look back in later life, particularly my last wife. Her walking out on me whilst in such a traumatic condition after those 59 days in the Intensive Care Unit was simply unforgivable.

There are certain things you simply cannot work out in life. Well there certainly are in mine. I say this because no matter what wrong she did, she will now be regretting it, even if it's just a tiny piece of remorse. Love just doesn't die like that, does it?

My job after returning from Bulgaria and, I remember it so well, was to quell this bad blood, even though I was still the youngest player in the Chelsea squad. For this reason, and there are others, I thought that although I was the junior of the team, I should have been made club captain, if only for having enough class not to urinate in the bath - yeah Dave, there was plenty you missed through those dodgy "minces" of yours. Only with things such as this, we all knew you turned the other one.

I would always have a drink with Oz on our return. And this time, I saw it as the get-out clause. We headed for Matthew Harding's local The Imperial Arms, where I actually calmed our hot-headed centre-forward down and, thank God I did, for can you imagine the tabloid press picking up on what would have been headlined: The Duel of the North Stand?

It would really have rocked the world of football. I just could not believe that our manager would see things this way. Why could he not see just how much Osgood had done for his team?

The season before, he scored in every round of that magnificent FA Cup success and, brought us back from the dead at Old Trafford. Now he was just about warming up to do the same, by breaking more records in Europe. If he added knocking Dave's head off behind the North Stand it would have not only have been a record, but made history, the kind of history that would make those schoolboy antics of Drogba, Terry and Cech against Scolari and Villa-Boas look like schoolboy stuff and, that is just what it reminds me of.

Everything Oz did on the pitch was totally calculated and, like a seasoned gunfighter he was always looking to gain the edge on his marker. When he wasn't winding up Jack Charlton, Mike England and Frank McLintock, it was Sexton, almost as if he was in training for the ultimate set-to and, had he and Dave came to blows that would have been the football equivalent to the Rumble in the Jungle.

With Oz, it was all just to shave the odds in his favour.

It was his incredible competitiveness and, calculated mind, plus his hair-trigger temper which made him so very dangerous. The situation with Sexton exploded and would so again and, although this looked serious it blew over, but there was never, ever a shadow of a doubt it was only on hold. The closest after that was at the Victoria Ground, when like against Burnley in the FA Cup, Dave pointed that finger dangerously close to the brink. I really don't know who wanted the rumble most?

But it would be a year or so before it really looked like the gloves were on again and, it was just another episode in this saga that was the deciding factor in the break-up of this very talented team.

Who would have won?

This was something I wasn't used to at Chelsea. I had seen fights on football pitches and, in pubs but Dave Sexton and Peter Osgood...

It's hard to call the result and, one I am delighted to say I have never had to say, "I told you so."

Oz was younger, of course and, a big strong lad who relished a bare-knuckle fight, having had many with his best pal Hutch. The manager came from a boxing background. We nicknamed him Stiff Neck because of his stance.

All managers have nicknames, although I was too young and, had too much respect early on to give Alf a nickname, especially when hearing him speak. He took elocution lessons, which I found about right, for it was very FA, which led to fucking atrocious.

In Seattle, I nicknamed Alan Hinton Clouseau after, of course, that brilliant Peter Sellers character and, Bill Asprey at Stoke City was Mr.

Bojangles, for impersonating Ron Atkinson with his wrists full of jewellery. You could hear him coming from the office to the dressing room.

I dare not go into the different names we had for Don Revie. The only exception I take to him is that he is still mentioned in rhyming slang when people talk about having a few bevies. You might hear someone say, "Do you fancy a Don Revie?"

Now, that's close to turning me off the hard stuff, but only close.

The name of Stiff Neck could also be used for Chris Eubank, who I see on TV with his similar posturing. Is it a coincidence that he is also from the fighting community?

I could never reconcile the mixture of Dave's boxing heritage and, his religious background. The two seemed in conflict with one another. Perhaps this was the crux of the problem. Osgood was the King of Stamford Bridge to his beloved and adoring followers. Anyone who ever stood in The Shed would have heard the famous carol adapted to suit Osgood's title. To this day, I cannot believe that those in the Shed allowed the club to sell their hero. When I first saw the Tottenham riots the other week (August 2011) I thought about those times and, that was how I saw Stamford Bridge after putting Osgood up for sale. It still has never sunk in with me. Even to this day, I remind the people of the Potteries just what they missed when Osgood reneged on the promise made to Tony. They would have had his statue up where Matthews now stands and, I would go as far to say that they might even have replaced Wedgewood with Chelsea's finest ever number nine and, had Ramsey not been on some kind of hallucinating drug in Mexico - with no disrespect to Jeff Astle - as I said earlier, he would have returned to England hailed as the 'Best on the Planet' which just happens to be our company name.

But back to the calamity of Stamford Bridge, Sexton committed regicide.

The first blow was struck then. Oz would never back down, like Raging Bull again.

Strangely enough I attended the funeral of Dennie (Tony) Mancini with Tommy Wisbey and Malcolm. In doing so, I found out that he was a regular churchgoer and, wondered about the connection of boxers and churchgoers?

Was it that they prayed for their opponents?

Years later as their pub crashed in a sea of debts, Oz gave Hutch a black eye in a dispute. That happened more than once, but they always made up and, watched each other's backs as if they were the only ones who could lay a hand on one another. You see the love/hate situation I just mentioned?

On the field they were exactly the same. If one got knocked the other would be first in. They were like a shield for one another.

The pressures off the field and the adjustment to facing up to life without football could be as great as any problems when you're still in the game. Wealth and glory throw a gentle hug around some players. Lineker embraced them and never abused them. Like teenage sweethearts, wealth and fame loved him back and, it became a lasting romance. For the Mavericks, though, it was different.

The fight, as I said, never took place. Thank God. The tabloids never got the kind of day they lived for. Tommy Docherty once said that when he was the manager of Chelsea, the problem was that Stamford Bridge was too open to the media. No secrets could be hidden. That is why they have always figured so prominently amongst the headlines. I found that out a couple of times in the mid-Nineties. After a couple of disagreements in the Chelsea players' tunnel, it was easy to see that the events which took place were blown out of all proportion. When I tried to explain to Ken Bates that it was absolutely nothing, he wouldn't listen, preferring to fire me after listening to others. What's new?

I always thought there were two sides to every story, but of course not.

This was Ken Bates.

The thing that also astounds me is that if he doesn't want to encourage such things, why have the Press Room in the tunnel?

It makes me wonder if he was putting the bait out there. You never knew with him. He was certainly a Jekyll and Hyde....and I didn't like either!

Webb - who had a spell of management under Bates - scored the all-important goal that saw off our Bulgarian opponents. Having done so, he returned to the back line to thwart their ever-dangerous forward line. This really was becoming very interesting both on and off the field. What with bust-ups with the manager, death threats, thrilling comebacks, divorces, all coming thick and fast, and, more importantly, we had the great belief that we had a great chance of breaking more new ground at Stamford Bridge. When you think of all that was going on in our lives, it is truly remarkable that we were in serious contention to win this competition, but that was all to come.

But if the FA Cup belonged to Houseman the Cup Winners Cup was the same for Weller and, that brings me onto when I hear players asking for time to settle in - Torres at Chelsea - Weller didn't waste no time at Chelsea and, was in inspirational form.

And here was living proof. The following weekend, after the near escape with the Fleet Street Gang, we went to Blackpool on Saturday 24 October 1970, where a crowd of 24,940 saw a match that was more like an Agatha Christie thriller. A Who Dunnit if you like. John Phillips (what a season in Europe he was to have) made his debut between the sticks, which became his nickname, though I am not so sure for what reason. It may have been because he was built like a stick insect, or was it because he stood between them, but that couldn't be, otherwise others would also have such a nickname.

Anyhow, Fred Pickering, a great warrior of old, hit his net a couple of times and, we found ourselves three goals behind at half-time.

It seemed like the Blackpool Tower was coming down on us.

Similar to those old floodlights in Bulgaria.

Going in three goals down was not something we were used to and, I thought of the teams last season in the FA Cup, who we had absolutely wiped the floor with. The one and only time I can recall this happening had been at Everton, but give them credit they were awesome. But this was Blackpool and, this was the score and, it remained that way until the 70th minute. Dave had changed things around, bringing Charlie on to replace Sponge, then moving Nobby to left back - a position in which he would finish his Chelsea career - whilst moving Chopper over to the other flank. Ronnie could play anywhere along the back line as long as he had a target. Paddy Mulligan moved to the centre of defence which allowed Webby to move up-front alongside Weller. This might look like a touch of genius, a complete fluke or even a minor miracle very soon. Whatever, between them they (Webb and Weller) pulled the three goals back and, we knew we could board the train having saved face. But it didn't end there, far from it. In the very last minute Charlie got the ball on the left touchline and, feigning to go to the by-line, cut inside onto his favoured right foot and slung a hopeful cross into the Blackpool box. Now the Tower was about to fall in, but not on us. With not a Chelsea player in sight Hatton hooked the ball high into the top corner of his own net, which made it a simply incredible end to a simply incredible match.

How delighted I was that Ian Holloway brought this great old club into the Premier League and, with such fantastic style. He has proved to be one hell of a manager, all of this at a time when we are screaming that there are none around.

Hence Sven and Fabio!

I tipped Blackpool to stay up after watching them put in a superb display at the Britannia Ground in the Carling Cup the season before. I told my pal Peter Fox, who was working at Blackpool at the time, that these were a terrific football team.

I think this result against Chelsea was the last time they were in the top flight, be it the old First Division. And I will tell you in a minute about another match on this old ground when the Old Bill saw me off the team bus and, into the dressing room. This time though, they were on my side.

They looked Premier League material in fact, the best football team I saw at Stoke City and, that included Arsenal (supposedly the best?) Liverpool, Chelsea and Man United!

The Great Escape had been achieved. We walked back to the half-way line looking at each other as if we had just bunked off school and, been given a gold star for doing so. It was definitely the strangest match I'd ever played in. The next time I was to walk into Bloomfield Road, I had a police escort awaiting me which made a change from arresting me.

Once again, I was innocent, but in real danger. Someone had telephoned the cops with a threat on my life. Obviously "shooting" sprung straight to mind. How else were they going to kill me?

As usual our lads were brilliant in such situations. They all rallied round to make it clear to keep away from them for the upcoming 90 minutes. It didn't bother me because as you know, if people are going to carry out such an act, they do it, they don't talk about it. The mind boggles in such times. I began thinking about knowing nobody in that part of the world, so my mind flashed to anywhere nearby, or did whoever it was come all of this way from London to throw the Old Bill off the scent?

No of course not. If anyone wanted to shoot me, they could have done so at any time in London, why wait to do it in a football match? Never dreaming all those years later, I would be targeted in a completely different fashion?

Had it been in my Stoke days then yeah, I might have understood it, but that was all to come. We were barely an hour down the motorway and, although I never made a habit of playing games with married women, I had been guilty once or twice. On my first night in The Place I met a lovely blonde, but that was okay because my wife was debating whether to follow me to the Potteries. She couldn't be behind this, surely?

No, of course not, but if she were, that would be two wives wanting me dead, so much for thinking I was a good husband?

Everything flies through your mind at such a time.

It was a little funny because either that season or the one before, I cannot recollect, the same thing happened at Old Trafford. Only it was one of my team-mates.

I could understand it happening in Manchester. The Chelsea lads were always pretty active in George's nightclub, Slack Alice, but the one who had been chosen for the 'hit' was one I did not understand. Me. There was Oz, of course, Hutch definitely, Webby the same. And then there was Sponge. Later Mulligan and, then there were Garland and Garner, who were all a hit with the girls.

That's what we called them, whereas the bands called them groupies, whilst today they are obviously thought of as piece of meat, which they roast.

If this was the norm, we would have needed police protection wherever we went and, as for going abroad, Interpol. When you think about it, we were sitting ducks, but if this was the case, George would have been the first player in history to have such an assassination carried out on him, although there are some odd-balls that would be, or might have been, quite proud to say that their wife had been sleeping with the best player in the world.

But there was one thing about George and, that was he didn't mess with married women, he didn't need to, but who does?

I say this, because a couple of years before I got into the Chelsea first team, Oz, along with a few of the boys, came to a party in the Chelsea Boys Club and, one of the locals, Johnny Elliott, who idolised him so much, said to him quite openly, "If you don't pull tonight you can take her."

It was his wife and, a different kind of Indecent Proposal.

Oz would say that he had more about him than Robert Redford.

But as I've said, after his performance with Raquel Welch, I don't think so!

On that particular day in Blackpool, I found out something about myself. I knew I was a good athlete even with my chronic ankle injury, but I did not know that I could actually keep on running even though everyone else had stopped for a dead ball, be it a corner, free-kick or goal-kick. Something I didn't do in that game though, was take any of them, for it was far too close to the crowd and, far too dangerous. I made sure most of my movements were made in the middle of the pitch. I think this was an FA Cup tie that we finally won 1-0, so with everybody getting off the pitch without a bullet mark on them, this was a very good day for us. We were not only all still in one piece, but in the hat for Monday's draw, which we would listen to in the forecourt.

The funniest thing at the time - to try to make light of it - I slipped Osgood's No 9 over my head and, hung my No 10 on his peg. This was hoping the gunman would obviously go by the team sheet, but Oz was having none of it.

If events in my first season were something incredible, then this was even more so. An FA Cup winners medal, selected for the World Cup, runner-up for the Footballer Writers award, playing in the Cup Winners Cup and, now I was watching out for a speeding bullet. It doesn't become more interesting than that. And I wasn't yet 20. It would make - not that I watch them - Coronation Street and

Eastenders look more stupid than what they really are. This was more Reality TV.

The only time I ever watched them was whilst holed out in hospital and I got hooked on Coronation Street and, tells you just how strong the morphine was.

21 SIMPLY THE BEST

When George wasn't pulling Miss Worlds, he was pulling defenders apart.
On this particular evening it was Chopper!

The in-flight bust-up was a microcosm of the whole soap opera that was to unfold like a soccer Brookside, though some of the Chelsea stars of today, notably John Terry and Ashley Cole, have brought a whole new meaning to it.

In comparison, there run-ins with management have benefitted all parties, whereas the players build up more power and strength in the dressing room whilst the manager walks away with several more millions to add to his bank balance. When I left I was out-of-work and on the dole queue before my car ordeal....

By the end of that momentous year of '71, we were third in the table still chasing Leeds United and, the eventual champions, Arsenal. In the autumn we had gone out of the League Cup to Manchester United, who for once had beaten us at Old Trafford. I did not play but I had a fantastic view of the winner scored by, you guessed it, George. And what an incredible one it was. I was sitting in the Stamford Bridge Arms opposite the ground. I was still building a great friendship with the then landlord Danny Gillen. It was one of the first big screens I can ever remember and, if ever a screen captured such an astonishing goal, this was it.

It was almost as if George knew about this screen and, saw me sitting there all alone waiting for something special to happen and, he certainly didn't disappoint.

The closest thing I have ever seen to such a goal was Maradona's incredible goal against England. He picked up the ball in his own half, spun on the ball, faced Shilton's goal and, set off on a wonderful run, which left my mate Peter Reid in his midstream and, had all the others in white shirts looking like Sunday morning pub players, just coming up to the tape at the end of the London Marathon.

Once reaching Shilton, he rounded him easily and, squeezed the ball into an empty net to score my favourite goal in any World Cup.

For you youngsters, if you have seen Lionel Messi, only he today could score such a goal!

I've told you all about Danny, who became top man on the chauffeuring front and, would even have Sinatra ask for him personally when in town for his concerts. Danny and I went to Cornwall one summer with our wives-to-be and, had an absolute ball, when I say that I always think of Alan. I was asked to present prizes by Mr. Harry, whose farm we stayed on and, Danny and I went along. It was hilarious as I told him, like being on Stars in their Eyes, that tonight he was to be Charlie Cooke. It was going swimmingly well, when one local sussed it out. Danny - remember the College - had to threaten him to keep his mouth shut and, he don't know how lucky he was, that he did.

Danny still owns the FA Cup medals of both Peter Osgood and Ian Hutchinson. It was their collateral for him helping them out financially in their pub in Windsor - I think it was the Union Inn. I went there one night with that beautiful girl I told you I left behind. She was from Luxemburg. The reason I mention Danny here is because it was whilst he had the pub opposite the ground, where we met and, not only that, it was where I watched the following goal on his big screen.

I was out injured and, will never forget sitting in his pub watching such magic!

I still can't believe George never received an FA Cup winners' medal, yet Osgood and Hutchinson got two each, for the FA replaced them, no, Oz get three if you added his Southampton one.

On that evening at Old Trafford, the surface was perfect, my kind of perfect, muddy perfect. George glided through the middle of the last third, but coming from another direction was Chopper, like a panther seeking his prize prey. And Ronnie looked upon George as exactly that. Like Greaves, George was phenomenal in such a position. He zoomed in on Bonetti's goal, only to be attacked savagely by a vicious Harris tackle that caught him around the waist. He buckled as the Chelsea captain hit the floor in amazement, if only for not believing George didn't join him. He said years later that, "Every time I watch that on Grandstand, I expect George to go down, thinking I had nailed him."

Well he definitely nailed him alright, but the nail somehow didn't go in.

Like La Motta again, George somehow kept not just his feet, but his head and, the kind of composure I spoke of earlier!

Next up was Catty, who came from his line like an Olympic sprinter and, flung himself down in the muddy goalmouth, but like with Messi, George's feet were gone, he had shimmied past him, like he did Harris. All I can say is that it was like watching an electric eel gliding through murky waters. The only thing that was murky here though was the attempted GBH of Chopper's scything tackle. He rarely missed his man. In fact he never missed his man. He was a professional marksman of a different kind. George was then free of the arguably toughest defender in the game. After simply waltzing around our keeper he was finally faced by Lou, who stood there on the goal-line like a man on Death Row, in front of the Stratford End. Marvin had got back having observed the evidence, only to find that he was stuck on the goal-line with a look of horror on his face and, once getting there, he stood as if standing in front of a firing squad. My first thought was George would stick it through his legs and, it wouldn't have surprised me if Lou had the self-same premonition. George spared Marvin and coolly slotted it out of his reach. You could see the relief on Marvin's face as the ball nestled into the back of the net. This all took place at the Stratford End.

This ground, now called The Theatre of Dreams, would definitely been on this night.

The Belfast Boy fell to his knees looking up as if to thank 'The Man' for his wonderful God-given talent. As for Lou, he just stood thanking the same man for something else, as for Bonetti and Harris they were still in the Manchester mud.

As I said, George was like Jimmy Greaves, though I am not so sure that Jimmy could have withstood such a thunderous tackle. He was majestic in every way, but he never got the better of Harris. George had done something that was quite new to the game. He had floored Harris and, along with him the keeper who was rated one of the best in the world. Can you also remember the goal he scored against his pal Pat Jennings - who was the best in the world - when he lobbed him at Old Trafford, with Phil Beal falling back in his own net trying to get to keep it out, but there was no way. It was simply fantastic.

This was my mate George at his most mercurial best, with his genius there for all to see. If the authorities had anything about them they would show this goal to players and referees in seminars, as to how to keep your feet and, your control. Mind you, when it came to such things, it would have been wasted on such people. Like Messi, defenders kicked George from pillar to post, but like all the wonderful players before them, they never, ever go down. Maradona is another who rides such ferocity with contempt, making those hatchet men look like park players.

One I cannot stand for his play-acting and cheating is Didier Drogba and, had Harris got him in the same way he got George he would still be there now and, that was 1971/72.

If Sir Alex should be sponsored by Wrigley's and referees by Specsavers then Drogba would do a fine job with Kleenex.

George, on the other hand, was a complete one-off. He was the most complete entertainer in the world. He had looks that movie stars would have plastic surgery to get. He had more top-class birds than Bernard Matthews and, of course, he came over from Belfast with the strangest name. This is the kind of name which those Hollywood icons would have to pay for. All superstars change their names and, one who springs to mind is Gerry Dorsey - Engelbert.

He sang a song that could have been mine at Chelsea in the not too distant future.

'Please Release Me Let Me Go for I don't love you anymore' and, I've felt that way ever since!

Talking of love, I just loved playing against George and, was fortunate that I never played in a match where he ripped us apart, although I must tell you that I had some say in this. For whenever I received the ball in our half, I would look to see where he was and, once doing so, took it to the other side of the field. I knew if the move was to break down, it would not be him who'd pick it up. If he was on our right, I'd take ball down our left. I know it frustrated him. Once again, this couldn't be coached. In fact I don't suppose Dave ever knew what I was doing. So when he would say to me, 'Why don't you pass to Peter more'?

I couldn't tell him this, could I?

I would say simply, "I thought the game was all about giving the ball to your best players."

That is not a knock at the other Peter, it is just a massive compliment to the main Peter and, I have no need to tell you who that was.

One particular Wednesday night at Old Trafford I told George, "You won't be seeing much of it tonight mate" - and he didn't. That was the night he jumped on my ankle. He would just shrug those shoulders of his and, flash that smile that knocked over so many beautiful women. Playing against him was like playing a game of chess. You see, I was a footballer, whereas he was the great entertainer. That was the difference between us. If only he had got his wish and played for us. That was one of my greatest regrets and, something else for which I never forgave our manager.

This is why Tony Waddington chose me to replace another chess player, George Eastham. As a Stoke City supporter said to me not so very long ago, "When we signed you, we didn't sign Alan Hudson, we signed a 22-year-old George Eastham."

We both saw it as a great challenge, chess, making all the right moves!

Now on top of my ankle, my shins were troubling me. I did not play again until near Christmas. I recall playing in an under-23 match in Wrexham against Wales and, put up quite a display, despite the pain of such an injury. But again, I was lucky for the rain came the day before and, because these were my conditions, a mud bath and, with my socks rolled down, I led the Welsh a merry dance. I also remember Alf Ramsey telling me afterwards not to cover so much ground to save my energy, which I found a little weird. I never, ever could work it out, for I thought one could never work too hard for his team.

However, my performance hit the London evening papers, who were shouting for my return to form and, first-team duty. After the usual post match drink and, a very late night - like in Europe - I was really excited when buying an Evening News and Standard at the news-stand at Sloane Square, to read the headline of HUDSON TURNS ON MAGIC AND IS READY TO RETURN TO FIRST TEAM...it gave me the kind of tingle that I had been missing for so long. Football is like sex, a drug and, as I said before, I love the foreplay and, the afterwards of celebrating knowing you had not only given your all, but satisfied all parties. Well, I was most definitely satisfied and, I felt my confidence coming back. I knew at this time that the only conditions that I could play on were, as they would put up on the board in the paddock at Cheltenham:

GOOD TO SOFT

What was good about this also, was that there was no Dave Sexton checking you out the following morning. At this time, I was getting on alright with Alf, but all the trouble was to come. It gave me great pleasure to play well for the England youngsters and, never more than alongside my favourite player Tony Currie - along with AB - and, on one particular occasion at the Baseball Ground when the young Scots couldn't get the ball off us. A couple of years ago, I was at a function with Steve Perryman and, he commented on that match for he was the third member of that midfield. He said that, "it was such a great pleasure sitting in midfield watching the two of you toy with the Scots."

I have always said that the perfect England midfield trio for England would have been Ball, Hudson and Currie, I believe we had it all and, enough amongst us to see England qualify in the 70's but...

I've always liked Steve (Perryman) since we first crossed swords at the Welsh Harp in '67 as 16-year-olds and, our paths crossed quite a few times, although by the time I was turning on at Stoke City he had dropped into the back four at Tottenham.

On my return from Wales, I was then substitute against West Ham. Oz scored both goals in a match that saw us squeeze through 2-1. He was finding goals a lot tougher to come by, probably the exertions of the year gone by, the heat of Mexico, the rows with Dave and, the disappointment of seeing Jeff Astle preferred to him. Oh, and of course, there was no Hutch. All of this possibly drained his power. Possibly, though more like probably.

And then of course there was Miss British Airways. He even had a favourite song for her, by Art Garfunkel. I think I had introduced it to him - and him to her. How very romantic, Oz was like that. Everything he did was a little OTT. A little like the Bryan Adams song, had he and Pippa been together when Bryan recorded Everything I Do, I Do It For You it would have been Oz singing to Pippa. You couldn't help but think the world of him. I think it was because every time I looked at him, I saw the magic on the field – and those incredible goals. I was the same with Bobby Moore and, that magical display in Mexico, but Bobby had more in his locker than Oz, when it came to class.

After all he was God!

In my talks in the pubs and clubs I mention constantly how much better the game was then and, on talking of Osgood and Moore proves a point, for West Ham have never seen the likes of Bobby again and, neither have Chelsea seen anything close to Osgood. At Arsenal they'll never be another Charlie George and QPR, a Stan Bowles and, I dare think where Huddersfield would find another Frank Worthington. I think after reading that you'll understand and, get my drift. And yeah, they were all home grown from Windsor to

Barking and Manchester to Islington. Huddersfield is on its own, although Frank will never be alone, for if he's not with his Carol, he'll be with Elvis.

But, as I said, I felt I was definitely on my way back, summer had long gone and, the rainy season was here and, it seemed after that match in Wales, so was I.

22 THE YEAR OF LIVING DANGEROUSLY

January '71 saw us defending the FA Cup and, it all came flooding back as the draw brought us together, yet again - unluckily for them - with Crystal Palace.
Oh how I wanted to go back to Wembley.
Only this time I wanted to actually be out there with my mates!

I had been out for quite a while but the Welsh match pit me back in the frame and, that match was against Manchester United where I scored on my return and, should have scored my first and only ever hat-trick.

Anyhow, once again those great big gates at the Bridge were closed, although nobody outside or inside knew that our opponents would be without George. That was except those in the Manchester United squad. He had missed the rattler from Manchester's Piccadilly Station and, was last seen with a young blonde actress. United reprimanded him. George shrugged his shoulders once again - no doubt. His love affair with United was coming to an end. All I can say is that for George to miss a Chelsea/Manchester United match, his latest flame must have been something else. If only we could have offered him the opportunity to regain his love with the game he played so magically - just as Waddington did with me a couple of years later.

Oz and Weller also missed this match.
With an hour gone I put us in front at the Shed End.
This was courtesy of someone who would become as special to me as Bobby Moore.
Well, almost. The great Paddy Crerand was to George what my mate Dennis Waterman was to Arthur Daley and Sponge was to Charlie. His Minder!

Paddy was a fantastic player. He was an old war horse of a wing-half, a wonderful distributor of the football and, a fantastic competitor. He was Sir Matt Busby's brains in the midfield area. Because of injuries to Oz and Keith and, with Sponge and Hutch also indisposed, we were short to say the least. So I was pushed up to the furthest part of the field and, relished it.

I loved this role and, with no pressure on me, I went out to enjoy myself. I had no problems playing there and, it wasn't as if I was playing up there against the Mean Machine of Leeds United. That was a back four who would be looking to put me out of the game in an entirely different way this Manchester United side.

My team-mates knew there was no point banging long balls forward to chase or high balls to compete aerially, plus definitely no Fiver-Balls - Dave's specialty. In a nutshell, I wanted everything into my feet, never knowing that my mate Pat would be the perfect supplier of such a thing. What on earth was he thinking?

I asked him one afternoon after a few drinks at a function in Trentham - of all places - but he chose to make out that he was more Schindlers than he actually was. I understood. I was only interested in how such a player had made such a hash of things. It was like he had a memory lapse as to what colours United were playing in.

Or just simply he felt sorry for me being up there all on my own. I jest!

Anyhow, he put the perfect pass on a plate for me, rather like Manuel in Alexandre, in fact, I did not even have to move a muscle, until I looked into Stepney's eyes, although I nearly made the cardinal sin of losing concentration because of it. But I gained my composure and side-footed past Alex and, into the left-hand corner of his net. It was a simple chance and, that is how I made it look.

This was the third goal I'd put past Alex, but the only one that counted!

Pat, the last I saw, was standing bent over with his hands on his knees shaking his head. How I wished it could have been a Bremner or a Giles that had done such a thing. I would have run by them and patted them on the backside as a 'thank you' gesture. Pat has many qualities I love most about great people...humility, honour, a sense of humour and, most important of all, again modesty.

He is still very close to Sir Alex Ferguson and, that speaks volumes for the Manchester United boss. Later, I should have scored with a header, but hit the bar from close range. Some people say that it was because I couldn't head the ball; others say that I preferred hitting the bar, but neither was true. It was because I was not used to being in such a position. I was usually setting up such plays.

The ground had absorbed so much cold that the rain made it very slippery, which I think led to their winner, but luckily for me that was all going to change as rain was on its way, but that was for the next match. United were not playing particularly well. They hadn't won for ages and, there was no doubt that with Oz we would have murdered them. With teams like United when you are in control you must kill them off, because they are always capable of finding something from somewhere and, that was what they did. We let them back in this match with Willie Morgan (who always reminded me of the Hollies singer Allan Clarke) scoring from the penalty spot. This came about after Denis Law had cleverly tricked Johnny Boyle into fouling him. I then missed that header, although I don't think it bothered me in later life.

My head, in fact, was to be battered by a big old oak tree, which led to that blood clot on the brain. Although doctors broke the news to my family that they had dispersed it a short while later, I was told by that wonderful lady and medium, Betty Shine, that she was responsible for doing so a few days prior. It was whilst reading the Daily Mail, over a cup of coffee, she read of my disaster and, I cried out to her for help. She then came to my aid. I met her some months later and found her an extraordinary lady, one who was on the same plateau as Maria Callas, as a singer. She had to make the choice between either opera or healing. She chose to help millions of people. I am glad she made such a decision, if only for having the pleasure to meet her. I was so looking forward to seeing her again, but after trying to contact her, found out that she had sadly passed away. She says in her book, The Infinite Mind that she was in contact with Bobby Moore and the Busby Babes, so I can only think by the time I get there they'll be Bobby, Tony, Leslie, my dad Bill, Harry Yewings, Tommy Nicholson all talking football, while, of course my mum, making the tea.

In the closing seconds United stole it, breaking away with a punch from Stepney that would have floored Ali. Alan Gowling - that big, tall, lanky and gangly forward - swallowed half the pitch up unchallenged before beating Catty.

Some years later he did the same thing against us at the Victoria Ground, chasing a Malcolm MacDonald through ball, but it was over hit by my old Arsenal team-mate and, with under a minute left on the clock, Peter Shilton ran out and, in an attempt to boot it out of the ground, he kicked the floor and lay there in a heap, as Gowling walked it into an empty net. It was a very important point dropped!

But here at the Bridge, Gowling got to the ball first and, although his first attempt was stopped by Bonetti, he could only block it and, the ball spun over the top of him like a ping pong ball. He then dived backwards (hence the nickname) and, scooped the ball out via the post. The referee pointed to the centre-circle. United had won 2-1. This was as ridiculous as my goal against Ipswich, so how could we complain?

Technology again!

What goes around comes around. When you think of that wonderful goal George had scored against us and, then you see this. I wondered at the time what he would have thought of it all and, at that moment I know I would rather have swapped places with him. A leggy blonde, though, was the furthest thing from my mind, as Gowling ran through our defence as if they weren't there. Which, they weren't.

This was eventually going to be our downfall, I would not have minded, but we were short of forwards on this particular day, but when the defenders were called on, they were nowhere to be seen.

If only Oz was playing, if only to get the blame?

Catty was gutted, but he had saved us on so many occasions, so there was no way anyone could point a finger. He was up there with the best of all-time.

I played in the following two league matches before being left out of the FA Cup match, though, I cannot remember why.

We desperately wanted to return to Wembley, after all, the club had still not won a final there, having beaten Leeds United in Manchester. We had tasted the wonderful taste of euphoria and, although it tasted differently from Pepe's steak, we still wanted more than ever before.

I just hoped we could stay in it whilst I was, hopefully, regaining my form, because the grounds were softening up and, with being side-lined for so long, I felt that the time was right for me to put things right, although I missed this all-important 3rd round tie against Manchester City, who were the holders of the competition we were in now, the European Cup Winners Cup, and they were still in it along with us, never knowing that we'd clash along the way.

But who knew where or when?

My greatest regret here was that the pitch was a quagmire and, although I had that match in Wales under my belt, Sexton saw it that I was not quite ready. I'm not sure if he was at Wrexham and, could only think that he weren't, because I had shown enough to regain my place.

This was to become one of the matches that hurt me most in my Chelsea career, as Manchester City took us to the cleaners and, we needed it, as the pitch was like a bog.

I had to stand in the East Stand Long Bar and watch Colin Bell absolutely run us ragged and, whilst doing so, knew that had Dave had seen that I was ready, I could have changed things dramatically.

This was my pitch and, I knew I was ready, however we got knocked out and, I was sick as a dog, in fact, vodka sick, although I think I had been knocking a few brandies back with Joe McKay and, with each goal it was as if like taking a blow from the doorman of Annabelles. You might say I would have left Stamford Bridge punch drunk. But I didn't, I walked out in a daze, if only just for knowing, no Wembley for me again this year.

Thanks Dave, but no thanks, it was like one of Alf's gaffes!

I can't even remember which pub I went to as I walked through those gates absolutely shell-shocked. Marvin Hinton had played in midfield, but as I told you earlier, he was not the man for such a job, especially as they called the man who was running riot, Nijinsky.

Well, a long distance runner, Lou was not.

Today, they might say, "Well, they're going for the bigger prize, the European Cup Winners Cup," but that was the last thing on my mind on this particular Saturday afternoon and, I think that terribly hurtful defeat spurred me on and, thought to myself, 'Well Al, it's now Europe or bust?'

This was a case of them knocking the holders of the FA Cup out, but later on we'd be knocking the holders of the Cup Winners Cup out. Touché!

And talking of hurt, who next but West Bromwich Albion, who I now hated the sight of, even to this day and, every time I see their ground, I look for that hole. I can't help myself, but every time the ball bounces about thirty yards from that goal, I look, even though I know that I will never see it.

So this was a double dare with destiny, the missing out of two FA Cup finals, as crazy as it sounds and, who was opposing me but the man who stood nearest me on that dreadful day last Easter, Asa Hartford.

But the good news was it was my pitch and, the longer the studs the better these days, although Ronnie would say that for different reasons.

We won with goals from Holly (twice) Hutch and a South African lad, Derek Smethurst - who actually played in Seattle with me also - but what I can remember most was walking into The Ifield Tavern about 5.30 and, after ordering a pint, telling my uncle that, "I am back George, I really am back," which for the first time since beating Watford, I was really happy, well, more like relieved.

I also recalled that I set up a rare goal for Hutch and that Smethurst was playing because Osgood was serving an incredible eight week long suspension - no not for missing a drugs test - but an accumulation of points.

So, nothing has changed at the FA, they are still morons!

Smethurst was introduced to Sexton by his mate Eddie Firmani, the old Charlton athletic manager and, that is about all I knew about the situation apart, from we missed him like mad - Osgood that was!

My nightmare, I knew was behind me and, how bloody good that felt. So my season began on Saturday 21 January 1971 in front of 26,874 Chelsea and WBA supporters and, how amazing that it was against this team, where I recaptured my form.

This really was to become my time of year, when pitches would have more of a cushion. How I loved the rainy season, but only a few days leading up to matches. The pitch that day was still suffering from the rainfall, much like I was suffering from that FA Cup defeat, however, it was nice and heavy and, I found a new lease of life. I don't know if that cup defeat hurt me so much that I wanted to ram it down Dave's throat, but I felt I needed to prove something once and for all. It was times like this that I wished I had not talked Osgood out of going behind the North Stand, but the outcome of that contest will forever remain a mystery.

I had been struggling with my shin splints and needed the rain more than I ever needed any drink. I was now getting to understand how these thoroughbred horses relied on certain grounds. I still watch certain horses plough through the mud and wonder if that is where the term you're Having a Lark came from. On this day that is what I had done, I was enjoying a mud-lark and, it was the most I'd enjoyed myself so very long.

I speak about such things to Graham Bradley - that brilliant National Hunt jump jockey - who brought over a special horse named Well Chief from Germany. When I asked him once if it would like the going, he replied that, "The more he can hear his feet rattle, the better."

Next was our first flight to a football league match, was Dave catching on that this was the best way to travel, or was it he'd rather spend 30 minutes on an aeroplane with us drinking than four hours on British Rail?

All I knew that after getting the only goal, I found celebrating at the Airport Bar far more stimulating than the one on British Rail and, years later it stood me in good stead for my jaunts all around the United States.

So, with my new found confidence, we flew out a few days later to Jamaica, leaving a freezing February behind us for the 85-degree heat of Kingston where we would play Santos of Brazil. After writing the original Ballet I spent more time in this wonderful place and, realised the magic was not just that of Pele.

So, it was from the beautiful surroundings of Kingston, the National Stadium and Pele to the forever windy Newcastle, St James' Park and

Barrowclough - no, not the one in Porridge - but the under 23 right-winger.

Talk about a complete culture shock, although I had been there before, Newcastle that is, when Chelsea lost 5-1 under Docherty, when I had my knee injury and was skip boy.

When I visited there for a second time, Jamaica this time, I treated the local bar staff to a night out and, also to Ali Campbell of UB40 fame - on the jukebox and, whilst looking over the beautiful ripples around us, I understood just why he wrote such a romantic song about this most incredible of places.

On a short boat trip along from our hotel we were showed the home where Ian Fleming wrote the Bond movies. On the beach going back to the boat, I pictured Ursula Andres coming out of the water towards me. Had that ever have happened - even in my wildest dreams - I would certainly have impressed her more than Oz did Raquel Welch.

Before deciding to rewrite this story I met Ali at Trentham Gardens with my mate Ranvir and the Brummie genius said hello to him in Punjabi. The reason I mention something that might sound so terribly trivial is that to my friend it was right out of the blue and thrilled him.

But on this first visit to Jamaica it was the genius and the magic of the Black Pearl that had me completely mesmerised. Pele was everything - and more - that I had ever imagined playing against.

They had another star player in Edu, whilst Douglas (no relation to the Blackburn winger) scored the only goal of a match dominated by Santos and, Pele in particular. It was totally amazing being on the same field as him, for he was, it seemed, as complete a player as you can ever imagine. Not very big but strong, very powerfully built, beautifully balanced, with a touch like an angel. Remember the goal he set up for Jairzinho in Mexico against England when the ball came to him like a speeding bullet?

He killed it stone dead under immense pressure and rolled it gently for the Brazilian winger to finish us off from about eight yards out. It was that piece of genius that allowed that wonderful right-winger to become the only player to score in every match of the most fantastic World Cup of all time. Can you imagine any England forward in our lifetime having the ability to do such a thing? This is why we cannot possibly win another World Cup.

And here we were, the Wingless Wonders!

Talking of fantastic wingers, I was at a function a few weeks ago with Jeff Powell in the Manchester Hilton. Whilst on stage I told the story about meeting Pele in the bar after this match in the wee small hours. One of my all-time favourite players, John Barnes came up to me afterwards and, he told me that he was at the match on that evening. He was a tiny 9-year-old ball boy. Pity our manager had not been told about John then, but then again he wouldn't have liked John for he would have fitted into our social team as perfectly as he would have fitted into our football team.

Whilst at a function at Olympia in London, I forgot to ask Jimmy Greaves about his trip to Ocho Rios. That one night I mentioned earlier, where in a mini cab, I was asking the cab driver about the local bars. Before dropping us off he told me he used to pick up a very famous English footballer. He said that he was the last one out, in fact the only one left each night and, it was Jimmy. All of these things went through my head whilst hospitalised, which really did help me fight to first get out of bed, then out of my wheelchair and, finally defy Frank Cross, and walk.

To give you an idea of what I went through, one night after 'lights out' I dropped the remote control, for the TV. I somehow managed to crawl down to the floor and get my hands on it before incredibly pulling myself back up to the pillow.

It took me an hour-and-a-half and I was completely exhausted.

God knows what damage I would have caused had I fallen out.

Whilst laying there paralysed, the only time I knew the time was by the street lights going on and off and, the sound of the first car engine starting up outside my window. After a long night suffering the dark this sound was so welcoming and, I knew right then the ward lights would soon bring my hell hole back to life.

In the space of a few months I had now played against the three best players on the planet. The 33,000 spectators that turned out to see this match - to watch Pele - was the biggest-ever gathering to watch a soccer match on the island. The majority of them spilt onto the pitch when Santos scored. The match was held up for 10 minutes before order was restored, such was the great excitement of the occasion. No-one was hurt. However, when we arrived back at Heathrow it seemed that the Carnival had been turned into a riot by the media. We were greeted back with headlines of: CHELSEA INVOLVED IN RIOT MATCH....which could not be further from the truth, there was no trouble, in fact, quite the opposite, for to see these locals get the opportunity to see their hero under such circumstances was fantastic and, I felt privileged to be a part of it. Had someone said to me a year prior, that I would be not only playing, but drinking afterwards with Pele in Kingston, Jamaica, I would have checked their drink. This trip was something to behold!

Kingston was the home of Robert Nesta Marley - better known as Bob!

He was football crazy and it was said that the cancer that took his life started with an untreated injury whilst playing. His toe was slashed by another player's pair of rusty spikes whilst playing on the Boys Town

Recreation Ground in Trench Town. Marley's best mate was Skill Joe - no relation to Joe - who played for the national side of Jamaica and in Brazil. Marley's team was Santos. He was a pal of Paulo Cesar, a Brazilian World Cup player. When Bob lived in London he could be seen playing every day over Bishop's Park at the back of Craven Cottage, just where you get off a 22 bus at the bottom of Putney Bridge. I would walk through there many, many times to watch Johnny Haynes. It was said that Marley wanted to be a player more than anything else, just like yours truly. Oh, to have pulled JH's number ten over my head!

Just say he had swapped with George, do you think my mate would have sung:

No Woman No Cry?

So the following Saturday, a few days after the fun and sun of Jamaica, we visited another beauty spot, St James' Park, Newcastle. It was like Chicago - windy!

We were certainly racking up the air miles, not that they existed then and, as I said, this was the first time that we flew to a Football League match and I remember it being more exciting than going on the rattler. In the years to come I would experience this by constantly flying all over the United States, one of things I loved most about playing in the NASL, as I told you earlier. I still get excited as I write about it. It is times such as these that I so wished we earned what they earn today, for I would have travelled the world, which would have been a little different from those today. I often wondered what it would have been like had I ever played in the same team as George, I suppose I would have had to plump for the Miss Word Runner-Up. Maybe!

Had we played together on a couple of hundred-grand-a-week, the mind boggles completely!

There are obvious things that you'd want to change in your life and, the obvious thing in ours (the 70s) would be the money of today, but the other thing is if only Bolt had been in Jamaica then, as he is now. A very young John Barnes was there on that night as a ball-boy. What a very talented nation they are!

Newcastle was Newcastle. As I said, it was incredibly windy and bloody cold. The excursions and exertions of Jamaica didn't seem to have taken their toll though and, no sign of trouble with our manager and, top scorer. Not even standing in the bar with the great Pele in the early hours of Thursday morning could stop us beating this team. And like against West Bromwich, I found I was still in form, scoring a great goal that won us the match. Eddie won a ball on the half-way line and knocked it forward for me to latch on to and, as I did, all I could see was the big frame of Bobby Moncur, their Scotland skipper, heading towards me. Flicking it over his head was simple. The difficult part was to follow. I was on the by-line and, after steadying myself, I looked up to see a very mean looking Hutch tearing towards the near post screaming at me to get it into him. I feigned to play it into his path but instead, right at the last moment noticing a tiny gap, tucked it between the near post and Ian McFaul, their goalkeeper.

I just screwed my foot around the ball at the very last moment and the ground fell silent.

It felt so surreal, as if the world had stopped for a few seconds. I thought of Pele!

And then the sound resumed but only at one end of the ground and, it was where our boys from The Shed had congregated. It was one of the only pictures I have ever seen of a goal where the scorer was not in it. Again, I didn't score many, but when I did....

After the match I wondered if being on the same field as Pele, being in the same bar, watching him walk in with a drink in one hand and a stunner in the other had anything to do with it. I knew one thing though, if it was good enough for him, it was good enough for me, although Dave wouldn't have seen it that way.

For it must have been about 2am in Jamaica and Sponge, myself and Johnny Boyle were reflecting on such a night; the beautiful place, the carnival atmosphere, the people, the life we had when all of a sudden it was like a mirage and, then in walked the Great Man with this most beautiful of blondes on his arm. This was the first time I had ever seen these two Playboys take absolutely no notice of such beauty. We stopped Pele and, insisted he had a drink with us. We also insisted we called him God; a word we used only when speaking of his mate Bobby Moore back home.

I'd now met four football Gods, three socially, if you add Bobby, George and Johan Cruyff, who would soon the take over from Pele and George as the greatest player on the planet!

Pele, like George and Bobby, was absolutely brilliant, a gentleman of the highest order and one who had that quality I spoke of earlier - modesty.

I had found at an early age, that the bigger the genius, the nicer the person.

My confidence was returning in a very big way now and Pele, there was no doubt, had given me a very timely lift - one that would get my season under way. There is no manager or coach that can do such a thing and, it proves that our game is all about players. Players can make you - and managers can break you - and I was soon to find this out in a very big way. I never knew that I was going to become the luckiest man in the world by changing the latter.

My first reaction from The Ifield Tavern was proving to be right and, as I said to my uncle, "George, I'm back" and, I was. I was selected to play in my second under-23 international, but I put that down to my performance in Wales. Even if Dave took no notice, at least Alf did. This time it was at Hampden Park though and, Hutch was also called up. This was a match I didn't enjoy and for some reason I can't put my finger on why I did not play well. But I was not really interested in those matches. I was more interested in getting Chelsea to the final of the Cup Winners Cup. With my form returning, now that the grounds were softening up, there was a fair chance of that happening. Having said that, we were about to meet possibly the best team in the competition, and how we got away with it, I'm still not quite sure.

I was still frequenting the local clothes shops. Stanley Adams, the Squire Shop, Lord Kitcheners and the Village Gate were now all the in-places to get kitted out.

Plus, they were only a short free-kick from both the Markham Arms and Alexandre.

Later that season a great big lad we bought from Slough Town made his debut. His name was Mickey Droy and, he was a man-mountain. We lost 1-0 at Wolves to a great strike by Kenny Hibbitt (a player who would join me in Seattle all those years later). He was a player who impressed me immensely while on loan with us. I always thought Kenny to be a very useful midfield player, but in the States he was magnificent. He was a natural footballer who played alongside me, scoring not only some superb goals but also several vital ones, like the one that took us to the Soccer Bowl. I had a lot of time for Kenny. He was another from a working-class background. His brother Terry, who played for Leeds United, died not long before he came over to us. He was still only very young.

Mickey didn't really establish himself in the team until after its break-up. He became a big player for Chelsea but while all the big names were there, he was a little overawed by it all (I think I am right in saying). The likes of Oz would constantly rib him about him not being physical enough and, I don't think it helped his confidence. Like so many young players he was launched into the stratosphere without breathing equipment. I was lucky from day one, for I had my father and my great self-belief in the ability The Man had blessed me with. But that really sank in after that match at The Lane.

Some years' later Chelsea abused a real great talent named Dale Jasper, who I mentioned earlier. It was my second time around at the Bridge when I saw enough of this youngster to know that he could, with the right guidance, become as big a player as any before him. When I moved back to Stoke City for a second time in the Eighties, this time on a month's loan (a little different from the £250,000 seven years earlier), I told our manager to bring him to the club. I suggested that if he brought Jasper to Stoke, this player would become as big as the names you will read about later at the Victoria Ground. The only problem was that Tony Waddington was no longer in charge. Instead, we had a clown named Bill Asprey. But after returning from the States, I found out that the game had been taken over by so many of these clowns dressed in tracksuits.

Spring came suddenly and with it my pitches.

We were paired against the team who, to this day, I don't know how we knocked them out. They were the Belgian Cup winners, Bruges. This was now the quarter-final stages of the European Cup Winners Cup and, we were slowly getting our act together and, once again we were going out into the unknown once again. They had the first player in the competition I'd ever heard of and, he was the brilliant Robbie Rensenbrink, possibly the closest thing I've seen on the field to George.

However, we had one problem.

We would be travelling to Belgium without Osgood.

He was still out suspended.

Since, you might say, it would be like Argentina going to the World Cup without Maradona and Messi (today), Holland without Cruyff, West Germany without Beckenbauer, France with no Platini and England without Emile Heskey - I jest!

That is basically the comparisons we've had to those nations over the years!

The time was 7.30 the date the 10 March and, the place, the DeKlokke Stadium, with 23,000 inside this tiny place. The result was a complete mauling, but somehow we got away from there with just a squeak of a chance of getting through. I remember that night we flew straight back and recall thinking to myself, 'Well, that's it mate, we're out and, then I thought of our lifeline, Osgood is back,' as I looked into the darkness of the night, with the only light flashing off the wings, and, whilst looking thought of Rensenbrink, he was simply magnificent. But had he done enough to knock us out?

Sitting on that flight I was so disappointed and had the loneliest feeling and, I don't know if it was because of this being our first defeat and, the trip being nothing like any before. We were used to getting the right result, going out afterwards carefree, having a drink and a laugh and, using our celebratory skills to the full and, this aeroplane was like bringing home the dead from Afghanistan. It was dark and miserable and, I had a feeling that this was the end of what looked like being another dream cup experience. But, as I said, tomorrow would be a new day and, I still had Osgood at the back of my mind, after all we had gone there with him and Hutch and, that really was all I could take out of it, that is, if you ignored the brilliance of young John Phillips in goal. If not for him, we would most definitely be out of this competition - he was absolutely incredible.

We respected Bruges, if only for getting this far, especially after getting past CSKA. But we really never knew just how good they were until a ball was kicked. We were soon to find out. They were unbeaten on their home soil in domestic competition in three long years. That was where we were heading first. Their two best players were Robbie Rensenbrink and Lambert. There manager was Frank de Munck. In that first leg they ripped into us in front of a crowd of only 23,000 (it was jam packed) and, I had never experienced such a hostile atmosphere. The closest in a ground such as this would have been last season at Derby County in the hostility of the Baseball Ground. At the Bridge we could play in front of 60,000 and, not get an ounce of that kind of atmosphere because our fans were too far away from the pitch.

But here they could strangle you as you took a throw-in. However, they did not need their supporters to do that, for they were doing it on the field. They simply battered us. Had it been in a boxing ring, Harry Gibbs would surely have stopped it, even though there was no blood. The noise was deafening and, they knocked the ball around with such blistering speed it was truly frightening.

I just wished that I had a video of this performance, for it was one of the greatest I'd ever seen, let alone played against.

They came out of the traps like it was the final of the Greyhound Derby at Wimbledon - and their fans were barking too. To make things tougher for us they grabbed an early lead. The place went totally bonkers. It was a dream start for them and, the beginning of a nightmare evening for us, although it could have been so much worse, if not for our keeper. Lambert flicked in a near-post header from Thio's corner. John Phillips, who was making his European debut, was powerless to stop it. And even though the big Belgian centre-forward was surrounded by several yellow shirts, he still managed to find our net easily.

This gave them a tremendous lift and belief. The onslaught had begun and, we could sense that we were in for a very long and unfruitful evening. They played a great passing game at full tilt, with the ball going in and out and from side to side. It was actually like watching a master on the pinball table. Or as Elton John might sing, a Pinball Wizard!

Then it would stop with Rensenbrink - a player of immense skill and pace who just loved taking on and pulling full-backs apart. He was the closest I had ever seen to that bloke Peter Thompson that I told you of earlier and, of course, as I just mentioned George.

We were the opposite, as we were stunned by the early blow and couldn't put two passes together, let alone string them. We missed Oz big time and, even though Sponge was fighting a brave fight alone up front, it was mainly chasing their defenders. He got no service whatsoever, whilst the rest of us were clinging on for dear life. The Bruges team strung their passes together with such ease. They had tremendous all-round skill. They were a team which had been well coached on how to play the game the right way. The ball hardly left their carpet of a pitch. They were also a team which would never attempt to play the Fiver Ball, something that will be relevant later on.

The thing about Osgood and Hutchinson was that even if we were under the most intense pressure, you could always hook one up to them and, they'd battle like mad for it. They could hold it up, which would always give us a little breathing space, but here we were desperate for someone up front to get a hold of the ball so that we could have that breather. This was not being critical of Tommy - he simply had no chance. Without those two we were being over-run and outplayed in every department. Thankfully, our debutant goalkeeper was making a mockery of his status.

It was in matches like this that you would have thought Dave would have realised just how much Osgood was worth to our team. After all, he was as the Shed boys sang, the King of Stamford Bridge!

With Oz you could always count on him getting a goal out of the blue, no matter how much pressure we were under and, no matter how well or not he was playing. To make things even worse, when we did create an opportunity, luck was nowhere to be seen. It looked like we were back in the match remembering the importance of an away goal when Weller found Tommy who headed it and, as he did so, Sanders (the Bruges keeper) was going the wrong way. Somehow, he threw up his arm and punched the ball against his own bar. Our lifeline had gone. It looked a certain goal and what a bonus an away goal would have been to take back to the Bridge for the second leg. The ball was scrambled away instead and that had me thinking on the aeroplane coming home that night that this save had cost us a place in the next round.

Just before half-time they scored a second, when another Thio corner found, the impressive Rensenbrink who powered it towards our goal. Their centre-forward Marmenout tried to get out of the way, but it struck him full in the face and ricocheted past Phillips and into the net. It would not only make it more difficult back in London, but was a cruel blow to our keeper after performing heroically.

We were stunned once again and from there on only the brilliance of our goalkeeper kept any hopes we had of reaching the semi-final alive. Sticks played absolutely superbly on this night of high drama.

Sponge went close late on when nearly sliding another cross past Sanders, but it just was not to be. We had been battered into oblivion - rather like me in the Mile End Road!

Since my arrival in the side, this was only the second time we had been totally mauled by the opposition after suffering at Goodison Park the previous Easter.

That was the worst Easter of my life, for reasons you have already heard, but the Christmas, years later, would rather put that in the shade when it came down to catastrophes.

But that day at Goodison Park, we knew exactly what we were up against and, they were the team with the best three midfield players in any one team. If you imagine Barcelona today, it might give you some kind of idea.

I suppose in many ways it was a good thing that we had not had these watched or been shown a video. After all, ninety minutes of torture was more than enough and, that was what was taking place right here on this tiny little ground called DeKlokke.

Trouble marred the end of the game. The Chelsea fans attacked the Bruges fans and there were some ugly scenes. Up until now our supporters had been exemplary, but here they were fighting. I can only think out of sheer frustration after watching their team getting a good hiding. Now maybe, they wanted to give their fans the same.

Those fans were then led by Mick Greenaway, a legendary figure and one whose legend lives on. He was a huge influence on his followers, being famous for his chant of Zigga, Zagga, Zigga, Zagga, Oi, Oi, Oi!

Often in quiet periods during games, or when we were up against it, he would unleash his war cry and it would go from The Shed around the dog track to finally reach and lift us. It seemed a lot more humorous then too. This was before the real violence of the mid-Eighties.

The northern fans were the pioneers of the aggression. I first experienced the Leeds United supporters raining down coins on us in The Shed in '66. This day I stood there never dreaming that one day I would be playing against this team in front of such fans. We had the sign over them, though, especially in the FA Cup as well as beating them in that League Cup match I told you of earlier. On this day of the coin throwing, a brilliant Bobby Tambling free-kick put them on their way back up the motorway with their tails between their legs and that was followed by a Tony Hateley header in a semi-final at Villa Park. We most certainly got the better of Leeds United in those FA Cup exchanges.

This was the time when Docherty was seen on TV hanging out of the 'pigeon loft' at the top of the East Stand screaming on his Diamonds and, so the Docherty Diamonds legend was born. The following season, after knocking out Leeds United in the FA Cup yet again (this time in the semi-final at Villa Park), I recall seeing a massive Docherty's Diamonds banner at Wembley for the final against Tottenham. After we had lost that match and, when I was walking down Wembley Way, I saw it in the gutter, all crumpled and torn like a discarded pennant in the aftermath of a medieval battle.

I have to stop saying we, for as you know by now, I was still Fulham!

But on this day at the Bridge (whilst we were being pelted by coins) Chelsea held on to beat their fiercest rivals, with Catty making a point blank save from Jack Charlton in the very last minute. When I heard some years later that my eldest son, Allen, stood among these kinds of supporters I had to have words with him. Of course, Chelsea fans were no angels even then, but like the gunfighters they attracted trouble. The media seemed puzzled when the hooliganism thing came back into vogue as Chelsea qualified again for European football. Of course it was a different generation and a different kind of hooligan.

Just as when Chelsea beat Bruges in the '95 Cup Winners Cup their side was not as good as our '71 side, as the hooligan was not in the same league as ours. In '71 it was boots and fists and lots of charging harmlessly around the back streets of Fulham. It had changed to Stanley knives, CS gas, mobile phones and arranged meets. Just as Bugsy Segal claimed in the Forties that his gangsters, "Only shoot one another!"

The bad boys who followed Chelsea only fought with other gangs: West Ham ICF, The Cockney Reds of Manchester United and Spurs' Park Lane Crew to name but a few. This is not to glamorize it, merely to explain the heritage behind it.

The Chelsea supporters never gave us a more fantastic backing than they did in the return leg against the Belgians.

But before that they backed us brilliantly at White Hart Lane, where they were amongst 49,192 fans that saw us lose 2-1 and, then in a 0-0 draw at Huddersfield which was the first time that I came across Frank Worthington and. Frank and I were to become very close in the Nineties.

But our most famous times were along with Alan Ball under Revie. He, Alan and I would skip Bingo and Carpet Bowls and go socialising down the road from the hotel at Bernie Winters home and, any other of Alan's friends who were at home that afternoon. Don, caught up with me and Alan one early evening as we sat in the hotel bar, although he wasn't man enough to ask where we'd been?

We were having a quiet drink when an arm came on our shoulder with a great big head following it in between us. Then Don said, "I just hope they are soft drinks?"

Like two little schoolboys - and Alan didn't need to get up - we said, in unison, "Of course Don," like we had been caught bunking off school and, were about to get the cane. Our respect for him was non-existent and, it was one of those situations where you almost wanted him to know, for one/to see what he'd tell the press and, two/to let the country know our side of his pathetic story. I mean Bingo and Carpet Bowls, can you imagine Maradona, Moore, Pele, Beckenbauer and Baxter sitting around spending time as if they were doing porridge.

Here is what Alan Ball had to say about the situation: Maybe I was too experienced in the ways of the world for him. Looking back I think I knew one or two things that might have annoyed him. He had a squad staying at the West Park Lodge Hotel in north London and in the afternoon, when there was nothing on the official agenda, it seemed like a good idea to go along to my friend Bernie Winters house, which was not far away. Bernie was a regular visitor to Arsenal and I often met him on nights out in London. I had struck up a good friendship with Alan Hudson and took him along to Bernie's, where we drank tea and chatted to while away the time. Players were often looking for things to do and I was quite open about it, but I am sure Revie got it in his head that we were going to Bernie's for two reasons: to drink something stronger than tea and, to indulge in some serious gambling using Bernie's telephone. When I told Bernie this, he said that he wanted to set the record straight and, wrote to the Football Association, setting out the reality of the cups of tea.

Well, that was Alan's story. Mine is different, I never ever drank a cup of tea in Bernie's home and neither did Frank Worthington and, the reason I tell you that is, if I wanted a cup of tea, I would have stayed in my hotel room. We had a few drinks over a few brilliant stories. I remember a marvellous story Bernie told me about Tom Jones, which I cannot divulge for it being personal, but it was absolutely amazing and, it was worth going there for that alone. I can also tell you gambling was never an issue. We simply stood at Bernie's bar and laughed away the afternoon.

When I played in Seattle, we played in Fort Lauderdale at a time when we were beating everyone out of sight. On this particular evening I left the changing room and saw Mike, Bernie's brother, standing outside and, because of Bernie's kind hospitality introduced myself and, dragged him into our dressing room and introduced him to all of our players, many of whom he obviously knew, the likes of Bruce Rioch, Jeff Bourne and Roger Davies from Clough's Derby and my favourite, David Nish although also from Derby County, but in a different league as a player.

The reason that I mention this is because this is what football is all about, bringing nice people together. Now, in my world, had I been England manager and, had known of Bernie living just down the road from the hotel, I would have invited him into meet the players.

I remember when Webby brought Marty Feldman and Michael Crawford into our dressing room at the Bridge, whilst I met many very well-known actors and actresses upstairs in the Long Bar, the one Dave hated. It was all a great part of being a player. Being backstage for entertainers was the same. I've been backstage with Elton, Jack Jones, Phil Collins, Supertramp and The Who. That doesn't make me a Groupie or a star-seeker, it's simply meeting people you admire and are a big fan of. I had all Phil's albums. I had all of Supertramp's too. I met Tony Bennett in Seattle and nobody had more of his albums than I did. I remember getting Elton's first album and from there I was a fan forever and had everything he'd ever recorded.

The biggest thrill was when meeting both Phil and Jack Jones I was with Bobby Moore and, my biggest regret I don't have the photographs for you in this book.

So, the point I am trying to get across is that I think Revie is not only shallow, but if he thought that players would rather play Bingo than meet these people then I am living on the wrong planet.

But back to the great and masterful Alan Ball, who used to call me Maestro. Now, even had we been drinking tea, which we weren't, the FA would have done nothing about it anyway. Bernie was a smashing bloke and, he entertained us wonderfully, I think Frank was with us on that occasion and, from there we dropped into another friend of Alan's where we broke into another bottle.

Alan was alive when he wrote this book and, I think had he been alive today and, we were on Parkinson or Jonathan Ross, I think he might tell a different story and, the one that is totally alright. After all I remember coming out of the Whiter Hart one morning at 5am, and, we were training at 10.30 and, on that evening Alan was on the subs bench.

Alan Ball, in my eyes, has absolutely nothing to hide and, that is the problem, because like Moore they were hounded by the likes of these type of England managers, who come in and want to introduce Bingo, Carpet Bowls, going to the movies and all that bollocks, Brian Clough took his Nottingham Forest team down the pub the night before a European Cup final for Goodness sake and, incredibly won the bloody thing.

How many European Cups had Revie won by playing fucking Bingo?

I remember Revie saying to Clough about him not playing these games with his players and Brian simply looked at him as if he was a complete idiot.

I still can't believe that I had the misfortune to come across such a man and, if Waddington ever come up with such pathetic ideas, I am certain he would have been certified. Can you imagine Tony sitting down Maurice Setters, Calvin Palmer, Eddie Stuart and Eddie Clamp on a Thursday afternoon to play Bingo?

You're having a laugh and, the terrible thing was that was what the England team were doing, whilst failing to reach the World Cup finals around that time and, if there had been a Bingo calling competition we might have had a world champion in our midst. No, I'm sorry, Revie had it all wrong and, the terrible truth of the matter was that he was the right man for the job, because they were all pathetic, every single one of them and, also there wasn't and, still isn't, a man amongst them.

But let's get back to a little matter of trying to work out how we were going to get back into that tie against those Belgians and, the first thing we needed to do was make sure Rensenbrink never had too much possession, for he was a complete master at work.

That was the only time I'd ever been to their ground and, how glad I am of that, but the only thing that still worries me is that I can't work out just how we escaped alive?

But it was now D-Day at the Bridge and, the biggest match of my career so far, having missed last seasons' FA Cup final and, the people inside the ground were in for a real treat, for this was possibly the best performance our Chelsea side ever gave under the circumstances as a collective unit. If you ask any Chelsea fan of that time and mention that match, I think you'll find they would agree. The tragedy again, was that it was never captured on film for posterity. A video of it would definitely make a best seller. It had absolutely everything you'd hope to see in a football match. It was real edge-of-the-seat stuff, not as violent as the FA Cup final replay with Leeds, or a Quentin Tarantino blockbuster, but a real classic. Pulp Football!

I could count the greatest five matches on my right hand without hesitation this was most certainly one of them. The other four were my debuts against Liverpool and the Germans. Then there was that other match against Liverpool, when Bill Shankly said it was the greatest individual performance he'd ever witnessed. Last but not least, when Stoke City stopped Revie's Leeds United from breaking the record number of matches unbeaten.

There was something about beating Leeds that gave you such a glow and, no matter how long my third life continues, the thoughts of them get sweeter and sweeter.

They don't sound so great when you say it like that, but that's the beauty of writing books and watching videos. When I look back, I look back with not only pride but such fantastic memories and, that is why with Chelsea, I have no time for them, because they have no time for both us and these matches.

They never even had a celebration for this most magnificent of seasons....

In front of 45,558 supporters Peter Houseman gave us a great start, just as Lambert did for the Belgians over there.

The referee, Petar Kostovski from Yugoslavia, looking back was hardly seen, and apart from Johnny Boyle replacing John Dempsey after 46 minutes all I can remember of this game was it having everything and more that you'd pay to go and see, that was unless you were Belgian of course. This goal lifted us as much as it did them in that first match. It also lifted the crowd and raised our hopes; as we knew from the start that this was going to be one long night and a real tough hill to climb. However, they were never flustered. They were a very confident team and one that was not going to give their lead away easily.

The one thing we had going for us and, that was that Oz was back in the side after eight long weeks.

In that time he took his frustration out on moving home and, once again he showed that it was a case of the bigger the match, the bigger the challenge, the bigger the player. That was Osgood!

Although we led early, we were still holding that slender advantage with, just under 10 minutes left on the referee's watch. We were a Houseman goal in front but still one behind. The crowd, led by our boys in The Shed, had been staggering. Sometimes in lesser matches they could be on our backs, but that was because their expectations were so high. They knew what we were capable of and they expected it. In the real big matches, though, especially when the odds were stacked so high against us, they seemed to have a completely different attitude. It was the same at Old Trafford in extra-time against Leeds when they propelled Chelsea on to score with the old mantra of - Chelsea! Chelsea! Chelsea!

On this night we could hear it coming down in waves from the back of The Shed, right across the stands and finally over that hindrance of a dog track and onto the pitch. Those incredible souls in The Shed will never know just what they meant to us and, had we had the stadium of today, we would have won the championship well before the great Jose Mourinho arrived.

I mention the dog track once again because it very much favoured the visitors. The first aim when playing away, especially in Europe, was to silence the home crowd and this was more difficult when they were on top of you. And in Bruges they were certainly on top. That piece of land surrounding our pitch was like the graveyard behind the East Stand. Had we had a stadium like today, I am certain our home record would have been far superior and the Chelsea fan would not have had to wait 50 years for another title.

I remember those days of cleaning the ground on a Monday morning, after 50-odd thousand had left their rubbish behind on a Saturday afternoon. Then there was Saturday night Greyhound Racing where they'd add to it. When I was having those nine months off through that knee injury, I would take a break from cleaning the boots, scrubbing the baths, showers, toilets and floors and watch the dogs spin round. The main grounds-man George Ansters would walk them round with his flag in his hand, whilst other members of the staff put them in the traps.

The stories were great, grabbing the nuts of trap 3 when their money was on the 2 dog, for instance.

These stories mostly came from old Arthur, a lovely little man who was a dentists dream. We used to say of his set of railings, "He only needs a white for a snooker set," but that was long before Jimmy White supported us, or was it?

Do you see the fun we used to have....it was one big happy family, why?

That was because we were all local, from Christine Matthews in the main office to Peter Houseman our left winger.

But tonight, with only the floodlights covering the field of play, the noise filled the terraces, the pitch and our very heads and hearts, it was simply electrifying. Bruges had played superbly, but it felt as if they sensed something incredible was going to happen, and it did. But it took time.

But when the time came, they began hacking the ball away, whereas in the last 170 minutes they had passed it neatly. What I just mentioned about them being confident and, composed was now changing under immense pressure - the kind that we experienced on their tiny ground.

We were nine minutes from oblivion when Osgood did what he always did in our hour of need. He scored! It was not one of his super goals, but its importance was unquestionable. In the context of this tie, this round, this competition, it was simply priceless. He had done it again. He was a genius. The big centre-forward turned in a shot by the far post whilst surrounded by, it seemed, an army of Belgians. But the old hand controlled it superbly, created that little extra space and, turned it home and, even though he wasn't properly fit it didn't matter, his positioning and timing were perfect and, once again, that's something you just cannot coach!

As I say repeatedly, he was in my view the best in the world around that time - if only Ramsey and Sexton saw it that way. What more had he to do to prove it to them?

Maybe his goal at Old Trafford was more emotional and it was also better crafted. Cooke setting it up beautifully, but this was the most cathartic moment in that particular team's history. We all thought that he had been treated harshly by the FA. He had. What's new at Lancaster Gate? But with him coming back and scoring such a vital goal, it unleashed hysteria, passion and frenzy.

These were all the good things in our game, no sleaze, no drugs or corruption. Fields of Gold, as the man sang. Oz ran off somewhere celebrating as only he did. Just as he had kept his record of scoring in every round of that incredible FA Cup success, he kept his word to the fans one more time. He said he would score. He did. How could they fail to love him?

He had scored from just under where the North Stand used to be and, after leaping that tiny little fence onto the dog track, he ended up in front of the benches. The crowd was streaming down to greet him, to share the moment, to mob him. In those days a hot-dog truck trundled around the perimeter and in matches nothing like as intoxicating as this, you could smell the burgers and onions. This was all pre-Big Macs and Burger Kings. Oz dived on to the trolley and the bus went flying, as the crowd engulfed him.

Sometimes in your life you can re-create certain moments and feelings. That was always a special moment for me. I think at that moment with Bruges absolutely out on their feet, we knew there was no way we were not going through to the semi-finals. His goal took this thriller into extra-time and the look on the faces of our opposition told the complete story.

They were talented, but on this night they showed that they were also gutsy.

The match was now ours for the taking - this was probably the greatest lifeline I'd (we'd) ever had the opportunity to be given. We seemed to spring into another gear, just simply a mental thing as relief flows through your body to replace the adrenalin. The relief of just having another half-an-hour in this great competition, but we wanted more. There was no way they were coming back at us. We had worked too hard and given far too much to get this far - you only had to look at the opposition to know you were a very good side. There are some matches you win and get changed and celebrate, then there are matches that you have to really dig deep, go beyond the norm and, then when coming off know you'd been in a real football match. This was one of them.

They must have known they had missed their chance in Belgium. They had us on the ropes. But they failed to kill us off. Again, I remember sitting on that aeroplane coming home thinking that there was no way back, but now it was their turn to take such a journey, only there was absolutely no way back, for they were going back to Belgium and staying there.

We were going to experience the self-same thing in the months to come, but now this was our greatest achievement to date as a team. Even as I write, I am still a little mystified as to just how we got through this one and, I am sure their players must have experienced the same feelings.

I still think Bruges might have been better coming out and having a go at us more. They probably thought that after we gave such an inept performance on their ground and, we were not capable of such a performance and, who can blame them, but as I said, I might have been inclined - if that was the case - to go for that all-important away goal. They obviously, a little like us with them, knew nothing about Osgood.

Unlike on Sky today, where you can see those Champions League matches and study teams and players, this was so different, playing in Europe for us was like going into the unknown on each and every occasion. They were by far the best team we played that season. They were like Leeds, Liverpool and Manchester United all rolled into one in that first match. The only thing they lacked was an Osgood. They had a Best in Robbie Rensenbrink, but had they had a real finisher, we would have been not only down, but out!

He was the closest thing to George we'd ever seen.
In that first 45 minutes in Belgium, I thought he was going to knock us out single-handedly!

We were now kicking into the Shed End for the second time and, it was quite fitting that was where we scored our third goal. It was as if it was definitely 'Meant to Be,' just for those supporters who had been with us throughout all our journey from Selhurst Park, Turf Moor, Loftus Road, Old Trafford, Bulgaria, Greece and then to Bruges in Belgium, our last port of call.
This had become quite a journey. In fact, it was more like a Magical Mystery Tour!
The third goal was a result of the Hudson and Osgood party piece. Where and whenever I got on the by-line he would make believe to rush into the near post. As his marker tried to get in front of him, he just put on the anchors and pulled out. I was standing there with the ball at my feet waiting for him to get into his scoring position. I laid it back and watched the Master at work. He pulled the trigger from a slight angle and from 15 yards out it nestled into the back of their net. Can you remember Deco scoring in the Champions League final for Porto?
It was exactly the same. He knocked the ball wide and then made his near-post run. He then pulled out and the ball was laid back to him. The defenders running in to defend the goal can do nothing about it, for they are simply flat-footed and lambs to the slaughter. That was exactly how we did it, forty years prior, and there was no doubt good players doing it forty years before us. It is not rocket science, it is good play by thinking players. Again, we didn't need coaching here, for it was simply Osgood and Hudson having a great understanding.

How many times today do you see players get to the line and panic?

I mention somewhere else about the quality of players when they get into crossing positions. I think I mention Weller, who at pace was as good as any. Jimmy Robertson and Geoff Salmons at Stoke were brilliant. And there was no better player than Brady at Arsenal when delivering his cross. George Armstrong at Highbury was also in a different class and, that was one of the main reasons why Arsenal won the Double.

A lovely piece of play involving Charlie, Oz and myself opened them up again for Sponge to put our toughest opponents to date out of their misery by making it 4-0 on the night. A result that must have made Europe sit up and wonder just who this team were, especially if they had seen Bruges play.

I remember weighing myself afterwards and had left 10 pounds on the Stamford Bridge playing pitch. I was so tired, weak and shattered that I couldn't even show my emotions. It was like floating through air, your body out there just looking down on the rest of the world. I have never experienced anything like it since, well, until coming down off that morphine after my 59 days in one kind of space or another.

We had a function for our visitors, although I can't recall what part of the ground it was held in. I was that shattered. Though I do recall sitting in the corner of this room trying to gather enough strength to get to my favourite post-match place of celebration, Alexandre. The place where I knew our friends (who were now more like family) would join in those celebrations. If ever I had earned my corn it was on this evening, as did all the rest of this incredible bunch of lads. Again, not bad for a bunch of Playboys!

This comeback was right up there alongside that at Old Trafford and that says it all about these players!

I also remember Charlie Cooke coming more into this match the more we asked questions of the Belgians. And in extra-time he was magnificent. Meanwhile, Sponge lived up to his nickname, soaking up as much work as he'd ever done and thoroughly deserving his goal and, then there was John Phillips, the one man who kept our faintest hopes alive over there and, in quite fantastic fashion.

Everyone also has an unsung hero, well we had several.

This was such a long way from watching my beloved Fulham and Johnny Haynes and, of course John Dempsey. Although my father was a Fulham supporter, he could tell you about most of the past greats from yesteryear, whether they played for Preston, like Tom Finney and Peter Doherty, Hull City, who had Raich Carter, Stanley Mathews at Stoke City or the player he felt was the best of the lot, Len Shackleton. He would make sure I knew about all of these players and he would always point me towards the best inside forwards to further my education. But I was never more educated than on the two nights of these battles, two entirely different ones, but absolutely memorable.

There was also a player named Hughie Gallagher, who was legendary at Newcastle United, scoring as many goals as the games he played (fifty odd) in their only championship-winning team. He was also the only man to ever score five goals for Scotland and, still holds the record for the most hat-tricks scored for his country. How good was he?

He was also quite a player at Stamford Bridge as well, for I heard that he could dribble like Cooke and score goals like Osgood, despite standing only 5ft 5in in his stocking feet. Like those players, too, he was a Big Match specialist, saving his best performances for special occasions. Chelsea still ignored such a great part of their history. When I turned up to the 100 Years Celebration in The Butchers Hook (The Stamford Bridge Arms) opposite the ground, it was laughable. For they had a chap there who was the oldest living former player. Not a soul - past and present - knew his name. It was embarrassing and, that alone just about summed up the present set-up.

That was the poorest PR job I have ever witnessed.

They treated him like royalty, fraudulently!

Back to real players and Gallagher, who was always in trouble off the pitch by getting into rows and overdoing the drinking, or so I have been told. Dave was lucky that he was born a long time before him taking over. I can only imagine Hughie joining Osgood, Cooke, Baldwin, Hutchinson and Hudson, not to mention George, for he would have put in for the part given to Jack Nicholson in the Cuckoo's Nest…..

He (Hughie) left the Bridge after a huge bust-up with management. Sound familiar? Tragedy followed him around - like me - and after some very dark days back in his home town of Gateshead, he took his own life. It was one of the saddest stories I have ever come across and one caused by the authorities.

Sound familiar?

After being wrongly hounded by them - for simply clipping his son round the ear - they threatened to take his kids away in an act of public humiliation of this wonderful man. He could not face such allegations so he walked the streets for days on end, before finally taking his life by walking in front of the Edinburgh to London express train.

Sponge still sees his two sons back in Gateshead and will often tell me they have grown into fine men. What a tragic story and one such people should be ashamed of. Just someone trying to make a name for them self - authorities be damned!

Gallagher should have been helped by Newcastle United and Chelsea but, as is the case, players gave everything for them, but when the boot was one the other foot?

That is why I really would have loved taking their money today, but that Bosman bloke came along far too late, I am sad to say!

On the Saturday after Bruges, our favourite opponents were back at the Bridge and, we had no right to beat them after such exertions, but we did. The Bruges match took so much out of me, so much so, that I can't tell you much about beating our fiercest of rivals. I was completely and totally knackered after the previous Wednesday. The Belgians, over those two matches, drained me and just before a match against Leeds United and, all I can remember is this:
Chelsea 3 Leeds United 1 and....

Oz scored yet another spectacular goal. This effectively finished their hopes of winning the championship and, this opened the way for Arsenal. So we had dented their hopes in the championship race, just as we did in the FA Cup the season before. Just how good it feels to tell you that is, difficult to put into words.

Can you imagine having to live with the opposite?

I really don't think I could have lived with meeting people north of Watford and listening to such a thing?

I don't think people realize just what a massive result that was in terms of the history of both clubs and, I can only think that when Chelsea nosedived dramatically - self inflation springs to mind - and were playing Sunday morning stuff in front of sparse crowds, that it was and is still not appreciated and, when I see those lads (now old chaps) I hug them with a passion never shown by the hangers-on who are there now and, believe me there are so many of them and, they are the reason I stay away. Some players make out they still support their old clubs and then there's the likes of me and, I must stress to you that there is no player having played the game more passionate than me, however, although the love has been totally knocked out of me my passion is still alive, if only for what I am telling you about. How can you lose such a passion?

It's like an incredible love in your life, whether a woman, a racehorse or a lovely grand-daughter, in my case the last two are stand-out loves and, both were are and still are 2-year-olds.

My Lifetime Lady trained by Reg Hollinshead was one of them and, Nancy is the other trained by my son Allen Hudson. My Lady won a couple of races and only time will tell what surprises Nancy has in store for me before I leave for the third and last time. She is just lined up for date with an Agency and, I have no doubt that like many I have mentioned within these pages, the Lady included, she'll be a star in her own right.

So, we had done Arsenal an almighty favour and thankfully they took full advantage of the situation and, walked away with the League and FA Cup Double in 1971 - and did so in great style. I would like to have been a fly on the wall in Revie's household as Frank McLintock picked up both trophies.

The Arsenal and Wenger of today are talked of in such hefty terms, but this Arsenal, coached brilliantly by Don Howe, was a wonderful team with some very under-rated individuals and, unlike today's team, they had guts.

George Armstrong was the shining and glowing example of that team. I remember being with him and I loved every minute of his Geordie no-nonsense attitude and, you must remember, at this time, that I was having a complete nightmare. So to get close to someone was difficult, but not with wee George. It was that bad that, although I was a good footballer, in all the time I was at Arsenal, I could not pass water. Plus, I could not pass a pub; much like Stan could not pass a betting shop.

However, I do remember playing very well at QPR on the Monday night after we beat Orient in the FA Cup semi-final and Stan stuck past Pat Jennings as to make him look quite average, which he was certainly not. I truly believe that the big Irishman WAS the best keeper in the world and, amazingly, that had Northern Ireland had just nine average players, they might have given anyone a game, but because they didn't poor old George had to go to Spain every four years.

That was how good Stanley (Bowles) was, I mean really good, no fantastic, when those Rangers fans talk of Rodney Marsh, they must have had blindfolds on. Bowles was the undisputed King of the Bush, like Osgood at the Bridge, Bobby at the Boleyn and Greaves at the Lane. I think that Charlie George was the greatest talent I have seen on the other side of north London. He was a total one off.

I watched Arsenal play Chelsea yesterday 22.4.2012 and with all Wenger's boasting, they were crying out for a Charlie.

And at this time, in 1971, our Charlie still wasn't doing too badly....

But now we were looking forward to the draw for the semi-finals of the Cup Winners Cup as our legends were growing.

Although I was nicknamed Huddy - which I don't like - I was mainly called Hud, which was originally going to be the title of the original Ballet, but you will understand after reading about so many fabulously talented players inside these pages that it just had to be Tony Waddington's idea of such a title and, that is why I just mentioned so many great players of those days of Bill and Tony's Working Class backgrounds.

If you watch George, Messi, Maradonna and Johan Cruyff and put it to music it is got to be

The Working Man's Ballet

As Tony puts it!

If you had an English jigsaw puzzle you'd always be missing one piece at least and, that is someone in charge - like in Parliament - that someone who knows exactly what they are doing, like pulling our young kids out of wars. If they want a war, they should go fight them themselves and, take their families with them, instead of lunching out, while young lads are being carried through the streets of Wootton Bassett.

In between writing, which has taken me a very long time, I have brushed up a little on U-Tube and watched George and Johan, and all it has done is confirm that we are second, no maybe, third class citizens in world football.

We have no more Bobby Moore's, Bobby Charlton's and Alan Ball's. We have loads of millionaires but no bloody footballers. They are all from other countries. I watched Match of the Day this morning and all the brilliance came from overseas and, we have the European Championships coming up with no manager, no best player and no chance.

HOW SAD
(22 April 2012)

I know I get criticised, quite a lot in fact, for digressing, but as I go over this book, I can't help but compare 1970/71 to today and, I am searching for an answer to that ongoing question. Where have all our good players gone?

Keeping in mind I watched Lionel Messi again three nights ago, wow!

But there is one glimmering ray of light and, that is Jack Wiltshere (although he is no Messi, but who is?) however, he is struggling with a bad injury and, how the Gunners need someone with a little guile and brain in midfield.

My mind flashes back to Brady....however he'd be no good, he was Irish!

They have gone six years without a trophy and I can see, with Wenger, that dismal run continuing, because there is simply no heart there. When I think that George Armstrong - bless him - died of a heart attack and, look at this lot, I cringe in despair and, my heart aches, for George that is, not Arsenal. When I think of George, I only had wished his heart had been as strong as mine whilst I was undergoing one operation after another in the Royal London Hospital and, although they thought that mine would not be strong enough they should have woken me up out of my coma and I would have told them to carry on,

Only that morning I had put myself enough in the gymnasium to give them the kind of answers they could not get on a heart machine.

But anyhow, back to George and, if there was one man in my playing days that I would have had a heart as strong as mine it would have been him. Standing alongside the likes of Alan Ball, Geordie was a giant in stature if not in size, I loved him dearly and, he was one of the great regrets that I had to walk out on Arsenal.

No heart!

I simply cannot stand Arsene Wenger, for he is simply an arrogant French Aristocrat of football, or so he thinks?

English football is all about the heart and he hasn't got one. He somehow believes he is a 'Professor of Football' and, to my great relief I am truly grateful that he did not operate on me. Professor Norman Williams did a job on me, one where he did not go on TV and talk a load of French cobblers; he simply got on with what he did best. What amazes me though is that football supporters still listen to him and are taken in by it all. The same goes with Harry, he talks, but the end result is nothing. All he has won is the FA Cup with Portsmouth - by beating Cardiff City (big deal) and all of a sudden he is the new Messiah, please give me a break, the FA Cup is not what it was in 1970, Manchester United did not even bother to enter it a few short years ago.

When you look back at what both Chelsea and Leeds put into those two matches at both Wembley and Old Trafford and, then think that the FA allowed Sir Alex to pull out of, what used to be, the greatest domestic cup competition on the planet, it tells you that our game is diminishing rapidly. Ask a young kid if he'd like to play in an FA Cup final and I don't think he'd say, "no, not this year."

George Best and Johnny Haynes would have loved to have played there the year Manchester United pulled out, I know because I asked George once....

So the game has changed and the goalposts have been moved on many, many occasions and, that is what you can do to a simple game if you have clout, however, the clout (money) in the game now has brought it down to a new low. The standard has dropped alarmingly since the great European club sides of the Fifties, Sixties and Seventies with no more players of such greatness. There are those that have blessed the competition along the way, but over all there is nothing today outside of Barcelona's calibre of football and, had it not been for the brilliance of Cech, the goalpost and, that crossbar which saved both the Czech and Chelsea after an uncharacteristic penalty by the world's greatest player, they would have carried it off for the fourth time in seven years.

The Real Madrid team between1955 to 1959 are the undisputed champions of Europe scoring eighteen times in front of an average attendance of 87,372 football lovers, in five consecutive seasons of carrying it back to Spain.

That was, of course the Puskas era, a man I was delighted to meet at Molineux on the opening of their new ground. Somewhere amongst the crowded bar that night was Billy Wright still looking for him after that drag-back at Wembley on 25 November 1953, when I was toddling about, as a 2-year-old, in our Elm Park Gardens flat just off the Fulham Road, just about three hundred yards from Stamford Bridge.

If only my father had known then, that one day I'd not only pull that number ten shirt on that Puskas, Haynes, Pele, Eastham, Suarez (of Real Madrid and Barcelona) and Law wore before me?

Baxter wore the number six and, Cruyff the first to make the 14 famous and, the most famous number 14 in that day was the bus passing by our gardens.

Now, that is something to talk about, not Chelsea defending for the majority of those three matches played against both Barcelona and Bayern Munich, who as you know, missed a penalty also.

You are not telling me that this was not written in the stars and, what made things even more crazier is that in that penalty shoot-out, former Chelsea hero, Arjen Robben, who was responsible for missing that penalty, refused to take one.

Which led to their goalkeeper grabbing the ball and, coolly slotting it past Cech, something that both Robben and Messi failed to do, something that made the final stages of the Champions League even more ridiculous than the final outcome.

But back to Puskas, who was invited by my boss Tony Waddington to play in Stanley Matthews' farewell match at the Victoria Ground and, he did so and, did so in great style. He was amongst an array of talent that included my hero, Johnny Haynes, on that incredible night for those living in and around the Potteries.

My point is that is what Waddington brought to the people of Stoke-on-Trent with no money and, yet here we are with a billionaire

Russian boasting about a win in the Champions League, which in terms of football, made me cringe.

It goes to show, in his case, money can't buy you football or love, or in his case again, neither!

The reason I give out the statistic about Real Madrid, is because Chelsea went to Munich with absolutely no intention of scoring. If that is the way that the game is going then I think my love for the most important thing in my life, apart from my family and, that has been closest to my heart and, been responsible for both fulfilling and wrecking my dreams, will have to be looked at far more seriously.

However Roman Abramovich will never know how champagne tastes, because there is a difference and, one I spoke of earlier, for there is winning and, as Brian Clough says, "winning with style," which was aimed at Don Revie. He also mentioned that he would change and, his team would win things "with a smile on their faces," and would "not cheat."

However, Clough took on the impossible, because these players, although talented, were brainwashed to a point, that there was not a single man on the outside that could follow, The Don.

Chelsea won, as they call it today, "ugly" a word I don't like in football or women.

Clough began his Leeds reign at the Victoria Ground where I made two of the three goals, which got him off to a rotten start and, the start that was to keep him at the club only 44 days.

That would have been a record for even Roman.

Anyhow Chelsea have become European champions, but as the great man said, "Not good champions!"

I have every opportunity to delete this after the Champions League success of Chelsea - but that would make me like them - and, like in 1966, they might find winning will harm them more than they understand. The Barcelona match was as much like a couple of matches that will come up in the latter part of these books. I have never seen such a one sided match as the Barcelona one and, it reminded me of our sensational defeat against the Swedes the year when we were going to retain the Cup Winners Cup.

I have always said to my son, who is a massive Chelsea fan, that Chelsea are the luckiest club in the country, whether it's with the cup draw or any deflections of one kind or another. Then you'll look at the Tottenham and Liverpool cup finals, with the last one being the Petr Cech save from Andy Carroll, a save that only he in the Premier, could have made.

Of course, I accept that goalkeeping is a part of the game, but with Abramovich making such a ridiculous statement after beating Bayern, that "we will win it seven times," had me thinking that he has been drinking his yacht fuel.

If the goalkeepers had been swapped in Chelsea's final ten matches, apart from when he missed that 4-1 defeat at Anfield, Chelsea would have limped hopelessly and, helplessly quietly out of the Nou Camp never to be seen again.

I know Chelsea supporters will be up in arms with my comments, but after what you have already read about my leaving Chelsea with Osgood - when Mears admitted he was wrong - they slaughtered the wrong people, because of their blindness of football and, their complete fickleness.

When I write my books I write them for football lovers, not football supporters, because the difference is monumental and, it is the difference between loving and adoring a beautiful woman or going with a hooker. Not that there aren't any beautiful hookers around!

All football clubs are like brothels, where they have no shame about charging their loyal fans through the nose, yeah, those people on the top floor who sit there thinking up ways of robbing the most important part of their club, the people who without, there would be no club.

It's called football prostitution and, like in any way, shape or form of prostitution, the paying customer, after being "rumped" in more ways than one, yet they walk away with empty pockets and false smiles on their faces.

And, in this moment in time, Chelsea supporters are smiling, but not for long, mark my words, for as I told you, in 1970 about England, and was proved right, by saying we would never see another final of any kind in my lifetime and, this is my third!

Lifetime!

And, although Chelsea's wonderful battling spirit, although it is a lot easier just sitting back like ten statues than coming out to play - which England did against Belgium yesterday 2.6.2012 – I have talked about our different kind of spirit and, of course I talk of all of the class players I admired with in this book and, of course George was my classic example, for as the saying goes, "don't **** on your own doorstep" which brings me back to the present day Chelsea team and, the whole truth is still to come and, what happens is it is a knock-on effect, where Wayne Bridge wouldn't go to South Africa and Rio Ferdinand refused to play with the England captain, now can you imagine Alan Ball or Bobby Charlton refusing to play with Bobby Moore?

You're having a laugh, for it was such an honour, whereas today, it's more of a bloody catastrophe that has seen our national team, not to mention Chelsea, becoming a laughing stock. Forget Munich, for as I said winning only papers over the cracks and here's a crack, something that would not happen in our team, where there was only one case of such a thing, but that was between Tommy Baldwin and Gabrielle Crawford, who didn't play for us.

Vanessa's flings with 5 Chelsea stars:
Terry's mistress ready to talk: Terry affair girl to 'sell' story!

John Terry's secret French lover scored with her very own five-a-side team of Chelsea stars, The Sun can reveal. Sexy underwear model Vanessa Perroncel had flings with strikers Adrian Mutu and Eidur Gudjohnsen, skipper Terry and his betrayed pal Wayne Bridge - plus a mystery fifth Blues player. A source close to Vanessa last night told The Sun, "To say she's a Chelsea Girl is a bit of an understatement. "Wayne knows that he was one of several Chelsea players who were close to Vanessa. Vanessa has always had a thing for footballers and set her heart on becoming a kind of super-WAG.

Matrix "During each affair she was always a single girl. "But by the time she got to John Terry she'd achieved her own five-a-side football team."

Revelations of Vanessa's flings will heap further embarrassment on defender Terry, 29, as he comes under pressure to quit as England captain. The star's heartbroken wife Toni, 28, was yesterday still coming to terms with his betrayal as she relaxed by the pool at a luxury hotel in Dubai. Terry last night led his Chelsea team to a 1-1 draw in their Premier League clash with Hull. Meanwhile Bridge - now at Manchester City = travelled the North for a tearful reunion with Vanessa and their three-year-old son Jaydon at the former family home in Oxshott, Surrey.

Vanessa's spokesman Max Clifford - who I know pretty well - said: "He has been on the phone constantly, but this is the first time they've seen each other since Friday. It was a very emotional reunion. There were lots of tears. It's been very upsetting for both of them and they are anxious to protect their little son Jaydon from this as much as possible."

Bridge and Vanessa split last summer, but the left-back is said to be devastated after it emerged that Terry, one of his best pals, had been sleeping with his now ex-girlfriend.

Bridge's meeting with his ex was their first since her affair was revealed. It took place amid reports that she is about to tell all in a £250,000 media deal. Vanessa, who claims to be 28, began her affair with married Eidur Gudjohnsen in 2003 after meeting him at the trendy Elysium nightclub in London, where she worked as a waitress. Dad-of-three Gudjohnsen spent the night with Vanessa at her Fulham home before sneaking out at 5am. Vanessa spent nine months working in the VIP area of the club - which has now closed - and was a favourite with the Chelsea players. The team regularly let their hair down at the club after games, and also held Christmas and birthday parties there.

As Vanessa grew closer to the players - and their wives and girlfriends - she joined the exclusive Chelsea Club, a private members' gym and fitness centre at Stamford Bridge.

A former colleague at Elysium said: "Vanessa worked three nights a week - always Wednesdays, Fridays and Saturdays when the players were around. The Chelsea boys loved her and always ordered Cristal champagne and vodka. They were big spenders and tipped lavishly. Vanessa earned £150 a night for working there and got about another £150 a night in tips. But the job really opened her eyes as to the possibilities.

"Gudjohnsen used to visit her at a flat she was living at near Stamford Bridge." Gudjohnsen, 31, left Chelsea in 2006 after six years - and has just joined London rivals Tottenham after spells with Barcelona and Monaco. The Icelandic ace was previously caught cheating on his wife in October 2002, when he had a torrid affair with blonde beauty Osk Norofjoro, 24. She claimed to have fallen pregnant, but Gudjohnsen dumped her.

Gudjohnsen has previously admitted gambling heavily while at Chelsea - losing £400,000 during a five-month injury lay-off. Terry has also been a heavy gambler, and sources believe Vanessa may have been attracted by their flash lifestyles. Sources close to Vanessa also revealed she had an "intense" relationship with shamed star Adrian Mutu. The fling came before the Romanian striker was sold by Chelsea and hit with a seven-month worldwide ban after testing positive for cocaine in 2004. Mutu, 31, is currently fighting a £15million court ruling against him after Chelsea sued him for breach of contract. Now at Italian side Fiorentina, he tested positive for a banned anti-obesity substance last month.

Vanessa also had a relationship with a fifth Chelsea star - who cannot be named - before meeting Bridge. There is no suggestion that any of the other players in the 2004 Champion's League line-up had a relationship with Vanessa.

There was a photograph alongside this article.

Bridge moved Vanessa into his £1million home when she fell pregnant with Jaydon. But she went on to have a four-month affair with Terry, who arranged for her to have an abortion when she became pregnant by him. The fling happened even though Vanessa also knew Terry's wife Toni because their partners were best friends off the field. Wronged wife Toni was showing the strain yesterday after jetting off to the Gulf with her two children and her mum Sue. Bikini-clad Toni looked gaunt and tense in the pool in Dubai. An onlooker said: "Toni is very attractive but it's clear she is suffering from the strain."

Terry is set to be given compassionate leave by Chelsea so that he can concentrate on saving his marriage. The Sun told yesterday how he is planning to fly to Dubai for a make-or-break Valentine's Day meeting with his wife.

Last night Gudjohnsen, who was here at Stoke City last season 2010/11, denied having any improper relationship with Vanessa.

23 GREECE IS THE WORD

The years can take away the looks, the money, the suits, the hangers-on, even the medals, but never the glory - never that. Memories: the living with them and, the killing of them.
That is what gives me such great pleasure, and of course, why I loved writing this book.

FROM THE PLAYING FIELDS 1970…..
TO THE KILLING FIELDS 2012

Before going any further, the following is what I wrote before Chelsea went into that Champions League match at The Nou Camp and, you'll see the difference, keeping in mind that after both the Bruges and Manchester City matches, I was enjoying my evening in Alexandre.

My bill was about £35 for six and, we always had a bottle on the house.

MILLIONS OR BILLIONS, DOES IT MATTER?

It's a far cry from when winning Chelsea's first European trophy in 1971. On the way to Athens we picked up a bonus of a few quid for every thousand fans that turned up at the Bridge for a Cup Winners Cup match and now this….

And funnily enough our last match, just like this Chelsea, would be against Real Madrid, if they were to overcome the fourth semi-finalist in the other match, I have not got a clue as to who they were facing, for being so wrapped up in our match with holders Manchester City, but if Chelsea go through tonight - which I doubt - all eyes will be on the other semi tomorrow between Madrid and Bayern Munich. I have fancied an all-Spanish final this year and, have no reason to change my mind as Real take an away goal to the Bernabeau after losing the first-leg 2-1, to a last minute goal, which needless to say, I backed the draw.

It has been reported that this Chelsea side go into tonight's blockbuster return against favourites Barcelona just two games away from owner Roman Abramovich's Holy Grail and, the Russian billionaire has set aside the sum in incentives for his squad and interim boss Roberto Di Matteo.

Each of the 25-man Euro playing squad will receive around £350,000 should they go all the way to glory at the Munich final on May 19 and that adds up to a cool £8.75m.

Di Matteo is yet to receive an overall increase in the £1.2m-a-year salary he was paid as No 2 to sacked Andre Villas-Boas and, the final terms of his bonus is also still under negotiation. But club insiders reckon the former Chelsea midfielder will receive £500,000 as a 'thank you' for turning around the club's season - even though it does not guarantee him the job on a permanent basis.

The backroom staff, too, will get extra cash for playing their part if Chelsea can hold onto their 1-0 first-leg lead and, then beat either Real Madrid or Bayern Munich in the final.

Di Matteo has lost just once in 14 games since succeeding axed AVB seven weeks ago.

He has guided them to the FA Cup final and, his impact has been remarkable even though a top-four finish in the Premier League looks unlikely.

What I don't understand is that this is not big news as that is only about two-to-three weeks' money for several of their top players and, that kind of incentive won't possibly change anything. To us, it meant nothing, as we approached each match and, all I can remember is the difference being that had we got through, I did not have a bank manager's letter on my carpet that following week.

So, after beating Leeds at the end of March '71, we went to Arsenal, where the biggest crowd of the season of more than 62,000 watched us lose 2-0 and, easily.

The previous biggest attendance had been when Tottenham had won by the same score-line at the Bridge the previous November. I remember that if only because they were now the only conditions I could perform on and, I'll tell you a story, although it was four years on, that is quite incredible.

Can you imagine Dave Sexton getting the Chelsea Fire Brigade in for me?

Well Tony did at Stoke City when I was just going to pull out of a match because we were having a drought in the Potteries and, the field was like that bank managers' heart - or Dave's drinks cabinet - dry and terribly hard.

Ouch!

Well, my front lawn was like the M6, but when I got to the Victoria Ground it was like Niagara Falls. So, to return the compliment, I put on my finest ever display again European Champions, Liverpool. Now, that is what I call real management.....

My shins were hurting even more as I walked like a man walking a tightrope without the netting below. I was numb. So on top of my ankle, I was doubly depressed; add missing such a big game and, these being my conditions, but I could do nothing about it, now that's bad management...

I had come to a stage where I wasn't bothered about missing matches on hard or firm pitches, but today would have suited me right down to that last drop of rainwater. The rain was torrential, like something out of Bladerunner.

But now I had the opportunity to show my feelings to both Dave and our opponents, who I loved playing against, since watching their brilliant Championship winning team at Craven Cottage in the late Sixties.

Our minds were now were firmly on that semi-final and, it looked like being a classic. Manchester City were holders of the trophy after two or three terrific years of success, but I thought that we were better than them and, I had a score to settle after them knocking us out of the FA Cup earlier in that mud-bath of a pitch where had I played I thought we would have gone through. I cannot explain how long it takes to get over such defeats, especially when you're not playing, but that one hurt, especially after missing the last final, knowing I had to wait another year to get another crack at playing at Wembley.

But little did I know that apart from my England debut, Wembley was to become a curse on me and, the reason I say that is that it is your dream and, then somehow it turns into a nightmare!

My first FA Cup nightmare was in the red shirt of Arsenal seven years on.

Did I break a mirror, as well as a rule?

It is one thing losing, but losing and playing badly is even more hurtful - like for Arsenal against Ipswich Town - but what was more hurtful at this time was missing so many vital and crucial matches.

But I was back again and after losing at Highbury we drew with Palace and beat Liverpool - which was a great result - thanks to an Alec Lindsay own-goal, in front of just under 40,000 (38,705 in fact) at the Bridge on the Monday before our big day.

But all eyes were on Manchester City, the holders of the Cup Winners Cup and, we wanted to not only wrestle it off them, but get revenge for that FA Cup defeat. It was more than a defeat; it was a complete disgrace in front of our own fans, those who had followed us from Selhurst Park to Salonika for our very first match on European soil.

My mind flashes back to that Bubble spitting at Osgood before kicking the ball off the penalty spot and, the look on the big centre-forwards face as he missed. It was a picture and, then, of course, as if planning it all, smashed our first European goal never knowing he'd do again in the final, which strangely enough was to be played in the same country.

That is why I cherish that photograph taken by the side of the aeroplane on the tarmac in Salonika.

It was the beginning of our incredible journey.

There was another great interest for me personally as Colin Bell was playing, for he was the one that ran the show when knocking us out of the FA Cup and, now I not only wanted revenge but get his England shirt from him as well. This made the match even more fascinating and, I say that because I know had I played in that earlier match, Colin Bell would not have had the freedom of Stamford Bridge, the one where I told you Dave played Lou in midfield - big mistake!

I said they were my conditions and, I was the one player, if fit, who could have matched him for his incredible work rate.

As I mentioned earlier, he was nicknamed Nijinsky, after the wonder-horse that was ridden quite brilliantly by Lester Piggott.

We would have preferred to have faced them in an all-English final, although I fancied us to beat them more over two legs. Had we met in the final it more than likely would have been swapped to Wembley, but that was by-the-by, for now we were meeting them at the Bridge first and, this was another first for us, because we had come all of this way by playing our first-leg away from home.

The attendance of 45,695 was just about eight thousand more than the Liverpool match two days earlier. This was also strange because, although we could never have imagined that we would be playing the actual final twice in two days - another complete fuck-up by the FA or UEFA or both, but nothing changes.

But the fortunate thing, for now, was that we were playing Manchester City twice and, not Liverpool and, quite frankly this City team were not the force they once were, when they had Lee, Summerbee, Bell, Young and Coleman in their forward line. That was one of the best front-lines in the history of the game, before Malcolm Allison messed it up my buying Marsh.

Those five I mentioned had everything. Well, all except great height, and, although Neil Young was tall and elegant he was not a prolific header of the ball although, afterwards they bought one of the great headers of the ball, in Wyn Davies.

Along with Young - not out of Crosby, Stills and Nash fame - they had the power of Franny Lee and Tony Coleman - who chinned me at Hillsborough - the long distance running of Bell and, the enterprising and dazzling Mike Summerbee.

It was a thrill playing against those five because I watched them destroy MY Fulham a couple of seasons earlier at The Cottage when winning the championship in such fine style and, their passing game was exceptional and, although I have told you before, I don't apologise, because they were the best football team in this country. They played the way Clough and Waddington wanted their teams to play and that was with a "smile on their faces" and, in those times they had plenty to smile about, as they won matches with such flair and imagination, moving the ball around a little like those teams I talked of just now, but not quite in that class, Real Madrid were on a different planet, like Barcelona today.

With the first match at home, for some unknown reason we both had to change strips.

Strange, but what's new in our game?

Whether it's the FA, UEFA or FIFA, there is absolutely no difference, as their right hand doesn't know what their left is doing, unless they are holding it out.

Anyhow, we wore our trusted yellow and blue, whilst City shocked everybody in the stadium when running out in shirts that could be mistaken for the table cloths in Alexandre. After the Bruges match this was to turn out to be something of an anti-climax, which may sound ridiculous being such a big match, but that was how it worked out.

We did not play well - though well enough to run out 1-0 winners. This was due to injuries to key players. Mickey Droy made his European debut and, our hero in Bruges, John Phillips, kept his place in goal. Derek Smethurst scrambled home the only goal of the night from just inside of the box in front of the North Stand - and Matthew Harding.

Now this result had our fans wondering if one goal would be enough to take us through to our first ever European final, but the return leg was in Manchester and, we all know what that brought. Boarding the train for the second-leg, I can still feel it now, that feeling of, "And now you're gonna believe us....just like the previous season, only Leeds United were a far tougher proposition, even, though it was a neutral venue on the other side of Manchester.

Ever the optimist - every Gemini knows that there are several ways to perceive any situation - I therefore figured Maine Road would suit us better. Their great big pitch would suit us fine. It would give us the opportunity to hit them on the break. I felt that the blind spot between their full-back Tony Book and centre-back Tommy Booth could be attacked. If we could get either Houseman or Weller against the ageing full-back we could take advantage of it. Book was coming up to 40, I think?

It worked a treat. Keith Weller scored the only goal from a free-kick in the first half, although it was given as an own-goal as Healey whilst clawing his way to the ball helped it into his net. But the damage was done by Keith.

In one of those strange fixture quirks we had played there in a league match just eleven days before. Weller scored in that match also - in front of 26,120 fans in a 1-1 draw - losing his boot in the process.

Tonight there were 43,663.

Weller was having a great season for us and, as I said before, gave us another attacking option.

Looking at it another way, I just wondered how teams looked at playing against us attacking them and, now that Manchester United were a spent force in this department and, I thought that we had the best front line in the business, although, Hutch's injury really did take the edge off of our full potential.

We had the intricate skills of Cooke and the speed and great crossing ability of Weller, whilst down the middle Osgood and Hutchinson were deadly once the ball was put in the right areas. And, then there was Houseman, the player who saved his best for when you least expected it.

Near the end of this match, he (Houseman) hit the post with an uncharacteristic flying header as we exposed them even more. My theory was right.

I thought that City were coming to the end, just like their neighbours would become the following year or so, all getting to the wrong side of thirty together.

My way of thinking this was that I'd seen them play as a school boy with Bill Boyce and, that is the way I saw it with most of those players of the Sixties. Many of my favourites were on the way out, making way for the likes of Currie, Bowles, Worthington and me, whereas Osgood had already made his mark and, when I arrived he had just gotten over that broken leg.

Some 10,000 Chelsea fans marched into Maine Road. Like us, they loved playing in Manchester. The last big cup-tie we played there had been the FA Cup final replay, almost a year to the night. There was a hell of a lot of trouble in the streets after the match as the Chelsea boys fought their way back to the train station. The trains were bricked as they pulled out of Manchester Piccadilly. Nothing had changed in that respect.

I remember the previous season their fans abusing us as we boarded the train from the same station, spitting and hurling obscenities. I recall Dave Sexton walking through with phlegm all down his overcoat; their fans did not have the class of the team they supported. George, Denis, Bobby and Pat deserved a better brand of following. And then there was Sir Matt.

When you think back at the Munich Air Disaster and all of those incredible emotions and, then you walked through the platform to see such behaviour it gives you a feeling of sadness.

Well, it did me!

As a youngster, I had been in The Shed with those yobs from Leeds United and, now this. I can understand small clubs with nothing to be very proud of, so they have to get in the headlines for these things, but Manchester United?

Years on when there was trouble at Heysel and Hillsborough and, it made you wonder if it sunk into such idiots. I was at Villa Park on the day of the tragedy at Sheffield and, it hit me hard and, it takes all the joy - not that the other semi-final at Villa Park was joyous - and the love and excitement out of our game. It annoys me, even more so now, that those on the streets with nothing better to do, can bring it into football grounds, after all, there young children and women there. I'm all for passionate supporters, but there's a limit!

Mind you, having said that, I am almost certain that the police were more in the wrong that any supporter. At the match I was at, I was walking through the streets and, once getting to the ground I saw police on horseback bumping into innocent and nervous Everton supporters and, I swear those fans behaviour was impeccable, So, what did you expect me to think, when I heard about this most tragic of incidents?

I watched a TV documentary and it was quite obvious that the police were not only to blame, but from that box on the corner of the ground, did not do the job they're paid to do.

Much like my case, whilst lying in a coma, I woke to find, although they made me guilty saying I walked drunk, with a mobile phone in my hand, in front of Fatehi, they had closed the case. How could they close it, if I was guilty?

Firstly, how could they know that if they were not there and, the only witness - who was my witness - was frightened off by them?

Why did they not interview me when out of my coma?

So, after finding their letter amongst all of my get well cards, I was mad and, I mean mad. How could they come to this equation?

I had not only been cruelly battered by Fatehi, but woke up to find that they said that I walked in front of his car and, were hoping because of my trauma that I would accept it. I don't think so and, apart from anything else I knew that there was something not right here as, for when I crossed that road I was safe as houses and then...

When the Tottenham riots took place the other week (7 August 2011) I realised that nothing really has changed. How can you make excuses for such behaviour?

And, again, where were the police?

After all, don't tell me that they didn't know this was going to happen?

But back to Manchester United, only their players and, as a kid the player I loved most before George came along, Denis Law and, to play against him at such a young age was such a thrill. I can remember being so close to him when on the terraces at the cottage, seeing his every mannerism from close range. With his shirt hanging out, something I would copy and, holding his shirt cuffs, something I'd never seen before, he'd be a handful for not only his marker, but the referee, always looking, like Osgood, for an edge. He was the cheekiest footballer I'd ever seen.

Clough again, playing "with a smile" on his face all the time, as if tomorrow never came, something that will always be with me. Unlike the likes of Joey Barton, today, he was what people paid good, hard earned money to watch. Those people, who had been at work all week and, had problems, forgot them when watching the Lawman.

As the song goes, "That's entertainment," and that was Denis and, that is why when George appeared, those Manchester United fans were in football heaven. Stick the thunderbolts of Bobby Charlton into this equation and, can you wonder why United they rated them the deadliest attack in the world. As I have said elsewhere had we signed George we would have taken over that and, unlike today, they were all British.

As I said, had Alf played Osgood in Mexico, he would have been hailed the greatest number nine in the world therefore, with George, Charlie - at his best - and me, the young pretender, I think we would most certainly have earned that title.

For they relied on George, Denis and Bobby and, I think we had five such players.

Paddy Crerand tells me that he (Denis) was Ferguson's favourite. I may have mentioned this elsewhere - if I have, I don't apologise - but on a memorable night in Manchester, only this time not in Slack Alice or at Old Trafford, but in the Hilton, I had the pleasure to be amongst him, Ossie Ardiles, John Giles, Tony Woodcock and John Barnes.

Sitting opposite Den, I had to ask him if it was true that he would make sure he got booked before the New Year so that he could go back and enjoy Hogmanay with his family?

With glazed eyes, he just gave me the look. You know the one he gave when sneaking a cheeky goal, like the back-heel that sent his beloved Manchester United scuttling out of the league they once dominated.

It's such a joy to be around the likes of Law and Best!

Now it was a joy to be in the final and, we had to finish the job. I would say that we were underdogs once again in our second big final in two years, if only on reputation. We had done brilliantly well to get past both CSKA and Bruges, but now we were faced with an entirely different proposition when facing the Spanish cup winners. A year earlier we came back from the jaws of defeat on three occasions and, we had to show exactly the same defiance and determination here in Athens on a very close (warm) Wednesday evening. We had already been in Greece once this season and, left with a 1-1 draw, but now there was no second leg. It was a one-off 90 minute match, or so we thought.

I knew it was going to be difficult and, that was exactly how it turned out. Again, we were faced a team wearing all-white, so that was a little eerie in a way. I believe Revie copied this teams playing strip, but they'd never become such a class act, if only because of their win-at-all-costs tactics. And again I don't apologise for stating Brian Clough once again, "you may you won those trophies, but you are not worthy champions," which could never be said of this football club. Their history is enough to send shivers down your spine, although there was no Puskas and Di Stefano, thank goodness.

We now had to do what we did against Leeds on that memorable night 12 months earlier. These were no doubt a very good side - otherwise they would not be there - but a mere shadow of their predecessors. I saw the early Sixties version when they made the European Cup their own personal property, as I documented earlier. Di Stefano, Puskas, Gento, Kopa and Santamaria - all were a football Hall of Fame. The team we met were short of such players and, were (dare I say it) far inferior, although certainly no pushovers. They played with a pessimistic outlook and were too traditional to please the more sophisticated fans.

I also said earlier, that they called Holland some kind of football Gods, but this Real team were superior, like Barcelona today.

In 1971 though, Real's best player was the midfielder Pirri, who was beautifully balanced and, played the game as I like it played; chess again, as he used his team-mates like pawns - working gambits. At the very highest level of a European competition, it really was like playing chess in a championship tournament; a battle without armour; a war without blood!

I usually relish playing against players like him but on such an important occasion there was no time to compare talents. However, I didn't know until about a quarter-of-an-hour into the match that he was such a special player. He began running the first half. I got concerned early on as he was in complete control.

If there was an upside to not knowing about the opposition, this was it, otherwise you might have got far too nervous and, sometimes that is not a good thing. I'd rather worry about how I perform, than the opposition and, I think that applies to most great players. Waddington never, ever spoke about our opponents, he knew that if we played, then he never needed to and, that is why he gave me my head and, to simply get as much of the ball as humanly possible. Whilst going over this, I have just watched England beat Belgium in Roy Hodgson's second match in charge and, the post-match panel, made it very clear that, one/we never had enough of the ball and, two/when we did have it we gave it away too cheaply.

This was not what Waddington would allow!

He would simply say, "Aye, Aye, Aye."

Well, I tell you this because that was Pirri, the man in possession was marvellous and, his passing immaculate.

However, although they had the best of the opening exchanges, for a split second I looked like being the first player in the history of the club to score in a European final, but thanks to a hefty tackle from a white-shirted Spaniard. I hit the deck. I thought it was a penalty, but the referee waved play on. But that wasn't the biggest problem as this tackle had left me with a damaged thigh, one we kids called a Dead Leg.

Harry Medhurst rushed to my aid, as I lay there thinking of the whites of the keeper's eyes as he came out sprawling at my feet. I was picking my spot. I was just about to squeeze it past him and, into the far corner of his net when, whack!

I felt it was as blatant a penalty as you'll ever see.

But I knew from watching European football on TV, that there was no point in arguing the toss with the man in black.

Fast forward again to 24.4.2012 and, the Nou Camp, where this time he did give a penalty, as the most unbalanced (quite the opposite of Pirri) and, clumsiest player over the 180 minutes - Didier Drogba - crashed unnecessarily into Fabregas. If there was any doubt in the referees' mind in Athens, there was absolutely none in Barcelona, as he pointed to the spot immediately. What was to follow was like watching an Alfred Hitchcock movie. I simply never thought I'd see the day, as Messi stepped up looking so surprisingly nervous, much like Dave Sexton going to his drinks cabinet and, after filling our glasses, spilled them onto the bar, before we could touch a drop.

The tiny little genius stepped up and uncharacteristically sent the ball agonisingly against the Chelsea crossbar = and, it was as if time stood still.

I stood in the bar of The Grapes, where one second I was totally exhilarated as he put the ball down and then...

I looked at this most incredible of players once the ball came back into play and if I had Roman Abramovich's billions, I would have gladly gave him a million of them to tell me, not only how he did such a thing, but how he felt at that precise moment?

Had the Argentine magician just handed Chelsea that place in the final?

For that would have made the score 3-1 and, edged the match back in Barcelona's favour, but after the Man of the Match - over these two matches - Petr Cech, touched another of his efforts onto the post, it seemed that the writing was well and truly, on the wall, as my mind flashed back to the Bridge on the night Iniesta snatched victory in the final minute and, as in our first match against Spanish opposition, it happened once again.

With the red and blue footballing machine still pushing and, probing the ball continuously around the edge of the Chelsea penalty area, it broke loose and, Fernando Torres, just like Zoco, 41 years ago, struck the ball into their net, only this time breaking Spanish hearts, but in all fairness the match was over - whereas with us, it merely sent it into a second match!

Overall, Barcelona had absolutely battered ten-man Chelsea into submission - Terry had seen red by childishly kneeing Alexis Sanchez off the ball - but as in London, the Spanish champions missed chances galore.

The drama - as did the chances - kept coming all night long only, Chelsea got two and, put them away. As I will say until I leave this world for a third time, I know the game is all about sticking it into the back of the net, but Barcelona...

The turning points were many and, one was when at 0-0 and, with only Cech to beat, Messi blasted the ball into his massive frame, which was reminiscent of Peter Schmeichel, the Great Dane of Manchester United. However this was the bouncing Cech of Chelsea and, the diminutive Argentine of Barcelona, the parallels were many, but the difference was, the result unjust.

Anyone who reads this and, disagrees either is daft, ignorant or both.

As I have mentioned about Waddington and Clough, football will always win, well in 999% times out of a hundred. No, this was not a misprint.

As I have said, when, in the year to come, we failed to overcome Atviderberg at the Bridge, they did not have a Schmeichel or a Cech, but they certainly had a power of a different kind. It was the first time I sat in a dressing room afterwards and wondered how we did not win this particular match and this was exactly the same, even as I write six weeks on.

And to make it even more weird, is that we missed a penalty, well not us, but Johnny Hollins and, I might say elsewhere, that every time I see him now, I see that ball skim the post at the end opposite The Shed, it is seriously weird.

Three matches that were so one-sided going to the team who didn't deserve to win them all had missed penalties.

And, I know that those results were simply meant to be, like me staying alive after such a bashing, something many doctors could not work out, well, I cannot work this out.

The moment Lionel missed that spot kick, it began sinking in - had it been another player I would have seen him a little unlucky - however, this was the 63-goal Messi, whose body language now seemed rather different, for usually it is so assured.

Cech is seen here saving yet another penalty, this time from Ivica Olic of Bayern Munich.

Messi just cannot find a way past the big Chelsea keeper, who, for me, won Chelsea the Champions League on his own.

I watched him about six weeks ago chip the goalkeeper twice in the same Champions League match and, just when I thought I was going to see him repeat such magic, he chose the wrong option and, whilst doing so he also chose the wrong moment to show the world he was mortal.

So, incredibly, Barcelona had failed to win in their last three matches and, how ironic it would be against Chelsea (twice) and Real Madrid who they would now more than likely meet in the final.

Only it will not be in Athens, but Munich.

I am not one for statistics, but the most incredible one is that Lionel Messi, who had had more touches and, went close on so many occasions over those two matches, had not scored against Chelsea in eight Champions League matches and, that alone tells a story of its own.

I would not say this was a good result for football, in fact, over the two matches, football lost, however, the best teams don't always win and, that takes me back to the beginning of the book and the year I signed apprenticeship terms, that being 1966 when winning The Jules Rimet Trophy (World Cup) and after doing so, what happened....

Anyhow, once watching that penalty miss I thought, 'say my penalty had been given?'

Maybe Osgood might have missed also and, the match swung in the opposite direction and, as I have said all through, unlike that night in Barcelona, there was no point in arguing, for we spoke different languages, so it was absolutely pointless.

When I see players today arguing, it makes me wonder where they get their brains from, if at all.

As for my injury, which was caused by a far heavier tackle than John Terry's on Sanchez, I knew one thing and, that was I was not going to miss the replay. What was in my favour, like in Barcelona, the hot night air, whereas on a cold night in the Fulham Road, no chance!

So I began driving myself harder, although worrying about the half-time break, which would be a hindrance.

I also had in the back of my mind the heartbreak of the previous year. That was enough to take my mind off the injury. It was very clear from the first whistle that Pirri was their main man as he started everything that gave us any problems. There was one thing for sure and, that was Charlie and I had to fight him, like we had done so many times with Giles and Bremner.

Oz once again, put us in front with another one of his beauties and, when it came to beauties, Osgood was ahead of George Best, only his didn't wear tiaras.

Wasn't it fitting that two of my all-time favourite goal were scored by those two and, both on the same ground, George against us and, Osgood against them - them, being Leeds United.

His goal here looked for a very long time, as if it would win us the match, but Pirri had other ideas by pushing on his troops with some masterly football. We had done well in Europe when in front and, once again, we were doing all right here.

But with 20 seconds left, they hit us with an equaliser as Zoco capitalised on a mistake by John Dempsey and, struck a great blow past Catty.

We had breathed the air of the Dragon.

Like most finals, they can pass you by and, I felt this one did me and, not only that, but it seemed to fly, much like Zoco's strike.

The final whistle went and, we were absolutely devastated after getting so very close to carrying that great old trophy around the Olympic Stadium. With this match being played on a Wednesday, our fans had come over just for the night and, had booked their return flights for straight after the match. They had booked special flights at somewhere around £24 for the whole package deal, which included a return flight on that night after the match. But then it was announced that the replay (can you imagine this happening today) was to be played on the Friday?

For the majority of fans it was a case of Plan B. They had done most of their 'spenders' just getting there, but pooled their funds, all helping one another out so they could stick together and, not miss the biggest match in the club's history.

This was just another case of those morons in high places and, nothing has changed with the likes of Blatter and Platini.

As I said earlier, the majority of those fans slept on the beach - what fans they were. They had been all over London the year prior, with just a long trip to Lancashire in between. That night in Burnley was as scary as any other night in my life, even more so than 15 December 1997, because that was a different kind of strike to the one that pegged us back.

It was more like the tackle, the one that is banned today.

Anyhow, back to those wonderful fans led by Mickey Greenaway, as like an army they could endure any hardship as long as they could be with their team. The atmosphere for those three days were a mixture of magic and mystery; the magic of breathing it all in and the mystery of the eventual outcome.

The pickpockets and the ladies of the night were on overtime and, the streets were full of jugglers (no not Charlie Cooke) and dancers to on-going music and, it was if they knew what was going on. Was that why Osgood, Cooke and Baldwin were partying the following day, could they have forgotten about the replay?

Whether they did or not they did not nothing seemed to bother them and the following night you just would not have known.

The whole city was buzzing, not only with flies, but with the merriment of everything that was going on around us and, then to my absolute amazement there was even more buzzing the following day in the Hilton.

Had Sexton had walked into this place, for the first time in this book; I could not tell you what would have happened, for it had been ordered as a day of complete rest. We had strict instructions - not that we needed them - from our manager, that although we needed liquid intake, he didn't mean the alcoholic kind. I went to the market with drinking the last thing on my mind. I was struggling with my thigh and, the thought of facing Pirri with a damaged thigh whilst nursing a hangover would have been not only very costly, but personal suicide. Much like I said with Dempsey and Webb facing Joe Royle, the last thing you need when colliding in mid-air with Big Joe is something like that.

Joe was a brute of a centre forward and one who took no prisoners and, I can remember being in the England under-23 squad with him and saw close-up that he was not aware of the danger he could easily do to you.

He was, though I have not seen him for a long time, a hell of a nice bloke.

Plus, it would be like facing Alan Ball at his best and, just the thought of that is terrifying enough when sober. I knew by now if we were going to go one step further than Wednesday, we had to prevent him (Pirri) either by a Ronnie Harris tackle or with better performances from me and Charlie.

The injured were told to report into a room made into a Mash-like treatment room and, I was there to have Harry Medhurst take a look. It was a far cry from that day at the Stamford Bridge, cigarette in hand, being asked if I was fit to play at Southampton, although it was very much similar in the Athens Hilton Hotel. It was not Barbarella, however, it was the place where three of the four players involved with my starting my first ever match were at it again.

Although I was playing it down, it was still very, very sore and, like against Southampton, had it been another match, I would have been declared myself unfit and, there was absolutely no doubt about that. I was about 60% fit and the toughest part was warming up before the match. I spent ages massages my thigh, whilst hoping that in the other dressing room was their superb inside-forward was not about to put in another master class of football.

I can only compare it to facing one of Barcelona's midfield players today, not Lionel Messi though, because there is no one man that can mark him out of the game.

Anyhow, there was absolutely no way I was going to miss the replay as, for a moment I thought that Dave was questioning me and, I had the feeling that he was trying to talk me out of playing.

Or was I simply imagining such a thing?

Or was I was getting paranoid now about missing cup finals?

Did he want to replace me with one of his favourites?

That was something we used to say, so with everything going through my mind at this time, I was most definitely getting paranoid, as to looking at every way that would keep me out of the biggest match of my life.

By now I was also sensing an all-out war with the club, although it was just the beginning without me knowing it and, as I said this European campaign had its pitfalls.

But again, was I imagining it all?

I really was in a state and, all I needed was to get to the ground although I was still hoping that nobody noticed me limping.

That long Thursday was solitary and almost surreal. I seemed to be caught up in so many different emotions, as I walked into the Hilton I thought of just how far not only me, but we had all come together in such a short space of time and, then I looked across the swimming pool area and, to my complete horror, saw something that had me thinking, that this was just another dream.

Or, was it a nightmare?

I had just been walking off, or attempting to walk off the knock, down the flea market and, I had

Found, that there were no fleas, no Squire Shop or Markham Arms.

But the latter didn't seem to bother the boys, because as I looked across I saw three of the four lads who had been responsible for my debut (about 16 months earlier) and, they were at it again, only this time, it was not Barbarella and, our opponents were a far cry from Southampton.

It must have been about 90 degrees and, there they were downing tropical punches like they were on an end-of-season tour or family holiday.

As I said just now, surely they couldn't have forgotten about tomorrow?

Here we were going into the most important match of any of our lives and, these three were throwing these drinks down them as if tomorrow never came. And had Dave been tipped off, like he was before, it never would have, for they would have been on the next flight home.

Now wouldn't that have been something?

Or would Dave have turned a blind eye?

It would have certainly have topped the Blackpool saga when Docherty sent eight players home!

I wondered what would have happened had the Spanish coaching staff walked in?

They would have been rubbing their hands together whilst throwing a few pesetas over the bar to, "Keep 'Em Coming, Senor."

There were so many unanswered questions and, I just wonder if Dave did know and, overlooked it and, kept it up his sleeve for another day, although, if he did, he never mentioned it.

The mind boggles!

These three were completely different characters and, the frightening thing about them was, if you put them all together, you had a very powerful concoction and, judging by what I saw on the table, plenty of the other concoction had been consumed.

I honestly could not believe it and, as I left, I was just praying that Dave would not get tipped off again and, I was thinking, 'Good job we were not in London,' because the blower would have went and, there could have been, "Bad news on your doorstep....

As for my leg that song was quite appropriate, "Bad news on your doorstep, I couldn't take one more step....which incredibly was the song we sang on all of our trips. American Pie!

For now though, had Dave had turned up it would not have been Bye, Bye, Miss American Pie...

As I said earlier, Charlie could be very obnoxious in drink. In fact, more times than not, Tommy was his best pal and Minder and, believe me he needed one. There are that go quietly and then there are those like Charlie.

I like a good drunk, one that laughs and, in those days forget their many cares and woes and, there were many of them.

Tommy was Mr. Nice Guy. Everybody loved him. They still do, in fact. He is one of the reasons I love talking and writing about our times together, when there's players such as him, Johnny Boyle, John Dempsey and Marvin Hinton about and, the reason I mention them is because they don't get enough recognition.

Well in Athens both John's did brilliantly, Dempsey getting that wonderful volley whilst the other John can boast that he marked the legendary Gento for a period of that famous replay. They were fantastic memories and, as for Sponge he was always involved with everything that was great about what we achieved. Marvin, on the other hand, if he had believed in himself, could have been absolutely world class. When I hear supporters talk about the likes of Desailly I tell them to, as the Eagles sang, Take It Easy!

Tommy remains a very special man in my life, even though we don't see enough of each other. Oz, on the other hand, had that affable nature on the surface.

I challenged him about his pre-match build up seeing the great importance of such a match. He simply sent me back to our hotel with my tail between my legs telling me to, "Go home and have an early night son and, leave it to me. I will win us the game!"

The result: He was true to his word!

He had the frightening confidence bordering on the ridiculous and, arrogance (self-belief) that was almost unbelievable, but he had done it time and time again. As I have told you before, absolutely nothing and, nobody fazed him. On that worrying Thursday - and did we have worries - he was wearing a striped shirt that I think he wore after the match the following night with a pair of Chelsea match shorts and sandals. As I left and he raised his glass again, "Rest your leg son and don't worry, leave it all to me."

He had such an incredible belief in his talent - such certainty. Charlie wore a flashy white jacket and carried sunglasses. I told you about Charlie, he wasn't quite like Osgood, for although he knew how good he was he never showed such a thing, he just took it all for granted - and was like a magician in possession.

They were two incredible talents from different worlds and, when both on song it was like two worlds colliding and, you would not want to be on the opposite end of what they could muster up, just like at Old Trafford when Charlie took the ball and, waltzed into space and, without looking, placed a ball so perfectly weighted into that space between all of those white shirts, one so beautifully executed, that they were totally bamboozled. It was if that Leeds United defence had never defended before, such was the delicate way Charlie set it up and, the then Osgood took over like as if in a relay team.

It was the perfect goal, out of absolutely nothing and nowhere and, as if magic.

Again, you can't coach such brilliance.

Well, anyone watching them by the pool could never have imagined that these lads were going to carry off the second biggest trophy in club football the following day, for it was totally unthinkable.

They must have stayed there until around eight, when the sun went down because I recall them walking into the hotel restaurant at about 8.30pm as large as life, as if they had just come from the cinema. If they had have been and, Dave had been in the movie, it would have been a War film, The Guns of Navarone or something similar.

I think had Dave known and caught up with them, the first blow would have been made in Greece, for it was coming slowly and, if did not happen by the pool on that afternoon, then I'd have known it never would.

I cringed at the thought of the manager approaching them and, in a strange spooky kind of way it felt like he knew something had been going on and, as I just said, it also entered my mind that he may have turned a blind eye

Alongside these three at the poolside was a lovely bloke from Chelsea who I mentioned in my introduction, Johnny Fennell, a scrap-metal dealer out of the back streets of Chelsea. Lots Road runs from the Embankment right around where Chelsea Harbour now stands and on to the Kings Road at the bottom of Stanley Bridge. Our prefab stood, it seemed, like a wagon train in the middle of things.

Looking out of the prefab and to the right was the Cage, the left was Ashburnham School and on the next corner the betting shop stood. This is where my gambling complaint began, as The Globe at the foot of my grandparent's building started my social disease. But back to our domain and along from the betting shop was the laundry and off licence. This is where all of us kids hung out. This is where I was to find out about lovely young ladies. Carol Hudson, Pat Dunne and Kathy Bannon were just three such lovelies. Although at that time, at school, I had a thing going with Jean Higgs from Fulham. She was a lovely young girl, full of life and all that was good in and around those wonderful times.

The strangest thing as kids back then, looking back, I often wonder what the likes of young Jean must have thought in that first season? We left school and that seemed to finish our childhood. It is one of the saddest things growing up as kids and caring about someone and then you never see them again. That's what I mean by strange!

Then you sign an apprenticeship and you move into a completely different world, a world with grown-ups and, that was where it all started to go right and wrong for me, mainly down The Kings Road.

Although, in fact, what changed my life socially was The Lord Palmerston in Fulham, for that is where I was swayed by my elders.

But as I have always said; I was brought up amongst all these people who seemed to love enjoying oneself and, once I got into that way of life, I loved it too. There was a party on every Saturday night after coming out of that pub, for it was like there was a rota of whose home we were partying at. If tomorrow never comes, neither did Christmas, because it was simply 25 December every Saturday night.

Having said that, through that car attacking me on 15 December 1997, I missed Santa for the first time in 46 years, however, I had a better one than my family, who lived through my battles with my Demons.

At the top, on the corner of Upcerne Road on the Kings Road was the Cook Bakery which stood next to our local paper shop and, its proprietor Tony Tobias. He was more famous than I was in those days, but not for long. And talking of long, he had a nose which went on forever. But the girls loved him, which makes you wonder if that saying is true, or was it the size of your feet?

In fact, I recall when Goldie the Eagle flew out of London Zoo.

It was a standing joke that TT was ambling across the road when someone threw a net over him shouting, "Where's my reward?"

There were some incredible characters all around us. My old man chased old man Tobias round his shop one day after he tried to fiddle my mum out of a packet of fags. He also chased Docherty around his office one day after promising to sign my brother as a professional and then reneging on the deal. This was just after The Doc sent those players home from Blackpool. My brother was on that trip, but did nothing wrong. The Doc saw it otherwise.

My dad, Bill, threatened to take me away from the club but was told in no uncertain terms that if he tried that, because of me being contracted, I would never get another club, now can you imagine that happening today.

Bosman springs to mind?

The following evening, Osgood was true to the word.

Was I surprised?

I had seen him do it and chuckle. I don't know about the Madrid keeper and, I don't really need to know about him, because I saw Osgood beat Shilton and Banks in 7 days with identical strikes and, look at me with the look of love, if you don't mind my mentioning another song, which was written by the absolutely phenomenal Burt Bacharach and sang beautifully by Dionne Warwick and Dusty Springfield, a lady who I was supposed to take out around this time, which still remains one of my greatest regrets.

Whilst on "greats" I could not resist looking up this man's achievements, for around that time I remember him being married to Angie Dickinson (Policewoman) who had close links to the Rat Pack and, of course Frank. The Look of Love was also introduced to a great movie of the 70's called Boys in the Band.

Burt Bacharach is, quite simply, one of the most accomplished composers of the 20th Century. In the '60s and '70s, Bacharach was a dominant figure in popular music, writing a remarkable 52 Top 40 hits. In terms of musical sophistication, Bacharach's compositions differed from much of the pop music of the era. Bacharach songs typically boasted memorable melodies, unconventional and shifting time signatures, and unique chord changes. Combining elements of jazz, pop, Brazilian music and rock, Bacharach created a unique new sound that was as contemporary as it was popular. Lyricist Hal David, Bacharach's primary collaborator, infused Bacharach's music with tart, melodramatic lyrics worthy of the best Tin Pan Alley composers. David's bittersweet, unsentimental lyrics were often in striking contrast to Bacharach's soaring melodies. While in the late 1970s Bacharach's name became synonymous with elevator music (due in great part to its sheer familiarity), a closer listening suggests that his meticulously crafted, technically sophisticated compositions are anything but easy listening.

The son of nationally syndicated columnist Bert Bacharach, Burt Freeman Bacharach was born in Kansas City, Mo., on May 12, 10928. In 1932, Bacharach's family moved to Kew Gardens in Queens, New York. At his mother's insistence, he studied cello, drums and then piano beginning at the age of 12. As a youth, Burt hated taking piano lessons. His dream was to play professional football, but his size, or lack thereof, kept him out of that field.

When he was 15, Bacharach started a 10-piece band with high school classmates. With Burt on piano, the group gained exposure playing parties and dances. After graduating from Forest Hills High School, Bacharach enrolled in the music studies program at McGill University in Montreal. It was there that Burt says he wrote his first song, "The Night Plane to Heaven."

From 1950-52 Bacharach served in the Army, playing piano at the officer's club on Governor Island and in concerts at Fort Dix. His performances then consisted primarily of improvisations and pop medleys of the day, although he was billed as a concert pianist.

In 1962, Bacharach collaborated with lyricist Bob Hilliard on "Any Day Now," which reached No. 23 for Chuck Jackson, but his greatest success was achieved in collaboration with Hal David, who co-wrote the No. 4 hit "The Man Who Shot Liberty Valance," inspired by the John Wayne/James Stewart movie, and the No. 2 hit "Only Love Can Break a Heart." Both were recorded by Gene Pitney. Bacharach & David also scored a hit that year with Jerry Butler's "Make It Easy on Yourself" which, reached No. 20.

Bacharach worked extensively with the Drifters during this period, arranging horns and strings and writing (with Bob Hilliard) the group's 1961 singles. "Mexican Divorce" and "Please Stay." It was at a Drifters session that Bacharach met Marie Dionne Warwick, a member of backup vocal group the Gospelaires and niece of vocalist Cissy Houston. It soon became apparent that Warwick possessed a remarkable ability to navigate even the most difficult of Bacharach's melodies and tempos.

I believe this is the link to Whitney Houston who tragically died last
year, 2011

She began cutting demo records for Bacharach & David, one of which
was for "Make It Easy on Yourself." Warwick mistakenly believed
that "Make It Easy on Yourself" would be her commercial debut, and
when the songwriters revealed that the song had been given to Jerry
Butler, she angrily shot back, "Don't make me over, man!" (slang for
don't lie to me). Warwick's angry response became the seed of her
first Top 40 hit, 1962's "Don't Make Me Over," which reached No.
21. Bacharach & David went on to write and produce 20 Top 40 hits
for Warwick over the next 10 years, seven of which went Top Ten:

!Anyone Who Had a Heart" (1963), "Walk On By" (1964), "Message to Michael" (1966), "I Say a Little Prayer" (1967), "Do You Know the Way to San Jose" (1968), "This Girl's in Love with You" (1969) and "I'll Never Fall in Love Again" (1969).

Besides their work writing and producing albums for Warwick, the team of Bacharach & David was also responsible for hits with other performers, including Herb Alpert ("This Guy's in Love with You"), Tom Jones ("What's New, Pussycat?"

Jack Jones ("Wives and Lovers"), Dusty Springfield ("The Look of Love") and B.J. Thomas ("Raindrops Keep Falling On My Head").

All of these songs were a great big part of my life turning from a young lad into a young man in the Kings Road.

I met Jack Jones along with Bobby Moore one evening after one of his shows and, as I just said, I was supposed to date Dusty. All these years held something different for me and, as I went from my school trouser years to my Kings Road Playboy ones, which were the most wonderful times of my life, until reaching Seattle.

Through his wife, screen star Angie Dickinson (whom he married in 1966 and divorced in 1980), Bacharach moved into film scores. His credits include the title song to Alfie, a hit for Cilla Black and Dionne Warwick, and film scores for What's New, Pussycat?, (its title song was a Top 5 hit for Tom Jones in 1965), After Casino Royale (which introduced "The Look of Love") and Butch Cassidy and the Sundance Kid, which spawned the No. 1 hit "Raindrops Keep Falling on My Head" and earned Bacharach a pair of Oscars (Best Score and Best Theme Song) as well as a Grammy for best score.

If a footballer, you might say Burt's strike rate was phenomenal and, talking of strikes, Osgood's was a great one and, then the one to follow was something else, so much so, that Osgood would have been proud to add it to his list of beauties. John Dempsey scored an absolutely stunning volley, which for a centre-half you might also call phenomenal, as I did Bacharach. Webb used to score plenty of goals for us but they were all pretty the same. He would score coming in late on the end of balls knocked in, making himself very difficult to pick up, in fact, almost impossible.

So, we thought we were home and dry as Johnny's shot bulged the back of the Real Madrid goal, but once again they came fighting back.

Sponge, playing instead of John Hollins, played him the ball and, taking it into his stride the master striker (Osgood) blasted a curling shot out of the reach of the Real keeper. As the ball nestled in the back of their net, I wondered, 'What has their keeper been drinking?'

That was Osgood's contribution for the night and, as usual he'd take his bow and come off and, for the next goal, Sponge was involved once again, by firing in an angled shot which keeper Borja tipped over. Charlie's delivery to Dempsey saw the centre-half make a mockery of his status as a defender. His volley was unstoppable, sublime, sailing high into the net and, that put us on our way. What a goal it was and, how he deserved it. He was our unsung hero in many ways and, it more than made up for being responsible for that late equaliser two nights earlier.

For the first time in those two big finals, a team had a two goal cushion and, thanks to Osgood and Dempsey it was us.

What I must add here was the wonderful sight of Pirri taking the field with a bandage, or cast, on his arm. I am certain this affected his display. Charlie and I sensed that this was our opportunity to take advantage and that's what really swung the match our way.

Pirri wasn't the same player as in game one, thank God!

Having said that he was better than that one-armed Luxemburg midfield player who made us all chuckle when attempting to take a throw-in but that was to come, the following season.

Dempsey had gone a long way to creating history and I was absolutely delighted for him, if only for him, as I said, being the one who made the mistake for the equaliser in the first match. He even survived a penalty appeal just before he scored the most important goal of his life. He only ever scored two goals for us, the one at Palace I told you of earlier being his first, another great volley, and this one, an even greater volley, with even greater importance, by far.

This was different from making our debuts together at Southampton - simply incredible!

We knew that from the first match that they wouldn't lay down and that was right as they gathered one last raid on our goal. If they had snatched one and then another, what the hell would UEFA come up with?

Just when it seemed that we were home and dry, with 15 minutes left Fleitas dispossessed Webb and ran about 20 yards before shooting magnificently past Bonetti. It was quite similar to their equaliser on Wednesday, which seemed another lifetime away as they picked up more momentum.

Webby was not a good full-back and, once again it was crystal clear for all to see, unless you were the manager.

I only have to mention Eddie Gray and Terry Conroy and those Chelsea supporters will understand just where I am coming from.

Oh no, not again, the heart began pounding. Bonetti made a last-minute save to keep them out with literally seconds on the clock and, then with our fans creeping towards the pitch, I picked up a ball on our right-hand side. I knew I had to get the ball as far up field as possible, so picking it up, I surged forward past our bench heading for the corner flag, skipping a lunging white-shirted tackle along the way. I reached my destination. I was going to take it into the corner-flag when out of the corner of my eye I saw Derek Smethurst running into a dangerous position.

I can remember clearly that I was in two minds, as it wasn't Oz or Sponge, I thought and, although it was tempting to keep it safe, it was also tempting to put the game beyond Real's reach by getting a third. I whipped a great cross into the path of Smeth, but to my horror he fluffed an opportunity to write his name into Chelsea folklore.

Thankfully, we were in front at the time, otherwise that miss would have haunted me and, we would have gone into extra-time one more time. The thought brings a twinge to my thigh!

The Athens Hilton Party had played magnificently under the circumstances. In fact they probably stole the show. They were involved with both the goals that put us on the brink of the club's first ever European success.

We had now broken new ground in both my first two seasons. Cooke played superbly; Sponge worked like the Trojan he had become, never knowing when to stop battling for the cause ahead. Then there was the Wizard of Oz, and what more can one say about this bloke? He limped off with a very bad ankle injury that had been plaguing him for some time and was replaced by Smethurst. Bonetti, who had been out for some time, played brilliantly as Sexton - I thought at the time - gambled on him, putting him in front of Phillips because of his vast experience. It was harsh on John, because he had played magnificently. However, it paid off. Dempsey, probably one of the most under-rated players I have ever come across, earned his eighty-odd-quid-a-week. He was fantastic.

My everlasting memory of this whole thing was - looking back at that great Real Madrid team I talked of - the sight of the legendary Gento entering the arena.

He was sent on to pull this tie out of the fire, but instead pulled off something else, for whilst running past the bench and confronted by Johnny Boyle, he realised that he was still wearing his wrist watch, so in full flow he whipped it off and, threw it to his bench and, had it not been such an important match, it would have been totally hilarious, unlike the one armed Luxemburg midfield player taking that throw-in at 16-0, on aggregate, we did not have time to stand around and have a laugh.

On returning to London the last thing I remember of Athens was sitting on the end of my bed, having had no sleep, looking out over the white-topped rooftops still wondering if I had dreamt all of this. And then I realised I had not as I was clutching my winners medal in one hand and in the other a photograph of me walking up to congratulate Oz after his goal. The goal he so confidently promised me. The following day there was an open-top bus awaiting us, only this time I was on it. It took us down the M4 and through Hammersmith and Fulham to the Town Hall opposite Fulham Broadway Underground Station. From there, completely knackered, I made my way to The Adelaide. This is where I blacked out on one of their small tables, where I sat alone, just like on the bed in Athens and, just like so many nights in hospital all those years later. Only I was reflecting on something completely different. All of the times over the years that I have needed to take sleeping tablets and, here I was all alone in my local asleep on that tiny table, with my European Cup Winners Cup winners' medal in my pocket. Not very romantic, but it told a great story of those three days since leaving Heathrow for Athens.

But even more importantly, although I can't remember the last thing on my mind, I can only imagine it might have been my mind flashing back to this bunch of players from all over Britain, coming together and pulling off something that only eighteen months ago would have been looked at as something completely out of this world. It was most definitely the kind of stuff that dreams are made of, but like everything else in my life, those dreams to turn to nightmares and, there was so many of those still to come.

But for those few minutes alone in one of my favourite pubs, again, I can only imagine that my thoughts were all about our incredible team spirit and, nowadays when people look at this piece of gold hanging round my neck they have the wrong impression.

Some people look at it as much as to say, "flash bastard" but they'll never know, for this is my memory of those magnificent times amongst those players that stuck together against all the odds.

Coming back against Leeds, after being behind three times was something special and, something these players can really be proud of and, something they've never been rewarded for, in terms of turning Chelsea Football Club into something they were in 1968, a nearly team.

Along with the Athens Drinking Team, those of us can say that we brought European success to Chelsea and, oh, how we did it....

What we also did was save my life. Because my time in hospital, just when I was at the crossroads would depend on whether to fight like at Old Trafford and Athens, or simply accept getting there, there being Treves Ward, once out of that coma.

Loneliness can break you. My loneliness was close to doing so.

But with these memories, so precious, if you think positive, they can pull you through, much like the therapy of writing this book for both you and me!

It was the last I can remember of that day. It had been an incredible journey throughout and, those last three days just about summed it all up. Who would have imagined when we entered Greece a few months earlier, that we would be returning for such a climax?

And even more weird, who would have thought when boarding that aeroplane on the Tuesday evening we would not be travelling back until the Saturday?

No wonder I totally blacked out in my local, for I was completely exhausted by it all. The strangest thing about times and matches such as these, is that they seem to pass you by, leaving you in a daze. And if that is how I felt, I often wonder just how the Athens Hilton Party must have felt.

That picture on the tarmac by the aeroplane - that Salonika player kicking the ball from the penalty spot and then spitting towards Peter Osgood for good luck - seemed light years away.

We arrived in Greece as no-hopers and, left there champions of Europe, albeit in the lesser competition of the two, however, even if it was not the premier tournament, I still fancy that Bruges would have given any team in Europe a run for their money, not to mention CSKA.

The following day, I received a telephone call and a voice told me that a good friend of mine was dying. They asked if I could visit him. I folded my royal blue European Cup Winners Cup shirt and headed to see Denis Darcy. I walked into a house in Fulham where there were a handful of people surrounding his wheelchair. They had that dreaded look on their faces. It was one of death!

After all I had been through after such joy and jubilation, there sat Denis. It wasn't fair. Life isn't. I handed him my shirt and I was happy, as he was to be buried in it. There are certain things in life we cannot account for, and this was one of them.

Where did this go?

Where did that go?

Why me?

This was, why Denis?

What had he done wrong?

This shirt went to the right place. Denis wanted to play for Chelsea.

He got his wish when he least expected it.

He died playing for them in a major European final.

A BBC 1970's show hosted by my friend Dennis Waterman barely touched on our great achievements over those 12 months. Winning the FA Cup and European Cup Winners Cup, and breaking new but stony and bumpy ground, we should have been recognised a little more. This should have been the launching pad for the stars for this team. We should have been given more credit from both the manager and the board of directors. But we weren't and for that everyone suffered.

It was different, unlike today, we were just a bunch of lads coming together to make Chelsea history, from a hundred yards up the road to Gateshead. And nobody loved Chelsea more than Tommy Baldwin. Again, unlike today, the French - oh how I dislike them - the Ivory Coast and those from all over the world can drive through the Kings Road, but it will never mean anything to them.

We were the Kings of the Kings Road, a road that meant something to all of us and, as for me, it all started and ended there.

AS far as I am concerned there is no Chelsea any more, as it was then and, that is why the club means nothing to me.

Both Frank and John Terry wanted to leave not too long ago, Frank to Jose when he was with his Spanish girlfriend and, JT to Manchester City, but allegedly, his Agent fucked the deal up. However, the point is, they still kiss the badge, as Elton John sang, I Wanna Kiss the Bride...that is just about how ludicrous it all is!

Going back to Osgood and I did not want to leave, more Osgood than me, but we were slaughtered for far less. Osgood never, ever wanted to leave Stamford Bridge, why would he?

As for me, it was a blessing in disguise, but once again, although I met Tony and, he injected that love for the game back into me, there just   wasn't   the   money.

Had we got paid what they get paid today, the Seventies would have been untouchable, in terms of the national game with those names I have already mentioned.

I was talking to the brilliant Tony Currie not so long ago and, he told me, he was sweeping the dressing room out at Sheffield United after the kids finished training and, he turned to the parents and said, "You'd never believe I once played for England, would you?"

The place fell in silence and my guts turns and I feel that so many of us were cheated.

Why?

Instead, it was the beginning of the end. We had another foot in the door after opening it a year earlier and, looking over to north London, we should have been a little more like Arsenal who won the Double that year. The difference was that they had people running the club that knew just what they were doing. Like, I have said so many times, they had a manager who could manage and, a coach who could coach.

Need I say any more?

Instead, we were led by people with their heads in the sand. I told Brian Mears years later that I blamed him and, meant it in no uncertain way. At first he chuckled and, then after a few seconds he realised that I was deadly serious.

You see, the problem with these people, like with some managers, it does not really matter to them, because their life goes on, but with us we pride ourselves on what we do in our career and, in those days, unlike today, it was a short one and, not very healthy financially.

So that is why I gave it to him, so it would sink in and, I think he got my point.

Had I not been so young then, I would have told him so in an entirely different way, but I was young, naive and actually thought that directors, like those at the FA, UEFA and FIFA knew what they were doing.

How daft was I?

He said after I had my say that he got caught up in all of our fantastic successes and, what that success brought with it. That was not a good enough reason, for he should have wiped the sand from his eyes. Had he, who knows just where all of this would have led?

Instead of being the end, it should have been the beginning.

Here are just two good reasons why the BBC's was the best morning show, but Chris quit in March of 2012 for pastures new and has continued to impress. Sian Williams (left) is equally impressive and I liked when they tried to cut her expenses down and, she reacted by saying, "I'll come on nude then" and, she was right. She and her co=female presenter Susanna Reid are absolutely delightful. Susanna was reprimanded for showing too much flesh (ridiculous) yet the BBC allow Lineker and Sue Barker to do those daft adverts. Lineker should be ashamed of himself, whilst Barker confuses me. I thought that you needed talent to get to the top?

Talking of adverts, I've thrown all Lionel Richie's music away since he did that Walkers crisp advert with the BBC presenter.

Can you imagine Frank Sinatra doing an advert for Shredded Wheat?

It was after forty years that I heard the following story as I sat watching Chris Hollins on BBC1 Sport one morning when talking about, I think, the Champions League final of 2011: When Chelsea and Real Madrid went into a replay in Athens - two days later - my mum (Linda) telephoned my dad (John) and told him

"You better get back home here we've got a wedding to go to, my dad said but Linda..."

Great stuff!

Because there was only one boss in that household and, thank God, for all three of them, otherwise they would have ended up like me, homeless!

Chris Hollins is a very, very talented young man and, is a lot like John in his style, but I would say, he might have been a better manager than his dad?

John would have done well in management had he had someone like me with him, much like playing, because I would have been like Waddington and, stuck with my belief to play the game the right way, whereas he was too much "long ball" (Charlie Hughes) and, one of the Lilleshall mob and, we all know how far they put our game back!

24 BEST BIRD PULLERS IN TOWN

The scene at the airport was not quite as exciting as the old footage of the Beatles returning after conquering America, but it was still a fantastic feeling.
If we had a ceiling, I would have been dancing on it.
Especially after my disaster a year earlier, when watching the boys go by on that open-top bus from the Stanley Arms.

Four decades have passed by since and, an awful lot of water has gone under that Bridge. But one thing I can remember vividly and, gladly this time as I travelled on that open-top bus was, that I was a part of it. I had been there, seen it and done it. Got the photograph, or at least had it and, lost it. The medal still hangs around my neck, not for Chelsea, but as a symbol of our team spirit. Whatever spirit we had, we built through the sheer joy of enjoying one another's company.

I have obviously been in other dressing rooms where the camaraderie was great, but this team was phenomenal. I know they sometimes pushed the boat out a little close to the horizon, but you'd never know it on a Saturday. The Athens Hilton squad was a great example. I mean, had three of Madrid's players been Schindlers the night before that replay, I think we would have won with the handbrake on!

Anyhow, I really did have the photograph. I still remember sitting on the edge of my bed watching the sun come up with my medal in one hand - the medal that Terry Ellis bought for his father in 2011 - and a photograph of me and Oz in the other. He was standing there hands aloft, while I was walking towards him after he had just scored yet another blinding goal. I remember the look between us, knowing exactly what he was thinking. "I told you so, I told you I'd score, son," and it was not the first time.

My mind flashed to not only the day before as the sun beat down on that table of an uncountable amount of glasses filled, half-filled and empty punches.

Well, Oz didn't pull any punches when it came to big matches; he simply did what players today cannot do, he matched his pre-match boast, although it wasn't boasting with him, it was sheer contempt and pure and utter self-belief.

I still, to this day, have never known anyone like him and, if it caused him any problems, it was he did it off the field and could not match the genius on it, but I forgave him for that, because he was a good bloke - who took massive liberties at times - and, whom without we would not have had the glory I am telling you about and also, that is why Alf deserved the sack, because of not seeing it my way.

I would not mind if it were difficult to see but...

I was telling my son, Allen, about when Frank McLintock's partner in the Caledonian pub, Harry Hicks, who took Lennie Peters to Highbury one day. We were in the Players Bar after the match and, he introduced him to me. I asked if he enjoyed the match and, he said he loved it and, I of course smiled, as you would.

Harry had him sat behind a pylon and, was commentating on the match for him, anyhow, the gist of the story is that even Lennie, with the aid of Harry's commentary, would have seen just how brilliant Osgood was.

Some players are just in a different league and, some managers just can't see it. Is it that coaching thing again, where they can't coach such genius?

I told you about him and, how the bigger the stage the more he loved it. And more than that, he always produced.

I had some good times in The Caledonian and, had a thing for Gill Gerrardo, who had a wonderful voice and, was quite a darling as well.

I liked the Caledonian, because Frank's a lovely bloke and, it reminded me of his run-ins with Osgood, which was quite funny, because it was nothing like the Leeds United/Chelsea battles, it was merely something I can't put my finger on, but that was Oz and, he was exactly the same with Mike England on the other side of north London.

Mike was in Seattle when I arrived and, was a bloody good player, but a little backwards coming forwards. He was nicknamed Bungalow, as he had nothing upstairs.

With that in mind, was it a surprise he did no good in management. My mate Mickey Thomas made me laugh when he was playing for Wales and Mike was manager and, when the lads come in at half-time after giving England a roasting, Mike said, "I don't know what to say, because I never saw this coming."

So, some nicknames were apt, in this case, definitely.

Like with Jack Charlton and Mike, Oz always, not only got the better of them but scored vital goals.

Oh how Alf messed up in Mexico, what was this man thinking?

I often think we might have been better with Harry and Lennie in charge, or Peters and Lee - no, not Martin and Frannie. After all we had Mercer and Allison, Clough and Taylor, Lennon and McCartney, Barry and Robin Gibb and, now todays answer to Morecambe and Wise are Ant and Dec, which I mention, because all else has gone downhill and, the way things are going these two Geordies might be as well running Soho Square, they get everywhere else.

There are no Les Dawsons Eric Morecambes, Tommy Coopers, Ronnie Barkers or Leonard Rossiters and, these stand-up comedians only get away with it because they swear more than I do. And, then there's our music, no Beatles, Bee Gees, Supertramp or Beach Boys, across the pond.

I was very fortunate the other day to meet John Hurt outside The Green Man in Berwick Street and, told him I was a big fan. Now, he stands alongside Anthony Hopkins, Cary Grant, Humphrey Bogart, Jack Nicholson and Jimmy Cagney in their field, although it's different, because unlike ours, it's not the killing fields.

Today Ray Winstone is my man, whilst back over that pond, Morgan Freeman, Tom Hanks and Denzel Washington, are my kind of people, on the big screen.

But going back to comedians, we had plenty in football management - and still do - but Alf and Don stand out for allowing the best players of my lifetime to rot on the side lines.

And, watching today, you look at Osgood, Chivers, Worthington, Bowles and Charlie George and, then look at Darren Bent and Emile Heskey and, it might tell you something about what that little Irishman said to George, "Where did it all go wrong," only this don't need much answering.

As for sheer footballers (inside-forwards) we have no Currie, Hoddle, Robson or Gascoigne, with only young Jack Wiltshere showing anything that resembles anything like them, however, he has a long way to go, although I must say I've been impressed.

Not long ago I was speaking to TC and, he told me that one day he was sweeping the Sheffield United dressing room out, after the kids had finished training and, whilst doing so, said to the parents there, "You wouldn't believe I used to play for England, would you?"

The place fell silent, for nobody knew Tony Currie, the greatest inside-forward in the club's history.

My heart falls silent, as this is one of the reasons I hate those people who have spent so many years at the place, on the back of Tony's fantastic performances. He was Sheffield United!

They're drinking their Gin and tonics in the boardroom whilst he's sweeping the bloody dressing room. Now do you see how we have it the wrong way round!

I say that about management then, because every single Englishman who knew anything about football would have told Oz to get his arse off that bench and, get us back into the match that put our game back years. By putting on inferior players, all you are doing is taking our game backwards and, that is what Alf did in Mexico and, Don did thereafter.

Even the Brazilians had no match for him. They had Pele, yeah, but Osgood was the ultimate centre-forward, in fact, they would not have been out of place together.

Pictures on the front of the open-top bus showed me wearing a blue and white striped shirt from Take Six, I can only imagine. As I hung onto the trophy alongside Keith Weller, Marvin Hinton and Johnny Boyle with the headline:

THE GREAT HUDSON BALANCING ACT

Since '97 my balance is virtually non-existent, but like Charlie Cooke's, it was once great - apart from outside of Barbarella – and, they can't take that away. Well they can, they have, but having lost my balance, I have gained so much more. And in writing this story you will know what I mean

I was still only 19 and should not yet have had the key of the door. But again, I skipped the queue.

That summer was uneventful.

Were things to stay the same?

Was this all a dream?

No, of course it wasn't, for I had now almost got over my nightmare from the previous year, but not quite. I never did until 1997.

Hutch was almost extinct - finished!

Enter Chris Garland, a player I liked on and off the field. He was the first-ever player to play for Chelsea with two such names. All I knew of him was that he was part of a two-pronged attack at Bristol City, the other half of this partnership was a bloke named John Galley. Chris, it seemed, had been playing forever because I remembered him as a kid, mainly because of the Garland/Galley names being a little different.

This time I think Dave bought the right one.

I looked at everything that was going on. I suppose that is a part of wanting to be a player, wondering how good he is, etc. Anyhow, Chris was the first in line to try to fill Hutch's boots. He was talented and, a lot better player than he was given credit for, in fact, he had much more natural ability than Hutch, but Ian had that special something, that special something my dad told me and my mum about in our prefab.

Was it something to do with Osgood again?

He (Chris) was also a good looking boy who could pull the birds. I suppose what helped him in this department was his Bristol charm and brogue. He wasted no time fitting in, proving a hit in the dressing room and, all the pubs surrounding it, although he and Hutch were more dangerous over Worcester Park way - The Plough, in fact.

No woman was safe with these two about and, it seemed we were now breeding Playboys like Docherty once bred footballers.

After all, Bristol was a Rocking Good City. I played there in the under-23 team and, experienced the light of day when leaving a night club there. I think Chris introduced me to it. It was called the Stage Door, a funny place, a little like people from that part of the world.

It reminded me of a place I went to recently. We were going towards a lovely Sports Bar where I did a One Man Show a few weeks later. This place also had a slope. This was the Crooked House in Crooked House Lane deep in the West Midlands. I can only imagine that in the early hours of the morning you had to question what you were drinking. But this was lunchtime and, was something new, strange new.

With my continued limp, it almost straightened me out. But we were still all over the place.

You had to get drunk to walk straight, but we didn't stay that long.

Chris reminded me of Ben Murphy out of the TV series, Alias Smith and Jones and, was what we call in London a Pretty Boy. We were to have quite a few of those over the years. In the bird-pulling stakes Chris was right up there with Alan Birchenall, Keith Weller, Ian Hutchinson, Bill Garner, Tommy Baldwin and of course, the one and only Peter Osgood, or so he believed!

Oz was always romancing, so much so it was like his lines were like something out of 'Only Fools and Horses' - remember Del Boy with the two girls in the downstairs Wine Bar - that could have been Oz?

I've mentioned him making a mess of meeting Raquel Welch. He should have really milked meeting this ravishing beauty, but failed the big test miserably. I watched the interview only the other week and had to chuckle, because he was like Rigsby with Miss Jones and, made a complete mess of it.

If only it had been me?

He was almost falling all over himself, something he never did on the field, for he left that for Drogba to compare him with and, on consistency alone, our centre-forward was far superior. Remember in those days defenders actually knew how to defend, today they are all over the place and, apart from referees being hopeless, that is the main reason for so many penalties.

He was trying to impress this gorgeous Hollywood icon with his Windsor humour. It was almost as if he was talking to Barbara Windsor.

Oz, you showed your true colours and they weren't blue, more like red.

On the field you were in a different class, but off of it?

These new players were also very popular with the crowd and, there is no doubt about it, they should have been on gate money if only for introducing the females to our matches. That is how it all began and, today the amount of women at football matches is astounding. Years ago, you would not see so many pretty young things amongst the crowd, now they dominate the screens. They not only brighten and, lighten up the place they also know what they are on about. They have even taken over the TV screens.

Where they were once weather girls, they are now football pundits. You can't knock it though, because the ex-players who dominate our screens leave a lot to be desired. Carry on girls - I'd rather look at you talking rubbish than them.

The difference is that you don't.

Now on the other hand there are what they call WAGs - the wives and girlfriends of the top players. And then there are those out there searching for the next upcoming star. Our WAGs were in a different class. My Maureen was a stunning brunette, as was John Hollins wife Linda. Peter Houseman had a very pretty wife Sally. Oh, how sad their deaths were!

Peter Bonetti had a very good-looking wife, although I can't remember her name. Bill Garner had a French beauty. Tommy Baldwin was dating a stunning blonde, but she, or he, disappeared before she could nail him.

Plus, you can never say they married us for our fortune and fame. Fame might have been something to do with it, but never the money. My missus, when I walked out, years later, on Arsenal, had to get a job otherwise we could not have paid our mortgage.

Yeah, they'd knock spots off today's WAGs and, they were safe amongst their husband's team-mates. Having said that, Sponge, as I have told you, ended up with Michael Crawford's wife Gabrielle, but that was after I had left for Stoke City.

Today's WAGs have become pop stars, models, even hosts of TV shows. George Best used to have Miss Worlds. The likes of Frank Worthington, Stan Bowles and I would not be far behind him. We were the Mavericks. Had we been around today with so much money in our pockets, I think we would have been on a different level from today's stars. I, for one, would have flown the most beautiful girls in the world into my Chelsea penthouse, well, one of my penthouses. Either that or I'd fly out to New York for the weekend. When you think you can be in Spain in a couple of hours and in a local bar quicker than getting to the other side of London. This country really is going downhill. But as long as the politicians are alright, that's okay! It would also have been a helicopter for me.

As for a car, my mate TD would have been my chauffeur.

When I see modern-day players misbehaving inside and outside public drinking clubs I cringe. Why oh why do they frequent drinking dens where they know there could be a very good chance that people will have a pop at them?

In my time playing, if I were to fight everyone who had a pop at me - for pure jealously - I would have been a contender because of all the practice I would have had. The media used to typecast us players who were burned out fast, but that was untrue. You only had to check us out in both those finals where all the odds were stacked against us.

Garland was brought in to give us more fire power up front and, he had a big job ahead of him, for Hutch was almost irreplaceable. As we all knew, he was close to the finishing line through sheer self-inflicted damage. In a nutshell, he was far too brave for his own good. To put your head where he put it was simply not sensible. As a young boy, if I had thought you had to play the game this way, I would have taken up cricket. His catalogue of injuries included two broken legs, two cartilage operations, a broken arm and broken nose that he sustained in one match alone. Only my team-mate Denis Smith at Stoke City could boast more self-inflicted broken bones.

Remember that incident I told you about earlier, it was just incredible. Nottingham Forest hard man Sammy Chapman - and I mean hard, tough as old boots hard - well this was just another day at the office for Hutch. Although Hutch looked indestructible, this episode proved he wasn't. You can't believe the TV series The Six Million Dollar Man where it starts out by saying, "We can rebuild this man."

What Hutch actually proved was that being like a football suicide bomber was not sensible. I cannot see the point of getting your head kicked in for scoring a goal and, as I was to find out, as he did, not being so ridiculously brave for your club. I feel that there are other ways of going about the job.

There is a fine line between bravery and lunacy - and Hutch crossed that line!

It was around this time, I read in the Evening News and Standard, that AC Milan was interested in signing me, which was very flattering.

Had I known what Sexton was about to do, I would have walked to Italy. I always wanted to play there because I had watched and admired Luis Suarez and Gianni Rivera, two fantastic inside-forwards who played in their league. I think the Spanish game today would have been more to my liking, but maybe the pitches might have been too firm for my ankle. Firstly the climate would have suited me and then the Spanish women, although when you get a beautiful Italian woman, wow. Ava Gardner flashes through my mind.

The only thing the Italian scene had that would have swayed me would have been the restaurants. As for the football, I fancy the quicker style of the Spanish game although I loved slowing the game down. That would have been another great challenge.

Suarez reminded me so much of Haynes. They were almost twins.

The body swerve, the swaying of the hips and, their immaculate passing.

They were mesmerising.

The Ballet!

Milan had obviously been monitoring my progress through our FA Cup run. Nowadays, with players having agents, they would have been on the case. At that time I looked at it and thought no more of it. Today, if you look at David Beckham, he does not miss any opportunity to move up that ladder, no matter how good or bad his form is. He should have invested in a removal business. He'd make a fortune on himself alone.

I watched a Beckham interview and he spoke of how his love for Manchester United still remains. I thought that Ryan Giggs and Paul Scholes fit that mould far better. This is not a dig at the former England captain, but don't take us all for complete idiots. United to Real Madrid to LA Galaxy to Milan does not really leave us thinking of any love affair anywhere. People who love each other stay together. Peter Osgood would have stayed at Chelsea his entire life if it wasn't for management and, if Chelsea had had a Waddington, I would have done likewise. Johnny Haynes could have taken his pick of any club around, but he stayed with his one love - Fulham. Bobby Moore never wanted to leave West Ham. It was only that Ron Greenwood let him down. No, I'm sorry I just don't buy that David. Why don't you just be honest?

In the end, it cost you a World Cup place!
I thought it a disgrace where Beckham lit the flame and that great
Olympian, Mary Rand had to pay for her own tickets.

He has won an award for his contribution to our game on the
Sportsman of the Year Show on BBC which, I switched off for the
sheer lunacy of it all. Not only has he never won the World Cup, he
helped mess up our attempt to hold the 2018 tournament. Here is a
player who we slaughtered in one World Cup for getting himself sent
off against Argentina, but here he was standing in front of a packed
auditorium to a five-minute standing ovation. Sickness is the only
word I can use to tell you how I felt! It took the gloss off AP McCoy
winning the trophy and the man from here in Stoke-on-Trent, Phil
Taylor, being the runner-up. Well done to the Potter.

You might say Beckham won this and won that, but who doesn't
under Ferguson?

I sometimes wonder what he would have achieved had he came into
the Victoria Ground. As I did!

Milan was obviously looking to import players and according to the
Evening News I was at the top of the list, though I heard nothing
about it. At that time I think I was probably right up there for the next
Captain of Chelsea, which I thought I should have been given. Had
things worked out for me and had Sexton wanted gone earlier the
move would have suited everyone. I would have been living in a 17th-
century palazzo with a rack of Armani suits and one of those nice
yellow sports cars in the drive. Well two or three more like it -
something that is not so incredible today. In Italy nobody wants to be
a train driver.

I am convinced a move there would have been great for me and, quite honestly I wanted to play abroad from a very young age. Something appealed to me more than playing here. Was it something inside of me that knew what was in store for me?

As a kid I was quiet and very easy going. I just wanted to go with the flow. I just wanted to play football. In other words, I was not prepared for what was coming my way. I could not handle management and the hierarchy. I hated them from an early age. Was it because I thought them to be fraudulent?

As a young boy, politics never interested me and, I knew that politicians were exactly the same and the same went for the police, as my dad knew the cop that was responsible for bringing my mate Tommy Wisbey in. His name was Jack Pritchard, or as Bill knew him, John.

I was going to say, bringing him to justice, but that would not be true.

I think it was because I was quite simply not impressed with any of them. Even on the first day I met Alf Ramsey - he may have won the World Cup - but he did absolutely nothing for me. Dave was the same. Tommy Doc also and Revie more so. And if you were not impressed with them, at an early age, just who would impress you?

Again, only players impressed me.

The only two who I have really admired has been Waddington and Jock Stein.

I always look back and wish we had been taught at school the most important lesson we would soon have face. Looking up to, and trusting the right people, for it was not until reaching Waddington that I knew that I had met the only man in the game I could trust, therefore, I played my heart out for him.

Tony Waddington, for me, stands alone!

Although I was impressed more with Inter Milan, they would have fitted the bill too. Both teams played my kind of football. You only had to look at Suarez (the Spaniard who played for 10 years at Inter after moving from Barcelona) and Rivera, who seemed to play for AC Milan forever. Suarez was nicknamed The Architect for his ability to construct the play. Sandro Mazzola was another genius of legendary status, a player who began as a striker before dropping into that scheming role.

I mentioned earlier my first ever trip on an aeroplane, it was to Switzerland for a youth tournament. Inter Milan were represented and, I was immediately impressed.

They looked the real business in their blue and black striped shirts, black shorts and blue and black stockings. I remember thinking, 'What class, they look as if they come from a different planet.'

I'm not surprised that Jose Mourinho took the Champions League with them.

The Doc wasn't there, but not long afterwards he chose that strip for his Diamonds. But after the boys wore it in the FA Cup semi-final defeat by Sheffield Wednesday in 1965-66, he gave it to John Hollins to give it to his pub or boys club team, so I believe.

In the first League match of my third season in 1971-72 we travelled across town to Arsenal, where they were showing off their Football League and FA Cup trophies from the previous season. We took our European Cup Winners Cup trophy with us. It was a fantastic start to the season on a red hot day which had me thinking of George Best in Spain. I should have been with him the way I played on this day. Nobody would have missed me. The ground was far too firm and, once again I was doing my Elvis impression, for being far too overweight.

But the lead up to the match was magnificent. Highbury was a fantastic place and it glistened on this day. It was not all because of the silverware on show. I had, and always will have, a very special place in my heart for this club, but one thing still astounds me. Why did they ever employ Terry Neill?

I was told a story about when Spurs contacted Hull City for his services. There was a letter ready to be posted telling the Irishman that he had been fired. But when the Spurs chairman got through they stopped it because they wanted compensation. You see what I mean about some people being lucky? In this case the luck of the Irish came into play.

That great feeling did not last long though, because Arsenal whipped us by three goals and in doing so showed we were in decline, while they were improving under Don Howe's wonderful coaching. Alan Ball once said at Arsenal that they did not need a manager, which was a pot-shot at Neill. Well they didn't really have one when winning the Double, they had a physiotherapist. But he was a man who could handle players.

That was Bertie Mee and, he was a master in the managers' office.

He was not a Waddington, Clough or Shankly, but he did not need to be because he had a great coach. All he did was to handle the players like men and when this does happen, you react and play like one. He was a real gentleman and when contracts were ready to be renewed, he sent them to my mate Ken Friar, who was secretary (Chief Executive). That was the best way because if you fell out with the manager over such things it was difficult to hold your respect for him and give him your all, the difference being, deep into extra-time you ask yourself, would he do this for me?

And when you had to run that extra mile it would enter your head, was he worth it?

This was a great time for my home town, London that is, displaying such wonderful finery. The old town had never seen such Tom Foolery in their midst. We could never get going under conditions better suited to a barbecue and beer, and it was as if we were on it this particular day. We got an absolute roasting whilst seemingly punch drunk. From the moment Frank McLintock headed them in front we were cooked and legless.

Our defence got caught napping so much that it was if they were dreaming of the past two seasons. Arsenal, on the other hand, were hungry for more than just a barbecue, they wanted more silverware. Our friend Ray Kennedy scored his obligatory goal.

Ray was the player that Sir Stanley Matthews let go from Port Vale, thinking that he wasn't good enough, well, it was a good job Stan could play because…

Osgood was transfer-listed after Manchester United beat us on our own patch in front of another closed-gate capacity crowd. It was like that night a couple of seasons ago at West Ham where the sun seemed to stay out forever, with the heat immense and, the beating hurtful. George got sent-off when we were in front, which led to a troubled season for him. Bobby Charlton lashed in one of his wonderful left-footed humdingers which, if it had hit the bar, would have shot upwards to the moon. Or had Sticks got any part of his anatomy to it, he would have followed.

Forty years on I am still trying to fathom out how Chelsea - which includes directors, coaching staff and supporters and, I do blame those fans - for allowing Chelsea to sell Osgood.

It would be like Barcelona letting Messi leave.

Charlton was an icon, but he disappointed me in those days. He did not stop moaning to the referee and that got my goat because he was such a special player. He and George never got on because The Belfast Boy would not pass to him, something George admitted. He once said, "All I wanted to do on getting a hold of the ball was to beat as many opponents as possible." I dread to think how many he beat.

This reminds me of 'Jinky' Jim Smith of Newcastle, an elegant Scot who played the game just for nutmegs. Jim did it against Arsenal 20-odd times, a record in any part of the world.

He was an incredibly talented player, who targeted that talent in the wrong direction. Had he been coached by a Don Howe and, channelled that kind of ability in the right manner, as Michael Parkinson said of me, just who knows what he might have achieved?

I played against Smith once and, it was a joke just how much skill this bloke had. However, I learnt at any early age that catching the ball on the back of your neck doesn't win you football matches. I have seen so many players in training doing this trick and, that trick, but just haven't a clue when to make the right pass. Joe Cole springs to mind and, I hate to say it but the same applied to my John's son, Billy. He was at Crewe after leaving Tottenham and, as much as I tried to drum it into him, he, it seemed, was too much like my brother.

I preferred to play the game the other way. Where you work on the other side of your game, which in my case was my fitness and, once you've got that cracked your natural ability would shine through. The same applied with Alan Ball and, that is why people looked at him as being a player who just ran around, but he was the best one-touch player I've ever seen.

In the end, winning is the feeling you want at 5-o'clock on a Saturday. Having said that, I just wonder how many people at St James' Park would rather watch him (Jim Smith) play, or watch the likes of Joey Barton in more recent times?

The crazy thing is that Newcastle's trophy cabinet over the years has been rather empty - which is a crime in itself - you just wonder if they might have done better by having the likes of Jimmy and opening a circus on their ground.

They have had the big name managers and players - not forgetting those fantastic supporters - but have always fell short for one reason or another. I mean Bobby Robson, Kevin Keegan and Alan Shearer in the managers' chair. They don't get any bigger, but big is not always best. My favourite all-time player was David Ginola, but KK messed that team up. I think Sir Alex had something to do with that when Newcastle looked like they had the championship in the bag and he simply wound Kevin up and, the Newcastle manager made a right "Wally" of himself in on front of millions of people on Sky TV.

Bobby Charlton had played in Mexico in '70 but was effectively a spent force. He wasn't the Charlton of '66. He got through on reputation and experience and, he definitely had plenty of that. But for my injury before the FA Cup final, I am sure and, I was told some years later, that I would have been his understudy. That meant I would have replaced him on the dreaded day against the Germans when we led 2-0 and, Alf Ramsey made a hash of the substitutions. How come Sir Alf can make such mistakes, yet I can't?

It just doesn't add up to me. Did he lose his marbles in the heat of Mexico?

I mean, Astle in front of Osgood? If that was not enough, he then pulled off Charlton to save him for the next match. That was the match that never came.

It set Beckenbauer free to damage us.

And I got a three-year ban for one mistake. Although I cannot see that I made a mistake. He should have listened and respected my decision because it was not only a football decision but a family decision also. Was he not a family man?

Although he was coming to the end of a glittering career, I knew that if I could hold my own against him (Bobby Charlton that is) I could go anywhere in this game. I played against George, Bobby and Denis at such an early age and, I more than held my own. It gave me a shot of confidence you can't get out of a needle in the Royal London Hospital - and boy did I have plenty of them!

One evening I threw a vampire out of my room when he failed after five attempts to find a vein!

Denis Law, who was my 'Man for all Seasons' saw Ron Harris as something of a bloodsucker, a marker who was as dangerous as any of those in Hammer Films. Ron said that Denis was his most difficult opponent. Law was smart, knowing that Ron would hack him to shreds if he got the ball played to his feet, so he cleverly got ball in the air. Ron Davies once told me, "They can't kick you up there," and, he was arguably the best of all time in terms of heading and his leaping ability.

Denis was the first superstar footballer, whilst George was the first pop-star footballer.

If Chelsea were a rock band they would have been the Rolling Stones, who just a couple of years earlier were living just around the corner from our prefab in Edith Grove and, played in the Wetherby Arms at the Worlds End, which is now a Paddy Power Betting Shop. I wonder, what odds you would have got that they would have sold so many albums?

This was the pub Ian Hutchinson took his first drink, one Christmas. It was a rum and black, and on that day we didn't know just how important a factor it would be in his life and his death!

Ronnie Wood, who moved from The Faces to join the Stones, is a big pal of Jimmy White - the greatest snooker player never to win at the dreaded Crucible. I was there one night with him when he was playing Steve Davis. I had dinner after one session with Jimmy, his father and Brian Madley of the Sunday People. Jimmy confessed that he was a Chelsea supporter. I was at the table for over half-an-hour before he realised it was me. He must have had his mind on other matters, not Steve, but the greyhounds at Wimbledon?

Law was the first player to wear his socks round his ankles, shirt outside his shorts and, was seen always holding his cuffs. He was simply unique in our game.

He lived up to the comic book hero Denis the Menace, where his influence over this generation could never be over-estimated.

So United had three of the greatest players in the world (unlike today).

I used to watch a young Rodney Marsh at Craven Cottage and, watched as he tried to emulate Denis. He was a talented player but a poor copy. The problem with him was he had an affair with the mirror. The one on the wall, that is!

Law was also the closest rival to Jimmy Greaves in the bicycle kick stakes, an art they also called the scissor kick. He perfected it during his days playing in Italy.

As I said, Law would come off Ron Harris and get the ball slung over top of him. It wasn't just the ball over his shoulder. Denis was brilliant in the air and, lethal from a standing jump!

The best I have seen in recent times is Ian Wright.

He was fantastic at coming towards the ball, then spinning and turning his marker. He also finished with such coolness and style. In our day, Sponge based him game on this.

Harris couldn't stand players who did that, for he loved them in his sights with the ball played up to them. That would give him time to position himself for that killing tackle.

This was something my father and, first coach always told me, "Never receive the ball with your back to an opponent." There were two occasions I ignored his advice and, both times I received terrible punishment. The first time Bruce Rioch broke my leg with a tackle from behind (a coward's tackle) at Derby and, on the other occasion Jim Steele snapped my knee ligaments with a similar tackle in Pittsburgh in a pre-season indoor friendly.

Was it a coincidence that they were two Scots?

One of the toughest defenders of all time was also one of the cleanest and, that was Dave Mackay. Was it a coincidence also that Brian Clough brought him into his Derby County team to clinch promotion to the top flight?

I mentioned about Clough having the best disciplinary record and once again this proves it, because Dave was toughest players in the history of the game. However, his record was impeccable!

Also, this 'turning my back' almost cost me my life in the Mile End Road!

Dennis Bergkamp was another player who loved coming off his marker and, spinning him and not only did he perfect that but once doing so was a fantastic finisher.

Remember that incredible goal he scored at Leicester. The ball travelled a long way and, as it did, his first touch was immaculate and, his second a goal, all in one fail swoop, which is something you won't see today.

Watching those players of today, how many can execute such an art, even though they supposedly abolished the tackle from behind. I have spoken to a couple of former Gunners who played with Bergkamp and, they said that he was the best player they had the privilege to play with. One was Paul Merson and, he was no mug when it came to playing the game Like Wright, he was a super talent.

He also scored a wonderful goal in a World Cup match against Argentina and, once again the ball had travelled an awful long way before executing it brilliantly.

We were now in the defence of the Cup Winners Cup. I hadn't heard of last season's first opponents and, this was no different. They were Jeunesse Hautcharage of Luxembourg and, we hit them for eight. In the return it really rained goals and, our 13-0 win set a new European record which still stands. It will never be beaten, if only because these teams no longer exist in such competitions. In the away leg Oz powered in a hat-trick and, promised to follow up with a record breaking tally. He did just that and, broke all European goal-scoring records. As I have told you on several occasions, the big elegant striker never promised anything he couldn't deliver.

As you know by now, I detest anyone boasting about how they are going to do this and that, but when Osgood said anything about what he was going to do, he never fell short of his prediction.

Houseman, back to his FA Cup form of '70, hit a couple. DJ, Sponge and Holly with a penalty all chipped in. It would not have mattered had John missed a penalty in this match, for it was when he took one later in the competition that broke our hearts. Jeunesse were amateurs and, had a captain with one arm. And no, he didn't play in goal and, wasn't any relation to Richard Kimble, played by David Jansen, I say that because he reminded me of the best coach I've ever had. My dad!

Every time I talk or think of this team I can't help but think back to the girl I left behind, or was it her leaving me? She was absolute stunning and came from this tiny country. Although, I wish I had met her around this time, a time where at the Bridge, I saw something quite hilarious.

This bloke ran onto the dog track where he picked up the ball and, in front of forty-odd thousand spectators, shaped up to take a throw-in. I wondered what Hutch was thinking as he watched this, for he could throw the thing out of the ground on a good day.

In Luxembourg, Oz also hit the post twice, which would have brought his tally to five. In the following match that is exactly what he did bag and, once again, he predicted it.

So after winning by eight, we fancied our chances. And what with away goals counting double, we were confident of going through. They were that bad that even I scored!

It was the biggest-ever Chelsea victory, smashing all aggregate records in European history. I have never felt so sorry for a bunch of people in football shirts, but we wanted to break as many records as we could. We were well into records around these times. We were the first Chelsea side to win both the FA Cup and European Cup Winners Cup, therefore breaking new ground. And now we had broken the goal-scoring record in Europe and Oz had broken the individual one.

And then my personal records, which included The Beatles, The Beach Boys and The Bee Gees and, then just coming onto the scene, Elton John - Reggie Dwight.

I was already a Sinatra lover, as I am Michael Buble today!

There was a great story about Reggie. I told Oz about this new singing sensation and, one night in our Liverpool hotel room, he came on to sing Your Song. I told Oz, "This is the bloke I told you about." He said, "I know him, that's Reggie the tea-boy at the studios where Linda Harris works. One day Terry Venables sent him off over the shops on an errand and, then some year's later Elton bumped into Terry at a party and, sent him to fetch him some champagne.

You just never know who you're talking to, as in this case Terry didn't know if it was Elton or Reggie?

Peter Houseman was getting some unfair stick from the West Stand. Peter was a deceptive player who ghosted in and out of matches. When getting to the by-line he would whip in great crosses with his educated left peg. Although having said that, there were times when I am sure Hutch turned a few bad ones into a good looking one and, that is not a knock at the crosses, just a reminder of how good Hutch was.

The tragic manner of Peter's death in a crash shook me to the roots of my soul. It was the last time I cried like a new-born baby and, the feeling remains as I write. He was a great, great lad who died on the M4 along with his wife Sally, when an out-of-control speeding car hit them head on. Had any one of eight of our players been in the headlines for this tragedy, the public would just have shrugged their shoulders.

Had it been Sponge or I, the reaction would have been, "What we expected. He had a good time. So long, sucker."

They always say, "Where were you when JFK, the President of the United States, got shot dead?"

Well I can't say, but I will never forget the news being given to me about Peter and Sally and, the same went for Matthew Harding and, amazingly I was in Matthew's old local, the Imperial Arms when the telephone behind the bar rang out for me.

Peter was at Oxford United whilst I was doing the business for Tony Waddington at Stoke City. I had just played in London and, was staying at the prefab that Saturday night. We had left Chelsea when the sea of life had started to flood the lads in all different directions, such is our game; eddies and currents had started to batter us.

At around 3.30pm the following day, the call came and, I was flooded with uncontrollable tears. My mother was the bearer of such incredible news whilst I was playing pool with my best mate Leslie, who himself would die so tragically young.

These were the days when pubs closed at two, but we stayed on every Sunday for Afters, as it was called then, a Lock-in these days. Her voice was hesitant. "Peter and Sally Houseman have died in a car crash," she said. I went into a spin. Like that Beatles song, A Day in the Life where he gets to the top stair of the bus and, the drug begins kicking in. I felt sick, vodka-sick, brandy-sick, champagne-sick, West Bromwich Albion-sick. Somebody I knew so little, yet so well, had died-sick.

I drowned my sorrows just like the Gemini I am. When you miss an FA Cup Final you smile, shrug your hurt away. Bust-up at Chelsea, shrug away your loss. Control, you see. Get a right-hander off the ball, smile at them and run them dizzy. Come out of a coma, think about it all and, get on with your life and, fight death with that life.

Again, you have two choices, for you either fight it or let it beat you. It's much like being behind three times against Leeds United in an FA Cup final!

Control, it's just that I could not even see at that moment. For Peter and Sally to die in a car accident was unbelievable. I began thinking, 'but he used to get the train home after some matches. I never once remembered him driving.' Not that it had mattered because he and, his very pretty wife were back-seat passengers.

My fondest memory of Peter was on a boat trip in the Caribbean. We all went fishing because the food was so bad in the hotel we decided to catch our own, whilst also getting out of the way of Dave so that we could really enjoy our end-of-season holiday. We could have drunk the ocean dry that most beautiful of days in Trinidad and Tobago. I think we tried. It was the first time Peter and I shared such an occasion and, he was delightful. His entire character came out on that particular day.

But the highlight of that day was when like a scene from Jaws, as the shark hits the side of Robert Shaw's sailing vessel, except that it was Mickey Droy who went overboard. It was hilarious as the boat sped for what seemed an eternity. The big centre-half must have felt we had either not noticed him leaving us, or were simply leaving him for a laugh. The last I saw of him, was whilst he was walloping a king size fish on the side of the boat when he lost his footing. Typical centre-half like. You have never seen two arms move as quickly as Oz was howling, 'Shark! Shark!'

Mind you, had a shark spotted him the thing might have had second thoughts and turned away!

Peter and I were sitting safely up front, our legs dangling in these magnificent waters with some of that punch from the Athens Hilton. Peter was completely chilled out and happy.

I drink mainly for the effect not the taste, unless it's the finest Bourbon or Coconut Rum.

This day it was that punch and, it worked. With inhibition gone, the conversation like the drink flowed. On that day I felt I had met Peter Houseman after five years of being at the same club as him. I found him to be a cracking bloke - one of life's real gems. I sensed he would have liked being that Peter Houseman more often. Maybe the restrictions placed on him made him so laid back and, so quiet.

Being accepted seemed to be enough for Nobby Houseman.

I wish that we could have had more drinks together, become closer and, become really good friends. It was a moment in time that had me thinking, 'Why don't we do this more often'?

Plus, 'Why is he not a part of our social team'?

If you were a stranger watching us you'd have thought us real great mates.

What a loss!

What a waste of two young lives and, what made things worse was leaving two youngsters behind.

At the end of all of this you'll probably say about me not liking Chelsea Football Club and, you won't be wrong. But here is just another case. What happened to those two young Houseman children? They should have had two season tickets for life, because that is what Peter gave to Chelsea. He was so important in winning the first ever FA Cup.

I wonder if anyone has ever mentioned this to Roman Abramovich.

Not that it would have mattered, for if he doesn't care about us when we're alive, what chance you got when you're dead?

We should never be together again - perhaps I knew that then on that boat?

Dave Sexton thought that because Peter was so quiet - an introvert - and, Oz and I were both extroverts, this was the reason we would not pass the ball to him more often. What cobblers!

Stuck out on the left touchline he would obviously seem neglected. Once again the manager confronted me saying, "You keep passing the ball to Osgood." I simply repeated that, "I thought the game was all about giving the ball to your best players."

That is how you win football matches. The team who has most possession nearly always wins and, the best players win you matches, by both creating goals and scoring them.

Although in that FA Cup run Peter did both brilliantly
Just watch Barcelona today. The team whose best players always perform and win.

It's not rocket science is it: If you had the ball at Old Trafford and, had two options, would you give the ball to George Best or John Aston?

Today, if you were looking for a winning goal would you pass to Defoe or Heskey?

Thinking back about that boat trip in these terms if we had hit anything or been hit by a freak storm, like the one that would blow the roof off the Butler Street Stand at Stoke City or, that speeding car in the Mile End Road, we would have all gone down with the captain. The only difference was that Chopper was not aboard.

We would have certainly all gone. Chelsea would be doing just that after that ridiculous decision to sell the two players, who at that time were their two best. Charlie was just about past his best, just.

Years afterwards I would dream about that boat trip and, always take one whenever I got the opportunity whilst abroad in an attempt to recapture such memories. The Silver Jubilee at Chelsea brought it all back. None of us spoke about Peter, although we hardly did when he was alive. But, although we didn't, it did not mean he was not one of us. He was very well respected as a player and, loved as a lad. He was simply shy. So shy, in fact, some days you would not recollect him being around. Maybe that was why he was known as The Ghost for the way he set up so many goals by sneaking by defenders to arrow in those crosses of his. It takes all types to make up a team. And in that Chelsea team there certainly were some different types. Ron Harris was neither one of them nor one of us. There were three different parts that made up our team: Peter, John Hollins and the other Peter, Bonetti. And then there were us, those you have read about, the drinking and womanising Playboys - for want of a better word. And there was the skipper, Ron Harris. I can only think he was captain because he had been there forever. He hardly spoke. I know at Spurs when things were going wrong, Dave Mackay would hold the half-time team meetings and, get stuck right into his team-mates. But in our dressing room all Ron did was bite his nails. Ron was a complete loner and, still is. As for being captain, I suppose some might say because he was tough that was a good enough reason. He was not a leader as such and, definitely no Dave Mackay, who was simply world class.

The media never told the real story of why Dave took the captaincy from Ron. It was through him urinating in the bath before Dave, after being warned, jumped in and washed his face and hair. I was watching from the shower. It was an accident waiting to happen, although no accident. I thought whilst watching just what the repercussions would be?

What would Dave do?

The club seemed to be in turmoil.

I know Ron had been captain for quite some time - since Venables left, in fact - but I found it a strange appointment.

This kind of player never captained other clubs, like Tommy Smith, Norman Hunter and Peter Storey - all similar to Ron - for they simply had a job to do and, we know what that was. Every team had one. Today, none of them would be on the field too long, which is a crying shame. It is a contact sport, a game for men.

It's very simple, you hit and get hit.

Bremner was captain material as was Haynes and Baxter, not your hatchet man and although they were three completely different players, they all were all wonderfully gifted ones!

On that upcoming Friday, just before we boarded the club bus for Euston Station, we were all hauled into the boardroom, where we were sat with pieces of paper and a pencil. Ron Stuart handed them out as we entered the room. It was funny. I would love to reinvent it, as a comedy, and it didn't need too much reinventing, it was really funny, stupid funny!

We were then asked to write down who we thought should take over the captaincy?

On the bus to Euston we were howling, as everyone was asking who voted for whom. When I was asked, I said myself, which was true!

Instead of selling me I believe I should have been made captain. I think that I was still learning, but although I liked a good time, I could be a good go-between for everyone. The problem we had with Dave was that everyone was drifting apart, because of a lack of man management!

Ultimately, people are remembered for what they are. For example, Marilyn Monroe is remembered for herself more than her acting. Similarly, Elvis is not remembered so much for his singing or acting, but for his overall image. I am not ranking Chelsea personalities of the Seventies on such a high plane, but in terms of football history and public consciousness - they are legends. When you go back years later and older fans see you, they make such a fuss and, it is not because of how you played then, or how good, great or indifferent you were, it is simply that they were the best times for them.

Like anything else in life the older you get, the better player you were. It's all in the mind!

I mention elsewhere about sitting around the table recently with likes of Tommy, the two John's, Boyle and Dempsey and Lou. I go numb with disappointment for what the club have not done for these chaps, especially in a year of winning the Cup Winners Cup. They did absolutely nothing!

I think having read of these fantastic matches and, the times we spent going into them and, also celebrating them together, you just might get my drift.

And, it's quite appropriate I mention it whilst on the subject of Peter Houseman.

There is no better feeling than being a part of such camaraderie. That is what wound me up about Dave Sexton. He just didn't see the spirit that was built through being simply ourselves. I would not mind if we cheated, or were left wanting for being not good enough in big matches, then he would have had a case. But when the chips were down, these lads could be counted on. Just ask Don Revie, Johnny Giles and Billy Bremner.

No matter what went on between these two clubs, I get the feeling when I come across them, there will always be a sense of great respect either way. I saw Johnny Giles the other week, and there is no doubt I am right. I was a massive fan of Giles, Bremner, Cooper and Gray. They were brilliant players and, that is why I loved playing against them and, beating them gave you the greatest feeling. That is what the game is all about!

Steve Kember made his debut at Sheffield United after signing from Palace. He was dazed by the ball early on. He'd never seen as much of it, when he was at Palace. The Blades had made a tremendous start to that season, almost as good statically as when Tottenham won the Double. Our nemesis Scullion - you'll recall him from the Watford side in our FA Cup Semi-final win - scored the only goal of the game.

In the last minute Webb, that oncoming reliable express train, headed one down to the unmarked Oz. He was literally on the goal-line. In one of the most bizarre and remarkable moments I have ever witnessed on a football field, this superbly talented striker somehow contrived to volley it over the bar. It was as you've heard the term so many times, "Easier to score than to miss." It looked impossible to miss, but somehow the scorer of so many breath taking goals did just that and, those missed chances would ruin our season and the following match was living proof of just that.

Next up were Atvidaberg from Sweden.

How we left Sweden with no goals to show for our supremacy was totally amazing and, what was to follow even more so. The pitch was awful, but I loved it, muddy as hell and, I ploughed through it and, on one occasion I once went through to thunder a shot that shook the bar. I thought at that moment we'd have to wait for the return leg, how wrong can one be?

My ankle hurt like hell afterwards, but that was nothing new, but that hurt turned into another kind of hurt, only it was nothing to with this on-going niggling career threatening injury.

The problem that I had was that nobody not only believed me, but seemed as if it didn't really matter, well it didn't to them, for it wasn't there ankle.

However, they expected you to do the business for them, never taking such things into consideration. Oz was another. The times I saw him on the treatment table with no chance of being fit, but come the next day, he was out there in front of his adoring fans. I said to him one Friday "That's it then mate," and he said, "What's that?" in which I said quite simply, "We'll miss you tomorrow," and, with that look of his in his eye, he said without any shadow of a doubt, "What are you on about, I'll be there tomorrow son."

He got off the table and could just about get his shoe over his foot.

We flew into Heathrow never considering that it would be our last flight into the unknown. It never once entered my mind that we could be going out of this competition. We could have done with an away goal, of course we could, for it is the cushion, the kind of cushion that my ankle enjoyed through this match.

But not scoring was to be our downfall.

Before the second leg I received a call from Christine Matthews at Chelsea. She said that she had someone on the phone asking if I would go to the hospital to see a kid who still lived in Elm Park

Gardens (my birthplace) whose name rang a bell immediately. It was Robert Drewitt. He went to the same school at a time when we kids were not even thinking about finding our way in life. We were simply growing out of our short trouser years and, moving on in no definite direction. Now, here I was going into a European Cup Winners Cup match as he lay dying.

I mentioned this to Hutch and without hesitation we were at his bedside.

At times like this you were not only helping the person wickedly struck down with illness, but also giving yourself the opportunity to thank your lucky stars and, appreciate the God-given talent you were born with. Robert had leukaemia. I remember him from school, of course, like all the kids, but I never really knew that he loved his local club. I suppose like anything else, you have your own mates, like Leslie and Bobby, Chris Maughan and Keith Davidson. Not to mention Mick, who wanted to blow-up his own home!

This was not only my sentimental side, but my realistic side also. On that night Robert, like Denis Darcy, also played for Chelsea, only this time it was at Stamford Bridge. In fact he went one better by scoring a superb volley, a ball that had goal written all over it as soon as it left my right foot. Surely, this would put us through. Then we were awarded a penalty, 'That's settled it,' I thought as soon as he pointed to the spot, I could hear the balls rattle in the machine, "Chelsea will play.....

Holly stepped forward and missed!

But we were still in the driving seat, banging away at their goal while never contemplating that they could break away to score and knock the holders out and, as sure as God made little Green Apples, that is exactly what they did.

I think at certain stages in your life The Man upstairs either sends people to you, or they cross your path to remind you of the fragility of life and, the uncertainty of it all. Well, this player was Roland Sandberg, a player I'd only seen in glimpses over in Sweden, but no danger to us, or so I thought.

I wonder if that is why our defenders were caught napping?

We absolutely dominated for 180 minutes and more, but finished as if we had never ever scored a goal before. All of those goals against the team from Luxemburg were no good to us right now, they counted for absolutely nothing.

After finishing the first part of The Playing Fields - with The Killing Fields still to come in book 2 - I had to look these chaps from Luxemburg up, if only for wondering what they are doing now and what their thoughts were about that night. It would be great have a party with them and cover over old ground and, I mean that in way

that, as I might have said, I have never felt sorry for an opponent in my life, apart from that night. Here is what I found on one site by Statman and, I put my own title with that Swedish match in mind:
IT STILL DOESN'T MAKE ANY SENSE!

A butcher, a baker but sadly no candlestick maker arrived at Stamford Bridge 40 years ago this week, along with a party of others from the small country of Luxembourg who played football for a hobby. By the time they left London they had against their names the biggest aggregate defeat over two legs in the history of European football competition.

Today 29.9.2011, is the anniversary of Chelsea's 13-0 win over Jeunesse Hautcharage in the first round second leg of the European Cup Winners Cup 1971/72, to this day our biggest win in a game in any competition. Two weeks earlier we had won the first leg 8-0 in Luxembourg and we had not rested on our laurels during the rematch.

'Lucky 13 as Chelsea Smash Record' shouted a newspaper headline after the Stamford Bridge second leg but although it was indeed an historic victory in world football, it must also be admitted that it was one of the great mismatches of all-time as well.

Chelsea in 1971/72 were the holders of the Cup Winners' Cup having beaten Real Madrid in the final in May and had finished sixth in the league the previous season. It was still very much the Kings of the King's Road side with Peter Osgood, Charlie Cooke, Alan Hudson, Peter Bonetti etc. on board, although the successful spell under manager Dave Sexton was coming to an end.

To say Jeunesse Hautcharage had been surprise winners of the Luxembourg Cup the previous season would be an understatement. A club from a village with just 704 inhabitants, they were in Luxembourg's third division when they stunned the country by winning the cup final 4-1 after extra-time against Jeunesse Esch, one of the country's biggest clubs, although they did win promotion to the second division by the end of the season as well. In the club's 52-year history they had only played in the top flight for one season and their previous best run in the cup had taken them to the quarter-finals. The local brewery celebrated the 1971 cup win by offering free beer to the village for three days and three nights but everyone had sobered up by the time Chelsea came calling in mid-September for the first European match in Hautcharage's history.

"I must admit that we didn't know much about them before we played. But it soon became clear it would be an easy game. We were obviously in a different class from them and it was their first time in Europe and we had a bit of experience of playing in Europe," Chelsea's Peter Bonetti told us.

461

Player/coach Romain Schoder was one Hautcharage team member who had played at a higher level in Luxembourg but that was as a goalkeeper. Now he was his team's sweeper. He, like the rest of the players, didn't earn a penny from football, as long as a wrist watch they were given to commemorate winning the cup didn't count. There were a couple of claimants to be the football dynasty in Hautcharage. Joseph Thill was the club chairman and Guy Thill was their youngest and most promising player, despite only having one arm. The club also had four Welscher brothers. Eddy, the oldest, was the captain.

Only 1,500 could have attended the first leg had it not been moved to Luxembourg's national stadium where a 13,000 crowd watched on. Had any of them harboured ludicrous hopes that the mother of all giant-killings might be possible then those were surely banished after just two minutes when Osgood scored. Peter Houseman then put away a second goal and, Ossie headed another to make it 3-0 inside half-an-hour.

He completed his hat-trick before half-time with Houseman again, Tommy Baldwin and John Hollins also on the score sheet before the interval. Baldwin and David Webb scored in the second half to complete the 8-0 win. Five of the goals were headers. Osgood, twice, and Baldwin, also struck woodwork. Had the return match been away from home rather than at the Bridge then the Chelsea players might have felt the temptation to go a little easy on the lambs who had been brought to the second-leg slaughter, but the Chelsea match programme for the game carried words on the need to 'put on a show' for the 27,621 supporters who had paid to see it, although it did speculate that the rarest of scorers Ron Harris could find the net on the night and, on the possibility that Bonetti would play in attack at some stage with David Webb going in goal.

The programme also made everyone aware of records that might be set. Chelsea's had not hit double figures in a single game before, and the previous best aggregate scoring by any club in a European tie was 18 goals with the best score by a British club 16-0. "Records were something I didn't even think about before the game. It was only when we had finished I thought blimey, we might have scored a record amount here but I couldn't have told you what the record score in Europe was anyway. It certainly didn't cross my mind for a minute going into that second leg. And I was never going to play elsewhere in the team. We weren't going to muck around. It was a serious game and to start changing positions wouldn't have been very professional. When you are playing a side like that who might not be as experienced as we were you can't let them off the leash, you have to go out and play your best because you have a duty to yourself and your team and to the fans. I don't think we took the mickey at all, we played our stuff and got the goals and were very professional about the whole situation," said Bonetti.

All four Welschers brother were in the Hautcharage team at the Bridge; there were also two Thills in the side and one of the visiting team wore glasses during the match. Osgood declared before the game that he would score six goals, which would have set a new best for a player in Europe, but was positively sluggish at the start compared with the first leg, taking four minutes to open the scoring although he had two goals by the sixth minute when keeper Lucien Fusilier dropped a cross. John Hollins's successful penalty meant the Blues were already 4-0 up after 13 minutes and as in the first leg, the half-time score was 6-0. As speculated in the programme, the sixth was scored by Harris.

The eighth goal gave Osgood his second hat-trick of the tie and it was Houseman who struck the historic 10th in the 77th minute, taking Chelsea beyond the nine-goal hauls put past Glossop and past Worksop way back in the first three seasons of the club's existence. When Osgood made it 11-0 Chelsea had set a new European record. Our no. 9 headed in goal no. 12 from a corner for a personal five goals on the night and there he would stick. Baldwin completed his second-half hat-trick with the last kick of the game and Chelsea had won 13-0.

It seems strange to talk of eight-goal Osgood falling short of targets but in 'only' scoring five in the second leg he had equalled rather than surpassed the eight-goal record for individual scoring in any European tie and, had also lost a bet with team-mate Bonetti. "Ossie had said to me in the dressing room before we went out that he was going get six having got three in the first leg, and I was winding him up by saying I bet you don't. In the end I said I'll bet you a fiver. Later on after the game he told people that when we got the penalty, I came up to him and said you can't take that because John Hollins is our penalty taker but I don't remember that at all. Fair enough though, he came into the dressing room and gave me a fiver straight away."

Hautcharage's Guy Thill told Chelsea's club historian Rick Glanvill in 2006, "I was a student and there were steel and railway workers, a hairdresser and a butcher in our team. None of our work experience was any use to us against Chelsea, not even the butcher's. We knew what to expect from Chelsea. I'd watched them beat Real Madrid in the final the previous season, which was a good game and, I remember we were really happy to be drawn to play Chelsea, a big London club. We never ever thought we would win the tie. The manager spoke to us before the game and told us to try not to lose too high. Chelsea were too strong for us obviously. We had hardly any opportunity even to shoot," the former midfielder recalled. I had one chance to test Bonetti, a free-kick, at 2-0 (in the first leg) - it would have been a sensation to score. He caught it. We had a good time in London, looking around, doing the big sights. The players were great with us and, signed autographs as we wished. It was a great atmosphere and, we never thought they'd be gentle with us and, they weren't. Thirteen goals to nil there, and 21-0 overall, it's quite a lot. We weren't upset that it went in the history books, though - Luxembourg teams, we are used to it. After the game there was a dinner, and we met all the players. None of them said "hard luck" though. We really enjoyed the day.'

Chelsea's outright European victory margin record lasted just a season. Feyenoord beat Rumelange from...you've guessed it... Luxembourg by the same score in the 1972/73 UEFA Cup first round, but we still hold that joint record to this day.

Jeunesse Hautcharage no longer exists as team name. The club merged with another some years ago and the new one holds its own in the Luxembourg top flight. It plays in a different, larger town. With hindsight, Chelsea's thumping of the minnows from the middle of Europe can be viewed as a last hurrah for Sexton's team that had captured the hearts of so many. In the next round of the Cup Winners Cup we did suffer a giant-killing, on away goals at the hands of Swedish club Atvidaberg. Although a far bigger team than Hautcharage (they were soon to be crowned national champions), Atvidaberg were part-timers. We wouldn't compete in Europe again until 1994. Before the 1971/72 season was out we were knocked out the FA Cup by second division Orient and the following weekend lost the League Cup Final at Wembley to underdogs Stoke, missing out on three different trophies in three years. Soon the team would break up, but they left behind winning margins in European competition which it is hard to imagine any Chelsea side of the future managing to surpass.

WHAT A THRILL!

I can only think that was quite a thrill and, something they can tell their grand-children when they watch Chelsea win the likes of the Champions League today, I know I do things like that, by saying, or thinking, 'I remember playing there when we beat them 4-3,' as I did the other week as Blackpool beat Birmingham in the Play-Offs.

It will be much like Sandberg - who experienced a different kind of thrill - when looking silently dangerous in Sweden, where his robust play should have told us that maybe we should watch out for him, just in case, having said that, even in hindsight that was not the case, for it was simply a case of us missing so many chances, including that penalty.

How today, could you say at 2-0 down in the Nou Camp that Chelsea would go through?

How could you say that when Messi stepped up against Cech that Chelsea would go through?

It was simply meant to be and, whether you talk about it until you go Blue in the face, you just cannot argue with that. I had never played in such a one-sided match and been beaten and, in those two legs against Spain, Barcelona had enough chances to win three matches, when hitting the post and crossbar more than once and, then there was the brilliance of Cech and, if that wasn't enough there was Messi, just like Hollins, missing that penalty. Like our match I have never seen such a one-sided match with the result favouring the team who looked absolutely shell-shocked, almost as if on Death Row, only it was if there was a power cut.

Well, for those of you who weren't amongst that Stamford Bridge crowd on that stunning night, I can tell you most definitely, that this was like watching a repeat performance.

We really should have completely buried them in Sweden and, needn't have to have worried about any of their players because this match should never have been a consideration. Had it been a boxing match, the man in the white shirt would have asked the judges if it was worth going to London for the second leg.

And, I was told, that like in The Royal London Hospital where those surgeons were so close to pulling the plug.

This was like the Great Train Robbery - only the Swedes got away with it!

This is who they were and unlike the team from Luxemburg they still exist: Åtvidabergs FF is a Swedish football club located in Åtvidaberg. The club was formed 1 July 1907 as Åtvidabergs IF, before changing to the present name before the 1935-1936 season and, were one of the strongest teams in Sweden during the 1970s, winning two league titles (in addition to being runners-up on two occasions) and the Swedish Cup twice. Not much of a history but it was enough to knock us out, so it had us wondering, after Beating Leeds United and Real Madrid, what the hell was going on?

We were stunned, to say the least and, after missing so many chances, like Barcelona again, we paid the price. Was John Hollins missing that penalty the writing on the wall?

As I write, I bow my head in disbelief. Holly, what were you thinking?

Whilst researching I played something on U-Tube and, a little piece of it was John blasting a penalty past Pat Jennings at the Bridge in one of those wonderful League Cup semi-finals. He put the ball down picked his spot and, simply blasted it with such precision past one of the greatest keepers of all-time. On this night, he scraped the outside of the post, oh John, what were you thinking?

I have asked myself that question so many times even to the point of making out I was John and, tried to find an answer. I suppose John can say, well, if Messi can miss, then I can?

This was the end of not only our fantastic European experience football wise, but the incredible experiences of seeing such places. I would not have minded had we been knocked out by Bruges or CSKA, but a Swedish team that were simply not in our league. They were second best at everything, oh John....

We would, I am almost certain, have gone on to retain the trophy, for we and, me in particular were getting better as the season wore on with the pitches getting heavier. My pitches!

Today, when you hear players or managers say "we were unlucky" take no notice, because you have just watched it on Sky. In this particular match we were not unlucky, we were cursed. I am just happy that night that we were playing at home because had we had to fly afterwards...

The strangest thing is that John is someone you just can't help but like, but every time I see him now I think of that penalty, even though we've since played against one another.

One time was when we both captained our sides at the Victoria Ground in our 1-0 win.

It was, I think, the first ever Sunday match, at our ground, when I won the penalty and, Geoff Hurst blasted it home. I thought of Sweden.

Geoff will know exactly how John felt, for he rarely missed a penalty, but he did in the other semi-final of the 1972 League Cup at Upton Park. This indirectly led to Stoke City getting through to beat us in the final. However, although Geoff missed, at least he hit the target, only to watch in horror, as his World Cup winning team-mate somehow turn it over the bar. Banks made a superlative one handed save which changed the direction of this match and, had he not, it would have become the first ever all-London League Cup final at Wembley.

I stood in disbelief and, the same kind of horror, as Sandberg ran onto a long through ball from Lars Andersson and beat Bonetti from close in. We were out. The Swedes somehow held out and, we crashed out of the competition in which we had played so magnificently throughout. Looking back, we had only been outplayed once throughout those two seasons in Europe and, that was in Belgium, strangely enough, when Oz was out of the team, Dave.

That is something to be proud of and I don't think Dave gave us chaps credit for that.

As I say elsewhere, Mr. Waddington would have let us known in no uncertain terms that we were doing him proud, and that included the club and those wonderful fans.

A little champagne here, champagne there, and knowing that after sweating it out, we would go back for more, silverware that is, not champagne?

Well, a little of both, knowing Tony!

I cannot in my wildest dreams imagine that had Osgood signed for Stoke City, Tony and him ever having a cross word. The manager would have been shouting from the roof-tops that England must not ignore Peter Osgood - as he did for me - and, never once contemplating wanting to fight him behind the North Stand.

After the Swedes, the following week we gave an almost repeat performance against Bolton Wanderers in the League Cup when again I hit a brilliant volley. This time we played the replay away from home. Bolton were a hard nut to crack at Burnden Park, far tougher than the Swedes. But those Swedes haunted us. I don't think I have ever played in such a one-sided match where we did not win. Now we were staring up the barrel of another cup exit. My pal from Seattle played against me on this night, although we never mentioned amongst all of our hours socialising, which you cannot blame him, for a six goal drubbing does not warrant a fun-loving conversation. He was Roy Greaves a very good, hard-working wing-half, with a very good football brain. He was perfect playing next to me. If I were wearing number ten I'd want a Roy Greaves, Johnny Hollins or John Mahoney wearing the number four shirt!

As for that night against the Germans - which was still to come - Colin Bell, Alan Ball and I worked perfectly together. It was a great combination.

This night in Bolton was like a remake of Jekyll and Hyde.

We swamped them from the very first whistle, like we did the Swedes, only this was the other side of Chelsea and, would turn out so very different, as everything we hit ended up in the back of the Bolton net. How we could have done with Sponge hitting a hat-trick in our 6-0 victory and, although it was a remake, someone had switched the scripts.

I scored again the following week, this time straight from a corner at Crystal Palace in a 3-2 win. Yet again Oz got the winner. He was John Jackson's biggest nightmare. If Jacko and Osgood lived in the same turning, as I said earlier, it would no doubt have been named Elm Street.

A few years later I scored again from a corner at the Victoria Ground, but it was disallowed. I would practice this, much like the winner at White Hart Lane in the semi-final of the League Cup. Although it wasn't a corner-kick, it was that close to the flag that most people think it was one!

In fact, it was in the second-leg of the following match....

A few days before Christmas we met Tottenham at the Bridge in the first-leg of the League Cup semi-final. It was our Christmas treat to our brilliant supporters. We opened up as if we would not need the second-leg, although it had to be played. We simply murdered them.

It was an absolutely brilliant match, the kind of classic cup-tie you'd expect from two such teams. Tottenham were very fortunate to get out of the Bridge without a severe hiding. We led 1-0 at the break, yet somehow within a couple of minutes of the restart we found ourselves trailing. Two goals hit us like a thunderbolt. Firstly, my mate Terry Naylor equalised and, then big Martin Chivers put them in front. Chivers was having a fantastic season for the visitors, mauling centre-halves up and down the country.

On this form he was the only one who could hold a candle to Osgood.

We were down but far from out. We seemed to step up a gear and, began tearing them apart once again, as if still having a hangover from that Swedish match. Not a hangover where you were suffering, but one where there was only one way to get it out of your system. We battered them with the kind of football that was delightful on the eye. Ralph Coates, previously a thorn in our side at Burnley, was showing signs of doing some damage, but a couple of whacks from our full-backs stopped him in his tracks.

This was no match for the faint-hearted!

Chris Garland and Cyril Knowles were having their very own private fight out on our right-hand side. Knowles was a cult figure at White Hart Lane, although Tommy Docherty once said that they had a lot of cults over that side of London. He once said they were, "The biggest cults in the game."

Cyril's kid brother Peter was the biggest mystery in my football lifetime.

He was supremely talented. He walked out on Wolves to become a Jehovah Witness, when he should have been walking out at Wembley for the 1966 World Cup and, the one to follow, which made him the biggest waste of talent in the history of the game. He was a player that would surely have played in Mexico '70. Had he, he would have become a household name in our game!

Talent like that comes along once in a Blue Moon and, there he was, for some incredible reason, walking away from a game he was born to play so brilliantly.

The only scenario I can think of worse, is if he were to do such a thing today?

Today, he would be one of those coining in £1m=a=month tax free, but the last I heard he was doing a job stacking shelves in Marks & Spencer. When you look at these situations, is it any wonder that we haven't been close to winning anything since '66?

There is one of the finest talents we ever had stacking shelves in a local supermarket.

Can you imagine that in Brazil or Argentina?

Messi would have been no good, for he couldn't reach the top shelf!

Charlie Cooke came on for his mate Tommy. The crowd went into a complete frenzy. Chris headed us level from yet another Houseman cut-back cross. As I said earlier, we would never really know just how good his crosses were. For when Hutch was playing, it seemed he could turn a hopeless-looking cross into a good one.

That was how scary or, should I say, how good, brave, stupid and totally irresistible he was. He'd throw his body into a sea of boots and elbows to make a half chance a goal scoring certainty. He did it for us, his pals in the dressing room and, those who followed us from the Fulham Road to Athens and, after doing so couldn't get a ticket for a home match.

Yeah, this was the man that Bates through out of the office one afternoon.

Hutch was simply waiting for two complimentary tickets!

He rose like an eagle when fit, but those days were now, few and far between - he was going downhill rapidly. He was too brave for his own good and, in the end it was very sad. Like me, to think that Chelsea turned him away years later and, wouldn't give him a ticket, as I just said. Ken Bates asked him who he was and, once Hutch replied, Captain Birdseye turned him away. This was Chelsea Football Club. Some years later I witnessed the same thing at Stoke City. I walked through the crowd to see, in horror, Mr. Waddington waiting outside in the rain for a ticket. I went totally berserk!

Can you imagine Manchester United doing this to Bobby, Denis or George?

Chelsea were and, have always been so class-less off the field and, now they boast such wealth they're even worse, but they are not English are they?

They're Russian and America.

To put it in a more simplistic way:

Did Brian Mears or Ken Bates ever put their head where Hutch did for the club?

Young Marcus comes back into my mind when writing to the PM.

Right at the end I found Paddy Mulligan out on the right and, went for the return pass. The Irishman chipped into the box and, as I ran on to it, my mate Terry Naylor handled. I wanted to take the penalty but Holly picked it up and, this time made absolute no mistake against one of the best keepers in the world. Pat Jennings.

Terry does the rounds now in the east End of London, his favourite being Sinatra!

Still, it didn't make up for the Swedish experience, but it did give us a tiny cushion for the second leg in north London. I'd rather have been boarding at Heathrow than a coach to Wembley for a League Cup final.

It is also funny, that once we were knocked out of Europe - with it hurting so much - you ignore the rest of the competition. Rather like a lost love, you split up and move on. Although getting knocked out hurt more than any love. With such matches you only have one opportunity, whereas with a love you get another chance to try to sort it out, although I find myself alone and, fretting more about that defeat against the Swedes more than any love that slipped through to the next round!

The Spurs match had been a tremendous advert for our game. The electric atmosphere we experienced that night was on a par with Bruges. It also reminded me of the night when Chelsea beat Roma a few years earlier. The night I touched on earlier, when Venables was instrumental in securing a magnificent victory whilst scoring an extraordinary hat-trick along the way. Although I was still a Fulham supporter then, I knew at that moment that I wanted his role as Chelsea captain, or so it seemed. Dreaming again, I suppose!

Oz had his usual running battle with Mike England who, along with Frank McLintock, was the player he loved rubbing up the wrong way. Was there something about north London?

Webby meanwhile, had five stitches in a cut which really made him a more frightening sight, although he didn't really need cuts.

If this was a great match, the return was even greater on a ground I just loved performing.

We had won there in that FA Cup semi-final, but this was not Watford.

Tottenham were up for it and, although they were playing well, we were fantastic.

We were putting on a performance which Venables told me the following day was,

"The best Chelsea performance I have ever seen."

After celebrating in Alexandre, the following morning we were off to court to watch the second leg of an entirely different kind, the Police versus Peter Osgood and Danny Gillen. We won that one also!

This match had everything and high drama was on top of the list, right up to the very last kick, and, that kick was mine. It was once again my kind of pitch, having rained constantly throughout the day. It was a pitch we had become so used to in big cup matches. It was a complete mess. It was our second semi-final there and, both matches were played under the most severe conditions.

The first against Watford was more like a beach, whereas this pitch was somewhere that those Afghan terrorists would not have a clue where to plant their IEDs.

However, what gave you the most pleasure was to be able to play such great football on such a surface!

This one was so outstanding for all the good things in our game. Tackles were going in all over the field, but never having any effect of the pace of the game. It was pinball stuff at its best. It really was a match which never let-up. When you see matches today, there are long pauses. This was a non-stop frenetic football at its very best. Again, Pulp Football!

I am gutted to this day that we have not got a video of this match because it had absolutely everything and, was one of those matches where neither team deserved to lose.

Although over the two-legs we were undoubtedly superior.

They threw everything at us, but we stood tall and firm with Dempsey and Webb magnificent in the heart of our defence. We looked like going in at half-time with that slender lead, but Coates got the ball, ran the line and, put in a cross which Martin Peters got a flick to. Running in behind him was the other Martin, the massive frame of Chivers. He tapped in an easy chance from close range. White Hart Lane opened up into song. It was a mixture of both sets of fans not going to be outdone, especially by such rival fans. That rivalry continues. It's now a toss-up between Leeds United and Spurs who Chelsea fans hated most. How both Ken Bates and Denis Wise could cross that great divide, I can never work out. Well, I can with Captain Birdseye, but Wise was such a bloody good player for Chelsea, I was surprised and disappointed in him for doing so. As Neil Diamond sang, Money Talks!

I could not for the life of me imagine pulling a Leeds shirt over my head and walking out of that Elland Road tunnel, not that they wanted me, for according to Revie they had the following: .

In that film Damned United, when Revie was interviewed with Clough, the former Leeds United manager accused the new one of disrupting all the great work that had been done. When Clough asked how he came to that conclusion, Revie said, "You have brought players in when we have world call players like Mick Bates here."

He was, of course talking about when Clough brought in John McGovern, who had captained both his Derby County and Nottingham Forest championship winning teams. Anyhow, Don Revie rated Mick Bates as "world class" something I only use when talking of Messi, Maradona, Pele, Johan Cruyff and George.

Now, this is the bloke who those at Lancaster Gate saw as an international manager.

How could he be?

He was rating a player who couldn't get into his club side as "world class" and, I think I must be boring you now with the times I have told you about those at the FA and, the managers they pull out of a hat and, isn't it about time that we had a rabbit, for we've had a turnip and a swede amongst other phonies.

I mean, how can they give Fabio Capello a two year extension on his contract before we got to South Africa for the last World Cup?

You give people extended contracts when they've shown they are capable of doing the job.

He had lost it before we boarded that aeroplane, yet still he got those two years, worth nearly £10million.

Well, at this moment in time, we were getting about £125-a-week and, the only difference was we earning every penny of it, yet the Italian walks away with a big fat cheque for, once again joining the queue of managers who have taken our national team back in time. For, the following match after he left this country Stuart Pearce, one of his backroom staff, made, Scott Parker, the next England captain. Can someone tell me why he wasn't on that plane to the World Cup, a few short months earlier?

After coming from behind against Leeds United three times in that '70 final and, bouncing back against Real Madrid, after the disappointment of being pegged back in the last minute by Madrid, we now had to come back and do it all over again against Spurs. We were now, once again, showing just incredible the character was in this team, or should I say this squad, although there was only about fifteen of us.

If only Dave could see it and give us the credit we deserved.

My mind also flashed back to Dave telling me to put six international caps on his desk before I asked for a raise and, I might have told you elsewhere, if that were the case, I would have been on £125-a-week for my entire playing days.

Just as well, he never told me that when I signed apprenticeship on a fiver week.

Unlike the strange feeling when we were last in this dressing room in a semi-final, we were buzzing, although slightly stunned. I knew this ground as well as the Bridge, or so it seemed. I loved it here as we were unbeaten and, knew we could go on and win here again. Some years later I played in an England match behind closed doors against a Spurs XI, which went a long way to getting me my first cap. It really was my favourite ground, though at that time Revie did not want to pick me. The only reason I was a part of his plans was that I was playing out of my skin for Stoke City.

And, Tony was forever banging the drum for me as I said earlier and, he would have told the world about Osgood, had he not reneged on a handshake with him, the day after I signed.

Anyhow, back to the action and, there was plenty as Garland scored a stunning goal - firing past Pat Jennings to make it even more stunning. Pat rarely got beat from such a distance. Cutting inside Cyril, Garland hit a fantastic left foot pile-driver into big Pat's left hand post. I was right behind it and, my eyes followed it every inch of the way. It was a goal good enough to win any match. This lifted us on to another plateau. We were playing the ball around beautifully when they scored through a freak piece of play.

Martin Chivers threw in a ball from the left side. It was on the side of this great ground where the clock sits at the top of that very steep stand. With the underfoot conditions treacherous, the ball skidded across it and, into my chest. "Handball" went right round the ground and, to my amazement, the referee responded to it.

He pointed to our penalty spot.

If the ground had opened, I'm sure a hand would have come out and dragged me into it.

And it would not have been the Hand of God!

It was harsh, very harsh, in fact a bad decision, but what is new with referees and, they've certainly got worse since our day. They have become like policemen. They are brash. They are arrogant. I saw a bus pull up outside Upton Park one Saturday afternoon and out jumped half-a-dozen official looking characters. I did recognise one, so I knew who they were. It was like watching a film where the minders jump out first, have a look about, before letting the President out. Who do they think they are?

I showed the man the mark on my chest, but he shrugged me aside. Up stepped Martin Peters, who coolly slotted it past Bonetti. We were all square once again and it was all down to me. Had I cost us another trip to Wembley?

As I mentioned earlier, in my first season, I swore at Jim Finney.

He simply told me exactly what he thought of me as well. That's how it's done!

When I heard they were going to bring out a ban for no swearing,

I thought, 'here we go again, are they serious, half the players in this country can't talk English.'

Anyhow I swear we were playing brilliantly and, as we did so often, we stormed back after the winner, coming down on their goal in droves. We were still playing swift inter-passing in such terrible conditions, my conditions. We were playing like the home team swarming all over them. Then in the very last seconds England brought down Osgood once again. It was so reminiscent of Charlton jumping all over him at Wembley which led to Hutch heading our late equaliser. I headed for the corner flag. Some supporters to this day still think it was a corner that I scored from. It was in fact a free-kick as close to the flag as possible without being one. I drilled it in hard and low, sending it through a forest of legs and, into the Tottenham net. If I said I meant it, it would have been the greatest goal of all time. But I would be a liar.

This was my ground now, as I watched it trickle into the back of the net. It went agonisingly through Cyril's legs.

Nice one Cyril went through my mind.

Agonisingly for poor old Cyril that is. Nice for us, that is. I then ran the entire length of the pitch right alongside the paddock where I used to sit on my dad's shoulders watching Greaves and Mackay.

I checked the Tottenham website out to see what they had to say and, this was how it read: League Cup heartbreak came in the last minute of this second-leg as Chelsea scored to go through to Wembley. Spurs had taken a 2-1 lead with goals from Chivers and Peters. Chelsea goals came through Chris Garland, but with the seconds ticking away a corner on the right was played in by Alan Hudson. It managed to skid by Cyril Knowles and into the Spurs net. Gate: 52,733.

As I said, everyone thought the free-kick I took was a corner. However, it was very close to the flag. It was that yard or so that gave me the angle to hit it through a sea of legs.

Thank God it skidded past Cyril. Nice One!

I often wonder just what extra-time might have brought?

We were at Wembley once again and oh, what a feeling. I could have danced on the ceiling, once again. Chris and I had our photograph sitting in the corner of the dressing room. We had got the goals that had taken us to the Twin Towers. It was a night that will stay forever in my head and, my heart, not just for my goal, or our victory, but because of the quality of our overall performance. I don't think I have seen a match in recent years so thrilling. It was a match where - although we were the better side - had they had come up with a late winner, instead of us, I would still be writing about it with such enthusiasm. Years later, I say that the Stoke City and Leeds match, where we stopped them breaking that record, was the best I've ever played in, but this was pushing it close. For sheer quality this match was second to no other I ever played in, but the importance and repercussions, had Leeds beaten us on that wonderful day at the Victoria Ground, would have been something I think about from time to time and think,' Oh my God…

This Spurs match was breath=taking and pulsating, whereas the Stoke/Leeds match was one where the result meant much more than the performance as the final whistle grew closer.

Venables may have been right, for The Spurs match was a truly special performance!

When you hear people speak today of the modern game, they start to compare and, talk about the pace of the game. It's a myth. This was at break-neck speed. What must not be forgotten is that these players were brought up in Chelsea, Windsor, Battersea, Bristol and Gateshead. Today I see local people all over players who, if they were not footballers playing for Chelsea, they would not give them the time of the day. I am just not one for hypocrisy. It is like in the United States where, although I love the country, they are so hypocritical.

They torch the blacks and yet a black boxing champion comes along and, he can eat at the White House (no pun intended).

They now honour the likes of Stevie Wonder (who now a special guest in the White House) and Ray Charles, no sorry, I can't have hypocrisy.

Either you do or you don't.

I have never been so happy, in political terms, than to see a black President. I was overwhelmed when Obama was elected because they have been treated absolutely shabbily over the years unless, of course, they were multi-talented. If it wasn't for the blacks the United States would not be half the country it is today, when you take into account the revenue the boxing, basketball, baseball, American Football and music brings in. I really would like to have had lunch with Obama and Stevie Wonder, within those walls and, break a bottle with them. Obama says if it wasn't for the genius of Blind Stevie his wife would not be by his side today. Wonder-full story - wonderful stuff! I remember when I first watched the TV show Roots my gut churned, my heart sank and, I prayed that one day something like this would happen. The Ku Klux Klan was so terribly brave, so much so they had to wear hoods.

I bet there are some licking Obama's boots now. How happy I am that the worm has turned and that the boot is on the other foot. And that is also getting licked. If it were not for the black man, the USA could never boast anywhere near half of what they have done over the years. Stevie Wonder has done more for that country than any one white man - except Frank, perhaps?

He has put more white men in work than any President. The only work the white man gave the black man was close to what Charriere had to go through.

Okay, I hear you say, "Shit happens."

But what if it were you?

Like FIFA and Sepp Blatter, Michel Platini, UEFA and the FA, they have power that abuses everything.

Like Platini when talking of the Champions League, saying he wanted Juventus in the Champions League.

Come on Michel, you're either taking the Michel, or you're not as smart without football kit on as you were with it?

After reaching Wembley again with Chelsea in 1972, there was only one place to celebrate and that was, of course, Alexandre, although I was shattered by the state of the pitch and, the drama that had taken its toll. Not forgetting emotions running sky high. We celebrated for what seemed like an eternity. Little did we know that the drama for the night was far from over, for when you put in a performance of such high quality, your adrenalin doesn't stop flowing at the final whistle, in fact, quite the opposite!

I get very high on a great performance. Give me a great performance, the best bourbon and a beautiful young woman and, my adrenalin level go through that ceiling I could have danced on.

The Chelsea fans once again were phenomenal. They, like me, loved winning there, I think more than any other ground. There is something about the Lane. There were over 52,000 fans inside the ground, but it sounded like twice that amount. We had now played in two semi-finals there in two years and won them both.

It was my ground and, our ground, a very special ground and, it had been a very special ground for me since watching their Double-winning team of the Sixties.

I was there (on my old man's shoulders) when they crushed Crewe Alexandre 13-2 in an FA Cup replay and, for many other fantastic games when they won that first Double for this country. It was as if every time I played there, Greaves and Mackay were on the pitch with me, or should I say against me?

As I told you earlier I played against Jimmy there, but never Dave, but I came eyeball to eyeball with him whilst he was at Derby County and, although he was past his best, he still had that incredible presence.

There are not many players over the years you meet later in life and think, 'blimey, he was something a bit special' and this was one.

When I was in his company with Tommy Docherty, the Doc was in awe, very similar to Matt Busby in the company of Tony Waddington.

That might sound bizarre, but I was there and, it's true, great people don't make mistakes. The stuff I told you about Bobby Moore, when Phil Collins - who loves his football - could not takes his eyes off of him and held on to every word was the same and, Phil's met greatness more times than Frank Sinatra's sang My Way, his least favourite song, allegedly.

Anyhow, back to Spurs, when a strange thing happened to me, whilst I was watching my nephew play at Crewe. I spoke of that match of fifteen goals and, someone told me that Crewe missed a sitter in the last minute of the first match which led to the replay.

It was actually scooped off the line at Gresty Road , which meant Spurs would have been out and there would have been no 13-2 in the history books and, that would have been one less dream. These were dreams because these Wednesday nights for me, were so very exciting and, a fantastic part of my wanting to be a player, especially with those players on show and, Greaves in particular.

Chelsea, for years to come, would make this a very lucky ground, much like Old Trafford when we won our first FA Cup. Manchester in general was good to us. In 2009/10, Chelsea won there in a match that decided the outcome of the championship. Although there were still several matches left, it was that match that knocked the stuffing out of the team chasing their fourth consecutive Premier League title. Some things, it seems, never change. In my first season I remember coming off the pitch there looking at Best, Law and Charlton thinking, "If I can make it here, I can make it anywhere," which some years later Frank sang about New York.

When I was first writing the original Ballet, a lot was being written about the cult of the LAD. Magazines were full of it and TV ransacked the Seventies for its shows. At that time Adam Faith was starring in the quintessential London Lad show - Budgie. Faith was a pal of Venables and Hollins. Richard O'Sullivan, who was in Man About the House, was once asked if he could be someone else who it would be. He answered "Alan Hudson."

I had a lot of time for Richard. We last had drinks in Terry Neill's Sports Bar in Holborn.

Rodney Bewes, another Alexandre party-goer, was a big Weller fan. Keith that was, not Paul. He was starring in The Likely Lads then, while my pal Dennis Waterman was in The Sweeney. That kind of metamorphosed into Minder. Michael Caine had already been in Alfie and, Patrick Mower was in Special Branch - these were all Chelsea-goers. I met Caine at David Frost's home one evening after a day at Royal Ascot with Alan Ball and, I liked him. Then when I approached him years later - in fact only about three years ago - I said hello in Langans and he rudely blanked me. Fuck him!

I liked Russell Harty, one of the first outstanding "camp" comedians and his performances against Elton was terrific, for he stood his ground as the verbal lashings flew across the kitchen.

I thought that Elton was going to put his tennis racket over his head at one stage.

But Elton showed there was another side to The Rocket Man.

Elton John was at the Frost home that night having a right old Gay Ding-Dong with Russell Harty. It was hilarious stuff. I spoke to Elton and said I would be at Wembley the following day to watch him and, he asked me what it was like playing there? I assured him that he would be okay, for Wembley was tailor-made for people as talented as him. The following day he followed The Eagles and The Beach Boys on stage and the first words out of his mouth were to wish me a Happy Birthday. The sad thing was that it was not captured on tape or video. He was magnificent, but he always is. Another Chelsea follower was Tom Courtenay, a man I thought to be a very special bloke, very unassuming and almost shy. He was, and still is, a brilliant actor. Today, although a Hammer, my mate is Ray Winstone, a giant of a man, as a human being that is, and he is as good an actor as anywhere in the world. Go out and purchase Love, Honour and Obey, because his Frank Sinatra impression is something to behold.

Another great regret was going into Elton's dressing room at Earl Court, after another magnificent performance. As I approached the tiny staircase which led to his dressing room - rather like the one we used at the Bridge, when they were building the stand that was responsible for to me and Osgood leaving.

I had the pleasure to have a quick kiss and cuddle with the lovely Shirley MacLaine. Thinking of it, I become breathless and, again, regrets, I've had a few....

But that does not make me one of the Rat Pack, unfortunately.

My great regret, looking back, is that I should have taken her in with me and on leaving invited her to Dinner. Franco's was only a minute walk!

She was standing there all alone to see Elton, when John Reid, his manager, called me in and, like missing Dusty this still rankles with me.

One common thread to all of these shows was the references to Chelsea. I cannot emphasise enough the showbiz connection. This is probably why Chelsea had such media attention over those years, even though trophies eluded them. They were such a part of the nation's consciousness. Programmes like Budgie were never understood up north.

He was seen as a fantastic figure, but in the capital you could actually bump into him everywhere you went, whereas there were several Budgies around the Worlds End, although around this time that wasn't the kind of bird I was interested in and then, of course, there was Goldie the Eagle.

Our shows were not understood in the USA either, whilst their comedies, like ours, are not understood here. I certainly understood and, loved them. Today they still stand out with Frasier becoming one, if not the greatest of them all. Kelsey Grammar lights the screen from his Seattle apartment, which overlooks the city I loved so much and, miss so terribly. I mention him being inspirational somewhere else in the book and, even weirder is that the great John Mahoney - my side-kick at Stoke City - played the part of his father in the show, his name is Marty Crane.

Neil Simon's writing of the hit comedy The Odd Couple with Jack Klugman and Tony Randall was nothing short of phenomenal, Frasier is on a par.

I think that these shows hit on the humorous part of a nation and, the writers are the pulse of such a thing. Take 'Only Fools and Horses' for instance. This is the perfect guide through London. If someone says, "He isn't streetwise," that means he hasn't seen Del Boy, Rodney, Uncle Albert, Trigger and Boysie in the Nags Head.

When I lived in Seattle the locals were intrigued by my attitude and, that was only because they had never seen a boy from the backstreets of Chelsea and, if they ever watch this programme today, I'm quite certain, their memory would flash back to our days together, especially my next door neighbours, the Barman's.

Del Boy was precious and, it was sad when the writer John Sullivan died last year!

As I said, I grew up surrounded by people like Budgie, some to be found in Scribes, the watering hole fronted by Venables years ago. I was with Stan Bowles recently and, we spoke of holding his book launch there. Stan remains a great character and, this country has never seen another player quite like the old QPR magician. Stan completely astounds me, as I have never known another player so disinterested in our game, especially one so fantastically gifted and talented. I suppose the saying "The Lord Giveth and the Lord Taketh Away" applied here, but still quite amazing.

Where Stan was brought up on the outskirts of Manchester, you know by now that I grew up down the Kings Road with the flash clothes, the fancy eating houses, boutiques and, beautiful sights of the new attire worn by those females that were always tantalising to me.

I just love things of beauty. The women, music, clothes, restaurants and beautiful people in general, for they will always be a part of my very own special package of life. Some people have photograph albums and, although I had them around the walls of me bar in Seattle, they were a part of the scene in that room. The blended into the music and, when I poured a drink I'd look around and, they'd jump out and stand at my bar with me.

I'd arrive home some early mornings, after a day out with my team-mates and, put on Frank and, pour myself my favourite Bourbon. I had been out all day long laughing, joking, telling stories and, enjoying my life amongst such a wonderful background of life and, I would sober up, as I thought back to where I started and where it had taken me.

It was those times when I missed Leslie and Tony more than anything else. It hurts even now, that we could not share this together and, whilst I lay paralysed in that hospital bed, I vowed that I would return and, I hope the sales of this book will help me reach my one last dream and then...

And then, there is the talent that goes with all of this. My fondest memories are all about places and people and, I have my father alone to thank for that and, I'm delighted to have shared a little of that with him.

When he first met Tony Waddington properly, in the Federation House restaurant, he shook his hand. Well, had it been a movie, there would have been sparks coming from that handshake. He never shook hands with people, for he trusted nobody he did not know and, although he'd never known Tony, he knew what he was doing for me was something that touched him greatly.

For me, it was much like Pele hugging Bobby Moore, where two worlds collided and fell to the ground in such an incredible way.

I turned to my mother and said, "Come on my mum, let's leave them alone," which didn't really matter to them, because they were in a trance.

My ambition and comfort with it grew out of being raised amidst the contrasts of a cosmopolitan life. That is why someone like Coates, stepping out of a community like Burnley, found Tottenham such a vortex.

They say that the brothers of Le Tissier were better prospects than the brilliant Saint?

That is pretty difficult to believe!

Matt once told me of his apprehension about joining a Bright Lights football club.

I'll always doubt his conviction, if not his ability, because he was, like Knowles, one of the greatest wasted talents in our times and, the reason I say "wasted" is because when you see people since, paying good money to see such mediocrity and, there's Matt playing in front of a sparse crowd somewhere down Hampshire way. To me, that is a total waste!

It is the same as I said about George. How could Sexton deprive all of those thousands upon thousands of football fans the right to watch something so incredible. He had no such right and, as I have pointed out, had it been Waddington, those fans would have seen George at Stamford Bridge more than once a season.

Chelsea would have had their very own Beatle, instead of Liverpool having five of them.

The Chelsea showbiz connection is still carried on today. My mate Suggs of Madness fame still hangs around the place, usually downing the odd pint in Finch's. Paul Weller, once of The Jam, is still seen around town in The Trafalgar or the Chelsea Potter. On the cover of his Stanley Road CD (painted by Peter Blake, the artist who constructed the cover of Sgt Pepper for the Beatles) Weller featured his hero Peter Osgood. When the artwork was completed the picture was scrapped because Blake had depicted Osgood in the red and white stripes of Southampton.

There were two famous Wellers going to the Bridge in the early 70's, one was a great signing from Millwall and the other a very talented musician - and a big Osgood fan.

I often see Eric Slow Hand Clapton walk the Kings Road with his baby in his pushchair and, automatically think of the tragedy of his other child. I sometime wanted to stop him and mention Phil (Collins) to him, but you sometimes never know what's on people's minds when out like that. It was devastating what happened to his young child and, it's remarkable how he has kept going with so much class.
I always try to remember what my physiotherapist, Claire Strickland, said to me, although I never needed telling, after my near fatal episode in the Mile End Road.
"Always keep your dignity, no matter what."
I see Robbie Williams there, or used to when he visited the AA, which stood in the grounds of the Worlds End where I once lived with my mother after my run-in with Fatehi. That led to another tragedy - me being evacuated by the council of Kensington and Chelsea because of it being a two-bedroom home. When I said my son was moving in with me to be 'my carer' they took me to court and, made a mockery of my disabilities. They won, of course, but who

wouldn't with such weight. Three black ladies very cleverly turned up with a white 'brief' and, I was thrown out to make way for more immigrants, those that fill the spaces of all our kids getting shot at and killed in Afghanistan. I wonder if those politicians have their sons and daughters lined up for such a future!

What's new?

I had no chance with Sexton, Ramsey and Revie, so what did I have with this lot?

There is lots of trouble in the news today 22.12.2011 over racism. Two cases, in fact, one being John Terry swearing at Anton Ferdinand, calling him whatever it is they call one another. Well, my case in the Worlds End was worse. Three black council workers walking into court with the look of the Devil on their faces was enough to tell me I could not win. But you had to applaud them, for they could have worn hoods. And they were smart, as they had a white lawyer. You don't have to use a four letter word to be racial. Has the whole system gone nuts?

The result I got thrown out onto the streets. I have never been offered a one bedroom flat by them. Had my father had been alive through both my car ordeal and this, I think quite a few people might have regretted their racial behaviour. In our prefab everyone was fed and, I mean everyone. Bill Boyce, Eric Bingham, two black lads from our part of the world. They were welcomed into our tiny prefab and, given the same warmth of our own family. Yet, here we have these council workers using their positions to nest their own. The country from Cameron, the gay Portillo, a man I went to see about my being evacuated - and a man who, handily for him, turned a blind eye. Like football, all the wrong people are in the important positions and, I don't mean on the playing fields, I mean the killing fields!

After our triumph at Tottenham, Osgood featured in a stormy fracas outside Alexandre, where he and Danny Gillen were taken away in a police wagon. That was the on-going drama I just told you about.

I find it quite interesting in many ways and, one is I wonder just what those coppers were doing whilst we were playing our part in entertaining nearly sixty thousand football lovers over the other side of London?

It will always be a case of pure jealousy. Instead of trying to lure Osgood into a fight they should have been shaking his hand, for what he had been doing for this area and, when there is trouble and, I mean real trouble on our streets, like the Tottenham Riots, I think of those policemen harassing Osgood and Danny Gillen and, think, 'there you go, get on with it,' and order another vodka and orange.

And they want help, I thought that is what they joined up for, to give our children and mothers and grandmothers protection and, now they want help.

Oh, and I'd like to have their pensions for pushing pens and, innocent people about.

I am living on the outskirts of Stoke-on-Trent and was told of how they messed up the Lesley Whittle case, but for the police, that poor girl would have been shopping in Tesco today. Instead she died horrifically down a shaft in the dead of night.

But back in Chelsea, after our stunning victory, we broke up our party at around 2.30am and, walking through the Kings Road, the Old Bill came down on us because we were still jubilant. They must have been called by a Yid who lived in on our manor, for we weren't doing anything wrong. I mean there was nobody but us in the street, so what was going on?

Anyhow, you know how the police can get with "flash footballers" and, all that, anyhow, Osgood loved being provoked and, confronted whether they were a centre-half, his manager or a copper. Danny, on the other hand was a cool customer, who if I were to gamble on this matter, I would have backed him to have wiped the floor with the lot of these men in blue with one hand tied behind his back. If only they had known just who they had picked on. There is not a human being in the police force that could stand toe-to-toe with my mate Danny. They could carry a baton, a gun and a knife and, that is what they'd end up with apart from a long stay in the Chelsea Westminster Hospital.

Danny would have need just a fair reason, no, not a fair reason, an unfair reason. He was a pussy cat, but if you stroked him the wrong way, he claw your eyes out and shove them up...

They are brave in numbers, whereas I have seen my mate take on three or four at a time and, come out not only unscathed but victorious.

And, unlike our players of today, never boasted about such trivial things, why should he, he never, ever began it.

I sometimes think what might have happened had Danny been any good up front and, also imagine him and Osgood against Charlton and Hunter. That really would have been something new for the two Leeds hard men.

Somehow, I don't think their shirts would have been white by the end of ninety minutes!

One night, after coming out the Fox and Pheasant, we were walking over the bridge near the Chelsea ground - he, Tony Frewin and me - when these four blokes on the other side of the road recognised me. The abuse began. One of them confronted Danny. Danny told me and Tony to walk away. We went upstairs to my uncle George who straight away headed for the front door. As he opened the door there was Dan.

Danny said, "Where you going George?" George said. "I'm coming to look for you."

He simply smiled and said, "It's all sorted mate don't worry, but thanks!"

The next day walking down the Fulham Road, I looked inside the gates of the college. I saw more claret than in the blood bank a hundred yards up the road in St Stephens Hospital - the Chelsea and Westminster now.

Anyhow, they came down on me, Chris Garland and the two lads just mentioned as if we were out to blow up the House of Commons. Given the chance!

I mean, seriously, when you look at all the troubles in the world, terrorism in particular and, then this situation and, you wonder why our country is in a mess. Plus, keeping our boys in Afghanistan in mind, we simply are useless at looking after our own. This is our country isn't it?

The police in Chelsea should have embraced us and said, "Well done this is great for the area, but instead, they were and, are the opposite.

Is it jealousy?

Of course it is, I have said that elsewhere and, I cannot think of any other reason.

Danny, my mate since the days running the Rising Sun - that pub I told you about opposite the gates of the Bridge - is now in Switzerland with Phil Collins and, this scene was like one of Phil's in Buster, when they arrested the train-robber, which saw Phil playing Buster Edwards. After returning from Spain, like us, he was surrounded by an army of police, squad cars and vans. About the only thing they did not send out of Scotland Yard was helicopters. We, like him, were treated shabbily. It was as if we were celebrating in White Hart Lane. We were in our domain, The Kings Road, the place where we had made so many people happy and proud of us. What did these people expect us to be doing after such a fantastic night?

Are their lives so shallow? Does the jealousy run so deep?

Or was this the beginning of those in the Kings Road not being from Chelsea?

I think that is the problem and, you walk down that street now and you'll be lucky to see a local. We are strangers, not only in our own country, but our very own back garden.

Oz took exception to this and a brief scuffle broke out. The night ended with the two boys spending the night in the comfort of Chelsea nick - something that the manager was not too pleased about. We really had done absolutely nothing wrong. We were still simply on a high, but this time not in the sky.

I can promise you one thing, as I just said, had any of these policeman wanted a one-on-one with Danny they would have had an even earlier retirement than they actually get and, of course, fully paid up, pension and all…

To this day, I just cannot see how and why this all came about and, when I watched the recent Tottenham Riots I laughed my head off. There was us going home happily after reaching Wembley and, were pounced on by the Old Bill. So, I got kick out of that. Call it payback time or as Betty says, "What goes around…

The newspapers wrote it as if Osgood had been doing some anti-Semitic chanting.

Today they would have made it into Schindler's List.

Later, Oz was found 'Not Guilty' of being Schindlers and Disorderly.

So now we were in another final, but this time against some Hicks from the Sticks managed by some bloke called Waddington. Little did I know that this would lead to my transfer to Stoke City and, that he would change my whole life in such an incredible way!

Even after my horrors of '97, I still feel so very fortunate. All things levelled out, that's how I feel about having come across and, played for this man. When I think what might have happened to my career had he not dragged me out of my Stamford Bridge misery, I think my retirement might have come a lot earlier. A little like George. As I said earlier, I prided myself on performance, like George again. When you look at the state of affairs at Manchester United, after what Busby did by winning the European Cup. The men in suits did not have a clue. They still had the very best footballer on the planet, yet brought managers in who could not "organise a piss up in a brewery." Yet, the only one who suffers is the genius.

Again, like I said at the Bridge, who do the supporters walk up to the turnstiles and, pay their money to be entertained. Not Brian Mears or Martin Edwards and, not Dave Sexton, but players like George, Bobby, Denis, Charlie and Ossie!

Around this time football was just beginning to change. The great managers were ageing and, the new ones were getting their coaching badges. Ouch!

They were as dangerous as driving licenses, that piece of paper that cost a fortune and means nothing and, if you did a survey in Coventry, Bradford or Wood Green, of who has and who hasn't a legitimate one, I think there'd be a Stewards Inquiry.

Only Ferguson today has kept the game in its right place. To follow a man like Busby, you have to reach a standard and, once reaching it maintain it. Only Ferguson, in modern day football, can boast such a thing. Look at the managers Chelsea, Manchester United, Manchester City, Tottenham, Newcastle United, Leeds United, West Ham and Arsenal have employed since those fantastic days of the Sixties.

At Stoke City, nobody could walk into Tony Waddington's office and turn on the lights.

They simply couldn't find the switch, let alone find a player, a team and, a way to play.

When you pass the Victoria Ground, where the fans hold so many incredible memories, there is rubble. A couple of years ago, I walked across this rubble and, I swear I could hear noises below my feet. It was eerie. Maybe it was my imagination, but whatever it was, there were noises below. I had to look down at my feet, for thinking a hand would appear and, pull me under. I shook. They were probably making those noises about the mess those above had made of it all. And, oh boy, some mess!

Talking of Stoke City is much like what I said about Chelsea and, of course, going back to 1966. They are now going through the best period for many a year with their robust style, the one that Arsene don't like playing against. Ah!

Well, those fans who, although are enjoying the fruits of the Premiership are being starved of real football and, they are close to being up-in-arms about it. Why?

Because the vast majority of them were brought up on Waddington and, the times when they could sit there on a Saturday afternoon and watch something so special in my life, magic!

The reason I bring this up, is because the laughter that success brings, blinds you and leads to tears, just you wait and see…

But this Stoke City side were not like today's, they didn't rely on dead-balls and throw-ins although that was how they got the opening goal, but in those days we were beginning to look a little suspect, even though we had beaten a very good Spurs team, but that was because of our exceptional attacking play.

So this was the last chance to rescue our season. We had been knocked out of two cups by two very inferior teams. Now we were strong favourites, but it was never going to be an easy match. We felt we were a better team than them, but after the Orient (an accident waiting to happen) and, the Swedes (the penalty was no accident) we were not confident of beating anybody.

Stoke had been terribly unlucky against Arsenal in two successive FA Cup semi-final replays, so it seemed to me that it just might be third time lucky.

And, putting it like that, it might have been quite the opposite for us, just maybe…

We'd won two major trophies in the last two seasons and, now we were on course to make it a treble, though I only drink doubles!

25 WHERE DID IT ALL GO WRONG?

The chalk marks that were drawn around us were already getting blurred by the rain.
It was '72 and Bowie was singing about The Man Who Sold the World (Ken Bates). Hurricane Higgins won the World Championship and £480.
The future looked so bright we should have worn ray-bans.
Well, that brightness could so easily turn into darkness and, although we were still all quietly confident, how could we not be, the candle was flickering!

That candle reminds me of Elton and, the night I saw him at Wembley and, now that was where we were heading against a team who with, I was to find my niche, but that was eighteen months and many, many humps and bumps along the way. The only surprise was that there were none on the faces of either Sexton or Osgood, for they never got their seemingly, desired bout behind the North Stand.

As I said, we were already through to Wembley, but we also had our eyes on the FA Cup again and, wanted more European glory. Blackpool and Bolton (our whipping boys that season, just as Palace had been before) had already been dismissed. We were drawn away to Orient in the fifth round. It looked easy, too easy, but so did Atvidaberg of Sweden in the second-leg of the Cup Winners Cup. If we had a problem, I really do think that a couple of our players might have been, for the want of a better saying, 'a little over the top.'

They had been great, but there were too many unforced errors creeping into their game. And this, what I am about to tell you, was as good an example as I can give and, I am not a coach or manager, where did it all go wrong?

The Orient tie would be the first time I would see my mate Ray Goddard since winning the National Federation of Boys Club trophy at Craven Cottage in '63. I was 12 then and, he was 14. That was the first time I had played at the Cottage and, the second and last time was in a reserve team match for Chelsea on my return there.

However, I played much better as a 12-year-old, when I played for Bill, my dad.

Winning the NABC trophy was the biggest trophy I'd win before the FA Cup, although I didn't make those finals. I like to think of the first one more, if only for Johnny Haynes presenting us with the silverware. In those days John was one of the finest inside-forwards in the world. I was seen looking up at him, as if in awe, but he was as usual in total control and, in those days I wasn't aware of the word "awe" and it didn't happen to me too many times in my life, even though I'd met some pretty fantastic people.

But the people that I respected more than anybody else were those in the Royal London Hospital.

Outside of playing brilliantly, I was told John was dating Petula Clarke at the time. I was a great fan of both of them. Pet - if I can call her that - lived just off the Kings Road where my mother once worked in a restaurant. This is where I got my information from, at such an early age.

Today, that would have been far bigger than David and Posh, Peter and Abbey and Wayne and Colleen. I won't mention John Terry for respecting him too much as a player.

John (Haynes) not only had class on the field, but off it also, for. Petula was as the Americans might say and, the song went, "A Living Doll."

This was around the time she recorded Downtown and, the time also, that John played one of his greatest matches, where he scored a hat-trick, in a 9-3 win over Scotland at Wembley.

I envied Ray - if only for being at Fulham with John - he was a smashing lad and, a good keeper, but never thought that our paths would cross again, especially not in a FA Cup tie. He left Fulham for Orient not long before this match and, after the save he made from me - that possibly changed the game - I wished he had stayed there.

Oh, how I wanted to play for Fulham and, more than anything and, pull Haynes white No 10 shirt over my head, both for Fulham and for England.

I remember looking at the photograph some years later and, there was me, a tiny creature looking up at the great Haynes like something I can't explain.

If only I had known then what I know now?

I would have asked him to take me under his wing, just like Bobby Moore did and, take me to Fulham with him. Just imagine a forward line of Hudson, Haynes, Hutchinson, MacDonald and Barrett, the mind boggles!

Had Les Barrett been at a big club, he would have been remembered and mentioned today. He had electrifying speed, but unlike most of today's players, when he used it, he took the ball with him.

I saw him one day selling flowers over Earlsfield way - that is around the corner from my old home in Southfields - and he was totally astonished to know that I recognised him. I embarrassed him by telling him I was a big fan, which I was very sincere about. But that again, tells you about the great players of yesteryear. Today, we have such average player's - who are earning fortunes - in our newspapers for what they do off the field more than off of it, and, the likes of Les selling flowers.

Joey Barton, after getting a 12 match bam for fighting on the field, was at it again yesterday 7.6.2012 only it was off the field, a different kind of killing field than mine.

Whilst watching the likes of Les and, wanting to play in the same team was a dream. My dream, which came true, though not at Fulham, had of course to be combined with a total nightmare. Again, Betty Shine believes that everything levels itself out. I don't agree.

Ask Papillon, Anthony Mason and, of course, myself after the Mile End Road. Nothing levels itself out. I know some people who have never caught a cold. I loved Betty Shine and, was hoping to see more of her and, also wanting to talk about this further, but she sadly died and, although I know she'll be doing her work somewhere else right now, I felt that after me calling out to her whilst in my coma, we had some unfinished business.

It was sad to hear not long ago that Ray Goddard had also passed away!

In the League, our form was improving; like M People sang, we were, Moving On Up. We beat Manchester United at Old Trafford, a ground that was becoming as lucky as Three Point Lane. Oz scored the only goal of the game after we tricked United with a one-two from a quick David Webb free-kick. United threw everything at us in the closing stages but we held out comfortably, as we always did at the Theatre of Dreams. We had knocked them off top spot. George was still taking terrible flak from the media, but it was all water off a duck's back for the Irish genius.

He was with yet another Miss World, this time Marjorie Wallace. I recall a lot of fuss and, scandal about a certain fur coat, but George cleared it all up with us afterwards in his club.

I told you I loved playing against George, but another reason was that he raised the bar and brought out the best in you. He also ran a great bar where his stories had our boys in fits of laughter. Some people are glued to Coronation Street and Eastenders and, there was us getting the real story and, a realistic one from, not only the great bird puller but entertainer in world football.

Now, do you see just how special our lives were and, these were our perks, unlike today, where they get a million here and a million there, however, if it weren't for the money, they'd be so much poorer than us, for where was there George Best?

We blitzed Everton 4-0 at the Bridge with Osgood hitting two. One was a screamer on the run from a John Hollins through-ball, similar to the classic he scored at QPR in that FA Cup tie. Without the real ball, Alan, who by now was playing brilliantly for Arsenal, it meant Everton lacked the driving force that he once gave them. They would become like Chelsea without me and Osgood.

They say that one man doesn't make a team and, in theory they're right, but I sometimes wonder...

A team without his presence and wonderful ability to play the game was obviously going to be weaker than before. He made them tick and, if you can imagine a clock without a second hand. That was what Everton had become without the little redhead and, as I said, the same applied at Chelsea without Oz and me. I still cannot believe Dave could not see it. Football is all about trying to assemble the best team around and, you can't do that by letting your best player's leave, especially if you cannot replace them. But even in those days the money seemed to be the most important motive for such dealings, although Dave was having a hard time trying to control the uncontrollable, for that is the way he saw it.

We were still cruising along in mid-table but looked to be running into peak form at the right time, especially with the big cup matches approaching.

I truly thought that we could and would win all three cups.

After all, we could not have asked for the draws to be kinder, Brighton, Ipswich and Sheffield Wednesday in the FA Cup, the unknown Atvidaberg in Europe and Stoke City in the final, at Wembley. After beating Leeds United and Real Madrid in the two previous finals and, a really decent Spurs side in the semi-final, you had to fancy the treble was on the cards?

Stoke City were a good side, but George Eastham, although a brilliant player was nearly as old as my father and, Peter Dobing weren't far behind him. Looking at the two teams, you'd have to fancy us.

George was only a couple of years off of being twice my age.

In the semi-final at White Hart Lane they had four top key players in vital positions. In goal Jennings was on a par with Banks - you could toss a coin - rather than argue about who was best. Mike England - a team-mate of mine in Seattle - was as good a centre-half as any in the business. Martin Peters was still a top notch midfield player and, Martin Chivers was second only to Osgood as their main striker.

And we had beaten them in brilliant fashion over two legs.

Stoke City's strength, which I found over my years there, were the players who were totally under-rated and overlooked. I have no need to tell you about Greenhoff.

Alan Bloor was magnificent and, a fit Terry Conroy was a handful for anyone and, poor old David Webb who was still having living nightmares about this last visit to Wembley, was out on that same patch again and, facing the twinkle-toed, cheeky Irishman.

What was Dave thinking?

It was like taking a beautiful girl out on a first date and, after it all going wrong, the last thing you'd do, if given another chance, is take her back to the same place.

Well, that is what Dave did, only this was the same place, only a different opponent, but one just as deadly. Is management that difficult?

I mean, if I could see this…

And then, later on, I was to find out about Alan Dodd and Steve Bould, both local talents who, had they have come through the London youth systems, who knows?

At around this time we cut a record that is still played at the Bridge. Blue is the Colour had all the period trappings, but still remains one of the most successful football records ever recorded. One of the few you could listen to without cringing. It got to No 5 in the charts and, was still rising as the League Cup final arrived. If we had won that final against Stoke City, it would surely have reached the number one spot.

Stoke City also cut one, written and produced by Tony Hatch and Jackie Trent - quite an appropriate name - called "We'll Be with You," which got nowhere. So, at least we could say we were better in that department.

I said that Osgood was not only a superior player to Jeff Astle but a better singer and, I'm certain he was also a better singer than this lot and, the only big regret was that he did not get to show the people of the Potteries just how good he was as a player, on a regular basis.

I think that Tony Hatch composed the Crossroads theme song?

And here we were at the crossroads, in football terms.

We were bound to be more forward in the recording business, because on the way to the studio, we crossed paths with The Bee Gees. We walked down Waldorf Street as one of my all-time favourite artists came from the other direction. All these years later their song

Staying Alive stands out for me, if only because that is something I did against all the odds, which is where Phil Collins might come in?

I still can't believe they play Blue is the Colour constantly and, yet we never got a penny for it, not even a ticket, bring back Bates. I cannot believe I said that?

To this day, I don't know if the club have the rights to such a song. I do know that a bloke named Larry Page was responsible for bringing it out, through his company Penny Farthing. Again George springs to mind for that was the name of one of his night clubs.

Getting nothing was nothing new though.

Signing for Chelsea as an apprentice - nothing!

Professional - nothing!

Transfer - nothing!

Number five record - nothing!

Testimonial - nothing!

And, that is why and what Chelsea mean to me – nothing!

The Bee Gees had just been in the studio, but unlike us what they had recorded never got in the charts. We couldn't beat the Swedes, but we could get higher in the charts than one of the greatest pop groups in the history of music, not Abba, but The Bee Gees.

With all else gone and only the League Cup to play for, I suppose you could say that we were also, Staying Alive, but not for long, although it was more like hanging on to what we got, which was obviously a Frankie Valli song, one called Let's Hang On, and, that was how it was becoming. We were once a team who fought back against the might of Leeds at the peak of their powers and, now we were hanging on against teams, we used to beat in a heartbeat.

QUITE SOMETHING

I warned you at the beginning about my love for all of the best things in life and, music is one of such great importance to me.

Our prefab was always filled with Sinatra and The Beatles, two very different types of music, but the best of both and, who would have thought back then that The Voice would not only record, but say on stage that George Harrison's love song, Something (in the way she moves), was the best ever written?

I remember whilst playing for Stoke City they showed me in motion, on Central TV, to Shirley Bassey singing this wonderful ballad, only she sang, Something in the way he moves, affects me like no other lover, something in the way he woos me, I don't want to leave him now, don't want to leave and how…

The only difference was Maureen didn't see it that way, but I suppose I had a new life in Stoke-on-Trent as meeting Waddington brought a whole new meaning to playing the game. Whereas at Chelsea, I played for my dad, my mum, my uncle George and my team-mates, but now I had added the man who like David Goodier not only saved my legs, but my life.

And then, there was, of course myself, because if you don't satisfy yourself, then you can't satisfy anyone else and, like all of those wonderful players that I have already mentioned, my standards were very high.

To be quite honest, very honest, or perfectly honest, I am privileged to put my name amongst them. It really has been the greatest honour in my life. When I see these people collecting OBEs and MBEs, I'm afraid that would mean nothing to me, as I look at those I Afghanistan and - thinking of my sons – those pieces of gold or silver, whatever they are worthless.

I'll stick with John Lennon and, I'd be happy to sit in a bar with him and say, well, "we did it John, we sent them back, after all what really do they really mean?"

I'm sure JL would have written and sang a song about the following.

My time meeting those young lads when they came back from the frontline taught me a lot, already I already knew enough, but it shook me to the roots and, when I see the way they're treated I know that I am right and, again, as young Marcus Kipling wrote to Cameron, "I am writing this letter because I am angry about the wages of a soldier. I think that soldiers that go to war should get more money in their wages. They risk their lives for their country. And, I get cross when I read of how much both footballers and politicians get paid, do they risk their lives for the country?"

That was an 8-year-old son of Tony, of the Yorkshire Regiment, who also questioned the equipment his dad had to take the fight to the enemy wearing. He also insisted a replay by saying, "If you were a good PM you would reply to my letter, as I deserved an answer, sincerely Marcus Kipling."

Well, when I was eight I wasn't even writing for trials, let alone writing to the PM. Mind you, my dad was out Asphalting whilst I was playing outside our prefab, working on my passing , dribbling and game in general, knowing that my dad would be home safe and, with that in mind, I say well done to you, young Marcus, you are an absolute credit to both your mother and father and, I also pray nothing happens to you dad, well I do, I hope your letter works and, he gets more money, which he won't, of course!

The video age was not quite with us yet and, only one photograph remains showing me in a white polo neck jumper with a cardigan on top of it, courtesy of Cecil Gee. My hair was still long, so going into the studio I at least looked the part.

The Bee Gees also wore their hair long and, it wasn't until a little later that I regretted not pulling them up and, introducing ourselves.

Had I done so, you can bet your life Osgood would have been all over Barry Gibb and, challenging him to a night on the karaoke in Windsor, or Epsom, where he now lived at that time.

His neighbour Willie Carson, a jockey I can't stand, if only for the way he rode My Lifetime Lady at Chepstow, The Lady came back as if she had just been marking Hutch for ninety minutes in the forecourt, Carson strangled her and, I could have strangled him but I couldn't reach and, my back was killing me.

Can you imagine Oz going out with Carson, they'd bring a new meaning to Little and Large and, Oz would no doubt have been giving it just that the following morning.

They would have never, however, have been The Righteous Brothers, because with Wee Willie there is definitely, no loving feeling between him and I.

Osgood had as much confidence with a microphone in his hand as he did with a ball at his feet.

I was beginning to make friends in the pop world, my first being Frank Allen of the Searchers. He was the George of pop, a great-looking bloke who, I often had to disappoint the girls about by telling them he was gay. He was, of course, although I would have told them that anyway. He was so good looking that I made sure I was never seen standing next to him. Frank would pull up outside the prefab in his open top E-Type Jaguar and, we'd cruise The Kings Road. We'd drop into the Bird's Nest before heading to The La Chasse Club where Keith Moon and Long John Baldry amongst others would be hanging out.

Moon, the drummer of The Who was a case!

He drove cars into swimming pools, threw televisions out of hotel windows and, legend has it that he could out-drink Ollie Reed, whilst leaving a trail of devastation and destruction behind him.

It sounds as if he would have fitted nicely into our squad of players.

Some years later, he bought a home a few doors along from another of my heroes, the legendary Steve McQueen, where he finally met his match and more.

Any trouble from Moon and the Hollywood legend would shoot his lights out - literally, for if Moon started any of his antics, Steve would get his rifle out and shoot out his spotlights overlooking his driveway. I simply adored McQueen and, if you an ardent reader, you must buy his book named simply McQUEEN.

However, I found him charming, but then I would as he was my kind of man - crazy, nuts crazy!

Driving a Rolls Royce into a pool was repeated by Jim Morrison of The Doors. Morrison was a dark, moody maniac under the influence of drink and drugs, but nevertheless a superstar with a massive following. His band had a very big hit with Light My Fire, later covered by Jose Feliciano. I only saw one door on the day of recording our song and, that was the one that Oz showed me after being a little worse for wear following an all-night 'wetting the head session' of my first son Allen.

If that's what it's called, wetting your child's head, then he is lucky to be alive and, as I write he has just had the first child of his own, along with his girlfriend Jo. Stevie-Marie came into the world at 5.3lbs on 9 May 2009, although she is Nancy to me and, always will be

It's amazing - though I'd never looked at it in this way - that's two and half times the bag of sugar my mother once bought into our prefab.

But that, sugar, was the last thing that I wanted at this time, because with my dodgy ankle, which made it very difficult for me to train properly I was having trouble with my weight - and, then there was the boozing sessions.

But these sessions were becoming a little less wonderful, as I was becoming a little moody because of my injury and, my marriage was going off the rails, which was something that seemed inevitable, looking back in hindsight and, was something that was always going to happen.

Whilst on Wembley, in her first year by arriving in Stoke at a special 1st birthday party for both her and, the FA Cup final, this little grown-up bag of sweetness was far sweeter than what was to follow against Manchester City. It took City over a hundred years to reach their first FA Cup final, whilst on 14 May 2010 it had taken Nancy just the one.

Also, like Nancy, it only took me a year, although I was fast approaching my 19th birthday. The reason I go on about FA Cup finals and, take up a lot of the first part of this book with our glorious achievement by winning one is, because as kids it was all of our dreams. To have achieved this in my first season was incredible, even though I missed both the final and replay. As I have said, it was absolutely incredible George never reached such a goal, whilst there are so many mediocre and inferior - weren't we all, players who have. However, that's cup football and, I love it. That is not a knock at inferior players, for it is just amazing my mate never made it there and, even unluckier, there was the World Cup finals.

In and around the times I played, the FA Cup was shared around much more, whereas today, it is mainly the top four.

Since Wimbledon beat Liverpool in 1988, only Portsmouth have lifted it outside of Manchester United, Liverpool and Chelsea (five times each) Arsenal (four times) Everton (twice) Tottenham and Manchester City.

Whereas in the year I was born, Newcastle won it and, then did so again twice afterwards, followed by WBA, Villa, Bolton, Forest, Wolves, WHU, Sunderland, Southampton (with Osgood a winner), Ipswich (with me a loser) and Coventry City.

So, you see where the game has gone and although it is true that "money rules" it takes so much away from the best domestic cup competition in the world, because all the fun of the fair (cup) has diminished, because all of that fun comes from the Giant Killings that dreams are made of.

Only a couple of years ago, Crawley Town went to the Theatre of Dreams and, nearly caused them their greatest living nightmare by hitting the bar in the final minute, which had it gone in, would have been no more than they deserved, for they were the better side.

It even had Sir Alex stop chewing!

And had that have happened, Crawley winning, it would have been the best thing ever to have happened in today's game, for it would have given all others hope and, that - as I could have told you from my hospital bed - is what life is all about.

If that would have been the best thing to have happened, the worst was when Manchester United was allowed to pull out to help a World Cup bid, a bid that was never on. That was absolutely out of order, belittling the greatest domestic cup competition going. I think that showed that money and money alone, had finally taken over our game.

It simply told us that dreaming was for those who have empty pockets.

However, going back to my new grand-daughter Nancy, I wrestled Jo to call her that name, 'The One with the Laughing Face,' the first wife and daughter of Francis Albert. To compromise, she is now Steve-Marie Nancy and, will be one of the most confused children ever when I'm around. It has begun already, for as she is passed over to me as Stevie-Marie, once in my arms she becomes my Nancy!

I think she knows though, for when inside Jo's belly, my son Allen, then 38 - he was obviously 8 when I first started writing the original Ballet - would place his mobile phone close to her and, play this most wonderful of songs.

Whilst talking of finals and, Stoke City the League Cup final was coming up. And although it did not seem to register until it was far too late, teams were now giving us more and more trouble than before. As I mentioned just now, was it that our defenders were getting a little too old together?

Or was it that Dave was not picking his best team?

I will mention that later, although I will mention right now, that after the roasting that Dave Webb got from Eddie Gray at Wembley in '70, Dave chose to play him there again.

This time in this final and, it was Terry Conroy of Stoke City that did the damage on his side of the field. Terry skipped past DJ for the winning goal to leave our right-back on his backside.

This was nowhere near the first time I had seen this happen.

Not long before that I remember George Armstrong giving Webb a right roasting, only this time at the Bridge. Now the reason I mention things like this, is because players get slaughtered by managers for their off-field behaviour - well, we did - yet they cannot see the obvious at a professional level.

Here's a great pose of one of the loveliest lads I have ever come across and, our time in Australia was memorable, as Supermac and I were sent home and George went to see the manager insisting he joined us. He was an incredible competitor and bloke, still so sadly missed.

I was in hospital when the sad news of his death got to me and I was devastated.

Dave was not a good full-back; he was a good centre-half, because in the middle you can afford to dive in a little more with other defenders there to pick up the pieces if you fail, but not down the touch lines on those wide open spaces at Wembley.

It would be like playing Bobby Moore right-back, he'd get slaughtered!

The theory about Chelsea losing matches they should have won in a canter and, snatching them when all seemed lost, was open to further discussion. Experts would say that the more Chelsea had the ball, the less they would do with it. But I don't buy that.

Possibly, just possibly, an element of predictability was now creeping into our game and, predictability comes with time. It's only like listening to a singer sing so many times and, you end up knowing them off by heart and, football is absolutely no different. Why do you think coaches and managers watch videos of the opposition?

Well, Stoke City's manager was nothing if not cute and, I say that almost apologising to his memory. He was, in fact, light years in front of all I had come across. Having said that, I can almost assure you that he never watched a video of our opponents, for his "magic" was that he concentrated on his team and, how they played and, that was his "key" to unlock the door, of their defences, if you like.

However, back to us and, it was becoming more evident that the loss of Hutch was hurting us more and more, especially against these lesser teams who hustled and bustled. We missed his incredible appetite for such battles. He had been through the Southern League, so he was a dab hand at giving out and, taking a pasting and, he took that as a compliment. But you would not want to have taken a compliment from him in this way, for he was like an over hungry boxer, who wasn't happy until his opponent was down and out on the canvas and, I'd seen quite a few. .

He thrived on such things. Up front we were unsettled, Smethurst had left for Millwall and, Tommy was in and out of the side, whilst Chris Garland was still adjusting to our way of playing. Having said that, Chris was having a brilliant run and improving with every outing, but we were still lacking that something special. He was our best player for several weeks. That wonderful goal against Spurs gave him that much-needed confidence.

I visited Bootle just recently (August 2011) and, did a show for my mate Matty, who is a big Everton fan. His mate was there and, I was delighted to meet him at last. I had heard so many great tales about him and, of course, he was a wonderful player. He would have been in the 1966 World Cup final had he not been locked up for throwing a match. That was Tony Kay - who was innocent - but had he been involved he might have had the keys thrown away.

He told me that whilst in court he explained, "How on earth could I have thrown the match, I got 9 out of 10 in one newspaper and, was Man of the Match in another."

This was not good for the future. Had Kaye been kept out of that prison, I have no doubt I would have one day have known him very well, for he was right down Waddington's street. He had all the qualifications of a player wanted at the Victoria Ground. That great ability to play the game and to go with vast experience - something Tony loved - he had an exceptional presence. Like George Eastham, they didn't need telling (coaching) how to play the game, unlike Mick Bates at Leeds United, Tony bought players who could already play the game. You might say, it made his life easier.

I knew that Tony Waddington was a very astute manager and, would have been rubbing his hands together at the thought of playing us at Wembley. I had seen his team at the Bridge at a very early age and, knew that they were a team on the up and, one that wanted to play the game properly. The one player who impressed me most in those early days was Alan Bloor, a big strong centre-back who came forward with surging runs, on my kind of pitches, those heavy ones. I first saw him in a League Cup tie at the Bridge one Wednesday night and thought immediately, 'Who's this bloke?'

What was it with Chelsea and Stoke City in League Cup ties and Chelsea and Leeds United in FA Cup ones?

On reaching them, I found this to be true, Bloor was everything and more, although his legs were getting weary, through the wear and tear of a players life in those days and, he was a big lad, powerfully built, with incredible upper body strength, however, on the ball he had a great touch. As I said many times, like Alan Dodd and Steve Bould, he was a tremendous player, one immensely under-rated!

NICK HANCOCK

Staying on Stoke City I am fortunate enough to have made a very special friendship with one of their most staunchest, of supporters, Nick Hancock of, They Think It's All Over fame and here is what he had to say about yours truly:

There have of course, been many great players down the years but for sheer skill, consistency and influence Hudson is my number One.

Eastham and Dobing shared his lightness of touch, Chamberlain and Conroy exhilarated, Greenhoff and Crooks scored thumping goals, but it was Hudson, always Hudson that conducted the orchestra.

Once at a game when we were top of the league Keith Humphreys, who was to become a senior figure at the club, said 'We're in danger of becoming a one man team here', and I knew just what he meant.

We had a team full of wonderful players, but it always felt like Alan was pulling the strings; He'd pick the ball from the keeper and edge his way forward, lending the ball to player after player and then receiving it back, often with arms outstretched to indicate where the ball or player should go next. It was wonderful to watch!

In some ways he ruined the game for me because for years I couldn't understand why the players who succeeded him faced with a packed defence, didn't just slip the ball between three opponents and, into the path of a player' making a previously unseen run. Eventually I realised that they just hadn't the gift, great players as many of them were, they had to me, one fatal flaw and, that was that they weren't Hudson!

This was why Alan Hudson was, to the fans, The Messiah - he had come to lead us to the Holly Land, and he very nearly did.

Like all good Messiahs should, Alan came back and, enjoyed his second spell almost as much as his first, with Alan, arm aloft as always, turning a ragtag team into a crisp unit that miraculously avoided relegation.

My favourite moment of that season was of Alan launching a long ball into a channel for Ian Painter to chase. The ball seemed to be going long and, Ian and his defender turned back; Alan stood indignant, rotating his head to indicate that the ball had backspin, it hit the ground and stopped virtually dead, it sat and for a few moments there was an unholy and, then an undignified dash for it by Ian, his marker and the keeper. It was cleared but what joy .what class!

I asked Nick to put s few words together for my book The Waddington Years and this is what he kindly wrote:

This book, it seems to me, is a hymn to a lost age. Not an age when the game was different, although that is not true, nor when the players and their lives were different, though that is true also.

It is a tribute to a time when football still had room for people instead personalities, when managers could speak to players without their agents present and when fans felt personal connection with their heroes.

I am sure there are still many great friendships forged in the game but the story of Alan Hudson and Tony Waddington is the story of such an unlikely fruitful and indeed tender bond that changing face of the world and football condemn it's like to history.

For those of us who stood behind the goal and watched the fruits of that friendship, I can only say Thank You for a beautiful, romantic dream that so nearly came true.

Nick Hancock Stoke-on-Trent March 2008.

If I was to tell you that Nick was one of the loveliest chaps you'll ever be likely to meet, then it might be something that I have completely spot on, he is just a complete one-off. He is on a par of Tony Banks, Allan Phillips and Matthew Harding, three football lovers who share the game and, the time with you, but the only difference is that it is sheer quality, as they are or, in Allan, Tony and Matthew's case, were – although they'll be looking down on us as I write.

The first time I came across him (Nick) was in Rome and, I was standing with Stan Bowles outside the stadium - on the night England needed a draw to qualify for the World Cup - and we watched in horror as about two hundred England fans came tearing past us. One had a red and white striped top on. It was Nick and, he just stopped instantly, looked me in the eye and, knelt down and kissed my feet. Well, as near as hell!

In the years that followed, Chelsea went from a superpower to a dreadful second division team better known for its hooligans than its football. The whole place became a rancid meat pie crawling with maggots. Then there was the Boardroom. The collapse of the club began when Sandberg hit that goal past us and, continued in east London.

If the Swedish match was the first nail in the coffin, what was to follow at Wembley was probably the last.

Perhaps we had been living dangerously, but to us it was the only way we knew, the only difference was now we were living dangerously in the wrong penalty box. Leeds at Wembley and Old Trafford, Real Madrid in Athens (twice) and of course, those two wonderful semis against our fierce rivals over in north London, not forgetting two amazing clashes with Bruges. Was it all drying up?

Was it coming to an end?

Frank springs to mind once again, but the only difference that was a song, whereas this was reality, however whatever way you looked at it, the end was near and, so I faced the final curtain, well not just me, but you know who...

There was an art to living dangerously. George Best did it, as did Steve McQueen. So did Papillion more than anybody and, then of course there was my good friend Tommy Wisbey - my Great-Train-Robber friend. It doesn't get much more dangerous than that, although Tommy got out of it far better than Steve, I think those solitary confinements finally took their toll.

I won't go into the details of the great man's death, because like several things inside this book, there are still a few discrepancies.

I mention Tommy so much because I have met several very special people in my life and, he is certainly amongst them. He did a lot of 'porridge' for something that he admits was a mistake in his life, yet you get these paedophiles walking the streets and, allowed to harm our children and grandchildren. This country has a lot to answer for!

And then there's those cheating bastards in Fleet Street, those hypocritical ones that write about us, then do the same, yet go home to their wives and put their feet up.

The talismanic quality of people like Hutchinson had gone. Nietzsche (I don't know who he played for) said that if you only live one life, it might as well be extraordinary and, that was my friend Ian Hutchinson and Osgood's best mate.

Well, there is absolutely no doubt that this was the most extraordinary period of my life, right up until 15 December '97, or more like waking in '98!

Webby, it could be said, was more worried about things going on at the other end of the pitch and, his becoming a stockbroker. Maybe it was that winner at Old Trafford that had gone to his goal-scoring head. That might be harsh, but I am searching for the right answers here.

The old drinking stories were now rife. Well, it is the easy way out. We were drinking whilst beating everything and anybody that came our way, but all of a sudden…

We were cocky like Docherty's team, but we never let vanity or our social programme get in front of success on the field. Even when we were out and about we always talked about the things that were going on around us. We loved winning things. Vanity is all about standing in front of the mirror - Rodney Marsh-like.

We were not guilty of anything like that, we wouldn't allow one another.

Yeah, we were guilty of enjoying the good times; guilty of being in the company of our showbiz friends and, beautiful women.

All I can say is put yourselves in our place.

You would be daft not to want all of these things at that particular time, for after all it was the Swinging Sixties bursting into the not-so Swinging Seventies for heaven's sake. The world was bursting at the seams. It was more difficult for me than anyone else because I lived in the middle of such a world. I always told youngsters I played with, work hard in training, give the game everything, but for God's sake, don't let your teenager years pass you by. You're only young once, so enjoy yourselves. Waddington insisted you enjoyed life. Nobody was more professional and, loved the game more, but once the whistle blew his defenders became animals and, his inside forward (artists) began prodding and probing, trying to find a way through such defences and, in those days they were tough, real tough.

At Chelsea our back four prided themselves on being able to mix it with the best and, I am not saying they were tougher, for when I get to Stoke City they were on a par. However, the most outstanding young player was Alan Dodd. I tried to take Alan under my wing a little, by trying to bring him out of his shell a little, but as they say in the States, "No Cigar!"

Not so long ago I went into a bar where he was trying to relive his youth.

My Indian friend and I watched him as he failed miserably.

On returning, he turned to me and said, "I should have listened to you years ago'
I think it's too late for me now."

We never had that problem at Chelsea, where we were sometimes accused of being poseurs, but that could never be further from the truth. We were simply a bunch of young men going about our daily life the best way we saw fit. After all, you didn't do what we did against Leeds and Real in 12 months and, all of a sudden become a load of wasters. We were also never fakes. Never!

People could never really figure me out.

Was I very complex?

Whether I was uncomplicated or complicated?

That seemed to be mainly those people on the top floor (those that are always behind all the trouble) and, as the saying goes, "The trouble begins at the top!"

A place we were no longer at.

I do get the hump about it all, especially as they were the ones responsible for the mess we were getting into. Had these people had half the talent in running that club as we did playing for it, there would never have been such a collapse!

The Mears were to blame for the most of it and, as I have already told you, I told Brian as much some years later. I told him that when Sexton began his running feud with Osgood, he should have listened to both sides of the story. Had they had a consensus and, asked those 50,000 supporters who should go, it would have been Sexton who would have gone, not us!

How many times do you see supporters watch managers destroy a team and, then call for their heads, well, our heads were now on the block and, I think Tony Waddington was quietly confident that the club (team) who had never won a major cup competition would beat a team who had just won two of the main trophies to be won.

However, it wasn't until getting to know Waddington that I came to this conclusion.

I liked Brian Mears.

But I am still trying to work out why he came to visit me in hospital?

Was it that he liked the kid from around the corner?

Or was it a guilty conscience?

Whatever, he was a lovely bloke, it was just he got caught up in the middle of Chelsea's finest hour. They had Gallagher, Bentley, and Greaves, but in all fairness, this was the Swinging Sixties and, things had changed rapidly, almost overnight, or so it seemed. One moment it seemed as if I was at school and the next I was in the middle of something I'd only ever seen on the big screen.

After all, if playing against George wasn't enough?

Now, here I was the youngest player in a side that was like the crew on a Boeing 747, only we were taking off from a standing position. There was no runway and, no warning and, that was how it all began. There was no time to take a breath and, even when I went down that hole - it hit me in my hospital bed, after coming out of that coma - that, this was the way it worked and, that time waited for nobody.

Top Man, Jose Mourinho, who Chelsea foolishly allowed to leave after bringing them their first championship in 50 years. I would have loved to have played for him!

The only difference in 1998 when experiencing such a diabolical act of injustice, I was thirty years older and, I had so much more time to not only take it all in, but analyse it all. ,

But right now, in 1972, we were going through a different kind of coma, as our defenders were caught napping on two occasions and, both of these proved to be what Frank sang about, only the curtain hadn't quite fell.

Going back to those fans, they came to the Bridge week in, week out to see Osgood, Cooke and Hudson - not Sexton. They weren't interested in what we did from Monday to the following Saturday. I thought this to be true then, but once joining Stoke City it simply confirmed it.

I recall one day a chap telephoned Tony to tell him about several of his players drinking in his pub before a match. The bloke thought he would be making a friend in Tony.

Well, he most certainly misjudged my boss, because Tony didn't like grasses and, he also didn't need telling, something that he already knew. Tony was not only smart and, wasn't interested in their social or their sex lives, he was above such people.

I remember playing in Charity match when Lou Macari was manager there and, after a drink with one of their players, I invited him elsewhere and, he turned down the invitation, because all pubs within a certain radius of the County Ground were a no go area. The publican would call the manager if one of his players were seen on his premises. I could not believe what he was telling me, but insisted that it was true. I had no doubt to doubt him; it was just that I found it to be quite incredible.

It was said that when signing one player he bought a home outside of that radius, so he could use his local pub and then there was Tony Waddington...

Tony was only interested in his players performing for Stoke City. In a nutshell, Tony was only interested in football and, that's why he would have walked a million miles to sign George Best and, put him in a red and white striped shirt.

Brian Mears - as we sat in an Old Street Restaurant - was quite taken back at my claims. I suppose he thought that over the years and, as time goes by, you mellow. Well I am still mad about all that went on inside the walls of Stamford Bridge. And to this day I don't think that the club appreciate our ground breaking contribution. As I said earlier, it's alright for them, they don't rely on their playing ability and, once your career is over you're simply like the newspaper they once used to wrap up their fish and chips.

Only recently, Leeds United beat QPR and on TV they interviewed Eddie Gray, Paul Reaney and Johnny Giles from inside the Elland Road restaurant where they had no doubt been entertaining their fans! Just what is it with Chelsea?

It's almost like Papillon where he visits that Leper Colony and, that's how I feel every time I walk through that walkway to meet Tony Millard in the old Shed Bar, which has now gone.

Every step I take, I look down to the ground that we had broken over the last two years - before facing Stoke City - and, the hurtful thing is that it was for all of those to reap the rewards. I feel nausea each and every time I walk through, yeah, I hear you way, well don't bother, ok, I'll take your advice, I won't anymore.

It was tragic!

It was unfair!

It was ludicrous!

It was unprofessional and, ignorant!

And they repeated this unprofessional manner and, ignorance, by the way they crucified and, lied about Eddie McCreadie's sacking as their manager.

What they did, was hide behind all that was good at the Bridge - the players!

With those big old walls covered by some kind of plant that decorated the offices, it became like Dracula's Castle. The blood dripped through those plants and, trickled slowly down onto the concrete where we would hold our Friday five-a-sides. In the end you could smell it and taste it. It was sickening. It was sour, and that was the way it ended. In the end, it was the end of a memorable period and, I defy anyone, anywhere to tell me any different!

However, for now, that final curtain was only just hanging on by a thread as we entered Wembley as unworthy favourites and, as I was told in years to come, they were as confident as we used to be when tackling Leeds, Real Madrid, Bruges and CSKA. Our confidence had been shaken by the likes of Orient and that Swedish team, or so it seemed, for when writing about those matches it is almost as if the final whistle has just blown and, I become rather lost.

Losing was once something that never entered the equation before matches and, now we looked a frightened outfit, although outfit is a little misleading.

By now, Dave had even sewn that button back onto his navy blue jacket, was that a sign?

You just could not help but love our characters though, unlike today, they were just an ordinary bunch of lads who sweated blood for one another. I don't apologise for repeating that we were all from the same place. And, unlike today also, nobody was better than his mate, we all had something to bring to the table and, I don't mean Alexandre.

I have been in the company of several supporters of the side in Abramovich's first couple of seasons and, on one particular night - in the Chelsea Hotel - after they had won the championship under Mourinho, and I am a massive fan of his, I was stunned to hear a bunch of them say they were sending their season tickets back, because of the attitude of not only the manager, but the whole club.

I don't think the main body of the side today see Chelsea supporters as that, I think they look at them of those that not only buy their shirts but are merely a vocal point of the team, but no part of the club. With us, they were looked at as a part of Chelsea Football Club.

This was the club that finally refused to pay me the 5% of my transfer fee. They had merely hit another low. I don't go on about this just because of being cheated or lied to, I do it because they got what they deserved when relegated.

They not only had lost control, but whilst doing so got found out, and, as I say many times elsewhere, you can hide behind results, when they're going your way.

Between 1972 and the end of 1973 Chelsea Football Club got found out and, those directors could not handle the aggravation. They were fine with all of their cronies in the boardroom, when we were doing the business in Manchester and Athens but now...

They lied again, and that was one thing I never did in all of my time at Stamford Bridge. I played with a chronic ankle injury, which today many players would finish with. And whilst doing so I spent the little money I received (my wages) from them, going throughout London trying to find a doctor to mend or repair it. But that was all in vain, I visited Faith Healers, Chiropractors, Hypnotists, Spiritualists and pubs. It seemed the latter was the closest to the cure I was looking for, but obviously, it returned once sobering up.

I know it is impossible to compare, but today, a player would be sent to the USA for the finest treatment. Although, it still really confuses me, for even after 59 days in a coma, after such intensive treatment and, after finding out I received multiple injuries, my ankle was still as bad. So, it just goes to show just how bad it was and, still is!

My ankle and luck is as consistent as Chelsea Football Club, but what they do best is what is essential in life, they never look back. In their case they never look back at just who made Chelsea the club it is, or should I say, was?

I even got a dressing down for going outside of the club for doing such a thing.

In those days our medical team was like watching Syd James, Hatti Jaques and the rest of the Carry On team, however, we would have welcomed Shirley Eaton in our treatment room and, had that been Osgood, would have, no doubt, spent more time there and, he needed it, for although his ankle wasn't nowhere near as chronic as mine, it was bad enough.

The one thing that astonishes me is how I live with that chronic ankle injury and, not the Osgood Schlatters disease, for that was the least he could have left me.

However, he did my liver enough damage.

In the 14 years just gone by, this all seems so trivial and, that is why I decided to update this book, if only to put everything into perspective. Having said that I needed to get this off of my chest, out of my head and, onto the paper you have in front of you. That's me, although I hardly talk about it, people need to know, if only when I walk, they will realise that I'm not totally pissed all the time. My balance is lethal, dangerous lethal and, here is the main reason: FASCIOTOMY or FASCIETOMY - is a surgical procedure where the fascia is cut to relieve tension or pressure (and treat the resulting loss of circulation to an area of tissue or muscle). Fasciotomy is a limb-saving procedure when used to treat acute compartment syndrome. It is also sometimes used to treat chronic compartment stress syndrome. The procedure has a high rate of success, with the most common problem being accidental damage to a nearby nerve.

Complications: Can also involve the formation of scar tissue after the operation. A thickening of the surgical scars can result in the loss of mobility of the joint involved. This can be addressed through occupational or physical therapy.

Process: Fasciotomy in the limbs is usually performed by a surgeon under general or regional anaesthesia. An incision is made in the skin, and a small area of fascia is removed where it will best relieve pressure. Plantar fasciotomy is an endoscopic procedure. The doctor makes two small incisions on either side of the heel. An endoscope is inserted in one incision to guide the doctor. A tiny knife is inserted in the other. A portion of the fascia near the heel is removed. The incisions then closed.

In addition to scar formation, there is a possibility that the surgeon may need to use a skin graft to close the wound. Sometimes when closing the fascia again in another surgical procedure, the muscle is still too large to close it completely. A small bulge is visible, but is not harmful.

I was told by one certain therapist that when I had both my legs completely opened up on all four sides that it was the most horrendous thing she'd ever witnessed in a hospital room. That was whilst in the ITU. It was to let all the blood and gangrene run out, which could have caused amputation. So my days of running the streets were over with that first incision, and plus, when you've covered every blade of grass of football pitches all over the world, it becomes a pretty traumatic experience to wake up to!

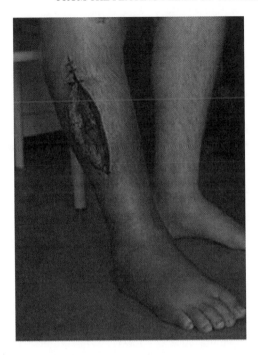

I never cheated my team-mates and our supporters.

Dave might re-direct that by saying you are cheating by going down The Kings Road when you should be tucked up in bed thinking of the following day's training. That again is the easy way out. I proved once joining Stoke City that when left alone to do what I am good at, I would produce the goods and, I did just that in 89 consecutive appearances before breaking my leg.

No, I am not a cheat. Dave once told the media that Alan Hudson was A Great Competitor and, has since told my great friend Dean Powell, of boxing fame, that "If there was one player I would have picked to survive that car accident, it would have been Alan."
Had I been a cheat, I would not have got out of the Intensive Trauma Unit.

No, I am not a cheat. The only things I cheated were death, and my first wife! I cheated on my wife, for which I apologise loosely, because she also cheated on me.
And far more importantly, I definitely don't apologise for cheating death.

When I apologise 'loosely' for that first wrong doing I must confess that I see marriage much like an affair with your football club. It is a two-way street. When people don't appreciate what you are putting into something then you tend to wander, looking for someone or something else. How many times do you see today, players - and managers and directors, come to that - move on to another club, affair or marriage - having given so little to the last one, yet get a bloody fortune!

The question about me still remains unanswered by so many, whether complex, uncomplicated or complicated?

Perhaps the answer lies behind that great Latin proverb, 'Ars est celare artem' (art lies in concealing the art). The image of us all as hell-bent hedonists, forever living on the edge, constantly chased by demons intent on destroying us, suited the media. Perhaps our talent was narcissistic.

Chelsea had won those first two trophies in magnificent style and, whilst doing so we never talked or boasted about it (today they are far better talkers than performers) we simply enjoyed it, and, I say this because we were not overpowered by all around us, we did so by, not only enjoying ourselves, but shared it with those around the area, by giving those surrounding my prefab so much enjoyment and, pleasure. It was like one big family then, now it's like a picture of spot the native and, I'm being far too polite. When I walked out of Stamford Bridge with the great Tony Banks and, was ignored by the Russian entourage surrounding Abramovich and, jumping on a number 14 bus, it flashed through my mind 'fuck you lot.' The only difference was I felt good about it all - I came from Chelsea and, now I wasn't accepted in the ground my dad walked me into as a 13-year-old and, even worse I was already a player when he did so. I had, had my apprenticeship whilst living in the prefab and, had been educated by him taking me to see all of those wonderful players around London in those days. This was mainly Tottenham, of course, which I have already told you about.

The media might write about, and think, it's some kind of a joke, but I don't, my dad worked his fingers to the bone and, made the ground work for those people who have now raped pillaged and laugh at my playground. This place whatever they think is still ours. They might have a yacht but ours won't ever sink or, have the wrong diesel put in it.

I had my first short pair of trousers put on me in Chelsea, where did Abramovich?

Yet he rules where many people in Chelsea not only care more, but knew more and, still do. Money Talks as Neil Diamond sang again. However, it also ruins!

You might have big houses, fantastic yachts and servants, but that brings a new meaning to living a false life. If he loved Chelsea so much why is he not seen on our River Thames downing his champagne with Frank Lampard - and his dad - John Terry, Gordon Ramsay, Bernie Ecclestone, Claudia Schiffer and all?

When are you Chelsea supporters going to get wise?

The River Thames is the place where Chelsea supporters used to walk or cross.

Those from Battersea, Victoria and a little further afield.

Remember the place where we were all born.

Of course I know that times have changed, but it has only changed because of all of those money grabbing strangers from out of town.

That is why when I began this book I told you at the tender young age of 18, I said we'd never win the World Cup, again, in my lifetime, let alone the European Championships. And as I go over my notes Switzerland have just reached the final of the Under 21 European Championships, which does not look too good for the future of English football. I mean, after all, they are not the nation that 'allegedly' invented the game.

A little while later a Swiss team, Basel, knocked the mighty Manchester United out of the Champions League.

Do you actually realise what that actually means?

Now do you see what damage all of these people in suits and, track suits have done to our game? If only my father had been given the opportunity to clean up our game, like he did people's walls and floors. My old man would not have had the likes of Emile Heskey and Carlton Palmer in his Sunday team. I shouldn't really be mentioning this type of player in The Ballet, but if I didn't you would not know the difference between winning and losing, but more importantly, class, and I mean real class, where have they gone?

But back to Chelsea, it is getting worse, I walk down the Fulham Road and, I cannot find a friendly face, it's like going abroad. It really is like being on holiday, only there's no sunshine!

Brian Clough and Enoch Powell rush to my head again.

The scary thing is if Matthew had still been here, Roman Abramovich would be at Tottenham and loving it - another false love! Mind you, if I had more billions than him I'd build my own island and, it would make Stamford Bridge look like Alcatraz, which it is not far off right now!

They don't have managers - Mourinho apart - they have inmates!

It simply amazes me. Maybe Richard King, 'another hanger-on' can tell me why?

We were all local and, because they were buoyant, so cocksure and, secure behind their brash displays, they now replace us and not only do they do that, but look down on us. I say fuck all that sail on you.

Me, and those that done the business in your hour of need will one day have one last trip and, you cannot share those memories of the real Chelsea shirt. We never kissed the badge, we sweated in it, that is absolutely bollocks and, you know it. As I have already told you, Frank wanted to leave for Mourinho and, Terry was going to fuck off to Manchester City but they still kiss the badge. Do they kiss the badge because of the worth of their contracts?

I think that's more like it. Don't get me wrong I am envious that our team never had the riches that they have today, but at least be honest about it all.

I read in a newspaper the other day that when asked, a foreign player said quite simply,

"I came to this country strictly for the money," at least that's being honest!

Yet you Chelsea supporters loved Bates, after he wanted to put an electric fence around you, like animals - and then he goes to Leeds, so how good a judge are you?

Had he had more of a say at the FA, he would have thought about doing the same at our national stadium and, that was where we were heading next. For in the first Saturday in March we went back to Wembley to face Stoke City and, although it looked like a foregone conclusion - after beating Leeds and Real Madrid - it was soon to become clear that we were not the team we once were.

These lads from the back streets from in and around Campbell Road - where they adopted players such as Conroy and Mahoney - were nothing like us Playboys from Chelsea and, also let us not forget this was not an unknown Swedish outfit. These were more than a very decent team and, of course, they had that Man Waddington guiding them. Not forgetting two of the '66 World Cup-winning squad, Gordon Banks and George Eastham, two men I would soon get very close to after my move north. Both are true legends in our game and, one of them I would have some of my toughest matches against.

Some Friday mornings in that old gymnasium at the back of the main stand at the Victoria Ground, George would become one of the greatest tests I have ever had to face.

Like Alan Ball, he was so deceiving and pound for pound he was one of the best players in the world. He was a complete genius!

He once told an old mate of mine that I was the best inside-forward he had ever seen after a display at Newcastle United. That was one that Jimmy Hill overlooked. Or did he ignore such a performance?

Or is it that he is a little illiterate about football?

I think it may be a little of all three.

George and Gordon played for the people of Stoke-on-Trent, the people who became such a great part of my second home, which has now become more my first. This final was their first taste of the big time as a club team for both Gordon and George - and of course the incomparable Jimmy Greenhoff. I am not ignoring Banks playing at Wembley for his former club Leicester City and, although that was a special occasion and, an FA Cup final, he will genuinely tell you that his love for the Potteries is far stronger. To prove it, he still lives in the area. Oh, and like me, he was cheated by his former club, his being Leicester City, mine being Chelsea.

And like me again, they never paid him, it was Tony Waddington who did.

I like Gordon, and he is worthily called world-class, like Bobby Moore, Bobby Charlton and Alan Ball. I first met him when arriving at the Victoria Ground, when I was with Bill - my father who I hope is still behind that cloud smiling at those good people amongst us - and although I had been in an England squad with him, I never, obviously, got close. You never do in such situations, although it was in one of these situations that Bobby Moore seemed like a magnet to me and, me to him. I don't know what he saw in me to this day, but it was like he wanted to be me. I don't mean that in a bragging sense in any way, he was, and still is, a giant compared to me. That is why we called him God - and he most certainly was just that. He didn't have to live up to it, like some players try to do today, or should I say, seem to believe that they are?

Anyhow, as I mention within these pages he wanted to take me under his wing and he, I still feel, is looking over me. The problem when I talk or write about this man is that I can go on forever, like Waddington, these were the two most important people I met throughout my entire football career. Without them it would not have been so very special. There is so much mediocrity in our game - like any other I suppose - so when someone like these two people come along you just realise you have met true greatness.

As for the blindness, ignorance and corruption within the FA, there lies the damage that has got this football nation into such a state.

Instead of making Bobby Moore the national manager - as other nations do - they go with people such as Charles Hughes who destroyed our game – how can that be?

As I found at Chelsea, the trouble starts and finishes at the top and, with Chelsea it seems nothing changes, as for those in Soho Square even the pimps can walk around with their heads held high!

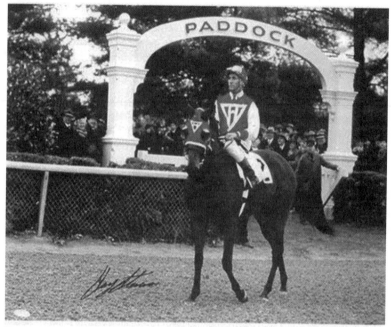

Here's the wonderful Seabiscuit with Gary Stevens aboard (in the movie).
I spent time with the legendary Stevens in Santa Anita for the Breeders Cup a few years back, for he's a good pal of my mate Jimmy Duggan.

As Jeff Powell says everyone needs their Svengali and, when watching Seabiscuit you'll know what I mean exactly, as Tom Parker brought him to his rightful place. As in a special manager who nurtures a natural talent, Parker saw that this most incredible of horses was neglected - me and Waddington again - and, would wither and die, if he didn't step in and help. He stepped in and the horse became something never to be seen again and, as in football today, just imagine the managers I tell you about having the money to build a team.

Had Lionel Messi been born in this country he would never have been seen or heard of and, that is exactly the reason why we are a hopeless nation, not just in football terms but organising our future.

How about this in the media, which is out of my other boo and, it just about sums the country up and, the politicians are behind most of it:

FINAL MEDIA SUMMATION

This was basically the main reason for me starting to write this book, with today's superstar players, managers, actors, actresses, models, singers and X-Factor contestants and, of course, those who sit judging them, including Simon Cowell, Louie Walsh and Cheryl Cole. And after this period, I thank whoever sent me this text message, I say whoever, because it came through to me under a Private Number:

Subject: With regret - who should we remember?

With regret, Whitney Houston's death, while a sad thing, was the direct result of very unwise life choices. It dominated the news. Charlie Sheen is 45 and, his story is all over the news because he is substance abuser, an adulterer, sexually promiscuous and, obnoxious. Lindsay Lohan is 24 and, her story is all over the news because she is a celebrity drug addict and, thief.

Amy Winehouse's story was all over the papers and, shoved down our throats as she was a singer and 'celebrity' and a substance abuser. Something as frivolous as Kim Kardashian's stupid wedding (and short-lived marriage) was shoved down our throats.

While the following Justin Allen 23

Brett Linley 29

Matthew Weikert 29

Justus Bartett 27

Dave Santos 21

Jesse Reed 26

Matthew Johnson 21

Zachary Fisher 24

Brandon King 23

Christopher Goeke 23 and Sheldon Tate 27, who were all British Royal Marines who gave their lives last month for you. There is no media for them; not even a mention of their names. Honour THEM by sending this on. I did, will you?

And then there was the young lad who lost his leg in Afghanistan and, they are arguing about giving him £81-a-week. Is what I am reading and, hearing really true, of course it is, it is just I have to ask myself over and over again.

WHY?

THE FA KEEP DOING IT ALL WRONG?

WELL, WE KNOW WHY, BUT IT'S TIME THEY

BROUGHT IN SOMEONE WITH BRAINS...

Why not a Branson or a Sugar?

Well, the problem is the same as why they would not employ Brian Clough, for he'd get the broom out and, that'll be the end for "me and all my pals," whose contribution to football, totally non-existent.

Do you know there are people on the FA payroll that have never, ever been to a football match, but get paid expenses for sitting down in the likes of St Ives, Penzance and Timbuktu.

As regards the managers they employ, they pay them off for being a complete failure, which makes me wonder if they are getting a bung for giving them the job?

When was the last time that they employed someone with any substance?

If Trevor Brooking knew all about this - and allegedly, he snubbed Harry Redknapp - why don't he take the job?

Trevor was my first room-mate with England at Hendon Hall back in 69/70 and, if you went to a party with him, I promise you he'd turn it into a wake. Is this why England are so boring?

Why don't they have a panel of "football people" who actually know about, not only the game, but what a football manager is all about, not one who will look like one and, act like one, simply be one. As I said Clough would have turned Lancaster Gate and Soho Square into the Chelsea Labour Exchange and, that's more than those morons deserved.

I also think that the managers should have a clause in their contract, whereas if they mess things up, they put a percentage into the kitty, to look after our boys and girls both in and, coming back from Afghanistan and, after all, they come here get paid fortunes and, then take it back to Italy, Sweden or wherever they have several homes - all paid for by the FA.

They aren't even British and, these young people are fighting a war for them. I wouldn't mind so much - well, I would - if their players fought for them, when they were messing things up?

We complain about there being no English managers that are any good, so we employ a couple of foreign mugs. I would have gone along with Ian Holloway, he takes no prisoners and, his team play as if their lives depend on it. He also plays the way we were brought up to play.

I was in Majorca recently in the Bristol Bar and, could have cried in my vodka and orange, when they didn't cash in on their chances against West Ham at Wembley. But that has been the season, a season, especially the last month, where all the best teams lost their all-important matches.

But back to England and, Eriksson as manager and how when he first took over he had a team for each half, "What a complete Wally," as Del Boy would say!

Eriksson was a complete joke, only the kind of one who keep walking away with millions of pounds for doing nothing, although he did quite a few things that became public like the weather girl, Ulrika -

who was also carrying on with Stan Collymore (I was a great fan of his), and Hunter from that show The Gladiators, or something like that. I met Hunter at a party and, he told me all about this as we stood in the kitchen having a drink and a laugh. I'm just glad I weren't Stan, for I would not have wanted a right hander of him! However, I like him a lot'

He also had some pretty decent perks in Lancaster Gate with Faria Alam being the best considering the following was reported by The Sun:

FARIA ALAM IS A SECRET £8,000-a-night HOOKER

The 40-year-old Asian beauty stripped to her bra and knickers and offered an undercover News of the World reporter sex for cash.

"I am pretty good at what I do," she said as she watched wads of £20 notes being counted out for her in an apartment in London's Mayfair.

She had demanded so much money she had difficulty stuffing it all into her designer handbag and, she also boasted of a wild cocaine-fuelled lesbian sex session she'd had as she desperately tried to seal the deal. Fresh from her appearances on TV discussing Jade Goody's allegedly racist attacks on CBB winner Shilpa Shetty, Faria was looking for something of a different nature.

Soon she unashamedly went into her sordid sales patter, bragging about her "party trick" - a sex act she carried out on Sven Goran Eriksson that she practices with an eight-inch candle.

The figure she demanded was a whopping £9,000 for just three hours - but she eventually settled for £8,000.

Her staggering fee of £8,000 for two hours worked out at £66.67 per minute, putting her in the same league as top footballers.

I reckon that she earns her money whereas the players don't, so don't knock her, for I'd rather have 90 minutes with her than watching what I did in South Africa and then there is the other side to the story, where Eriksson walks away with a fortune whilst he has to go in hiding, whereas I thought it would be the other way round.

IN THE INTERNATIONAL WILDERNESS FARIA, I KNOW HOW YOU FEEL LOVE!

Living in exile, consumed by bitterness, why Faria Alam can't escape the toxic legacy of her affair with Sven-Goran Eriksson by Helen Weathers.

These days, Faria Alam's life could not be further removed from the scandal-drenched existence she left behind in Britain, fleeing as she did with her reputation beyond repair. Home is now a rented house in Calgary, overlooking the Canadian Rockies, where people are largely unaware that she was once the notorious mistress of former England football coach Sven-Goran Eriksson.

Here, Faria does not rush to tell new acquaintances that in 2004, as the former PA to the Football Association's then executive director David Davies, she became embroiled in the most embarrassing scandal in the FA's 140-year history.

Swede memories: Faria Alam has now moved to Canada and said she is no longer in contact with Sven-Goran Eriksson. Now aged 43, she insists she is happy to live alone, quietly, embracing whatever anonymity she can claw back, which she admits isn't easy - even in Canada - when her past is there for all to see on the internet in all its sordid, humiliating detail.

But that is what happens, as she has learned to her considerable cost, when you kiss and tell about one of the most high-profile of sporting figures in the most startlingly graphic, toe-curling sexual detail for a reported £410,000.

Regrets?

Faria, now effectively living in self-imposed exile, has more than just a few. "When I look back, I regret the whole thing. If I could go back, I would do everything differently. For a start, I would never have accepted that job at the FA in the first place. When I became involved with Sven, I didn't realise the magnitude of what I was getting myself into. I can see now that the whole lifestyle I bought into in Britain was rubbish. I thought it was glamorous and exciting, but it's not'

This is Faria's first in-depth interview in almost six years. She tells me she is happier now than she has ever been, but throughout our conversation anger simmers beneath the surface.

She says she 'takes responsibility' for the mistakes she made, has learned her lesson, rediscovered her Islamic faith and, bears no malice towards those who she feels hung her out to dry, but the occasional flashes of bitterness suggest otherwise. "I don't miss Britain one little bit, she said.

"And I am sure Britain doesn't miss me either. "I don't care what people say or think about me anymore. I have been able to reinvent myself over here. My life is so different now. I am much more contented. From my window I can see the Rockies, blue sky and sunshine. I go hiking, canoeing on the lakes, I meditate, pray, do yoga and Pilates. I eat well, exercise and lead a healthy life. Today, I feel as though everything that happened with Sven and the FA happened to someone else. My life has turned 360 degrees and I am back to where I want to be.

Betrayed: Nancy Dell'Olio with the former England coach - Faria claims she wasn't with him when they were still together

"Here, there isn't a nightlife culture. I don't go out. I can go for a whole week without seeing anyone."

All I can say is he not only messed up our national team, but her life also, although she obviously takes some blame. Plus, he had a better eye for a woman than he did a player!

It's just as well that Wayne Rooney never knew about it at the time…

It all sounds rather lonely, but Faria insists she loves the solitude. For a while after the scandal she tried to carve out some sort of career via reality TV, appearing on Celebrity Big Brother, because, she says, 'who was going to give me an office job?'

In 2005 she lost her sexual discrimination case against the FA when her claims of sexual harassment, unfair dismissal and breach of contract were rejected by an employment tribunal.

She fled Britain in 2007 to study for a master's degree in Canada and be nearer her mother living in the U.S., after a red-top tabloid exposed her as an alleged high-class hooker, who offered to sleep with an undercover reporter for £8,000 a night.

"I've been accused of all kinds of things, everything, you name it, I've been accused of it," she says wearily. "What I said was a joke. Women often say things they don't mean. What woman hasn't said at some time, "I'd sleep with so and so for £8,000?"

Not many of my acquaintance, but perhaps Faria moves in different circles.

"Women often say things they don't mean. What woman hasn't said at some time "I'd sleep with so and so for £8,000?"'

Working now as a marketing and fundraising consultant, she says she makes a good living, splitting her time between Calgary and an apartment she owns in Vancouver, but it all sounds rather ad hoc. There appear to be yawning gaps between marketing jobs, which she fills in with voluntary work with children, chasing new clients and even, on occasion, dog walking. She admits she has suffered bouts of depression in the past two years, when, she says, "I wanted to die," but has been helped through her crises by her family and friends. Certainly, it's all a far cry from those heady days spent in London's champagne bars, mixing with football royalty, where Faria - nicknamed 'Ferrari' - attracted the eye of not only Sven but the FA's chief executive Mark Palios, with whom she also had a brief affair. But as Faria says now: "I can see now that the whole lifestyle I bought into in Britain was rubbish. I thought it was glamorous and exciting, but it's not.'

There are those who will always regard Faria as the worst kind of attention-seeker. If she now craves anonymity, what is she doing raising her head above the parapet again?

Can it be a coincidence that she is talking about her acting debut, as a cat suit-wearing assassin in the new British movie Cash and Curry, the very week her ex-lover Sven - coach for the Ivory Coast national team - was in the frame for the vacant Fulham football club manager's post?

"I haven't had any contact with Sven for years, but I wish him well. I don't love him anymore, but I care that he does well and is happy. He's getting on with his life and I'm getting on with mine," she says.

"I had no idea there'd be so much interest in the film. It was just a walk-on part, a bit of fun for me when my life had become so serious. I am not chasing fame, I am under no illusion that it will lead to more acting parts."

Reality TV star: Faria appeared on Celebrity Big Brother in 2003 on the back of the affair scandal

Born in Bangladesh, one of four children to a devoutly Muslim family, Faria never thought for one second that this would be her fate. She admits that her late father, a Pakistani bank employee, who emigrated with his family to the North of England in 1970, would have been appalled by the way her life has turned out.

As a teenager Faria went through an unhappy arranged marriage in Bangladesh, which was later annulled, and when her mother moved to Seattle after divorcing her father, Faria headed to London. There, she worked as a part-time model and supplemented her income by working as a secretary, in PR or as a freelance IT consultant before being offered the job as a personal assistant at the FA. How she wishes now that she'd turned it down. "I didn't sit there on my first day thinking, 'I'm going to have an affair with Sven-Goran Eriksson.'

It just happened. I was a single woman, enjoying my life, dating guys in London," she recalls.

"Sven was always very charming, very polite, a gentleman through and through, and when he first showed an interest in me, I'd say, "I'm seeing someone else."

One of the people Faria was seeing was divorced chief executive Mark Palios, who according to her kiss-and-tell was no great lover and rather cool in his affections. Faria, it must be said, emerged as a good-time girl who targeted powerful men, bewitching them with her sultry looks, but she insists it was the other way round.

"I know he loved me. He told me he did. At the time he loved me. I don't care what anyone else says. I know I am not deluded. When someone is persistent, they get through eventually and Sven was very persistent. If a woman did that she'd be a stalker, but when a man does it people say: "Oh, he's crazy about the girl." They have great names for guys, but when a woman does it she's a slut, she's this, she's that, all negative. All I knew was that I was falling in love with this man. I wasn't thinking about marriage, I didn't know what I wanted, I was just thinking about getting the relationship started. I don't know why he liked me, and I refuse to accept he regarded me as a fling."

But what about Sven's partner, Nancy Dell'Olio?

What about television presenter Ulrika Jonsson, with who Sven was caught out having an affair prior to starting another with Faria?

Surely Faria must have known what she was playing with fire.

"I know the man loved me. I know he did. He told me he did. At the time he loved me. I don't care what anyone else says. I know I am not deluded," she says, her voice rising.

Perhaps he did; or perhaps it's simply easier for her to believe so.

"He liked the fact that I was normal, down-to earth, a jeans-and-T-shirt girl who didn't care about her appearance or powdering her nose every two seconds. He could talk to me. I don't know if he realised that he was taking a huge risk, but I certainly didn't at the time. As far as I was concerned, we were two single, adult people. When we were having a relationship, he wasn't with Nancy, despite what she told all and sundry afterwards. Whenever I went to see him, she was never with him. She was out of the country half the time. Sven wasn't with her, certainly not mentally."

In the spotlight: Faria claims she is happier now she is away from the media glare and, has nothing positive to say about the way the FA handled the scandal, initially denying any affair between Sven and the

PA, then admitting it was true. When the story broke, the FA's then director of communications Colin Gibson reportedly offered the Press Faria's full kiss-and-tell on Sven if they agreed to save Mark Palios from further embarrassment.

"I had no intention of selling my story, but the FA wanted me to go public and protect Palios and discredit Sven, while Sven was also telling me to do it, because he wanted people to know what the FA were doing, He was very annoyed. If the FA had simply said "this is a personal matter between two adults" I might have been hounded privately, but I could have kept silent and run away. Instead, I felt a gun was being held to my head and I was told "you will give verse, line and chapter this Saturday". I wish I'd never done it.'

In her interview, in which she revealed the Sven to be an "ice-cool Swede and a red-hot lover" who liked to load the dishwasher before sex, she claimed Sven's calls to her had stopped and she felt "abandoned and I felt he is like all the other men in my life who have let me down."

On a later television interview on Tonight with Trevor McDonald, Faria broke down in tears when asked by reporter Fiona Foster if she was in love with Eriksson.

"I wasn't then, I am now," she said, before revealing that she didn't think he'd ever been in love with her. Now, however, she tells a rather different story.

"Now, when I see him on television or in the Press I don't think of what ifs or if onlys - it brings back uncomfortable memories of all that happened. We were in touch for a whole year after the scandal. I don't think Sven really cared about what I'd said, and why would he feel betrayed? He wanted me to do it. There was nothing for him to forgive. I still had my feelings and he had his. He would call me every day, and we'd talk about getting back together, but it was impossible to meet because we knew there would be a media frenzy."

After the scandal, Faria secured a job with the UK arm of a fashion label, which meant to-ing and fro-ing between Britain and the U.S., where it was her job to set up trade fair events, but she dreaded returning to Britain. "I said to Sven on the phone one day that I was thinking of leaving the country. I said: "I can't do this anymore. It's killing me," and he said, "Don't go yet, please don't go." He wanted me to stay and thought we could find a way to see each other again. But I'd reached the point where I wanted to give up, so I decided to go. I couldn't stand it anymore. If I'd stayed, it would have killed me. When I left I deleted all the numbers I had for Sven and his email address, because psychologically it helped me cut the ties with the past. As far as I'm aware, he never tried to contact me. Your feelings fade when you can't see someone. Now, when I see him on television or in the Press I don't think of what ifs or if onlys - it brings back uncomfortable memories of all that happened.'

Nowadays, Faria says she is in a relationship with a 49-year-old Los Angeles-based divorcee who runs a film production company. They met in 2006, and she says that he knows about her past and 'doesn't give a damn'.

They meet up every few weeks, but Faria has no desire to get married or have children of her own. Through her voluntary work, however, she has discovered she has a natural affinity with youngsters and is thinking of adopting in Canada as a single parent. "People here would describe me as hard-working, fun and bright. I never lie about the past if people ask me, but not one single person has ever said to me, "I don't want to know you because of your past,"' she says. "I made a mistake. Everyone makes mistakes. No one's perfect. Who hasn't at some time thought: "Oh God, I wish I hadn't done that?"

'There are times when I sit here, all alone, and ask myself, "What the hell happened?" I'm a different person now.'

So, the FA are not really any good at employing anyone any good and, that is a knock at Faria, because she is very attractive. What I meant was in the right position - if you'll excuse me putting it that way.

In the end, the FA are there for the taking, so you cannot blame anyone for taking their money, they throw it at idiot managers, so, I say, 'jump on the bandwagon, for there are so many hundreds of people on their payroll who do absolutely nothing, so why not?

I feel for Faria, for it seems she is carrying the can for all of those others who have made a mint out of both Lancaster Gate and Soho Square, yet they walk away to their comfortable lifestyle, paid by the FA and, live to tell a different story.

So, one last time, that is exactly what the FA brought to our country and, what makes me smile is thinking, 'Do they actually have anyone there who does any homework?'

Anyhow on with the story and, the reasons why this is nonsense, is because had I been playing it would have been as foreign to me as he was, as my game depended on lasting 90 minutes and more, I trained to go two hours and, like Ball, was running on at the end of matches when my marker was flagging.

That was what training was for and, apart from having a nightmare at Highbury, through a stomach injury I trained for the marathon, not the sprint.

If my understanding with Osgood was something special - I could pick him out in the dark - then the one to follow was stunning and, you can ask any Stoke City fan, even now and, they are still lost for words to describe such an understanding. The craziest thing about it all was that we were not good buddies. We hardly ever spoke to one another, but that was not because we never got on. Jimmy was the complete introvert, whereas I was the opposite. And who said that people from Leeds and Chelsea never got on?

We were the epitome of the extrovert and introvert, on the field, the perfect match.

He was simply a genius!

Wonderful, Magical, real Supertramp stuff!

When he was interviewed on a Stoke City video Jimmy said that, "Years ago players like Alan were looked at as clowns, but now Gascoigne is doing his thing and is loved and, Alan was better player than him."

However, this was all still to come. On this day in March 1972 Jimmy and I were on opposite sides, never knowing that there were two players on that Wembley turf that one day would, in football terms, become one.

As for Chelsea, we needed to right so many wrongs. We were like 11 big bears with many sore heads and, I don't mean hangovers.

But it was as if these bears had turned into Santa Clauses, only this was March and, not December.

We were a team who needed to show our fans that there was still some life left inside of us all.

This was our Last Chance Saloon.

And you know just how much we loved saloons.

In fact, we would have fitted in nicely with Jesse James and Billy the Kid or in Osgood's case,

Wyatt Earp.

I can't remember the build-up to this match too well, but I can remember my first touch and, I thought it was heading for Stan Bowles over at the White City dog track. I hit a long ball out to Nobby and, it went towards the North Circular Road. I thought that, 'things can only get better' but they didn't, they got worse, for after a mix-up in and around our box, they got a throw-in and, their captain Peter Dobing wiped the ball on his shirt, Ian Hutchinson-style.

Today, Rory Delap at the Britannia Stadium, which Tony Pulis built on to frighten the living daylights out of the likes of Arsenal. It worked, but unlike the way the other Tony, our Tony loved playing, it's not pretty, but then again, neither is Wenger.

A few seconds later and, after more confusion in our penalty area, the red-headed Terry Conroy scored a very rare headed goal. Now I mention rare for the simple reason that people were scoring goals against us that they never did against other teams and, although I did not know too much about Terry, I did know through watching Match of the Day, I never recollected him scoring with his ginger-nut. But, we were Chelsea and, were now becoming a team that no longer were tough to score against. I mean we played brilliantly against Spurs in the semi-final, but they still scored four times against us. We had lost our reputation, where teams dreaded playing against Harris and McCreadie and, then there was Webb and Dempsey, who were still formidable, if played in a back four where the manager had it right, however, as I said, Webby should have been in the centre of defence or down in Alexandre.

Around this time John Dempsey was without a doubt our best and, most reliable defender and, then there was that goal he scored in Athens, which was no fluke.

At the other end of the field Chris Garland, our best player on that day, was showing the same form as at White Hart Lane and, was running at them like he was running for his life, which has me thinking of that day at Blackpool when:
I was supposedly going to have the first attempt on mine.

Anyhow, Chris had many nicknames - many unprintable - but the obvious one was Judy, although he was far from being one of them.

He was making powerful runs into their half to give Mike Pejic plenty to think about. The Stoke City left-back brought him down as he broke through and, received a booking. Then Alan Bloor, as I just said - what a great player he was - was booked for a similar offence. I thought at the time that we were in control, but after watching the video, I felt that Stoke were always comfortable, if at times a little wayward.

That is what a cup final at Wembley does to you. It is a very harrowing experience if you are new to it all. But the biggest weapon in Stoke City's armoury was of course the goalkeeper, Banks. He was the coolest man, along with Osgood, inside this famous old stadium.

Just before half-time we equalised. And it was him again, Oz. He had scored in the FA Cup and European equivalent. Now he put us back on level terms in yet another final. It went through my mind once again and, as it has for years, why did Dave always make a beeline for him when things were not going our way?

It continues to baffle me and I suppose it always will.
Not many things do about our game.
They are simple to work out, but this thing with Sexton and Osgood?
It has been one of the biggest mysteries of my life, something that I've never been able to work out.

If their goal was scrappy, this was its equal. Cooke found Osgood inside the box. The big fella stumbled. He was floored, although he wasn't touched. He somehow scored. You remember how I mentioned earlier on about some players getting themselves into a position before picking their spot?

Well, Osgood was lying on the floor sideways when beating Banks!

He never ceased to amaze me. Now I thought the match was well within our grasp and, I also thought there would only be one result. You cannot score at a better time, especially in such a big match. Stoke looked like we did against the Swedes, devastated!

This should have elevated us to our third major trophy in three years, but as our friend Lou Christie sang, at our post-match party, Lightning Strikes Again!

Paddy Mulligan went off at half-time after his studs got caught in the Wembley turf. Tommy Baldwin came on and Peter Houseman went to left-back, but we continued to press and, began looking like the more likely to get that all-important second goal. I set up Tommy who missed. Later, as he burst into the box, another strong tackle decked him.

No penalty!

As I would find out later on, the Stoke back line were tough, very tough, Ronnie Harris tough, meaning they would go to any lengths to deck you. Sorry, I mean stop you scoring.

The best piece of play led to the winning goal and, on this alone, Stoke City deserved it. Again I blame the manager. Once again, as I mentioned earlier, Webb went to ground, 'Keep your feet, DJ,' is all you have to do, but Conroy skipped past him. Once doing so, looking up to the far post, he hit John Ritchie with a raking cross. The very experienced No 9 simply cushioned the ball with his forehead (something he had off to a fine art) and, Greenhoff pounced.

Jimmy, I felt, only half hit it - I told him so in a radio show we did in the week of the 2011 FA Cup final - although he hit it pretty well, it was by far a Greenhoff classic.

I have seen him hit better, far better, far sweeter and with more venom.

Catty, I felt again, should have caught it, but he didn't. Shades of Mexico '70. The ball fell from his palms to the feet of the veteran George Eastham. The oldest man on the field side-footed home from six yards and, the Potters had one hand on their first major trophy. One second I was standing next to George, but when I saw it heading towards Catty, I moved away and, was looking for a throw-out thinking Catty would save it easily.

I thought we'd hit them on the break, but instead the break fell their way.

But before they went up to collect it, they had one last scare as Mike Bernard, another warhorse, and a great lad, misjudged a pass from almost the half-way line. Garland sped through the middle, like a five-furlong specialist at Chester, and just as he was about to clip it over Gordon, the keeper spread himself immaculately to make sure that the League Cup went back to what would soon become my new home.

Chris swears to this day it was a penalty.

The great Banks also made a superb reflex save from a Tommy Baldwin header, but it was no more, than you'd expect from him. Finally, the whistle blew as we were throwing everything at them, which made it the third big cup defeat in a very short space of time.

And now the end is near and so I face the final curtain.

Never knowing at that time, how close it was to closing!

This was a time for support from the manager, but once again nothing. I think that he should have sat down with us and had it all out. At least we might have respected him for at least trying to understand us. After all, he took all the 'pats on the back' for what these players did at Old Trafford and Athens when they dug deeper than any ocean. But as the song goes: That's How It Goes!

It was the fourth time Chelsea had failed to win at Wembley and, they had never scored first in any of those finals. It was Stoke City's first major honour in a hundred years of existence.

109 years in fact.

And unless Banks, Eastham, Greenhoff, Matthews and I can find some kind of time machine, it might be another 109 years before they do again!

As I said earlier, it really didn't hit me until I got to the hotel for our celebratory party where some bright spark - and that is not a pun - brought Lou Christie in to perform the cabaret. This is where he sang his greatest ever hit: Lightning Strikes Again!

That was when it all hit home. The following day it poured with rain, which had me thinking just as well we lost because it wouldn't have been nice on an open-top bus. Anything to ease the pain and, also I can't remember where I went on that Sunday. When I went to Wembley six years later with Arsenal, I know exactly. It was The Duke of Wellington. I was fine all through the lunchtime session. I must have been in a state of shock - although nothing like in 1998 - for when I got back to my home in Sispara Gardens, as Maureen was serving up lunch, I broke down as if I had just received some tragic news.

Well she had, I was on my way home!

The day before leaving Wembley I remember me and TD sitting in the Wembley tunnel on the front of our team bus, wondering how we could have played so badly. And then, on the way back to our Mayfair hotel, the Dorchester I think, Sammy Nelson burst into tears and I thought 'what's that all about?'

Strange thing emotions, the highs and lows of this game cannot be explained. However, I never cried after this defeat against Stoke City and, little did I know that it would all lead to the best thing that ever happened to me. In my football life, that is.

That odd breakdown once returning home, looking back, might just have been a reaction to all that had gone on at Highbury.

When we reached Wembley I was so proud to go there with such a great club, especially after my on-going nightmare both on and off the playing fields.

But then the disappointment of that final must have hit me harder than I thought.

Not just the disappointment of losing, but the overall performance!

We played out the season like a team who had just come back from the moon - as if we had been lost in space and, when things are going wrong space becomes hard to find, unless you want to hide, that is.

But at this moment in time, with the things the way we were the only way out of it was to work our way out of it. It was not so much the space, but others who, once losing confidence, don't see it. You can find that all-important space and once finding it you don't receive the ball and, that is when you know that things are not going well. When things are going well you do things that become second nature but then, you hesitate and that space closes down

That was why Ball was such a special player, he'd find space so quickly, making himself available and, when you got to him - to close him down - he had been given the ball and knocked it on. You might say, like most brilliant footballers, he was one step ahead

We had lost everything we had gained in those magnificent cup successes, and more. It was if they didn't exist anymore.

I was to experience such a loss in hospital, losing 59 days, a year of my life, losing the use of my legs, although I only just kept them.

It's amazing, just like a fantastic love affair.

When it all goes wrong all the great times are forgotten.

This is the part of the book I don't remember much about because of being so beat up by both cup defeats, although the Orient one was far worse than the one at Wembley for I thought it was our time to go back for an FA Cup final. I had this thing about the FA Cup, so much so, it was almost an obsession, but although I don't know or can't explain it, I think it might be because of the one I missed in '70?

And then there as Dave leaving me out of the match against Manchester City the following year and, as I always have said, life is too short and that maybe another reason, for looking at my first three seasons, the first I got there and missed it, then there was the one I just mentioned and, now that Orient match when we were 2-0 up and cruising when, crash!

And only a few days before being beaten by Stoke City at Wembley, but as I said, the Orient match hurt more, in fact, much more. The way I saw it and, still do, is that give me one FA Cup and you can have two, three or four League Cups. It is like comparing Sharon Stone to Steve Stone.

After that Wembley defeat we drew against Liverpool before recording four straight wins, which must have been some kind of miracle, for one/I can't remember one of those matches and two/how could we do so, when we had just let some really silly goals in against both Leyton Orient and Stoke City. After the Liverpool match we beat Forest, Manchester City, West Ham and Sheffield United before losing at Portman Road, oh how I disliked Ipswich Town.

About six weeks after Stoke City won the League Cup at our expense, we completed the double over them by beating them 2-0 at the Bridge.

However, there was none of the old Chelsea and, no glitter, no gold, no passion, no love and, no more of that dash that led to so many good times.

We were becoming the Chelsea of old and, I did not like that and, it may have been alright for the hierarchy, but I found it difficult coming to terms with the break-up of such a great bunch of lads and, the post-match celebrations were drifting away like John Lennon from Paul McCartney and Maureen and me, although it was at an early stage, much like Osgood's on-going feud with Dave.

As I just said, the post-match drink tasted different, the winning taste had gone.

Where we once looked very much on course for three cups, we were now looking like being pot-less, like in years to come, personally. If you're not winning and, not winning with style, the aftermath seems to be a waste of time. It is like having sex without foreplay, wham, bam thank you...

We were going into these matches with no confidence, yet getting results that were unimportant and then you realise the seriousness of the state we were in. These ordinary Football league matches meant nothing. For once you've tasted those matches in Bruges and Old Trafford when the stakes were high it seemed that life was dull.

The team had lost it's everything. We used to be able to read one another, now all we were reading was about the break-up of such a team. The greatest tragedy was Hutch and, looking back, our team unit was much like him, for apart from falling apart, we also were breaking down. Although we didn't realise it then, after all, we won the Cup Winners Cup without him, which was some achievement, but that just showed the depth of our inner spirit. Whenever Sponge, Chris or Bill came in, they gave us something different and, were all good players, but Hutch was Hutch.

All players have different attributes and, could boast their own special qualities and, they gave the team them, where some players are more worried about themselves. However, none of these could follow Hutch. Don't get me wrong he was not a great footballer, who could hold the ball up for you, but alongside Osgood, it was as if they were going to take the match to the opposition on their own. Sponge gave everything and, was terrific in the box, with a great eye for goal and, nobody had a bigger heart than Chris and, I felt that he never reached his full potential, like Bill, because of the team declining. I think the disappearance of the impressive Weller was another nail in our coffin. It seemed everything was falling apart. And, as I say many times, the fighting between Dave and Osgood was the major factor to all of our misfortunes.

I search for answers and, can't find them. On reaching Stoke City, for instance, I could tell you the problems within the side, and the club, within a month of my arrival, although I had problems there at the beginning, within the dressing room.

It seemed that they resented me, but I didn't care, for I was there to resurrect my career and, although my marriage was on the rocks, I needed to sort that out and, a lot more. But as I have always stated, if I am on top of my football, I am on top of my life and, with Waddington that was how it proved, but right now it was an entirely different ball game.

So, I had gone from a completely different kind of surroundings, but the difference was Tony wasn't bothered about that side of it, as I said earlier, he was only concerned about Saturday afternoon.

Unlike Dave, he put his energy into the playing side of things, knowing boys will be boys and, the Potteries is a very small place and, if you believe everything you heard you'd go nuts, plus there were those in the area who loved making trouble for certain players.

It was said in the Sixties that Eddie Clamp, a real hard nut from Wolves, used to leave my mate's pub, The Staff of Life, at a quarter to three and, walk down to the ground with those fans. That was ok in those days, because they were the only team in the whole of the Football League that kicked off at 3.15 and, this was to give the folk in the Pot Banks the time to have a quick pint before the match. Eddie made use of such a thing and, Tony whether knowing or not would not budge an eyelid as long as he was performing.

Can you imagine Dave standing for such a thing?

After all, Eddie, like several other players of his time of life, were given an extra year or two by Tony, which was beneficial to both parties. Tony got the kind of experience he needed to see the club through, whilst the likes of Eddie and Maurice Setters were happy to muck in, as the club fought off relegation and, these players were not shy, when it came to a fight. I remember watching Setters and, I don't think I'd be wrong in saying he was the last of a dying breed.

I know from my mate Brendan O'Callaghan, who played at Doncaster under his management, that if you mentioned Waddington, it better be with the utmost respect.

This time became weird to me, for it was the first time we were not in contention in all of my time in the first team. At this time of the season we were warming up for the big run-in, whether it at home or abroad and, although it was only my third season, it seemed like forever, such was what we had all been through together.

Where we were fancying our chances in all the cups, we were now struggling. We had lost that zip. Eddie was struggling, Charlie too. Webb was to leave for QPR whilst Holly left for Arsenal. Only the new boys stayed and, if they couldn't cut it with the likes of Oz, Charlie and me, then they were going nowhere.

The sale of Osgood seems more ridiculous the more I think about it, the more I write about it and, the more I talk about it. Oz even made the wrong move, because, as I tell the people of the Potteries, had he followed me to Stoke City there would be no statue of Stanley Matthews. His teaming up with Greenhoff and, his old mate would have captured the city like wild fire. Where we ended up nearly winning the championship, with him, we would definitely have done so. The other tragedy of that time - and one of a very different kind - was that year when we were having our problems with management, Gordon Banks, had his problem on a bend in Newcastle-under-Lyme, which led to him losing his eye.

My car ordeal was quite some time off, but I can begin to share it with you now by telling you that by the time I have finished off part two this will tell a totally different story as to the way it started. There are some incredible revelations and, news of the way it all came about. So, I take this time in between books to find out more and wait for certain people to get back to me about what was the real truth about the 15 December 1997, where I was seen to be walking in front of Ashgar Fatehi's motor vehicle.

As I have told you, there was only one witness and he saw it as it was, but was frightened off by the Bow Police. Why?

Well that is the main reason for deciding to rewrite The Ballet, as this all happened just six months afterwards and, once waking up in The Royal London Hospital and, reading the book once again, it put things into a different light. The injury at WBA, had become like a runny nose, whereas before it had haunted me, now whoever was behind all of this does.

For now, I can tell you absolutely no more than that. There is, obviously, much more about my unfinished business in the game. There are also my times at Arsenal, Seattle and, my run-ins with both Revie and Clough, not forgetting Terry Neill. You have heard of my relationship with Tony Waddington, but there's much more to come and, then the wonderful players I played both with and against in the North American Soccer League. When I began writing the Ballet Harry Redknapp had not long left Seattle and, here we are reading about him being linked with the England job. Okay, it was thirty years ago, but taking all things into account don't you think the world of football has gone berserk.

When I left Chelsea for Stoke City I signed for £200-a-week and, after that signing for Arsenal, after the roof blew off, for a hundred pounds more.

When first signing for Chelsea in 1966 directors were not even seen, let alone heard, but I returned and signed for a man who wanted to put an electric fence around the ground where I was brought up.

My international ban was still to come and, with it the incredible disappearance of our national team in the World Cup finals throughout that period. If the Sixties was the greatest period in English football the Seventies was by far the worst, in terms of not qualifying. In that time Denmark has won the European Championships as a wild-card, whilst we haven't even sniffed a final.

My hometown club has been taken over by a Russian, with an American Chairman whilst being managed by a couple of Portuguese, a Brazilian, a Dutchman, a couple of Italians and a Jew.

I would like to say to them thanks to someone at Chelsea, for the get well card I received whilst hospitalised for the entirety of 1998, but I can't, because I never received one.

Going back over this book I was asked for my monthly column in The Voice. This was on the 13/4/2012 and here was my reply....
DIFFERENT MEANING TO EUROS
With all that is going on around us, the rumblings at the FA since the John Terry and Wayne Bridge issue still pretty much fresh in our minds, followed by Wayne Rooney's hookers, Peter Crouch's mystery woman and, the never-to-be-forgotten Rio Ferdinand drug test failure......yeah, they still exist and, although have taken back seat to Capello leaving and, Harry and Rosie taking over, the Euros are, whether the FA like it or not, almost here and, here we are manager-less and hopeless in regards, of our record in competition and, recent

World Cup performances being worse than the jury in Harry's court case. If Harry was innocent after opening an account in his dogs' name then sell your house, your car and, get your divorce settlement and, rush down to Paddy Power and bung it all on us to win the upcoming European Championships, well either that or, shoot off to Vegas and put it all on red. You'll be out of your misery a hell of a lot quicker! Anyhow, with the Euro's in mind, it seems that the press (media) and, the FA seem to have forgotten the most important competition since1966 is nearly amongst us. I know that sounds a little dramatic, but that, in reality, is what it is. You hear the cliché's of all of these well-educated footballers "We'll take one match at a time" and, it reminds you of a young man in Khaki agreeing that "we'll take one war at a time" only you can trust that they'll return, not all of them, with such pride and honour, that you can hold your head up high, but there, is a big difference, unlike those "superstar losers" they won't be coming back to their stunning WAG's, their all-inclusive mansions with three of four up-to-date motor cars in their drives and, no-limit credit cards waiting in the glove box. Sounds like an episode of Dallas doesn't it.....boo, it's true!

Anyhow, here's the bad news, Joe Hart is still our best goalkeeper (Spain don't need one) Micah Richards can't get a look in, Ashley Cole has stopped taking photographs of himself in front of that two way mirror, Frank Lampard's scored more with his new girlfriend than from free play, Steve Gerrard is still believing that Benitez will come good eventually (great sense of humour those Scousers) Scott Parker will leave Thunderbirds and take the captaincy full-time, Emile Heskey and Peter Crouch will go on a strict no-nonsense diet so they will fit into Lionel Messi's shirt, While leaving their existing one for Jermain Defoe, so all in all, you might say, or was it Stan Laurel, it's another fine mess?

And, we're just around the corner.....what hope, Bob Hope, meaning, none.

So, for you gamblers, like me, don't gamble, take the bets, because William Hill, (Joe) Coral who I've boycotted for cheating again, Paddy Power and Ladbroke will all be rubbing their hands together and, then holding them out as those mug English punters pile on once again, when will you ever learn?

The good news (for the opposition) is that England still have this incredible habit of leaving their best players out, remember Osgood, Greenhoff, Currie, George, Bowles, Worthington and yours truly?

Well I know that was the 70's and, apart from Bryan Robson, Glenn Hoddle and Paul Gascoigne since, there is not too much to talk about, unless you wish to talk about Carlton Palmer, David Batty, Terry Butcher, Terry Fenwick, Steve Hodge, Mark Chamberlain and my all-time favourite goalkeeper Peter Shilton, yeah, he was the one who let it under his body for the Polish goal that got us knocked out in '74, let it over his head against Brazil and, was late getting to it when the 5ft 5in Diego Maradona out-jumped him some time later, the only difference was that our goalkeeper forgot to use his hands where Diego didn't, now do you see just how far advanced the opposition are?

Did I say good news?

No, nothing has changed and, the only reason I am putting it this way is, don't be foolish like those that cancelled their well-earned summer holidays on the beaches of Spain and Portugal and wasted their time, money and emotions in South Africa, so my suggestion to those who did is, get to the best possible beach that your money will take you and, if it takes your fancy switch a TV set on and, if like as usual we are showing the world that we are no longer a force in world football, switch it off and enjoy yourselves. I do it every two years, whereas George did it every four!

Only in the last World Cup I sat in The Grapes in lovely company watching the Germans wipe the floor with us, whilst those poor people I just mentioned, flew half way round the world to suffer.

"Not me, buddy," as my old mate Don Shanks might say.

As an ex-England international I can give you some inside information - if you don't already know- these people, Sven Goran Eriksson, Steve McLaren, Graham and Peter Taylor, Bobby Robson (who only picked Gascoigne because Plan A wasn't working) and Fabio Capello know as much about winning international competitions as Rosie does about opening bank accounts, it makes me barking mad!

And the shame of it all, Robert Frederick Chelsea Moore was born in Barking, is that a coincidence or what?

The greatest England captain in our lifetime coming from the same place as Rosie and, the only difference being the wonderful Moore, never had an apartment in Marbella.

Bobby captained England ninety-odd times including the only time we won anything - that obviously being the Jules Rimet Trophy - which we did with the help of a Russian linesman (they hate the Germans more than they hate us) and, in the quarter-final, those "animals" as Alf called them were reduced to ten men, when another dodgy referee sent off their captain Rattin.

Had he sent off Bobby we would have the BBC would have closed down the show after that match.

This is how it read on Wikipedia: Meanwhile in the other two games, Ferenc Bene's late goal for Hungary against the USSR, who were led by Lev Yashin's stellar goalkeeping, proved little more than a consolation as they crashed out 2–1, and the only goal between Argentina and England came courtesy of England's Geoff Hurst. During that controversial game, Argentina's Antonio Rattin became the first player to be sent off in a senior international football match at Wembley. Rattín at first refused to leave the field and, eventually had to be escorted by several policemen. After 30 minutes England scored the only goal of the match. This game, even today, is called el robo del siglo (the robbery of the century) in Argentina

And my mate Tommy Wisbey, the Great Train Robber, was involved in The Crime of the Century another great number by Supertramp and, I wonder if they had Tommy in mind?

The reason I mention this is because our nation is one that is always using excuses and, The Hand of God incident, although was wrong, is our greatest excuse of them all. It happens every week in the Premier League and, it's called "cheating". Thierry Henry did it against the Irish but we don't hear the Irish keeping on about it and, of course, there are those referees, who are completely inconsistent, unreliable and, in all fairness, hopeless and, what makes annoys me is that they are deciding more matches with their infuriating blunders than any incompetent keeper or blindfolded goal scorers.

As I write, you might say that if Yakubu (Blackburn), had he not scored afterwards, he backed Liverpool judging by the way he took that first penalty. Had it been in Columbia he would have either got done for match fixing or took a bullet in the back of the head by one of those fanatical fans of theirs.

So, the point I'm trying to make here is it seems that results are all down to cheating or disgusting (and Roberto Martinez agrees) refereeing decisions.

I have two suggestions that were both laughed at in my local, first one being that penalty shoot-outs should be taken before the match,

Why? I hear you say. Firstly, it would make for a good spectacle for the supporter before they decide which way they are going to kick. Then, when, or if, the match is fizzling out to a bore-draw, one team has to do something about it. How many times do we see the weaker team play for penalties? Often, is the answer to that one!

It would stop this immediately. Fans pay good money to get entertained and, I'm afraid that is not entertainment, plus pubs and households pay SKY fees to see good entertaining football, but find themselves being cheated once shelling out. At least try the penalty shoot-out before the match. Nothing to lose, it might just catch on...

There's one thing, at least the player cannot blame the pressure if he doesn't know the result, because he still has ninety minutes to redeem himself if he misses, which again makes for better viewing.

Lastly, as there are no players to really talk about (English that is) unless Jack Wlitshere bucks himself up, I suggest that we go to the Championships without a manager; because we can't do any worse than what we have done with one. Alan Ball, a World Cup winner, once told me at Arsenal that "we don't need a manager, because all we need is keeping fit, because managers complicate things."

And, I make him right. Does Messi need telling, did Greenhoff need telling what to do, no, and, that is why Waddington bought him, because he knew what to do, as for myself, as Tony once said, simply, " I never told Alan Hudson what to do because he already knew," I rest my case!

And talking of the European Championships, it is the first time we approach it without a manager, again, what a mess the FA create. But we can be thankful for one thing and that means all of Europe - and that is Lionel Messi is not Spanish otherwise it would not be worth anyone else turning up, unless we leave Spain out and, all play for second place, just food for thought!

The most successful manager in the history of our game had not yet reached Manchester United. Bobby Moore, George Best and John Haynes were still alive and, although they've left us, they have given me a reason, and a good one, to rewrite this book.

As for when I first began writing the original Ballet, I said then we'd not only never win the World Cup again, but reach a final, and that is still how it still stands 14 years and, four World Cups on.

But the most important reason is to find out just who was behind my near demise and, as I say, this is all being looked into and, hopefully this book will help me find out more. I have all the pieces to this jigsaw puzzle, but cannot piece them together, so this will help.

I am reminded by all of this every minute of the day and, as we come up to the Summer of 2012 (did I say Summer?) I await two more visits to the Operating Theatre. As David Goodier told me, "You will never improve and, your legs will get worse - which is my main problem - but be thankful you never lost them."

I have been fortunate that those early days are gone, as to my falling because of my foot drop, but nevertheless, my balance and, my knees are no better and, unlike in my playing days I walk better now when I an drunk that when I'm sober and, that is because I put it to the back of my mind, out of my mind even. But the nightmare continues and, that is why I must find out and, I wonder if that was what Miss Betty Shine was on about, "You have some unfinished business down here," when my dad and Leslie laugh at my passing cloud.

I'm still searching and waiting for a sign, although the first sign was that young man in the pub telling my son's friend, that "Alan Hudson was lucky, the driver messed up."

The Working Man's Ballet and its playing fields have turned into the killing fields, so as they say, watch this space....

However, it all comes back to my all-time favourite player and man, a man who like they sang about me at the Victoria Ground, "Walks on Water" in my playing days, only Bobby did this outside of those 90 minutes. His advice to me was, "Alan, play for your country, don't ever put your club first, which I ignored because of the treatment I received from Alf and, then he was behind my signing for Seattle. Had it not been for him, I would not have taken such advice. But more important than anything every time I saw him he was absolutely delightful, even when he was looking unwell and, it was obvious he was going to leave us. However, that kind of wonderful presence he always had, never left him even though his health was enough to knock the stuffing out of a bull.

I never told him the reason why I could not do as he told me and, in the end oddly, it was me who was right (I think) when you look at just how they treated him, those that lived off his incredible work he did for them. When you look at Trevor Brooking, Geoff Hurst, Ray Clemence and David Beckham, it is a poor story of how far we have gone backwards. None of them have his heart and soul, if only for not standing up and, saying the kind of things that are in this book. I know there will be people who read this and say, "Well, it's obvious, he's pissed his readies up the wall by drinking, gambling and womanising and, now he's got nothing, he's bitter," well, all I can say to those people is, if you want to live your life so shallow, keep banging that drum for your heroes, those who continue to let you down and, I ask you one thing, "How can you call them heroes?"

Heroes are role models to youngsters, they are winners and, they are great human beings who share their greatness, just as Bobby did. Beckham is friends with Tom Cruise in Disneyland, who names his kids after American bridges, whereas Bobby called his son simply, Dean.

If we were standing in a pub in Liverpool, Manchester or London and talked of icons only Bobby and George Best names would be spoken, unless you have had too much to drink or simply brain dead, or both.

Can you imagine Bobby showing such petulance, that Beckham did, against Argentina, when leaving us in the lurch with ten men and, now we see him standing alongside Royalty in a desperate attempt to land a World Cup.

They might have shown the incident against the Argies, for it might have told the real story and, when I see the following, I realise that when I finally leave, not only this sport, but the country will be left in the kind of hands that have seen us continually not only pull the wool over the public eye but simply blindfold them, however, if they are foolish enough, then they deserve no better.

I will say one thing though, the whole of the world are laughing at us, because if David Beckham is an Ambassador for England, what the hell is he doing in Los Angeles?

He is one of those who talks a good game and, that is the kind of game that cost lives, he mixes in all the circles where vultures wouldn't go, which takes me back to John Lennon, can you imagine seeing him standing beside those who castrated him and then, of course, would you see Henri Charriere up on a rostrum with those that sent him to Solitary for a murder he did not commit?

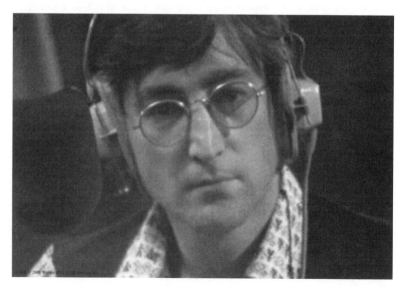

Here is a man who would be ashamed of some of our stars like Beckham, those who continue to jump on bandwagons, Lennon would ignore them all.

This is all weak and, it makes the beginning of my book look and feel to me like a barge load of lies and, dreams that I made up. Ask me if I'd like to change places with David Beckham and, I'd have to apologise for not being one of the in-crowd, those in that crowded room, where David Cameron and all of his chums reckon up whatever they reckon up?

I now realise just why we don't have Summers anymore, because this country is getting more and more miserable and, a place where all of the wrong people seem to be running everything that goes wrong and, as I said a few pages ago, get a real man into do the job, someone who actually knows what he's doing.

If David Beckham was the man he thinks he is and, making himself out to be, he better take a long hard look in the mirror and, of course keep his eyes off those young girls who dance personally for him on the side lines of those LA Lakers matches. It would not surprise me if he thinks they're pole dancers and, if he does, maybe someone in Parliament might let him know?

This is the most sickening part of the book...in fact, quite the opposite of how my life all began and, how can you forget, "When I was young I thought that life was so wonderful, magical....

According to Chapter One, Article 2 of the Olympic Movement and its Action, the mission of the International Olympic Committee 'includes upholding ethics in sports, encouraging participation in sports, ensuring the Olympics Games take place on a regular schedule, protecting the Olympic Movement, and encouraging and supporting the development of sport.'

With the exception of Pele, there are few footballers who have done as much to promote the image of the sport, throughout their careers as Beckham - yeah, even they've forgotten that World Cup, and, by the way, Pele won 3 World Cups and was never sent-off in any one of the four he played in.

Are you actually comparing all of that with this: Edson Arantes do Nascimento (name given as Edison on birth certificate, born 21 October 1940 (however, Pelé himself claims that he was born on 23 October), known by his nickname Pelé (Brazilian Portuguese pronunciation is a Pele a retired Brazilian footballer. He is widely regarded as the best football player of all time.

In 1999, he was voted Football Player of the Century by the IFFHS International Federation of Football History and Statistics. In the same year French weekly magazine France-Football consulted their former "Ballon D'Or" winners to elect the Football Player of the Century. Pelé came in first place.

In 1999 the International Olympic Committee named Pelé the "Athlete of the Century".

In his career he scored 760 official goals. He is also the most successful Top Division goal scorer of all time with 541 League goals.

In total Pelé scored 1281 goals in 1363 games.

In his native Brazil, Pelé is hailed as a national hero.

He is known for his accomplishments and contributions to the game of football.

He is also acknowledged for his vocal support of policies to improve the social conditions of the poor (when he scored his 1,000th goal he dedicated it to the poor children of Brazil).

During his career, he became known as "The King of Football" (O Rei do Futebol), "The King Pelé" or, simply "The King."

This is the difference - Beckham has been an ambassador throughout a career that has taken him to Manchester United, Real Madrid and AC Milan, three of the biggest clubs in world football. Beckham won 115 caps for his country, winning his place back in the squad after he was initially axed by Steve McClaren in 2006 and, breaking into Fabio Capello's plans before injury ruled him out of the 2010 World Cup.

CAMEO ROLES ARE NOT ACCEPTABLE - ASK BOBBY MOORE AND BOBBY CHARLTON!

They haven't mentioned how many of those caps were cameo roles, where they brought him on in the last few minutes so we could celebrate him breaking the record. It's called cheating, but that is what we are good at.

Bobby Moore was never once a substitute.

With the exception of his two red cards for his country, he is regarded as one of the game's iconic characters, always immaculately dressed on England duty - wouldn't you be?

After all, he earns over a £1million-a-month.

In his role as captain, he wore his England suit to press conferences, well aware that the images would be broadcast around the world - I wore better suits in 1970, tailored by Hayward.

He has always promoted the sport, speaking of his schoolboy love for the greatest game and retracing his roots back to Leytonstone during his frequent journeys back in time - John Dempsey looks after the handicapped.

There are 1.4m unsold tickets for the Olympic football events and Beckham's selection in the squad can help shift a vast number of them - he'll have to dig Stan Flashman up.

He will be joined in the Team GB squad by Ryan Giggs, another member of that famous Manchester United dressing room during that glorious, treble-winning era - all they need is the England coach, Gary Neville, with them.

Experience: Ryan Giggs could also join Beckham at the Olympics - fantastic, his brother will be delighted.

Giggs will bring some sparkle to Team GB, another big name capable of drawing big crowds at a time when most of the attention will be on the athletes - Natasha says he's a wonderful athlete.

Beckham's presence at the Olympics will promote the sport, drawing attention to football and adding to its appeal at London 2012. Team GB will tune up for the tournament with a friendly against Brazil at the Riverside on July 20, taking to the field after Hope Powell's female team face Sweden - I suppose like Manchester United pulling out of the FA Cup, England will no longer enter the European Championships and World Cup, for they'll now make the Olympics the number one competition.

Beckham will add a splash of colour to the occasion, embracing the Olympic ideal and raising football's profile again after the country takes a short break following Euro 2012 - could be a longer break than you think!.

At 37 his international career with England has come to a close, applauded on to the turf at Wembley last weekend when he received a special cap as one of the country's 'Centurions'.

If Team GB make it to the final at Wembley on August 11, he will deserve one last walk around the stadium to salute 90,000 supporters - it will remind me of Ben Hur.

After a career like this and, all that he's earned, maybe he'll donate it all to Afghanistan.

This reminds me of a TV Movie, where the authorities let out the most evil paedophile and give him the Head Masters' job at the biggest primary school in the world and then...

WILL THE REAL DAVID BECKHAM STAND UP - OR IS THERE TWO OF THEM?
THESE PEOPLE IN HIGH PLACES COULDN'T SINK ANY LOWER, OR BE MORE IGNORANT!
England (0) 1 Austria (0) 0

The madness and gross irresponsibility that led to David Beckham's sending-off at such a crucial stage of this crucial World Cup qualifier should mean that it was his last act as England captain.

It was not as if we had not been here before. Beckham, angry at being booked for a foul on Austrian defender Andreas Ibertsberger in the 58th minute, was suddenly engulfed by the red mist that experience and the responsibilities of captaincy and fatherhood were supposed to have removed from his game.

After first shaking his new hairstyle in anger at the yellow card, he then sought immediate retribution on the same player when play resumed. Not once, but twice within a minute and though referee Luis Medina Cantalejo perhaps leniently ignored the first, he could not allow Beckham to stay on the field after the second.

Although he seemed to get the ball, he caught Ibertsberger afterwards and though the latter responded with an over-theatrical dive, there was absolutely no need for such rashness under the eye of the referee. Ill-judged would be the kindest way of describing Beckham's conduct in becoming both the first England captain to be sent off and the first to be dismissed twice, though his manager, Sven-Goran Eriksson, said afterwards that an appeal was being considered.

It was St Etienne all over again, when Beckham was sent off against Argentina for an act of petulance in the 1998 World Cup finals and England were knocked out on penalties. But on the pitch that was once home and where he delivered 2002 World Cup qualification four years ago with a sublime free kick against Greece, Beckham could have put England's hopes of going to Germany next summer in the gravest of peril.

Unrepentant after the second yellow was flashed under his nose, Beckham showed all the maturity of the missing Wayne Rooney, by running across to Ibertsberger and shaking his hand. It was not an act worthy of any player sent from the field of play and, certainly not one befitting an England captain.

Beckham, of course, always finds some way to make himself the story. Just as he did when getting booked against Wales here a year ago, claiming afterwards that he had done it deliberately to make sure he missed the following game in Azerbaijan rather than a more meaningful encounter.

Can you imagine that when Harry was playing, because he reckons he can't add up?

His yellow here (WR) was enough to ensure that he will not even be in the wings for England's final World Cup qualifier against Poland on this ground on Wednesday. But he should have made sure he completed the full 90 minutes here.

IN MEMORY OF BOBBY

I have been writing this book for a very long time and, that is why it is in two parts, however, in all of that time, I have never come across anything like this.

I've seen brilliance and tragedies, some that are inside of these pages, but now I know it is time to go to print, for I can't wait any longer for more information as to who was behind the "hit".

But do you know the most terrible and, misleading thing about all of this is, people who unaware of people like Beckham - and it's getting worse since his halo has been lifted higher than Simon Templar's - for they put them into a category that is, for me, ludicrous.

David takes a great free-kick, which has been made easier by coaches continually blinding the goalkeeper with a six man wall, and crosses the ball to near perfection, but so did Alan Hinton, John Robertson, Keith Weller, George Armstrong and John Barnes, before Alf scrapped wide players and then we started all over again. It is only because we have players today who are useless crossers of the ball that makes David stand-out.

Is it so difficult?

I couldn't play out wide but when I got there, if I could not pick out one of my own players, I would not bother going there. Going back to my apprenticeship, take George Cohen - a World Cup winner - who I watched for years as a kid at Fulham, for when he got out wide at the Cottage, we'd all duck behind the goal. When he started his run I'd turn to Bill Boyce and say, "Bill, careful mate, here comes George."

If the ground had been facing the other way, there would have been more balls in The River Thames than rowing boats.

What gets me about Beckham is, how can you become an icon for simply taking a free-kick or crossing a ball, two things that I could get someone off the street to do, given time. He was a talented player, but George Best, Diego Maradona, Lionel Messi and, I only mention them for the simple reason, of getting carried away again in this country where "world class" is thrown around more than confetti by an over excited pub-crawler.

This recent Olympic Games (July 2012) I truly feel has shown just what a shallow nation we are, by allowing him to be some kind of Ambassador. It is a little like allowing Bin Laden to open a Kiddies Playschool. Talking of children, crucified by his childish antics against Argentina, thrown out by Ferguson, for not being able to control "'er indoors" at Old Trafford and being set-up for 'cameo roles' by the FA, is like watching a poor movie. I mentioned "shallow" and we will remain that way until someone puts a stop to all of this. That's why I speak of Bobby, a person who was not only ten times a David Beckham, but absolutely adored and totally respected by his peers and, right there you'll find the difference.

In my times looking to try and improve myself - and to see if I am right - I put on You-Tube and watch Puskas and Haynes from the

Fifties and Sixties right through to Zidane and today, Messi and, can only tell those in high places to do the same. In a different book I am writing Harry Redknapp says, "We must find a Pirlo", who walked around our players in Poland (or was it Ukraine?) an Italian, who would not get a game in the Premier League and, Harry himself certainly wouldn't put up with him, for he couldn't control Joe Cole.

The point is: Why are we looking for a Pirlo?

If that is too difficult a question for you, put Coronation Street on...

Again, we are the best nation of misleading and then, afterwards making excuses and, if Beckham was any good at what he is doing, why didn't he and The Prince succeed on their last escapade?

I just wonder exactly what Pele must think when he reads that David Beckham is right up there alongside him and to make thing worse, just before I go to print, Roy Hodgson has put Wayne Rooney alongside him also. Has the entire world gone totally nuts?

It is like saying that one of those Gallaghers were alongside John Lennon or William Roache got an Oscar in front of Cary Grant!

Oh how our standards have dropped. I can understand Simon Cowell earning zillions from average pop stars, but at the FA, the country waits in anticipation for some kind of inspiration.

That I'm afraid, is far too late and our latest chance died with Bobby Moore and, when I watched Beckenbauer interviewed the other day, talking about the incompetence of the same thing in Germany in those days, it simply reminds me of just why the Germans are a superior nation. They do something about such things. While Germany were employing Franz, the English FA were listening to Bobby Moore on Radio Gaga with Jonathan Pearce.

Disgusting!

It is and always will be a case of "I'm Alright Jack" and trust me, they are!

I am beginning to feel weak as I write this piece because I enjoy writing and, feel good about it, but this last piece has been sickening, so I'll get off the subject of Beckham.

The one and only reason I do this is, because of the way he (Bobby) was so shabbily treated by those people who lived off his performances like blood suckers and, yet when he was under house arrest (in Bogota) before his magnificent 1970 World Cup, they were nowhere to be seen and, should have employed him once he hanged up his boots. Like most things in life, this is somehow being told that you're doing it all wrong and, then try to put it right, only it's far too late, you missed the boat and, that boat had Bobby on it - and, all alone, with the FA having their feet up with brandy in hand.

The only person who put himself out was my other hero, Jimmy Greaves, who was out in that part of the world taking part in a car rally.

The story goes that Jimmy went to see him but once getting to the house saw that it was covered by journalists, so I'll let him tell you the story:

"I got there and because the front was crowded, I went round the back and climbed over a wall and onto a tree. I then found my way into the room where Bob was, by going through the kitchen and luckily after looking through the hall, saw him sitting at a table drinking a cup of tea. He looked up and said, "James, what you doing here?"

I said, "I've come to see you mate, I've been worried about you," and, as I said it, a woman came in and asked who I was and what I was doing there? She also asked, "How on earth did you get in?"

I told her that I jumped over that wall and onto that tree before finding my way through the kitchen and she told me that I should not be there, or even if I wanted to come and see Bobby, I should have rung the bell like everyone else. She then led me to the front door like a naughty school kid, you know that head mistress in The Fenn Street Gang, or was it Please Sir?

I walked outside and she closed the door. I rang the bell and she answered the door immediately and asked who I was and what I wanted. I said that I was Jimmy Greaves and wanted to see my friend Bobby Moore.

She then took me to Bobby. I walked in again and we said exactly what we said first time. She then left us together and Bobby asked if I wanted a cup of tea and I said, "No thanks, mate I've got a couple of cans of lager here." "

Jimmy also told the story of when they were in the World Cup and Bobby was with West Ham and he was at Spurs. They promised one another wherever they were on a Saturday night after a match (and whoever they were playing for) they'd always meet at a certain pub in the east End of London.

Again, that is the difference between then and today, simply ask Wayne Bridge!

BOBBY MOORE
After football...

Moore retired from playing professionally in 1978, and had a short relatively unsuccessful spell in football management at Eastern AA in Hong Kong, Oxford City and Southend United.

He became manager of Southend United in 1984. In his first full season, 1984–85, Southend narrowly avoided having to apply for re-election to the Football League amidst severe financial difficulties. However, the side was gradually rebuilt and in the 1985–86 season, Southend started well and were in the promotion race until the new year before eventually finishing 9th. His successor, David Webb - that incoming express train - built upon those foundations to win promotion the following year. Moore agreed to serve on the board of the club and held this role until his death.

His life after football was eventful and difficult, with poor business dealings and his marriage ending. Many saw Moore's acceptance of a role as a columnist for the salacious tabloid newspaper, the Sunday Sport, as a sign of how low he had been forced to go. Moore's supporters said that the Football Association could have given a role to Moore, as the only Englishman to captain a FIFA World Cup winning team. Moore himself kept a dignified silence.

Moore joined London radio station Capital Gold as a football analyst and commentator in 1990. Moore married 42-year-old Stephanie Parlane-Moore (her real maiden name) on 4 December 1991.

He had a son and a daughter from his first marriage, to Christina (Tina) Dean. They were married on 30 June 1960, after a four-year relationship which had started when they were both 15, but the marriage ended in divorce in 1986 after 26 years.

My son was with Bobby's son, Dean, a few days before he took his life and, was going to take him out. We were trying to get him involved with something that we were trying to set-up, so the news was twice as devastating and, had Bobby been here it would have been just one more heartbreak, although I think such a thing would not have happened. I would have contacted Bobby and know that he would have sorted this out, for it was only because of his own illness that he lost control of things and, you don't need that explaining to you.

Had Bobby had been alive today, so would Dean, which is just another question about the authorities, for don't you tell me that they didn't know that the son of the captain of our only ever World Cup winning team was living in a bedsit?

As for the FA not giving him a job when they treat David Beckham, Trevor Brooking, Geoff Hurst like some kind of football Gods, it is absolutely sickening and then, there's Ray Clemence....the FA continue to not only screw-up, but cheat and lie. They, like those in Parliament, cheat on expenses whilst Bobby was working for that newspaper and radio show, to simply "make ends meet."

If I detest them for what they did for me, what they did to my friend was totally unforgivable and, will live in my heart and my head forever and, the latest episode of the John Terry and Fabio Capello story is just another reminder of just how this country sucks at such a level!

Illness and death….

In April 1991, Moore underwent an emergency operation for suspected colon cancer, though at the time it was just reported that he had undergone an "emergency stomach operation".

On 14 February 1993, he publicly announced he was suffering from bowel and liver cancer; by this stage the cancer had spread. Three days later, he commentated on an England match against San Marino at Wembley, alongside his friend Jonathan Pearce. That was to be his final public appearance, just seven days later on 24 February, at 6.36 am, he died at the age of 51.

He was the first member of the England World Cup winning side to die, the second being Alan Ball 14 years later. Moore was also outlived by the coach of the side, Harold Shepherdson, who died in September 1995, and the manager of the side, Alf Ramsey, who died in April 1999.

Bobby Moore's funeral was held on 2 March 1993 at Putney Vale Crematorium, and his ashes were buried in a plot with his father Robert Edward Moore (who died in 1978) and his mother Doris Joyce Moore, who had only died the previous year.

However, he'll be in the great company of Betty Shine - who keeps them in touch of what going on down here - Tony Waddington and Bill Hudson, the other two men who I loved so much and, like Bobby, was such a great influence in my playing days both on and off the field.

His former England team-mate, Jack Charlton, on a BBC documentary of Moore's life in and outside of football, said of Moore's death, "Well, I only ever cried over two people, Billy Bremner and Bob (long pause). He was a lovely man."

On 28 June 1993 his memorial service was held in Westminster Abbey, attended by all the other members of the 1966 World Cup Team. He was only the second sportsman to be so honoured, the first being the West Indian cricketer Sir Frank Worrell.

Here are some of things that important people thought about Bobby:

"My captain, my leader, my right-hand man, who was the spirit and the heartbeat of the team and, a cool, calculating footballer I could trust with my life. He was the supreme professional, the best I ever worked with. Without him England would never have won the World Cup," - Alf Ramsey

"He was my friend as well as the greatest defender I ever played against. The world has lost one of its greatest football players and an honourable gentleman," - Pelé

"Bobby Moore was a real gentleman and a true friend," - Franz Beckenbauer

"Moore was the best defender I have ever seen," - Sir Alex Ferguson

"Bobby Moore was the best defender in the history of the game," - Franz Beckenbauer

"There should be a law against him. He knows what's happening 20 minutes before everyone else." Jock Stein

"Ask me to talk about Bobby Moore the footballer and I will talk for days. Ask me about the man and I will dry up in a minute," Ron Greenwood

The only evidence of The Working Man's Ballet was left in Spain, with Lionel Messi and, his Barcelona amigos. This country has ignored all of its greatest talents both on and off the playing fields over the years and, now the result is that we are a third class nation in more ways than one. When Montenegro give you a game and our best player is doing his David Beckham impression - by getting himself sent-off - you know you are no longer up there where Bobby Moore stood. I think when it all sunk in, is when I put on the TV and, saw Beckham standing alongside Prince Harry, or was it William?

I thought of Bobby sitting in the freezing cold with Jonathan Pearce.

As I said The Ballet has gone but lives on with Waddington and my father and, as I watch matches today, I am reminded of their loss, or my loss and, the thought of just how badly they were treated. Football, I have always said, football is a great game for bringing people

together, however, it seems that it is no different from life, the wrong ones always seem to win….my mind flashes to Henri Charriere, for he stands alongside the ones who have been so mistreated!

PS: THIS IS WHERE I CAME IN….WHAT REALLY IS GOING ON AT CHELSEA?

THEY HAVE BECOME A CLUB, BUT NOT A FOOTBALL CLUB…..THE MONEY REALLY IS STARTING TO STINK - WHEN DI MATTEO DOESN'T WANT THE JOB?

Only ten days before the biggest match in the clubs' history to date this occurs in one of the nationals: Di Matteo blew his Anfield selection - and his shot of being Chelsea boss, for the Blues' brass are furious after under-strength side's loss to Liverpool guaranteed club's worst league finish of the Abramovich era, after Di Matteo's team was thrashed by Liverpool only a few days after celebrating their FA Cup success.

I truly believe that this man doesn't want the job, but can walk away with his head held high and, how many of Abramovich's managers' can do that?

Getty: The Book of Revelations states that the last days will be heralded by the Four Horsemen of the Apocalypse. But while the quartet of Chelsea top-brass who entered the sombre visiting dressing room at Anfield were not Pestilence, War, Famine and Death, the end-game for Roberto Di Matteo may have begun.

Watching a 4-1 capitulation to a side they had conquered in the FA Cup Final at Wembley three days earlier had not been in the script for the Stamford Bridge hierarchy. The heaviest defeat of the Roman Abramovich era also confirmed that Chelsea will finish sixth, their lowest position in the nine years since the Russian took over the club, and with their worst tally - by, at best, seven points - too.

Anything other than an against-the-odds victory over Bayern Munich in the Champions League Final on May 19 will condemn the Blues to Europa League football, becoming a Thursday night (on Channel 5 or elsewhere) afterthought while all eyes are drawn to its big brother.

No wonder, then, that the faces of chairman Bruce Buck, chief executive Ron Gourlay, secretary David Barnard and technical director Michael Emenalo were thunderous after the final whistle at Anfield.

Who's the boss?

Nothing will be said in the coming days that might disrupt preparations ahead of the season-defining game in the Allianz Arena, but the team Di Matteo selected on Merseyside may become seen as the straw that broke the camel's back. Abramovich's lieutenants had anticipated a few changes after the FA Cup Final, but with Chelsea still in with an outside chance of finishing third, let alone fourth, the expectation was that Di Matteo would field a strong side. After all, the Italian had been made aware of the annoyance and unhappiness in the upper echelons when he fielded a shadow team at Arsenal between the two legs of the Champions League semi against Barcelona - although subsequent events in the Camp Nou were seen by Di Matteo as abundant justification of his decision. The nature of the Blues' subsidence at Anfield, though, was not good enough, irrespective of Di Matteo's legitimate citing of the fact that Chelsea had played a staggering 19 games in 63 days, starting with his first match at Birmingham on March 6. Squirming in their seats, shaking their heads in disbelief, this was not what the Chelsea leadership envisaged. Di Matteo may have changed the mood music around the club since replacing Andre Villas-Boas but, in the Premier League at least, he has not significantly altered results. Just four wins in 10 games - one of those the decidedly lucky 2-1 home victory over Wigan - and defeats at the hands of Manchester City, Newcastle and Liverpool plus draws against Spurs and Arsenal total15 points out of 30.

By Chelsea's standards, that is simply not sufficient.

Di Matteo would be a popular choice in the dressing room - the same dressing room warned by Abramovich that the players were responsible for the failure of Villas-Boas - but the men who count do not care about the players.

Although Pep Guardiola has turned Abramovich down twice already, it seems unlikely there will not be a third approach to the Catalan, while Germany coach Joachim Loew is out of contract after Euro 2012.

Another pop at Pep: Chelsea will surely try a third time to tempt Guardiola?

Senior figures at the Bridge maintain there will be no rush to make a public statement at the end of the season, so Di Matteo faces being left hanging on, waiting to hear his fate and, that will, at least, give him hope, unlike Claudio Ranieri, Avram Grant - sacked three days after Champions League Final defeat in 2008 - or Carlo Ancelotti, who received his marching orders in a Goodison Park stairwell within minutes of the end of last season, however, Di Matteo's only realistic chance of being made permanent rather than merely "interim" manager seems to be if Abramovich cannot get any of his targets and, even then he would be seen as merely keeping the seat warm. In the meantime, Di Matteo has to try to put together a team to tackle Bayern, with his options hugely restricted by the suspensions ruling out John Terry, Branislav Ivanovic, Ramires and Raul Meireles and reliant massively on his medical staff. Gary Cahill looks to be running out of time to recover from his hamstring injury although fellow centre-back David Luiz, out since pulling up lame against Spurs on April 15, could return to face doomed Blackburn in the final home game of the campaign on Sunday, which left the Italian saying, "We will check their progress and see how well they develop, We're obviously working towards their fitness and trying to get them back. But I can't answer if they will play on Sunday. Ideally we'd like everybody available but we will have to see."

The midfield absences made Tuesday's game a Champions League audition for Michael Essien, Oriol Romeu and Florent Malouda, where Essien looked exactly like a man who's been wrecked by three major knee ligament operations in two and a half years. Knee injuries have taken a huge toll on Essien. Romeu also floundered, leaving Malouda, set to leave this summer, the favourite to play by default and, Essien - lucky not to see red for a shocker on Andy Carroll - will increase Chelsea's desire to land Newcastle's powerhouse Cheick Tiote, despite the £25million valuation placed on the midfielder by the Tynesiders. After the game, Di Matteo blew out his cheeks before conceding: "Michael has been out for a long time. It takes a bit of time to get back into the rhythm. I'm sure that next year, with a full pre-season, he will start next season fine. I will have to think about the team for Munich. We have these suspensions and I have to think about how to play and which players fit best into our set-up for the final."

CRISIS WHAT CRISIS?

This was a great album by the best band since The Beatles, Supertramp.....and as our boys and girls still face tremendous turmoil in Afghanistan, something that is far too often overlooked, I come to this: As the two teams that had the biggest influence on me back in 1969 face just that. As you have just read Chelsea are, although going into the biggest club match in domestic football, are at the crossroads, where they simply have no idea of their future and, that is all because of the constant chopping and changing of management by Russian Oligarch Roman Abramovich, something I said all along would be not only so damaging, but become his downfall. They now also face the following, something my great pal, Martin Knight told me about some months ago and, it all revolves around the one giant stumbling block - the CPO (Chelsea Pitch Owners) - something that Ken Bates began, never knowing after selling out to the Russian that it would be of such great importance. Or did he?

I can only tell you after my chat with Martin that Bruce Buck is behind the buying of these shares back from those loyal supporters by conning them. After telling me about all of this, I asked Martin to let me know when the next meeting will take place because I know many of those fans who are now being held at gunpoint, in fact, like I have told you throughout, it is something that will never change at my local club. I am still waiting...for Martin, that is!

BRIDGE OF SIGHS: Chelsea fans loathe the idea of having to give up on a stadium they love. Supporters always feel an emotional attachment to their home ground but for Chelsea fans the link with Stamford Bridge may have a deeper resonance than most.

The Chelsea owner Roman Abramovich has shown more respect for the club's tradition than the unlamented Bates regime but he will not be around forever and, Chelsea's chairman, Bruce Buck, has compared it to a little "financial housekeeping" that should have been cleared up years ago, a state of affairs no longer appropriate for a club now wholly owned by Roman Abramovich. For Chelsea fans, though, the club's offer to buy back the freehold on the land the stadium is built on from the supporter group which owns it is a hugely emotive issue.

Chelsea Pitch Owners was formed back in the 1990s as a result of the prolonged and bitter battle fought by the club's pugnacious chairman, Ken Bates, against property developers who wished to knock down the stadium and build luxury flats on the site. Few doubted that the club's very existence was on the line. Through a combination of a fortuitous slump in the property market and the cussed determination of Bates, Chelsea won back the deeds to their own ground and, to ensure that the club would never again fall victim to the developers, the idea was that fans would own patches of turf ensuring that any prospective buyer would have to negotiate with thousands of individual owners. Chelsea Pitch Owners could function only thanks to a loan from the club but still it was one of the earliest and most imaginative examples of supporter participation in football. Legend has it - we cannot know for sure because Abramovich never speaks publicly - that the sight from the oligarch's helicopter of the green oasis of Stamford Bridge, so close to the centre of London, is what led the Russian billionaire to buy Chelsea for £17m from Bates in 2003 and absorb its huge debts. Supporters always feel an emotional attachment to their home ground but for Chelsea fans the link has perhaps a deeper resonance than most. Chelsea Football Club was founded to occupy Stamford Bridge rather than the other way around when in 1905 Fulham declined Gus Mears's offer for them to play their home games there. In the days when what is now the West stand was one huge bank Stamford Bridge drew vast crowds. The 82,905 people who watched Chelsea take on Arsenal in 1935 remains the second-highest attendance ever for an English league match and it is estimated that when Moscow Dynamo visited just after the Second World War more than 100,000 crammed in, some literally hanging from the rafters.

Less happily, the new East stand (now the oldest part of the ground) is widely held to have hastened the demise of Chelsea's stylish early 70s side as construction costs soared out of control, and before redevelopment the stadium's running track, which once hosted greyhound racing, had a deadening effect on the atmosphere. Nevertheless, the sight of the stands and, in the old days, the floodlights rising above the local streets as the supporters took over Fulham Road on a match day embodied tradition and pride in the club.

At the height of the battle for the Bridge in the 1980s most supporters would have found the idea of leaving their traditional home inconceivable. Times, though, have changed. Chelsea then were in a precarious state, bouncing between the top two divisions. Now they are one of the top sides in Europe, with a wage bill to match and, Arsenal, having left Highbury behind for a bigger ground, pull in significantly more cash from every home game than Chelsea. Many clubs have moved to new stadiums and demonstrated that the unthinkable is in fact doable and that life goes on (although in Arsenal's case they have not won a trophy since switching to Ashburton Grove).

But the great news for Arsenal fans is that he (Wenger) has the good sense to hire Steve Bould, the player I was very much responsible for him becoming an Arsenal player in the 80s. Steve has been promoted to the first team following the retirement of Pat Rice. I have been absolutely stunned as for all the time Pat was assistant they have not had a decent back four and, that will change with Bould around. I have spoken to Steve about this; as I did Frank McLintock, and we are all agree on this. Anyhow, I take this book to wish Pat a good retirement and, Steve a very successful time as the Frenchman's right-hand man…..and, thereafter, I'm certain he will one day make a great Arsenal manager. The sooner the better, if Arsenal are finally going to get back to winning ways!

Modern safety concerns appear to rule out the possibility of an enlarged capacity at Stamford Bridge, although that is the option most fans would surely prefer. When nearby sites have emerged as potential new homes for the club in recent years - Earl's Court, Battersea power station, for example - the mood among Chelsea fans has been broadly receptive. Supporters have tasted success and want to continue to compete at the top level. Financial fair play rules will increase the pressure on the club to pay its way without its sugar daddy's largesse.

And yet … the impulse behind the formation of Chelsea Pitch Owners remains valid. Who better than the supporters to safeguard the long-term interests of their club? Buck has assured fans that the club will not move further than three miles from Stamford Bridge before 2020.

But what about after 2020?

The difficulty of finding a suitable site in London is well-known. Could Chelsea end up playing in Slough, Guildford or Milton Keynes? And who will own the club by then? Abramovich has shown more respect for the club's tradition than the unlamented Bates regime but he will not be around forever and his successor may not be as generous or benign towards the club.

Chelsea Pitch Owners is being asked to take a great deal on trust.

I have the perfect solution. How about simply start building on the end of the runway at London's Heathrow Airport, for the future of the club is in the import and export business, with the days of an Alan Hudson, Peter Osgood, Jimmy Greaves or Frank Lampard, long gone. Long live the King….which was, of course Osgood, no matter how many times Didier Drogba scores at Wembley?

YOU CAN HAVE CHELSEA HARBOUR - BUT NOT THE POWER STATION - NOT EVEN BATTERSEA

Well as I told you, they took away Upcerne Road and, our prefab and along with it our Cage, then built Chelsea Harbour, a place where you have to be wealthy, whereas in our time you had to be one of us, in the main. So, it's great to see that Battersea, one of the places I mention about where those once faithful "real" Chelsea came from have knocked the Russian and American back. Why?

Because, you just can't keep taking. When we lived there and made it the place it became we never took, we gave...   BATTERSEA BLOW FOR CHELSEA

Chelsea have failed in their bid to build a new stadium at Battersea Power Station. Last month the Blues revealed that they had submitted an application to move to the 39-acre site in Wandsworth, but administrators revealed on Thursday morning that a joint bid by two Malaysian companies - SP Setia and Sime Darby - had been chosen instead. A statement from Ernst & Young read: "Following an extensive global marketing campaign, undertaken by Ernst & Young Real Estate Corporate Finance and Knight Frank LLP, the Joint Administrators are pleased to announce that on Wednesday 6 June 2012 they entered into an exclusivity agreement with SP Setia and Sime Darby and are working towards a timely exchange and completion of the site and associated land."

The European champions are considering moving away from their Stamford Bridge home as their current capacity of around 42,000 is preventing them from bringing in the kind of match day revenue enjoyed by the likes of Arsenal and Manchester United, who have much bigger stadiums. Chelsea revealed in plans last month that they intended to transform the Grade II listed building on the south bank of the River Thames in to "one of the most iconic football stadiums in the world".

Their plan for Battersea was to develop it into a 60,000-seater ground that included the power station's four chimneys. When they released their plans, Chelsea insisted that they had definitely not committed themselves to leaving Stamford Bridge, although they also claimed it was not economically viable to redevelop their current west London home.

The Blues have also been linked with other sites in south-west London.

SP Setia and Sime Derby revealed in a release to the Malaysian stock exchange this morning that their £400million "multi-use real estate regeneration project" bid had been successful. They also plan to build a tube station on the premises that will connect to the Northern Line.

A 28-day period of due diligence will now follow, but the hopes Chelsea had of relocating to the site of one of London's most iconic landmarks are seemingly over.

Last October the fans' group who own the freehold of Stamford Bride, Chelsea Pitch Owners (CPO), rejected an offer from the club's owner Roman Abramovich, to buy their shares. CPO shareholders have accused Chelsea of failing to fully explore the prospect of revamping Stamford Bridge, while Hammersmith and Fulham Council have disputed the club's claims that doing so would be far more expensive that moving.

Wandsworth Council, meanwhile, were happy with the administrators' decision over Battersea. Council leader Ravi Govindia said: "There is still some way to go but this is potentially very good news. The power station is one of the biggest development opportunities in Nine Elms and key to extending the Northern Line into Battersea. "We're making tremendous progress towards transforming this old industrial stretch of the South Bank which will provide up to 25,000 new jobs for London. It's important that this site and its iconic building are not left behind and that a developer is brought in who understands our vision for the new Nine Elms."

Chelsea said on Thursday afternoon that they were disappointed with the decision over Battersea but confirmed they are still looking at other options for a new home when a club statement read: "We are disappointed not to be selected as the preferred bidder for Battersea Power Station, as we believe we can create an iconic and architecturally significant stadium on the site in a scheme which is commercially viable and of great benefit to the Wandsworth community and London generally. We have been clear throughout this process that Battersea is one of a limited number of options the club is considering."

As I heard this great news it took me back to the Sixties when I was a young boy living just across the water from that great dark old building, which is mirrored with the Chelsea equivalent. And as you know I love a song, which always seems to be so apt, sang by the Rolling Stones, who used to play in the Wetherby Arms, which went like this:

YOU CAN'T AWAYS GET WHAT YOU WANT
WHILST AROUND THE CORNER

How lucky we were in the Sixties and, me especially, for I remember going to Park Lane, down Curzon Street to see Ken Adam, who was my agent from 1970 and, then to Shepherds Market before meeting up in the Playboy Club, yeah, when only nineteen. The place was buzzing with faces from all around the world and, stars galore, because it was the best time and, although we did not know it then, we most certainly had the best of everything. There was The London Hilton on a Monday night with Allan Phillips, a place where every London club was represented for a monthly Boxing Card put on by The Sporting Club and, then Allan would take us into the 007 Bar before the Playboy Club, oh, if only we earned what they do today, if only to repay Allan, who was on a par with Matthew Harding and

Tony Banks, simply Chelsea through and through and, like them also, so sadly missed. But now this...

Hundreds upon hundreds of unkempt Romanian vagabonds have swept into the affluent Park Lane area of the capital and also infested nearby Marble Arch. They have been turning up since the beginning of last month and now Westminster Council are worried 'several hundred' more could soon arrive. Most of the men while away their time drinking copious amounts of vodka and laying about while the women divvy food out from their cheap plastic bags. In disgusting circumstances, street cleaners are left to remove human excrement left by the intruders. They are usually seen hanging around showrooms which sell expensive cars. A gardener who works in the area, Selma Chaib, said, "The problem's been getting worse as more turn up. I've seen them coming out of Sainsbury's in Marble Arch with big bottles of vodka at 9am. They leave bottles, bags and their own mess all over the place - it's disgusting. I saw 50 of them playing dice for about 300 pound coins laid down on the ground."

Another worker Abdul Mohammed, 36, said: "I've seen them in KFC begging for food" and also shopkeeper Said Aly, 60, said: "They sleep in underpasses and leave lots of mess."

One of the Romanians was quoted as saying "The houses here are very nice. I came here from Romania today. We left Romania to find work. We can have a better life here."

Nickie Aiken, a Westminster councillor said many were enticed by tricksters pledging employment and a home saying, "They're dropped at Park Lane, given a map and dumped. It's sad. We need to stop coaches from Romania. It's 73 days until the Olympics and the International Olympic Committee will be staying in hotels on Park Lane where people are now sleeping rough. It presents a bad image, in the last six weeks we have seen this influx. These are very desperate people - something is happening in Romania. We think we are dealing with a couple of hundred so far. If we don't get on top of the problem we could end up with several hundred more."

Police confirmed they were trying to work with both the council and the UK Border Agency to prevent crime and anti-social behaviour linked to the recent intake of gypsies.

Dear Miss Aiken, how on earth did you get into politics? "We have to do something about this," I think that you and all of your friends are a little too late once again. I am the person who wrote The Working Man's Ballet a book for those people who were local and, came from working backgrounds, not from Romania or Poland, Oh and by the way, my son, who was born in the heart of London, Princess Beatrice Hospital, in fact, was attacked by two Polish immigrants about a month ago and, it was a good job he hadn't his 2-

year-old daughter with him, for he would have slit their throats and, got a long prison sentence for being racial, so maybe you can stop that as well. We are simply wasting our time here in this country, well it's not ours now is it, while you lot, I am afraid are living in the dark ages whilst getting richer for being there. This has gone too far and, there's nothing you can do to stop it, so like our footballers, keep your mouth shut and your eyes open, because you might be next.

Alan Hudson, unfortunately living here - if only you could kindly get me deported and give me what you give these people who enter our country, for that would be my answer, as for you, forget it love!

SIR ALEX'S CRISIS

Back to the game and a second crisis which is taking place approximately 200 miles north of Watford as Manchester face the biggest dilemma since George Best walked out - at the age of 26 - and Sir Alex Ferguson had to revamp his team by ousting Norman Whiteside and Paul McGrath, although keeping Bryan Robson after taking that massive gamble by building his team around Ryan Giggs, David Beckham, Paul Scholes, Gary and Phil Neville and Nicky Butt. Had that move not have paid off the club would have been finished, but no matter what Alan Hansen says, you can get success with youth, but only if your senior players are of a special quality and, luckily they were, unlike today. They have no Cantona, Sheringham or Van Nistelrooy to make all the right decisions when their midfield players are in possession. The kid Welbeck looks like he's got a good future, but it is difficult to place him any category and, when say that, the three players I have just mentioned were top drawer and, that was because they did not show their class every now and then, they were incredible consistent. Rooney for me is a long way behind in that department and, is nowhere near as consistent and, his temperament is definitely suspect. I could forgive him early on for thinking he'd grow up, but after watching his antics in Montenegro, he continues to show that he can be very unreliable. Truly great players such as Teddy were in a different class and, could set the pace of attacks by holding it up and, bringing people in the game at just the right time.

Here's a man with great class both on and off the field, he followed Cantona and shut a lot of people up…

As I write on 11.5.12, that time has returned, where the most successful man in the history of the game faces crisis number three - in the case of Old Trafford. After experiencing the most inept and limp performance against fiercest rivals, and new champions-elect, come Sunday, Manchester City, Sir Alex faces yet another crossroad, for this Manchester United squad and, team in particular, is simply the worst since he took over the reins and, began rebuilding. What he has achieved is mindboggling, but the one thing he has never done is put all his eggs in one basket and, that egg, Wayne Rooney, does not lay enough gold to carry this team through. Oh how they cry out for a Teddy Sheringham to hold the ball up with such craft, assurance, confidence and know-how. Dare I say it - although this is a bad Premier League - United are in tremendous trouble of losing their grip on something that was once theirs for all to take off of them.

That is my update with the European Championships coming up and, once again, turmoil, although in Roy Hodgson they have a man who finally has everything in the right place. This has always been his main objective and, now he can take his very own team to the tournament, which he has begun by rightfully leaving out Rio Ferdinand. If Alf Ramsey had one thing right it was the leadership of Bobby Moore, something we lack today. As I said when missing out of the 1970 World Cup and, England's failure to qualify throughout that decade, we still have absolutely no chance.

I just hope the media are not too rough on Hodgson, as they were Swede, Turnip and, the Wally with the Brolly. With Harry - keeping in mind - we were in Seattle together when I was contemplating writing The Ballet, having shot himself in the foot, regarding the England position, he now faces a tough task in holding onto his Tottenham job. I believe that he has done far too much talking in the capacity of both manager and Sun columnist and, has overstepped the mark as Daniel Levy will take into account him wanting to walk away for Soho Square and, then after the court case several things began going wrong for him. I am interested in him speaking to Alan Sugar, for if he asked for the Lord's opinion, I am pretty certain, the former Spurs chairman would say, "He was ready to walk out on you and leave you in the lurch and, you can't be loyal to someone who is disloyal."

We must always keep in mind that these people might be idiots that run our game, but when it comes to watching their own positions, they are far from it. Harry has always had a great sense of humour, but I think the whole country found the bank account in Monaco, a little too funny, especially when there are politicians constantly cheating and lying, whilst our boys and girls are getting shot at in Afghanistan on a daily basis.

I finish this book in Majorca, where I can hardly get up and down the hill to watch the final couple of matches of the season, although I will get a taxi on Saturday for the Champions League final from Magaluf.

I have many happy memories of Palma Nova and Santa Ponca when I was visiting here before many of my operations under Professor Williams, Professor Mundy and David Ralph in the Royal London, Middlesex and University College Hospitals.

Along with David Goodier, Claire Strickland and Otto Chan, I think about them every now and then and, thank them, especially David, who pieced back my pelvis, insisted on stronger management and, then finally - along with the C-Clamp - saved my legs from amputation.

I can't leave this without telling you about my trips to this island, one where packed my bags one day and, whilst doing so, decided that I would return without my walking sticks. So one night I went out to my local bar in Santa Ponca - where the barman, Smiler, was once again having them in fits of tears - and on leaving there in the early hours threw away the two things that I had been so dependent on. Well, I had beaten the wheelchair in the pub opposite the hospital and, now I had beaten the sticks in a bar on Majorca and, they say you can't do business in pubs?

I beg to differ!

But seeing you have been patient reading of my favourite moments, so far, in the game, my most favourite moment on this island and, always will be, was on the First of May, which is day that has all my times with Leslie come flooding back. I sat by the waters' edge, the only man on earth, and lifted my glass to both Leslie and The Bee Gees, as their song of the same name went through my head over and over and over again.

There is a song that goes, 'I wish it could be Christmas every day.' Well, I wish it could be the 1st of May. That is my song for my best mate who died so young and, so tragically. The only consolation is that I know that he's with Bill, because I saw them both behind that cloud. As for when I'll see them again, I'll just have to wait and see what Betty Shine meant when she said, "It's not your time, you still have some unfinished business," well, Betty I'm still waiting.

Although my life began in Elm Park Gardens on 21 June 1951, The Ballet, aptly named by Mr. Waddington, was born in Seattle exactly thirty years on. I enjoyed writing the original book immensely, although I was under a lot of pressure, which led to me near death, which was a failed attempt on my life by Ashgar Fatehi and, all I can say to whoever was behind it is, that they should have got a local driver, but they obviously they couldn't, because like that fella in the pub, they knew that drink talks and, people like Fatehi don't drink and, even if he did, he doesn't talk in our native tongue when out with his pals. I know, and feel, like this has turned from a wonderful story about a young boy who fulfilled his dream of becoming a professional footballer to one of such sinister and more evil than good. I think that a lot to do with all of this is the environment where it all took place, in the east end of London.

Who said the days of the Krays were over?

This would never have happened in Chelsea, Wimbledon, Stoke-on-Trent or Seattle, where I resided before meeting my wife. However, after all said and done, although the experience has wrecked my life in so many ways - something that the culprit should be happy with really - because had it been me, I'd rather my enemy live in constant pain, than die instantly and, for this I am thankful and sincerely grateful to them for being like the FA and employing an idiot to do the job of a professional.

The love I had for my second wife was real and serious and, I was devastated to see her chair moving further and further away from my hospital bed by the day. I cannot stress enough that I loved her so very much and, am still trying to work it all out, as to how this all came about. Ann, was a stunningly beautiful lady, but could also, like so many other women, swing like a sharp edged pendulum. However, as you do when having someone you cherish and, I did, like with a great run on the horses or, an incredible purple patch playing the game, you never see it coming to an end. Again, however, I never dreamed of such an ending. Well, not one in a pine box and, as someone famous said on his headstone, "If I knew I was going to look so good, I wouldn't have went," well, with me, if I had known they were planning on killing me, I would not have put so much hard work into my final training session on that incredible of days, which led into an even more incredible night.

So, where I put Sinatra on my stereo and, poured myself a Crown Royal Deluxe Bourbon over a crystal glass of crushed ice, with a slice of orange, I finish 31 years on, far more disillusioned than when Frank hit his first note. It seems a little strange that Francis Albert Sinatra, should die whilst I was escaping my maker and, I still remember the news slowly coming through to my hospital room. And then a copy of the Sun was brought in with the headline so simple SINATRA DEAD which had me thinking, is that all, which was a Tony Bennett song that goes: Is that all there is, for if that's all there is my friend, then let's keep on dancing, then we'll get out the booze and, have a ball, if that's all there is?

My immediate future is to concentrate on that other book of mine, Don't Shoot the Taliban...You'll Wake the Locals and, wait to see how this one goes before writing the follow-up, although I have almost got it done and, the only reason, I split it in two was one/it was too many pages, for one book and, two/hopefully someone somewhere in another pub might just give us a little more information on just who was behind all of this. If I can tell them one thing and, that is, you have given me the most incredible pain and amazing discomfort in my standing, walking, sitting, sleeping and all-in-all, my everyday life. However, what you also have done is given me the greatest challenge of a life, I found very demanding and, one where I have always felt the odds have been against me, not to mention, those people I have mentioned in this book, hence, the Killing Fields. You gave me an incredible boost when I was at my lowest ebb, for some people crack and, then there are people like me. The cross countries were never long enough for me, I just couldn't get enough of them. Even after the longest of sessions, I knew when going through those sessions that I would have to pull out all of the stops the following day. It was always in my mind, as Willie Nelson, would sing.

But most of all, it was when I was given all of the news of my multiple injuries, which led to me never walking again and so on and so on. A nerve man tested my legs one day and shook his head, unplugged his machine and, simply walked out. They told David, that they were wasting everyone's time and, there were people waiting that had a chance of living and, had David not walked round to see me in the ICU and, decided that they were wrong, I was cooked. All of this coming back to me gave me as much ammunition as they have taken over to the front in Afghanistan. When my friends and family looked at me with some kind of pity it wound me up and, drove me on. I wanted to start all over again, with not only my life, but my career. I wanted to go to all those wonderful places again. New York, San Diego, Tampa Bay, Jamaica - and Ocho Rios in particular - and then I wanted one last sniff of Hoolihans and Benjamins in Seattle. These were my goals, just like Osgood was hungry for his, I was hungry for mine. Once this book is printed, I just hope that I can fulfil those dreams and, then there was this wonderful little baby coming into our lives and, wanting her to see such places - and, that is when Nancy really will have a smiling face, trust me!

Although those odds were stacked so very high against my living, where those early exchanges in the Intensive Care Unit saw me through such an incredible amount of cutting and patching up, but unknowingly to me, I was in the hands of David Goodier, who without, I might be looking down laughing with my dad, my mum, Tony Waddington, Bobby Moore, Geordie Armstrong, Leslie and Harry Yewings, all people I loved so very much and, for a change, cannot put into words.

And then, as you know by now, there was Osgood and Hutchinson, who will always be together and, by one another's side. All of these people were the main reasons behind my sitting down on that beautiful Seattle night - much like in the Mile End Road, even though June was different from December - however, the night was still and, nobody knew where it would lead to. Well, they didn't in Seattle and, although they did in east London, they never thought that they'd be reading this?

No, I was absolutely choked when that great big fat bastard Anderson took over Seattle Sounders and, I put him to the sword much like those Chelsea players do Abramovich, the only difference being, although they are not in his league moneywise, it would make absolutely no difference had they had been given the same treatment that I received. Had I been wealthy, like Matthew say, Anderson would not have been able to spoil my life, for I would have done my utmost to get that first knife in, something I was just about learning about when reaching the Great North West,

Whilst on the subject of my times in Seattle, which is all in Book Two, one of the greatest characters of my time there has just died. On 5.6.2012 the following happened and, you'll read about Steve in the follow-up, but as I write, I could not finish this book on a sadder note. Before hearing of this, I was so happy to have finished this book, but now I have hit a low:

STEVE BUTTLE, THE FANS FAVOURITE, DIES AGED 59

"He was all heart and soul," said Alan Hinton, who coached the NASL Sounders from 1980-82. He wasn't a big guy and had a wonky left knee. You wouldn't have thought he could play at all the way he strolled onto the field at the introductions, but as soon as the game started, he probably had the fastest brain on the field."

Popular for his No. 15 uniform, skill and nonstop hustle, Buttle totalled 15 goals and 44 assists as a versatile midfielder for the Sounders. He helped lead Seattle to the 1977 Soccer Bowl, where it lost to the Pele-led New York Cosmos.

Buttle played his last seasons with the Pittsburgh Spirit of the Major Indoor Soccer League, before joining the team as an assistant coach upon retirement. In 1987, Hinton - who loved Buttle's sense of humour - hired his former player as an assistant coach for the MISL's Tacoma Stars. Both were fired a couple years later, and Buttle moved back to England in 1991.

His soccer legacy lives on through his son, John, who played a couple seasons in college and coaches at Juanita High School in Kirkland.

"Since a very young age, all I remember was being around soccer," said John Buttle, who credits his love of the game to his father.

Steve Buttle, who was diagnosed with terminal bowel cancer a few months ago, is survived by his ex-wife, Jen Sheeley, their two children - John, of Seattle, and Sarah, of Omaha, Neb. - and four grandchildren. Buttle was an only child and his parents, Freda and Arthur, live in Norwich and cared for him in his final days.

"It's a sad day that we've lost him so young," said Hinton, "but he kept battling, just like he did all the days of his life."

Also, along with those wonderful times both on and off the field with Steve - in the follow-up - you'll find out about me travelling to the Potteries to not only play my best football, after my England ban was dropped, following the sacking of Ramsey and, then being so unfortunate to experience Don Revie taking over. Talk of out of the frying pan…

So the sparks were still flying, so to speak and, I had not given up hope of receiving that first England cap. My life was still very much a roller-coaster ride before that car nearly finished me off, but as you can see, I am still alive, although far from kicking.

My greatest regret was still to come and, that came when I was about to become the Stoke City manager. I met with the chairman on the Friday night and, he asked me to see him at the Victoria Ground the following Monday, where we would "sort it out" and, once getting off the train and, onto the platform, I telephoned to find out that Mr.

Frank Edwards had died, just a few hours earlier n - in the early hours of the morning, in fact.

I truly don't know what I did from that train station?

Even after my career was cut short by injury and, being in and out of the game for long periods, which led to my off field antics taking on new meanings in different parts of the world. You might say, from The Town House to The Tin Pan Alley or where my final curtain began to come down, in Vagabonds, the place where I met my wife and, CID, John Mullally, the owner. But, as luck would have it, as you now know, the driver messed up and, that final curtain was, as Frank sang, closing in on me. This is where Tommy Nicholson, TD and I had so many wonderful afternoons and, the place which would end up being responsible for my near demise. The first day that I walked in, I had a feeling that something would happen with Ann, although we were both married. I was living in Seattle and back here on vacation and, visiting Fleet Street, where Brian Madley worked and, then all of a sudden there seemed to something in the air. As I have mentioned, Ann was the cream of the crop and, it was just when we looked at each other, it seemed inevitable we would end up together. But it was not on my mind when I returned to Seattle, but when I did Maureen and I had a big row and, after thinking that she did not appreciate the life I had given her, I contacted Ann, to simply keep in touch and told her what I thought about her and, it was all really innocent. By the time I went back to England the next time, my marriage was deteriorating and, I am one of those people who act on my first gut feeling. To make things tougher, Ann was a beautiful girl and, it seemed, like in the movie Sleepless there was that "magic" the first time I touched her. This "magic" though, was to almost cost me my life.

On a lighter note, Ainsley Harriet was the Head Chef, a man Ann always told me insisted that he'd be a star, I only ate there a couple of times and, he certainly had that side of it right. One afternoon my mate George Byatt and I were joined by Brian Madley, who was still with the Sunday People then and, the great Freddie Trueman, one of my all-time favourite sportsmen, who was working for the same newspaper.

If only he was as quick to the bar as he was as he ran up to the crease, not mention once the ball left his hand.

He was something else and, I loved following him and his Yorkshire team as a kid every time they came and, slaughtered both Surrey and Middlesex, where I was a regular at both The Oval and Lords. In those days, I opened the batting with my Geoff Boycott bat, along with Bill Boyce, Bill was the cousin of Keith, the Essex and West

Indian all-rounder and, had Bill a father like mine to guide him, I have no doubt he would have made it, like I did, in our game.

Bill was the best cricketer and sprinter while I was the best footballer and long distance runner in west London as 14-year-olds at Kingsley.

Bill was the reason I was introduced to racism. The first time I came across such a thing, it was because of him. We were in Chiswick one evening for net practice with Lofty Herman, an old player, who I think was umpiring at that time and, after one session he invited me to Lords for a trial and, after he asked me, I said, "Great, we'd love to come." He said, "Who's we?" In which I replied "Billy and me." He made it very clear that my mate weren't welcome and, for me it was, "welcome to the real world, Al."

I, of course, would not go without Bill, for as I said to Herman, "My mates' different class to me." But he was simply the wrong colour.

Talking of run-ups, there are still more run-ins to come and, by the time I begin going through it again, I will have had a few more, of that you can be sure, but until I do, I must tell you that Sir Alex is also another who crossed me, but that's all to come and, it amused me more than anything. I like Sir Alex, but if you catch him on a bad day, it don't matter who you are, you'll get it. I smiled afterwards, because he's mugged of Beckham, Van Nistelrooy and Jap Stam, so I looked at it as if I was in decent company. There is one thing for sure and, that is I could definitely have played for him, but not in the same team as Bryan Robson, who I think was absolutely fantastic. I jest about being in the same team as him, if only getting the Paul McGrath and Norman Whiteside treatment from Sir Alex. Christ, they were two unbelievable players, but if you not going to play ball with Alex you're out. I watched McGrath many times at Villa and he was not only immaculate, but the best player on the field, every time I went there.

As a manager there is no doubt he is the best, even though this past season, I believe has had his worst team since having a clear-out, when bringing in the kids. As for management, with Mr. Edwards, I saw that as my last chance to fulfil another dream, one of becoming a manager although, the only other time was when coming out of hospital and, going to Harry's Book Launch in the Barbican. He asked me to join him on the staff at Upton Park, but I told him to wait until I had thrown away my crutches. I heard no more. But the very last time was when Alan Ball promised me the assistant managers' job at Stoke City just before he took over, again no cigar!

I would have been a brilliant assistant to Alan, for it would have been much like Clough and Taylor who had the simple "Good cop, Bad Cop" approach and, that would have been the way I saw it. Alan was like a bull in a China Shop, whereas, I stand back and, weigh it all up. I recall one day my mate Fox telling me that he would go mad on the training field because players could not do what he did so simply, much like Glenn Hoddle's downfall. When the answer is improving the player you have, for I believe in making a bad player a useful one, a useful player a good one and, a good one, a great one. Sounds ridiculous, but it really is that simple and, I might have said before, football is a simple game complicated by idiots. But what do you expect when you have idiots running the clubs and, the FA running them?

It is a wonder I am so complimentary about him after that, but I hold no grudges, people are what they are and, Alan will always be remembered by me as, one of the truly great inside forwards of all-time.

The thing that disappointed me about that scenario is that I was told that certain board members were against me and, I know who they are, they are the ones who were smoking cigars and sipping champagne with all of their cronies when Jimmy Greenhoff and I were charming the birds from out of the trees in the Potteries, and one or two are still there having taken the club through the dregs of the Trent since Waddington left and, I still will never forgive them for the way they treated him, let alone me. As the saying goes, "I wouldn't give them a nod in the desert."

THROWN OUT BY CHELSEA AND KENSINGTON COUNCIL

On the 28 April 2004 The Evening Standard reported that, former Chelsea star Alan Hudson is in danger of being evicted from his flat near the Stamford Bridge stadium.

A gifted player in the swashbuckling side of the Seventies, he was among the first of the soccer superstars. But his career was blighted by alcohol and gambling and he then suffered appalling leg and pelvic injuries after being hit by a car while crossing the road.

Now Chelsea and Kensington council has given him notice to move out of his late mother's two bedroomed flat. Hudson, 52, has lived there for six years after moving in after the accident and the break-up of his second marriage. He has been in dispute with the council since it ordered him to leave within two days of his mother's death last year. The council wants him to move to a one-bedroom flat but Hudson says he cannot because his son Allen lives with him as his registered carer. Hudson said today, "This is my home. All my family are around me and Allen stays here with me. Without him and my family nearby I do not know how I am going to cope. I suffered appalling injuries when I was knocked down and, I've lost count of the number of operations I've had. I've got to go for another next week. This stress is the last thing I need."

His surgeon, Dr. David Goodier, said Hudson should not be moved given his present condition.

Hudson joined Chelsea as a 13-year-old and was sold for £225,000 to Stoke in 1974 before moving to Arsenal. He also played for England. Chelsea spokesman Neil Barnett said, "Alan is a Chelsea legend and will always be one. He is part of our family and, we are looking at ways of helping former players with problems like Alan."

Today the council said, "While we sympathise with Mr. Hudson's situation, his claim for a succession to his mother's tenancy does not meet the conditions laid out."

The spokesman said Hudson had consistently failed to provide proof of his right to the flat.

The Council lied. I received a telephone call a couple of days after my mothers' death, whilst walking down the Kings Road, on my crutches, to the gymnasium and, had this woman telling me that I was going to be thrown out and, what made things worse - if anything could be worse than losing your mother - was that my son had just complete gutted the flat and laid new floors in. Now, these immigrants get to enjoy all the good work he did, so I am fighting the case. I have been so see Portillo who said he'd help, but he had no intention whatsoever, for although I have tried to contact him, nothing, absolutely nothing. What good is he?

So, the Authorities win again, they always do and, always will, whether the FA, UEFA, FIFA or the Government, that had me thrown out of my mothers' flat and, into the street I was born, those that include Michael Portillo and, those who work just at the back of High Street Kensington, where their jobs are safe and, their code of morals and ethics, are none. If I could come back as something else, I'd like to come back as their electric blanket for that one woman so wicked - she doesn't need naming, for she knows who she is - as for making me homeless and, if they ever, ever come to pick up this book, I can assure them that I have not forgotten them, in fact, I think about them when I'm in the cold and, in the warmth and comfort of the nearest public house. Yeah, it is not only the great people that keep me warm, for those rats are as big a part of my life as those greats, for without the cold you would not appreciate the warmth, without by rain you would not appreciate the sun and, without the bad you wouldn't appreciate the good, or in this book, the great - people that in more cases than not I have had the great fortune to come across.

I like to let them think that they have won, but there is no way. As I have said before, winning is not measured by a result, like in 1966 when winning the only World Cup and, this year Chelsea winning the Champions League is like winning a war, wherever it may be, there are always repercussions and, that will always be the way. It does not mean that if you won the lottery, it would bring you complete happiness. I know you'll laugh, but many have suffered by doing so. My car ordeal has brought me so many problems, the kind that when I was doing my Forest Gump impression around the streets of Chelsea, Wimbledon, Barlaston, Bellevue (Seattle) and Greenwich Park, my favourite of them all, if only for not having to do it and apart from the amazing views, it finally kept me alive. I might have said elsewhere, that I truly believe that my final training session on the morning of the fifteenth saved my life.

That is what I call winning. It does not mean that you are the best, in fact, far from it and, it is very dangerous in thinking that you are. In the case of Chelsea, they have dug a big hole for themselves, because by becoming a better team without the ball, they now have, if they are ever to be looked as true champions by the real football people of our world, to simply prove it by playing the game as champions do. Like Brian Clough said to Revie, "With a smile on your face and win better." They now have to find a way to be the best team when in possession. Like, as I mentioned about the Real Madrid of the Fifties, followed by the brilliant Dutch champions, Ajax, and Bayern Munich in the 70s and now, whether you like it or not, Barcelona, still remembering Lionel Messi is still the age that I was when leaving Chelsea for Stoke City, Tony's youngest, best and most bravest signing at 23 years and six months.

How can I say that? Well, he might have made many great signings, which he did, but with me, had it all have gone pear shaped and, I had turned out to be like so many other big money flops, he would have been put up against the wall, with no bullets spared. It was truly uncanny; his signing of me, as if he knew exactly what it took to take a player rapidly in decline and, piecing him all together again, like Tom Parker did with Seabiscuit and, I must include David Goodier here. All he did was understand his problems and, then he took those problems and, put them all in the right order. As I have said of Tony, he taught me that everything I was doing was alright, but I was not doing it in the right order and, that may sound easy, but nobody before him had bothered. Was it because they didn't know?

Well, a little bit of both really, one/they didn't know and, two/ they couldn't care less. But that is the way it worked, because Tony wanted me to become the player that he was searching for and, he needed to change things with my life, although, with him it was more a case of kidology, although he really cared and, because of that, we had the best relationship any player and his manager ever had. How do I know? Because, I do!

Managers today, in comparison, simply haven't got a clue in that department. All they do is throw a lot of money at it and, when it all looks like it was a bad move, they simply make excuses. When Chelsea signed Torres and he looked like he'd never kicked a football before, they got out of it by saying "give him time," well, I had 90 minutes at the Victoria Ground, otherwise Jeff Powell, Nigel Clarke, Hugh Jamieson, Bob Driscoll, Ian Gibb and Ken Jones would have torn him limb from limb for going anywhere near me, The Fleet Street Gang, in those days were far superior to today's up market scribblers and, they understood because they drank with us and, therefore knew what was going in inside the clubs with certain players and their managers.

Look at George at Old Trafford, when Busby sat him down and gave him - like Ferguson did with Giggs and his mates - a lesson in the art of living, George knew exactly how many flowers there were on his office wall.

I mean, what ever happened to Joe Cole, a player who Harry Redknapp said was the "greatest young player I've ever seen" well, what happened then? He should now be approaching his prime, yet still doesn't understand the basics of the game. You've heard me talk about Alan Ball and, when I saw him play for Blackpool at seventeen, he looked played the game as if he had been here before. That's greatness!

I know I have said so much about Waddington, but my times with him are still to come and as I anticipate my next book, I get excited as to bringing him back to life again and, I just wish the a club would employ me, so I could pass this kind of experience onto the new breed, although I don't think they'll understand. So, there's plenty more still to come and, as I say that, tomorrow, England go into their opening match against France in Donetsk in Ukraine and, I see it another case of what manager will follow Hodgson?

I am looking forward to writing about all of my run-ins for you, but regret that many of my opponents (wrong-doers) are no longer with us and, the only thing I can say about that, is most of the, were when I was going through the most daunting stages of my three lives. I just hope I see it out long enough, which I think I will, for I am still waiting for what Betty Shone promised me and, unlike many I have written about, I trust her implicitly.

And then, last but not least which is quite astonishing, after seeing a photograph of the car and, the smashed-in windscreen, the driver, who they told me, asked a passer-by, "Did, I hit you?"

Well he didn't hit him he had hit me, as this bloke pointed to my battered body lying under that old oak tree. However, when the police arrived at the scene of the crime they, like Kenneth Wolstenholme, also got it all wrong, thinking it was all over, well it isn't yet...

The Manson Family

In 1968, Beach Boy Dennis Wilson introduced Melcher to ex-con and aspiring musician Charles Manson. Manson and his 'family' had been living in Wilson's house on Sunset Boulevard after Wilson had picked up Patricia Krenwinkel and Ella Jo Bailey from the family hitchhiking. Wilson expressed interest in Manson's music and even recorded two of Manson's songs with The Beach Boys. For a time, Melcher was interested in recording Manson's music, as well as making a movie about the 'family' and their 'hippie commune' existence. Manson met Melcher at 10050 Cielo Drive, the home Melcher shared with his girlfriend, actress Candice Bergen. Manson eventually auditioned for Melcher, but Melcher declined to sign him. There was still talk of a documentary being made about Manson's music, but Melcher abandoned the project after witnessing his subject become embroiled in a fight with a drunken stuntman at Spahn Ranch. Both Wilson and Melcher severed their ties with Manson, a move that angered Manson.

Not long after severing ties with Manson, Melcher and Bergen moved out of the Cielo Drive home. The house's owner, Rudi Altobelli, then leased it to film director Roman Polanski and his wife, actress Sharon Tate. Manson visited the house looking for Melcher, but was turned away as Melcher had moved. On August 9, 1969, the house was the site of the murders of Sharon Tate (who was eight months pregnant at the time), coffee heiress Abigail Folger (known as Gibby to her friends), hairdresser Jay Sebring, writer Wojciech Frykowski, and Steven Parent, by members of Manson's 'family'. Some authors and law enforcement personnel have theorized that 10050 Cielo Drive was targeted by Manson as revenge for Melcher's rejection, and that Manson did not believe that Melcher and Bergen had moved. However, Manson Family member Tex Watson states that Manson and the Family did know that Melcher was no longer living there.

At that time, Melcher was producing singer Jimmy Boyd for A&M Records. After initial tracks were recorded, the Manson murders took place, prompting Melcher to go into seclusion, and the session was never completed. When Manson was arrested, it was widely reported that he had sent his followers to the house to kill Melcher and Bergen. Manson family member Susan Atkins, who admitted her part in the murders, stated to police and before a grand jury that the house was chosen as the scene for the murders "to instil fear into Terry Melcher because Terry had given us his word on a few things and never came through with them". In this aim, the Manson Family was successful. Melcher took to employing a bodyguard and told Manson prosecutor Vincent Bugliosi that his fear was so great, he had been undergoing psychiatric treatment. Melcher was the most frightened of the witnesses at the trial, even though Bugliosi assured him that "Manson knew you were no longer living (on Cielo Drive)".

Later years

Melcher again acted as producer for The Byrds on Ballad of Easy Rider, their eighth album, released in November 1969 (see 1969 in music). The album peaked at No. 36 on the Billboard charts. At the time it was met with mixed reviews but is today regarded as one of the band's stronger albums from the latter half of their career.

In the early 1970s, Melcher was the producer of The Byrds' 10th album Byrdmaniax, but the results were not well received; one critic referred to the album as "Melcher's Folly". During this time, he also dabbled in real estate and served as the executive producer on his mother's CBS series, The Doris Day Show. He later recorded two solo albums, Terry Melcher and Royal Flush. In 1985, Terry co-produced the cable show, Doris Day's Best Friends, and worked as the director and vice president of the Doris Day Animal Foundation. He and his mother, to whom he remained close throughout his life, also co-owned the Cypress Inn, a small hotel in Carmel-by-the-Sea, California.

In 1988, Melcher earned a Golden Globe nomination for co-writing the song "Kokomo" with John Phillips, Scott McKenzie and Mike Love. Recorded by The Beach Boys, the song was featured in the 1988 Tom Cruise film Cocktail, and hit No. 1 (the band's career fourth overall) on the Billboard Hot 100. The single was certified gold for U.S. sales of more than a million copies. Melcher also produced the band's 1992 studio record, Summer in Paradise, which was the first record produced digitally on Pro Tools.

Death

On November 19, 2004, Terry Melcher died at his home after a long battle with melanoma. He was 62. He is survived by his wife Terese, son Ryan Melcher and his mother, Doris Day.

---o---

PS…But what I would like to know, after watching Beckham open the Games and his wife close it, did those people that organise it, finally contact Mary Rand, the lady who won three Gold medals in Tokyo, yet had to pay for the tickets of her daughters and herself?
If you cannot remember

Well, I remember Mary, even if they don't!

ABOUT THE AUTHOR

Alan Hudson is the former Chelsea, Stoke City, Arsenal, Seattle Sounders and England international footballer. He was the darling of Stamford Bridge, the quixotic maestro at the midfield hub of Chelsea's supreme team of the seventies. He was England's prodigal genius, the rebellious young man about the Kings Road at its trendiest. Now Mr. Hudson is an author whose glittering instinct for the beautiful game and indulgence in the good life makes an extraordinary transition from the playing pitch to the printed page. Never orthodox or predictable in his passing, Hudson's writing is also a genre of its own. In his own way idiosyncratic, off-the-wall, quirky, often bizarre, sometimes surreal, he offers a weird and wonderful insight into the world of flowing football and life in the London fast lane during the roaring seventies, and comparisons with today's game and its personalities. It is as much a perceptive social document as it is a kaleidoscope flashback to the heyday of Osgood, Cooke, Tambling, Baldwin the Sponge, Bonetti the Cat, Chopper Harris and... Alan Hudson.

Follow Alan @alanhudson28 and http://alanhudson.blogspot.co.uk/